THE FORMATION OF CHRISTENDOM

The Formation of Christendom

JUDITH HERRIN

BASIL BLACKWELL

Copyright © Judith Herrin 1987

First published 1987

Basil Blackwell Ltd
108 Cowley Road, Oxford, OX4 1JF, UK

British Library Cataloguing in Publication Data

Herrin, Judith
  The formation of Christendom.
  1. Church history—Primitive and early
  church, ca. 30-600   2. Church history—
  Middle Ages, 600-1500   3. Europe—Church
  history
  209'.4   BR160

  ISBN 0-631-15186-9

Typeset in 11 on 12 pt. Linotron Garamond by Princeton University Press, Princeton, New Jersey

Second Printing, 1989, in the
United States of America by
Princeton University Press

For Anthony

Contents

CONTENTS

LIST OF MAPS

Acknowledgements

IN A BOOK of this length, errors of fact and judgement are inevitable. Not only are they all mine, but they would have been even more numerous but for the vigilance and care of friends and colleagues. I am glad to thank them in print and at the same time absolve them of responsibility for the final outcome.

The following read the whole manuscript at some stage: Anthony Barnett, Guy Boanas, Hugh Brody, Peter Brown, Anthony Bryer, Patricia Crone, David Ganz, Christopher Hill, Eleanor Herrin, Jinty Nelson, Lyndal Roper, and Gareth Stedman Jones. In particular, I pestered Patricia Crone and Jinty Nelson with telephone calls, which they always answered without complaint. Specific queries were also addressed to Sebastian Brock, Donald Bullough, John Haldon, and Cyril Mango, and I am grateful for their expertise. My overwhelming debt is to Anthony Barnett; may he also share in the book's published life.

I want to express my appreciation of encouragement and assistance of different kinds, provided over a long time, by Robert Browning, Averil Cameron, Philip Grierson, George Huxley, Elisabeth Soler, Davinia Truby, Greta Ilott (particularly for her skill when confronted by numerous changes in the text), and especially Tamara Kate, who stood on the parcel when the manuscript was finally dispatched to the publisher. There, I am grateful to my editor, Joanna Hitchcock, and to Sherry Wert for her scrupulous copyediting. For the careful execution of the maps I thank Keith Bennett, and for advice on problems of cartography Mark Elvin.

When I began this study in 1977 at the Warburg Institute, University of London, its final shape was by no means clear. The magnificent library there helped me to define its central preoccupations, as the stacks revealed the sources for a broad comparative treatment of early medieval cultures. It is a pleasure to thank the director, Joe Trapp, the librarian, Will Ryan, and the staff of both the photographic and book collections. In 1980-81 I was helped by Olga Vrana and the staff at the Society for the Humanities, at Cornell University. In 1982-83 the British Academy gave me a travel grant, which enabled me to consult manuscripts in Rome and Paris, and I thank Franco Moretti and Vera von Falkenhausen (Rome), David Jacoby and Avigdor Posèq (Jerusalem), and Ernest Hawkins and Taciser and Murat Belge (Istanbul), for making me feel at home in these ancient cities that I so much enjoy visiting and writing about.

With all this help I should have been able to finish sooner. But it was only thanks to a Senior Simon Research Fellowship at the University of Manchester in 1983-84 that a draft of the whole text was finally completed. The critical appraisal of members of the history department, who attended a seminar based on the book, particularly Terence Ranger and Rosemary Morris, improved it in many ways. The staff of the John Rylands University Library in Manchester join a number of other librarians, at the British Library in London, the Bodleian in Oxford, and the Olin in Cornell, to all of whom I am indebted. Over the years I have also been fortunate to receive copies of periodicals and books not generally available, provided by Alan Cameron, Michael Hendy, Oistein Hjort, Alexander Kazhdan, Margaret Mullett, Andrzej Poppe, Michael Rogers, Paul Speck, David Winfield, and Ian Wood.

An invitation from the Shelby Cullom Davis Center to spend a semester at Princeton in one of the liveliest of history departments allowed me to take advantage of Peter Brown's immense knowledge of Late Antiquity. His suggestions led to many improvements to the text in its ultimate stage. I also learnt much from Roy Mottahedeh and from Paula Sanders's infectious enthusiasm for some of the less accessible aspects of Islamic culture, and was privileged to consult Otto Neugebauer at the Institute for Advanced Study on matters of dating.

I have not always taken the advice or accepted the opinions generously offered. Nor, despite this help, have all the problems raised by my research been resolved. But they remain in the text as evidence of my own fallibility, and perhaps occasionally as testimony to the never-concluding and even irresolvable nature of historical investigation.

Oxford, March 1986

THE FORMATION OF CHRISTENDOM

Introduction

THE CHRISTIAN way of dating by numbering years from the Incarnation, "in the Year of the Lord," *Anno Domini* (A.D.), is perhaps the only such chronology currently recognised throughout the world. But while A.D. dating takes the birth of Jesus of Nazareth as its starting point, the system itself only came into use much later. For many centuries Christians continued to use pagan and Jewish chronologies and dates. This was a natural consequence of their Judaic inheritance, which provided them with a timescale stretching back to the Garden of Eden. The Old Testament embodied a millennial eschatology, in which the years of the world *Anni Mundi* (A.M.) linked Jews and Christians to the divine act of Creation, recorded in the Book of Genesis.

The method of counting by generations was also a common one, and it too bore Biblical authority from the First Book of Chronicles: "So all Israel were reckoned by genealogies . . ." (1 Chr. 9.1). For dates in their own lives, the early Christians used some of the many Greco-Roman methods then current: the regnal year of emperor or local ruler; the succession of Roman consuls; or the ancient four-year cycle of Olympiads, going back to the first pan-Hellenic games held at Olympia in Southern Greece. A plethora of local eras were in use; in Spain, the Roman conquest of 40 B.C. was commemorated through a distinctive *aera*; in Syria, the Seleucid era persisted. Later, the accession of Diocletian in A.D. 284 became the starting point of an era widely used in Egypt. Another novel system introduced under the same emperor, originally for taxation purposes, became very widespread: the fifteen-year cycle of indictions. Similarly, not only did the early Christians use the pagan months as we still do, but in areas subject to intensive Roman influence they also identified days of the month in the manner established by Julius Caesar, counting back from the Kalends, Nones, and Ides. With such a variety of dating methods available, it is not surprising that the followers of Jesus did not consider the introduction of another one. In any case, they were not concerned to document the present as much as to prepare for the future. For the transitory nature of life on earth had been emphasised, and they knew that the Second Coming (*Parousia*) and Day of Judgement were at hand.

From an early stage in their debates with the pagans, however, the Christians were concerned to prove the antiquity of their faith relative to secular history. In the early third century, Sextus Julianus Africanus set out

to demonstrate the superiority of the Judaeo-Christian faith by fitting the
established events of ancient Persian and Greek chronology into the record
of the Old Testament. A Christian chronographer of the Alexandrian
school working in Palestine, Africanus took the Bible as the record of a preconceived destiny being worked out according to divine dispensation. Calculating the years of the world since the creation of Adam, and using as a
model the seven days of Creation and the 70 weeks of the Book of Daniel,
he united all world history in seven millenia: the first five covered Biblical
history from Creation to the Babylonian captivity (A.M. 1-4999); the sixth
consisted of 500 years of preparation for the advent of Christ—dated to the
symbolic mid-point at A.M. 5500—and 500 years of subsequent Christian
history that would end with the sixth millenium in A.M. 5999. The year
6000 would witness the Second Coming and the Apocalypse described in
the Book of Revelations. It would usher in the seventh and final millenium
of the Kingdom of Heaven. This chiliastic account of human history established fixed points for Christians: the date of the birth of Jesus, and the
precise moment at which the *Parousia* would occur. It thereby provided a
clear eschatology of Christian existence, and countered pagan predictions
that the Christian faith would endure for only 365 years (a claim St. Augustine was pleased to see refuted).

From the early third century, therefore, the notion of a Christian age had
been established, although its dates continued to be recorded in the year of
the world. Africanus provided the basis for an even more elaborate demonstration of Christian superiority in historical chronology, drawn up one
hunded years later by Eusebios of Caesarea. Eusebios refused to try and calculate the precise number of years between Creation and the Flood, because
the Old Testament evidence was too scanty, and differed with Africanus
over the precise date of the birth of Jesus, which he realised was out by two
years. Nonetheless he retained both the millenial system and the symbolic
mid-point of the sixth millenium as the hinge between all time before
Christ and the remaining 500 years after Him. The chronology and canon
tables established by Eusebios summarised the most sophisticated understanding of Christian history at that time and were translated from Greek
into both Armenian and Latin soon after their completion.

The year of the world 6000 came and went, however, without change,
despite Christian expectations of the Day of Judgement. The *Parousia* had
obviously been delayed. Christians were instructed not to reduce their
preparations for what might occur at any moment, but the millenial point
had passed, and inevitably the theories of Africanus lost some of their authority.

Only 25 years later (in "A.M. 6025"), an eastern monk named Dionysios
saw a way of drawing upon the chronology developed by Africanus to re-

name the Christian era and to identify it by "the years of the Lord," *Anni Domini*. He had been asked by a friend, a western bishop, to explain the complex problems of computation involved in calculating the date of Easter by the Alexandrian method. The task of establishing the correct date for this, the most important moveable festival of the church, had previously been entrusted to the Church of Alexandria by the First Oecumenical Council at Nicaea (325). So Dionysios translated into Latin the authoritative Easter tables drawn up by St. Cyril in the middle of the fifth century, together with the computistic canons and methods of calculation used in the East. As he worked on his own tables for the future celebration of Easter, projected through a 95-year period, he realised that 28 nineteen-year cycles would soon have passed since the year traditionally attributed to the birth of Christ. He was able to conclude that he was living in the 525th year since the Incarnation. He had found a system that would allow a truly Christian calendar to be elaborated, and rejoiced that he would no longer have to use one that commemorated Diocletian, the pagan persecutor of the Christians.

Dionysios's Easter tables, and with them the possibility of using A.D. dating, remained relatively unknown, despite initial papal enthusiasm. The untimely death of Pope John I in May 526 unleashed an anti-Greek reaction in Rome that was responsible for the death of Boethius and the disgrace of his eastern associates, among them Dionysios. The Christian system of dating that we use today was another of the casualties, for Rome had long harboured hostility towards the powerful see of Alexandria. Although Dionysios's manuscript on Easter calculation passed to Cassiodorus, who described how to convert A.M. dates to A.D. dates, there was no shift to dating from the Incarnation, even at the famous monastery founded by Cassiodorus at Vivarium.

It was nearly two hundred years, in fact, before the system was put into regular use, and then by Bede, an Anglo-Saxon monk in remote Northumbria. His *Ecclesiastical History of the English People*, completed in A.D. 731, is dated throughout by years reckoned from the Incarnation, coupled with the regnal years of local and more distant rulers. Although Bede was an expert at computation and chronology, as his own Easter tables show, he remained quite unknown in the East and without influence there. In the West, however, he was quickly followed. Many eighth-century chronicles adopted the same method of dating, and Charles the Great, known to us as Charlemagne, made the system familiar in many parts of Europe by using it for some of his acts of government.

Meanwhile, in the Greek East, the Byzantines adopted the system of dating from the Incarnation, but only side-by-side with ancient systems, which remained dominant. Old Testament chronology in the form elaborated by Eusebios continued to date universal history by the year of the world, while the year of the emperor reigning in Constantinople and the 15-year indiction cycle served to identify more recent events. In Rome the ecclesiastical authorities continued to use traditional methods, also dating their documents by indiction and imperial year, until the middle of the eighth century. And when they did change, it was not to the A.D. method exclusively; they substituted the year of Charles's rule for the Byzantine imperial year, adding the pontifical year also. Secular dates thus remained the norm in Rome, even if these became firmly axed on the realities of western power, while the A.D. system was gradually becoming established in much of northern Europe.

In striking contrast to this lengthy process of devising and implementing a Christian dating system independent of any ruler, Islam found its own particular method within a decade of the Prophet's death in A.D. 632. Muslim society took Muhammad's flight (Hijri) from Mecca to Medina as the basis of its new calendar. The year of the Hijri (A.H.), complete with its lunar months adapted from the Jewish system but renamed in Arabic, was introduced. It remains a chronology employed in many parts of the world today.

The emergence of an Islamic dating system was thus as brief and intense as the Christian was extended and disrupted. Yet these two world calendars were first diffused as authoritative methods of counting the years in the same period: the tumultuous centuries that span the transition between the late Roman and early medieval epochs. Modern times began in those dark ages—and not only with respect to our present styles of dating.[1]

EVER SINCE the seminal work of Henri Pirenne on the consequences of the eruption of Islam, the seventh century has been recognised as decisive in the development of the Middle Ages.[2] Despite the paucity of evidence, which does not facilitate close investigation, it is clear that the political unity of the Mediterranean world was irrevocably lost at that time. Roman imperial forms of government, often adapted to novel purposes in the non-

[1] E. J. Bickermann, *Chronology of the Ancient World*, 2nd ed. (London, 1980); J. H. Breasted, "The Beginnings of Time-Measurement and the Origins of Our Calendar," in *Time and Its Mysteries*, 1st series (New York, 1935), 59-94; J. T. Shotwell, "Time and Historical Perspective," in *Time and Its Mysteries*, 3rd series (New York, 1949), 63-91. Cf. R. L. Poole, *Medieval Reckonings of Time* (London, 1918), a very brief and useful introduction, and his *Studies in Chronology and History* (Oxford, 1934).

[2] See particularly Henri Pirenne, *Mohammad and Charlemagne* (London, 1939), and idem, *Economic and Social History of Medieval Europe* (London, 1936), both volumes frequently reprinted since.

Roman kingdoms of the West, began to give way to medieval ones. In particular, the rise of feudalism distinguished western Europe from the two other successors of ancient Rome: Byzantium and the Caliphate. The tripartite division has been of lasting significance for the modern world, and it is in the interaction of the three component parts that the initial particularity of the West can be located. I cannot resolve, nor have I addressed, the "structural dynamic" of this transition to feudalism.[3] An adequate historical theory will probably need to be articulated within a much broader framework of comparison, which will also identify patterns of imperial decline and succession, for example, in China, India, and Japan. But by investigating the transformation of the ancient world in its entirety and the three heirs of Rome in their shared Mediterranean context, I have tried to expand the empirical base for further theoretical work.

Although political and economic elements of the transition from Antiquity to the Middle Ages may be determinate, they are here subordinated to a study of the development of Christian faith. This is approached not through the well-known features of ecclesiastical history, but through an analysis of medieval faith as a material force. Nor do I begin with the physical substance of the church, its properties, its accumulated wealth, and its economic role in dispensing charity, which will form the subject of a companion volume. The following study will, instead, examine the structural role of faith in early medieval society. It may appear perverse to tackle the cultural parameters of Christendom before its economic dimension. But the capacity of faith to mobilise, frequently manifested in the seventh and eighth centuries, is indicative of a force that may determine other factors, particularly at times of political failure and economic crisis.

Belief is often taken for granted as a given fact, whose characteristics can be assumed at all levels of society, the most sophisticated and least educated. Rather than make that assumption, I prefer to try and examine the meanings of belief for early medieval believers. This is a delicate business not only because of the inherent difficulty of grasping the significance of faith for people so distant from us, but also because medieval religion is sometimes conceived, and criticised, as the chief support of an unchanging and fixed social order. While beliefs certainly did unite and restrict medieval Christendom, they seem to me infinitely more complex than they are often thought. There are a great many subversive aspects to belief, and medieval culture was more varied than ecclesiastical leaders cared to admit. So

[3] P. Anderson, *Passages from Antiquity to Feudalism* (London, 1974); C. Wickham, "The Other Transition: From the Ancient World to Feudalism," *Past and Present* 103 (1984): 3-36.

I make no apology for studying religion from the viewpoint of a non-be-
liever; the history of faith is far too important to be left to adherents alone.

The Formation of Christendom addresses both the Christian and the Muslim inheritors of the Roman Empire and asks how it was that they came to
define their world solely in religious terms. As the ancient world collapsed,
faith rather than imperial rule became the feature that identified the universe, what Christians called the oikoumene, and Muslims, Dar al Islam. Religion had fused the political, social, and cultural into self-contained systems, separated by their differences of faith. Other regions beyond these
spheres were of course known, but were branded as barbarian, pagan, heretical, and hence inferior. Such groups might even intrude into the Christian and Islamic worlds, as the Jewish communities did, always condemned and only tolerated under certain conditions. Paradoxically,
however, Christianity, and in its turn, Islam, was formed in reaction to
other faiths and creeds, Judaism primarily, but also the cults of pagan
Greece and Rome, the panoply of Egyptian deities, Persian Zoroastrian-
ism, Mithraism, and others. The history of the growth of Christian faith at
the expense of these, and then of Islam in reaction to Christian as well as
Judaic practice, does not require another general study. Instead of assum-
ing a universal potential within the first Christian communities of the East
Mediterranean, where Islam now predominates, I have asked how Christianity developed a dominant position and status in Europe, of which the
term Christendom could justifiably be used. Concomitantly, I have looked
closely at the religious rivalry that resulted in the transfer to Muslim allegiance of those areas where Christianity first flourished.

The term "Christendom" is recorded in late ninth-century Anglo-Saxon
England and has no exact parallel in the Latin or Greek words used previously to designate Christian adherence, Christianitas or oikoumene.[4] It thus
enters European vocabulary at the time when King Alfred was translating
works of Augustine, Boethius, and Pope Gregory the Great into Anglo-
Saxon. But this first known use does not reflect the reality of the late ninth
century, a troubled period of Viking raids, which familiarised Christians
in the West with Nordic paganism. On the contrary, the Anglo-Saxon concept of Christendom derives from an earlier period, when Charles the Great
created a notion of Christian universality in his Holy Roman Empire.[5]

    [4] "Cristendome" is used by Alfred himself in 893 (in his revisions of the World History by
Orosius), see A New English Dictionary, ed. J. A. H. Murray (Oxford, 1893), II(i). Contem-
porary twentieth-century use continues this meaning, "the state or condition of being
Christian"; see, for instance, B. A. Gerrish, ed., The Faith of Christendom (Cleveland/New
York, 1963).
    [5] See J. Fischer, Oriens, Occidens, Europa (Wiesbaden, 1957), 78-79, on the equivalence
of orbis-mundis and orbis-ecclesia in the late eighth century.

In this analysis of faith and the struggle between Christianity and Islam, the Muslim challenge is crucial, because it threatened the legitimacy of both the theological and political dimensions of Christianity. Although Christian authorities might identify Muhammad as another heretic, albeit with an extremely large and devout following, his claims to be the ultimate prophet of God explicitly contested the orthodoxy of their own faith. Islam was proposed to believers as the strict observance of monotheism: "There is no God but Allah and Muhammad is his Prophet," as the Muslim profession of faith states. Like Christianity, it broke from the primitive, tribal claims of the Israelites, while it too recognised the enduring force of Mosaic Law. Islam, however, insisted upon a monotheism unconfused by Trinitarian problems. Both faiths believed in the same God, and each claimed to fulfil the promises of the Jewish Old Testament: Christians through the New Testament, which proclaimed the Messiah and spread the faith among Jews and Gentiles alike; Muslims through the Koran, which identified Muhammad as the final prophet of God, whose instructions replaced all previous ones.

The extent to which Islam considered that it had surpassed both the older religions is symbolised by the building of the Dome of the Rock in Jerusalem. On the site of the Temple Mount, the holiest of Jewish holy places, Caliph Abd al Malik commissioned a mosque over the rock from which Muhammad had ascended into heaven. The octagonal building, constructed in white marble with reused Roman columns and decorated in glittering floral mosaics by Christian craftsmen, is surmounted by a golden dome typical of classical and early Christian architecture. According to the long Koranic inscription that runs around the interior, it was completed in A.H. 71 (A.D. 691-92) as a celebration of Allah, the God of both Jews and Gentiles who now favoured the Muslims above all others.

It was under the impact of these Islamic claims that Christians developed new means to ensure their survival. They also abandoned several pagan features inherited from the ancient world and adopted Christian ones—the introduction of dating from the Incarnation being an outstanding example. The simultaneous emergence of Islamic and Christian calendars was no coincidence. In rejecting Muslim belief, however, the eastern and western churches redefined their faith in different ways. Faced with Islamic monotheism, they each attempted to regulate their Christian belief and practice in accordance with their own interpretation of the Old Testament. In the East, the entirely novel doctrine of iconoclasm was elaborated, as a means of preventing the worship of man-made objects, to be replaced forty years later by the elevation of icons to an integrated position within worship. In the West, both the destruction and the veneration of religious pictures was condemned by the emergent Christian leadership of northern

Europe, where Charles was identified as a New David and his subjects as a New Israel. The division of Christendom, marked by the synod of Frankfurt in 794, finalised a long tendency towards separation, and set the churches of West and East on different courses.

Long before Muhammad began dictating his revelations, however, internal factors had confirmed tendencies towards a division of the ancient world. To draw attention to those elements, linguistic, cultural, and artistic, that separated East from West, is not to deny the unity of the Mediterranean. Following Braudel's magisterial work it is impossible to ignore the special environment shared by those regions united under imperial rule around the Roman lake.[6] Within this fixed physical framework, marked by a common pattern of ancient structures and systems of belief, parallel and simultaneous but distinct processes were responsible for the development of three particular heirs: the reconstituted empire of the East, the Arabic Caliphate of the South, and the self-conscious unit of western "Europe"— the modern sense attached to this term originates at the time of Charles the Great. Despite the lasting divisions established by the year A.D. 800, these regions remained bound together by their shared inheritance as well as by their geographical setting. Precisely because these bonds were real, there were constant attempts to recreate a past unity, attempts as varied as the movements for political union usually based on crusading force, or those for religious union based on theological compromise.

Throughout the following study, the terms "East" and "West" are used as a shorthand for the Greek regions of the eastern Mediterranean and the Latin areas of the West respectively.[7] These terms are of course Eurocentric. But they correspond roughly to the regions where the two major classical languages were spoken. Their meaning is fairly clear, they are in widespread use today, and I have not found any better general designations. The historian, after all, can try to allow for, but should not seek to escape, her time.

Linguistic factors held the key to the process of differentiation between an "Eastern" and a "Western" sphere during the early Christian period. For as the unity of the Mediterranean became less meaningful to its inhabitants, East and West were locked into ever-increasing mutual incomprehension. In the first great history of the faith by Eusebios (263-340), the Christian church is always singular, yet the existence of many churches formed by Christians scattered throughout the Roman Empire, and their geographical separation, is recognised. Eusebios himself personified the Greek

---

[6] F. Braudel, *The Mediterranean and the Mediterranean World in the Age of Philip II*, 2 vols. (London, 1972-73), 2:763-71.

[7] Fischer, *Oriens*, 26-39.

sense of superiority; he knew no Latin, and he depended upon the careful translations of others to render his work comprehensible to western Christians. One hundred years later, a considerable body of Greek patristic thought had been made available in Latin, but the West never had access to the full range of early Christian writings from the East: nor was the work of western authors like St. Augustine accessible to Greek speakers.

In the East, however, this was not felt as a loss. As Momigliano has shown in his panoramic sweep of ancient culture, the Greeks and their Christian descendants remained impervious to scholarship transmitted in a medium other than their own.[8] After the turn of the sixth century, when knowledge of Latin became rare at the imperial court of Constantinople, the Greek-speaking world closed itself off from western thought. While translation skills were not maintained in the West either, scholars there did not forget the existence of Greek, and they revealed a continuing curiosity about it. The non-classical world of the North, the Irish in particular, remained open to new channels of information in unfamiliar languages, especially the three sacred tongues, Hebrew, Greek, and Latin, in which Scripture was preserved. In this respect they reacted like the Syriac-speaking population of the Near East, who had cultivated the art of translation from an early date. Syriac versions of Greek writings provided a vital link with the ancient world, for it was through this medium that the Arabs gained access to Greek science and philosophy, as well as early Christian works that they found interesting.[9]

The long-term effects of the Greek refusal to look beyond their own heritage became evident in the twelfth century, when western scholars began to benefit from the Arabic medium of transmission. From Baghdad, where Syriac versions had first been rendered into Arabic, the basic works of Aristotle, Ptolemy, Euclid, and many applied subjects had been disseminated throughout the Islamic world. In the caliphate of Cordova (Spain) and the trilingual culture of southern Italy and Norman Sicily, clerics trained in translation skills provided Latin texts.[10] The twelfth-century discovery of Greek thought and its accompanying stimulation of western intellectual endeavour had no parallel in Byzantium, though the period witnessed a lively cultural and artistic development. There was no concerted effort at

---

[8] A. Momigliano, *Alien Wisdom: The Limits of Hellenization* (Cambridge, 1975); idem, "The Faults of the Greeks," in *Proceedings of the American Academy of Arts and Sciences* 104 (2) (1975): 9-19, reprinted in his *Essays in Ancient and Modern Historiography* (Oxford, 1977).

[9] S. Brock, "Aspects of Translation Technique in Antiquity," *GRBS* 20 (1979): 69-87.

[10] R. Walzer, "Arabic Transmission of Greek Thought to Medieval Europe," *Bulletin of the John Rylands Library* 29 (1945): 3-26; M.-T. d'Alverny, "Translations and Translators," in R. L. Benson and G. Constable, eds., *Renaissance and Renewal in the Twelfth Century* (Oxford, 1982), 421-62.

understanding Latin culture until the late thirteenth and fourteenth centuries, when parts of St. Augustine, some of the Roman classics, and St. Thomas Aquinas's *Summa Theologica* were finally translated into Greek. It was already too late for the East to catch up with the more adventurous scholarship of the West.

A further element of separation within the Mediterranean world that can be traced back to the period of transition lies in the development of distinctive artistic traditions. From a shared heritage of Late Antique skills and a common environment decorated with classical buildings and ancient statuary, the three heirs of Rome faced the problem of representation and resolved it in very different ways. In addressing this matter, the West was guided by the dictum of Pope Gregory I that pictures are the bibles of the illiterate, while the East adapted the ancient tradition of portraiture for the lifelike representation of holy people in icons. Western art came to be dominated by a pedagogic function, not ignored in the East but there supplemented by the use of icons as an aid to veneration. Through veneration, icons came to act as intercessors between God and men in a fashion barely known in the West. This contrast in Christian art forms must be set beside the Islamic prohibition of sacred art altogether. In enforcing the Mosaic commandment against the worship of man-made objects, Muhammad established the basic framework for a purely decorative art suitable for Islam. No scenes from the life of the Prophet or his companions were to be illustrated, human portraits were banished, even graves were unmarked (proscriptions that were not observed to the letter). Instead, inscriptions of Koranic verses formed an elaborate calligraphic art visible on ceramic, leather, and wooden objects, in mosques as well as on official seals and coins. The question of what could or should not be shown in artistic terms was tackled in completely different ways, which only assumed their settled form after the iconoclast movements of the eighth and ninth centuries.

Despite the turbulence of the early medieval period, it witnessed the establishment of Christianity as the fundamental belief of the vast majority of people in eastern and western Europe. Edmund Bishop once described the period between Caesarius of Arles (in the early sixth century) and Alcuin (in the late eighth) as the darkest of western European history. He went on: "Yet it is precisely in those three centuries that took place the evolution definitely fixing the religion of medieval and a large part of modern Europe . . . when popular piety that has listened to the word of the preachers makes the ideas they express . . . its own; and that piety in its slow and silent workings generates by and by a common and accepted belief."[11] The very obvious role of Christian institutions in sustaining belief

[11] Edmund Bishop, " 'Spanish Symptoms'," *JTS* 8 (1906/7): 278-94, 430; reprinted in

and maintaining at least a part of ancient culture into the modern period should not make us forget this other, less discernible role, which made Christians of entire peoples previously devoted to the cults of Woden or the moon, sacred trees and pagan goddesses.[12] It is a much harder subject, for converts did not record their thoughts and were often accused of sliding back into ancestor worship (or worse); yet it is equally worthy of analysis.

In examining this history of the formative period of Christendom, I have tried to provide the general reader with an overall view of the period that links ancient Rome with Charlemagne and later European history. While different aspects are familiar enough—the decline of the Roman Empire, the importance of Christianity during the "Dark Ages," feudalism, Bede, Moorish Spain, medieval cathedrals, voyages of discovery, and the Renaissance—the connections between them are frequently unclear. The rebirth of classical interests during the Renaissance, for instance, could hardly have taken place without prior developments, but these remain abstruse, partly because they are not usually set in their proper context: the entire Mediterranean, Islamic as well as Christian, which had its centre in the East. Byzantium is of fundamental importance in this process. I have, therefore, had to write a history of the Mediterranean between about A.D. 550 and 850 to document the transformation that occurred, the consequences of which remain embodied in the area to this day.

While the book has become long and perhaps difficult, I have tried to use English translations of source material wherever possible, though evidence in original languages is also provided. My hope is that a persistent general reader will find the result as exciting as scholars familiar with the field. While studying early medieval faith, I have become aware of the complex interlockings of belief with cultural factors, as well as with those elements of social and political development that have been deliberately excluded from this study. These extensive interconnections are very evident, whether one is reading the seemingly endless theological tracts and ecclesiastical histories that form the basic sources, or the archaeological, literary, and artistic studies that are an essential supplement. I am only too conscious not only of my own limitations, but also of the patchy and unsatisfactory nature of the material, its uneven distribution and inherent difficulties. Yet it seems churlish to condemn it as inadequate; we have to make the best of it. My reading has necessarily been selective—it would

---

his *Liturgica Historica* (Oxford, 1918), 165-202. In connection with the first article, G. Mercati added a note, "More Spanish Symptoms," 423-30, which is also included in Bishop's later volume.

[12] H.-I. Marrou, "La place du haut Moyen Age dans l'histoire du christianisme," *Settimane* 9 (Spoleto, 1962): 595-630; cf. Anderson, *Passages*, 131-39, on the church as the "indispensable bridge between two epochs."

probably be impossible to read all the available material, and in any case I am not equipped to do so. The approach outlined above requires a consideration of Islam and early Arabic history that cannot wait for me to master its medium. If my interpretation appears overconfident, it is because I have covered my hesitation with firmness, a firmness based on the conviction that the formation of Christendom in this period is a subject of immense interest and relevance that demands fresh investigation, whatever the risks and dangers.

I

LATE ANTIQUITY

YORK

BRITAIN

LONDON

TRIER ▣   REGENSBURG   PASSAU

PARIS   GAUL   *R. Danube*   *Noricum*

R. Seine   *R. Rhine*   *Rhaetia*   PANNONIA

AUTUN   AQUILEIA   SIRMIUM

R. Loire   TOURS   *Istria*   *Dalmatia*

POITIERS   LYON   MILAN   *R. Po*

Aquitaine   VERCELLI   ITALY   RAVENNA   SPLIT

BORDEAUX   *R. Garonne*   VIENNE   PISA   *APENNINES*   SPOLETO

OVIEDO   TOULOUSE   ARLES   MARSEILLES   ROME ▣

CANTABRIAN MTS.   NARBONNE

PYRENEES   *Corsica*   NAPLES   AMALFI

Galicia   SARAGOSSA   BARCELONA   GAETA

BRAGA   PALENCIA

RECCOPOLIS   *Sardinia*   *Sicily*   SYRACUSE

TOLEDO   SPAIN   VALENCIA

MÉRIDA   *R. Guadiana*

CORDOVA   HIPPO   CARTHAGE

SEVILLE   *R. Guadalquivir*   BASTI   CARTHAGENA   HADRUMETUM

MALAGA   *Numidia*   RUSPE

CEUTA   AFRICA

SPAIN   TRIPOLI

Mauretania

MOESIA   Dioceses of Diocletian
---------   Diocesan boundaries
—"—"—"—   Division of empire
Galicia   Region
▣   Imperial residence
•   City

0   100   200   300   400   500 miles

MAP 1

The World of Late Antiquity

CHERSON

CAUCASUS MTS.

Lazikè

SINOPE · TREBIZOND

Armenia

R. Danube

DUNUM
MARGUS
NIŠ · NICOPOLIS
ERDICA · THRACE
CONSTANTINOPLE
ADRIANOPLE · NICOMEDIA
PONTOS
R. Halys
MELITENE
CAESAREA · AMIDA
R. Tigris
PHILIPPI · EDESSA
THESSALONIKE
PERGAMON
IKONION · TAURUS MTS.
KIRKISSION
Persia
THEBES · ASIA · TARSOS
ANTIOCH · DURA-EUROPOS
R. Euphrates
Chios · EPHESOS
APAMEA
CTESIPHON
ATHENS · CORINTH · Kos
BABYLON
MPIA · Rhodes
Cyprus
Crete
BEIRUT · DAMASCUS
GORTYNA
TYRE
ORIENS
CAESAREA
JERUSALEM
GAZA
CYRENE · ALEXANDRIA · PETRA
Libya · Egypt
ORIENS
R. Nile
Arabia

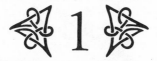

1

Romans and Non-Romans

IN THE FIFTH century A.D., the western half of the Roman Empire finally ceased to have a formal existence. The sack of Rome by Alaric the Goth in 410 and the removal of the boy-emperor, Romulus Augustulus, in 476 are just two of the best-known points in the process. But the invaders who burnt, looted, and destroyed also perpetuated many features of Rome rule, so that to speak of the "disappearance" of the empire would be misleading. All the Germanic and eastern tribes that settled on Roman territory were greatly influenced by imperial administration, law, education, and art, some more than others. Most of their leaders sought to gain approval of their occupation through diplomatic relations with the eastern capital of Constantinople. When the Herulian general, Odovacer, justified his deposition of Romulus Augustulus, he asked Emperor Zeno for the title of patrician, normally granted to powerful non-Roman allies, and expected to govern in the emperor's name. The barbarian impact did not therefore involve an immediate and total destruction of Roman traditions: imperial patterns of government survived and were even preserved by the newcomers.

This survival has long been noted and is recognised by even the most "catastrophic" theories of Rome's decline. It has given rise to the term "Late Antiquity," coined to cover the period from the third or fourth century to the late sixth or early seventh, a period scorned by classicists as being too late and inadequately "classical" for their scholarship, and neglected by medievalists as too early for theirs.[1] The historical continuity im-

---

[1] European scholars have been studying Late Antiquity for nearly a century, but their work has only recently become familiar in the English-speaking world through the 1971 publication by Peter Brown, *The World of Late Antiquity* (London). This book went further in opening new perspectives on the period, and has generated a flurry of research, notably on Christian features of Late Antiquity. Since 1971 the field has expanded enormously; see, for instance, H.-I. Marrou, *Décadence romaine ou antiquité tardive? IIIe-VIe siècle* (Paris, 1977); S. Mazzarino, *Antico, tardoantico ed erà costantiniana* (Rome, 1974); E. Cerulli, ed., *Passagio dal Mondo Antico al Medio Evo, da Teodosio a San Gregorio Magno* (Rome, 1980); E. Patlagean, *Pauvreté économique et pauvreté sociale à Byzance, 4e-7e siècles* (Paris/The Hague, 1977). For a

plicit in this identification has further reduced the need to pin the "fall" of
Rome to any one particular date, though the long-term causes and consequences of imperial decline are singled out for special investigation.[2] It has
also drawn attention to the period's integrated cultural unity, which survived until at least the sixth century and flourished in the Mediterranean
environment of Late Antiquity.

This notion, that what the Romans called *mare nostrum*, "our sea," not
merely joined all parts of the empire but also united them in some way, is
fundamental to the concept of Late Antiquity.[3] At a time when transport
by sea and river was much cheaper than by land, and when the rocks and
currents of the Mediterranean had been successfully mastered, this vast inland lake encouraged direct lines of communication between its different
shores. For the purposes of trade, this ease of access was tremendously important; it permitted the shipment of basic supplies around the empire, it
fed its littoral and riparian cities with grain from Africa, oil and dried fish
from the Iberian peninsula, wine, pepper, and spices from the East, and a
host of other supplies. But it did not necessarily mean that the communities that provided these commodities felt themselves to be united with the
others, or with Rome. Political unity around the shores of the Mediterranean had been imposed by force, as the Jewish inhabitants of Palestine discovered in A.D. 70 when the Temple was destroyed, and had been maintained by force ever since.[4] Following that event, however, when the last
fervent resistance to Roman rule was crushed, the Jews scattered to new
settlements around the Mediterranean. Alexandria was already largely a
Jewish colony, highly cultured and Hellenised, a Greek-speaking city typical of the eastern Mediterranean. Other coastal settlements that gained
their Jewish quarters at this time were already linked by trading patterns.

---

useful survey of the concept of Late Antiquity, see M. Gelzer, "Altertumswissenschaft und
Spätantike," *HZ* 135 (1927): 173-87.

[2] A. Momigliano, "Christianity and the Decline of the Roman Empire," in the volume
edited by him, *The Conflict Between Paganism and Christianity in the Fourth Century* (Oxford,
1963), 1-16, stresses the importance of Christianity and the impossibility of fixing on any
one date.

[3] This Roman unity was a product of the first three centuries of the empire according to
F. Millar, *The Roman Empire and Its Neighbours*, 2nd ed. (London, 1981), 1-12. See also his
article, "The Mediterranean and the Roman Revolution: Politics, War and the Economy,"
Past and Present 102 (1982): 3-24, and the observation by M. I. Finley, *Ancient Slavery and
Modern Ideology* (Harmondsworth, 1983), 79, that the Roman Empire was "in Wallerstein's
conceptual scheme . . . a 'world-empire,' not a 'world-system'; a structure in which different labour-regimes and modes of production co-existed and were tied together politically
rather than economically." P. Anderson, *Passages from Antiquity to Feudalism* (London,
1974), 20-21, stresses the unifying nature of the Mediterranean waters.

[4] Josephus, *De Bello Judaico* 6.9.3; in *The Complete Works of Josephus*, trans. H. St. J.
Thackeray et al., 10 vols. (London, 1926-65), 3:497-501.

The commercial unity of the Mediterranean under Roman rule would permit a great volume of cultural exchange in the early centuries A.D.[5]

Chief among the cultural artefacts and ideas that thus penetrated to all parts of the Mediterranean world were religious beliefs. The cults of the ancient Egyptian gods and goddesses, those of Persia and lands further east, as well as those of Greece, made familiar in their Latin guise, engendered shrines, statues, and temples dedicated to Mithras and Serapis, Diana, Jupiter, Hecate, Isis, and the Phoenician Baal in different parts of the West. Under a powerful tendency to syncretism, many of these were worshipped together, as joint dedications to Zeus, Helios, Serapis, and Mithras record.[6] In contrast, the Jews of the diaspora created an awareness of monotheism with their belief in one God, Yahweh. But it was the God of the Christians that made a remarkable number of converts in the world of Late Antiquity. Born in reaction to the extension of Roman authority over the Hellenistic kingdoms of Syria and Palestine, yet brought to power by the imperial structures themselves, the Christian faith was both non-Roman and Roman. Its precise role in perpetuating the life of the empire is much debated. But there can be no doubt that Christianity became one of the most significant elements in the world of Late Antiquity. It permeated and transformed the inherited culture of Greece and Rome, providing a crucial link in the transmission of the ancient past to a medieval future. In its Christian medium, Late Antique culture helped to prolong the "sub-Roman" successor states of the West long into the seventh century, and extended ancient traditions far beyond their original habitat.[7] The faith embraced by Constantine I and established as the Roman state religion by his late fourth-century successor, Theodosius I, certainly delayed the empire's decline, and in some ways emerged as its most powerful heir. To understand how this could have happened, it is necessary to examine the context in which Christianity became the dominant belief in both Roman

---

[5] M. Grant, *The World of Rome* (London, 1960), 61-64; J. D'Arms and E. C. Kopff, eds., *The Seaborne Commerce of Ancient Rome*, Memoirs of the American Academy in Rome 36 (Rome, 1980). On the diaspora of Jewish communities, see J. Juster, *Les Juifs dans l'empire romain*, 2 vols. (Paris, 1914); E. Schürer, *Geschichte des jüdisches Volks im Altertum*, 3rd ed., 3 vols. (Leipzig, 1901-1909), 3:2-37; P. Battifol, *L'Eglise naissante et le catholicisme*, 2nd ed. (Paris, 1971), 1-20.

[6] F. Cumont, *Oriental Religions in Roman Paganism*, 2nd ed. (London, 1911, reprinted New York, 1956); A. D. Nock, *Essays on Religion and the Ancient World*, ed. Z. Stewart, 2 vols. (Oxford, 1972); E. R. Dodds, *Pagan and Christian in an Age of Anxiety* (Cambridge, 1965).

[7] The classic statement of this claim was made by H. Pirenne, *Mohammed and Charlemagne* (London, 1939), 3-47; see also S. Mazzarino, *The End of the Ancient World* (London, 1966), 75-76, and the time chart that includes both Pope Gregory I and Isidore of Seville, thus extending to 636.

and non-Roman circles, and the way in which it ultimately contributed to
the division of what had been a purely Roman lake.

The first part of this book is therefore devoted to an analysis of the culture of Late Antiquity, which is so often held responsible for the survival
of Roman traditions. And because this study is an investigation of the formation of Christendom in the following centuries, I must begin by asking
the question, "To what extent was there a unity of Mediterranean culture
in the middle of the sixth century?"[8]

THE WORLD of Late Antiquity drew on a variety of elements inherited
from earlier civilisations in the Mediterranean basin: Ancient Greece and
Egypt, the Phoenician and Hellenistic empires, the indigenous cultures of
pre-Roman Europe and, of course, Rome itself. Not surprisingly, the most
recent, namely the Roman Empire, had imposed a physical framework
within which concepts and ideas specific to Late Antiquity developed. Although geographical notions of "East" and "West" may not have been
clearly defined at the time, they existed naturally in the physical formation
of the Mediterranean. A glance at Map 1 (pp. 16-17) will indicate the two
unequal basins that comprise this landlocked sea, with the island of Sicily
placed strategically between them. The compact western basin formed a
unit separate from the much larger eastern one, which extended through
the Aegean and into the Black Sea as well as southeast to Alexandria, including the rugged coastlines of Asia Minor, the myriad archipelago of the
Adriatic, and the long shore of Egypt and Libya.

At the end of the third century, when Diocletian devised an official par-
tition of the empire, these two basins became the core of each half.[9] The
dividing line ran from Singidunum (modern Belgrade on the Danube)
south to the Adriatic coastline (north of Dyrrachion, Durazzo in modern
Albania) and across the East Mediterranean to the Gulf of Sirte (present-
day Libya) (see Map 1). Most of modern Yugoslavia was firmly associated
with the West, linked to Istria and the lagoons at the head of the Adriatic,
the Alps, and Italy. Similarly, western Libya was united with Carthage and
the highly populated regions of present-day Tunisia. In Roman parlance,

[8] The claim for a unity of Mediterranean monastic culture was made by P. Riché, *Education and Culture in the Barbarian West* (Columbia, S. C., 1976), 109, and amplified by
P. Brown, "Eastern and Western Christendom in Late Antiquity: A Parting of the Ways,"
in D. Baker, ed., *The Orthodox Churches and the West*, SCH 13 (1976): 1-24, esp. 6-7 on the
Mediterranean *koinè* of Christian piety.

[9] E. Kornemann, *Doppelprinzipät und Reichsteilung im Imperium Romanum* (Leipzig, 1930),
78-134; E. Demougeot, *La formation de l'Europe et les invasions barbares de l'avènement de Dio-
clétien au début du VIe siècle*, 2 vols. (Paris, 1969-79), 2:9-55; idem, *De l'unité à la division de
l'Empire romain 395-410* (Paris, 1951).

"Africa" is always this western half of the north African coastline, while the eastern half is "Egypt." Correspondingly, most of the Balkan peninsula, all the territory between the Danube, and the Aegean and Black Sea littoral falls into the East, as does eastern Libya. The Mediterranean is thus naturally divided by the Italian peninsula and Sicily. Diocletian partitioned the empire along this geographical divide, the vertical line that separated the two sea basins, but that also confirmed the integrating function of the Mediterranean waters. His purpose was to increase the strength of centralised Roman government. Yet the longer-term effect laid the foundation for a post-Roman separation between the western and eastern parts.

THE TETRARCHY: WEST AND EAST IN THE ROMAN EMPIRE

With this formal division of territory, Diocletian established a new system of imperial government, the Tetrarchy.[10] It involved the creation of two equal emperors, each assisted by a co-emperor (or junior emperor), making four in all; they shared in imperial authority, but had responsibility only for their respective halves of the empire. The system aimed to resolve the problem of imperial succession by designating the junior emperors as heirs of their senior colleagues, while preserving the unity of the empire through Roman law, with new laws and all official documents being issued in the joint names of all four rulers.

Originally, Diocletian established 12 large dioceses throughout the empire: Britain, Gaul, Vienne, Spain, Africa, Italy, Pannonia, Moesia, Thrace, Asia, Pontos, and Oriens.[11] In the West, the significance of Italy was indicated by the provision of two governors (called "vicars," *vicarii*), one for the North and one for the South, the latter based on Rome. Africa's importance in the empire's economy was also signalled by the particular administration of that large province. In the East, the diocese of Oriens, which comprised the entire East Mediterranean hinterland and Egypt, was by far the largest. Until the early fourth century, there was no supreme capital; imperial residences at Nicomedia (richly endowed by Diocletian), Antioch, and Thessalonike served in turn. An equivalent number of important cities in the West—Trier, Milan, and Ravenna among them—were recognised as provincial capitals, but Rome remained the established capital city and metropolis. Overall, the Roman Empire was governed by one law, decreed by semi-divine leaders who were assisted by aristocratic sen-

---

[10] A. H. M. Jones, *LRE*, 1:40-42, 49-51, 325-326.

[11] Jones, *LRE*, 1:46-48; 3:382-89 (Appendix III). Cf. T. D. Barnes, *The New Empire of Diocletian and Constantine* (Cambridge, Mass., 1982), 195-225.

ates of largely honorific standing, and by military hierarchies with real power, the whole being administered by a centralised bureaucracy.

In practice, however, the Tetrarchy did not work so equitably. The separation into two halves gradually created two empires, distinct in their resources and capacities as well as in their geographical characteristics. The process of differentiation was deepened by political failure; after the joint resignation of Diocletian and Maximian in 305, the peaceful succession of co-emperors was never achieved. In addition, the principle of divided responsibility tended to confine particular loyalties to one half or the other. These tendencies became clearer during the civil wars between Constantine and Maxentius, and between Constantine and Licinius, which resulted in the reunification of empire (324) and the choice of Byzantion as a new imperial residence in the East.[12]

Constantine's decision to rebuild the Greek colony on the Bosphoros, to which he gave his own name, no doubt reflected the need for an eastern metropolis. But New Rome, as it was also called, was not only a counterweight to the old western capital; it was also designed to replace it. Partly because the Roman Senate and praetorian guard had acclaimed Maxentius in the civil wars, Constantine was determined to reduce their power. After his victory at the Milvian Bridge (312), he dissolved the guard, which was never to be re-formed, and left Rome without an emperor. In contrast, Constantine's own city became the imperial capital *par excellence*. Set on the bridgehead between Europe and Asia, it was enlarged, fortified, provided with all the public buildings necessary for a capital, and adorned with the most famous pieces of classical statuary that the emperor could remove from other cities (like Rome). It was dedicated on 11 May 330, in ceremonies both traditional and new, which foreshadowed the specifically Christian character of Constantinople only realised in later years. In every way, New Rome marked a departure, one that heralded the separation of East from West within the Roman world.

Other factors confirmed the distinct character of the East Roman Empire. In population, language, terrain, climate, and soil, the dioceses governed from Constantinople were unlike the imperial homeland in Italy.[13] Long exposure to hellenising influences had made Greek a common tongue throughout the East Mediterranean, even though many different languages and local dialects were still in use. In the degree of urbanisation and density of population, the ancient centres of the East had always outweighed those of the West, with the exception of Rome itself and the most prosperous

[12] G. Dagron, *Naissance d'une capitale: Constantinople et ses institutions de 330 à 451* (Paris, 1974), 13-27.

[13] See C. Mango, *Byzantium, The Empire of New Rome* (London, 1980), 13-23, for a succinct survey of these differences in about the middle of the sixth century.

parts of Africa. Traditions of public service, higher education, and literacy were also more developed. The most distinguished schools of philosophy, law, and sciences were in such cities as Athens, Beirut, and Alexandria. Although drought was common, systems of irrigation made most of the East Mediterranean lands fertile and relatively wealthy. Apart from very large estates belonging to such families as the Apions of Egypt, most landowners controlled only modest holdings, and independent smallholders were common. The particular importance of Egypt, which provided grain to feed the population of Constantinople, was recognised in about 367, when it became a separate diocese. This development confirmed the imbalance of resources in the Roman world. The resilience and lasting power of the East would be highlighted when the empire came under threat in the late fourth century.

THE BARBARIAN INVASIONS

Centuries before the Huns began to exert their pressure on the Gothic tribes that had settled to the north and east of the Black Sea, the Rhine and Danube provinces of the empire had experienced unexpected Germanic raids. But it was the Hunnic disturbances of the 370s that seem to have unleashed the first serious disruptions of imperial control.[14] These continued in haphazard actions throughout the fifth century and into the sixth. Depending on the severity, the Roman authorities would try to muster an effective force to confront the advance, or might offer to buy off a direct attack. At the first significant clash, however, the intruders succeeded in killing the emperor and shattering his army, at Adrianople in 378. After the death of Valens I in such ignominious circumstances, the surviving Roman generals selected a military officer from the West, Theodosius, to lead the campaign against the victorious Visigoths. He was not able to check their hostile activities in the Balkans, but he was proclaimed emperor nonetheless. The situation was finally resolved by a treaty, which represented a recognition by the authorities in Constantinople that direct force might not suffice. This treaty permitted the Visigoths to occupy imperial lands south of the Danube for the first time.[15] It was a major concession.

Some accommodation must have resulted, for despite looting and other disorders, Visigoths were settled in large numbers within the empire. Many had already adopted Christianity, albeit in a heretical form. In 394, under their leader, Alaric, a Gothic contingent participated in Theodo-

---

[14] Demougeot, *La formation de l'Europe*, 2:368-93; L. Musset, *The Germanic Invasions: The Making of Europe*, A.D. 400-600 (London, 1975), 73-76. Contemporary authors noted with horror the Huns' extreme savageness, lack of religion, and passion for gold.

[15] Jones, *LRE*, 1:153-54, 156-58.

sius's campaign against a western usurper. On the emperor's deathbed in Milan (January 395), Theodosius designated his two sons, Arcadius and Honorius, then aged 17 or 18 and 10 respectively, as his heirs. So when Alaric decided to alter the Goths' status as loyal allies, he rebelled against Arcadius, emperor of the East. Instead of returning to the established Gothic "homelands," he led his people south to Athens, plundered many cities in Greece, and evaded a Roman force sent from the West under Stilicho (a half-Vandal, half-Roman general).

In these circumstances, the second major concession was made: Alaric was recognised as *magister militum* (397) and given the right to draw taxes or tribute from the cities of Illyricum.[16] This Roman admission of weakness would result, eventually, in the mutually advantageous arrangement of permitting tribes to occupy imperial territory in both East and West as federates or allies, *foederati*. Their leaders would be granted imperial titles and expected to keep the peace. Often their sons were kept as hostages and given a thoroughly Roman education at an imperial court—for instance, in the case of Theodoric the Ostrogoth. But the potential dangers inherent in such arrangements were rapidly made clear. After four years in southern Illyricum, Alaric led the Visigoths north and west into Italy (401). They captured Aquileia at the head of the Adriatic, threatened the court at Milan, and forced Honorius, the western emperor, to flee to Ravenna, a safer base because of its marshy surroundings where the sole direct access was from the sea via the port of Classis.[17] From there Honorius sought in vain to frustrate the Gothic campaign. Alaric's aim, to judge from the sparse and prejudiced records, was to gain a more fertile and permanent home for his people, for he opened negotiations immediately. He wanted guarantees that the Goths might live peacefully in Istria, Rhaetia, or Noricum. Honorius, however, declined to make concessions. His rejection of these proposals, coupled with the Roman Senate's adamant refusal to buy off the threat, resulted after eight long years in the sack of Rome (August 410).[18] The more moderate camp of diplomatic compromise, represented by Stilicho, lost out to the aggressive anti-Gothic party. During the decade of uncertain fighting and talking, usurpers in Britain took advantage of the disorders in the West to detach the Gallic prefecture, while Vandals,

[16] Ibid., 1:183-84.

[17] Procopius, *Wars* 5.1.16-23; J. F. Matthews, *Western Aristocracies and the Imperial Court*, A.D. *364-425* (Oxford, 1975), 273-74.

[18] C. D. Gordon, *The Age of Attila: Fifth Century Byzantium and the Barbarians* (Ann Arbor, 1972), 32-35 (including translations of Olympiodoros, frags. 3, 4, 6, 13); R. C. Blockley, *The Fragmentary Classicising Historians of the Late Roman Empire*, 2 vols. (Liverpool 1981-83), 2:156-69 (text and translation); P. Courcelle, *Histoire littéraire des grandes invasions germaniques*, 3rd ed. (Paris, 1964), 45-56.

Alans, Burgundians, and Sueves crossed the Rhine frontier and advanced across the empire to Spain. It is not an exaggeration to say that while Alaric negotiated, Roman control in the West was lost.

The dramatic capture of Rome and its brutal if short sack did cause an immense stir of anxiety throughout the Late Antique world. Never before had the imperial walls been breached to allow barbarians to loot, rape, burn, kill, and steal with impunity. Contemporaries blamed the family of the Anicii, by far the wealthiest of the city, who owned extensive property near the Porta Salaria, through which the invaders entered. They pointed to the fact that Proba, widow of the urban prefect Probus, escaped from Rome with her daughter and granddaughter by ship for Africa, and that the family was not ruined by the attack. But it is more likely that other elements within the besieged city opened the gate by arrangement with Alaric. For the population had only just withstood a dreadful siege in the winter of 409-10, when many thousands of slaves (presumably of Gothic origin) had joined the Visigothic forces encamped outside. Food supplies were very scarce even in the storerooms of the grandest palaces. In the course of the looting, Alaric is alleged to have ordered the treasures of St. Peter's church to be spared; those of the senatorial aristocracy were not so fortunate. Among the prisoners taken hostage was Honorius's half-sister, Galla Placidia, an imperial princess, who was later married to Athaulf, Alaric's successor. The wedding, which took place in Narbonne in 414, was celebrated in traditional Roman style with fine rhetorical speeches and wedding gifts that were said to include, on the groom's side, 50 elegant Roman youths dressed in silk—another relic from the sack of 410.[19] The event enraged Honorius so much that he tried to blockade the Goths and provoke a famine in southern Gaul. In this he was successful, and the Goths were forced to move further west to Toulouse, which finally became the capital of a Visigothic kingdom. But in the agreement of 418, Honorius had to make the concession he had previously resisted: the Gothic right to settle Aquitaine, which involved the permanent loss of large areas of the empire.[20]

In other regions Honorius might delude himself into believing that imperial control might be restored. But Trier, which had served as the chief imperial residence for much of the fourth century, had to be abandoned; in its place, Arles was to become the metropolitan centre of Roman admin-

[19] Olympiodoros, frag. 24; Gordon, *Age of Attila*, 40-41; Blockley, *Fragmentary*, 2:186-89.
[20] M. Rouche, *L'Aquitaine des Wisigoths aux Arabes, 418-781: Naissance d'une région* (Paris, 1979), 19-27.

istration in what remained of Gaul.[21] Bordeaux was devastated in an attack recorded by Paulinus of Pella: "The Goths, who on the order of their king, Athaulf, were due to leave our city, where they had been admitted in peace, inflicted on us the most cruel hardships, just as if we were a people vanquished in war, and reduced our city to ashes."[22] Similarly, much of Spain was overrun by Vandals and Sueves. Despite the court's efforts to play off one group of non-Romans against another, their various occupations of imperial territory were not to be reversed. And in the case of Britain, there is evidence that Honorius himself realised that the withdrawal of Roman forces in 407 was final.[23] The dioceses of the West were effectively reduced to Italy, though many Romans continued to live in areas occupied by non-Romans.

The net result of Visigothic pressure on East and West seems not dissimilar—in both cases non-Romans were permitted to settle on imperial lands. But the treaties of 382 and 418 were made in very different situations. Although the first was agreed to after a disastrous imperial defeat, its terms were carried out fairly successfully and peacefully. Theodosius kept his new Gothic allies under control with the help of other non-Roman allies. Honorius, however, had been struggling to dominate Alaric and his successors for 16 years when he agreed to their occupation of Aquitaine. Cities had been captured, the court moved, and vast areas devastated in the long period of struggle. Worse, the chaos and confusion engendered in both Roman governing and military circles had provoked numerous other non-Romans to seize imperial lands for themselves. As Paulinus complained, "Much more frightening than the hostile horde spread out all around [were] a troop of slaves joined by some wicked youths of free birth but incensed with fury, who directed murderous attacks chiefly against the nobles."[24] While both parts of the empire were harmed, the West suffered from the Visigoths in a qualitatively more severe manner than the East.

Modes of Integration

This first large-scale westward migration reveals three important processes at work in the relations between Romans and non-Romans. The first sprang from an imperial tradition of employing mercenary fighting forces, which allowed certain non-Roman leaders to be incorporated into the em-

[21] A. Chastagnol, "Le repli sur Arles des services administratifs gaulois en l'an 407 de notre ère," RH 249 (1973): 23-40.

[22] Paulinus of Pella, Eucharisticos, verses 311-14; in C. Moussy, ed., Poème d'Action et de Grâces et Prière (Paris, 1974), 78-79, with French translation.

[23] P. Salway, Roman Britain (Oxford, 1981), 426-44; Matthews, Western Aristocracies, 320.

[24] Paulinus, Eucharisticos, verses 330-36 (in Moussy, Poème d'Action, 80-81).

pire's military and social order. The second was due to the barbarian adoption of Arian Christianity. And the third concerns the non-Roman awareness of differences between the Roman East and West and corresponding imperial rivalries symbolised by the competition between Constantinople and Rome.

Looking first at the means whereby ethnic commanders (and their followers) could assume a rather imperial style, it is important to remember that by the end of the fourth century, Germanic leaders held nearly all the highest military positions in the empire, and commanded a variety of non-Roman contingents.[25] Most emperors depended on them, as Honorius relied on Stilicho. As *magister militum*, Stilicho had defended Italy against numerous invading forces in a competent manner. His campaign against Alaric in Greece may not have been entirely successful, but there was no doubting his capabilities. Having won Theodosius's approval for his marriage to the emperor's niece, Serena, he celebated his authority in the West by marrying his own daughter to Honorius.[26] By such means, military commanders of non-Roman origins tried to become respectable and rise in Roman society. Their aspirations, however, did not alter the fact that barbarian fighting forces dominated the nominally Roman armies; the traditional legionary had been almost completely replaced by mercenaries, slave and prisoner recruits, and bands of federates led by their own ethnic leaders. In their skilful manipulation of imperial candidates, Arbogastes (a Frank), Stilicho (Vandal), Ricimer (Sueve), and Odovacer (Herulian) usurped more effective control than most usurpers.

As a result of Germanic incorporation and intermarriage, the clear-cut distinction between Roman and non-Roman began to blur. The fact that Galla Placidia, daughter of Theodosius I, did not appear to object to her enforced alliance with the Visigoth Athaulf, and that their firstborn was christened Theodosius after his grandfather, suggests that had the child survived he would have been accepted as imperial. After Athaulf's death, Galla made endless difficulties over the proposed remarriage to a respectable Roman called Constantius.[27] Apart from those ancient senatorial families who prided themselves on inbred and endogamous unions, most mem-

---

[25] Jones, *LRE*, 1:159-60.

[26] S. Mazzarino, *Stilichone e la crisi imperiale dopo Teodosio* (Rome, 1942); S. I. Oost, *Galla Placidia Augusta* (Chicago, 1968), 99-101. Theodosius had adopted Serena as his own daughter. Olympiodoros, frag. 2 concerning Stilicho can be found in Gordon, *Age of Attila*, 25-26; Blockley, *Fragmentary*, 2:152-55.

[27] Oost, *Galla Placidia*, 106-108, 127-30, 133-34; Olympiodoros, frag. 6, the death of Galla's son, Theodosius; cf. frag. 33, her opposition to Constantius, in Gordon, *Age of Attila*, 41-42, 43; Blockley, *Fragmentary* 2:188-89, 196-97. On the continuing importance of such marriage alliances, see R. C. Blockley, "Roman-Barbarian Marriages in the Late Empire," *Florilegium* 4 (1982): 63-79.

bers of governing circles had experienced a certain amount of intermarriage
by the fifth century. Among military and court families, especially, this
was emphasized by the custom of sending hostages to the enemy to ensure
that terms were honoured. From the Roman side, for example, Aetius had
been sent as a hostage to Alaric; he married a Gothic lady and later sent
their son, Carpileon, as hostage to the Huns.[28] Similarly, the sons of barbarian chieftains often spent part of their youth in the confines of an imperial palace, a custom that generally influenced their outlook. As a result
of this prolonged experience of intermarriage, both "Roman" troops and
their leaders had become in effect a series of mixed factions warring for control. Each claimed to be more "Roman" than the others, yet no one candidate had significantly greater authenticity than the next.

This process was not restricted to the West. An identical development
of dependence had brought non-Roman forces into the armies of the East
Roman Empire and even into ruling circles. Fravitta, the Gothic general
who served Theodosius I, was followed by Gainas, another Goth, as *magister militum*. Then, after a twenty-year gap, the Germans Ardaburius and
Areobindus shared with two Romans the command of the Persian campaign of 421-22.[29] From the mid-fifth century, however, a line of soldier-
emperors established a novel type of rule. They took care to marry into imperial circles and to balance the prominence of one ethnic group at court by
favouring others. And in contrast to the West, imperial administration
continued to function in traditional fashion despite this non-Roman intrusion. Eastern success in absorbing ethnic federates and allies was greatly
assisted by a firm continuity in the imperial civil service, which maintained
basic control through the collection of taxes and provision of governmental
services. This was also helped by a closer supervision of fighting forces,
their more regular pay, training, and inspiration to overcome direct assault, as in the case of the Huns, for example. Hunnish attacks in the early
fifth century, comparable in strength and ferocity to those of similar tribes
in the West at that time, had a less permanently damaging effect. East Roman forces managed to counterattack, checking the advances on Constantinople in 448 and using all possible diplomatic skills and financial in-
ducements to turn Attila away.[30] The fact that these forces were largely of
non-Roman origin confirms and illustrates the integrative powers of the
East, which still preserved a Roman identity.

If these means of incorporation rendered military leaders acceptably
"Roman," then their faith made them welcome in the Christian circles of

[28] Gordon, *Age of Attila*, 48-49.
[29] Jones, *LRE*, 1:178-82.
[30] Ibid., 1:193-94.

the empire. The Goths, like the Vandals and Burgundians further west, had converted in the course of the fourth century, adopting the Arian beliefs supported by most eastern emperors after Constantine I. Military service under these emperors, regular contact with Roman traders across the Danube frontier, and Arian missionaries from the eastern empire all played a part in promoting this second process of incorporation. In Bishop Ulfila (341-81), the Visigoths of Nicopolis had a powerful spiritual and temporal leader, who translated the Bible into their own tongue, using a newly devised Gothic alphabet.[31] When Theodosius refused to allow the Arians to hold services within the city walls of Constantinople, the Goths sang the psalms in Gothic. Two hundred years later, some Gothic mercenaries, now characterised as a "barbarian people from the West" (i.e. Italy), appealed to the emperor to set aside a church outside the walls where their wives and children could celebrate. Even though Arian dogma had been condemned as heretical (in 325, 381, and at many later dates), Gothic adherents were recognised as Christian heretics rather than pagans, and their Christian heroes who had suffered martyrdom at pagan hands were celebrated throughout the empire.[32] Although the Gothic Bible did not remain in use for very long, the sixth-century *Codex Argenteus*, now preserved at Uppsala, indicates that luxury copies were made. The magnificent purple parchment manuscript with gold and silver letters was probably produced in Ravenna, where the Gothic cathedral of St. Anastasia was served by a large clerical and lay association in the mid-sixth century.[33]

Thus when Alaric arrived in the West seeking a permanent and fertile settlement for his Visigoths, he came as a Christian with long exposure to Roman traditions. The western court had been moved in 383, from Trier to Milan, where a vigorous Christian community under Bishop Ambrose (374-97) influenced all its activities. As a staunch opponent of Arianism, Ambrose was not predisposed towards the Goths, though he recognised the importance of a barbarian commitment to Christianity. But Milan, like several other western cities, was sharply divided by pro-Nicaea Christians and Arian Christians, stubbornly opposed to the Nicaean Council, a factor

[31] E. A. Thompson, *The Visigoths in the Time of Ulfila* (Oxford, 1966); H. Wolfram, "Gotische Studien II," *Mitteilungen des Instituts für Österreichische Geschichtsforschung* 83 (1975): 289-324.

[32] *Codex Theodosianus* 16.5.15, cf. 13; John of Ephesos, *Ecclesiastical History*, 3.26; Thompson, *Visigoths*, 95, 99.

[33] J. O. Tjäder, "Der Codex argenteus in Uppsala und der Buchmeister Viliaric in Ravenna," in *Studia Gotica*, ed. U. E. Hagberg (Stockholm, 1972), 144-64; cf. G. Kampers, "Anmerkungen zum lateinisch-gotischen Ravennater Papyrus von 551," *HJ* 101 (1981): 141-51.

that impeded the progress of the new faith.[34] It also made only slow headway against the traditional observance of pagan rites, especially in the ancient capital. Deprived of a permanent imperial presence since the time of
Constantine I, pagan administration was perpetuated there without
change. Rome remained the largest and richest city of the West, where
Christianity had few adherents of any power. Excluded from the life of the
court and imperial power, the aristocratic families of the metropolis devoted themselves to their own city and their leisure—duties frequently
combined by holding public office and performing services such as work on
civic buildings, the provision of entertainment for the population, and the
commemoration of pagan protectors in religious rites.[35] Maintaining the
old traditions was their response to the changes going on in the Roman
world, and they had the means to do so. Unlike many aristocratic elites,
their wealth in land, scattered through several parts of the empire, and their
powers of patronage secured a lasting dominance. New ideas, whether in
matters of belief or diplomacy, penetrated slowly; the pressures of Christians and barbarians alike were often ignored.

Given this marked contrast between a firmly pagan Rome and an increasingly Christian imperial court in Constantinople, it is not surprising
that relations between the Senate and emperor should be strained. The debate over the Visigoths, specifically how to deal with Alaric, exaggerated
these differences. For had the Roman Senate listened to the arguments for
buying him off and cooperated with those realists at court, Rome would
have been spared. But early in 408, when Honorius and Stilicho went from
Ravenna to inform the Senate that they needed 4,000 lbs. of gold, they
were rebuffed. It was not the sum that was criticised: an individual senator
like Symmachus spent half that amount on his son's praetorian games in
401, and Maximus would spend exactly the same sum to purchase his son's
praetorship.[36] It was the principle of accepting the barbarian's terms rather
than fighting. So by temporising over Stilicho's diplomatic initiative, the
Senate unwittingly encouraged the coup d'état that would overthrow him
and bring Alaric to the gates of Rome. And when the siege of 408-409 was
finally lifted, the terms for peace were more costly; Rome had to provide
5,000 lbs. of gold, 30,000 lbs. of silver, and great quantities of spices and
clothing for the Visigoth.[37] Nor did this arrangement last; just over a year
later Alaric was back, again frustrated by Rome's refusal to negotiate.

[34] Matthews, *Western Aristocracies*, 383-87, cf. 183-222; R. Krautheimer, *Three Christian Capitals* (Berkeley, 1983), 69-92.

[35] B. Croke and J. Harries, *Religious Conflict in Fourth-Century Rome: A Documentary Study* (Sydney, 1982), esp. 98-121; L. Cracco Ruggini, "Simboli di battaglia ideologica nel tardo ellenismo," in *Studia Storia O. Bertolini* (Pisa, 1972), 1:177-251.

[36] Matthews, *Western Aristocracies*, 277-78, 384.

[37] Ibid., 287-89.

The third process at work in the migration period is harder to identify and is less immediately linked to Roman/non-Roman relations. It concerns the relative strengths of West and East within the empire, the growing dominance of Constantinople over Rome or any other imperial residence (Milan, Ravenna), and the slow transfer of supreme authority to the eastern court.[38] Non-Romans, however, were intimately involved in this process. Alaric participated in Theodosius's second expedition to the West to put down a usurper, and witnessed the fact that imperial authority there was evidently less secure. Honorius's long reign (395-423) did nothing to correct this western pattern of weak government. The emperor showed consistently poor judgement, vacillated, and allowed himself to be persuaded by a Gothic bandit, Sarus, to make war on Alaric. He was no doubt overwhelmed by the variety of problems facing imperial administration in the West, but when he had experienced advisers like Stilicho urging a moderate course, he chose to ignore them, and refused to stand by them when other factions sought their downfall.

In the matter of accommodating non-Romans, the West was always at a disadvantage. For the lure of fertile lands further west provided the East with an additional and powerful instrument for reducing barbarian pressures. The promise of territories available in the less densely populated western half of the empire, whose wealth was doubtless exaggerated by eastern diplomats and non-Roman embassies alike, persuaded the Visigoths and many who came after them to move on westward. Through this device, the initial passage of Alaric's Goths was to be repeated several times, its last employment resulting in the triumphant settlement of the Ostrogoths in northern Italy at the end of the fifth century. Such possibilities did not exist in the West. As all the invaders had come from the East or the North via Illyricum, Moesia, and the Rhine and Danube provinces, they were familiar with conditions there and could not be persuaded to return. Inter-tribal rivalry and warfare enabled western officials to play off one band against another, but such competition rarely resulted in increased security.

In 416, for instance, the Visigothic king, Wallia, negotiated "permission" from Honorius to re-establish "Roman" authority in Spain, then occupied by Sueves and Vandals. As a consequence, the Visigoths overran the Iberian peninsula (which they held until the Arab conquest of 711). This in turn forced the Vandals into Mauretania (429) and began the conquest of North Africa, certainly the richest of the western provinces and one that had almost avoided non-Roman threats to that date. By 431 Genseric had

[38] S. G. MacCormack, "Roma, Constantinopolis, the Emperor and His Genius," *Classical Quarterly*, n.s., 25 (1975): 131-50. Even before 378, elite troops had been withdrawn from the West; see D. Hoffmann, *Das Spätrömische Bewegungsheer und die Notitia dignitatum*, 2 vols. (Dusseldorf, 1969), 1:379-88, 425-37, 440-49, 458-68.

captured Hippo (St. Augustine died during the long siege in the summer of 430), and eight years later the capital, Carthage, fell to Vandal control.[39] The loss of Africa was a far more serious and lasting blow to the western empire than the prolonged warfare in Gaul and Italy, for it established an aggressive Arian power that persecuted orthodox Christians and pagan Romans equally; it also threatened the western basin of the Mediterranean. Sicily, frequently raided, was overrun in 468; and when Genseric sacked Rome (in 455, forty-five years after Alaric), he inflicted a destruction commemorated in western vocabulary as "vandalism."[40] But it is not often realised that the Vandals came from the south. Through a combination of firmer governmental control, greater financial resources, and diplomatic experience, imperial officials in the East managed to ease the passage of successive non-Roman forces westward. And finding a lack of precisely those qualities among most western administrators, successive groups settled within the empire wherever they could. The disruption of imperial order, sometimes accompanied by heavy loss of life and property, could only exacerbate an inherent weakness in the West and reduce its status relative to the East. In the course of Honorius's, reign, a permanent superiority was consolidated in Constantinople. Western emperors would henceforth be kept in a position of inferiority as junior to their colleagues in the East, while the transfer of supreme authority from Old Rome to New Rome was completed.

The Consolidation of Barbarian Assimilation

While the Vandals remained noted for their antagonism to Roman rule, once other newcomers were settled on imperial lands they gradually began to take over Roman institutions. They all, even the Vandals, tried to maintain the by-now weakened financial system of taxation. But since they did not need to recruit and pay troops—the major expense of Late Antique rulers in the West—taxation was not of such importance as before.[41] Gradually, as they became more confident of their own autonomy, the newcomers adapted Roman administration, coinage, ceremonial, and patronage for their own use. Imperial influence is particularly visible in the barbarian law codes written down in the late fifth and early sixth centuries. And the Vis-

---

[39] C. Courtois, *Les Vandales et l'Afrique* (Paris, 1955).

[40] Ibid., 58-64.

[41] On the debate over barbarian attitudes towards imperial taxation, see C. Wickham, "The Other Transition: From the Ancient World to Feudalism," *Past and Present* 103 (1984): 3-36, esp. 19-22; cf. W. Goffart, *Barbarians and Romans* A.D. *418-584* (Princeton, 1980). See also the review-article by M. Cesa, "Hospitalitas o oltre 'techniques of accomodation'? A proposito di un libro recent," *Archivio Storico Italiano* 140 (1982): 539-52.

igothic codification of Roman law, known as the *Breviary of Alaric* (506), deepened and extended this throughout the West.[42]

One of the most successful and lasting fusions of Roman and barbarian elements was achieved by the Ostrogothic kingdom of Theodoric, who ruled from 497 to 526. Like many non-Roman princes, he had been a child hostage at the eastern court, where long exposure to imperial customs and court intrigues gave him an excellent preparation for Late Antique government. And like many who challenged imperial power, he gained the rank of *magister militum* from Emperor Zeno and permission to lead his people into Moesia to spare the eastern provinces additional insecurity and looting. Theodoric's Italian campaign of 488-93 followed a familiar pattern and settled the last of the Germanic peoples within the old boundaries of the empire. It culminated in a successful three-year siege of Ravenna, previously deemed almost impregnable, after which Odovacer and his supporters were killed. Four years later, Emperor Anastasios (491-518) recognised Theodoric as king and granted him authority to share in appointing consuls in the West—a more substantial form of "Roman" control than ever previously conceded.[43] No Goth was ever nominated as consul, however: a dual system of administration was preserved, whereby the Ostrogoths governed the Gothic population (and whatever other non-Roman kingdoms they could bring into their sphere of influence) while Roman officials governed the Roman population. But despite the distinction, a flourishing culture coalesced and lasted for over 50 years.[44] In the imperial environment of Ravenna, to which Theodoric added his own monuments, the Gothic king reigned as a very impressive "sub-emperor." He also made a point of allying his family with all the major non-Roman powers in the West—Franks in northern Gaul, Burgundians, Thuringians, Visigoths, and Vandals—as if to re-create a semblance of unity through Gothic domination and intermarriage.[45] Whatever personal skills he brought to this achievement, his long apprenticeship in the eastern court and arguments with Zeno probably influenced him decisively.

But it was not only those candidates most familiar with Roman customs who aspired to imperial recognition. Some who had witnessed the Roman way of life in its disjointed and threatened western form during the fifth century were still attracted. The manner in which Clovis, king of the Franks, celebrated his nomination by Emperor Anastasios to the position

---

[42] E. A. Thompson, *The Goths in Spain* (Oxford, 1969), 13-14,114-18, 134-39, 156.

[43] Procopius, *Wars* 5.1.9-15, 24-29; W. Ensslin, *Theodorich der Grosse*, 2nd ed. (Munich, 1959); fragments of Priscus, Malchus, and John of Antioch, in Gordon, *Age of Attila*, 157-83; cf. Blockley, *Fragmentary*, for Priscus and Malchus.

[44] B. Ward-Perkins, *From Classical Antiquity to the Middle Ages* (Oxford, 1984), 160-66.

[45] R. Folz et al., *De l'Antiquité au Monde mediéval* (Paris, 1972), 71.

of honorary consul in 508 reveals this appeal. After ceremoniously putting on the purple costume restricted to the holders of this office, Clovis entered Tours in state, observing the imperial "Adventus" (arrival) ritual and scattering coins among the crowd. Whether he considered himself more as a dutiful son or as an equal ally of the eastern ruler, he did not want to miss the opportunity to show off his new title correctly.[46] Thus, within a century of their settlement in Gaul north of the Loire, Clovis had accepted for the Franks this Roman title and honourable position within the empire.

Such a form of incorporation, however, could not conceal the fact that Clovis ruled as an independent king in northern Gaul, whereas Anastasios governed the still intact eastern half of the Roman Empire. The emperor had to deal with threats of invasion and constructed the Long Walls between the Black Sea and the Dardanelles to deter marauding bands of Bulgars.[47] But his capital was never sacked, and he had sufficient resources to counter the much more serious rivalry of the Persian Empire in a long campaign (502-506). The East had been spared much of the devastation that enfeebled the West and had grown proportionately stronger, creating a greater imbalance between the two halves.

EAST AND WEST AT THE ACCESSION OF JUSTINIAN (527)

When Justinian succeeded his uncle Justin as emperor, the area under his direct control remained more or less what it had been in Diocletian's time. Of the original dioceses, Moesia had been subdivided to create two, Dacia and Macedonia, which were also identified as Eastern Illyricum (Western Illyricum was basically the ancient diocese of Pannonia); and Egypt had been separated from Oriens. Berber incursions into Libya and Egypt had reduced the security of non-fortified settlements, and pressures on the eastern and Danubian frontiers caused a certain instability, but no major losses had been registered.

In contrast, the seven dioceses of the West were shared between non-Roman rulers and in some cases obliterated. Britain was totally abandoned to Celtic and Saxon occupants; parts of Africa had been taken over by desert nomads, primarily the extreme west and a thin coastal strip between Carthage and Libya; and Western Illyricum had been so deeply scarred by persistent military activity that it had almost ceased to function as a unit of imperial administration. In Italy, Gaul, Burgundy, Spain, and central North Africa, barbarian kings ruled, sometimes in the name of Rome, but with unrestricted independence in fact. They pursued what has been called

[46] Gregory of Tours, *HF* 2.38 (English translation, 154); Courcelle, *Histoire littéraire*, 239-50; A. Angenendt, *Kaiserherrschaft und Königstaufe* (Berlin/New York, 1984), 165-74.
[47] Jones, *LRE*, 1:231; Procopius, *Buildings* 4.9.6.

a "sub-Roman" way of life, conditioned by a symbiotic relationship with the culture they had conquered, facilitated by the use of Latin, which supplanted tribal vernaculars as the official language, and by the adoption of Christianity. Thus, paradoxically alien forces had become respectable allies and were perpetuating many ancient traditions. Although they could not be counted on to act in Constantinople's interests, the most striking feature of their settlement in the West became its Roman nature.

In areas beyond the Mediterranean world that had never been conquered by Caesar's legionaries, imperial culture was still influential. Contacts made by Alexander in the Persian East, which had been extended by Trajan to the Indian subcontinent, appear to have continued into the sixth century, because the commercial basis for them still prevailed. In the far northwest of Europe, a similar mechanism seems to have been responsible for drawing Ireland into the Roman sphere of trade. The import of oil, wine, pottery, and precious metals into Ireland, in exchange for indigenous metals, fitted into the pattern of Roman trading in Ceylon.[48] In addition, during the fifth and sixth centuries, Ireland provided a safe haven for refugees from warfare in Gaul and Britain. It abandoned its native ogham alphabet for Latin, a development that was to prove of momentous importance for the survival of Late Antique culture in Western Europe. But at that time these were the only direct Roman influences upon Ireland, which remained completely peripheral.[49] While Ceylon was equally distant from the Mediterranean, it was a recognised trading post between Rome and the unknown but existent world of China, linked to the Mediterranean by established maritime routes. Through Ceylon, Far Eastern silks, ceramics, spices, jewels, and other luxuries passed into the Persian Gulf as well as the eastern Mediterranean. The traders who maintained this flow dealt in both the gold coinage of Constantinople and the silver of Ctesiphon; they were more like international middlemen, fluent in many tongues, than the natives of "the islands of Britain" (?Ireland) who provided tin for Egyptian ships.[50]

[48] R. E. M. Wheeler, *Rome Beyond the Imperial Frontier* (London, 1954), 112-71; M. and L. de Paor, *Early Christian Ireland*, 2nd ed. (London, 1978), 15-48; L. Bieler, *Ireland, Harbinger of the Middle Ages* (London, 1963).

[49] De Paor and de Paor, *Early Christian Ireland*, 62 (Ogham alphabet); J. MacNeill, "The Beginnings of Latin Culture in Ireland," *Studies: An Irish Quarterly Review* 20 (1931): 39-48; K. Meyer, *Learning in Ireland in the Fifth Century and the Transmission of Letters* (Dublin, 1913).

[50] N. Pigulewskaja, *Byzanz auf den Wegen nach Indien* (Amsterdam, 1969), 70-87, 134-49; Wheeler, *Rome Beyond*, 172-75; A. D. H. Bivar, "The History of Eastern Iran," in *Cambridge History of Iran*, vol. 3 (1) (1983), 198-217; cf. V. G. Lukonin, "Industry, Commerce, Communications," in ibid., vol. 3 (2) (1983), 738-44; H. Miyakawa and A. Kollautz, "Ein Dokument zum Fernhandel zwischen Byzanz und China zur Zeit Theophylakts," *BZ* 77

Constantinople was well placed to take advantage of the ancient trading routes as well as to develop new ones (across the Black Sea to the river estuaries of the Caucasus, and overland to the Far East). But in the centuries since its foundation, the "Queen City," now the undisputed eastern capital, had been increasingly preoccupied with two non-Roman forces, both of eastern origin. The first force was the material threat posed by Sasanian Persia; the second, the spiritual challenge of Christianity. Ancient Iran had historically been the main rival of both Greece and Rome and had always disputed their claims to universal rule. The dangers posed by the revived Sasanian dynasty of Ctesiphon dominated most fifth- and sixth-century eastern emperors.[51] As they aspired to the imperial tradition that Rome held sway throughout the known world, rulers such as Anastasios had to take the Persian challenge seriously; it was essential to confine the Zoroastrian fire-worshippers to their own sphere. Despite its greater resources and stability, Constantinople had to come to terms with its powerful neighbour. Co-existence with Iran undermined its own cherished ideology of superiority. In this way, the tradition was gradually modified to allow the dominance of other powers in regions distant from and foreign to Rome. "Universalism" continued in theory but was limited in practice.

Christianity, on the other hand, presented a threat to the official pagan worship of the empire, which had been combined in classical Rome with a developed emperor cult. During the period of Late Antiquity, as the new faith spread deeper roots and won respect in all regions of the empire, favoured by imperial support, a Christian role for the emperor commensurate with his past pagan status as a god had to be devised. Two hundred years before the time of Justinian, the basic accommodation was achieved by Eusebios, bishop of Caesarea (315-40), who developed the notion of a human viceroy dispensing Divine justice on earth in God's name with Constantine I in mind.[52] As the first overtly Christian emperor, Constantine was well suited for this role, which also drew on Old Testament models. Eusebios's record of his reign, preserved in the *Life of Constantine* and the eulogistic oration delivered on the thirtieth anniversary of his accession (the *Tricen-*

(1984): 6-19; on tin from the islands of Britain, see Leontios, *Vita Iohannis*, ch. 10, ed. H. Gelzer (Leipzig, 1893), 19; ed. with French translation by A.-J. Festugière (Paris, 1974), 453; English translation in E. Dawes and N. H. Baynes, *Three Byzantine Saints* (Oxford, 1948), 217.

[51] D. Oates, "Beyond the Frontiers of Rome: The Rise and Fall of Sasanian Iran," in D. Talbot Rice, ed., *The Dark Ages* (London, 1965), 15-38; *Cambridge History of Iran*, vol. 3 (1 and 2).

[52] W. Ensslin, *Gottkaiser und Kaiser von Gottes Gnaden*, Sitzungsberichte der philos.-hist. Abt. der Bayerischen Akademie der Wissenschaften zu München (1943): Heft 6; J. Sansterre, "Eusèbe de Césarée et la naissance de la théorie césaropapiste," *B* 42 (1972): 131-95, 532-94; T. D. Barnes, *Constantine and Eusebius* (Cambridge, Mass., 1981).

nalia of 336), enabled later writers to elevate Constantine to the position of a saint.[53] But it is not clear whether the imperial image was immediately as powerful in its new Christian guise as it had been under Caesar and Augustus. And what power it had derived from the incorporation of Christianity into a pagan role and relationship to the emperor, rather than from a true conversion of the emperor.

The combination of the two forces reinforced their tendency to reduce imperial authority, the one at the level of political reality (by imposing on New Rome a rival of equal sophistication and military strength), the other at the level of religious and hence political belief (by establishing a Supreme Judge over the life to come). In the two hundred years that passed between Constantine I and Justinian, the rulers of Sasanian Iran had consolidated their authority over a vast area surrounding the Fertile Crescent, while the Christian church had extended obedience to its faith so widely that it might claim to be "universal." Since the Persians maintained traditions as ancient as those claimed by Constantinople, they had to be treated with respect. Yet when the King of Kings, Kavadh, asked Justin I to adopt his favourite son, Chosroes, the emperor replied that Roman law did not permit such a thing. Only an adoption according to barbarian custom could be offered. The emperor's nephew, Justinian, undoubtedly approved of this insult, which could only result in war.[54] But at Justinian's accession in 527 he quickly arranged a ceasefire, and after much frontier skirmishing this was finalised as the "everlasting" peace, signed in 532. Justinian regularly dismissed Zoroastrian pagan beliefs, while he insisted on controlling the precise definitions of Christian faith.

In these respects, therefore, Justinian reigned in traditional Roman style, quite unhampered by the restrictions implied by the changed circumstances of the sixth century.[55] Much older, biblical models also provided inspiration for his grandiose schemes. Whether or not he consciously competed with the Old Testament lawgivers and judges, Moses and Solomon, his determination to be measured by their scale and achievement is very clear. While this standard of comparison had never been absent from Christian thinking, with Justinian it assumed a more general currency. Today he is probably remembered most for his codification of Roman law, the

---

[53] *De Vita Constantini*, in *Eusebius: Werke*, ed. F. Winkelmann, Band I (Berlin, 1975), see especially 2.1-4 and 7.12 (199, 215); F. Winkelmann, "Das hagiographische Bild Konstantins I im mittelbyzantiner Zeit," in *Beiträge zur byzantinischen Geschichte im 9.-11. Jahrhundert*, ed. V. Vavřínek (Prague, 1978), 179-203.

[54] Procopius, *Wars* 1.11 (The Persian War) (English translation, 1:83-95); R. Browning, *Justinian and Theodora* (London, 1971), 52-53.

[55] Jones, *LRE*, 1:270, describes Justinian as "a Roman to the core"; cf. T. Honoré, *Tribonian* (London, 1978).

Codex Justinianus issued in 529 and revised in 534, to which he subsequently added further new laws, *Novellae*, the first Roman rulings written originally in Greek. Justinian is also known as a great builder, not only of fortifications, castles, and public buildings (cisterns, colonnades, stoas, etc.), but also of churches. The domed church of Holy Wisdom (St. Sophia), which still stands in Istanbul, was completed at his orders in 536. If an apocryphal tale is to be believed, the emperor had intended the new building to rival even the Temple of Solomon, for at the dedication ceremony he is supposed to have fallen to his knees, saying, "Solomon, I have surpassed thee," and visitors to St. Sophia today might well concur. This pervasive dominance of the ancient world is also revealed in the church of St. Polyeuktos (524-27), constructed by Juliana Anicia, one of the richest individuals in Constantinople. She was a member of the distinguished Roman family of the Anicii in the East. Her church was built to exactly the same dimensions as the original Temple, using the same royal foot of measurement, and decorated with identical symbols of ancient royal authority, which aroused Justinian's envy.[56]

Although the emperor paid particular attention to the needs of the capital—provision of fresh water supplies, free distribution of grain, and public entertainment (the bread and circuses traditional to Roman city life)—he also built extensively in many other centres of the empire, dedicating churches to the Virgin in some of the more remote cities, as well as magnificent new buildings in Jerusalem, Ravenna, Carthage, and many others. In conjunction with his concern for imperial splendour, Justinian reorganised the elaborate ceremonies of the eastern court, which were recorded by an official, Peter the patrician. He also attempted to promote an exclusively Christian form of education, which removed all traces of pagan philosophy and practice, and to regulate the beliefs of the entire Christian world through an oecumenical council. Such attention to correct teaching and doctrine was typical of the imperial ideal of total mastery, which had been practised by Justinian's pagan predecessors in a very similar fashion. In the early sixth century, however, it represented a much greater degree of control than was customary in the West, where few traces of such a highly centralised autocratic system of government remained.[57]

[56] Gregory of Tours, *Liber in gloria martyrum beatorum*, ed. B. Krusch, in *MGH, SSRM*, vol. 1 (Hannover, 1885), 102; R. M. Harrison, "The Church of St. Polyeuktos in Istanbul and the Temple of Solomon," in *Okeanos: Essays Presented to Ihor Ševčenko, Harvard Ukrainian Studies* 7 (1983): 276-79.

[57] Procopius, *Buildings*; Averil Cameron, "Images of Authority: Elites and Icons in Late Sixth Century Byzantium," *Past and Present* 84 (1979): 3-35, esp. 7-10; S. MacCormack, *Art and Ceremonial in Late Antiquity* (Berkeley, 1981), 222-66.

Justinian's Conquests in the West

Despite the transformation of the West, even 250 years after the first impact of the incursions, many features of Roman life survived and continued to mould the barbarian occupation. Needless to say, these Roman aspects were not identical with equivalent features in the eastern half of the empire. But they did spring from the same tradition and were recognisably from the same endurant system. Justinian could justifiably claim to perpetuate them in a more thoroughly Roman fashion, being the sole Roman emperor, ruling from New Rome over Roman citizens (*Romani*, in Greek *Rômaioi*). It was with this confidence in the ancient traditions that he launched his campaign to bring the western Mediterranean back under imperial control; to reassert Rome's right, now transferred to the Bosphoros, to rule over its lake.

His ambitious plans were not fully realised, but in large parts of Africa, Sicily, Italy, and southeastern Spain, direct rule from Constantinople was established by the 550s. The cost to the East, however, was very heavy, especially as the imperial treasury had already been depleted by Justinian's eastern campaigns and extravagant building projects. In the case of Vandal Africa, a rapid success made Carthage the base and centre of supplies for the Italian campaign. Although the imperial commander Belisarios was welcomed into Rome in 536, he made little headway against the Goths based in Ravenna; local resistance prevented a repeat of the African performance.[58] From within Naples, the Jewish residents financed a strenuous defence against the forces of Constantinople. So what should have been a triumphant reconquest became instead a twenty-year struggle, marked by as many setbacks as victories, and more importantly, by the devastation of Italy. At the lowest point Rome was besieged for one year, sacked by Totila and left empty (546); his Gothic troops preferred to camp outside the walls.[59] To an eastern contemporary, the writer who continued the *Chronicle* of Zachariah of Mitylene, the proverbial wealth of Rome was still something extraordinary; he lists in awe the number of palaces, houses, markets, theatres, public lavatories, free-standing statues in gold, bronze, and marble, churches, and myriad other facilities (which had been ruined by

[58] For a summary of the conquests, see Jones, *LRE*, 1:273-78, 288-91, 292-93. Procopius gives a detailed account in *The Gothic War*, books 5-8 of his *Wars* (English translation, vols. 3-5).

[59] See Procopius, *Wars* 5.8.41; 5.10.24-26, on the Jews of Naples; cf. L. Cracco Ruggini, "Tolleranza e Intolleranza nella società tardo-antica: il caso degli Ebrei," *Ricerche di storia sociale e religiosa* 23 (1983): 27-43. On the long siege and fall of Rome, see Procopius, *Wars* 7.10-36; Zachariah of Mitylene, *Syriac Chronicle*, 10.15.

Totila). And he concludes with the assurance that the eternal city will recover this immense prosperity precisely because Rome will last forever.[60]

As it turned out, this confidence was misplaced. Although the western
capital had survived sacks and pillages before, its destruction by Totila was
a turning point. Bad relations between the old Roman aristocracy, which
had preserved a semblance of its former power in the autonomous management of the Senate, and the eastern court, which represented a parvenu
capital, a recent creation, did nothing to help. As far as Justinian was concerned, this distaste may have been mutual, for the indefatigable builder
provided no major constructions for the city when it was finally reoccupied.
His commander Narses repaired the walls, aqueducts, and bridges, and individual eastern officials patronised the building of new churches.[61] In general, however, the old metropolis was allowed to fall into decay while Ravenna, the city favoured by the Goths, continued as the effective capital of
the reconquered diocese of Italy. Ravenna, in fact, would survive as an imperial stronghold for 200 years; even Carthage would enjoy a fairly prosperous existence for over a century; but Rome was not revitalised. The emperor abandoned it, and only indigenous Christian forces were to prevent
it later from passing under permanent Lombard control.

Whether hostility to the East was widespread in central and northwestern Italy and added to the length and bitterness of the campaign is hard to
judge.[62] But one result of the war was precisely a heightened sense of antagonism to officials from Constantinople, starting with tax agents, which
provoked a resistance akin to that generated by civil war. Another was the
poverty and hunger that followed on the outbreaks of plague and disruption of agriculture, a development exacerbated by the flight of many well-
to-do families to the East. After the capture of King Witiges in 540 and
his removal as an honoured hostage to Constantinople, most high-placed
Goths and families of senatorial standing left. Those like Cassiodorus who
had served in the Gothic administration could see that it was ruined and
sought positions in the East, some with considerable success. A small number turned north instead, offering their services to other kingdoms where
perhaps they had ties with ruling families. But to all who wished to maintain a proximity to Roman and imperial ways, the obvious place to go was
Constantinople, which had become the sole centre of government and patronage. The city acted as a magnet for those with resources and skills,

[60] Zachariah, 10.16.

[61] R. Krautheimer, *Rome: Profile of a City, 312-1308* (Princeton, 1980), 64, 94; on the
decline of the Senate of Rome, see T. S. Brown, *Gentlemen and Officers* (London, 1984), 21-
30; on the neglect of its monuments, see Ward-Perkins, *From Classical Antiquity*, 47-48.

[62] J. Moorehead, "Italian Loyalties During Justinian's Gothic War," *B* 53 (1983): 575-
96, suggests general support for Constantinople.

while at the same time it became the focus for resentment and hatred amongst those who had no choice but to remain in Italy.[63]

The ultimate failure of Justinian's reconquest was indicative of the changed character of empire, as well as the subtle influences of non-Roman elements in those regions brought back into imperial orbit. There was no possibility of re-establishing the western empire of the third century, nor was Justinian ruling over the same empire as Constantine. His empire was now one political system among many, and one Roman system among others that also claimed to rule in the name of Rome. Its imperial status could be more easily proved, its descent from the absolute authority of ancient rulers was direct, but its power was not equivalent to its claims upon the past. Challenged from a variety of geographical directions and by very different enemies, Justinian's reaction was to fortify and garrison the immense frontiers that defined his empire. This appreciation of weaknesses led him to build walls and fortresses in central Greece, Nubia, North Africa, and Kirkission in eastern Mesopotamia, to no avail. There was no way that every Roman border in the reconstituted empire of the mid-sixth century could be effectively defended against the disciplined forces of Persia, or against the Arab and Berber nomads, Slavic tribes, and organised Lombard bands that would shortly break through.

Justinian, however, remained scornful of western barbarian threats, treating only the Sasanian emperor as a serious rival. While this was traditional, it also reveals an assumption about the West, namely that newcomers could be handled by the same combination of imperial diplomacy and bribes that had worked in the past. They also continued to be considered barbarian; an inscription from Carthagena (southern Spain) commemorates the fortifications built by an eastern military commander sent to subdue the "barbarian enemy" in 589-90.[64] Although it is not clear that Justinian employed it consciously, Late Antique culture was another factor, a sort of secret weapon in the imperial arsenal. For through the efforts of lay teachers and clergy, non-Roman elements had been absorbed into the imperial system from the third century onwards. The essential stages of acquiring Latin and adopting Christianity had been undertaken by all those who successfully set up their own states in the West. In their turn, they would influence newly arrived non-Romans along the same paths, assisted from time to time by demonstrations of the superiority of this culture from the East. Justinian's intention of supporting education in the reconquered

[63] Procopius's account of the Gothic War, while written from the East, is pervaded with these contradictory sentiments. Cf. J. J. O'Donnell, *Cassiodorus* (Berkeley, 1979); idem, "Liberius the Patrician," *Traditio* 37 (1981): 31-72.

[64] J. Vives, *Inscripciones Cristianas de la España Romana y Visigoda*, 2nd ed. (Barcelona, 1969), no. 363: "contra hostes barbaros."

areas of the West is made clear in his provision for professors of the basic subjects of ancient study. In Ravenna, Rome, Sicily, and Africa, schools were maintained; elsewhere, private tutors were employed to educate in the traditional style. While the evident incorporation of non-Roman newcomers could thus be continued, Justinian's forced unity in fact proved to be the prelude to the final disintegration of Rome's Mediterranean world.

CLASSICAL SURVIVAL: THE ECONOMIC ASPECT

The classical inheritance of Late Antiquity can be seen most clearly in the organisation of its economy and in its social structure. Here the fundamental framework developed in Greece and adapted by the Hellenistic kingdoms and Rome continued to exercise a decisive influence, the origin of which can be traced back to the Greek city (*polis*). Through their assertion that urban life was superior to any other form, the ancients bequeathed to Late Antiquity a principle of lasting significance. It did not obliterate the mainly Roman ideal of leisured rural peace, characterised by the spacious villas and hunting lodges that have been excavated throughout the empire. But it determined the priority of cities.

Since the Greek city or city-state was primarily a political and social unit, its economic independence had to be guaranteed at least in part by provision of basic foodstuffs from the surrounding countryside. On this systematic subordination of the country to the city, a complex mechanism of extraction had been constructed, which developed in Roman times into an exchange of products between various parts of the Mediterranean. In the case of very large concentrations of people, in Antioch, Alexandria, and Rome for example, supplies reached the city from different continents as well as areas not within easy reach, some in lieu of taxes. Urban tentacles extended particularly into the richest grain-producing regions of the southern Mediterranean, notably Egypt and Africa, from which Rome and later Constantinople filled their capacious granaries through annual grain fleets. As free distributions of bread and other basic necessities were also built into metropolitan life, city officials had to make sure that adequate supplies and reserves were maintained. The building of granaries, as of aqueducts and cisterns, was therefore an essential civic responsibility.[65]

[65] The ongoing debate on the ancient economy is summarised by K. Hopkins in *The Role of Trade in the Ancient Economy*, ed. P. Garnsey, K. Hopkins, and C. Whittaker (Berkeley, 1983), Introduction. On the grain trade, see G. E. Rickman, *Roman Granaries and Store Buildings* (Cambridge, 1971); idem, *The Corn Supply of Ancient Rome* (Oxford, 1980); E. Tengstrom, *Bread for the People: Studies of the Corn Supply of Rome During the Late Empire* (Stockholm, 1974). For the provision of free distributions and their effects on the economy,

By the time of Augustus (27 B.C.–A.D. 14), Rome had incorporated the Hellenistic states of Asia Minor, Syria, Palestine, and Pharaonic Egypt. As a result of these additions, the empire may have had a population of around 50 million, a figure that appears to have remained stable until the disastrous decline of the third century.[66] The distribution of population was uneven, however, with the most dense concentrations in the eastern half of the empire, where all the major cities apart from Rome were sited. While the capital continued to attract rural inhabitants, newly rich senatorial candidates, craftsmen, and entertainers from all parts of the Roman world, the cities of the West were chiefly recent foundations on a much smaller scale than their eastern equivalents. The provinces too were sparsely populated. There the main addition derived from the influx of enslaved prisoners of war, who were established as an unfree labour force on the estates of the western aristocracy. And as the source of slaves dried up from the late second century onwards—Trajan's campaigns against insurgents in the Dacian and Germanic provinces completed the process of Roman expansion—even their numbers declined. In conjunction with several other factors, this demographic decline had serious consequences, economic, social, and legal, which cannot be detailed here. Suffice it to say that the total population of the empire probably never attained the earlier level, although individual centres such as Constantinople continued to grow. Eastern cities manifested a considerable prosperity in the fourth and fifth centuries, in marked contrast to those of the West. But all suffered equally from the ravages of bubonic plague, which reached Egypt from the Far East in the 540s. From Alexandria it was carried to the eastern capital and thence to Italy, leaving countless dead not only in the cities, where people went to be sure of being buried if they succumbed, but also throughout the countryside. Recurrent attacks of the plague may have reduced the entire population by as much as a third, and left survivors fearful and despairing of the future.[67]

Prior to this devastation, however, the inheritance of the ancient world was clearly visible in the economy of the sixth century. Cities still functioned mainly as commercial entrepôts where a variety of foodstuffs, raw materials, manufactures, and luxury goods were imported and re-exported.

see Jones, *LRE*, 2:696-701; J. M. Carrié, "Les distributions alimentaires dans les cités de l'empire romain tardif," *MEFR, Antiquité* 87 (1975): 995-1101.

[66] This is the figure assumed by R. Duncan-Jones in his detailed examination of population growth during the Principate; see *The Economy of the Roman Empire: Quantitative Studies*, 2nd ed. (Cambridge, 1974).

[67] Procopius, *Wars* 2.22-23 (English translation, 1:451-73); J. B. Bury, *History of the Later Roman Empire (395-565)*, 2 vols. (London, 1923), 2:62-66; on the plague of 541-42 as a watershed between epochs, see E. Patlagean, *Pauvreté économique et pauvreté sociale à Byzance 4e-7e siècles* (Paris/The Hague, 1977), 84-92, 427-30.

This economic function had completely overtaken the original political role of the Greek *polis*, with a consequent loss of citizen democracy. Despite increasing investment in land, there was a continuing preference for urban life, and the exchange of Mediterranean products remained basic. Different goods were transported by sea on established naval routes, some as tax dues, others to be sold for profit. A developed network of maritime shippers (*navicularii*) and the ubiquitous use of imperial coinage as the medium of exchange helped to maintain the system through the third-century crisis of inflation and economic reorganisation. Under Diocletian (284-305), laws to fix prices, ensure the continuity of craft guilds, and guarantee the succession of sons to their fathers' senatorial duties attempted to stabilise the economy on traditional lines. A reformed currency, renewed army, and greatly expanded imperial bureaucracy were designed to assist in this process, which had a certain success, especially in the more prosperous regions of the East. Measures that permitted the introduction of taxation in kind rather than coin tended to undermine the system by encouraging a less monetarised and commercialised economy. Trade was not as developed in the fourth as in the second century, but it continued.[68]

Nor was the system confined to the Mediterranean. Navigation down the Red Sea, from East Africa to the Malabar coast of India, and from the Pillars of Hercules around the Bay of Biscay to northern Europe, drew raw materials and luxury products of the east and north into the Roman orbit. By the fourth century, this trade was often run by Alexandrian, Syrian, and Jewish merchants, from communities scattered through Mediterranean ports and cities, and sometimes beyond the empire. Their main profit derived from the provision of luxury goods for the richest urban dwellers and well-to-do landowners. And it was by this means that the more exotic aspects of Roman diet and fashion, such as the taste for spices, dates, figs, pearls, and silks, was extended to Visigothic Spain and Merovingian Gaul. The bulk of goods carried within the Roman world, however, continued to be those staples of ancient life: oil, wine, grain, salt, and pepper; the traditional writing material, papyrus; and the supreme metals, gold and silver. Archaeological evidence in the form of shipwrecked amphoras, made in their thousands to carry products such as Gaza wine, Spanish fish paste, or North African olive oil to a multitude of destinations, supplements the meagre literary evidence for this trade. Although the number of shipwrecks with cargoes of this type declines from the third century onwards, it is clear that international commerce went on into the sixth and seventh, even when the cities so supplied had long passed out of Roman control. Local supplies

---

[68] On the *navicularii*, see Jones, *LRE*, 2:827-29; on continuing trade, K. Hopkins, "Taxes and Trade in the Roman Empire (200 BC-AD 400)," *JRS* 70 (1980): 101-125.

replaced some goods previously acquired through this trade in some parts
of the West. But urban demand persisted, and the system continued to
meet it.[69]

Meanwhile other factors were subtly modifying the ancients' dismissive
attitude towards the countryside. While the lands of the eastern empire
were generally cultivated by small farmers, tenants, and free peasants, from
the third century onwards individual landowners in parts of Egypt, Africa,
and the West tended to invest in rural estates as a stable source of income.
This development was accompanied by the decision of many wealthy families to leave the cities and settle permanently on their country estates, a
move that was both a function and cause of urban decline. In contrast to
the collective political life of cities, in which an individual would have
many competitors, rural existence might permit one particular landowner
to establish a regional dominance, particularly visible in Italy. A family
could concentrate its control over a greater agricultural area, usually in
scattered estates rather than as one continuous bloc, thus extending the
cultivation of crops that require time to mature, notably vines and olives,
in addition to cereals. This rationalisation of agricultural productivity was
accompanied, inevitably, by an increasing stratification of the rural population. As tenant farmers of nominally free status found their resources inadequate to the competition and sought protection from imperial tax
agents on the estates of a powerful patron, they were drawn down to a position remarkably similar to that of the slaves. By the sixth century, the
coloni whose status had been depressed in this way were barely distinguish-
able from the *servi*, original slaves. The development took place against an
increasingly lawless situation, where western imperial officials lost effective control and the private armies of local notables assumed a partisan responsibility for social peace.[70]

Elsewhere, slow changes in the economy meant that some could increase
their independence. Among the work force engaged in industrial production, a greater degree of artisanal initiative may be observed, for instance

[69] The continuity of international trade was firmly argued by Pirenne, *Mohammad and
Charlemagne*, 49-82, and is supported by the growing evidence of underwater archaeology;
see for instance J. Paterson, " 'Salvation from the Sea': Amphorae and Trade in the Roman
West," *JRS* 72 (1982): 146-57, and articles in Garnsey, Hopkins, and Whittaker, *Role of
Trade*, and in D'Arms and Kopff, *The Seaborne Commerce*.

[70] Finley, *Ancient Slavery and Modern Ideology*, 140-41; P. Dockes, *Medieval Slavery and
Liberation* (London, 1982), 49-90; G. de Ste. Croix, *The Class Struggle in the Ancient Greek
World* (London, 1981), 133-74, 249-55, 373-74. R. MacMullen, *Roman Social Relations,
50 BC to AD 284* (Cambridge, Mass., 1974) traces the even earlier development of private
armies, which drove so many peasants to seek the protection of a wealthy patron; cf. B. D.
Shaw, "Bandits in the Roman Empire," *Past and Present* 105 (1984): 3-52.

in documents related to the organisation of Egyptian potteries.[71] Leases on kilns negotiated by illiterate potters in the mid-third century establish an annual payment of 15,000 jars to the owner plus smaller quantities of other sorts of pot. While they required a scribe to draw up these terms, the tenant potters were possibly benefiting from the boom in overseas trade, which put them as suppliers of the essential containers in a seller's market. The degree of autonomy should not be overestimated. The economy of the ancient world was restricted by severe parameters, which inhibited accumulation of wealth. Those who made money from trade were generally merchants acting as outfitters of large-tonnage ships, as insurance agents for risky ventures, and as negotiators for desirable luxury goods of high value. Many who succeeded in these roles sought to cast off the despised identification with commerce and did in fact gain access to the senatorial ranks as men of leisure.[72] Even aristocratic families may have indulged in a little speculation in trade when their landed estates failed to provide sufficient income. But the old bias against commerce remained a defining feature of the Roman world and did nothing to encourage economic growth and ingenuity. The system remained hedged with limitations, and investment in land continued to play the most important role.

CLASSICAL SURVIVAL: THE SOCIAL ASPECT

In conjunction with this economic legacy, Late Antiquity inherited a social organisation, which obviously relates to the survival of cities and their significance in Roman life. The ancient Greek city had depended on the loyalty and wealth of its citizen body, from which the ruling council (*curia*) was elected. These governing circles of *curiales* of different ranks assumed responsibility for the basic running of the city, established the distribution of taxation, and administered its collection. In the East, where traditions of council service were most developed, loyalty to and identification by one's particular city was a defining social factor. Even in the third and fourth centuries, when curial status brought heavy duties as well as honours, local people still aspired to it. But during that inflationary period, pressures on those in the lower ranks of curial orders resulted in a decreasing number of candidates willing and able to meet the expenses of city government.[73] The falling-off in public building and in the frequency of pub-

[71] H. Cockle, "Pottery Manufacture in Roman Egypt: A New Papyrus," *JRS* 71 (1981): 87-97. Cf. W. V. Harris, "Roman Terracotta Lamps: The Organization of an Industry," *JRS* 70 (1980): 126-45.

[72] J. D. D'Arms, *Commerce and Social Standing in Ancient Rome* (Cambridge, Mass., 1980).

[73] P. Garnsey, "Aspects of the Decline of the Urban Aristocracy in the Empire," in *Auf-*

lic entertainment reflects a growing crisis. Many who had a hereditary duty to fulfill curial service sought exemption from it, chiefly by flight into the army or imperial civil service. Evasion became so pronounced in some areas that richer *curiales* tried to reduce their own contributions by shifting responsibility onto their weaker and junior members, who were even less able to manage. The consequence of such ploys among the ruling classes was a growing inefficiency of city administration and concomitant emiseration of the urban and rural poor, tenant farmers, and tied peasants who provided food for the city.

City autonomy was further weakened by the centralising drive of the Later Roman Empire, as provincial governors and officials from the metropolitan administration were introduced as rival authorities. Through such means the empire tried to impose its own dictates into city organisation and to lay its hands on urban resources. The actual business of government—collection of taxes and maintenance of public order, regional defence, and prosperity—was gradually removed from the councils, who nonetheless had to pay for these services. Local *curiales* also found themselves obliged to fund extravagant entertainments in amphitheatres and hippodromes, to build public monuments, and to support conspicuous displays of imperial propaganda. As they progressively lost control over essential aspects of local administration, so their functions became more honorific, and wealth was elevated to the highest qualification for council service.[74]

These circumstances encouraged a development towards the slow ruralisation of the empire. As it became harder for the *curiales* to maintain their urban standing, many retired to their country villas and devoted their energies to agriculture. The maintenance of such rural retreats in addition to metropolitan residences was a marked feature of the West, and of Rome in particular. Established senatorial families all derived their basic incomes from extensive country estates. So when the western cities were threatened by the fifth-century breakdown of imperial security, this retreat to the country villa became more pronounced, leaving the urban curial orders much weaker. In the accompanying disorder, few families managed to maintain all their wealth, lands, and properties undamaged. Numerous imperial edicts ordered their return to the cities, now suffering from considerable underpopulation as well as lack of resources. But many refused and remained in the country. Some linked their fate with that of the church, becoming guardians of the Christian faith and patrons of new mo-

---

stieg und Niedergang der Römischen Welt, ed. H. Temporini, vol. 2, *Principät*, Band I (Berlin/New York, 1974), 229-52.

[74] De Ste. Croix, *Class Struggle*, 465-74.

nastic establishments. Only in Rome, where deeply conservative forces nurtured senatorial traditions, was a semblance of aristocratic control, corresponding to ancient curial self-management, preserved. And this did not prevent the scattering of noble families with famous pedigrees through rural Italy.

A similar tendency for the rich to adopt a more rural existence can be observed in parts of the East, where Abedrapsas, for instance, took pleasure in living on his rural estates. His epitaph from Frikya, Syria (dated 325) records the proud claim, "I freed myself from having to go down to the city," as well as the family's devotion to an ancestral god, Arkesilaos.[75] Despite the prosperity of urban life, fortified villas at the centre of country estates became a more common base. In late fourth-century Asia Minor, the widowed mother of St. Macrina, St. Basil, and St. Gregory ran her extensive landed properties from such a villa near the Iris River on the borders between Cappodocia, Armenia, and Pontos.[76] Although the family was descended on both sides from senatorial ranks, the children's early life was entirely rural with no local city focus. Basil was of course sent to Athens to complete his education, a tradition among such families, and Gregory became a teacher of rhetoric in Constantinople for a time. Eventually, however, they were both appointed bishops in cities not far distant from their country home. On their mother's death the family estates were divided between the nine brothers and sisters, several of whom also went into the church, taking their inheritance with them. In this way one particular family ended its tradition of curial service and dispersed its land and wealth chiefly to the benefit of the church. The pattern was novel in the late fourth century and never became as common in the East as in the West, but it presaged a future development of importance in the gradual ruralisation of the entire empire and overall decline of *curiales*.

The process was a very slow one, held up by the relatively prosperous character of eastern cities into the late sixth century, when it was still considered socially desirable to maintain both an urban establishment and the honorific duties of the curial classes. Public service, especially in one's own city, is regularly recorded in official inscriptions to benefactors and in personal statements on funerary monuments. But the balance between rich and poor in the cities tended to shift towards a predominance of the latter. As growing economic pressures produced indigence and deprivation on the land, people sought refuge in the major urban centres. The increase swelled the numbers dependent on city food distributions and imperial largesse, a

[75] *IGLS*, vol. 4 (Paris, 1955), no. 1410 (119-20).
[76] Gregory of Nyssa, *Vie de Sainte Macrine*, ed. and trans. P. Maraval (Paris, 1971), paras. 5, 7, 11, and 160-61 n. 1.

phenomenon noted by contemporaries as one that put an additional strain on resources, while at the same time elevating urban status.[77] Cities therefore attracted an influx of poorer inhabitants and simultaneously began to lose their wealthier citizens—a contrary movement of population that could only impoverish them.

It was, however, through the cities rather than the countryside that non-Romans became aware of imperial traditions and adopted Roman styles of administration, building, art, fashion, education, and law. The official linguistic usage of the cities (Latin and Greek) and their faith (Christianity) provided the media for this accommodation. Gothic and other vernaculars continued in spoken use for a while (the Visigoth Euric used a translator in his peace negotiations of 475), but declined rapidly as the newcomers extended their control over previously Roman areas and abandoned their Arian beliefs for orthodoxy. Of the barbarian vernacular tongues, only Gothic had ever had a written form, and this appears to have been replaced by Latin when the Goths converted.[78] The fact that Latin and Greek were the official languages of both the state and the church, and that Latin was an essential tool in the propagation of law (even among those not subject to Roman law in the West), ensured the supremacy of the classical languages. New social relations based on imperial and Christian patterns similarly replaced tribal organisation. Civil and military titles were taken over unofficially or bestowed by emperors who wished to settle the invaders as allies. And through the intimate connection of cities and ecclesiastical organisation, the episcopacy (frequently recruited from the aristocracy) played a major role in promoting integrated urban life-styles in the new "sub-Roman" culture of the West.[79] As a result, military leaders distributed titles and honours to their followers, patronised craftsmen, teachers, and rhetoricians at their courts, and had themselves commemorated in statues and remembered by their public works in strictly traditional Roman fashion. In 577, for instance, Chilperic "was busy building amphitheatres in Soissons and Paris, for he was keen to offer spectacles to the citizens," and he therefore ignored a challenge from his cousins, Guntram and Childebert.[80]

---

[77] Patlagean, *Pauvreté économique et pauvreté sociale*, 25-35.

[78] H. Roe, "Rome and the Early Germans: Some Sociolinguistic Observations," *Florilegium* 2 (1980): 102-120; E. A. Thompson, "Christianity and the Northern Barbarians," in *The Conflict between Paganism and Christianity in the Fourth Century*, ed. A. Momigliano (Oxford, 1963), 56-78; on spoken Gothic, see P. D. King, *Law and Society in the Visigothic Kingdom* (Cambridge, 1972), 4, and also the discussion in Chapter 6 below.

[79] F. Prinz, "Aristocracy and Christianity in Merovingian Gaul," in *Gesellschaft, Kultur, Literatur: Rezeption und Originalität im Wachsen einer europäischen Literatur und Geistigkeit: Festschrift L. Wallach*, ed. K. Bosl (Stuttgart, 1975), 153-65; G. Scheibelreiter, "Der frühfränkische Episkopat," *Frühmittelalterliche Studien* 17 (1983): 131-47.

[80] Gregory of Tours, *HF* 5.17 (English translation, 275).

CLASSICAL SURVIVAL: THE ARTISTIC ASPECT

While the poor and non-Roman were attracted to cities, and depressed *curiales* were trying to leave them, a uniform style of Christian art pervaded both urban and rural settings alike. In particular, the art of Late Antiquity exemplifies the capacity to attract and unite non-Roman forces within certain limitations. Like its culture in general, this art draws heavily on Roman models, but by the sixth century it has developed a variety of architectural forms often determined by function, and a wealth of decorative and symbolic patterns celebrated in a range of media—fresco, mosaic, sculpture, metalwork, weaving, and book illustration. These styles are the common property of the entire Mediterranean world and are imitated in regions outside the Roman frontiers. Under Justinian, craftsmen with particular skills are sent all around the empire to adorn his buildings, and everywhere they influence local artists who wish to emulate the latest metropolitan fashions.[81] The Byzantine capital undoubtedly disposes of the greatest resources and is always a setter of trends, rather than a follower. But in the mid-sixth century, the brilliance of New Rome does not diminish artistic unity. Even the poorest pilgrim to the Holy Land returns home with a small flask produced in the East, in clay rather than precious metal. Patrons commission illuminated Gospel books and liturgical silver in the styles in vogue in the established centres of Christianity, sometimes employing a pattern book but also relying on verbal descriptions of especially impressive objects. In these ways Christian art forms were spread throughout the world of Late Antiquity.[82]

There is no doubt that the non-Romans of northern Europe were very much impressed by both imperial and ecclesiastical art. Frankish metalworkers, for example, produced imitative coinage and reliquaries based on eastern models, using traditional materials, gold, and garnets (and ancient cameos) with a skill unrivalled in the West. They absorbed the heritage of early Christian art, putting it to use in their churches and royal tombs.[83]

[81] A. Grabar, *Byzantium from the Death of Theodosius to the Rise of Islam* (London, 1966); A. P. Kazhdan and A. Cutler, "Continuity and Discontinuity in Byzantine History," *B* 52 (1982): 462, cite "the 'universal' body of decorations" found in the sixth century, but not found again until the eleventh (in relation to mosaic floors, but with implications for the entire range of Late Antique art). Similarly, see J. Hubert, J. Porcher, and W. F. Volbach, *Europe in the Dark Ages* (London, 1969), 245, on the new Byzantine style that pervaded all the lands of the old empire.

[82] A. Grabar, *Les Ampoules de Terre Sainte (Monza-Bobbio)* (Paris, 1958); K. Weitzmann, " 'Loca Sancta' and the Representational Art of Palestine," *DOP* 28 (1974): 31-55.

[83] Hubert, Porcher, and Volbach, *Europe in the Dark Ages*; cf. M. Brozzi, C. Calderini, and M. and M. Rotili, *Longobardi* (Milan, 1980); on Irish and Anglo-Saxon art, see

But they could not find an immediate function for those pagan elements that persisted in sixth-century secular art. Nor could they appreciate the artistic adaptation and re-use of ancient myths and deities of the pre-Christian world, in short, the survival of a pagan culture. Of course, it is not clear to what extent those patrons who ordered sets of tableware in silver decorated with scenes of Bacchic revelry, nymphs, and Silenus wished to preserve a non-Christian iconography.[84] Perhaps it was just a tradition. But such a commission presented no problem to craftsmen trained in the execution of pagan motifs, who knew the characters of the ancient mythology, their festivals and stories. The striking persistence of pagan images into the sixth century serves as a reminder that early Christian art by no means obliterated its Greco-Roman predecessor.

OBVIOUSLY this artistic inheritance, like all the other aspects of Late Antique culture, could not remove clashes between Roman and non-Roman any more than it could erase the latent rivalry between country and city, but it certainly facilitated a greater degree of harmonisation. Tremendous areas of friction remained: old senatorial leaders complained bitterly about the destruction of their way of life even as the barbarians adopted it.[85] Rural dwellers, trapped in the seasonal rhythm of the countryside, envied the calendar of urban life, punctuated by ceremonies to commemorate past victories, triumphs, imperial births, marriages, and deaths, which were nearly always marked by distributions of money and foodstuffs. Nor did the means of integrating the newcomers turn them into Romans overnight; there were reversals and long delays. Yet engrained methods of economic and social organisation guided the whole period of settlement and had a lasting effect in the changed circumstances of Late Antiquity. And the artistic achievements of the period reflect a certain underlying unity, which carried great weight in the transition from a classical to a clerical culture. It was, however, the church that played the decisive role, and it is to the Christian influence in Late Antique culture that we must now turn.

R. Bruce-Mitford, "The Reception by the Anglo-Saxons of Medieval Art, Following Their Conversion from Ireland and Rome," *Settimane* 14 (1967): 797-825.

[84] On the continuous use of pagan forms, see P. R. L. Brown "Art and Society in Late Antiquity," in *The Age of Spirituality: A Symposium*, ed. K. Weitzmann (New York/Princeton, 1980), 17-27; cf. G. M. A. Hanfmann, "The Continuity of Classical Art: Culture, Myth and Faith," in Weitzmann, *The Age of Spirituality*, 75-99, and the exhibition catalogue, *Age of Spirituality*, ed. K. Weitzmann, Metropolitan Museum of Art, New York (Princeton, 1979). See also H.-I. Marrou, *ΜΟΥΣΙΚΟC ΑΝΗΡ* (Grenoble, 1937); M. Simon, *La civilisation de l'Antiquité et le Christianisme* (Paris, 1972), 361-96.

[85] See for example the *Eucharisticos* of Paulinus of Pella; cf. Courcelle, *Histoire littéraire*, 92-95.

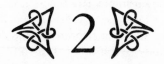

Christian Influence in Late Antique Culture

By THE SIXTH century, Christian elements pervaded almost every sector of the Late Antique world, yet they were not part of the classical inheritance. On the contrary, Christianity represented a new belief—new relative to the established cults of the ancient gods, the deities that protected ancient cities, the healing powers of Aesclepius, or the Sibylline oracles, and most obviously new relative to Judaism—which it developed by recognising Jesus as the Messiah. But Christianity was also propagated in reaction to the extension of Roman rule to the East Mediterranean during the first century B.C., and arose within the cultures of Antiquity and through antique structures. The complex relationships that developed in the early period A.D. between the faith and the empire, and between the faith and other beliefs, cannot be addressed here. Instead, I shall pick out various forms of Christianity identifiable by the early fourth century, when the conversion of Constantine I gave them greater prominence among antique systems of belief. This approach cannot do justice to the fascinating and complicated history of the early Christian communities, but it will provide at least a minimal sketch of the background from which the faith came to dominate Late Antique culture.

The Multiform Growth of Christianity

One of the difficulties in discussing the early history of Christian development springs from a tendency to reconstruct its growth in the light of subsequent world domination. The greatest church historian, Eusebios of Caesarea (ca. 260-340), who stands as the most important single guide and will be frequently quoted in this chapter, inaugurated the trend.[1] But in

[1] Eusebios, *HE*; cf. R. M. Grant, *Eusebios as Church Historian* (Oxford, 1980); G. F. Chesnut, *The First Christian Histories: Eusebios, Socrates, Sozomen, Theodoret and Evagrius* (Paris, 1977); T. D. Barnes, *Constantine and Eusebios* (Cambridge, Mass., 1981). In contrast to the many churches, however, Eusebios regularly stresses the importance of church unity, for instance in his denunciation of Novatus (Novatian) for dividing the church, *HE* 7.8.

his use of the plural, "churches," and their internal disputes, he betrays a sense of the autarkic nature of this development. I shall perhaps lay greater stress than is normal on the tentative and hesitant, divisive and competitive aspects of early Christian communities, their idiosyncracies in practice and belief, in short, the relative lack of uniformity. This is an attempt to place the new religion in its historic context, cut off from the received wisdom of hindsight, which treats it as embryonic to a later dominance. The very terms "Christian," "Christianity," and "the early church" become awkward, because they are overloaded with connotations of a subsequent development.[2] Instead, I shall try to employ a vocabulary that corresponds to the actual situation of the early Christian groups, emphasising the multiplicity of churches (rather than one) and the variety of Christian experience (rather than its unity).[3] This plurality dominates the entire history of early Christian practice and becomes embarrassingly evident at the meeting of the first general (oecumenical) council, held at Nicaea in 325.

At the time of Constantine I's so-called Edict of Toleration (313), which established the Christian faith on an equal footing with others and gave it important legal rights, the doctrines of Arios (d. 336) had introduced serious sectarian rivalry.[4] This deacon of the Alexandrian church attempted to define the exact nature of Christ, His divinity and humanity, and His relation to God. Arios believed that the Son was subordinate to the Father being created by a pre-existing force. He could not therefore be identical with God and must be less than God, an argument that stressed His essentially human nature and denied the Incarnation of God as Man. Christian communities throughout the Mediterranean world were greatly exercised by this matter. At the same time, they had no agreed system for calculating the date of Easter, the most important moveable feast in their annual calendar.[5] Since the second century, argument had raged over the dates of the fast (Lent) to be observed before the celebration of the Resurrection. In key

---

[2] The debate over the term *"Christianos,"* as used in the Acts of the Apostles, is conveniently summarised by E. Bickerman, "The Name of Christians," *Harvard Theological Review* 42 (1949): 109-124; cf. C. H. Roberts, *Manuscript, Society and Belief in Early Christian Egypt* (London, 1979), 3; *"Christianos"* was not used in Egypt before 256, when a papyrus record orders the arrest of a believer.

[3] P. Battifol, *L'Eglise naissante et le catholicisme*, 2nd ed. (Paris, 1971), 87-88, on the term for "church" (*ekklesia*, in Greek); 387-97, on Origen's insistent use of the plural.

[4] E. Boularand, *L'Heresie d'Arius et la "Foi" de Nicée* (Paris, 1972); R. Lorenz, *Arius judaizans?* (Göttingen, 1979); G. C. Stead, "The *Thalia* of Arius and the Testimony of Athanasius," *JTS* 29 (1978): 20-52.

[5] C. C. Richardson, "A New Solution to the Quartodecimen Riddle," *JTS* 24 (1973): 74-84. On the variety and complexity of systems in use in the early fourth century, see M. Richard, "Le comput pascal par octaéteris," *Le Muséon* 87 (1974): 307-339.

aspects of both belief and practice, therefore, Christians were divided, though overall they presented a united front against other faiths.

The first council of the entire Christian world met in 325 to try and resolve these matters. Arios's beliefs were subjected to critical debate, and a basic statement of correct belief, or creed, was drawn up. (In its slightly modified form it is still the *credo*, "I believe," of the Catholic church.) It defined Christ as being of the same essence, *homoousios*, as the Father, and consubstantial with Him; Jesus was further described as unbegotten, the uncreated Son.[6] Arios and his persistent supporters were branded as heretics and sent into exile. But their doctrines continued to command respect within certain sectors of the eastern churches and among the Gothic and Germanic tribes living beyond the Danube frontier and north of the Black Sea. Arianism was also favoured by several later fourth-century emperors. So the dogmatic problem was not resolved.

Neither was the practical problem of celebrating Easter, the commemoration of Christ's resurrection, which promises the redemption of all. Some communities still clung to a Jewish system of celebrating on the 14th day of Nisan that brought their Easter into line with the Passover; others denounced this as Judaising and determined to celebrate at a later date; yet others used their own way of calculating the phases of the moon in a manner different from the established Alexandrian system. In an effort to achieve the desired unity, the council authorised the church of Alexandria to work out the correct date, which would be communicated to all Christians. Yet even this decision to entrust the experts of Alexandria with the difficult computation involved, did not guarantee uniformity.[7] Both credal and Easter differences, however trivial they may seem, were fiercely observed as "correct," and their condemnation caused real anguish, because the event celebrated was central to the Christian belief in the heavenly hereafter. Thus "wrong" belief and "wrong" practice were both built into the early history of Christianity.

In using this example of disunity, however, I do not want to imply that the Christian world was utterly dominated by bishops and metropolitans,

[6] As the First Oecumenical Council did not issue a record of its proceedings, historians are dependent upon the subjective accounts preserved by two participants: Eusebios of Caesarea and Athanasios of Alexandria. These sources, the *credo*, and the council will be discussed in Chapter 3.

[7] As an example of the significance of Easter in early Christian thought, one can read the sermons preached on the Sunday of the Resurrection, e.g., Gregory of Nyssa, *The Easter Sermons, Translation and Commentary*, ed. A. Spira and C. Klock (Philadelphia, 1981); F. Graffin, "Exhortation d'un supérieur de monastère sur la Résurrection: Extrait d'un Homéliaire syriaque du Ve-VIe siècle," *Mélanges de l'Université S. Joseph* 49 (1975-76): 605-616. For dating problems, see Richardson, "A New Solution," and C. W. Jones, "The Victorian and Dionysiac Paschal Tables," *Speculum* 9 (1934): 408-421.

a hierarchy of church leaders. Local councils and meetings of believers had developed organically as a means of regulating certain matters. But in addition, a whole range of activities remained largely unregulated, spontaneously generating separate forms of organisation and existing independently of any consecrated "official." To overlook the extent of private initiative would be to ignore a major impulse to early Christian expansion.[8] In homes, whole families adopted a style of life modelled on that of the Apostles; some devoted themselves to missionary work, others to charitable deeds among the outcasts of Roman society—lepers and others identified as "unclean," vagabonds, prostitutes, the homeless and destitute. Some took vows of chastity and seclusion, dedicating themselves to prayer in what were in effect house monasteries. Still others left their homes completely and sought to escape from the temptations of the world by abandoning all human contact. In innumerable different ways, converts expressed their commitment to the new faith. Few became its public spokesmen; the great majority defended it in private, among their families and friends, in small groups and in the isolation of the wilderness. From its earliest days Christianity drew on these spontaneous expressions of faith, which were just as significant as those directed by recognised leaders. In what follows, it is important not to forget that private and public facets of Christianity co-existed to their mutual benefit.

The Expansion of Christian Belief in Cities

While Jesus preached primarily to the villages and country-dwellers of Galilee in the Roman province of Palestine, his followers took the message of the new faith to the cities of the Mediterranean.[9] From the *Acts of the Apostles* and the Pauline *Epistles*, in particular, one gets the impression that all the early believers lived in cities. It was in the urban centres of the empire that the new faith gradually spread in the first centuries A.D., and there that the first "churches" were formed. Antioch, Alexandria, and Rome, the three most famous apostolic foundations, were undoubtedly the most important cities of the Mediterranean. In each, groups of Christian believers chose their own elders, or welcomed people recommended to

[8] S. Barton, "Paul, Religion and Society," paper given at the Religion and Society History Workshop, London, July 1983, in *Disciplines of Faith: Studies in Religion, Politics, and Patriarchy*, ed. J. Obelkevich, L. Roper, and R. Samuel (London, 1986); W. A. Meeks, *The First Urban Christians* (New Haven/London, 1983); see Battifol, *L'Eglise naissante*, 34-45, on the "*religio illicita*" of the cities.

[9] G. E. M. de Ste. Croix, *The Class Struggle in the Ancient Greek World* (London, 1981), 427-33; Meeks, *The First Urban Christians*; D. Baker, ed., *The Christians in Town and Countryside, SCH* 16 (1979); R. MacMullen, *Christianizing the Roman Empire* (New Haven, 1984).

them as leaders. Like most dissident societies, they found it necessary to have a spokesman who could deal with the often hostile authorities. From this humble beginning as the nominee of a particular community, the position of bishop developed into a more exalted one, with a special rank in the hierarchy of the whole community of Christians. The expansion of this role took place during the centuries of persecution, and many bishops were martyred with their congregations. By the time Constantine I recognized Christianity as an official religion, the public image of this faith was emphatically episcopal. The bishop was the obvious representative who could be empowered to administer property and wealth bequeathed to the church and to preside over an ecclesiastical court. So the emperor confirmed the standing of bishops by giving them these duties, while he also exempted the entire clergy from civilian duties (such as curial service) that might conflict with their Christian obligations. In view of the strains already afflicting city government, this was a valuable privilege, rapidly exploited by the faithful. [10]

With imperial support and protection from persecution, the faith now experienced a great expansion. Calculating the numbers that might have embraced Christianity, both as a percentage of the overall population and in relation to other cults, is almost impossible. [11] This in itself compounds the difficulty of understanding the early spread of Christianity, for without any figures on the proportional distribution of beliefs we cannot counter the generally prevailing tendency to chronicle only Christianity's successful expansion. It is evident, however, that the Persian cult of Mithras had made many converts, not only among legionaries and mercenaries serving with the Roman armies, but also in cities, and later in Rome itself, where Mithraeums founded by aristocratic followers have been excavated. [12] Similarly, the mysteries of Serapis and other Egyptian gods were widely observed in the Roman Empire at this time. Nor were the old pagan beliefs dead; Stoicism had been raised to new heights by the philosophy of Marcus Aurelius (161-80), and largely incorporated into Christianity by Clement of Alexandria (d. after 215). Christianity was only one among many thriving cults. It appears to have spread easily among the urban poor, who were doubtless attracted by its egalitarian insistence on the worth of every individual, regardless of descent and position in society. But it also commanded the loyalty of highly placed officials; witness the conversion of Ter-

[10] H. Chadwick, *The Role of the Christian Bishop in Ancient Society* (Berkeley, 1980); G. Dix, *Jurisdiction in the Early Church, Episcopal and Papal*, 2nd ed. (London, 1975), 11-46; P. Brown, *The Making of Late Antiquity* (Cambridge, Mass./London, 1978), 54-80.

[11] P. Brown, *The Making of Late Antiquity*, 57 and passim.

[12] C. M. Daniels, "The Role of the Roman Army in the Spread and Practice of Mithraism," in *Mithraic Studies*, ed. J. R. Hinnells, 2 vols. (Manchester, 1975), 2:249-74.

tullian.[13] Through their guidance and often under their leadership, the urban communities of Christians made steady advances.

After the years of persecution, shared with adherents of other cults also, the acceptance of Christianity as a legitimate faith allowed the churches to celebrate openly without fear of reprisals. Special basilicas were constructed in most cities of the empire for this purpose, giving the Christians a more prominent presence. While the faithful frequently provided the means for such buildings, their bishops were seen to officiate in them. The communal nature of Christian groups in the earliest times was replaced, ever so slowly, by a ranked society, in which the congregation formed the base from which officials were elected to the various stages of office advancing to the episcopacy. In time this urban and episcopal character created an ecclesiastical government in parallel with the secular one and, like it, based in the most important cities.[14] All bishops were in charge of a city and its territory, which formed a diocese, roughly equivalent to the province of civilian administration. The official church thus became very much the religious counterpart of imperial government and brought bishops into close relations with Roman administrators. They all shared a vested interest in the survival of ancient patterns of social organisation, founded in the city, and they frequently collaborated in the enforcement of imperial decrees. Due to its urban environment and administrative responsibilities, the episcopal church was destined, inevitably, to grow further and further away from the Christian teaching of poverty and the denial of worldly goods. It became more like an additional arm of secular administration, the power responsible for sending heretics into exile, when they were not condemned to worse.

The Rural Expansion of Christianity

While this organised and most visible feature of Christianity continued to grow, a quite different form of expansion was under way in the countryside, in the wildest and most deserted parts of the empire, furthest away from urban civilisation.[15] It sprang from a desire to shun the world and all its evils, to escape to the desert and commune with God alone. The practice had older pre-Christian roots, which were taken over by Christians seeking to live by Christ's command: "Leave all thou hast and follow me." Given the model of His renunciation of possessions and commitment to poverty,

[13] H. Chadwick, *The Early Church* (Harmondsworth, 1967), 95-100; T. D. Barnes, *Tertullian: A Historical and Literary Study* (Oxford, 1971), 57-59, 67-73.

[14] Jones, *LRE*, 2:875.

[15] P. Brown, *The Making of Late Antiquity*, 81-101; A. Vööbus, *A History of Asceticism in the Syrian Orient*, 2 vols. (Louvain, 1958-60), claims a primacy for the Syrian development as opposed to the Egyptian, made familiar by D. Chitty, *The Desert a City* (Oxford, 1966).

they abandoned family and material things, usually causing scandals that are glowingly recorded in some of the early accounts of martyrdom. Saint Thecla, for example, was said to have been converted by St. Paul's preaching in her hometown of Ikonion. She then followed the Christian, eluding her parents' attempts to bring her back to an arranged marriage and shaking off the bad names shouted after her with the fervour of her faith. After a mock trial, she was sentenced to death in a wild animal show that broke down. "This most good lioness . . . not only did not touch the sacred and all holy body [of Thecla], but lay down at the virgin's feet and assured her protection from the other wild beasts."[16] Clearly, these early accounts were elaborated in each subsequent telling—this one dates from the fifth century—but they preserve a strain of that heroic period of casting off the world and all its vainglories for Christian poverty.

From a decision to abandon human company and withdraw from the world (called *anachoresis* in Greek, from which "anchorite" derives), the pursuit of ascetic ideals followed naturally. Disciples of the deity Serapis had developed this practice through the custom of becoming a recluse (*katachos*) dedicated to the god, and adherents of other pagan cults and of Judaism adopted similar techniques.[17] But among Christians this sort of withdrawal became very widespread in the late third century. In Egypt it was set in motion by a young man called Antony, who was moved by a Gospel reading to follow Christ; he withdrew from the world under the instruction of an old hermit in the desert of the east bank of the Nile.[18] There he cultivated a solitary life-style of extreme asceticism and self-denial, which attracted followers despite his repudiation of human company. When they would not leave him in peace, he moved further into the desert in an attempt to shake them off. But his lonely struggle for Christian virtues, again elaborated by rumours of his power against poisonous serpents, lions, and the lack of water, continued to draw others to the same life. Similar developments in northeastern Syria had produced a comparable situa-

---

[16] G. Dagron, *Vie et Miracles de Sainte Thècle* (Brussels, 1978), ch. 19, 244-47.

[17] For a Jewish example, see W. S. Green, "Palestinian Holy Men: Charismatic Leadership and Rabbinic Tradition," in *Aufstieg und Niedergang der Römischen Welt*, ed. H. Temporini, 2, *Principät*, 19, pt. 2 (Berlin/New York, 1979), 619-47.

[18] *Athanasios: The Life of Antony and The Letter to Marcellus*, translated and introduced by R. C. Gregg (London, 1980), paras. 2-3, 31-32. The Greek text is in *PG* 26:833-976, with the Latin translation by Evagrios (also in *PL* 73:125-70). A strong case has been made against Athanasios's authorship of the original *Life*, which was probably composed in Coptic by a monk in Antony's monastery, and is preserved in an early Syriac translation: see R. Draguet, *La Vie primitive de S. Antoine conservée en syriaque* (Louvain, 1980). Cf. P. Brown, *The Making of Late Antiquity*, 81-90. On the spiritual education Antony might have received, see J.-C. Guy, "Educational Innovation in the Desert Fathers," *Eastern Churches Review* 6 (1974): 44-51.

tion when Jacob of Nisibis adopted the ascetic practices of local hermits.[19] In addition, groups of Christians, branded as heretics for their support of non-orthodox Marcion and Meletios, were living in a more communal form of withdrawal in late third- and early fourth-century Syria.

Early Christian asceticism was not a new, originally Christian force (it had a pagan background), nor was it confined to Egypt (there were many other desert areas in the East Mediterranean). Yet the novel organisation and direction of Christian ascetic communities that produced monasticism was achieved in Egypt. It was the work of Pachom (St. Pachomios, ca. 292-346), who had been attracted to the faith while serving in the army. He was baptised in the Thebaid of central Egypt and put himself under the discipline of an old man called Palamon, who dressed him in a rough garment (*schema*) later adopted as the monastic habit. In about 320 Pachom moved to Tabennesis, a deserted village near the Nile, where he established a community under the authority of the neighbouring bishop of Tentyra.[20] In this settlement he expected disciples to cultivate the surrounding land as well as to plait mats and baskets (the traditional work of desert holymen), probably because the area could not support life without systematic agricultural work. Unlike other loosely connected groups of hermits in the richer Nile Delta, Tabennesis had to be organised to provide adequate food and shelter; it would not demand the total self-denial practised by the most severe solitaries. In due course, boats were built to transport surplus produce to Alexandria, and thus Pachomian monasticism remained linked to the world, involved in exchange and sale, rather than setting itself quite apart. This was partly the result of a tremendously rapid growth; in ca. 337 when Pachom moved to Pavou, there were already four associated communities, and fifty years later, when John Cassian visited the area, there were 5,000 monks. The growth in turn was due partly to Pachom's regulation of communal living, which set new standards for the inmates. By insisting on both manual labour in the fields and mental work in learning to read and performing the liturgy, Pachom established the combination that would direct the course of Christian monasticism for centuries.[21]

Almost contemporaneously with Pachom, Saint Ammoun established the first community of monks in the Nitrian desert, south of Alexandria,

---

[19] Theodoret de Cyr, *Histoire des Moines de Syrie: "Histoire Philothée,"* ed. P. Canivet and A. Leroy-Molingen, 2 vols. (Paris, 1977-79), vol. 1, no. 1; cf. Vööbus, *A History of Asceticism*, 1: 141-44, 151.

[20] H. van Cranenburgh, *La Vie latine de S. Pachôme traduite du grec par Denys le Petit* (Brussels, 1969), gives a critical edition of the Latin version with the second Greek *Life* facing. Cf. P. Brown, *The Making of Late Antiquity*, 92-101.

[21] A. Veilleux, *La liturgie dans le cénobitism pachômien au quatrième siècle,* Studia Anselmiana, vol. 57 (Rome, 1968).

which was extended in ca. 340 when he and St. Antony moved to a more distant retreat. But these settlements of Nitria and Sketis were like a scattered association of individual monks, as the name "Monastery of the Cells" implies.[22] Because the hermits did not necessarily have regular supplies of water and bread, they would usually meet once a week for services on Sundays, when they would collect their rations. Itinerant and illiterate holy men joined them from time to time and were taught the Scriptures by heart (though in the case of Pambo, Ammoun instructed him so thoroughly in the skills of reading and writing that he later became a priest and served Athanasios of Alexandria). The emphasis of the Nitrian communities remained on the ascetic practice of the isolated holy man, his individual communion with God and endurance of bodily deprivation. These were the exploits made famous by John Cassian, Rufinus, Palladios, and others who visited the Desert Fathers;[23] their collections of "Sayings" inspired many different types of withdrawal in other parts of the Late Antique world.[24] While Pachom shared this background, he also tried to incorporate its discipline into a collective life, through which the brothers would support each other in a centralised community. The *coenobium* (Greek *koinobion*) meant life in common, not just as a training for ascetic existence, but forever. With this shift in the organisation of Egyptian hermits, the Pachomian type of monasticism, rather than Antony's, gained a lasting hold on the Christian imagination.

Conflict Between the Rural and Urban Forms of Christianity?

Even before the establishment of an ecclesiastical hierarchy, Egyptian holy men had displayed a fierce hostility to ordination, even at the lowest rank of priest; they preferred a personal dedication to God rather than one dependent upon the regular administration of the sacraments. Many therefore sought total solitude and refused to have anything to do with urban communities. When a city delegation came to inform Ammonios that they had chosen him as their bishop, he went and cut off his own ear, claiming that no mutilated man could serve as a church leader.[25] And when he was criticised for his "Jewish" attitude, he threatened to cut out his tongue as well.

[22] Chitty, *The Desert a City*, 11.

[23] Cassian's *Institutes* and *Conferences*, Rufinus's *History of the Monks in Egypt*, and Palladios's *Lausiac History* provide detailed information about the hermits.

[24] B. Ward, *The Sayings of the Desert Fathers: The Alphabetical Collection* (London, 1975); J. Dion and G. Oury, *Les Sentences des Pères du Désert*, 4 vols. (Solesmes, 1966-81), includes the alphabetic arrangement as well as the collection made by Pelagius and John in sixth-century Rome.

[25] Chitty, *The Desert a City*, 53-54.

This reaction did not, however, prevent Christian communities from choosing desert hermits as their leaders. They appreciated the specially holy qualities developed in ascetic struggle and wished to import it to their own urban surroundings. Not surprisingly, many holy men refused outright, or showed great reluctance, for the desert notion of peace, *hesycheia*, could not easily be transposed to the city. Sarapion the Sindonite was one of the few who practised asceticism in all circumstances, when visiting Athens or Rome, as well as in the countryside.[26] After persistent pleading, and sometimes under threat of forceful abduction, many hermits were appointed to bishoprics and adjusted their lives to cope with the new challenges of political involvement and church administration. In order to be promoted to episcopal office, the unordained holy man had to be admitted to all stages of the priesthood in rapid succession. Although ecclesiastical lawyers did not always approve of this uncanonical progress, they usually bowed to the Christian community's right to elect its own leader and to suffer the consequences of promotion overnight. Popular acclaim brought Eutychios from his monastic community to the local see of Amaseia in ca. 550; it was, however, under imperial orders that he journeyed to Constantinople to be invested as the leading bishop (patriarch) of the eastern empire.[27]

Since the time of Constantine I, emperors had exercised a significant authority in the selection of candidates for the position of bishop of Constantinople through an ecclesiastical procedure whereby the diocesan clergy presented three names for imperial consideration. And even this residual element of communal choice was frequently overruled by the imposition of an outsider favoured by the emperor.[28] So the foremost episcopal sees in the late antique world, those of Jerusalem, Antioch, Alexandria, Rome, and Constantinople, were generally filled by candidates acceptable to the secular authorities, and these were often representatives of the monastic rather than the urban church. In the absence of any particularly favoured candidate, however, the choice of the congregation and clergy of the church might be decisive. The most celebrated example of such acclamation is undoubtedly the election of Ambrose to the see of Milan in 374, for the candidate was not even a baptised Christian.[29] As a Roman provincial governor of senatorial standing, he commanded such respect that even this disqual-

---

[26] P. Brown, *The Making of Late Antiquity*, 11-26, 86-98; cf. Palladios, *Lausiac History*, ch. 37 (trans. R. T. Meyer, *Palladius: The Lausiac History* [Washington, D.C., 1965], 105-110).

[27] Eustratios, *Vita Eutychii, PG* 86 (ii), chs. 2 and 3, 2287-2306.

[28] Jones, *LRE*, 2:919-20 (reducing imperial intervention).

[29] Ibid., 1:151; cf. F. H. Dudden, *The Life and Times of St. Ambrose*, 2 vols. (Oxford, 1935), 1:57-74.

ification was overlooked. The unusual selection was also completely justified by St. Ambrose's success in the episcopal role: not only did he bring a
profound sense of ancient philosophy and ethics to the job, but a commitment to the spiritual authority of the church, which he developed in a famous dispute with Theodosius I.[30] After a massacre in Thessalonike, in
which about 7,000 people were said to have been killed in reprisal for an
insurrection, the emperor was forced by Ambrose to perform public penance for this crime. The superiority of the church in such matters was
thereby reinforced.

Symbiosis Through Holiness and Celibacy. As Ambrose's election shows, when
Christian communities needed a new leader, their choice could sometimes
be determined by personal qualities regardless of qualifications. And in
Ambrose they found a truly Roman leader. Their decision reflects the fusion of imperial and Christian concerns that was taking place within society. Through their insistence that bishops should also have the necessary
charisma of holiness, a wide range of candidates were appointed to guide
the urban churches, most of them distinguished. The philosopher Synesios
made it a condition of his elevation to the see of Cyrene that he might continue to live with his wife and pursue his intellectual interests.[31] Dioskoros,
a monk from Nitria and brother of Ammonios, became bishop of Her-
mopolis without protest.[32] Most bishops, if married, tried to persuade
their wives to leave them and go into a convent, because the celibate life
was becoming intimately connected with holiness. And through the commitment to celibacy, the apparent contradictions between rural and urban
forms of Christianity were gradually removed.

It was within monastic circles that celibacy was first elevated to a com-
manding position, from which it came to dominate the Christian world.
St. Ammoun (ca. 295-352) is known as one of the first Desert Fathers to
have lived with his wife for 18 years in total abstinence.[33] This occurred as
the result of an arranged marriage from which Ammoun could not escape.
Instead, he persuaded his bride that they should lead an ascetic existence as
brother and sister, avoiding all sexual contact. Ammoun, however, later
felt the need to withdraw from the world completely and left his "sister"

[30] Dudden, *Life and Times*, 2:381-92; H.-J. Diesner, "Kirche und Staat im ausgehenden
vierten Jahrhundert: Ambrosius von Mailand," in *Kirche und Staat im Spätrömischen Reich*
(Berlin, 1963), 22-45, reprinted in *Das frühe Christentum im römischen Staat*, ed. R. Klein
(Darmstadt, 1971).
[31] J. Bregman, *Synesius of Cyrene—Philosopher-Bishop* (Berkeley, 1982), 155-63; C. H.
Coster, *Late Roman Studies* (Cambridge, 1968), 248-51.
[32] Chitty, *The Desert a City*, 53-54.
[33] Ibid., 11.

to settle in the Nitrian desert. There other young men fleeing from exactly the same tradition of arranged marriages, as well as older men retiring from married life, joined him in ascetic pursuits. Occasionally, whole families would arrive, the father and sons to become hermits, the wives and daughters to enter a female community. Although women were never welcomed in the desert, their needs were met by the establishment of parallel female houses. Some dedicated young women succeeded in living as holy men, disguised by their loose rough clothing and passing as eunuchs.[34] But most came to the desert communities trying to retrieve their sons or find their husbands. In the case of Theodore of Latopolis, who had been admitted to Pachom's monastery at the age of 14, his despairing mother was persuaded to join the female community established by Pachom's sister, where she would at least be close to him.[35]

Celibacy was therefore nurtured in the monasteries and the informal settlements of male hermits scattered throughout the desert regions of Egypt, Palestine, Syria, and central Asia Minor. But celibacy too had pre-Christian and pagan traditions, from which Christ's model behaviour and Paul's advice on the superiority of singleness did not differ greatly. Many Christians had observed a similar restraint privately before the eremitic communities came into existence. It seems to have been the stories circulating about organised celibacy that were responsible for a dramatic upsurge in the mid-fourth century. Paradoxically, such tales were confirmed in the West by a firm exponent of the city-based churches, St. Athanasios, bishop of Alexandria, who was banished to Trier by Constantine I (335-37), and exiled again to Rome (339-46).[36] During these visits Athanasios met with leading western bishops and discussed theological problems, such as the precise wording of the creed, and matters relating to the growth of the churches. Among these matters, desert asceticism must have featured prominently, for many individuals attest the significance of Athanasios's accounts in their own adoption of a celibate life.[37] The devotion of certain

---

[34] E. Patlagean, "L'Histoire de la femme deguisée en moine . . . ," *Studi Medievali*, ser. 3, 17 (1976), 597-623 (reprinted London, 1981); J. Anson, "The Female Transvestite in Early Monasticism . . . ," *Viator* 5 (1974), 1-32; see Ward, *The Sayings*, 34, apophthegma 4, on the solitary of Lycopolis, who was not identified as a woman until her death.

[35] *Sancti Pachomii vitae graecae*, ed. F. Halkin, *Subsidia Hagiographica* 19 (Brussels, 1932), chs. 26, 35-37. English translation with Greek text in A. A. Athanassakis, *The Life of Pachomius: Vita prima Graeca* (Missoula, 1975). St. Antony reinforced the tradition of separate communities for women when he settled his sister with a group of trusted virgins, who had independently adopted the celibate life; *Life of Antony*, para. 3.

[36] N. H. Baynes, "Athanasiana," *Journal of Egyptian Archaeology* 11 (1925): 56-69; Athanasios was, however, known as a great ascetic above all.

[37] R. Lorenz, "Die Anfänge des abendländischen Mönchtums im 4. Jahrhundert," *Zeitschrift für Kirchengeschichte* 77 (1966): 1-61; E. A. Judge, "The Earliest Use of Monachos for

Roman ladies to virginity was undoubtedly encouraged, as in the case of
Marcella, who established a female house after 339. Athanasios was well
informed about St. Antony, who paid one of his extremely rare visits to
Alexandria in about 338, when the bishop was attacked for illegal occupation of his see. During his third long and involuntary absence from the
city (356?-362?), Athanasios sought refuge in the desert and strengthened
his friendship with Antony. On the latter's death in ca. 356, Athanasios
received a personal legacy of his cloak and a sheepskin.[38]

It was then that Athanasios wrote the most influential account to that
date of Egyptian monasticism, a *Life* of St. Antony. This was not the first,
as a member of his circle appears to have written a Coptic *Life* earlier, probably for use among the desert communities. But this Greek version of ca.
357 was the first in a Mediterranean tongue, quickly translated into Latin
and immediately in demand.[39] It was addressed, "To the monks in foreign
parts," who are praised in the introduction: "You have entered on a fine
contest with the monks in Egypt, intending as you do to measure up to or
even to surpass them in your discipline of virtue."[40] These monks are probably to be identified as ecclesiastics in the West, trying to impose a celibate life and better organisation on their clergy, or to individual hermits:
Eusebius of Vercelli, for instance, instituted an ascetic routine within his
episcopal residence before he was exiled to the East (355-63) for supporting
Athanasios against Constantius II. He might have come across the idea in
Rome where he had been a reader (*lector*) prior to his appointment to Vercelli. During his exile near Antioch, he met holy men engaged in a quasi-
monastic commitment to silence, solitude, and prayer (i.e., otherwise uni-
dentified hermits whose aims were the same as his own). Similarly, Hilary
of Poitiers witnessed in the East what he had heard about from Athanasios
personally; it confirmed him in his determination to establish similar monastic institutions in the West on his return.[41]

'Monk' (P. Coll. Youtie 77) and the Origins of Monasticism," *JAC* 20 (1977): 72-89;
F. Prinz, *Askese und Kultur: vor- und frühbenediktinisches Mönchtum an der Wiege Europas* (Munich, 1980), 13-27.

[38] *Life of Antony*, paras. 69, 91 (82, 97); the cloak was one Athanasios had given new to
Antony. Another sheepskin was bequeathed to Bishop Serapion, while the two companions
who witnessed his death (and spared him the horror of public burial rites with mummifi-
cation and subsequent cult) received his hair shirt.

[39] Athanasios presumably had access to the Coptic *Life*, which he used for the long verbatim speeches in his Greek version. A Latin translation of the Greek was prepared very soon
after and probably preceded the elegant version made by Evagrios, which is addressed to
Pope Innocent I (401-417); see G. Garitte, *Un témoin important du texte de la Vie
de S. Antoine par S. Athanase: La version Latine inédite des archives du Chapitre de S. Pierre à Rome*
(Brussels/Rome, 1939).

[40] *Life of Antony*, Introduction, in Gregg, *Athanasios*, 29. The pressure on Athanasios to
record Antony's life clearly came at least in part from these monks abroad.

[41] Lorenz, "Die Anfänge"; see P. Rousseau, "The Spiritual Authority of the 'Monk-

The fact that Athanasios represented the urban church of Alexandria as well as propagated the ideals of the rural and monastic churches of the desert reveals the degree of symbiosis between them. Antony even overcame his loathing of the city in order to defend his friend's reputation, a clear indication of the strength of mutual support that existed at about the middle of the fourth century. Although some fanatical monks would continue to deny episcopal authority, to condemn the church hierarchy as essentially worldly and corrupt, and to urge a celibate life on all Christians, most accepted urban communities. Many made the transition from monastery to episcopal palace, maintaining their desert training and discipline in the cities. Others, like Agapetos of Apamea, who had been instructed by a hermit in the desert of Kyrros, founded monasteries near the city and promoted celibacy in this way. There was a remarkable impact of not just rural, but often desert, asceticism on the urban churches of the Mediterranean during the fourth century.

A parallel type of desert asceticism was practised by the Jewish community at Qumran and by Gnostic groups at Nag Hammadi, both sites of immense importance because of their extraordinarily preserved records, the Dead Sea Scrolls and the Nag Hammadi library. But in contrast to these groups and most religions of the ancient Near East, Christian asceticism demanded strict celibacy. This set it apart, particularly from Judaism, which demanded procreation and kept its religious leaders married. A group of inscriptions from Apamea in northern Syria records the endowment of new mosaics in 391, including one that runs: "Under Nehemias the hazzan, also called deacon, the floor of the porch of the sanctuary was paved in mosaic ⟨N. did this⟩ in completion of a vow with his wife and children."[42] Such evidence also serves as a reminder that the Jewish communities of the East Mediterranean flourished in the fourth century, despite sporadic persecution, and provided a constant rivalry with Christianity.

The Spread of Monasticism in the West

From its multiple and idiosyncratic origins in different parts of the East to its more formal Egyptian models, the ascetic celibacy of the early hermits challenged Christians everywhere to live by their ideals. Some had already found their own independent paths to a peaceful seclusion from the world, notably a number of aristocratic ladies of considerable wealth such as Asella

---

Bishop': Eastern Elements in Some Western Hagiography of the Fourth and Fifth Centuries," *JTS* 22 (1971): 380-419, on the ferment of ideas that passed between East and West.

[42] *IGLS*, vol. 4 (Paris, 1955), nos. 1319-37, especially no. 1321 (66-67); *hazzan* designates the role of chanter. I thank Léonie Archer and Fergus Millar for their advice on this point. For Agapetos of Apamea, see Vööbus, *A History of Asceticism*, 2:140-41.

in Rome and Marciana in Africa. Others took up the challenge in a more collective fashion as groups of hermits living on islands cut off from social contact with the world, at Gallinaria, Capraria, and Lérins, for example, but without the excessive asceticism of eastern monks. The example of St. Antony was instrumental in Augustine's conversion, and he records clear evidence of the direct influence of Athanasios's *Life*, which inspired some of "the emperor's friends," to become "friends of God." This story, which is set in Trier, may even record the precise moment when Jerome and his friend Bonosus decided to abandon imperial service. It certainly reflects the appeal of the desert.[43]

But it was probably later, in the early fifth century, that clear instructions for the organisation of monasteries became available in the West. Here Jerome's Latin version of the *Rule* of St. Pachom, which he produced for western monks at Canopus near Alexandria, and John Cassian's *Institutions* were very influential.[44] The two authors had lived in monasteries near Jerusalem founded on Pachomian lines by refugees from Egypt and had a wide experience of desert asceticism. Like Rufinus, Jerome's rival, and translator, possibly even author, of the *History of the Monks of Egypt*, they had been on pilgrimages to the holy sites.[45] In Cassian's case he seems to have spent over a decade among the Desert Fathers of Sketis and Nitria (ca. 388-400), recording a number of their authentic *Sayings* (*Apophthegmata*), which appear in his *Collationes* (*Conferences*) of ca. 429.[46] Through these writings, a mass of information about the holy men of Egypt was put into circulation and had a formative impact on the development of nascent monasticism in southern Gaul.

Honoratus and his companion Eucherius had already established their retreat at Lérins, on an inaccessible part of the coast of Provence, when

[43] Augustine's conversion is recorded in his *Confessions* 8.6. The intriguing account of the officials' abandonment of imperial service occurs in the same section and is commented on by P. Courcelle, *Recherches sur les Confessions de S. Augustin* (Paris, 1968), 181-87.

[44] Jerome prepared a Greek edition of the *Rule* of Pachom and then translated it into Latin; P. Courcelle, *Late Latin Writers and their Greek Sources* (Cambridge, Mass., 1969), 237. Cassian's *Institutes, PL* 49-50 (text and French translation by J.-C. Guy, *Institutions cénobitiques* [Paris, 1965]). Other texts deriving from Egypt but composed in the West circulated widely in the fifth and sixth centuries; see C. V. Franklin, I. Havener, and J. A. Francis, eds., *Early Monastic Rules: The Rules of the Fathers and the Regula Orientalis* (Collegeville, Minn., 1982).

[45] A.-J. Festugière, who edited the Greek version of the *History*, which Rufinus translated, believed it to be the original and Rufinus himself the author; see *Historia monachorum in Aegypto* (Brussels, 1961).

[46] The *Conferences* are also in *PL* 49-50 (French edition and translation by E. Pichery [Paris, 1964-65], an English translation by E. Gibson, *Eremita: The Works of John Cassian* [New York, 1895]). The final text of importance was Palladios's *Lausiac History* (see note 26 above).

Cassian arrived at Marseille to set up his own houses. Bishop Castor of Apt was anxious to learn from him, for he too was in the process of creating a monastery. At his request Cassian compiled the *Institutions*, a complete guide to the organisation of monastic living on Egyptian lines. For the two at Lérins, Cassian prepared his second series of *Conferences*, which he dedicated to them. In this way a very direct link was made between the eastern and western basins of the Mediterranean; those who would never move from Provence were guided by the experiences of the much-travelled pilgrim and bilingual writer, John Cassian. Their foundation at Lérins, in fact, was to prove more enduring and of greater influence in the western ascetic tradition than either Castor's or Cassian's. For like the communities of Apamea, Cappodocia, and Mount Izla, near Nisibis, Lérins would provide numerous candidates for episcopal sees, thus extending desert asceticism into many urban ecclesiastical institutions and confirming the mutual reinforcement of both.[47]

The first western monastery founded entirely on eastern lines was probably that established by St. Martin, later bishop of Tours (372-97).[48] He had been in the East and had seen for himself the spectacular growth of monasticism. Inspired by Hilary of Poitiers's teaching, he moved from Italy to Gaul and set up his first community at Marmoutier on the Loire. He clearly felt himself primarily a monk and only reluctantly agreed to fill the vacant see of Tours, where he continued to observe a monastic routine. Due to his activities, Tours developed into a major centre of Christianity in the late fourth century, where ascetic and episcopal roles were totally intertwined. After his death, his tomb rapidly became a site of miraculous cures and responses to prayer, and attracted pilgrims from all parts of Europe.

The Practice of Celibacy

The same combination of secular and devotional forms of Christianity was practised by many later western leaders, notably Ambrose of Milan, whose sister Marcellina had set him a powerful ascetic example before his election as bishop. Ambrose also knew of a *Rule* of St. Basil, which had been translated by Rufinus.[49] Saints Victricius of Rouen (386-ca. 409) and Augustine

[47] P. Rousseau, *Ascetics, Authority and the Church in the Age of Jerome and Cassian* (Oxford, 1978); A. Rouselle, "Aspects sociaux du recrutement ecclésiastique au IVe siècle," *Mélanges d'Archéologie et d'Histoire, Antiquité* 89, no. 1 (1977): 333-70 (Lérins provided ten bishops for Gaul in the fifth century); O. Chadwick, *John Cassian*, 2nd ed. (Oxford, 1968), 37, 50-81.

[48] Sulpicius Severus, *Vie de St. Martin*, ch. 10 (ed. J. Fontaine, 3 vols. [Paris, 1967-69], 1: 272-75).

[49] On Rufinus's translations of the Cappadocian Fathers, see W. Berschin, *Griechisch-Lateinisches Mittelalter* (Berne/Munich, 1980), 63-64.

of Hippo (397-430) pursued the same commitment to asceticism as bishops. Their example effectively resolved the dichotomy, more apparent than real, and so much more visible in the wilder, even demonic, landscape of the East, where the first "athletes of God" had "made war on the Enemy."[50] The example of the Desert Fathers was always at hand, but rarely provoked the most exaggerated forms of self-deprivation known in Egypt. This was partly due to the fact that in the West, communal asceticism was more general than solitary withdrawal. And from an early date ascetic bishops were closely associated with monasteries, often as their founders and patrons. Through this integrated practice of Christian virginity, the western clergy enshrined the celibate ideal more firmly than in the East. For paradoxically, the monastic emphasis on celibacy had less impact on the eastern clergy, and married men were always admitted to the priesthood (and still are). Thus, the denial of marriage that had grown out of the original search for seclusion from the world was elevated in the West into a guiding principle of the entire church.

In the fourth and fifth centuries, however, the majority of Christian monks and bishops were married men who had family responsibilities that antedated their adoption of a celibate life. (Later, the practice of dedicating children to the church would spread, and many Christians thus dedicated would avoid marriage altogether.)[51] As Christian marital vows were deemed perpetual, "until death do us part," wives could not simply be rejected when their husbands were selected as bishops. Some, like the wife of St. Paulinus of Nola, adopted celibacy and lived with their spouses in a spiritual union; others entered nunneries, not always in an entirely voluntary manner.[52] Sons and daughters also had to be provided for by their father before he could retire into a monastery or assume the office of bishop. In this matter the possibility of promoting a blood relation to ecclesiastical positions (nepotism) opened up an avenue of abuse common to both the episcopal church and the monastic world.

A glance at the genealogy of Gregory, bishop of Tours (573-94), who wrote the *Ten Books of Histories*, known as the *History of the Franks*, reveals the type of hereditary family concern that could be built up through these connections.[53] On both sides Gregory had uncles who had been appointed

[50] Vööbus, *A History of Asceticism*, 1:149.

[51] L. S. B. MacCoull, "Child Donations and Child Saints in Coptic Egypt," *Abstracts of Papers, Byzantine Studies Conference* 3 (1977): 33.

[52] J. T. Lienhard, *Paulinus of Nola and Early Western Monasticism* (Cologne/Bonn, 1977), esp. 137-38. Paulinus's wife, Therasia, may have influenced his decision to convert; after the death of their infant son she seems to have been content to adopt the role of sister rather than wife, 102, 106.

[53] Gregory of Tours, *HF* 5:49, claims that 13 of the previous 18 bishops of Tours were

to episcopal sees by relatives; some had promoted their own sons, others their nephews or more distant relatives by marriage. A kinship network linked the bishoprics of central France throughout the sixth century and gave Gregory family contacts in many urban centres. Although these contacts were repeatedly condemned, nepotism continued to provoke scandals and dismay at the worldy concerns of the episcopate throughout Christendom. While celibacy was constantly stressed as a desirable state, it was only gradually instituted in practice, and never completely evaded the dangers of confusing kinship in this world with promotion to high office within the spiritual world of the church. Eventually, however, by a process that is difficult to specify, the stigma of non-celibate priests became even stronger than that of clerical exploitation of blood relationships.

The Decline of Eastern Asceticism

By their nature, communities of hermits and isolated holy men form an easier prey to hostile forces than fortified urban settlements. So the repeated Berber attacks on many parts of Egypt and North Africa from the later fourth century onwards naturally took a greater toll on the monastic church. They constituted an element of the new pattern of disturbance that reflected the Roman failure to defend imperial frontiers. At Cyrene in 405, Synesios was able to organise the city's defence, but two years later the Mazikes swept over the Nitrian desert, murdering those who did not flee before them.[54] Although some of the larger monasteries built fortifications to keep out the intruders, after three devastations (407-408, 434, and 444) most of the surviving monks decided to move permanently to Palestine, Syria, and places further north. The Pachomian communities gradually abandoned the Thebaid and settled at sites like Canopus, which were nearer Alexandria and imperial assistance.[55] A century later, faced with similar conditions, the little group of monks remaining in the Sinai Desert petitioned Justinian to protect them and must have been somewhat amazed

---

his blood relatives, and elsewhere refers to his uncle Gallus and grand-uncle Nicetius, both bishops. His genealogy is plotted in the English translation by L. Thorpe (Harmondsworth, 1974), 11; cf. J. Daniélou and H. Marrou, *The Christian Centuries*, vol. 1, *The First Six Hundred Years* (London, 1964), 441.

[54] C. H. Coster, "A Curialis of the Time of the Emperor Arcadius," in *Late Roman Studies*, 145-82, cf. 218-68; J. Bregman, *Synesius of Cyrene—Philosopher-Bishop* (Berkeley, 1982), 168-70.

[55] The attack of the Mazikes constituted the first devastation, which forced many Desert Fathers to take refuge in more secure monasteries, see Ward, *The Sayings*, 28, 72. On Canopus, see Chitty, *The Desert a City*, 66, 68; on the desert monasteries of Esna (Latopolis), which continued in use for centuries, see S. Sauneron and J. Jacquet, *Les Ermitages Chrétiens du désert d'Esna*, Institut français d'archéologie orientale du Caire, Fouilles vol. 29, 3 vols. (Cairo, 1972).

to learn that a complete monastic fortress and garrison would be established.[56] This is the complex that still survives at the foot of the Holy Mountain. The Sinai monks, however, were exceptional, and they appealed to a ruler who loved to plan and execute the most costly and ambitious constructions.

By the middle of the sixth century, few ascetic groups still maintained the customs of the Desert Fathers in Egypt. They were scattered all over the known world and had proclaimed their founders' "Sayings" (*Apophthegmata*) in the remotest corners. Widespread diffusion abroad was, however, based on decline in the homeland. The loose-knit character of Pachomian monasticism also prevented a dominant institutional form from emerging, a form strong enough to resist attack and make permanent claims on the desert sand. The sites themselves were never forgotten and continued to exercise a profound attraction: once the Arab conquest had brought a certain Islamic stability to the area, many of the monasteries revived and developed precisely the endurant forms that would ensure their existence into the Ottoman period. Through the White Monastery near Sohag and the monasteries of Makarios and Antony, among others, the Coptic church was not only kept alive there, but was also supported in parts of Ethiopia and Nubia, where Christianity had always been very isolated.[57]

Ecclesiastical Responsibilities for Urban Survival

But in the period of Late Antiquity the desert communities gradually dwindled away, while conversely the city-based churches flourished. Urban survival at the expense of rural monasticism? Not entirely, for in some areas ascetic traditions took far deeper root than the ecclesiastical hierarchy, while in others cities were overrun and whole Christian church groups transplanted like the Nitrian monasteries to more favourable terrain. Clearly the fate of urban Christianity was intimately connected with the fate of Roman rule. Only in those parts of the empire where administration based on the city was perpetuated did the urban church expand. And ecclesiastical leaders played an important role in the survival of this traditional form of government, for it was in their interest also to protect the major urban centres from attack, in order to preserve their economic role and ruling character. The defence organised at Nisibis by its bishop, Jacob, in the 340s is an early and classic example.[58] As provincial government and city councils declined, such instances would be multiplied when church

[56] Procopius, *Buildings* 5.8.4-9; Saracen attacks on Palestine are cited as the major reason for the fortification.

[57] H. G. Evelyn White, *The Monasteries of the Wadi'n Natrun*, parts 1 and 2 (New York, 1926-32); H. E. Winlock and W. E. Crum, *The Monastery of Epiphanius*, part 2 (New York, 1926), provide evidence for the tenacity of these holy places.

[58] Theodoret de Cyr, *Histoire des Moines*, vol. 1, no. 1.

leaders took over civilian duties, organising military forces, negotiating with the enemy, ransoming prisoners through the sale of ecclesiastical plate, and even leading the city population into combat. In addition, when the imperial authorities or *curiales*, who should have been responsible, failed to repair damage to public utilities, such as the supply of drinking water, bishops assumed yet another secular duty. At times of crisis brought about by natural disasters, flooding, drought, or crop failure, bishops are increasingly found in charge of relief measures. In 535-36 Bishop Datius of Milan was instructed to arrange the distribution of grain from the stores of Milan and to establish fixed prices for other commodities during the Gothic War.[59] Church leaders were well placed to stand in for their civilian counterparts and had been doing so for many years before this. Indeed, their capacity to take over city administration constituted a vital link between the ancient and medieval worlds—a significant stone in the Late Antique bridge.

The process took on particular importance at Rome, as the pagan aspect of senatorial authority slowly gave way to Christian influence, often under the guidance of female exponents of the faith. Resistance to conversion was deeply rooted in the luxurious life-style of the wealthiest families of the empire, who like Symmachus (the pagan leader of the late fourth-century Senate) owned a dozen villas in different parts of Italy, plus landed estates beyond, as well as a large residence in the capital. Since the time when Constantine I deprived them of an emperor, they had been left to their own devices and had devoted themselves increasingly to the pursuit of an indulgent leisure and the holding of public office. Their landed wealth was not consumed by inflation, though they might need ten years' notice to save up for one of the really impressive public displays of racing or fighting required for a son's entry into public office as prefect. And as public office also demanded the maintenance of pagan rites, which were built into the city's history as necessary for its protection, the senators continued to perform them. When, under Ambrose's persistent urging, Theodosius I forced the Senate to remove the altar of Victory at which such rites took place, Symmachus wrote eloquently to reprove him. It is noteworthy that at the same time, Damasus, bishop of Rome, wrote in the name of the Christian senators to congratulate the emperor.[60]

Throughout the fifth century, although the antagonistic and unequal relationship between the church and Senate of Rome did not appear to change greatly, ecclesiastical influence gained ground while pagan de-

---

[59] L. Ruggini, *Economia e Società nell' "Italia Annonaria"* (Milan, 1961), 327-30; cf. 330-35 on the powers of bishops in general.

[60] S. Mazzarino, *Antico, tardoantico ed erà costantiniana* (Rome, 1974), 339-77; Dudden, *Life and Times*, 1:256-69. The two letters are translated in B. Croke and J. Harries, *Religious Conflict in Fourth-Century Rome: A Documentary Study* (Sydney, 1982), 35-50.

clined. Bishops had always provided the city with most of its new churches, but during this century Celestinus, Xystus (Sixtus III), Leo I, and Hilary were responsible for some of the grandest basilicas yet erected.[61] They were also beginning to turn their attention to public monuments as the Senate failed to repair and maintain older buildings. For the individual patron it was much more satisfying to commence a new construction, which would be known by his name, rather than consolidate (or even finish) the work of others. Into the gap bishops of Rome began to step, rebuilding the banks of the Tiber to prevent flooding (a perennial worry) and restoring hostels when they fell into ruin. They also began to participate in diplomatic activity on Rome's behalf: Innocent I accompanied the senatorial embassy of 409 to Alaric, and in 452 Leo I led the mission that went out to negotiate with Attila the Hun. By a familiar mixture of bribery and promises of an imperial bride, the threat to the city was removed. On this occasion, however, the bishop had been responsible, and the poorer, Christian population rejoiced in their *papa* (pope).[62]

Further north on the Danube frontier, Saint Severinus spent many years combining the roles of missionary, bishop, and warrior in his fight to maintain the forts between Regensburg and Passau and their Roman inhabitants.[63] After his death in about 488, however, these settlements were abandoned. The saint's disciples carried his bones with them as they joined the organised migration to Italy. They buried them at a site near Naples (Lucullanum), where they founded a monastery in his name. This failure only highlights the perceived role of church leaders—to support their cities. That the Danube region would eventually pass out of Roman control was probably inevitable—the "cities" along the frontier were more like fortified village camps—but most bishops carried out the uphill task as best they could. Instances of defection are recorded—for instance, the bishop of Margus who betrayed that city to the Huns in 442—but these are rare.[64]

[61] R. Krautheimer, *Rome: Profile of a City, 312-1308* (Princeton, 1980), 45-53. The churches of St. Sabina (425-32), St. Maria Maggiore (completed 440), the Lateran Baptistery, and St. Croce (both rebuilt) date from this period; cf. idem, *Three Christian Capitals* (Berkeley, 1983), 103-121.

[62] Olympiodoros, frag. 8 in R. C. Blockley, *The Fragmentary Classicising Historians of the Late Roman Empire*, 2 vols. (Liverpool, 1981-83), 2:160-63 on Innocent I; Priscus, frag. 22 in Blockley, *Fragmentary*, 2:310-22 on Leo I. On the term *papa*, see J. Moorehead, "*Papa* as 'bishop of Rome,' " *JEH* 36 (1985): 337-50.

[63] F. Lotter, *Severinus von Noricum: Legende und historische Wirklichkeit* (Stuttgart, 1976); but cf. E. A. Thompson, *Romans and Barbarians* (Wisconsin, 1982), 113-33, and the masterful review-article by M. van Uytfanghe, "Les Atavars contemporains de 'l'Hagiologie,' " *Francia* 5 (1977): 639-71.

[64] Priscus, frag. 6 in Blockley, *Fragmentary*, 2:230-31; E. A. Thompson, "Roman Collaborators and Barbarians," *Florilegium* 2 (1980): 71-88.

In general, church leaders found it natural to work for the survival of their close relationship with the Roman civil authorities, even when the latter were doomed to defeat.

In fifth-century, Gaul, where urban ecclesiastics faced various forms of non-Roman threat, they were often deprived of even an elementary military presence by the disorganisation of "Roman" fighting forces of the time. With the flight of the praetorian prefect from Northern Gaul, civil administration became chaotic, as new governors appointed by unknown usurpers or non-Roman powers demanded taxes and grain supplies for their troops. In such circumstances people turned to their churchmen for advice; whether these were holy men, bishops, or monks, they were often of local origin, members of the Gallo-Roman aristocracy.[65] Local loyalties and regional identification superseded any lingering concept of Roman belonging; and the Gallo-Roman church slowly became identified as the accepted organ of guidance in public affairs. From its ranks leaders emerged, and to its number the sons of surviving aristocratic families aspired. In a narrowing spiral of supply and demand, secular education in Gaul was replaced by a new "proto-medieval" syllabus, directed by and for the needs of the church. Christian learning replaced pagan, but very slowly, and without ever eradicating a Roman attachment to Latin poets and classical rhetoric. Through private tutors, sometimes slaves, families committed to this Late Antique culture educated their sons (and more rarely their daughters) in the works of Virgil and Caesar down to the seventh century.[66] By that date, however, the church had assumed the leading role in public education; it was clearly the main force behind the employment of artists and an important source of patronage, and it was taking a tougher line against pagan customs.

CHRISTIAN VERSUS PAGAN CULTURE

The tension between Christian truth based on Scripture and profane learning, which was evident during the fourth and fifth centuries, developed towards a heightened antagonism by the early sixth. A linguistic problem lay

[65] M. Heinzelmann, *Bischofsherrschaft in Gallien, Zur Kontinuität römischer Führungsschichten vom 4ten bis zum 7ten Jahrhundert* (Munich, 1976), esp. parts 2 and 3; R. Mathisen, "Epistolography, Literary Circles and Family Ties in Late Roman Gaul," *Transactions of the American Philological Association* 111 (1981): 95-109; E. James, *The Origins of France* (London, 1982), 49-60.

[66] On the competition for episcopal sees, see R. Mathisen, "Hilarius, Germanus and Lupus: The Aristocratic Background of the Chelidonius Affair," *Phoinix* 33 (1979): 160-69; on education, see P. Riché, *Education and Culture in the Barbarian West* (Columbia, S.C., 1976), 185-93, 311-20, 335-50; D. Illmer, *Formen der Erziehung und Wissensvermittlung im frühen Mittelalter* (Munich, 1971), 150-89.

at the root of the matter—the fact that Greek was barely known in the West and had been increasingly little-understood from the beginning of the period.[67] Neo-Platonist philosophy was, therefore, largely confined to the East, where it flourished. Jerome's mastery of both classical tongues had given him access to a vast range of literature and scholarship, much of it connected with or influenced by pagan thought. In addition, he thoroughly enjoyed reading it. In his lifetime a large number of bilingual scholars worked as translators to make Greek thought available to those limited to Latin. They justified knowledge of pagan authors as a necessary weapon against non-Christians. With Augustine, however, a very short time later, the effort to learn Greek is already apparent, and ease of translation, not to mention inherent pleasure, much more distant. Yet Augustine had been inspired by Cicero's *Hortensius* to study philosophy and felt before his conversion that he could not bear to give up such delight.[68] Thereafter those who knew and loved Greek literature were few and far between in the West. Sidonius Apollinaris, Boethius, and Cassiodorus stand out as exceptional. In general, and among churchmen especially, there was a wariness and suspicion of what was termed "wisdom from outside." It was contrasted with the safe wisdom of the Christian faith, the revealed truths of the Bible.[69]

By the sixth century, therefore, western bishops ceased to recommend a knowledge of pagan authors and turned instead to denounce it. They neither wanted to understand it, nor did their dominant social position permit them to allow others to indulge it. For the growing criticism of pagan cults was partly due to Christian pressure for conformity—ecclesiastics had to ensure that their flock did not stray into the old paths of pagan "superstition." Ancient cults, usually emptied of their original belief, persisted nonetheless, perhaps because people had always celebrated the end of the wine harvest and looked forward to the festivities. This was harmless revelry associated with the name of Bacchus, but no more concerned with a strict pagan cult than the habit of throwing spilt salt over one's shoulder. But clerics thought otherwise and continued to rail against well-established pleasures and superstitions. For Caesarius, bishop of Arles (502-42), non-Christian literature and superstitious practice were viewed with the same deep hostility, though his slightly younger contemporary, Ennodius, bishop of Pavia (511-21), indulged a passion for Latin poetry. Few of their

[67] P. P. Courcelle, *Late Latin Writers and Their Greek Sources* (Cambridge, Mass., 1969), 148-208.

[68] Augustine, *Confessions*, 3.4.

[69] See for instance, Avitus *"exterioribus studiis eruditus," Vita Bonitii*, in *MGH, SSRM*, 6, 121; cf. P. Riché, "L'instruction des laïcs en Gaule merovingienne au VIIe siècle," *Settimane* 5 (1955): 2:873-88; P. Brown, *Augustine of Hippo* (London, 1967), 40-45.

congregations were likely to have been reading Apuleius, however, so it was the watered-down survivals of paganism that churchmen generally attacked.[70]

It was in the East where a continuity of language made ancient writings so much more accessible that serious commitment to paganism could live on, albeit among very tiny circles of intellectuals who were no threat to the church. Pagan holy men attracted support in the same way as Christians: their ascetic habits impressed and were held capable of attaining a proximity to divine power. Pagan philosophers also attracted students, who wished to extend their understanding of ancient texts still studied in school.[71] Among clerics, however, the established parameters of Scripture, commentaries, and other writings of the Church Fathers were rarely overstepped. Most received a purely Christian education. Some never mastered the intricate theological arguments of early Christian debates, which were certainly lost on many western ecclesiastics. Fulgentius, bishop of Ruspe in North Africa (507-27), maintained an exceptional balance, writing with equal command on the finer points of theological and mythological exegesis.[72] These skills reflect his bilingual background and the rich monastic libraries in which he read. And even Fulgentius is a pale shadow of the great Jerome. Few could accede to the most elementary stages of this tradition by the beginning of the sixth century, and together with growing ignorance, hostility to paganism increased.

The Closure of the Academy

Justinian brought this to a head with his decree prohibiting pagans from holding positions of public education financed by city councils (529).[73] The measure struck the Neo-Platonic Academy of Athens particularly by confiscating its lands and traditional means of support. For centuries the chief exponent of pagan philosophy, the *diadochos* (literally, "successor") had imparted the wisdom of the ancients to an audience of the brightest young men from all regions of the East Mediterranean. The post, together with other teaching positions, was maintained from income derived from the original landed endowment and subsequent additions. In the fourth

[70] Riché, *Education and Culture*, 86-90, 93-94.

[71] G. Fowden, "The Pagan Holy Man in Late Antique Society," *JHS* 102 (1982): 33-59; P. Brown, *The Making of Late Antiquity*, 11-26, 54-72; on Libanius as teacher, see A.-J. Festugière, *Antioche paienne et chrétienne* (Paris, 1959), 91-119.

[72] H.-J. Diesner, *Fulgentius von Ruspe als Theologe und Kirchenpolitiker* (Stuttgart, 1966).

[73] *Codex Justinianus* (ed. P. Krueger [Berlin, 1877]) 1.11.10; cf. 1.5.18.4, against heretics, Jews, or pagans serving in the administration or holding any sort of dignity. On the closure of the Academy, see A. Cameron, "The Last Days of the Academy at Athens," *Proceedings of the Cambridge Philological Society* 196 (1969): 7-29.

and fifth centuries, philosophers like Proclus had continued to attract young intellectuals to their courses in the Pythagorean and Chaldean mysteries.[74] The Alexandrian school, on the other hand, had developed a certain synthesis of Christian and pagan thought under such masters as John Philoponos and was permitted to continue.

Two motives seem to lie behind this reinforcement of Christian learning: first, the church's growing intolerance, and second, the dominance of Constantinople. At one stroke the state attempted to remove the influence of the most overtly pagan school in the East Mediterranean and establish Christianity in its place, while it elevated the position of the capital above all other centres of education. In both respects the decline of Athens had been a slow one, extending from Theodosius II's restrictions on pagan teaching to Justinian's ruling. And even though it lost its philosophers and ultimately succumbed to economic and military pressures in the late sixth century, its classical fame survived long into the medieval period. In the middle of the eighth century when Athens was no more than a village settlement clustered around the Acropolis, with a small part of the Parthenon converted into a church dedicated to the Virgin, western authors could earnestly believe that Theodore of Tarsos had been educated there.[75] Knowledge of Greek and higher learning were automatically associated with the Attic home of the philosophers, despite the fact that Theodore had never visited the abandoned shrines of pagan wisdom.

The contradictory nature of the alliance between Christianity and classical learning can be summarised as follows: the new faith had a narrower focus but was spread wider. It was both more expansive *and* more limiting than its predecessor and rival. Thus, once it had established a strong hold on the religious life of the late empire, it proceeded to an unavoidable restriction and adaptation of Roman culture—the two developments could not be separated. Classical learning, being dependent upon imperial and civic support for its propagation, also had to accommodate the new belief that so rapidly altered the religious allegiance of its paymasters. But in so doing, it lost its monopoly on teaching and provoked the opposition of ecclesiastical culture. This eventually reduced its traditions to the type of literary riddle and poetic obscurity produced by the Irish grammarian, Virgilius Maro (flourished ca. 600-650).[76] The prolonged life of classical forms

---

[74] See the *Life* of Proclus by Marinus, ed. J. F. Boissonade (Leipzig, 1814, reprinted Amsterdam, 1966).

[75] So Pope Zacharias informed St. Boniface, see Letter 80, in *MGH, Epistolae selectae*, 1: 172-80 (English translation by E. Emerton, *The Letters of St. Boniface* [New York, 1940], 143).

[76] L. Holtz, "Irish Grammarians and the Continent in the Seventh Century," *Columbanus and Merovingian Monasticism*, ed. H. B. Clarke and M. Brennan (Oxford, 1981), 137-44,

of writings, devoid of any serious content, can be seen in some of the more preposterous etymological derivations of Isidore of Seville (570-636). Yet the work of this Visigothic bishop was of fundamental importance for the Middle Ages, as we will see in Chapter 6.

The Pedagogic Structure of Late Antique Culture

It is in the educational system of the sixth century that this complex synthesis of pagan and Christian elements is most clearly revealed. For despite the church's opposition to the most "dangerous" parts of the ancient trivium and quadrivium (or seven liberal arts), the classical syllabus continued to be studied. Some of the overtly pagan aspects had been removed, others rendered less inimical by the "harmonising" efforts of Clement and Origen, third-century Alexandrian theologians. Their authoritative writings on the common basis of certain Platonic and Christian philosophical ideas protected the teaching of pagan thought, mythology, and literature to a degree. But by the sixth century, Christians were much less receptive to ancient philosophy (as we have seen), and much less able to study Greek thought in the original.

Christian influence reinforced this decline in the ubiquitous employment of Greek by elevating Latin and Syriac as the medium of churches in the West and a large part of the East Mediterranean respectively. While the exact proportion of Greek to Syriac speakers in the East is impossible to determine, the quantity of translations made from the fourth century onwards implies a very large area in Syria and western Mesopotamia where Greek was not a first language. There, as in the West, the ancient syllabus was taught in translation. A figure like Boethius is quite exceptional, both in his interest in ancient Greek philosophy and in his capacity to study the original texts.[77] Through his distinguished translations and his own commentaries and philosophical writings, part of the Aristotelian corpus was preserved for medieval Europe, while 100 years later, Athanasios of Baladh provided a similar translation service for the Syriac-speaking East.[78]

147; M. Herren, "Some Light on the Life of Virgilius Maro Grammaticus," *Proceedings of the Royal Irish Academy* 79C, no. 2 (1979): 27-71; G. Polara and L. Carusio, eds., *Virgilio Marone grammatico, epitomi ed epistole* (Naples, 1979).

[77] Courcelle, *Late Latin Writers*, 274-318; J. Shiel, "Boethius' Commentaries on Aristotle," *Medieval and Renaissance Studies* 4 (1958): 217-44; H. Chadwick, *Boethius, The Consolations of Music, Logic, Theology and Philosophy* (Oxford, 1981). Cf. the essays collected in *Boethius*, ed. M. Gibson (Oxford, 1981).

[78] R. Duval, *La littérature syriaque*, 3rd ed. (Paris, 1907), 251-52; Athanasios was Jacobite Patriarch of Antioch from 683 to 686. He completed a Syriac translation of Porphyry's *Introduction* to Aristotle and another anonymous Greek one in 645; see G. Furlani "L'introduzione di Atanasio di Bâlâdh alla logia e sillogistica aristotelica tradotta dal syriaco," *Atti del reale Istituto di Scienze, Lettere ed Arte* 85 (2) (1926): 319-44.

This was more significant for the ultimate preservation of Aristotle's work, in that it provided a working text for ninth-century Arabic translators in Baghdad.

In the West, Cassiodorus played a major role in maintaining the traditions of classical education; his efforts reveal the strengths and weaknesses of Late Antique culture in the predominantly Christian environment of sixth-century Italy. Cassiodorus firmly believed that a classical training in the seven liberal arts was both the best preparation for higher studies in Christian theology and the best form of defence against non-Christian attacks on the church. His first attempt to establish some sort of Christian university to serve these purposes failed. It was a project organised jointly with Pope Agapitus in the years 535-36, which was barely set up before the civil disturbance of Justinian's re-conquest destroyed it.[79] Shortly afterwards Cassiodorus went to Constantinople, where he seems to have come into contact with Junilius, an African civil servant, who held the legal position of *quaestor* and was concerned with pedagogical problems. The two men thus shared a common background, a bilingual training and an interest in education. Junilius was responsible for translating from Greek a manual of basic theological exegesis written in the traditional style of the school of Nisibis. It was probably prepared by Paul the Persian as an elementary introduction to philosophical thinking, and Cassiodorus found in it a useful guide to the methods of the eastern school.[80] When he returned to the West he brought a copy of Junilius's *Instituta regularia divinae legis* along with many other eastern texts, which he placed in the library of Vivarium, the monastery he founded on family estates in Southern Italy (near Squillace).

It is in the *Institutions*, which he wrote to instruct the monks of Vivarium, that Cassiodorus's pedagogic principles are most clearly revealed.[81] He encouraged them to study profane as well as ecclesiastical authors, to develop their intellectual skills by reading pagan literature as well as the works of the church fathers. As a model of historical writing, he recommended Josephus (the *History of the Wars* in translation) and had a Latin version of the *Jewish Antiquities* specially prepared. For examples of correct grammar and elegant style, he regularly cited classical authors and used ancient examples to indicate how best to punctuate a Christian text. As the

[79] M. L. W. Laistner, *The Intellectual Heritage of the Early Middle Ages* (Ithaca/New York, 1957), 22-39; A. Momigliano, "Cassiodorus and the Italian Culture of His Time," *Proceedings of the British Academy* 41 (1955): 218-45; Illmer, *Formen der Erziehung*, 49-78.

[80] D. Gutas, "Paul the Persian on the Classification of Aristotle's Philosophy: A Milestone Between Alexandria and Bagdâd," *Der Islam* 60 (1983): 231-67.

[81] R. A. B. Mynors, *Cassiodori Senatoris Institutiones Divinae* (Oxford, 1937); Riché, *Education and Culture*, 163-69.

copying of manuscripts was a major task of the Vivarium monks, Cassiodorus prepared a manual for them, *De Orthographia*, which dealt with many problems encountered in the transmission of texts. While his own particular interest in grammar and literary matters is more pronounced than any philosophical concern, his attention to the training of copyists is a basic pedagogic feature of classical education, one echoed as far afield as the Nestorian monastery of Beth Abhe.[82]

In addition to this educational function, Cassiodorus intended that his monastery should transmit eastern learning in Greek to the Latin-speaking West, although there were only 15 Greek manuscripts in the library at Vivarium. To this end, he compiled a medical corpus from certain works of Dioscorides (the *Herbal*), Galen, and Hippocrates, accompanied by a sixth-century Greek commentary by Stephen of Athens; he also selected passages from eastern continuations of Eusebios's famous *Ecclesiastical History*, which were then translated under his direction. For obvious reasons the medical text continued to serve an important practical purpose and can be traced to the revival of medical studies in the eleventh-century school of Salerno. Similarly, the *Historia Tripartita*, so called because it is made up of three parts by three separate authors, became a valuable source for later Christians trying to study the early history of the church.[83] These historical and medical translations distinguished Vivarium from other monastic scriptoria in much the same way that Cassiodorus's familiarity with classical literature set him apart from his contemporaries. For his long life spans the period when knowledge of Greek became a thing of the past and the western church increased its grip over higher education, with a corresponding decline in secular schooling.

At the very time when Cassiodorus was attempting to instill the principles of traditional education among his monks, another Westerner was studying the same principles in Constantinople. John of Biclar, a Visigoth from Spain, seems to have spent seven years in the capital in the 560s and 570s, following the classical syllabus as it was taught by professors still financed by the state.[84] The reasons for his move from Spain to the eastern

[82] Eusebios, *HE* 5.20, quoting St. Irenaeus on the vital importance of copying correctly; Riché, *Education and Culture*, 163, 164-65; on Beth Abhe, see *The Book of the Governors: The Historia Monastica of Thomas, Bishop of Marga*, A.D. 840, ed. and tr. E. A. Wallis Budge, 2 vols. (London, 1893), 1: lix-lxiv, 2: passim.

[83] Courcelle, *Late Latin Winters*, 319 n. 7; on the medical texts and their future use, see ibid., 403, 408; on the *Historia Tripertita*, see Momigliano, "Cassiodorus," and Laistner, *Intellectual Heritage*.

[84] Isidore of Seville, *De viris illustribus*, ed. C. Cordoñer Merida (Salamanca, 1964), no. 31, 151-52. The manuscripts are unclear on the number of years spent in the East, some giving 17, others seven. On the basis of the *Chronicle* and its first-person observations of the plague in ?573 (in *MGH, AA*, vol. 11 (2), 213, line 17), the latter seems more likely. On

end of the Mediterranean are obscure; the suggestion that his mother may have been of Roman origin and therefore also a Catholic as opposed to the Arian Visigoths would help to account for it and for his un-Gothic name, but unfortunately we are totally uninformed about his parentage and upbringing. It was probably as a young man that he began to study in one of the most distinguished "schools" of Late Antiquity. There he mastered the classical languages and studied those texts that formed the backbone of the seven liberal arts. He may also have gained a familiarity with the civilisation of the East Roman Empire, its secular as well as Christian traditions. On his return to Spain, which remained under Arian control until 589, John founded a Catholic monastery at Biclar and wrote a rule for his monks (which does not survive). After the conversion of King Reccared to orthodoxy, John was promoted to the episcopal see of Gerona and ended his career in a manner typical of educated clerics of the sixth century.

What is, however, unusual for a Christian Goth of this time, is John's prolonged exposure to eastern culture, which gave him access to theological, historical, and probably monastic writings in Greek. The influence of these studies is evident in his own surviving work, a continuation of the *Chronicle* of Eusebios, Jerome, Prosper, and Victor of Tonnena, from the year 565 to 590.[85] This history, in Latin, reveals an awareness of contemporary Byzantine historiography; it employs a system of dating by regnal year (both of emperor and Visigothic monarch) and includes some lively observations of important secular events in the capital, written in the first person. Striking descriptions of embassies, from the *Maccurritarum* and *Sarracenorum*, and of the triumph celebrated after Tiberios II's victory over the Persians, complete with 23 elephants, are coupled with John's accounts of the plague and of Avar and Slav raids in Thrace, which provide an impression of daily life in the capital. This is all in marked contrast to the purely ecclesiastical section of the *Chronicle* contributed by the African cleric, Victor of Tonnena, and shows a greater attention to the problems of writing history than any contemporary western chronicler. To his younger admirer, Isidore of Seville, John of Biclar was one of the most distinguished men of his time: "He went to Constantinople and there was nurtured on Greek and Latin erudition. . . ."[86] With hindsight, we can see that he was one of the last Westerners of Late Antiquity who understood the rich depths of its culture.

John of Biclar's birth, see J. Fontaine, *Isidore de Séville et la culture classique dans l'Espagne wisigothique*, 2 vols. (Paris, 1959), 2:848 n. 2.

[85] T. Mommsen, ed., *Chronica minora saec. IV-VII*, in *MGH. AA*, vol.11 (20), 207-20.

[86] *MGH. AA*, vol.11 (20), 213.21-22; 214.29-31; 214.7-16; 214.30-33; 215.7; 215.24; 216.14. See also, note 84 above.

The Survival of Classical Oratory. While John shrouded his culture in an overtly religious guise, other writers of the period represent a more strictly classical vein. Thus we can cite several instances of public oratory, a highly secular and ancient practice, being employed at relatively minor courts. One of the most striking concerns the public recitation of the *Iohannis*, a Latin epic in eight cantos, given by the author, Corippus, in the governor's palace in Carthage in about 548, after the Byzantine reconquest. This celebrated the feats of a particular military general, John Troglita, appointed by Justinian to lead the campaign. It is a witness to the survival of classical traditions of official speech writing and heroic declamation, efforts barely justified by the subject matter. Corippus gained much greater fame as the official panegyricist of Justin II in Constantinople; his *In Laudem Iustini augusti minoris* of nearly 20 years later (566-67) is an interesting example of Late Antique rhetorical art, one of the last written in Latin for the Byzantine court and possibly one of the last in the established ancient style. A striking contrast is provided by the Greek panegyric delivered by Dioskoros of Aphrodito, when Justin sent his imperial portrait to Antinoë, the administrative capital of central Egypt, in 566.[87]

A rather different occasion provided the pretext for Venantius Fortunatus to compose a poem of equally classical proportions. The event was the marriage of the Visigothic princess, Brunhild, to King Sigebert of Austrasia in Metz in 566; it demanded an *epithalamium*, nuptial celebration, and the Italian poet, who happened to be there at the time, complied.[88] The offering was probably most appreciated by the young bride, who had apparently received a fairly rigorous traditional education. And even if the Latin verse was lost on the audience, they must have known that such speechifying was the correct way for marriages to be commemorated for posterity. For Venantius, however, the *epithalamium* was just another of the classical forms that he had mastered in the schools of Ravenna and Pavia in the 550s; he simply turned his fertile imagination to a new topic and wrote in the requisite metre. With such a complete Late Antique formation, it is somewhat surprising to find Venantius finally ensconsed as bishop of Poitiers—the ecclesiastical component of his education had been rather inadequate for such a position. But he came to it with the support and advice of Saint Radegund, who had detained him in Poitiers so that their conversations about classical literature might not be interrupted. Whether he was equally competent as a bishop and as a versifier is not clear; certainly he

---

[87] Corippus, *Iohannis*, ed. J. Diggle and F. R. D. Goodyear (Cambridge, 1970); *In laudem Iustini minoris*, ed. Averil Cameron (London, 1976); L. MacCoull, "The Panegyric of Justin II by Dioscurus of Aphrodito," *B* 54 (1984): 575-85.

[88] F. J. E. Raby, *A History of Secular Latin Poetry in the Middle Ages*, 2nd ed., 2 vols. (Oxford, 1957), 1:128-41, esp. 130.

became a great hymnographer while he enjoyed the friendship and cultivated discourse of the abbess of the convent of the Holy Cross.

One final instance of mid-sixth-century oratory must be mentioned
here, despite its very different nature. As Rome was being fought over by
Byzantine and Gothic forces in 544, Pope Vigilius ordered his subdeacon,
Arator, to give a public recitation of his verse paraphrase of the *Acts of the
Apostles*.[89] This four-day performance took place in the church of Saint Peter ad Vincula in front of a lay and clerical audience. It transposed the classical principle of court rhetoric to an entirely Christian setting and elevated
the then-popular attempt to render Scriptural teaching in a cultivated and
recognisably classical mode to an authoritative position. The same peculiar
combination had been tried in North Africa earlier; this was its first and
last appearance in Rome. But interestingly, Carolingian poets found Arator's work a source of considerable inspiration in their attempts to revive
classical verse forms. Like Venantius, Arator had been educated in the
grammar and law schools of Milan and Pavia. His command of Latin and
affection for the classical poets in particular is very evident, even though
his style is sometimes contrived and rather clumsy. He appears to have
served in the Gothic administration in Italy before becoming a cleric and
shared with Venantius an enthusiasm for literature rather than theology.
Yet both ended up in the service of the church, a fact that confirms the
ubiquitous spread of Christian forms of social organisation at the expense
of civilian ones. For people of culture the church increasingly presented the
most suitable type of employment.

Ecclesiastical Patronage of Learning

The church was also a refuge for many whose lives had been disrupted by
the violence of the mid-sixth century. The young Thuringian princess,
Radegund, orphaned and thrust upon the mercy of Chlotar I of the Franks,
ultimately found her vocation in the service of Christianity. Prior to this,
however, she was utterly dependent upon the king, who made sure that she
received a decent education and then made her his third wife. Although she
thus secured a high social status and gained a genuine feeling for Latin literature, her first love remained the church, and it was to the local bishop
that she turned to be released from her marriage in order to found a nunnery. Having chosen to place her foundation under the protection of the
True Cross, she then wrote to the Emperor Justin II requesting a fragment
of this treasured object, and the relic, probably housed in the magnificent
case that survives in part, was sent to Gaul. Although the correspondence

[89] Arator, *De Actibus Apostolorum*, ed. A. P. McKinley (Vienna, 1951); cf. A. P. Mc-
Kinley, *Arator: The Codices* (Cambridge, Mass., 1942), 104-118.

surrounding this transfer is full of formulaic praise and appreciation, it reveals an awareness of sixth-century realities.[90] Radegund knew that the see of Constantinople was not as celebrated as apostolic foundations such as Antioch or Alexandria, but she realised that the eastern emperor could provide what she wanted. So she applied to Constantinople, and it was probably from the capital that additional pieces of liturgical furniture were also dispatched to Poitiers. By the middle of the sixth century, Byzantium was both the repository of a great number of important relics and the centre of a highly developed artistic style, executed chiefly in imperial workshops under the direct patronage of the palace. In her determination to have the best for her own royal foundation, Radegund manifested a clear understanding of Constantinople's function as a city that combined both Roman and Christian traditions.

While the eastern capital maintained the bilingual skills required by a traditional classical education, in Rome steps had to be taken to preserve a working knowledge of Greek. These tended to serve the particular needs of the church, rather than the pedagogic structures of ancient wisdom. Even in the late fifth century, ignorance of Greek had proved a handicap to the church of Rome, and Pope Gelasius (492-96) installed an eastern monk whom he knew from Constantinople to translate documents in the papal archive.[91] Dionysios (Dionysius *exiguus*, "the small," to the Romans) prepared Latin versions of correspondence with Greek prelates and doctrinal debates of the eastern church; he also corrected a faulty translation of established church law (the *codex canonum ecclesiasticorum*) and prepared a treatise on the calculation of Easter by Alexandrian methods, which eventually replaced the western system devised by Victor of Aquitaine. Until his death in the 530s he was constantly in demand, receiving commissions to translate the *Life* of Pachomios and other eastern hagiographical works, as well as Gregory of Nyssa's philosophical text *On the Condition of Man*, requested by Abbot Eugippius of Lucullanum. This pressure to make accessible Latin versions of important ecclesiastical writings was the main force behind Dionysios's work, which Cassiodorus greatly admired. But it served a practical purpose in the life of the western church rather than perpetuating classical learning and pedagogic principle.

It was this same force that motivated the equally impressive work of

[90] Radegund's culture is praised by Venantius Fortunatus, who also composed the letter-poem to Justin and Sophia, in *MGH, AA,* 4 (1), Appendix II, 275-78; cf. *Vita Radegundi* 2.16, in *MGH, SSRM,* vol. 2 (Hannover, 1888), 388; and Gregory of Tours, *HF* 9.40. Part of the reliquary and other liturgical objects sent from Byzantium survive at the monastery of the Holy Cross at Poitiers; see P. Lasko, *The Kingdom of the Franks* (London, 1971), 74-75.
[91] Dionysius *exiguus*, works in *PL* 67; *Praefationes*, ed. F. Gloire, *CCL* 85 (Turnhout, 1972); cf. Courcelle, *Late Latin Writers*, 313-15.

Saint Martin of Braga in the second half of the sixth century.[92] Like Dionysios, Martin was of eastern origin and was familiar with the monastic world of Palestine and Egypt. He established an ascetic community in northwest Spain at Dumio, acting as missionary to the Arian Sueves and eventually becoming bishop of Braga. In establishing the orthodox church in this recently converted area, he presided at several important local councils, wrote treatises on topics of immediate significance (such as baptism and the calculation of Easter), and in answer to the request of a subordinate bishop, wrote a sermon against pagan and idolatrous practices. These writings alone would ensure the honoured position of Martin in the Spanish church. But he also translated two Greek collections into Latin, one of *Sayings* of the Desert Fathers, and another of eastern church rulings, the 84 *Capitula Martini*, selected from councils held in the East Mediterranean. These were intended to provide instruction for another subordinate bishop and therefore had a practical purpose. In addition, under the patronage of King Miro of the Sueves, Martin prepared a selection from the writings of Seneca, the *Formula vitae honestae*, which was to prove enormously popular with medieval scholars. This was the only purely classical work to come out of the monastery established by Martin. Its isolation is a further indication of the developed Christian culture that gradually squeezed out pagan literature and learning from the syllabus.

Despite Cassiodorus's intentions, the same exclusively Christian tendency frustrated his revival of classical studies at Vivarium.[93] The study of Greek was not deeply engrained; translators worked slowly and often without a real command of both languages, and the intellectual capacity of the monks was directed much more towards matters of Christian theology than ancient learning. Even during Cassiodorus's lifetime, the majority of Greek texts translated at Vivarium were of patristic or canonical writings, relating to questions of church organisation, discipline, and authoritative interpretations of Scripture. The principle of a sound classical education (in the old-fashioned pagan sense) as the best preparation for a Christian life could not survive in the restricted and narrow culture of late sixth-century Italy. Although Vivarium continued, its academic programme was abandoned and its library eventually dispersed to enrich the collections of the papacy and of the Northumbrian monasteries of Monkwearmouth/Jarrow.

In the East, meanwhile, the relative ease of access to ancient Greek philosophy meant that it had always been an integral part of higher education, whatever ecclesiastics might say to disparage it. A formal training in the

---

[92] *Martini Episcopi Bracarensis Opera Omnia*, ed. C. W. Barlow (New Haven, 1950), translated by Barlow, *Fathers of the Church*, vol. 62 (Washington, D.C., 1969).

[93] See Courcelle, *Late Latin Writers*, 354-403; and Riché, *Education and Culture*, 66-69.

seven liberal arts was considered essential for all professional careers and public positions within the empire. Official instruction in the ancient syllabus was, however, overlaid with a Christian interpretation, and the oldest centres of pagan learning had declined at the expense of the overtly Christian schools of Constantinople and Alexandria. While commentaries on most aspects of Greek science and philosophy were still written, they paid at least lip service to the dominant faith and official position of Christianity.

The "Christian Topography" of Cosmas Indicopleustes. A most revealing example of this synthesis of Christian and ancient learning is provided by the debate between John Philoponos and Cosmas Indicopleustes, which raged in Alexandria in the middle of the sixth century.[94] It pitted a literate, observant, and intelligent merchant (Cosmas) against one of the most outstanding teachers of philosophy (John); and the subject of their debate was no less a problem than the origin of the world. On either side, the contributions of different ancient authors were adduced and assimilated to basically Christian interpretations, again different, to produce a debate couched almost entirely in religious terms. In his *Christian Topography* Cosmas presented the world as a square building, a concept derived from Nestorian exegesis of the Old Testament description of the tabernacle, and he combined this with certain physical laws of Greek science. His flat earth, for instance, progressed through degrees of inclination relative to the sun, which explained the divisions of day and night as well as such phenomena as eclipses. While many ecclesiastics had imagined the universe as a flat surface under a vaulted sky, Cosmas was the first writer to try and prove how this structure had come into being and how it functioned. He wrote against the Aristotelian and Monophysite interpretation of John Philoponos, which had adopted the spherical world and a considerable body of ancient theory about its movement. John's rebuttal, in a text entitled *De Opificio Mundi*, clearly has science on its side, and indeed became the dominant interpretation in sixth-century Alexandria.[95] But before we dismiss Cosmas as a failure, it is worth looking at his history.

As a merchant based in Alexandria, Cosmas was involved in that long-distance trade which was characteristic of the ancient world. Although it may be doubted whether he ever reached India, as his nickname suggests, he was familiar with trading stations in the Red Sea and on the Persian

[94] W. Conus-Wolska, *Recherches sur la "Topographie chrétienne" de Cosmas Indicopleustes: Théologie et Science au VI siècle* (Paris, 1962), esp. 161-83; idem, ed., *Cosmas Indicopleustes, La Topographie chrétienne*, 3 vols. (Paris, 1968-73); English translation by J. W. McCrindle, *The Christian Topography of Cosmas, An Egyptian Monk* (London, 1897).

[95] John Philoponos, *De Opificio Mundi*, ed. G. Reichardt (Leipzig, 1897).

Gulf, which made him widely travelled for his time. He also displayed a curiosity about things he saw and heard about on his journeys, recording them and discussing them with friends in the lively cosmopolitan circles of Alexandria. He knew of the Christian communities in Persia that were independent of Constantinople and the three other eastern patriarchates. And in investigating their theology in the Nestorian texts available to him, he discovered theories that made sense of the creation of the universe. The writings of Theodore of Mopsuestia, in particular, provided a total subordination of cosmology to Nestorian philosophy.[96] From this Cosmas then tried to develop a complete system for the physical functioning of the universe, a scientific explanation based on his theological assumptions. The resulting unity of religious thought and ancient learning was typical of the sixth-century East Mediterranean Christianising of science. And it was the work of a self-taught merchant who had little formal education and simply pursued matters of spiritual importance at an unusually high level. While John Philoponos was well equipped to counter these arguments and succeeded in removing Cosmas from serious consideration in Alexandria, what is more significant is that such a battle had ever taken place.

For the debate reveals that laymen with no particular training in difficult subjects could master aspects of Greek science and philosophy and blend them with contemporary Christian polemic. This achievement presupposes a much higher level of basic literacy, a wider reading and access to texts as well as a conscious sense of enquiry about fundamental philosophical questions than that preserved in the contemporary West. Although Cosmas has a quite obsessive concern with correct Christian doctrines, which reduces the conflict with Philoponos into a sectarian one at times, his investigation is much broader than western clerical enquiry. But then, there is no western equivalent of the *Christian Topography*. The circumstances that made it possible for Cosmas to take on an established professor of philosophy in Alexandria simply did not exist in the western Mediterranean. This difference gave the East an advantage and pointed to a real inequality of inheritance in the two halves of the world of Late Antiquity.

It is tempting to relate this inequality to the historic formation of ancient Greek culture, which was spread throughout the Near East via the Hellenistic kingdoms while the Etruscans were independently laying the base for later Roman culture. But this would be to ignore the long centuries of interaction, bilingual practice, and mutual influence that produced a common intellectual culture and a genuine sense of shared background. By the middle of the sixth century it might be wearing very thin, but in

---

[96] Conus-Wolska, *Recherches*, 63-85. Both Monophysite and Nestorian theologies will be discussed in Chapter 3.

the work of individuals as different as Cosmas, John of Biclar, Arator, and Martin of Braga we are dealing with different aspects of the same cultural heritage. Significantly, the three who settled in the West all adopted an ecclesiastical mode; Cosmas is alone in tackling theological problems from a lay standpoint, and for all we know he too may have ended his days in some Nestorian monastery.

FROM INSIGNIFICANT beginnings the Christian faith had gradually established itself as the most commonly observed religion of the Mediterranean and an integral part of Late Antique culture. The imperial cult had been adapted to fit, and the worship of ancient gods was all but obliterated. In many cases, particular rituals were taken over and rendered innocuous by Christianity; others were relegated by the churches to the sphere of superstition and repeatedly condemned. The formation of a Late Antique cultural unity, based on the almost ubiquitous adoption of the Christian faith, thus involved losses, particularly in the West, but it also preserved undeniable strengths. For it created the medium whereby ancient skills and techniques could be inherited, in education, oratory and rhetoric, legal practice, and artistic traditions. In visual terms this unity made a real impact, even when a comparison is made between the wealthiest city of the Mediterranean, Constantinople, and small provincial centres both in the East and West. The classical heritage had been preserved and could flourish even in the predominantly Christian ambience of the sixth century. Equally, Christianity was actively shaping, restricting, and reworking this inheritance, which it also transmitted to non-Mediterranean regions. So we must now turn to examine the communities of Christians, who were directly involved in this process.

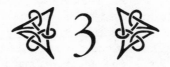

The Churches in the Sixth Century:
The Council of 553

ALTHOUGH Christianity provided the medium for both the unity of faith and the unity of culture in the Late Antique world, it was by no means a monolithic and uniform force. On the contrary, it was immensely varied and reflected the different regions into which it had spread in the course of six centuries. Over such a long time span and vast area, local particularities that distinguished one regional church from others were bound to develop, especially when Christendom consisted more of a loose confederation of believers than a tightly regulated organisation. In this process political and geographical factors, and autonomous and disparate growth combined. If these are ignored or given insufficient weight, we lose sight of the central dynamism of Christianity, which rests precisely on a unity through variety. In the early centuries Christians developed their own idiosyncratic and independent types of devotion; episcopal, patriarchal, and papal authority were established very slowly, and communities reserved the highest degree of loyalty, obedience, and affection for their local leaders, often monks. Thus uniformity of ritual and even of belief was impossible, indeed in some cases it was undesirable. For missionaries who could adapt Christianity to the particular needs of a region were much more likely to make converts than those who tried to impose a strict doctrinaire organisation. In the light of this diversity, which had assisted in such an enormous expansion of the faith, it is now necessary to examine the condition of the sixth-century churches.

THE THREE SACRED LANGUAGES

The first notable restriction to Christian uniformity sprang from the variety of languages in which the Scriptures had been transmitted. Aramaic was of course the original spoken tongue of Jesus and its predecessor, Hebrew, the medium of the Old Testament.[1] This was available in several Greek versions, of which the Septuagint, probably made in the third century B.C. for Greek-speaking Jews in Alexandria, was the most widely known. Because of this close connection with Semitic languages, Judaeo-Christian circles had access to many alleged sayings of Christ and the Apostles that circulated in both Greek and Aramaic. Such sayings held a special significance for communities inspired by oral rather than written traditions, as were many early Christian groups with a direct ascent to apostolic times.[2] The books of the New Testament, which did not emerge in its modern form for many centuries, were written in a simple Greek, known as *koine*, and frequently translated into Latin from the first century onwards. As Greek continued to be used for the Christian liturgy in Rome until the early third century, other centres in Italy or North Africa may have been responsible for these Old Latin versions of the New Testament.[3] At Pope Damasus's request, St. Jerome revised the many texts in use when he made a corrected translation from the oldest Greek manuscripts, and revised the Latin Psalter (prior to 384). Later this great *vir trilinguis* ("trilingual man") retranslated the Old Testament from Hebrew, and the complete Latin Bible that resulted is what we know as the Vulgate.[4] (It was not called this until the sixteenth century, nor was it generally accepted as the official version until well into the eighth; people familiar with the previous Latin wording were reluctant to give it up, and in the case of the Psalms Jerome himself recognised this problem, incorporating the Old Latin rather than his new translation into the Vulgate.) Although a standard text was thus available from the early fifth century, complete Bibles remained extremely rare, being bulky and very expensive manuscripts. More often, sections of the Bible circulated on their own—the Psalms and the Law of Moses (the Pentateuch, the first five books) from the Old Testament, the

[1] *Cambridge History of the Bible*, vol. 1, *From the Beginnings to Jerome*, ed. P. R. Ackroyd and C. F. Evans (Cambridge, 1970); G. Bardy *La question des langues dans l'église ancienne*, vol. 1 (Paris, 1948); J. A. Emerton, "The Problem of Vernacular Hebrew in the First Century A.D. and the Language of Jesus," *JTS* 24 (1973): 1-23.

[2] *Cambridge History of the Bible*, 1:286-95; cf. E. H. Pagels, *The Gnostic Gospels* (London, 1980). A similar stress on the direct links between Jesus and later times is displayed in the Gospel accounts of His genealogy; see R. T. Hood, "The Genealogies of Jesus," in A. Wikgren, ed., *Early Christian Origins*, Studies in Honour of H. R. Willougby (Chicago, 1961), 1-15. The oral tradition may be observed in the teaching of St. Polycarp of Smyrna, who transmitted to his students (including St. Irenaeus, later bishop of Lyon) an interpretation of Christian faith handed down orally from Apostolic times; see Eusebios, *HE* 5.20.4-7; cf. the oral teaching of Justin, in H. von Campenhausen, *Ecclesiastical Authority and Spiritual Power* (London, 1969), 192-96.

[3] B. M. Metzger, *The Early Versions of the New Testament* (Oxford, 1977), 285-329.

[4] *Cambridge History of the Bible*, 1:510-41; W. Berschin, *Griechisch-Lateinisches Mittelalter* (Berne/Munich, 1980), 63-69.

individual Gospels, some of the Epistles of St. Paul, or the Acts of the Apostles from the New.

Apart from the three holy languages, Hebrew, Greek, and Latin, the Bible or parts of it were known in many others.[5] Before the end of the second century, Sahidic versions of both the Old and New Testaments were available to the Copts. Antony heard the Gospel of St. Matthew read in Coptic, and in the early fourth century Pachom's monks would have employed a translation rather than the original Greek. Later the Armenian church had its own version, possibly made from the Old Syriac; Georgian, Ethiopic, and Persian translations followed. But in the East, Syriac (a type of Aramaic) was the main literary and liturgical language other than Greek, and through Syriac, Christianity was spread to the Far East. The authority of the Old Syriac version of the Old Testament, elaborated by many distinguished patristic commentaries either written in Syriac or rapidly translated, led to a medieval belief that Syriac rather than Hebrew was the original holy tongue used by Abraham in his conversation with God.[6] The *Diatessaron* of Tatian (ca. 170) introduced a harmonised version of the four Gospels in Syriac, and an Old Syriac version of the separate Gospels probably circulated as early as ca. 200. There were frequent later translations and revisions, such as that which produced the Peshitta, the standard text of the Syriac church.[7] The language provided an important intermediary between Greek and Arabic for the transmission of much ancient scientific and philosophical writing, and persists as a scriptural medium to this day.

In the West, as noted above, Gothic was the only barbarian language that resisted the supremacy of Latin, and the fourth-century Gothic Bible produced by Bishop Ulfila was the sole attempt to render Scripture into a vernacular.[8] By the late sixth century, the Latin Bible was generally employed, and it retained its monopoly on the scriptural medium throughout later missionary activity in northern Europe. In this way Latin became a supranational tongue, connecting the church with culture and learning in general, and the indispensable instrument for the extension of Christianity to non-Roman regions. Although Greek held roughly an equivalent posi-

[5] Metzger, *Early Versions*, 3-256; cf. Isidore of Seville, *Etymologies*, 9.1.3, ed. W. M. Lindsay, 2 vols. (Oxford, 1911); Berschin, *Griechisch-Lateinisches Mittlelalter*, 31-38.

[6] In the mid-ninth century, Ishodad of Merv, patriarch of the East Syrian (Nestorian) church, summarised this view in his commentary on the book of Genesis; see C. Van den Eynde, *Commentaire d'Iso'dad de Merv sur l'Ancien Testament* I (Louvain, 1955), 21; cf. 146-48 on the primacy of Syriac. I would like to thank Sebastian Brock for directing me to this fascinating text.

[7] On Tatian, see A. Vööbus, *A History of Asceticism in the Syrian Orient*, 2 vols. (Louvain, 1958-60), 1:31-39.

[8] Metzger, *Early Versions*, 375-93.

tion in the culture of the East, it never gained the same supremacy in ecclesiastical ritual. The existence of established Syriac, Armenian, and Georgian liturgies, to name only the most obvious, made it much easier for the Byzantines to concur in later Bulgarian and Russian requests for their own versions of Scripture. Indeed, through the efforts of Saints Cyril and Methodios, a Glagolitic alphabet was devised in the ninth century to record spoken Slavonic and another one was prepared by Cyril, appropriately called Cyrillic, for medieval Russian.[9]

Difficulties in Establishing an "Authorised" Biblical Text

A second and far greater problem than the number of different Biblical translations available in the early Christian world was raised by disagreement over their content (the canon of Scripture). Given Christian dependence on oral traditions preserved in a chain descending from apostolic times, this problem occurred even before the first New Testament texts were written down. It was particularly acute among the Gnostic followers of Jesus, who claimed to preserve and transmit a secret knowledge, *gnosis*. Canonical difficulties afflicted both Judaic and Christian sacred texts. Although Hebrew Scripture was accepted by the Christians and was generally identified as the Law of Moses and the books of Solomon, the Prophets, and the Psalms, the precise content of the Old Testament was not fixed by the first century A.D. The final destruction of the Temple in 70 acted as a spur to Rabbinic determination to settle it, yet the Qumran community of that time accepted certain psalms unknown in later orthodox lists. Surviving early papyri and manuscripts reveal considerable variety over the content, order, and wording of received books.[10] Even in the mid-third century, Origen, the greatest Christian Old Testament scholar, included many disputed writings that were denied canonical status by Jewish authorities. They classed these so-called "deuterocanonical" books ("of second rank")— Tobit, Judith, Wisdom of Solomon, Ecclesiasticus, Maccabees 1 and 2, Baruch, and the Greek parts of Esther and Daniel—as apocryphal. Until ca. 390, Jerome too had followed Origen. But once in Palestine with access both to Origen's six-column edition, the *Hexapla*, and to learned Rabbinic

---

[9] See *Cambridge History of the Bible*, vol. 2, *The West from the Fathers to the Reformation*, ed. G. W. H. Lampe (Cambridge, 1969), 102-120, on the gradual acceptance and dominance of the Latin Bible; see Metzger, *Early Versions*, 394-442, on the Old Church Slavonic versions.

[10] On Old Testament canon, see *Cambridge History of the Bible*, 1:67-199, and on the psalms in use at Qumran, see 1:151-53. Eusebios preserves a letter written by Melito of Sardis in response to a query about the books of the Old Testament and their correct order; see *HE* 4.26.13-14.

interpretation, he changed his mind; consequently these writings do not feature in the Vulgate edition.[11]

If Hebrew Scripture remained unsettled for so long, it is hardly surprising that the early Christians experienced similar difficulties in establishing the canon of their own belief. In particular, the importance attached to preaching and thus the emphasis laid on Christ's very words and those of the Apostles reinforced a powerful oral tradition that had little use for texts. As this world was doomed and Christians had to prepare to build the new Jerusalem, conversion and spreading the Word was a matter of urgency. Some apostolic sayings, later recorded in the Gospels attributed to Thomas and Philip (preserved at Nag Hammadi in Coptic translations), are recognised as Gnostic writings. Their appeal and apparent legitimacy may be gauged from the opening words of the Gospel of Thomas: "Here are the secret words which Jesus the Living spoke and which Didymus Jude Thomas wrote down."[12] Others, like the *Shepherd of Hermas* and the *Epistle of Barnabas*, were accepted by Clement of Alexandria and Origen and included in the third-century Bible manuscript, the *Codex Sinaiticus*, but later were rejected as uncanonical. During the first three centuries they circulated widely and were often considered just as authentic as other apostolic teaching. Similarly, many apocalyptic descriptions of the end of the world existed and, like the Christian apocrypha, varied from one community to another.[13]

Although St. Paul had contrasted the new convenant of Jesus Christ with the old Judaic covenant or testament, the technical use of the term "New Testament" for the corpus of Christian thought was first formulated by Tertullian in the late second century. He himself championed the prophesies of Montanos, which were not generally accepted. But his anti-Gnostic writings remained very influential, especially in the development of Trinitarian theology, and assisted in the establishment of the New Testament canon at the end of the second century. The exclusion of two Gnostic texts, the *Gospel According to the Hebrews* and the *Protevangelium* of James, did not, however, prevent the latter from remaining extraordinarily popular, for it purported to describe the Virgin's childhood, a subject conspic-

---

[11] *Cambridge History of the Bible*, 1:454-89; A. Vööbus, *The Pentateuch in the Version of the Syro-Hexapla* (Louvain, 1975). The Hexapla consisted of the traditional Hebrew text, and its transliteration into Greek letters, plus four Greek versions in parallel columns, and is recognised as one of the greatest achievements of ancient textual criticism.

[12] J. M. Robinson, ed., *The Nag Hammadi Library in English* (Leiden, 1977), 355, appendix 2; cf. J. Doresse, *The Secret Books of the Egyptian Gnostics* (London, 1960).

[13] B. M. Metzger, *The Text of the New Testament, Its Transmission, Corruption and Restoration*, 2nd ed. (Oxford, 1968), 42-46, on the Sinaiticus. Eusebios, *HE* 5.7, on Irenaeus's idea of New Testament canon. G. Bardy, "Faux et fraudes littéraires dans l'antiquité chrétienne," *Revue d'Histoire ecclésiastique* 32 (1936): 5-23, 275-302.

uously omitted from the New Testament. In this gradual definition of doctrine, appeals to emperors, debates with pagans and Jews, and disputes with heretical Christians played an important part. Justin's *Dialogue with Trypho* and Irenaeus's *Treatise Against Heretics* reveal how traditional skills of philosophical argument, logical training, and persuasive reasoning were brought to the defence of Christian dogma and to the aid of the faithful under persecution.[14] The public presence of scattered Christian communities was enormously strengthened by these firm statements and the flowering of apologetic material. But each group probably had access to a few texts only, hearing of others by title and remaining ignorant of those written in unfamiliar languages. In the use and interpretation of the New Testament, local and regional traditions frequently perpetuated diverse practice and belief. Although Eusebios had treated the *Revelation of Peter* as a book of uncertain status in the fourth century, it was still in use one hundred years later for readings on Good Friday in certain Palestinian churches.[15] So even the most authoritative relegation to the list of disputed writings did not necessarily guarantee their removal. In both East and West the number and variety of biblical texts employed continued to cause divergences. As these still prevent a secure modern reconstruction of the New Testament text used by Patriarch Photios in late ninth-century Constantinople, we should not overlook the problems they were likely to have caused contemporaries.[16]

Interpretations of Scripture

In addition to linguistic and canonical variety, questions of Biblical exegesis or interpretation were bound to raise even more differences. The inherent difficulty of making sense of complicated passages and contradictory references to the same event in the life of Jesus produced many harmonised versions of the Gospel stories, a symptom of the problems experienced in using the New Testament as a Christian guide.[17] While the superiority of one particular witness could be argued, the fact remained that four distinct

[14] H. Chadwick, *Early Christian Thought and the Classical Tradition* (Oxford, 1966); S. R.-C. Lilla, *Clement of Alexandria* (London, 1971); M. Simon, *Verus Israel* (Paris, 1948), 166-238.

[15] The text had already had a stormy history. In the second century, Bishop Serapion of Antioch allowed the community of Rhossos to continue using it, only to withdraw this permission when its non-canonical status was argued, see Eusebios, *HE* 6.12.4.

[16] J. N. Birdsall, "The Text of the Gospels in Photius," *JTS*, n.s., 7 (1956), 42-55, 190-98; idem, "The Text of the Acts and the Epistles in Photius," *JTS*, n.s., 9 (1958), 278-91.

[17] For a fascinating overview of the problems, see F. Kermode, *The Genesis of Secrecy* (Cambridge, Mass. and London, 1979). On the immense popularity of the *Diatessaron*, see *DACL*, IV (1921), 747-70 (by H. Leclercq): in the fifth century Theodoretos found it was being read in 200 parishes and tried to impose the Gospels instead.

accounts emerged with significant differences. They only hinted at the Old Testament premonitions of Christ's coming and did not give a clear picture of the end of the world and the Last Judgement. Even with the attempts of St. Paul to direct and systematise the activity of early Christian communities, there was room for justifiable variation in both organisation and belief. Occasionally this sprang from a principled disagreement, for example in the ascetic emphasis on renunciation of the world. In other cases, embodied in much sectarian and heretical development, it grew spontaneously out of an overzealous commitment to particular aspects of the faith. Marcion, for instance, reduced the New Testament canon to the Epistles of St. Paul and the Gospel of Luke, which he rewrote to bring it more closely in line with Pauline teaching. For these innovations he was excommunicated by the church of Rome in A.D. 144, and his attempt to separate the Christian God from the Jewish Yahweh was vigorously countered by Irenaeus and others. In a similar fashion, Montanism elevated the prophetic and apocalyptic revelations of its founder in order to prepare Christians for the second coming at the expense of all other practices. Despite frequent condemnations and efforts to force baptism upon them, the Montanists continued to be a force in rural Phrygia until the eighth century at least.[18] The history of the early church is full of such experiments, which frequently provoked a tighter definition of what was permissible within the church and what constituted grounds for expulsion from the faith.

The original mystery and central tenet of Christianity, God's Incarnation as man and the salvation of all men by His death and resurrection, was responsible for much theological speculation. The elucidation of Trinitarian problems (the precise relationship between God the Father, God the Son, and God the Holy Ghost) and of the links between the Old and New Testaments provoked further arguments. In all these matters Christians trained in pagan philosophy, as so many of the eastern church fathers were, found it natural to employ their skills in the elaboration of systems of belief designed to explain the Christian mystery to non-believers.[19] In the hands

[18] On these later identified as heretical movements, see H. Chadwick, *The Early Church* (Harmondsworth, 1967), 38-40, 52-53. E. C. Blackman, *Marcion and His Influence* (London, 1948); J. Pelikan, *The Christian Tradition*, 4 vols. (Chicago, 1971-83), vol. 1, *The Emergence of the Catholic Tradition (100-600)*, 72-79, 97-108; J. Pargoire, *L'église byzantine de 527 à 847*, 3rd ed. (Paris, 1923), 180-81. W. Bauer, *Orthodoxy and Heresy in Earliest Christianity* (London/Philadelphia, 1971), Introduction, xxi-xxv, is particularly clear on the problems of studying these movements from the generally prejudiced sources that survive.

[19] H. Chadwick, *Origen contra Celsum*, 3rd ed. (Oxford, 1979); E. Amand de Mendieta, "The Official Attitude of Basil of Caesarea as a Christian Bishop Towards Greek Philosophy and Science," in D. Baker, ed., *The Orthodox Churches and the West*, SCH 13 (1976): 25-49; M. L. W. Laistner, *Christian and Pagan Culture in the Late Roman Empire* (Ithaca, 1951), 49-

of theologians like Origen or Clement of Alexandria, this process was a highly intellectual one that confirmed and emphasised the philosophising capacity engendered by secular learning. It was based on a close reading of scriptural passages and commentaries on them, which often appeared as *scholia* written in the margins of manuscripts. By accumulating a great mass of citations to support one interpretation, a protagonist would hope to convince his opponent and ultimately to have his own view enshrined as the authoritative one. The pagan inheritance of this disputatious theology was of immense importance to the faith; it permitted a skilful handling of theoretical possibilities and encouraged hypothetical arguments that refined and defined Christian belief. Although some of the distinctions made in the second and third centuries may today appear insignificant, and some of the verbal subtleties are almost lost in translation—the shift in meaning between *homoousios*, "of the same substance" (i.e. consubstantial), and *homoiousios*, "of like substance"[20]—these disputes were conducted at a level of sophisticated reasoning and passionate involvement. They reflect the impact of Christianity in the Greek world, debated with the full armoury of philosophical weapons.

These three fields, the language, canon, and interpretation of Scripture, presented great scope for differences of opinion between Christian communities. In times of persecution, in particular, the strains of diversity would show. Although apostasy was always condemned, many leaders felt that to exclude from the faith forever all those who gave in to imperial orders was too harsh. The charity urged by Dionysios of Alexandria, for instance, was violently opposed during the persecution of Decius (249-51) by Novatian, a presbyter of the church of Rome.[21] He maintained a strict policy of eternal damnation for those who lapsed, and admitted only the pure (*cathari*, from the Greek, *katharos*) to communion. His views were opposed by a local synod held in Carthage in 251, confirmed at Rome late in the same year. This opened a direct conflict between Novatian and his bishop, Cornelius, which echoed round the church for many years. For in expressing the need for healing through "the medicines of repentance," Dionysios raised the related question of how those who genuinely wished to be readmitted to the church should be received. Was it sufficient for them to give proof of their repentance and for the bishop to lay his hands on them, or was a new baptism required? While Cyprian of Carthage maintained the

---

73. See also the special issue of *Civiltà classica e cristiana* 6 (1985), which is devoted to this topic.

[20] C. Stead, *Divine Substance* (Oxford, 1977), 190-222; R. Klein, *Constantius II und die christliche Kirche* (Darmstadt, 1977), 23-29.

[21] Eusebios, *HE* 6.43; T. E. Gregory, "Novatianism: A Rigorist Sect in the Christian Roman Empire," *Byzantine Studies/Etudes byzantines* 2(i) (1975): 1-18.

necessity of re-baptism, others thought that a single baptism secured entry to the faith and could not be repeated in any circumstances.[22] In turn, this debate drew attention to the variety of baptismal rites in use. Because many were baptised by sects that used their own formulas of admission, and did not teach the catechism, they too requested rebaptism once aware of their past heresy. The "ungodly baptism of the heretics" provoked much distress and anxiety, as well as a flurry of inter-episcopal correspondence in the third century. Nor did the matter end there, although Novatian's strict discipline was rejected. Precisely the same problems arose with later heresies, notably the Donatist movement in Africa that divided the church there for many years.[23]

On all these points, local decisions and contrary opinions circulated, frequently through Rome, which acted as a clearing house for West/East communication. The advice of successive bishops of Rome was also sought, though perhaps no more than that of other recognised leaders. The superior theological skills of Irenaeus of Lyon or Clement of Alexandria made them more respected than any bishop of Rome in their own lifetime. And it was not just in their original writings that this authority was vested; it also stemmed from their wide knowledge of the material identified as the received teaching of earlier Christians, going back to Christ and the Apostles. For all decisions were ultimately related to past experience or to hints in the authentic "Sayings" of apostolic times. This was the supreme test for Christians, that their rulings did not contravene the Scriptures.

Conciliar Definitions of Belief and Practice

Ecclesiastical synods constituted the customary method of resolving these issues. In the early centuries a collective authority vested in the presbyters of each community guided it, through instructions, prohibitions, and recommendations.[24] When problems arose, all the Christians in one city might meet together to smooth out disagreements and establish a uniform attitude to local disturbances. Such gatherings might draw on the members of many different communities and could be summoned on the initiative of various authorities: individual presbyters or bishops, groups of elders, particular holy men. Occasionally, appeals might be made to a greatly

[22] Eusebios, *HE* 6.42.6 (on the return of *lapsi*); 7.2-5 and 7.9 (on baptism). J. A. Fischer, "Die Konzilien zu Karthago und Rom im Jahr 251," *Annuarium Historiae Conciliorum* 11 (2) (1979): 263-86; von Campenhausen, *Ecclesiastical Authority*, 265-92.

[23] Eusebios, *HE* 7.9 (on the ungodly baptism); W. H. C. Frend, *The Donatist Church* (Oxford, 1952), 167-68, 227-99, 315-32.

[24] Gregory Dix, *Jurisdiction in the Early Church, Episcopal and Papal*, 2nd ed. (London, 1975), 28-32; von Campenhausen, *Ecclesiastical Authority*, 76-123 (on elders), 149-77 (on bishops and apostolic succession).

respected figure; when the community of Rhossos consulted Bishop Serapion of Antioch over the *Revelation of Peter*, for instance. Only in the East, however, in the regions around Antioch and Alexandria, did some form of recognised episcopal authority develop. In general, regional autonomy and traditions founded in the teaching of a local martyr, holy man, or patron sustained diversity. The rulings of local synods were rarely communicated to other churches and hardly ever became known beyond the geographical area represented. Direct personal contact could provide an exceptional instance of broader dissemination, as in the case of Irenaeus, bishop of Lyon, who retained ties with his native church in western Asia Minor long after his appointment to Gaul.[25]

Nonetheless, the mechanism for settling such vexatious matters as the readmittance of lapsed Christians existed by the third century and had already been put to use when Novatian was condemned. Councils and synods were prepared to identify heresy as wrong belief and decide correct procedure and punishment. When the era of persecution was ended by Constantine I, however, Christian communities everywhere were in disarray and in no position to regulate their reconstitution in the novel and more favourable circumstances. Thus it was the emperor who undertook the next obvious step, to gather representatives of the entire body of believers in one general council, which would speak for all the different churches. As we have seen, the beliefs of Arios and the date of Easter were among the pressing matters that required an authoritative resolution. The readmittance of those who had succumbed to civilian threats during Diocletian's persecution was another. So under imperial protection and with imperial financial support the First Oecumenical Council met in 325 at Nicaea (in western Asia Minor).[26] Constantine himself presided over the assembly, which is unlikely to have numbered as many as 318 bishops, the traditional figure, and took part in its proceedings. These were carried on in both Greek and Latin.[27] After the opening speech in Greek, probably delivered by Eusebios of Caesarea, and incomprehensible to some of the Westerners, the emperor replied in Latin, a language of which Eusebios was ignorant. A bilingual transcript of the decisions taken was prepared to prevent any misunder-

---

[25] Eusebios, *HE* 5.20.4-7, on St. Irenaeus, who provided the personal link; cf. W. H. C. Frend, "A Note on the Influence of Greek Immigrants on the Spread of Christianity in the West," in *Mullus: Festschrift T. Klauser* (Münster, 1964), 125-29.

[26] H. Chadwick, "The Origin of the Title 'Oecumenical Council'," *JTS* 23 (1972): 132-35.

[27] Eusebios, *Vita Constantini*, ed. F. Winkelmann (Berlin, 1975), 2:61-3:24; on the number of bishops present, Athanasios claims 318, Eusebios, over 250; Chadwick, *The Early Church*, 130, suggests about 220.

standing of rulings considered binding on all Christians everywhere (though this record was never widely diffused in the West).

The gathering clearly felt a responsibility to resolve problems afflicting the churches and set about the task in due seriousness. Although the Arian theology commanded widespread support, its condemnation as heresy was agreed by all but two bishops from Libya, and the opposing interpretation of Alexander of Alexandria was incorporated into a declaration of faith. It was also established that the creed should be taught and recited by the faithful during church services.[28] Further measures taken to ensure greater uniformity of Christian practice were set down in the form of canons, the first laws made for the entire community of believers.[29] They pertained to a number of different aspects of the faith and its ministers, with a notable emphasis on what customs should be removed; for example, the first canon forbade self-mutilation or castration, especially of a cleric. Thus ecclesiastical law made its hesitant beginnings.

Four aspects of the first council need to be stressed here. First, from the outset the emperor was intimately associated with it, an association deepened by the fact that subsequent universal councils were always held in the East at imperial initiative—Constantine I had established the model. Second, the eastern venue of the first council (as of the next eight, all classified as oecumenical) produced an imbalance in geographical representation; participants from the West found themselves a tiny minority among the eastern bishops. Third, and despite inadequate western representation, the councils gradually became recognised as the supreme authority for all Christians. Conciliar decisions on dogma and discipline attained an elevated status, far above that of local synods or an individual ruling, which gave the churches a truly universal judicial body.[30] Christianity could be seen to be a totalising faith with its own international organisation (even if councils were held infrequently and under secular restraints). But finally, these claims for the universality of the faith were seriously impaired by the failure to ensure knowledge of council proceedings throughout all Christian regions. Official transcripts were lost, lists of canons remained untranslated, and inaccurate versions circulated as authentic.

[28] Bishops Theonas of Marmarica and Secundus of Ptolemais accompanied Arios himself into exile in Nicomedia, and were joined later by Eusebios of Nicomedia and Theognis of Nicaea; Arios was pardoned in about 328, see R. MacMullen, *Constantine* (New York, 1969), 175, 179. On the first creed, see G. L. Dossetti, *Il Simbolo di Nicea e di Costantinopoli* (Rome, 1967); J. N. D. Kelly, *Early Christian Creeds*, 3rd ed. (London, 1972).

[29] P. P. Joannou, *Discipline générale antique (II-IXe siècles)*, vol. 1, part 1, *Les canons des Conciles Oecumeniques* (Rome, 1962), 22-23.

[30] At the second council held in 381, the first canon established the unalterable nature of ecclesiastical rulings, which had to be observed by all on pain of excommunication; see Joannou, *Discipline*, 1:69.

Some of the resulting problems can be illustrated by the synod of Carthage held in 419.[31] At this meeting the Roman delegates produced a document, the *Canones Nicaeni*, purporting to be the canons of the First Oecumenical Council of 325. It did not concord with the version in use in Africa, which had been brought back to Carthage by its bishop, Caecilian, after the council. (It was in fact a separate version of the 325 canons combined with those decreed by the council of Serdica and by another African council.) St. Augustine appealed to Constantinople for an authentic text of the canons and received from Bishop Attikos a translation from the original Greek, together with a Greek introduction, the *regula formatarum* (which may not have been part of the 325 council documentation). This proved that the Roman text was a composite one and established the correct canons of Nicaea.

St. Augustine's determination to clarify the canons of Nicaea was typical of his efforts to order and unite the Christian churches. Had he lived to attend the Third Oecumenical Council held in Ephesos in 431, he would have experienced the deep divisions then prevalent in the East. What would he have thought of the two rival meetings that anathematised each other's leaders and threatened their supporters? If Augustine had witnessed Cyril of Alexandria's deposition of Nestorios, who denied that Jesus was the Son of God, and Theodore of Mopsuestia's defence, the Christological arguments that dominated the council might have been better understood in the West.[32] But in the event, the invitation to go to Ephesos arrived too late, a few months after Augustine's death in the summer of 430. The sole representatives of western Christianity at the council were the papal delegates, another symptom of the increased "eastern" character of general councils.

St. Augustine's Contribution. This imbalance, which meant that dogma and discipline were defined in the East and in Greek, was countered in part by Augustine's personal attempt to construct a systematic Christian theology in Latin. While his own mastery of Greek was hard won, he was perfectly well versed in classical philosophy and not antagonistic to secular learning. But he directed his scholarship to a more spiritual and metaphysical realm, developing an allegorical interpretation of the Bible, without so much recourse to philosophical speculation. This resulted in an extremely compelling synthesis, the *City of God* (413-26), which guided the western churches for centuries.[33] It did not demand a complete understanding of all

[31] Berschin, *Griechisch-Lateinisches Mittelalter*, 91-93; Mansi, 4.401-415.

[32] P. Brown, *Augustine of Hippo* (London, 1967), 287-329.

[33] H.-X. Arquillière, *L'Augustinisme politique: Essai sur la formation des théories politiques du moyen âge*, 2nd ed. (Paris, 1955); Y. M.-J. Congar, *L'Ecclésiologie du haut moyen âge* (Paris,

the debates and complexities of eastern theology; it fitted the less developed thought-patterns current in the West; and it was both cause and effect of the decline of Greek philosophical study, which still dominated the East.

Augustine was by no means the only western church leader whose writings contributed to an identifiable theology of the Latin West, separate from that of the Greek East. His first mentor, St. Ambrose (340-97), bishop of Milan, Sts. Hilary, Cyprian, and a host of others assisted in the process of establishing a distinct western corpus of theology. But in Augustine we can see a number of strands united. His autobiographical writings, the *Confessions*, provide a unique insight, revealing the significance of Athanasios's *Life* of Antony (which converted the young Augustine to ascetic Christianity) and the powerful appeal of Manichaeanism (which he renounced). Perhaps it was because of his wide experience of fourth-century thought, pagan, dualist, philosophical, and Christian, that he could provide such a satisfying and discriminating interpretation of ecclesiastical learning. He understood the contribution of desert monasticism to the church, but abandoned the idea of going on a pilgrimage to Egypt for the more demanding task of administration in the strong but divided church of Africa. He remained a product and a part of the West, and it was there that his attempts to render the accumulated wisdom of the past in a securely rooted tradition were rewarded.[34]

Indirectly, however, Augustine influenced the growth of a universal faith as defined by general councils. The occasion occurred twenty years after his death when Pope Leo I (440-61) made a decisive contribution to the council of Chalcedon, the fourth, held in 451. His famous *Tomus*, the letter addressed to Patriarch Flavian of Constantinople on the question of the precise union of Christ's two natures, became the agreed doctrinal definition of this gathering of over 500 bishops, who invested the Roman document with supreme authority.[35] The extent to which Leo was indebted to

---

1968), 121-22, 331; J. O'Meara, *Charter of Christendom: The Significance of the City of God* (New York, 1961); G. B. Ladner, *The Idea of Reform, Its Impact on Christian Thought and Action in the Age of the Fathers* (Cambridge, Mass., 1959), 239-83.

[34] Congar, *L'Ecclésiologie*, 371-72; Ladner, *The Idea of Reform*, 153-238; P. Brown, *Augustine*, 412; H.-I. Marrou, "La place du haut Moyen Age dans l'histoire du christianisme," *Settimane* 9 (Spoleto, 1962): 626-27.

[35] H. J. Sieben, *Die Konzilsidee der alten Kirche* (Paderborn, 1979), 103-147; M. Wojtowytsch, *Papsttum und Konzile von den Anfängen bis zu Leo I (440-61)* (Stuttgart, 1981). For the *Tomus* of Leo (letter 28 to Flavian of Constantinople), see E. Schwartz, ed., *Concilium Chalcedonense*, vol. 1 (i) (Berlin/New York, 1933), 10-20 (the Greek version as read at the third session of the council, ibid., 81); *PL* 54, 756-82; English translation in C. L. Feltoe, trans., *Select Letters and Sermons of Leo I* (Oxford/New York, 1895), 38-43. Y. M. Duval,

other thinkers, John Cassian's anti-Nestorian treatise or Flavian's condemnation of Eutyches (the founder of the Monophysite school), may be debated; other authors, Prosper of Aquitaine and Gaudentius of Brescia, certainly influenced the work. What is not in question is the large part played by Augustinian writings in Leo's understanding. For the first time Rome took a determining role in the definition of Christian dogma. Opposition to it was widespread in the East, as is shown by the very delayed acceptance of the acts of Chalcedon by the bishops of Egypt and the primate of Alexandria, but Leo's *Tomus* was spread throughout Christendom. It became the statement on which later attempts to reunite the Monophysite factions with the majority were made. In years to come the western churches in particular were to cling to this fame and the increased theological standing that Leo (and behind him Augustine) brought to the see of Rome.

Roman Primacy

Other factors contributed to an increased confidence in the position and role of bishops of Rome within the Christian world. The final defeat of an obdurate pagan faction in the Senate in the last years of the fourth and early years of the fifth century left Rome's bishop as a natural leader in a city now predominantly Christian.[36] Like other bishops, he gradually took over aspects of secular government, negotiating with hostile forces, maintaining food supplies, and succouring the population in times of plague and floods. Under Innocent I (401-417) and Celestine I (422-32), the powers of St. Peter as custodian and founding rock of the church, and his intimate connections with later bishops of Rome, were emphasised. The significance of this particular apostolic tradition was drawn out to endow the see with authority over other bishops, an authority occasionally recognised in the past by the custom of appealing to Rome in cases of prolonged ecclesiastical disputes. Such supreme jurisdiction was gradually systematised by additional theoretical arguments. It did not mean that Roman decisions could be imposed on other churches, for local autonomy was cherished, and the eastern patriarchs also vied for supremacy. At the council of Ephesos (431), Alexandria appeared to have won. But by the time of Chalcedon, Constantinople succeeded in reversing this position. Canon 28 of the Fourth Council

---

"Quelques emprunts de S. Léon à S. Augustin," *Mélanges de science religieuse* 15 (1958): 85-94, esp. 86.

[36] C. Pietri, *Roma Christiana: Recherches sur l'Eglise de Rome, son organisation, sa politique, son idéologie de Miltiade à Sixte III (311-440)*, 2 vols. (Rome, 1976), 1:405-460. B. Croke and J. Harries, *Religious Conflict in Fourth-Century Rome: A Documentary Study* (Sydney, 1982), 73-97.

recognised the primacy of honour due to the see of St. Peter, while elevating New Rome to equal status with Old Rome.[37]

In matters of ecclesiastical discipline and liturgical practice also, Leo I was very active in promoting papal authority, instructing Dioskoros of Alexandria, Anastasios of Thessalonike (papal vicar in Illyricum), Hilary of Arles (who held an equivalent position in Gaul for a short time), and the bishops of Sicily on a variety of topics. The battle against heresy commanded his detailed attention, and he directed the churches of northern Italy and Spain to hold local synods condemning Pelagian and Priscillian survivals. Twice in the 450s, when Rome was threatened by military disasters, he defended the city as best he could and certainly spared it excessive Gothic and Vandal reprisals.[38] This combination of universal and local concern, an ability to confront both complex points of theology and direct physical challenges, made Leo an effective organiser. He was worldly enough to employ imperial power against heretics and had sufficient moral authority to settle civilian disputes in the name of Valentinian III. His surviving sermons reveal a preoccupation with instruction delivered in a simple and concise style, avoiding the more artificial rhetorical language in fashion, and many of the prayers and sections of the Roman liturgy attributed to Leo echo this rich but sober dignity.[39] While this linguistic heritage was to contribute to the development of a purely Latin rite, which gave the papacy its own distinctive liturgy, Leo's concern for the moral standing of Rome within the Christian world laid the basis for later independence. Pope Gelasius (492-96) developed this further with the claim that priestly authority, *auctoritas sacrata*, was superior to the power of kings, *regalis potestas*. On this basis Petrine authority in spiritual matters would later be elevated still higher.[40]

In spite of this increased standing, Roman authority was hedged by restrictions. As few bishops of Rome had bilingual skills, they were increasingly dependent on Latin translations of Greek theological texts. Although canon law was recognised as fundamental to a universal faith, Rome had no complete Latin version of the decisions of the first four oecumenical coun-

[37] Joannou, *Discipline*, 1:90-93.

[38] T. Jalland, *The Life and Times of St. Leo the Great* (London/New York, 1941). M. Jugie, "Interventions de S. Léon le Grand dans les affairs intérieurs des Eglises orientales," *Lateranum*, n.s., 14 (1948): 77-94; P. Stockmeier, "Leo der Grosse und die Anfänge seiner synodalen Tätigkeit," *Annuarium Historiae Conciliorum* 12 (1980): 38-46.

[39] *PL* 54; Feltoe, *Select Letters and Sermons*.

[40] W. Ullmann, "Leo I and the Theme of Papal Primacy," *JTS* 11 (1960): 25-51; J. L. Nelson, "Gelasius I's Doctrine of Responsibility," *JTS* 18 (1967): 154-62; R. L. Benson, "The Gelasian Doctrine: Uses and Transformations," in G. Makdisi, ed., *La notion d'autorité au Moyen Age: Islam, Byzance, Occident* (Paris, 1978), 13-44, stressing that Gelasius's formulation was not used until the ninth century.

cils until the early sixth century. Full participation in the process of defining dogma and establishing ecclesiastical discipline was therefore denied to the see of St. Peter, for without a complete knowledge of past rulings it was powerless. Meanwhile, at the regional level, the universal nature of conciliar decisions was tempered both by their availability and local tradition, which normally had no basis in council authority. Even officials designated as Rome's representatives sometimes made no headway against enshrined customs of this sort. The conversion of Clovis at the turn of the fifth-sixth century, for instance, brought the Franks to the Catholic (as opposed to the Arian) faith, and they entered the church of Gaul run by the descendants of Gallo-Roman families, men of senatorial standing with a concern for education and some knowledge of the classics.[41] However welcome the event, it brought neither greater Petrine influence nor canonical practice to this particular region of Christendom—in the early sixth century, the papal vicar for Gaul was rebuffed on more than one occasion.

Yet the Frankish adoption of the faith points to the field in which Roman primacy would eventually make most impact. For it was among the new converts, generally from northern Europe where there was no intermediary (often heretical) expression of Christianity, that the cult of St. Peter and devotion to his see would prove strongest. As with so many aspects of early Christian history, it is important not to read back into Late Antiquity a concept of Roman primacy more suitable to the reformed Gregorian papacy of the eleventh century. Roman authority in the West was built up very slowly. But it often met with greater success (or at least less opposition) among peoples who had been converted directly to Christianity, sometimes by missionaries sent from Rome. In such cases Roman custom generally prevailed. Roman use of canon law was adopted, and additional rulings sought from the holy see, because Rome was the source of dogma and discipline, the supreme authority of appeal in controversial matters. And because the Late Antique culture acquired by the new converts was purely Latin-based, any awareness of eastern interpretations of the faith and of early Christian activities recorded in Greek sources came via translations or collections of texts (such as those prepared by Cassian or Cassiodorus). In particular, Augustine's synthesis of past theology assumed a hegemonic position, which held sway over all western ecclesiastics. Thus the West's de-

---

[41] J. Le Goff, "Clerical Culture and Folklore Traditions in Merovingian Civilization," translated in his *Time, Work and Culture in the Middle Ages* (Chicago, 1980), 153-88; J. M. Wallace-Hadrill, *The Frankish Church* (Oxford, 1983), 1-27; M. Heinzelmann, *Bischofsherrschaft in Gallien, Zur Kontinuität römischer Führungsschichten vom 4. bis zum 7. Jahrhundert* (Munich, 1976). On Clovis's baptism, traditionally dated to 496 but probably at least a decade later, see I. N. Wood, "Gregory of Tours and Clovis," *Revue Belge de Philologie et d'Histoire* 63 (1985): 249-72.

pendency on translations of Greek patristic writings, hagiography, and history combined with the emergent leadership of Rome to provide converts with a distinctive Latin faith, administered by the see of St. Peter. This faith was, of course, moulded by many non-Romans—for example, Caesarius of Arles, whose sermons continued to be studied and read in churches long after his death in 543.[42] From the late sixth century onwards, these particular circumstances began to form the western churches in a novel fashion.

VARIETY WITHIN THE CHURCHES OF THE MID-SIXTH CENTURY

But any survey of the state of Christendom during the pontificate of Vigilius (537-55) would reveal only hints of this new process.[43] Division, disunity, and schism rendered official by excommunication intensified old differences, while ignorance and autarkic growth permitted others. In northern Europe, Anglo-Saxon invaders had driven the Christians into the westernmost corners of England and Wales, where they barely survived.[44] St. Patrick's mission to Ireland made a number of conversions in the fifth century, but it was probably the arrival of refugees from Gaul that provided the greatest stimulus to Irish Christianity. From the monastic centre of Clonard, St. Columba set out in about 563 to spread the desert style of Christian devotion (bequeathed by St. Martin of Tours and brought thence to Ireland) to the Picts. He founded the community at Iona that played a vital role in the conversion of Caledonia later in the century and ensured its autonomous development within the faith.[45] In other parts of northern Europe, pagan practices prevailed and exercised a constant pressure on Christian churches by the regular westward movement of their barbarian adherents. From the sixth to the ninth centuries and beyond, the Alemans, Frisians, Saxons, and Vikings would pose a series of challenges to the faith.

Within the nominally Christian kingdoms of the south there was considerable variation of belief, as the Sueves and the Goths in the Spanish

---

[42] Wallace-Hadrill, *The Frankish Church*, 110-22; Caesarius's sermons are edited by G. Morin, *CCL* 103-104 (Turnhout, 1953), and translated by M. M. Mueller, *Saint Caesarius of Arles: Sermons and Admonitions*, 2 vols. (New York, 1956-64).

[43] L. Duchesne, *L'église au sixième siècle* (Paris, 1925).

[44] N. K. Chadwick, ed., *Studies in the Early British Church* (Cambridge, 1958), 12, characterises this obscure period in Celtic history as the heroic age, during which the legends of Arthur germinated among a people in defeat. I am grateful to Wendy Davies for assistance in matters Celtic.

[45] L. Bieler, *The Patrician Texts in the Book of Armagh* (Dublin, 1979); K. Meyer, *Learning in Ireland in the Fifth Century and the Transmission of Letters* (Dublin, 1913); K. Hughes, *Early Christianity in Pictland* (Jarrow Lecture, 1971); N. K. Chadwick, *Studies in Early British History* (Cambridge, 1954), 193-238.

peninsula maintained their loyalty to Arianism until 561 and 589, respectively, and the churches of northern Italy refused to accept the ruling of Rome in the Three Chapters controversy. The Lombards who were to take over this area in the second half of the sixth century further complicated its affiliation by their own pagan or Arian doctrines.[46] For many years some cities would find themselves with both an Arian *and* a Catholic bishop (a situation paralleled in Visigothic Spain and in Syria, where the Jacobite Monophysite church vied with the Orthodox Chalcedonian episcopal structure). In southern Italy, meanwhile, one of the results of the Byzantine reconquest (completed in 554) was a tightening of eastern administration; but until the early eighth century the ecclesiastical dioceses remained under papal control. From this area popes often drew on clerics who were well trained and frequently bilingual who could act as advisers and envoys from Rome to the East, and who played a significant part in mediating some of the misunderstandings and disagreements that were a marked feature of East/West communication. A similar role had traditionally been performed by the churches of Illyricum and Africa, which occupied a midway position analogous to that of Sicily and southern Italy. While the Christian communities of North Africa continued to provide a link between the churches of the East Mediterranean and those of the West, especially of Spain, many of those in Illyricum were overrun in the sixth century and never revived.[47] Groups of Christians resettled themselves in safe cities where they could, but the destruction of the major Balkan and Danubian centres of urban living was extremely deleterious for Christianity.

Finally, in the East the four great patriarchates subsumed within their borders Christians of many non-orthodox persuasions. One of the main heretical groups was centred in the diocese of Antioch and had its own hierarchy of Monophysite bishops throughout northern Syria, with numerous supporters in Palestine and Egypt.[48] These adherents of the one nature (*mono-physis*) of Christ rejected the council of Chalcedon and Pope Leo's *Tomus*. In place of the belief that two perfect natures, divine and human, combined in the person of Jesus, they held that these two natures united into one divine nature at the Incarnation. This theology had been provoked in

[46] E. A. Thompson, *The Goths in Spain* (Oxford, 1966), 88-91, 94-98; M. Simonetti, "Arianesimo latino," *Studi Medievali*, series 3, no. 8 (1967): 663-744, esp. 695-744; S. C. Fanning, "Lombard Arianism Reconsidered," *Speculum* 56 (1981): 241-58.

[47] L. Cracco Ruggini, *La Sicilia tra Roma e Bisanzio, Storia della Sicilia*, vol. 3 (Naples, 1980); Averil Cameron, "Byzantine Africa—the Literary Evidence," in *Excavations at Carthage*, vol. 7 (Ann Arbor, 1982), esp. 29-53; cf. V. Velkov, *Cities in Thrace and Dacia in Late Antiquity* (Amsterdam, 1977).

[48] R. Devréesse, *Le patriarchat d'Antioche depuis la paix de l'Eglise jusqu' à la conquête arabe* (Paris, 1945); cf. S. L. Greenslade, *Schism in the Early Church*, 2nd ed. (London, 1964), 62-66.

part by the stress on Christ's human nature, elaborated by the school of Antioch and Nestorios.[49] And Nestorios's concern over this matter had in turn
been generated in part by the growing cult of the Virgin Mary, addressed
in the East as Mother of God (*Theotokos*), a title that Nestorios corrected to
Christotokos (Mother of Christ). In thus reducing the Virgin's role, he inevitably elevated the human qualities of Her Son, as the two were inextri-
cably entwined. Such theological disputes raged throughout the East and
continued to command widespread loyalty even after oecumenical denunciation, Nestorios's formulations at Ephesos (431), and *both* Nestorian and
Monophysite exegesis at Chalcedon (451).[50] Under this attack the Monophysite faction had retired to its strongholds in the East, the largest grouping inspired by the teaching of Severos, bishop of Antioch (d. 538). By the
middle of the sixth century, even after severe bouts of persecution, the
Monophysites represented a very large number among the overall population, although split into two factions, the Severan and Jacobite (so named
after Severos and James Baradaios, who secretely ordained a rival hierarchy
of very active bishops in Asia Minor and Syria). The heresy showed no signs
of abating.[51]

Even before the council of Ephesos found Nestorios a heretic, his supporters had been driven out of Syria into Sasanian Persia.[52] Though removed from the Byzantine sphere, they continued to exercise a profound
influence through their independent church and the theological school of
Nisibis. One of its students, Mar Aba, who became *katholikos* (patriarch) of
the Nestorian church in 540, had made a pilgrimage to Palestine and
Egypt; studied and taught in Alexandria; and visited Corinth, Athens, and
Constantinople, where he witnessed a public debate between his co-reli-
gionary, Paul the Persian, and Photinos, a Manichaean, in 527. Cosmas
Indicopleustes acknowledged the importance of Mar Aba's exposition of
Theodore of Mopsuestia's theology, which influenced his own writing so
deeply.[53] The Nestorian church suffered under Justinian's determination to

[49] Chadwick, *The Early Church*, 192-205; R. Devréesse, *Essai sur Théodore de Mopsueste*
(Rome, 1948).

[50] T. E. Gregory, *Vox Populi: Popular Opinion and Violence in the Religious Controversies of the
Fifth Century* A.D. (Columbus, Ohio, 1979).

[51] W. H. C. Frend, "The Monophysites and the Transition between the Ancient World
and the Middle Ages," in E. Cerulli, ed., *Passagio dal Mondo Antico al Medio Evo* (Rome,
1980), 339-65.

[52] L. I. Scipioni, "La controversia nestoriana," in Cerulli, *Passagio*, 381-413; J. Labourt,
Le Christianisme dans l'empire perse sous la dynastie sassanide (224-632) (Paris, 1904); Daniélou
and Marrou, *The First Christian Centuries*, 369-72.

[53] A. Guillaumont, "Justinien et l'Eglise de Perse," *DOP* 23/4 (1969/70): 39-66; R. Macina, "L'homme à l'école de Dieu d'Antioche à Nisibe: profil herméneutique, théologique

have the writings of certain theologians, including Theodore, condemned
as heretical. Because this imperial drive was largely successful in destroying
the evidence, and the Nestorians subsequently had little presence in the
West, we tend to ignore their achievements. But this Eurocentric view
overlooks one of the most dynamic missionary movements in Christian history—the first conversion of the Far East—as well as the scholarly accom-
plishments of the Syriac church under Persian and Islamic rule.[54]

Even amongst Christians who subscribed to the orthodoxy defined by
Constantinople, there was no predetermined consistency. The patriarchs of
Jerusalem and Alexandria formally agreed, but could not impose identical
beliefs on the monasteries in their jurisdictions. In particular, individual
holy men continued to escape their control and to attract disciples to their
own cults within Christianity. Similarly, healing shrines and especially revered relics or icons might command the loyalty of the faithful.[55] Sometimes these centres represented not so much a doctrinal variation as an alternative source of authority that threatened the established position of the
bishop. Such problems were endemic throughout the Christian world, but
were more developed in the East. A western ascetic, the Lombard Wulfolaic, was inspired by St. Martin of Tours to convert the people near Trier to
Christianity. He imported the stylite tradition, building a column close to
a statue of Diana. "I kept telling them that Diana was powerless, that her
statues were useless, and that the rites they practised were vain and
empty." Eventually, with the help of his prayers, the idol was pulled down
and destroyed. But Wulfolaic was criticised by local bishops who told him
he was too obscure to imitate the famous fifth-century Syrian column saint,
St. Symeon Stylites; besides, the climate of Gaul was quite unsuitable for
stylite asceticism. When he had climbed down and joined his disciples in
a monastery, one of the bishops had his column destroyed. At this, Wulfolaic wept bitterly but bowed to episcopal authority, for "it is considered

---

et kerygmatique du mouvement scoliaste nestorien," part 1, *Proche Orient chrétien* 32 (1982):
86-121, summarises a work in progress.

[54] A. S. Atiya, *A History of Eastern Christianity* (London, 1968), 252-66; W. Hage, "Der
Weg nach Asien: Die Ostsyrische Missionskirche," in K. Schäferdiek, ed., *Die Kirche des
früheren Mittelalters*, Band II/1, (Munich, 1978), 267-302.

[55] P. Brown, *The Cult of the Saints* (Chicago, 1981) examines the situation in the West;
cf. his article, "The Rise and Function of the Holy Man in Late Antiquity," *JRS* 61 (1971),
80-101 (reprinted in his *Society and the Holy in Late Antiquity* [London, 1982]); V. Saxer,
Morts, Martyrs, Reliques en Afrique chrétienne aux premiers siècles (Paris, 1980); E. Kitzinger,
"The Cult of Images in the Age Before Iconoclasm," *DOP* 8 (1958): 83-150. In the West
Syrian church, the cult of relics was so developed that several canons warn against monks,
presbyters, deacons, and even laymen, who carried bags of bones around the countryside;
see A. Vööbus, ed., *The Synodikon in the West Syrian Tradition*, 2 vols. (Louvain, 1975), 2:5-
6 (no. 15), 13 (no. 20). I am grateful to Andrew Palmer for this reference.

a sin not to obey bishops."[56] Appeals could not have dislodged his model, St. Symeon, whose example continued to inspire later stylites, dendrites (tree saints), and more conventional holy men in the East for centuries.

Another common problem for Christian authorities everywhere was the survival of pagan practices, astrological predictions, and magic charms, which were regularly associated with "outsiders"—heretics, holy women, Jews, witches, druids, and sorcerers.[57] Although these constituted more of a disciplinary than a doctrinal challenge, they frequently sprang from some lingering heretical movement or Manichaean inspiration. By the middle of the sixth century, the established churches had perforce developed the means to refute and remove such non-Christian elements. Naturally, they did so in the name of one faith, but that faith was still anything but uniform.

The Christian Liturgy

Tremendous variations can be detected in the physical celebration of the faith. The liturgy was by no means a fixed and unalterable rite in the sixth century, and it varied not only according to the language and service books employed, but also according to architectural setting, congregational participation, chanting, vestments and plate, liturgical furniture, and the number of officiating clergy.[58] While some of these factors can be traced directly to the resources of the particular church, whether it had a wealthy patron and an ancient endowment, some were intimately linked to local traditions. The use of singers or chanters was mainly an eastern feature, developed in Rome in the sixth century and later spread to parts of northern Europe. But within the eastern tradition there were styles of chanting that reflected regional developments. Similarly, clerical dress was not standardised throughout the church, although the principle of a declining hierarchy of extravagant and colourful garments was generally followed. The arrival in fifth-century Gaul of foreign pilgrims who refused to adopt the customary apparel of a bishop when they were elected to episcopal sees angered

[56] Gregory of Tours, HF 8.15 (English translation, 447).

[57] M. Simon, Verus Israel (Paris, 1948), 394-431; J. A. McNamara, A New Song: Celibate Women in the First Three Centuries (New York, 1983), 65-84, 107-125; M. L. W. Laistner, "The Western Church and Astrology in the Early Middle Ages," Harvard Theological Review 34 (1941): 251-75; J. Gouillard, "L'hérésie dans l'empire byzantin," TM 1 (1965): 299-324, esp. 300-307.

[58] Daniélou and Marrou, The First Christian Centuries, 431-33; A. Baumstark, Comparative Liturgy, 3rd ed., revised by B. Botte and edited by F. L. Cross (London, 1958), 15-30; E. Griffe, "Aux origines de la liturgie gallicane," Bulletin de littérature ecclésiastique 52 (1951): 17-43.

Pope Celestine.[59] To persist in the use of a loincloth and cloak when an established and more dignified uniform was required offended him and increased his opposition to the promotion of these outsiders over the local clergy.

Some variation in church services must surely be related to doctrinal divisions within Christianity—for instance, the wording of the creed; but others, such as its use in church and, if so, its place in the liturgy, sprang from local custom. A lack of service books, plate, or personnel might force adaptations; churchmen had to make do with their own limited resources. Although the Psalms and Gospels were read in every church, readings might not follow the same order, and certain prayers and responses might vary. The commemoration of local martyrs, patron saints, and church founders contributed additional variety to the cycle of feasts and holy days.

Easter Observance

The most serious barrier to unity of liturgical observance, however, arose over the celebration of Easter, the chief moveable feast of the church, on which all the others depended. Because several methods of calculation were used in different parts of Christendom, there was not one common ecclesiastical calendar but many, and in some years Easter was celebrated on three different dates. While the crucifixion was known to have taken place at the time of the Jewish Passover (always held on the 14th day of the month of Nisan), from an early date some Christians tried to avoid celebrating Easter on the same day. They preferred to wait until the Sunday after the vernal full moon, a delay that had already caused fearsome problems in the second century.[60] The church of Alexandria's expertise at computing the correct date, acknowledged at Nicaea (325), did not prevent the circulation of different calculations. In the mid-fifth century, Pope Leo I was forced to withdraw the western proposal in favour of the date established by Cyril of Alexandria, a move that was made in the interest of unity but which left an angry hostility towards the East's presumed superiority. In his anxiety to avoid a recurrence of the problem, Leo ordered the compilation of western Easter tables in line with Alexandrian practice, a task that was entrusted to Victor of Aquitaine. The new tables, published in 457, abandoned the 84-year lunar cycle previously used in the West in favour of the 19-year cycle of Alexandria. But Victor failed to understand the

[59] N. K. Chadwick and M. Dillon, eds., *The Celtic Realms* (London, 1967), 167.

[60] A. Strobel, *Ursprung und Geschichte des frühchristlichen Osterkalenders*, Texte und Untersuchungen, 121 (Berlin, 1977); idem, *Texte zur Geschichte des frühchristlichen Osterkalenders* (Münster, 1984), citing the earlier works of E. Schwartz, which remain fundamental. Cf. E. J. Bickerman, *Chronology of the Ancient World*, 2nd ed. (London, 1980).

eastern system of calculating lunar epacts, the *saltus lunae*, and therefore
produced dates at variance with eastern predictions in the first six years of
the lunar cycle. These alternative dates for Easter were published as "Latin"
(though in fact they were the correct dates observed in the East) beside
"Greek" dates that were in fact a complete fiction, observed nowhere.
Faced with such a difficult choice, western churches frequently requested
clarification from Rome. But even with papal authorisation for one date,
others might still be observed, as Gregory of Tours noted in 590. Within
each diocese the bishop communicated the dates of the most important
church feasts by an Easter letter.[61] In 577 the Spanish church celebrated
Easter on 21 March by its own (in this case) incorrect calculation—Easter
should never fall on the spring equinox itself—the papacy observed Easter
on 18 April, and the churches using the Alexandrian system waited until
25 April.[62]

Yet Dionysios, the eastern monk who translated works from Greek to
Latin in early sixth-century Rome, had already established Alexandrian
Easter tables using a Great Paschal cycle of 532 years, which would eventually compel a uniform observance among western churches. While the
battle for uniformity is best known from the Celtic/Roman clashes of seventh-century England, loyalty to a local system persisted in many communities. In the East a unique and anonymous work, appropriately called
the *Easter Chronicle*, combined a traditional chronology from the beginning
of time with a means of calculating dates, particularly the dates of Easter.
The entire text turns on this problem with much greater emphasis on the
methods to be used than is evident from early seventh-century manuals of
computation.[63] Despite its elaborate explanations and diagrams, disputes
over the correct date of Easter continued. In the middle of the eighth century, great disturbances occurred when the "orthodox" observed Lent from
18 February to 6 April and the "heretics" began a week later. According to
a Syrian source some greedy people shortened their fast by beginning with
the "heretics" on February 25 and ending a week early with the "orthodox."[64] Similarly, in seventh-century Francia, debates over Easter re-

---

[61] C. W. Jones, "The Victorian and Dionysiac Paschal Tables," *Speculum* 9 (1934): 408-
421; Gregory of Tours, *HF* 10.23 (English translation, 581-82). Easter letters often became
a vehicle for important communications on other matters as well, see Eusebios, *HE* 7.20-
22; L. T. Lefort, ed., *Lettres festales et pastorales en copte* (Louvain, 1955).

[62] Gregory of Tours, *HF* 5.17 (English translation, 274); cf. K. Hughes, "The Celtic
Church and the Papacy," in C. H. Lawrence, ed., *The English Church and the Papacy in the
Middle Ages* (London, 1965), 1-28.

[63] J. Beaucamp et al., "Le prologue de la *Chronique pascale*," *TM* 7 (1979): 223-302;
J. Beaucamp et al., "La Chronique Pascale: le temps approprié," in C. Pietri, ed., *Le temps
chrétien de la fin de l'Antiquité au Moyen Age (IIIᵉ-XIIIᵉs.)* (Paris, 1984), 451-68.

[64] Theophanes, 431; the details are supplied by Denys of Tell Mahre, *Chronique*, ed.
J. B. Chabot (Paris, 1895), 63.

mained a cause for regret, and in Spain the dates of Easter sometimes differed from one diocese to another, a confusion frequently censured by church councils.[65] Regional particularism in the use of Victor's tables not only delayed general knowledge of those by Dionysios, but also prevented Christians from realising one of the greatest advantages of his system, dating from the Incarnation (i.e. the *Annus Domini*, year of the Lord).[66]

Monastic and Architectural Variety. The lack of uniformity in public worship was exacerbated by the range of monastic observance and the existence of many private churches, founded to maintain an individual's tomb or to perform particular services for the salvation of one family. While many monasteries were based on ascetic practices developed in Egypt, there was no single model that provided for a uniform pattern of inheritance. From one source of inspiration many codes of eremitic behaviour were developed. Even after the composition of monastic rules by Sts. Basil and Benedict, these rules were not rigidly followed but were adapted and elaborated. Some communities grew up haphazardly around the cell of a holy man, others were established in urban homes and country villas. The transplanting of Pachomian ideals to the West also involved unavoidable changes due to the indigenous climate and terrain of Spain, Gaul, and Ireland, and to the changed political situation and the facilities available. So it is hardly surprising that the communities of Skellig Michael looked quite different from those of the Nitrian desert.[67]

For urban groups, the early Christian basilica provided a common architectural setting for ecclesiastical ritual.[68] This Roman style of construction, employing columns and capitals to support a flat or low-pitched roof, was adapted in the fourth century to create a rectangular church oriented towards the altar at the east end. The basic form was widely used throughout the empire, modified by local materials, building traditions, and topographical factors. From surviving examples, such as the churches of St. Maria Maggiore and St. Sabina in Rome, St. Apollinare in Classe (near Ravenna), or St. Demetrios in Thessalonike, we can get a sense of the im-

[65] J. M. Wallace-Hadrill, ed., *The Fourth Book of the Chronicle of Fredegar with its Continuations* (London, 1960), 97, para. 23.

[66] Bickerman, *Chronology of the Ancient World*, 79, 81.

[67] J. Gascou, "P. Fouad. 87: Les monastères pachômiens et l'Etat byzantin," *Bulletin de l'Institut français d'Archéologie orientale* 76 (1976): 157-84, for an analysis of the complex relations between monasteries near Antinoupolis and the local Byzantine authorities. In contrast, G. Ferrari, "Sources for the Early Iconography of St. Anthony," *Studia Anselmiana* 38 (1956): 248-53, shows how Irish devotion to Egyptian asceticism promoted artistic development and transported ideals to the most distant parts of the Celtic realms.

[68] R. Krautheimer et al., *Corpus Basilicarum Christianarum Romae* (Vatican City, 1939 onwards); R. Krautheimer, *Early Christian and Byzantine Architecture* (Harmondsworth, 1965), 45-65.

pact of the liturgy celebrated in such a setting. The capacity of these buildings suggests a congregation of hundreds, though there is no way of proving that scale was related to local needs. As the cities had many other
churches, the foundation of new basilicas may have been due to ecclesiastical or individual vainglory and the desire to honour a local saint (in the
case of St. Demetrios) rather than functional requirements. From smaller
basilicas uncovered by archaeology in less-populated areas, however, we
often find the same grandiose scale—in the churches of Philippi, for instance, or those of Cyprus and Syria.[69] Early Christian architecture was
clearly designed to impress, and to this end the use of different coloured
marbles, stone, brick, fresco, mosaic, and painted sculpture were judi-
ciously combined.

In addition to this traditional form of building, by the middle of the
sixth century a whole range of Christian architecture had developed, partly
dependent on function (such as the baptistery or small oratory) and partly
on indigenous skill in construction. From the East circular forms often associated with churches founded on tombs or around baptismal fonts spread
to the West, bringing the principles of the vault and dome. Because these
forms demanded quite complex technical ability, they were not so generally employed in northern Europe. But bearing in mind the lack of developed building traditions amongst the non-Roman invaders, what is remarkable is the degree of acculturation, which permitted the continuation
and development of Christian construction under their patronage. Simpler
churches built by ascetics reflect restricted resources and abilities, but
among Merovingian patrons of the mid-sixth century there is an awareness
of the type of Mediterranean art that should adorn a church or tomb. The
assimilation of Roman and Christian traditions to Merovingian styles and
techniques is evident in the official burial of Childebert I in Paris.[70]

Church-State Relations in Merovingian Francia . . .

But despite this successful attempt to incorporate older traditions, the
Merovingian kings remained recent converts to Christianity, whose familiarity with Latin culture, both secular and religious, was no more than a
few generations deep at the time of Childebert. They depended upon ecclesiastics to run the affairs of the church and carry through the conversion

[69] Krautheimer, *Early Christian Architecture*, 90-101, 116-20; P. Lemerle, *Philippes et la
Macédoine orientale* (Paris, 1946), 283-518; J. Lassus, *Sanctuaires chrétiens du Syrie* (Paris,
1947).

[70] K. H. Kruger, *Königsgrabkirchen* (Munich, 1971); J. Werner, "Frankish Royal Tombs
in the Cathedrals of Cologne and Saint-Denis," *Antiquity* 38 (1964): 201-261; P. Lasko, *The
Kingdom of the Franks* (London, 1971), 25-32, 46-62.

of Franks in rural areas that still clung to the old pagan ways.[71] And their primary concerns remained the pacification of northern Gaul and the extension of Merovingian rule to other parts of Europe (i.e. military consolidation). Under Chlotar I, who was himself well educated and intelligent enough to provide some training for the orphan Radegund, the territories conquered by Clovis's successors were briefly united. But at his death (561), the kingdom was divided in traditional Frankish (barbarian) custom between his four sons, who then fought bitterly against each other to negate the principle of shared inheritance. These fratricidal battles proved to be a persistent characteristic of Frankish rule and greatly weakened the political unity of northern Europe.

In such conditions Christian institutions developed autonomously in Gaul, often in independence of each other as well as of any secular authority. Since the fifth-century disorders, ecclesiastics had become accustomed to fend for themselves, and the continuing lack of organised protection encouraged this tendency. Of course, bishops were frequently drawn into political quarrels—not even the isolated monasteries could avoid taking sides—and this involvement meant that clerics were not immune from royal punishments and rewards. There was less sense of separation between sacred and secular roles to the point at which ecclesiastics were asked to wear their distinctive dress in order to be identifiable.[72] Although popes occasionally tried to intervene in this somewhat anarchic state of affairs, Roman legates were not usually welcomed. Only when it suited the aim of a particular bishop was the name of Rome invoked, for example when papal protection for a monastic foundation was required. Caesarius of Arles, who employed this tactic to ensure that his own monasteries would be totally independent of his episcopal successors, had no success as a papal vicar in southern Gaul.[73] The Merovingian church kept its distance from Rome and developed along local lines, determined by previous history and regional politics, rather than in accordance with any preconceived plan (papal, royal, or episcopal).

[71] Le Goff, "Clerical Culture"; Wallace-Hadrill, *The Frankish Church*, 75-109; F. Prinz, "The Frankish Nobility and the Territories East of the Rhine," in H. B. Clarke and M. Brennan, eds., *Columbanus and Merovingian Monasticism* (Oxford, 1981), 73-87, esp. 79: "the leading Franks were finally christianized under Dagobert I (629-39)."

[72] F. Prinz, *Klerus und Krieg im früheren Mittelalter* (Stuttgart, 1971), 8-21.

[73] Jaffé, no. 864 (dated 514/23); G. Morin, "Le Testament de S. Césaire d'Arles et la critique de M. Krusch," *Revue Bénédictine* 16 (1899): 97-112. On the numerous disputes between bishops and monasteries, see E. Ewig, "Beobachtungen zu den Klosterprivilegien des 7. und frühen 8. Jahrhunderts," in *Adel und Kirche*, Festschrift G. Tellenbach (Freiburg, 1968), 52-65, reprinted in *Spätantikes und fränkisches Gallien*, vol. 2 (Munich, 1979); E. James, *The Origins of France* (London, 1982), 107-111.

. . . And in the East

In contrast, the church of Constantinople had been moulded into a very close-fitting relationship with the secular government, which allowed for little autonomy even in matters of doctrine. Since the time of Constantine the Great, imperial control over patriarchal appointments and influence in theological definitions had given the secular authorities a legitimate role in Christian institutions. This was felt most immediately in ecclesiastical circles close to the capital and in the major bishoprics of the eastern churches. But through the practice established by Constantine when he summoned and presided over the First Oecumenical Council of the church at Nicaea (325), this imperial supervision was extended to the whole of Christendom. For despite disclaimers to the effect that it was the assembled clerics who determined Christian dogma, civilian officials made sure that imperial definitions of orthodoxy carried their full weight in these meetings.[74] During much of the fourth century, the imperial family's commitment to Arianism protected this doctrine and drove its opponents into exile. Similarly, churchmen both in the West and the East who consistently opposed imperial views generally paid a price for their principled stand. This heavy non-sacerdotal force was built into the relationship between the civil and ecclesiastical governments and was recognised by both parties.[75]

In discussing this structural subordination of the patriarch of Constantinople to the eastern emperor, it is quite easy to overlook the historical circumstances that created such a relationship. This results in a confused understanding of church/state contacts, sometimes expressed in the phrase "Byzantine caesaropapism." It is more helpful to recall the fact that Constantine established a new imperial residence on the Bosphoros *partly* because the city of Rome was too closely associated with pagan cults and pre-Christian history. Old Rome continued to look like a pagan capital for centuries, dominated by its temples, imperial buildings, arenas, baths, theatres, arches, and fora, all associated with the non-Christian past. Because the Christian monuments were at first underground or suburban, no decisive change was made within the city walls for many years. Pilgrims visiting Rome in the eighth century followed an itinerary that took them

[74] The presence and intervention of imperial representatives, generally civilian officials, is a marked feature of conciliar activity and is obviously related to the emperor's directing role in such meetings. See E. K. Chrysos, "Konzilspräsident und Konzils-Vorstand. Zur Frage des Vorsitzes in den Konzilen der byzantinischen Reichskirche," *Annuarium Historiae Conciliorum* 11 (i) (1979): 1-17.

[75] Dix, *Jurisdiction*, 65-95, laments the rather miserable process of secularisation set in motion by Constantine I; cf. J.-M. Sansterre, "Eusèbe de Césarée et la naissance de la théorie 'césaropapiste'," *B* 42 (1972), 131-95, 532-93; K. M. Girardet, *Kaisergericht und Bischofsgericht* (Bonn, 1975).

around the city, outside the walls; there were few major Christian sites in the centre.[76]

In marked contrast, Constantinople, from its first rebuilding (324-30), was endowed with Christian monuments.[77] The church of the Holy Apostles, which became the mausoleum of the imperial family, was founded by Constantine I. His son, Constantius, was probably responsible for the first church of Holy Wisdom (St. Sophia), built next to the imperial palace, the Senate, and the Hippodrome in the very centre of the city. (This was a basilica, destroyed in the Nika riots of 532 and replaced at Justinian's orders by the present domed church.) Throughout the city, churches and monasteries existed beside public buildings, pagan monuments, and other structures necessary to any fourth-century imperial city. A Christian presence was built into New Rome, emphasising the combination of past imperial traditions with the new faith.

These novel circumstances also served to highlight the magnanimity of the emperor who had freed Christians from the fear of persecution and granted them an official position within the empire. His role was acknowledged and celebrated in the imperial *laudes*, chanted by the assembled representatives of the faith at Nicaea and at subsequent councils. Just because the church was able to seize this opportunity to expand its public image, we should not forget that it remained dependent upon imperial privilege. Julian revoked that protection in his attempt to revive the pagan cults, and the Christians were powerless in the face of his personal decision. Had he reigned like his cousin, Constantius, for twenty years, he might have succeeded in reducing Christianity to one among many faiths again. His attempts to reinstate the teaching of philosophy reveal a clear understanding of the key role of public instruction.[78] But in the three years of his rule he could do no lasting damage, though he gave encouragement to those loyal to the old pagan cults. At the end of the fourth century, the church faced violent opposition in Rome, organised by aristocratic senators, and less obvious pagan survivals continued to disturb ecclesiastical authorities throughout the empire even into the seventh century. Neither challenge, however, succeeded in curbing the growth and dominance of Christian belief in Late Antique society.

So the particular relationship between the eastern churches and the emperor was not the result of some usurpation of ecclesiastical power by the secular state; it was rather an indigenous development from the imperial

---

[76] R. Valentini and G. Zuchetti, *Codice topografico della città di Roma*, 4 vols. (Rome, 1940-53), 2: 72-99 (*Notitia ecclesiarum urbis Romae*).

[77] G. Dagron, *Naissance d'une capitale* (Paris, 1974); idem, "Le christianisme dans la ville byzantine," *DOP* 31 (1977): 3-25.

[78] C. N. Cochrane, *Christianity and Classical Culture* (Oxford, 1940), 261-91.

establishment of Christianity as the dominant faith of the new eastern capital. Protected, endowed, and given extensive privileges in the Late Antique world, the church was bound to imperial control in specific ways. For geographic and strategic reasons, those Christian communities furthest removed from the orbit of Constantinople could sometimes escape it. The church of Spain, for example, was barely affected by the personal beliefs of fifth- and sixth-century eastern emperors, while these were dramatically imposed on the churches of Jerusalem, Alexandria, Antioch, Constantinople, and even Rome. In general, it was the patriarch of the eastern capital who suffered most from proximity to the emperor; his subordination to secular control was a distinguishing feature of Byzantine society that weakened the independence of the Constantinopolitan church and caused many disputes with the other centres of Christianity. Conversely, the full authority of the emperor could be put at the service of the patriarch, in the eradication of heresy, for example, whereas other church leaders lacked such considerable material force to impose their own interpretations of the faith.

Many factors, therefore, combined to distinguish the different churches that together made up the community of Christian believers in the sixth century. The sense of a shared community is clear nonetheless, and may be illustrated by the place of pilgrimage in the Christian faith.[79] Of course, people went on pilgrimages for reasons that were not solely religious—matters of prestige, fashion, social standing, and ill-health among them. But in their accounts of visiting the Holy Places, whether those of Jerusalem, Jordan, and Bethlehem connected with Christ's life on earth, or the Old Testament sites, or those of local martyrs and particular holy men, they all describe the same desire to experience the power of holy relics and of sites made famous in the days of persecution. Many travelled with a non-Christian expectation of marvels and wonders apparently performed at these shrines, and recorded their gratitude in monuments erected back home. And nearly all commented on the variety of tongues heard, clothes, hair styles, and customs observed among other pilgrims drawn from every part of Christendom. Those from the West could not understand the Armenian rites, Coptic prayers, or Syriac readings performed at the shrine of the Holy Sepulchre, while Egyptians could not follow the Roman liturgy at the tomb of St. Peter. But basically they went on pilgrimages to bear witness to the Christian faith and joined in this practice with zealous en-

---

[79] J. J. Wilkinson, *Jerusalem Pilgrims Before the Crusades* (Warminster, 1977); B. Kötting, *Peregrinatio religiosa: Wallfahrten in der Antike und das Pilgerwesen in der alten Kirche* (Regensburg, 1950); E. D. Hunt, "St. Sylvia of Aquitaine: The Role of a Theodosian Pilgrim in the Society of East and West," *JTS* 23 (1972): 351-73.

thusiasm. The universal character of their belief and its defeat of all rivals was a reassuring feature of sixth-century Christianity.

THE FIFTH OECUMENICAL COUNCIL (553)

These strengths were severely tested by the mid-century crisis over the Three Chapters, which was used by Emperor Justinian as an excuse for the Fifth Oecumenical Council of Constantinople. The dispute is frequently dismissed as one of those obscure arguments cherished by eastern theologians but without serious foundation. This characterisation, however, fails to grasp the implications of the debate, which threatened the entire organisation of Christendom. It is with these wider ramifications in mind that the events leading up to the council will be analysed.

The Three Chapters were texts by three fifth-century bishops, Theodore of Mopsuestia, Ibas of Edessa, and Theodoretos of Kyrros, all suspected of heretical tendencies towards Nestorianism but cleared by the council of Chalcedon (451). Ibas and Theodoretos had appeared in person before this gathering, had condemned Nestorios, and had therefore been restored to their sees.[80] Their writings might then have been accepted as orthodox and the discussion closed. But the doctrine of Nestorianism and the fame of Theodore of Mopsuestia, Nestorios's teacher who had died in 428, continued to attract adherents. Its growth in turn fuelled the opposing Monophysite tendency, which put forward its own doctrine of the one nature of Christ.

This resurgence of anti-Nestorian conviction in the churches nearly a century after Chalcedon seemed to Justinian to present an opportunity to reunite Monophysite tendencies with Constantinople. Since 532 the emperor had explored the possibility. But Pope Agapitus (535-36) persuaded him of the dangerously heretical nature of the Monophysite party, and he turned instead to persecution. (Justinian's concern with correct Christian dogma made him very hostile to non-believers of many varieties; he persecuted Jews, Samaritans, pagans, and heretical Christian sects with equal vigour.)[81] When force did not prevail, he sought another method of reconciliation. Since it was the formulation of the council of Chalcedon that had forced the Monophysites into schism, Justinian tried to find a way of removing this barrier to unity, and since all parties could agree on an emphatic condemnation of Nestorianism, branded as heretical at Ephesos and Chalcedon, this became the chosen weapon, and the Three Chapters the

---

[80] E. Schwartz, ed., *Concilium Chalcedonense*, vol. 1 (iii) (Berlin/New York, 1935), actio 9, pp. 9-11; actiones 10-11, pp. 13-42.

[81] J. B. Bury, *History of the Later Roman Empire* (A.D. *395 to* A.D. *565*), 2 vols. (London, 1923), 2: 360-61, 364-72, 377-78.

particular instrument. In this calculation the emperor thought he could win over the more moderate group of Monophysites, the so-called *Akephaloi*, followers of Severos, ex-patriarch of Antioch. The others would follow suit when they realised that unity was possible through the attack on Nestorianism.[82]

Although this ingenious solution was first proposed by a cleric, it was put into effect by a layman, the emperor. Justinian drew up an imperial edict in 543-44 condemning Theodore, Ibas, and Theodoretos as Nestorians.[83] It was sent to the five leading ecclesiastics for their approval, and under the usual threat of force the four eastern patriarchs signed. Later Zoilas of Alexandria had second thoughts and was therefore replaced by a more pliant patriarch. Of the clerics in Constantinople at the time, only two (both Westerners) expressed their doubts as to the edict's validity: Datius of Milan, who returned home to inform the pope, and Stephen, the papal legate who remained in the East. When Pope Vigilius (537-55) procrastinated, he was forcibly removed to Constantinople (November 545) and obliged to convene a council to debate the issue. Under close imperial supervision he condemned the Three Chapters in 548, provoking enormous protests in the West.[84] Justinian meanwhile assumed that he had convinced sufficient numbers to make his redefinition of orthodox belief binding. He issued a confession of True Faith in 551 (*Expositio rectae fidei*) and proceeded with the plan to summon an oecumenical council to meet in Constantinople and give ecclesiastical approval.[85] He had not counted on any serious opposition. But in this he had underestimated the vitality and independence of sections of the western churches.

[82] M. V. Anastos, "The Immutability of Christ and Justinian's Condemnation of Theodore of Mopsuestia," *DOP* 6 (1951): 125-60; P. Battifol, "L'empereur Justinian et la siège apostolique," *Recherches des sciences religieuses* 16 (1926): 193-264, remains a clear, useful summary.

[83] The edict does not survive; see E. K. Chrysos, *He ekklesiastike politike tou Ioustinianou* (Thessalonike, 1969), 20-32; E. Schwartz, *Drei dogmatische Schriften Iustinians*, Abhandlungen der Bayerischen Akademie der Wissenschaften, Philos.-hist. Abteilung, Heft 18 (Munich, 1939), no. 2, 47-69 and 114-16; cf. M. Amelotti and L. M. Zingale, *Scritti teologici ed ecclesiasticii de Giustiniano* (Milan, 1977).

[84] Fragments of Pope Vigilius's *Iudicatum* are preserved, Mansi, 9.181, 104-105; Chrysos, *He ekklesiastike politike*, 58-72. Western opposition had been manifested in 545 and was extended by Facundus of Hermiane's *Defense of the Three Chapters and Other Writings*; see Duchesne, *L'église au sixième siècle*, 179-80, 184-91.

[85] The *Expositio*, with a further condemnation of the Three Chapters, is published by Schwartz, *Drei dogmatische Schriften*, no. 3, 72-111; cf. R. Schieffer, "Zur lateinischen Überlieferung von Kaiser Justinians Ὁμολογία τῆς ὀρθῆς πίστεως (Edictum de recta fide)," *Kleronomia* 3 (1971): 285-302. It was to be reused in the seventh century.

Western Opposition

In the middle of the sixth century, ecclesiastical dioceses as far apart as Septimania (extending from northeastern Spain into southern Gaul), Carthage (North Africa), Illyricum (the Danube provinces and the Balkan peninsula), Crete, Sicily, and Dalmatia and Istria (the eastern and northern shores of the Adriatic) were all classed as western and fell under the nominal authority of Rome. This authority was very often quite unreal, as the churches led entirely separate and independent lives. In particular, the dioceses of North Africa maintained their own traditions, supported by a high level of theological training and a distinguished history of ecclesiastical scholarship. From this area, as well as from northern Italy, Istria, Dalmatia, and Illyricum, prelates protested against the imperial edict and Pope Vigilius's acceptance of it. Their opposition, well informed on the doctrinal details of the Monophysite/Nestorian clash, sprang from a fundamental support for the oecumenical council as the highest authority within the church. Thus, they were not prepared to see the decisions of Chalcedon impugned as unorthodox; they subscribed to its definitions of dogma and recited its creed. By re-opening the question of Nestorian influence in the writings known as the Three Chapters, Justinian provoked a serious battle with western clerics who would not tolerate such obvious interference in the established doctrine of the church.

The diocese of Illyricum, for instance, refused to endorse the imperial scheme on the grounds that its whole purpose was against the faith. Instead, the Balkan bishops held their own council in 550 to denounce Justinian's position and to uphold the decisions of Chalcedon.[86] When summoned to attend in 553, only nine Illyrians went to Constantinople: one from Dacia and eight from Macedonia. Three other Dacian representatives supported Pope Vigilius, who had retracted his statement of support and refused to participate in the council. The metropolitans of Milan and Salona (Dalmatia), on the other hand, felt obliged to attend in order to prevent the incorrect condemnation of the Three Chapters.[87] In taking this step they were following the example of the African church, which sent nine of its leaders; a large number of its most skilful theologians under Facundus, abbot of Hermiane, also went to Constantinople to combat the imperial plan. African antagonism was so extreme that the civil government removed some bishops from their positions and replaced them with manipu-

[86] Victor of Tonnena, *Chronicle*, a.549, ed. T. Mommsen, in *MHG, AA*, vol. 11, pt. 2, 202. Vigilius reports the same in his letter to Rusticus and Sebastian, two disloyal deacons; see *PL* 69, 45.

[87] E. Chrysos, *Die Bischöfslisten des V. Ökumenischen Konzils (553)* (Bonn, 1966), 128-38.

lable clerics. The council met from May to June 553 and was attended by 165 bishops.[88] Pope Vigilius protested quite legitimately that the western churches were underrepresented; apart from Milan and Rome, no Italian or Sicilian bishops were present, nor any from other churches further west. From Arles, Bishop Aurelian sent a legate to find out what was happening, but he took no part in the council. Throughout its proceedings (and since 547 in effect) the pope remained under house arrest, with Reparatus, metropolitan of Carthage, and Verecundus, bishop of Junca, who shared his seven-year ordeal. Verecundus died in captivity in the capital, and Reparatus was subjected to another decade of exile and deprivation before he too died. Justinian's persecution of the African prelates is an eloquent testimonial to their determined and forceful opposition, which spread the dispute through all Christian communities and prolonged it for many years.

Vigilius, however, was unable to withstand continual imperial pressure and finally issued a document of support for the council he had never attended. He had witnessed the deaths of Datius and Verecundus in 552 when they were all imprisoned in the church of St. Euphemia. He himself had been subjected to the most ferocious threats, harassment, and bodily violence, which probably brought about his death in Sicily during the return journey to Rome. In addition, he could not have foreseen either the divisive heritage of the Fifth Council or the continuing martyrdom of its opponents. But by capitulating to well-orchestrated theological and imperial arguments, Vigilius did not achieve the oecumenical unity he so much desired (and which was the Constantinopolitan justification for his signing). On the contrary, his agreement with the council produced only greater schism and confusion in the West.

Although the bishops of northern Europe had not been involved in the dispute and did not normally concern themselves with the little-known heresies of Nestorianism and Monophysitism, they subscribed to the ecclesiastical principle that doctrine was defined by church councils and accepted the canons of Chalcedon as binding. The Fourth Council had become a symbol of orthodoxy in the West, upheld at Orléans in 549, when the representatives of 71 bishops reaffirmed papal condemnation of Eutyches and Nestorios.[89] The council of 553, therefore, became an embarrassment for them and was in general ignored. The diocese of Dalmatia, whose metropolitan, Frontius, died in exile in the Egyptian Thebaid (along with Bishop Victor of Tonnena and other African prelates), may have been responsible for a document denouncing the 553 rulings as a means of sat-

[88] Ibid., 138-44; J. Straub, ed., *Concilium Universale Constantinopolitanum sub Iustiniano Habitum* (Berlin/New York, 1971). On Facundus, see H. J. Sieben, *Die Konzilsidee der alten Kirche* (Paderborn, 1979), 282-300.

[89] Mansi, 9.127-38; canon 1, 129A-B.

isfying the Monophysite faction within the church.[90] In this letter addressed to the emperor, the Dalmatians perceived the political motive behind the condemnation of the Three Chapters and indicated an awareness of its complex background. In contrast, when Bishop Aurelian's envoy to the East eventually returned, he had been converted and approved of the council.[91] But for most church leaders in the West, the main problem was Vigilius's acquiescence, which his successor Pope Pelagius felt obliged to support. For nearly twenty years the church of Milan remained out of communion with Rome, while in Istria the metropolitan of Aquileia used this disagreement to extend his control over Grado and to raise his own position to that of patriarch in a schism finally resolved in the early seventh century.[92] The only source of support for papal policy over 553 came from Metropolitan Primosus of Carthage, the disloyal legate of Reparatus, and Primasius of Hadrumetum, both of whom had adopted Justinian's policy in order to further their clerical careers. Their decision to enforce the condemnation of the Three Chapters in Africa was resented and resisted by other clerics of Chalcedonian faith and weakened the African church. Another imperial supporter, Metropolitan Firmus of Numidia, did not succeed in winning over his diocese until Primosus presented the consequences of continued opposition at a local council held in 554.[93] All in all, the extremely unpopular imposition of Justinian's religious policy in Africa gave the papacy no comfort and little material assistance, while it rendered imperial administration less attractive to the indigenous inhabitants.

Meanwhile, the Severan Monophysite church in the East Mediterranean was unmoved by the condemnation of the Three Chapters and remained in schism with the Chalcedonian majority. So the primary objective of the council was not achieved despite patriarchal and papal ratification. Further east, in the Syriac church of Persia, the 553 denunciation of Theodore of Mopsuestia in particular had important repercussions: under Patriarch Joseph, elected in 554, a council was held to renew the canons of the church and took the opportunity to reaffirm its Nestorian theology of Duophysitism.[94] This meeting at Seleucia/Ctesiphon reflected the thriving state of Persian Christianity. It was attended by eighteen bishops, a further seventeen sending their adherence by letter and seal. Thirty years later the

[90] Ibid., 9.589-646.

[91] Reported in the Italian clerics' letter to Vigilius, PL 69, 118.

[92] G. Cuscito, "Aquileia e Bisanzio nella controversia dei Tre Capitoli," Atti dell'Antico Adriatico 12 (1977): 231-62.

[93] Victor of Tonnena, Chronicle, aa. 551, 552, 554 (pp. 204-205); PL 69, 116; cf. Duchesne, L'église au sixième siècle, 215-16.

[94] J.-B. Chabot, "Synodikon orientale, ou Recueil de synodes nestoriens," Notices et Extraits des Manuscrits de la Bibliothèque Nationale 37 (1902): 352-67.

bishops formulated their defence of Theodore of Mopsuestia and condemned Justinian as a heretic.[95] While their number may seem insignificant, the geographical extent of the church revealed in their distribution is
striking. From the eastern borders of the Byzantine Empire to the Caspian
and the mountains of Afghanistan, and south to the Persian Gulf, Oman,
and trading posts on the route to southern India, this Nestorian faith was
securely rooted. Like other churches, it suffered from problems of simony
among bishops and political pressure from imperial authorities (Sasanian in
this case). But it was an equally valid inheritor of the Christian faith and
proved to be one of the most resourceful in its evangelical missions.[96]

The council of 553 thus represents a hollow triumph of political intrigue
and imperial intervention. Because of its ultimate failure and the extended
opposition to its rulings, the Three Chapters controversy intensified clerical concern about the relationship between the sacred and the secular, while
elevating previous oecumenical councils to a sovereign position within the
church. Although the eastern patriarchs had accepted Justinian's claim to
impose an imperial edict as ecclesiastical doctrine, western antagonism to
this tradition was contagious. By the late seventh and early eighth centuries
despite imperial attempts to continue in the old way, the eastern churches
also maintained that doctrine could be changed only by a council of the
whole church. For those who had opposed Justinian, often at great cost, it
was the emperor's decision to alter the definitions of Chalcedon that provoked their lasting hostility. Subsequent leaders of the western churches
often excused Pope Vigilius's apparent support for the council and consigned its decisions to oblivion; even Pope Gregory I (594-605) on occasion
advised acceptance of the first four oecumenical councils only. But a vigorous critic, like Columbanus, could attack Vigilius, who "was not very
vigilant," and his successor, Pope Boniface IV (608-615), as partisans of
heretics for supporting the council.[97] In addition to this awkwardness over
the canons of 553, an inevitable distrust of imperial power developed in the
West, together with a tendency to dismiss eastern theological debate. Instead of accepting Greek doctrinal definitions, western churches would in
future draw on the Augustinian corpus that had created a comparable Latin
authority of their own. The Fifth Council had diminished the previously
accepted standing of eastern customs and opened a breach in the ecclesiastical *oikoumene*, which would never be repaired.

In every respect, therefore, the controversy sharpened and deepened regional variations in church practice and dogma. It further alienated the

---

[95] Ibid., 390-424, esp. canon 2, 398-400; cf. Guillaumont, "Justinien et l'église de
Perse," 54-62.

[96] See Guillaumont, "Justinien et l'église de Perse," and Macina, "L'homme à l'école."

[97] *Sancti Columbani Opera*, ed. G. S. M. Walker (Dublin, 1957), 36-57 (letter 5).

churches of the West and the Severan and Nestorian churches of the East
from Constantinople, and thus gave them greater distance intellectually
from one of the most flourishing centres of Late Antiquity. It hastened a
new Christian form of separation between the two halves of the Mediterranean, confirming both an eastern sense of Greek superiority and a western
assertion of Latin identity. Crucially, it revealed that the papacy could no
longer keep pace with the Christological disputes endemic in the East.
Rather than pursue such matters and risk further imperial punishment, Pelagius I and his immediate successors withdrew into the war-torn and unsettled city of Rome to provide for its loyal population in times of need and
to establish a political base in central Italy. In this they built on Rome's
claims to an apostolic foundation, which had been developed by Popes Leo
I and Gelasius I. The shift was provoked in reaction to a humiliation imposed by Constantinople, not selected consciously in an attempt to create
an alternative source of regional support. But it was to have important consequences for papal development in the late sixth and seventh centuries.

Although these consequences follow clearly from the Fifth Oecumenical
Council, they were not recognised either in 553 or later. Both emperors
and popes continued to act out their traditional roles as if the council had
successfully accomplished its duty. Thus Herakleios, Constans II, Constantine IV, and Justinian II would attempt to impose a doctrinal imperialism on the church at different points through the seventh century. And
Popes Honorius, Martin I, Agatho, and Constantine I would respond to
such interventions in ecclesiastical belief in the same manner as Vigilius,
some with greater success than others. In the case of Pope Martin, whose
intellectual opposition to the doctrine of Montheletism was securely
founded and passionately defended, the full range of Byzantine political authority—kidnap, torture, mock trial, humiliation, and exile—ensured a
martyr's crown. Others escaped with compromise formulas that satisfied
the emperors' determination to intervene in ecclesiastical matters. But the
constant striving for total control over the church, inherent in their imperial office, and regular recourse to physical force when theological argument failed, reveal the impossibility of this aim. Christianity could not be
directed as the older pagan cults had been; it had established an internal
authority of its own. Under threats of violence this might be tamed, but in
the hands of a great Christian leader like Martin, it could resist and would
frustrate imperial designs for the church.

CONCLUSION

The Fifth Oecumenical Council thus marks a significant stage in growing
western disaffection from the East, and it parallels a political estrangement

visible from the second half of the sixth century. Both tendencies herald the breakdown of Late Antique cultural unity, most immediately in the decline of bilingual ability, and most seriously in the rise of local identities of greater import and coherence. There is no sharp break. But in discussing the unity of Late Antique culture, a turning point in about the middle of the sixth century cannot be passed over. The rejection of ecclesiastical discourse after 553 is symptomatic of a fundamental shift in the allegiances and cultural identities of the two halves of the Mediterranean world.

Thus, from the third until at least the middle of the sixth century there was indeed a common Mediterranean culture, which justifies and demands the study of Late Antiquity. But one of the most distinctive features of this culture was its employment of a relatively recent faith, Christianity. In turn, Christianity was dependent on classical pagan learning and Roman political power. From these sources, however, the churches sponsored both the cultural unity that buried pagan rites and the internal authority that defied imperial manipulation, thus removing two essential aspects of the Greco-Roman inheritance, secular learning (including philosophical speculation) and imperial dictatorship.

The Christian component of Late Antique culture was therefore a two-edged sword, capable of securing a dominant position. As the political unity of the empire became a thing of the past, Christian unity took its place. In the same way, it replaced the obnoxious aspects of Greco-Roman scholarship with its own brand of theological learning. Because it had developed in a manner designed to preserve so many features of the imperial heritage, it *appeared* as its natural extension. There is a sense in which the Christian faith, rather than the barbarian kingdoms, constituted the successor of the Roman Empire in the West. As a universal and fundamentally extra-territorial system, it could and did unite the various imperial remnants and non-Roman governments of the mid-sixth century. It could also extend Christian control to areas beyond the old imperial orbit—southern India, the Persian Gulf, Ireland, and the remoter parts of the British Isles. But precisely because it was a form of substitution, an adaptation of an older system with new elements grafted on to it, this Christian unity was both less and more than its predecessor. It could not claim the exclusive political allegiance of all inhabitants of the known world, for there were still military leaders and rival social groups demanding an immediate loyalty, but at the same time it offered the promise of a better life to come to those who gave it their spiritual allegiance. The novelty of Christianity lay in this systematic guarantee of deferred reward.

But in the world of Late Antiquity, it was the impact of growing theological division that permitted a cultural division to be expressed. The process of transition from a recognisably classical Mediterranean to one shorn of its antique character accelerates after the breakdown of Christian unity over the Three Chapters. It is a slow and gradual transformation not achieved until the ninth century, but already at work in the middle of the sixth when the cultural unity of the Late Antique world comes to an end.

II

FROM CHRISTIAN SCHISM
TO DIVISION

MAP 2

The East Mediterranean

SERDICA •
PHILIPPOPOLIS •
MONTE CASSINO +
SALERNO •
• BENEVENTO
Calabria
DYRRACHION
THESSALONIKE •
LARISSA •
• BERROIA *THRACE*
CONSTANTINOPLE
HERAKLEIA
MACEDONIA
THESSALONIKE
• ANCH
KYZIKOS
OPS
• ABYDO
• PERGAMON
Lesbos • SARDIS
Euboia
EPHESOS
• TARANTO
DYRRACHION
+ VIVARIUM
HELLAS
KEPHALONIA
• PATRAS
PELOPONNESOS
SPARTA •
Mani
• MONEMVASIA
• Thera
• REGGIO
SICILY
Kc
(654
□ SYRACUSE
CRETE • KNOSS
GORTYNA
• CARTHAGE (698)
• KAIROUAN (670)
Libya (647) ◀

HELLAS Byzantine *Themata*
—॥—॥—॥— *Themata* boundaries (very approximate)
Calabria Region
◉ Imperial residence
• City
+ Ascetic settlement
◀— Arab advance

0 50 100   200   300 miles

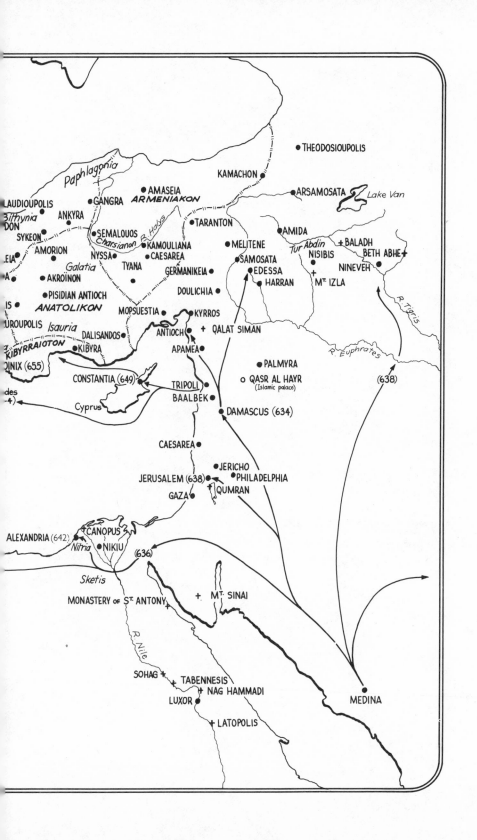

THEODOSIOUPOLIS

KAMACHON

ARSAMOSATA   *Lake Van*

Paphlagonia

AMASEIA
GANGRA   *ARMENIAKON*

LAUDIOUPOLIS

Bithynia   ANKYRA   AMIDA
DON
SYKEON   SEMALOUOS   MELITENE   *Tur Abdin*   + BALADH
        Charsianon   NISIBIS   BETH ABHE +
EIA   AMORION   KAMOULIANA   SAMOSATA
        NYSSA   *CAESAREA*   GERMANIKEIA   EDESSA   NINEVEH
A   AKROÏNON   TYANA   HARRAN   Mᵀ IZLA
        Galatia
IS   PISIDIAN ANTIOCH   DOULICHIA
        ANATOLIKON   MOPSUESTIA   KYRROS   *R. Euphrates*
UROUPOLIS   *Isauria*   ANTIOCH   + QALAT SIMAN   *R. Tigris*
        DALISANDOS   APAMEA
KIBYRRAIOTON   KIBYRA   PALMYRA   (638)
INIX (655)
        CONSTANTIA (649)   TRIPOLI   O QASR AL HAYR
des   BAALBEK   *(Islamic palace)*
4)   *Cyprus*   DAMASCUS (634)

        TARANTON

                CAESAREA

                        JERICHO
        JERUSALEM (638)   PHILADELPHIA
        GAZA   QUMRAN

ALEXANDRIA (642)   CANOPUS
        Nitria   NIKIU   (636)
        Sketis

                + Mᵀ SINAI
MONASTERY OF Sᵀ ANTONY

        R. Nile

        SOHAG   TABENNESIS
                + NAG HAMMADI
        LUXOR
                        MEDINA
                + LATOPOLIS

THE SEVENTH century is justifiably regarded as a "dark age."[1] In all parts of the Mediterranean, economic decline accompanied political instability. Levels of culture and standards of literacy fell as people ceased to learn, build, paint, and write in the traditional fashion. This development is reflected in the historical sources for the period, which are generally poor, especially for Byzantium, Rome, and the Frankish kingdoms, in part a symptom of the inability to record contemporary events. What written, archaeological, and artistic evidence there is, however, suggests that this century was a crucial bridge in the transition from a definably Late Antique world to a medieval one.[2] Classical and post-classical forms related to ancient Mediterranean traditions are gradually so adapted and changed that they become "proto-medieval." Perhaps the tensions of the period contributed to the silences. But as is so often the case, precisely because it was a formative transition, its history has to be reconstructed from very partial evidence.

This reconstruction should begin from the fact that Justinian's attempt to unite the western Mediterranean under Constantinopolitan control failed. The eastern empire could no longer claim to be the sole heir of Rome; other forces were in a position to contest the inheritance of the ancient world. These included the diverse secular powers of the West— Frankish, Visigothic, Celtic, or Lombard—and the purely spiritual authority of Old Rome, now a fully Christian city but no longer a political capital. To these indigenous rivals, a totally new one was added by the

[1] W. P. Ker, *The Dark Ages* (London, 1904), 1-23, categorised the seventh to tenth centuries as a separate and particularly dark interlude between Antiquity and the Middle Ages. Since then the epithet has stuck, despite attempts to dispel it, for instance, by D. Talbot Rice, "The Myth of the Dark Ages," in the volume edited by him, a useful survey of artistic developments, paradoxically titled *The Dark Ages* (London, 1965), or by F.-G. Maier, "Die Legende der 'Dark Ages'," in *Die Verwandlung der Mittelmeerwelt* (Frankfurt am Main, 1968), 10-20. For most recent use, see R. C. Hodges, *Dark Age Economics* (London, 1982); cf. K. Bosl, "Die Anfänge der europäischen Gesellschaft und Kultur (6.-8. Jahrhundert)," in *Die Gesellschaft in der Geschichte des Mittelalters* (Göttingen, 1966), on the importance of the seventh century.

[2] P. Riché, "L'instruction des laïcs en Gaule mérovingienne au VIIᵉ siècle," and P. Lehmann, "Panorama des literarischen Kultur des Abendlandes im 7. Jahrhundert," both in *Settimane* 5 (1958), 2:878-88, 845-71; Talbot Rice, *The Dark Ages*.

mid-seventh century eruption of Arabia into the Mediterranean. Within fifty years, the Caliphate of Damascus gained control of the eastern and southern shores in a tripartite division, which left the Byzantine northeast and European northwest as separate sectors. Under the same Arab impact, a parallel theological division produced two distinct Christian spheres, eastern and western Christendom, flanked by the rival faith of Islam.

The significance of this transformation was highlighted by Henri Pirenne, who may have exaggerated the economic effects of Islamic expansion. Nonetheless, his thesis that the advent of Islam in the Mediterranean sealed the end of Late Antiquity remains valid.[3] To say this is not to endorse every aspect of Pirenne's fundamental analysis. But obviously his memorable dictum—"Without Mohammed, Charlemagne would have been inconceivable"[4]—is correct, if we take it to mean that Charlemagne's coronation by Pope Leo III on Christmas Day, 800, would have been unthinkable had not Islam reduced Byzantium to a novel position of weakness. Had Constantinople continued to rule over the Roman lake, or had the Muslims realised their ambition of taking the Queen City for their capital, the creation of an emperor for the West could not have occurred. Part II of this study is devoted to the developments of the late sixth and seventh centuries, which set in motion this combination of political and religious division.

While forces external to the ancient world witnessed the division and hastened its resolution into permanent barriers across the universe once dominated by Rome, that world was already disintegrating (as we have seen in Part I). With the decline of self-governing cities and their senatorial orders of *curiales*, urban predominance gave way to a rural style of living. In Asia Minor this process was completed by intensive Persian campaigns of the years 614-19. But the invasions did not bring about the end of Late Antiquity, as is sometimes claimed.[5] Classical cities everywhere, even in the distant regions of Crimea and Africa, were in crisis during the late sixth and seventh centuries. Increasingly, ruralisation and the concomitant loss of imperial identity resulted in political and geographical fragmentation— a number of splinter societies, introverted and isolated, with limited economic and cultural resources. Although the Christian faith provided a common bond, spiritual unity could not compensate for the disappearance

---

[3] P. Brown, *"Mohammed and Charlemagne* by Henri Pirenne," *Daedalus* 103 (1974): 25-33, reprinted in his *Society and the Holy in Late Antiquity* (London, 1982).

[4] H. Pirenne, *Mohammed and Charlemagne* (London, 1939), 234.

[5] C. Foss, "The Destruction of Sardis in 616 and the Value of Evidence," *JÖB* 24 (1975): 11-22; idem, "The Persians in Asia Minor and the End of Antiquity," *EHR* 90 (1975): 721-47.

of empire; it was too fragile, and subject to local pressure and secular manipulation.

The military activity of non-Roman forces not only reinforced these inherent tendencies towards fragmentation, but also prevented a reconstruction of the Greco-Roman world under any one authority. Following the fall of two ancient cities on the Danube frontier, Sirmium (Sremski Karlovci) in 582 and Singidunum (Belgrade) in 584, the Balkans and Greece were slowly overrun by Avar and Slavonic tribes from the north. From these important bases Serdica, Philippopolis, and Anchialos were threatened, and before the end of the decade Byzantine authors recorded Slavonic settlements in northern and central Greece.[6] But like the Germanic tribes east of the Rhine who attacked the Franks in Neustria and East Burgundy, the Slavonic forces that entered the Balkans had a very undeveloped state formation. Once established within imperial frontiers, they appear to have pursued pastoral activities and fishing. Their allies and perhaps leaders, the Avars, were better prepared to take over cities and rule occupied territory. On the central European plain they established an empire that challenged both the Byzantines and the Franks.

Imperial control over the homeland of classical traditions was thus reduced to parts of Thrace, the Aegean littoral, and a few islands. Further west, Carthage, Syracuse, and Ravenna remained Byzantine, centres of Constantinopolitan administration of varying strength and loyalty. Far from constituting the major cities of a western empire, they manifested desires for local autonomy in direct conflict with the eastern capital. Nor did they provide much support for the Byzantine duchy of Rome, again an area under nominal imperial control, though increasingly an independent ecclesiastical centre. Throughout northern Italy and Transalpine Europe, non-Roman powers preserved their own authority with no more than a diplomatic gesture of respect towards the East. The Arian Lombards continued to dominate from their palaces in Pavia, Milan, and Monza, while the Frankish dynasties in Neustria, Austrasia, and Burgundy fought each other for supreme control over northern Europe. Spain asserted a more "national" character through its well-regulated church, which cooperated with a rather unstable but prestigious Visigothic monarchy. Beyond the Channel, the Celts and Anglo-Saxons vied for domination in the British Isles. Only in Ireland and Scotland, far removed from the world of ancient Rome, did a lively literature, a creative art, and an educated monastic clergy reveal sources of early medieval culture.[7]

[6] John of Ephesos, *Ecclesiastical History* 3.25; 6.30-32, 45-48; cf. the efforts of Emperor Maurice to make peace with the invaders, Theophylact Simocatta, 1.3-8.

[7] On Irish classical culture, see the detailed survey by E. Coccia, "La cultura irlandese precarolingia: Miracolo o mito?" *Studi medievali*, 3d ser., no. 8 (1967): 257-420; M. Her-

The destruction of imperial authority in the East Mediterranean was even more marked. In a campaign as sudden as it was successful, cities that predated even the rise of Greek civilisation—Damascus, Tyre, Jerusalem, Gaza, and Babylon—capitulated to the Arab forces of Islam. In the 630s and 640s, Persia and Byzantium suffered alike; while the Zoroastrian state collapsed completely, the Christian was reduced to the heartland of Asia Minor with the loss of Syria, Palestine, and Egypt. By the end of the seventh century, North Africa was overrun. The Arab leap from Ceuta across the Straits of Gibraltar into Visigothic Spain met little defence: King Roderick faced an internal revolt that gave assistance to the invaders, and had no determined strategy that could oppose the Berber proponents of the Islamic holy war. Thus by 711 the Caliphate established at Damascus extended as far west as Cordova and east into central Asia, a whole world united in the service of Allah and the pilgrimage to Mecca.[8]

Clearly, these new invaders were not solely responsible for seventh-century developments. The states they attacked were weak, enfeebled, and ill-prepared to meet such a challenge. Byzantium and Persia had been engaged in mutual warfare for about half a century, on and off—a six-year campaign by Emperor Herakleios against Chosroes II (622-28) exhausted both parties. In addition to their inherent feebleness, there may be another reason for the defeat of Persia, the eastern and African provinces of Byzantium, and Visigothic Spain: their antique state forms. Both the Zoroastrian and Christian empires inherited imperial traditions of great antiquity, while the Visigoths had adopted so many aspects of the Roman model of government that they may be seen as Romans manqués. These three polities shared common factors: a trained and educated class of government administrators, maintaining an established political structure; an elitist clergy interpreting a complex theology in which the secular ruler played a significant role; and a social formation shaped by tradition, not open to change, even technical change in a matter such as warfare, and structured by a sophisticated culture among ruling circles, not easily understood by the mass of uneducated subjects. In contrast, Islamic society from its inception was united by a relatively simple Monotheism and by rituals performed by all—the daily prayers, washing, avoidance of certain food and drink, and the Meccan pilgrimage.[9] Conversion to Islam meant joining in the holy

---

ren, "Classical and Secular Learning Among the Irish Before the Carolingian Renaissance," *Florilegium* 3 (1981): 118-57. On indigenous poetic traditions, see P. MacCana, "Regnum and Sacerdotium: Notes on Irish Tradition," *Proceedings of the British Academy* 65 (1979): 443-49. I am grateful to Julia Smith for assistance on this topic.

[8] J. Wellhausen, *The Arab Kingdom and Its Fall* (London, 1927, reprinted 1973), 15-26; F. Donner, *The Early Islamic Conquests* (Princeton, 1981), 82-90, 112-46, 173-220.

[9] M. Ruthven, *Islam in the World* (Harmondsworth, 1984), 82-89; cf. R. P. Mottahedeh,

war and participating in the campaigns of the 630s and 640s. The faith was open to new converts of all stations; profound learning or lengthy education were not required. The administrative structures of Muslim society were adapted from the old Persian and Byzantine ones in place in the first conquered territories. Even the system of Muslim clerical rule developed slowly and did not immediately become an elite one. Because it was such a novel force, Islam welcomed secular ideas and customs from established societies, including the desert nomads who became its most vociferous exponents. Military leaders were recruited from the most obscure regions and from thoroughly subordinate social positions.[10]

This comparison is of course very simple and ignores many differences in both the older societies and the new force of Islam. But it may help to demonstrate the lack of competent resistance to the Arabs in either the East or West. For nearly a century they met only limited opposition. Yet by 733-40 they had been effectively checked, at the Pyrenees in the West and the Taurus in the East, by new and tougher enemies. These new opponents belonged to the medieval rather than the ancient world; like the Muslims themselves they were not bound by the old conventions. Nobody would dispute that the remarkable success of Charles Martel at Poitiers in 733 represented a vigorous non-Roman force in the West, an alliance of Frankish horsemen organised for war.[11] But the Byzantines under Leo III who defeated Maslama and Suleiman at Akroïnon in 740 called themselves *Romaioi*, not quite Romans but close enough. By what definition can they be understood as newcomers in the ancient world?

This question raises a fundamental point about the transitional nature of the seventh century, for it is generally agreed that during this period Byzantium was transformed into a medieval state.[12] In the process of territorial loss, economic shrinkage, cultural decay, and overall militarisation, its very foundations were altered. What emerged in the third decade of the eighth century was a renewed and transformed society, capable of defeating the Muslims and rebuilding the empire on a different basis. This new By-

---

Loyalty and Leadership in an Early Islamic Society (Princeton, 1980), 20-21, on the "orthopraxis" rather than "orthodoxy" of the five Islamic pillars; and I. Goldziher, *Muslim Studies*, vol. 2 (London, 1971), 39-40, on the ignorance among early converts to Islam in Syria and Iraq.

[10] Wellhausen, *The Arab Kingdom*, 28-32; M. Cook, *Muhammad* (Oxford, 1983), 45-50; P. Crone, *Slaves on Horses* (Cambridge, 1980), 18-33.

[11] On the date, traditionally 732, see J.-H. Roy and J. Deviosse, *La Bataille de Poitiers—Octobre 733* (Paris, 1966).

[12] On the seventh-century sources, see A. Stratos, *Byzantium in the Seventh Century*, 5 vols. (Amsterdam, 1968-80); P. Lemerle, "Les répercussions de la crise de l'Empire d'Orient au vii siècle sur les pays d'Occident," *Settimane* 5 (Spoleto, 1958): 713-32; C. Mango, *Byzantium: The Empire of New Rome* (London, 1980), 4-5, 7-8.

zantium had grown from a series of measures, the first taken by Herakleios a century before Leo III, to consolidate and preserve the much-reduced eastern empire. In this process, most of the traditions linked with classical Rome lost their clear definition and gave way to medieval variants: from a basis of slave cultivation, a free peasantry emerged; from a city-based society, one of rural villages and small market towns protected by castles. Only the capital or Queen City, Constantinople, survived to become the source of all wealth and patronage. From a civilian administration involving the provincial aristocracy and men of substance, to a military government open to merit and based on imperial patronage; from a bilingual society with many dialects to a Greek-speaking one; from a plethora of Christian beliefs and religious practices to an exclusive Christian faith, all-embracing and intolerant of deviance and pre-Christian survivals. Contemporaries, however, persisted in identifying themselves as Romans, even if they used the Greek term *Romaioi*.

While these developments can be distinctly identified when the later sixth century is compared to the early eighth, it is still hard to document the individual steps and stages in the process of change. The difficulties can be illustrated by a simple question: When did the Byzantine Empire begin? The *Cambridge Medieval History* took the accession of Leo III in 717 as its starting point, recognising the unequivocally medieval nature of the eighth-century state. But J. B. Bury, its brilliant editor, knew that Byzantium could not be understood without its classical past, and Volume 4 therefore includes a general introduction on Christian East Rome.[13] While some historians have identified the reign of Herakleios as a crucial period in the inception of medieval Byzantium, others have gone back to Justinian, and yet others to Constantine or Diocletian.[14] Of course, the debate is artificial as there can be no one date in such a process of internal transformation, but it does at least pose the problem of tracing the shift from clas-

[13] J. B. Bury, ed., *Cambridge Medieval History*, vol. 4 (Cambridge, 1923). His introduction is reprinted in the 1966 revised edition, where the new editor, J. M. Hussey, states that "few scholars would still consider 717 to be the best starting point for a history of the Byzantine Empire," p. ix.

[14] Romilly Jenkins justified his characterisation of the period 610-1071 as "imperial Byzantium" by reference to the tripartite division of Byzantine history, into a first "Late Roman" epoch from the fourth to the seventh centuries; a second "Middle Byzantine" epoch, seventh to eleventh; and a "Late" epoch, which "can scarcely be called 'imperial,' except by courtesy"; see *Byzantium: The Imperial Centuries* A.D. *610-1071* (London, 1966), Preface. G. Ostrogorsky, in his classic study of the Byzantine state, also began his history proper with the reign of Herakleios, prefaced by one chapter on the early period, 324-610; see *History of the Byzantine State* (Oxford, 1956). J. Kulakovskii, on the other hand, treated the early period in great detail, starting with the official division of the Roman Empire in 395; his three-volume *History of Byzantium* (in Russian) extends only to 717.

sical to medieval. By looking at the seventh century as a whole, I am trying
to emphasise the long evolution of multiple changes rather than pointing
to a particular period. To fix one year within this development would be
arbitrary, and such pseudo-precision should be avoided.

While the eastern empire was undergoing its vital reorganisation, the
Frankish states of northwest Europe experienced a movement from fratricidal conflict and extreme disunity to greater unity under one prince, originally mayor of the Austrasian palace.[15] After repeated rivalries, conflict,
and instability, the two major kingdoms north and east of the Loire were
united in 687 by King Thierry III. The effective ruler of this state was Pippin, mayor of the palace and leader of the Frankish nobility. It was his bas-
tard son, Charles, who checked the Islamic raids from Septimania in a major defeat near Poitiers (733). Eudo, duke of Aquitaine, who assisted
Charles, recognised his overlordship, and the Frankish expansion into Frisia, Saxony, and Provence began. At the death of Thierry IV in 737 the
throne was left vacant; Charles had been addressed as duke and prince of
the Franks for some time and now took the place of the monarch. His authority was recognised by the papacy when Gregory III appealed for help
against the Lombards (739-40).[16] Although Charles had plundered the
church and those senatorial families who maintained local centres of Christianity, he protected Sts. Clement and Boniface in their missionary work
east of the Rhine. So while the papacy deplored the corrupt and feeble state
of the Frankish church, it appreciated the secular assistance given to Anglo-Saxon missionaries, who were later to help in reforming the church in
the Frankish kingdom. The mayors may have had limited culture and little
time for Christianity, but they did have what was necessary to halt the Islamic advance into northwest Europe—effective military power.

Thus, although Leo III and Charles Martel belonged to very different
worlds, they both emerged from newly militarised social formations to
hold their own against the Arabs. However significant their victories over
the Muslims in European development, these were by no means their only
achievements. Nor were their triumphs strictly comparable. For Byzantium, Islam had presented a continuous threat since the 640s. The 717-18
siege of Constantinople was the third—the culmination of many years of
annual raiding (700-714)—and despite Islam's defeat, warfare resumed
immediately afterwards.[17] From 720-40 the Arabs attacked annually al-

[15] R. Folz et al., *De l'Antiquité au Monde médiéval* (Paris, 1972), provides a concise guide;
cf. J. M. Wallace-Hadrill, *The Barbarian West*, 4th ed. (Oxford, 1985), 64-86; E. Ewig,
"Die fränkische Teilreiche im 7. Jahrhundert (613-714)," *Trierer Zeitschrift* 22 (1953): 85-
144, reprinted in *Spätantikes und fränkisches Gallien*, vol. 1 (Munich, 1976).

[16] *Codex Carolinus*, in *MHG*, Ep., vol. 3, letters 1 and 2.

[17] This will be discussed further in Chapter 8.

most without a break, persistent in their desire to make Constantinople their own Islamic capital. In contrast, the Spanish emirs who raided north of the Pyrenees in 714 were leading exploratory campaigns into unfamiliar territory and were largely unknown to the Franks of Aquitaine and Provence. These first raids sacked several important cities: Narbonne (720), Carcassonne, Nîmes, Lyon, Autun (725), and Bordeaux (729). It was to prevent a serious repetition of this last attack on Gascony that Eudo of Aquitaine solicited Charles Martel's help in 733 and thus secured Muslim withdrawal. Thereafter Frankish relations with the Muslim world were almost limited to Saracen piracy in the West Mediterranean and Frankish raids across the Pyrenees. There was very little familiarity with, concern about, or awareness of Islam for many centuries.

In the East, however, the Arabs were already a well-known enemy, and Islamic ambitions continued to command the attention of Constantinople. Direct confrontation continued even beyond the Abbasid revolution (750), which removed the capital from Damascus to Baghdad. This shaped Byzantium's development and contributed decisively to the militarisation already underway. But the Muslim challenge was by no means the only pressure that contributed to the transformation of the empire: internal factors had determined structural changes, particularly in the economic sphere. A whole way of life, in fact, was becoming obsolete in the early seventh century. Fifty years later it was barely a memory in the West and a memory only just kept alive in the East. While the Franks owed little to the classical world, the seventh-century *Romaioi* merged their ancient heritage with novel forms of government, rural settlement, and a military preoccupation with the Arabs. The combination produced an empire simultaneously Roman, Christian, and medieval—what we think of as Byzantium.

In this transformation the religious authorities of Constantinople played a very active role. Indeed, their support for and collaboration with the secular administration was crucial in the development of the medieval Byzantine "character." Since close relations between court and patriarchate already defined the position of the metropolitan church, this alliance evolved naturally. But during the seventh and eighth centuries it was brought into greater prominence, as Byzantium attempted to exclude deviant beliefs and dissident behaviour from its now-limited territories. It both reflected and stimulated a narrower and more restricted world view, and a leadership directed against subversive influence and divisive practice, especially when these could be traced to political rivalry or heresy. Under the threat of Muslim invaders, who gave visible form to such tendencies, lay and clerical interests were elided in defence of the Christian heritage of the East. While this process is particularly significant in the empire, a similar development can be observed in Spain, where officially-defined dogma and political thought was imposed with greater determination (against the public activities of Jews, for example). In fact, throughout the Mediterranean, "national" interests and regional concerns arose as part of the general fragmentation, a process that Christianity could not resist. Political division entrained the growth of regional churches, more committed to local issues than to the overall unity of Christendom.[18]

These pressures towards a local unity of ecclesiastical and civilian powers produced the most severe tensions in Rome, now no longer a centre of political authority, but evidently an important bishopric. The city's anomalous position had been greatly exaggerated by Justinian's policies. Constantinople's patronage of Ravenna at Rome's expense, combined with the military devastation of central Italy, deprived the reconstituted empire in the West of its natural heartland. No other area could serve as the imperial lynchpin between East and West, or as the uniting bond between the two ends of the peninsula. The failure to re-establish Old Rome as a political centre therefore may be seen as a symbol of the larger failure of Justinian's attempt at reconquest. By leaving the city isolated, integrated neither with Sicily and the south nor with Ravenna and the north, the emperor created in microcosm the fragmentation that marked the end of Late Antiquity. He also made Rome the weak link in imperial defence in the West, a development that encouraged the Lombard invaders to press on south towards the ancient capital.[19]

So while the bishops of Rome continued to consider themselves faithful subjects of the emperor—indeed, they had no alternative—their concern for the see of St. Peter and its immediate needs produced divided loyalties. Local issues, predominantly the Lombard threat, drew attention constantly to the inadequate protection provided by Constantinople: inadequate military forces, food supplies, and assistance with the maintenance of vast city walls and other essential buildings. In these tense circumstances, it was the great achievement of Pope Gregory the Great (590-604) to establish a *modus vivendi*, which recognised eastern authority while providing for the city's urgent needs. This compromise set a pattern for almost a century and

[18] F. Winkelmann, "Staat und Ideologie beim Übergang von der Spätantike zum byzantinischen Feudalismus," in H. Köpstein, ed., *Besonderheiten des byzantinischen Feudalentwicklung* (Berlin, 1983), 77-84 (on church-state relations, not feudalism); cf. G. Ostrogorsky, "Das Verhältnis von Staat und Kirche in Byzanz," *Seminarium Kondakovianum* 4 (1931): 121-32 (in Russian with German summary, 133-34). On the post-Chalcedon divisions within Christianity, see H. J. Sieben, *Die Konzilsidee der alten Kirche* (Paderborn, 1979), 275-91; J. Pelikan, *The Christian Tradition*, vol. 2, *The Spirit of Eastern Christendom* (Chicago, 1974), 8-90.

[19] T. S. Brown, *Gentlemen and Officers* (London, 1984), 21-37, on the decline of the Roman Senate; B. Ward-Perkins, *From Classical Antiquity to the Middle Ages* (Oxford, 1984), 47-48.

a half, and permitted Rome to rebuild its authority on a spiritual basis. By the time of Constans II's visit of 662, the success of this policy was quite evident. Despite severe theological disagreements, the emperor was accorded a most circumspect reception, for no one doubted that he was the master of Old Rome. Yet the inbuilt tensions that pulled the city in contrary directions remained and continued to find expression in religious terms. Only in the middle of the eighth century would they be finally resolved by a rejection of Byzantine control.

Pope Gregory's solution of immediate problems lay in the creation of independent ecclesiastical resources that could guarantee the city's survival. This reorganisation was part of a more general transformation of Late Antique society, which had completely altered the position of Christian institutions. In place of the ancient pattern of civic philanthropy, based on the generosity of local benefactors, senators, philosophers, and pagan holy men, Christian charity now dominated the same spheres of welfare, hospitality, poor relief, medical aid, and even education. As Patlagean has shown, private wealth was increasingly channelled to Christian rather than city authorities, and a new system of circulation and distribution developed based on donations.[20] These bequests and gifts were then directed towards charitable outlets in the form of hostels for pilgrims, hospitals, almshouses, and orphanages, and towards the maintenance of civic functions such as burial services and distributions of food to the poor. In comparison with the most prosperous days of ancient philanthropy, there may have been less wealth in circulation, but the most significant change was that this now moved through a different arc—from the individual donor to the church and on to the poor, rather than via the city. Since the resources of St. Peter's see far outstripped any other in the West, Rome was well placed to oversee such a transformation. But it was the farsighted arrangements made by Gregory I that permitted the city to make a successful move from ancient political capital to ecclesiastical centre.

In one respect, however, the expansion of Christian charity followed the ancient model: it tended to reinforce local concerns and cater to local needs. Individual sites thus became famous for their "special" services, in the same way that holy objects "specialised" in particular cures. Pilgrims arranged their travels accordingly, albeit within the increasingly limited circumference of their already restricted world. The universal character of Christianity was reduced, together with the respect nominally accorded to all parts of Christendom. In this process, the standing of oecumenical councils as supreme arbiters of the faith was frequently subordinated to a

---

[20] E. Patlagean, *Pauvreté économique et pauvreté sociale à Byzance 4e-7e siècles* (Paris/The Hague, 1977), 181-96.

more familiar, localised authority, that of the nearest metropolitan or of the bishop of Rome for Christians in the West. The failure of the Fifth Oecumenical gathering and Justinian's treatment of western ecclesiastics probably contributed to this depreciation of conciliar status.[21]

The elevation of alternate sources of authority, particularly collections of local council rulings and papal decretals, also emphasised the largely eastern nature of past universal councils and western unwillingness to accept them alone. In this preference for a closer, and often clearer arbitration of their problems, western Christians reflected the exclusively Latin culture of a clerical elite, which emerged in all the successor states of the West. Although they might be divided into "national" churches, each with its own particular concerns, these ecclesiastics shared and were partly defined by a common formation, transmitted in the highly respected works of pontiffs like Gregory I and scholars such as Isidore of Seville. Their "localism" in relation to the East was also an embryonic form of the much broader western culture characteristic of medieval Europe.[22]

Despite these growing differences, Christian institutions in general had developed to a point of such predominance throughout the ancient world that they inevitably transformed it. In the long term, as Gibbon revealed, the faith could be identified as a fundamental cause of the decline of the Roman Empire.[23] Under the impact of Christian expansion, the old system was strained to breaking point; while *curiales* fled from their civic duties to imperial or ecclesiastical service, and peasants to monasteries for protection or to major cities for employment, barbarian devastation, falling productivity, and restricted horizons combined to narrow the potential of daily life. Notions of wealth and the use of money shifted away from the private

---

[21] Sieben, *Die Konzilsidee*, 291-305.

[22] On the early medieval churches of the West, see *Settimane* 7 (1960), *Le chiese nei regni dell'Europa occidentale e i loro rapporti con Roma Fino all' 800*; and 28 (1982), *Cristianizzazione ed organizzazione ecclesiastica delle campagne nell'Alto Medioevo: espansione e resistenze*. On the development of early medieval Latin culture, see J. Le Goff, "Clerical Culture and Folklore Traditions in Merovingian Civilization," and "Ecclesiastical Culture and Folklore of the Middle Ages: Saint Marcellus of Paris and the Dragon," both in his *Time, Work and Culture in the Middle Ages* (Chicago, 1980), 153-88, 324-41; Riché, "Les instruction des laïcs"; Lehmann, "Panorama des literarischen Kultur."

[23] *The History of the Decline and Fall of the Roman Empire*, ed. J. B. Bury, 7 vols. (London, 1909-14), 3:1-148 (chs. 15 and 16); cf. 4:175 (the conclusion of ch. 38). After severe criticism from ecclesiastics, Gibbon issued *A Vindication* of his two chapters (London, 1779, reprinted with a preface by H. Trevor-Roper, Oxford, 1961), which proved very successful. For a very different and basically sympathetic critique, see A. Momigliano, "After Gibbon's Decline and Fall," in *The Age of Spirituality: A Symposium*, ed. K. Weitzmann (New York/Princeton, 1980), 7-16, emphasising the combination of factors that permitted Christianity to replace paganism, and thus to create a choice of career (between imperial consulship and Christian bishopric). This heralded the onset of the medieval period.

consumption and public display typical of antiquity. Christianity demanded a total reorganisation, drawing on individual bequests, endowments, and official benefactions to alter the hierarchy of status and value in its own terms. This shift from curial to ecclesiastical authority and the rise of celibate monasticism corresponded to a deeply felt need, one apparently shared at all levels of Late Antique society, notably the concern to secure personal salvation and life after death. In this complex fashion, the myriad "idle mouths" of non-labouring clergy and monks became established as an integral and essential element of society.[24] They both exploited it by extracting tithes, soliciting gifts, and removing themselves from productive work, and they simultaneously nurtured its life force by protecting spiritual activity. The gradual establishment of a social order devoted to those who pray thus completed the Christianisation of the ancient world.

[24] As Gibbon put it originally, "soldiers' pay was lavished on a useless multitude of both sexes, who could only plead the merits of abstinence and chastity" (*Decline and Fall*, 4:175). This is expanded in Jones, *LRE*, 2:933: "The huge army of clergy and monks were for the most part idle mouths, living upon offerings, endowments and state subsidies." The extent to which the church actually drained imperial resources may be questioned; private donations began to account for much of the income of monasteries, individual churches, and holy shrines, initiating a process of transformation, which would completely alter the ancient system of charity; see Patlagean, *Pauvreté économique et pauvreté sociale*.

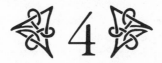

The Achievement of Gregory
the Great

Italy in the Mid-Sixth Century

BY THE Pragmatic Sanction, issued on 13 August 554, Justinian attempted to re-establish imperial administration in the reconquered provinces of Italy.[1] These were reunited with the empire and Constantinople, thus abolishing the patterns of civilian Roman government maintained by the Ostrogoths in the West. The traditional division between military and civilian sectors was modified in one important respect by a recognition of the leading role of the church. Bishops were empowered to participate in the choice of provincial governors; the bishop and Senate of Rome were made responsible for the employment of correct weights and measures. In other respects the old system was re-imposed as if nothing had happened. Provincial governors under the praetorian prefect were to collect taxation and provide public services, while four *magistri militum* under Narses attended to Alpine defence. Despite emphasising the devastation caused by the past twenty years of warfare, and denouncing the last Ostrogothic rulers, Totila in particular, the 27 articles of the Pragmatic Sanction insisted on a return to pre-war conditions.

Clearly, this was not possible. Neither the old ruling classes, the *curiales* and aristocrats of senatorial rank, nor the landed peasantry, tenant farmers, and serfs who had worked their estates, existed as before. Cultivation had been constantly disrupted by the passage of armies, especially in central Italy, and agricultural production was very limited. In the wake of those senatorial families who had left Italy with Witiges in 540, or who had retired from Rome when it was threatened by Totila, the labour force had fled, taking the opportunity to seek freedom and safety. Few large estates can have been functioning effectively in 554. Possibly some in southern Italy belonging to the church or to the remaining aristocratic landowners man-

---

[1] *Corpus Iuris Civilis*, vol. III, *Novellae*, ed. R. Schoek and R. Kroll (Berlin, 1895), Appendix vii (the only law of the 550s to be issued in Latin); Jones, *LRE*, 1:291-92.

aged to continue regular production. But as a whole, neither economy nor society could furnish the means to implement the Pragmatic Sanction.

It was therefore unfortunate that the law envisaged the restoration of pre-Gothic property ownership; all of Totila's donations, alienations, and grants of office and rank were to be nullified, though not those of earlier Gothic rulers.[2] But by insisting that property should be returned to its original owners, slaves and *coloni* to their original masters, and equipment and livestock to their place of origin (or that compensation should be paid), the provisions for Italy created even greater antagonism towards Constantinople. Section 15, which stipulated that those slaves who had married free women during the disturbances could be forcibly separated from their wives and might lose their sons (who could follow their mother's free status) can hardly have been popular among the husbands. As Totila had welcomed slaves into his armies and treated the rural population with some consideration, they would not be likely to tolerate the removal of their relative freedoms and small improvements.[3] The worst demand of the Pragmatic Sanction, however, concerned the collection of taxes, not only those due to Constantinople, which included provisions for numerous army units, but also those not paid to the Goths during past upheavals. From the rulings that the *coemptio* (compulsory purchase of supplies for the army) was to be levied only in provinces with an abundance, or that collectors were not to oppress people with their avarice (section 18), taken together with prohibitions of the sale of offices and the hampering of naval commerce (again, closely related to the matter of army supplies), it is evident that these demands were oppressive.

Throughout Italy, Byzantine officials were feared and loathed, but in Rome particularly, the new administration was experienced as a substitution of hardship for past imperial munificence. True, the corn dole was re-established, as well as the salaries of professors and doctors, but little was done to make good the damage inflicted on the city. It seems that its population had dropped to about 30,000 after Totila's siege and sack of 546-47, from a figure of about 100,000 at the beginning of the century (depending on the very rough estimates available).[4] And since most of the senators and wealthy merchants had fled, taking their moveables with

---

[2] As note 1 above; cf. T. S. Brown, *Gentlemen and Officers* (London, 1984), 5-10.

[3] Procopius, *Wars* 7.22.20-23; cf. 7.13.1. Books 5-8 are devoted to the Gothic War.

[4] R. Krautheimer, *Rome: Profile of a City, 312-1308* (Princeton, 1980), 65 (but compare the much more reliable figures for imperial Rome in the early fourth century, ibid., 4). Procopius, *Wars* 8.22.19 describes Totila's determination to leave Rome completely deserted, and his vain effort to restore the city later, 7.36.29-7.37.4. For the archaeological evidence, see R. Hodges and D. Whitehouse, *Mohammed, Charlemagne and the Origins of Europe* (London, 1983), 39-42, 48-52.

them, the population was largely poor. In addition, it had been attacked by outbreaks of plague (the same bubonic plague that had afflicted the eastern Mediterranean in the 540s) and suffered from inadequate food supplies. While the Italian campaigns may have resulted in a victory for the Byzantines, the Romans probably experienced the "triumph" of Narses in 552 quite differently. For them, the wars of Justinian had been the cause of tumult and disorder, while his theological innovations were deplored, a combination that was unlikely to make the eastern commander-in-chief welcome in the city.

Roman Opposition

To understand why there should have been such opposition to the Byzantine army, it is necessary to recall the events of the 540s. While warfare continued and Totila got ever closer to capturing Rome, eastern soldiers arrived in the city to remove Pope Vigilius. In November 545 he was unceremoniously bundled out of St. Caecilia in Trastevere and put on a ship for Sicily.[5] Realising that he would have to make the journey to Constantinople to discuss the question of the Three Chapters, Vigilius appointed a council of regents to keep order in Rome during his absence. The effective administrator in charge, however, was Pelagius, who had been papal legate (*apocrisiarius*) at the eastern court and had impressed the emperor. When Totila's threats to sack the city were clearly going to be realised, it was Pelagius who intervened and negotiated with the Goths. In turn, Totila sent him to Constantinople to put the Gothic terms to Justinian.[6] While Pelagius got caught up in the religious controversy there, Rome was governed by a priest, Mareas, who built up a large following among the population by his outright opposition to Justinian's theology and his defence of the Three Chapters. As accounts of imperial pressure on the pope reached the city, this antagonism was stiffened. Nor was it undercut by the news of Vigilius's collapse and agreement with the emperor. Had the pope returned to Rome, he would certainly have received a rough welcome. Instead, his death in Sicily (June 555) meant that Narses could impose the imperial choice of pope, Pelagius, against local opposition, which demanded Mareas. The priest's untimely death later that summer enabled the new pontiff to take over, though he was not consecrated formally until the

---

[5] *LP* 1.297; Procopius, *Wars* 7.15.9 and 7.16.1, merely states that Vigilius was in Sicily when Justinian summoned him.

[6] Procopius, *Wars* 7.16.4-32; 7.21.17-18. Pelagius carried a letter containing Totila's request for the emperor to restore the peaceful relations between Goths and Byzantines that had pertained earlier. It cited the imperial *"paternitas"* that had governed the alliance between Emperor Anastasios and Theodoric; *Wars* 7.21.23-24.

following Easter because of episcopal antagonism.[7] Since he was obliged both to support his predecessor's stand against the Three Chapters and to cooperate with the hated "army of occupation," it was a long time before he secured support among the clergy and people of Rome.

Thus, both the ecclesiastical and military authorities in Rome in the 550s were suspect in the eyes of the local population, hardly propitious conditions in which to impose the reunification of Italy with the eastern empire. For those of senatorial standing, the abolition of a separate western imperial administration meant that they had to seek jobs in the East (and see eastern officials appointed to what they regarded as "their" jobs in the West). The sole position that remained within their control was that of prefect of the city, a position revived, like the Senate and the vicar of Rome, by the terms of the Pragmatic Sanction. As leader of the Senate, the city prefect administered justice in quite a large area round Rome. The post carried considerable prestige and authority, as well as privileges such as the maintenance of a four-horse chariot for official duties. The reconstituted Senate, on the other hand, was always a ghost of its past form; in the 580s it even ceased to meet. While some aristocratic families restored their homes with material taken from ruined classical monuments, the concentration of senatorial residences was never re-established. On the contrary, large areas of Rome became deserted, given over to wasteland, a few vines, and plots of cultivated crops. Building was limited to essential repairs to the walls, aqueducts, and bridges serving the city, although Narses may also have assisted with the construction of a church dedicated to Sts. Philip and James, later known as the Santi Apostoli.[8] The image of Rome as a ruined and abandoned city, made famous by Edward Gibbon's description of the Forum, dates back to this time.[9]

The Position of Ravenna

In contrast to Rome, the old Ostrogothic capital of Ravenna flourished under Byzantine rule. It had been fought over but had survived as a distinguished centre of learning and commerce. Although western emperors had resided there since the time of Honorius (395-423), when Alaric forced the court to move from Milan, it was only under Theodoric the Ostrogoth that the city had taken on the appearance of a capital. After the victory of 540, Justinian's appointees, Archbishops Maximian and Agnellus, endowed it

---

[7] *LP* 1.299, 303.

[8] Krautheimer, *Rome*, 67-68, 70, 75; P. Courcelle, *Histoire littéraire des grandes invasions germaniques*, 3rd ed. (Paris, 1964), 231-33.

[9] Edward Gibbon, *Memoirs of My Life and Writings* (Dublin, 1796), 1:129, recording the journey of 15 October 1764, to the Forum.

with new buildings and magnificent decoration, such as the mosaics of San Vitale and St. Apollinare in Classe, completed in 546 and 549, and the redecoration of St. Apollinare Nuovo. The emperor presented Maximian with an ivory throne, which survives.[10] Government offices were rebuilt, and a separate palace ("of the exarch") was added to Theodoric's. Ravenna remained the sole administrative centre in the West that regularly used Egyptian papyrus for its records, and one of the few that maintained the art of classical epigraphy, visible in funerary monuments. It enjoyed direct links with Constantinople through the port of Classis and was provided with stronger defensive forces than Rome. Its bishops supported the Fifth Oecumenical Council and the eastern imperial government, whose representative, the praetorian prefect, chose to be based there rather than in Rome from 567. Justinian exploited all these features in an anti-Roman policy designed to downgrade the old capital and elevate Ravenna.[11] The shift was made clear in the sparkling mosaic portraits of the emperor and empress on the walls of its churches, which reflected both the city's favoured status and its position at the centre of imperial patronage in the West. To anyone looking at Byzantine Italy in the 550s, therefore, Ravenna was obviously the capital, while Rome and other major cities like Milan, Genoa, and Naples were neglected. Only in Ravenna could the governmental patterns implied in the Pragmatic Sanction be realised; perhaps there its terms were celebrated.

The Role of the Church

Elsewhere, the new administration depended for support on those bishops who accepted the imperial policy on the Three Chapters, led by Ravenna and Rome. In Tuscany, northern Italy, and Istria, however, the strength of opposition to the Fifth Council provoked hostility to all things eastern. When he tried to win over the schismatic bishops of Tuscany, Pelagius was careful to cite only the first four councils and Pope Leo I's *Tomus* as defining statements of Christian belief.[12] He was quite unsuccessful. All bishops, regardless of their theology, nonetheless had a common role, to care for their congregations and provide for those in hunger and sickness. In this

[10] S. MacCormack, *Art and Ceremonial in Late Antiquity* (Berkeley, 1981), 259-66, esp. 238 n. 365 on St. Apollinare Nuovo, a basilica formerly dedicated to St. Martin and altered by Bishop Agnellus, who also removed the figures from a mosaic arcade on the wall so as to leave the imperial palace empty and awaiting the emperor, "a perfect illustration of the changing status of Ravenna under Ostrogothic and Byzantine rule."

[11] J. Richards, *The Popes and the Papacy in the Early Middle Ages, 476-752* (London, 1979), 154-56.

[12] Pelagius I, *Epistulae quae supersunt*, ed. P. M. Gasso and C. M. Batlle (Montserrat, 1956), no. 10.

respect, their traditional duties were simply exacerbated by the devastation of the wars, which left large areas unproductive, caused famine, and permitted plague to kill many. Because of its superior resources, less well endowed bishops appealed to the see of St. Peter for assistance and received supplies of food, clothing, and sometimes church plate.[13] In the vacuum left by senatorial flight, the church became a directing force in and around Rome, securing supplies and distributions of food to the poor as best it could. As bishops of Rome had been doing this since the fifth century at least, it followed an established pattern and was expected by the local population. But the failure of other authorities to assist was more marked. It was to their bishop that Romans looked for the city's protection and their own well-being. When other, older traditions failed, the city turned to its Christian past and apostolic foundation.

Physically, this involved an important change in the daily life of Rome. For the bishops, being based on the Lateran palace constructed for them by Constantine I in the southeast of the city, were isolated from the predominantly pagan city centre.[14] They were cut off from the shrine of St. Peter outside the northwest sector of the walls, which had also been endowed with a vast basilica by the first Christian emperor. As they took up a more dominating role in the city's administration, they progressed regularly between the two as well as preaching in the two other churches served by the Lateran clergy, St. Paul's beyond the walls and St. Maria Maggiore.[15] This drew attention away from the Forum and the ancient monuments of pagan Rome, towards the Christian buildings concentrated on the periphery. Most of the important pilgrim churches were outside the walls at sites associated with martyrdom or burial in the catacombs, such as St. Lorenzo's, where Pelagius II built a new shrine in the 580s. Other major Christian monuments were generally on the perimeter of the city, close to the walls, for instance the church of St. Giovanni a Porta Latina, rededicated in the 550s.[16] Only a few occupied previously pagan structures in the heart of the metropolis. The church of Sts. Cosmas and Damian overlooking the Forum, converted under Pope Felix (526-30), and the monastic community on the Capitol later associated with the Aracoeli church, were exceptional.[17] And although Narses may have resided at the palace on the Forum, later transformed into the church of St. Maria Antiqua, his succes-

---

[13] Ibid., nos. 17, 51, 82; S. Loewenfeld, *Epistolae Pontificum Romanum ineditae* (Leipzig, 1885), no. 39 (20-21), in which Pelagius condemns the sale of church plate, a measure to be reserved for the redemption of captives.

[14] Krautheimer, *Rome*, 24, 26, 30-31, 37.

[15] Ibid., 58.

[16] Ibid., 67-68, 97.

[17] Ibid., 71.

sor Longinus moved to Ravenna. The centre of Rome was full of ruins and empty buildings, temples, baths, and theatres no longer used. It was into this decaying capital that Gregory, later Pope Gregory the Great, was born in about A.D. 540.

GREGORY'S EARLY LIFE IN ROME

Gregory's parents were devout Christians of senatorial standing who thus combined a pride in civic traditions of Roman government with a belief in the power of their patron saint. Although much is made of the apparent contradiction between *Romanitas* and *Christianitas* in sixth-century Rome, Gregory does not seem to have experienced it so profoundly.[18] Initially, he appears to have followed a once-traditional career in the civil administration, being nominated by the Senate to the position of city prefect between about 572 and 574; later he turned to a purely religious life. The change was very common and gave him no more problems than it did Ambrose, for instance. It was only later, when he reached the position of bishop, that Gregory's loyalty to Rome (now intimately linked to the eastern empire) might occasionally conflict with his loyalty to Christianity. And these competing pressures arose from the very particular position of Rome in the late sixth century. Had Gregory been brought up in Ravenna, it is possible that he might have pursued a civilian career longer, but in Rome there was hardly a satisfying career to pursue. In addition, his mother and aunts had already embraced the monastic life and apparently did not resist his plans to convert the family residence into a monastery.

He therefore withdrew from secular duties and adopted an ascetic routine in his monastery of St. Andrew, founded in the mid-570s. Later, when he felt burdened by the demands and difficulties of episcopal office, he would recall with particular pleasure the years of solitude, spiritual development, and biblical study in the monastic community.[19] Gregory appears not to have commented upon the major political change of this decade— the entry of the Lombards to northern Italy. From 568 onwards they threatened the Venetia; in 569 they captured Milan, and three years later, after stiff resistance, Ticinum (Pavia) was taken. A major expedition from the East failed to check their advance, and in 576 the Lombards moved

---

[18] J. Richards, *Consul of God* (London, 1980), 51-53.

[19] Gregory I, *Registrum epistularum*, in *MGH, Ep.*, vols. 1-2 (all references will be to this edition by section and letter number, unless otherwise stated); also D. Norberg, ed., *CCL*, vols. 140-140A (Turnhout, 1982); v.53a (Norberg, v. 53); cf. the dedicatory letter to Leander of Seville, *Moralia in Iob*, ed. M. Adriaen, *CCL*, vols. 143-143A (Turnhout, 1979), 1-7, esp. 1-2.

south to threaten Rome.[20] The city then sent its prefect, Pamphronius, to Constantinople to appeal for military aid. While Tiberios II recommended bribery rather than fighting and suggested an alliance with the Franks, he did send a grain fleet to relieve the famine, which had caused many deaths under Pope Benedict I (575-79). Despite this, the famine continued, accompanied as usual by an outbreak of plague and worsened by heavy rainfall and the flooding of the Tiber. At this moment the Lombard Farwald, first duke of Spoleto, laid siege to the city (579), and Pope Benedict died.[21] His successor, Pelagius II, immediately set about dealing with a combination of formidable problems, without waiting for imperial confirmation of his election. Perhaps the papal background of the surviving sources exaggerates the authority of successive pontiffs in coping with these crises, but there is little indication that any other official was involved in defending Rome, and the Romans expected their bishop to lead them. In the absence of an effective civil or military administration, and starved of funds by the rulers of distant Constantinople, the city had come to regard its pope as the natural spokesman and protector.

Pelagius II accordingly took charge. He determined to send an even more impressive embassy to plead the cause of Rome at the imperial court. Representatives of the church, the Senate, and the city prefect were selected to make the journey, among them Gregory, who was to take up the post of papal legate in Constantinople.[22] Since the end of the Acacian schism in 519, the papacy had maintained an ambassador in the East, nearly always a deacon of the church of Rome, who had an official residence in the Placidia palace and a formal position at the eastern court. These legates held considerable influence as a conduit for both public and covert communication between the supreme ecclesiastic of the West and the supreme secular authority of the Late Roman Empire. Two popes had been elevated from their ranks (Vigilius and Pelagius I), so that it was an established stage in a clerical career. It was to this position that Gregory, then aged about 40, was appointed by Pelagius II; he remained for six years in the eastern capital.

[20] G. P. Bognetti, *L'Età longobarda*, 4 vols. (Milan, 1966-68), 2:110-40. John of Biclar records the Byzantine defeat in his *Chronicle*, 214.

[21] Menander, frag. 49, in *Historici graeci minores*, ed. L. Dindorf, 2 vols. (Leipzig, 1870-71), 2:100-101; trans. R. C. Blockley, *The Fragments of Menander the Guardsman* (Liverpool, 1985), 196-97; P. Goubert, *Byzance avant l'Islam*, 2 vols. (Paris, 1951-65), vol. 2, pt. 2, 17-18.

[22] Paul the deacon, *Vita Gregorii*, para. 7; John the deacon, *Vita Gregorii Magni*, 1.26; both in *PL* 75, 44, 72; cf. Pelagius II, *Epistulae*, no. 1, *PL* 72, 703-705. Gregory may have accompanied the important embassy of 579-80, Menander, frag. 62, in Dindorf, 2:120 (cf. Blockley, *Menander the Guardsman*, 216-17).

The Situation in the East

After the death of Justinian in 565, his nephew Justin II reigned for nearly a decade before attacks of insanity rendered him incapable. He and his wife Sophia shared a devotion to the Virgin Mary, whose cult grew steadily in Constantinople from this period on.[23] They also ordered an outstanding icon of Christ, allegedly a portrait preserved on a towel that was miraculously transferred to a wooden painting, to be brought to the capital. This Kamouliana icon was housed in a special shrine, like the precious relics of the Virgin at Blachernai. In addition to their religious passions, Justin and Sophia patronised artists and architects. They were responsible for commissioning statues of themselves and their daughters and a number of new buildings in Constantinople, though not on the same scale as Justinian. Their concentration on the "Queen City," as the eastern capital came to be known, may be seen as a reflection of the gradual decline of other urban centres, for it was during the second half of the sixth century that the old traditions of city self-government finally died out. Officials appointed from Constantinople, whether as provincial governors, military leaders, or judicial and financial administrators, gradually took over roles previously reserved for local *curiales* and replaced regional autonomy by central government. In the field of military defence, such centralisation had become imperative due to the repeated failure of provincial troops to prevent foreign incursions. The fall of Dara to the Persians in 573, while provoked by Justin's refusal to maintain the costly peace established by his predecessor, was a serious blow to the security of the eastern frontier. And it was matched by a simultaneous failure to maintain the Danube border, overrun by Avar and Slav bands, who even captured the major city of Sirmium in 582.[24]

In the face of such evident failings in the old system of both civil and military government, the *caesar* (junior emperor) Tiberios tried to reorganise imperial resources. From 574, he was the effective ruler; he married into the imperial family and became sole emperor on Justin's death in 578. As a soldier by training he may have been aware of the difficulty of obtaining taxes, payments in kind towards the upkeep of the troops, and other dues designed to maintain imperial roads, bridges, and defences. The solutions developed to meet the new challenges, however, grew from a gradual militarisation of Byzantine society as a whole. For despite Justinian's fortifications and provision of garrison towns, neither local citizen militias nor troops commanded from the capital provided efficient armed forces. Fre-

---

[23] Averil Cameron, "The Artistic Patronage of Justin II," *B* 50 (1980): 62-84; cf. idem, "The Empress Sophia," ibid. 45 (1975), 5-21.
[24] Jones, *LRE*, 1:306-307.

quently, the Goths, Huns, Gepids, and even Lombards who served as mercenaries under "Roman" generals were prone to treacherous collusion with the enemy, or were simply ill-prepared for lengthy and strenuous campaigning, such as that demanded by twenty years of war with Persia. Few military units were as professional, loyal, and competent as the 300 veterans regrouped by Belisarios in 561, when the Kutrigur Huns threatened Constantinople.[25] Precisely because they had served under him in Italy through protracted and bitter fighting, they could follow his ingenious strategy and defeat a much larger force. The aged commander had been called out of retirement to demonstrate his superior skills, and, at the same time, the needs of the empire. Twenty years later Tiberios seems to have recognised this point and to have taken steps to correct further decline in Byzantine troop efficiency. By 582 he had recruited a crack force of 15,000 *foederati* and had appointed an experienced general, Maurice, as their leader.[26]

The Militarisation of the Empire. While he probably did not rate the needs of Italy higher than those of the Balkan and eastern Mesopotamian provinces, Tiberios may well have planned the important changes in western administration that came into effect between 572 and 584. Basically, these resulted in the consolidation of Byzantine possessions in Africa and northern Italy into two exarchates, each governed by an exarch who combined full military and civil powers.[27] Considerable uncertainty plagues attempts to reconstruct this shift, which went against the Late Roman tradition in permitting individual governors to accumulate powers in all fields of administration. It seems to have been an effort to resolve the special problems of the reconquered territories: the difficulty of communication with the capital, the distance over which supplies, men, and equipment had to be transported, and the continuing activity of hostile forces. In the 570s, Berbers in north Africa drove monks into Spain, while Lombard incursions had already severely disrupted most of northern Italy. These disturbances were compounded by the ecclesiastical opposition of Africa, Istria, and Milan, the most vociferous critics of the Fifth Oecumenical Council.

The novelty of the system lay in its concentration of authority in the

[25] Ibid., 1:293.

[26] Ibid., 1:308.

[27] C. Diehl, *L'Afrique byzantine*, 2 vols. (Paris, 1896); idem, *Etudes sur l'administration byzantine dans l'exarchat de Ravenne (568-751)* (Paris, 1888); A. Guillou, *Régionalisme et indépendance dans l'Empire byzantin: l'exemple de l'Exarchat et de la Pentapole d'Italie* (Rome, 1969); G. Ostrogorsky, "Sur la date de la composition du Livre des Thèmes et sur l'époque de la constitution des premiers thèmes d'Asie Mineur," *B* 23 (1953): 31-66; T. S. Brown, *Gentlemen and Officers*, 46-53.

hands of one official, the emperor's representative, who held supreme power within the exarchate. Through such concentration, the entire resources of each region could be disposed to obtain maximum military efficiency and secure government. The centralisation implied by these reforms was only one feature of the total militarisation of the empire.[28] But it was a particularly important one, which would later be extended to the eastern provinces through the system of *thema* administration (see the discussion in Chapter 5). Had the East Roman Empire suffered as greatly as the West from barbarian incursions and economic decline in the fifth and early sixth centuries, it could hardly have provided the resources to support such a reorganisation. The fact that it could is both a measure of past success in withstanding external pressure and the inherent wealth of the provinces of the East.

Although Tiberios and his successor Maurice both married daughters of the ruling imperial family and thus gained credentials among the eastern aristocracy, their promotion is symbolic of the increasing military preoccupations of the East. The Senate of Constantinople did not try to impose a civilian candidate from its own ranks; it recognised the need for competent army leadership. While aristocratic support for such candidates was not a new phenomenon—Marcian (450-57), Leo I (457-74), and Justin I (518-27) were all generals—in the late sixth century it reflected the failure of traditional government. It also established a pattern of army officer rule, which transformed the office of emperor and brought the army into politics in a novel fashion. In the past, successful generals had frequently seized the imperial position—the examples of Julius Caesar, Septimius Severus, Constantine I, and Theodosius I might be cited—but they all had to come to terms with the established bureaucracy of the empire and the vested interests of autonomous cities and self-governing regions. The military always remained one factor among many vying for predominance in ruling circles. The changes that occurred in the late sixth and seventh centuries, however, permitted the army to realise its ambition of dominance, at the expense of civilian forms of government. Not that the imperial bureaucracy disappeared or the cities ceased to desire self-rule. But an overwhelming concern for survival determined their subordination to the army. The example of late sixth-century soldier-emperors was followed by Herakleios in the seventh century and the Syrian dynasty in the eighth. As a result, the imperial office became permanently militarised and remained under constant pressure from successful army leaders until the final conquest of Constantinople

---

[28] E. Darko, "La militarizzazione dell'Impero bizantino," *SBN* 5 (1939): 88-99, esp. 91-95; *Atti del V Congresso Internazionale di Studi byzantini* (Rome, 1936); T. S. Brown, *Gentlemen and Officers*, 46-48.

by the Ottoman Turks in 1453. And precisely because this military dominance became an integral part of imperial government, it both preserved and simultaneously transformed the eastern empire.

The Results of Imperial Reorganisation in the West

Between 572 and 582, the surviving provinces of Byzantine Africa, Mauretania, Numidia, Carthagena, and Tripolitana were united under an exarch. By October 584, Decius held an equivalent position in northern Italy as exarch of Ravenna. But the provinces of central and southern Italy could not be included in the exarchate and continued to be administered in the old style. This meant that Rome remained isolated, linked to Ravenna by a corridor through Lombard territory, rather than integrated into the new system. In effect, the exarchate consolidated Byzantine control in the northeast but admitted Lombard authority over key cities in the northwest (Milan, Pavia, Monza) and in the duchies of Spoleto and Benevento in central Italy.[29] Previously Constantinople had tried to ignore Lombard claims to rule these areas; now it was concerned to limit their spheres of influence. This left Rome in an unsatisfactory position, dependent on Ravenna to protect it from the threats of Lombard forces established further south and constantly nearer. So as papal legate in the East, one of Gregory's primary tasks was to lobby the emperor for additional military support for Rome. In 579, Tiberios promised troops and probably began to plan the implementation of his reorganisation. But Pelagius II got no help from Decius in 584 and therefore instructed Gregory to make further representations to Emperor Maurice (582-602). He requested that Rome should become the base for a military commander with a permanent garrison and a staff to deal with recruitment, pay, and maintenance.[30] Without some regular army presence he feared that the city would be captured by Lombard forces. After a ten-year interregnum, their notables had elected Authari (584) as king and were moving steadily south from Pavia, their capital.

Gregory found that Maurice, like his predecessor, preferred to purchase a diplomatic alliance with the Franks rather than transfer troops from the eastern or Balkan fronts to Italy. But the isolation of Rome so far south of the Ravenna exarchate eventually vindicated Pelagius's demands: by 592, the *magister militum* who undertook the city's defence against an attack by Ariulf was probably Castus, later identified as duke of Rome. In March 595, he presided over the distribution of pay (*rogai*) to the soldiers, a firm

---

[29] C. Wickham, *Early Medieval Italy* (London, 1981), 28-33.
[30] Pelagius II, *Epistulae*, no. 1, *PL* 72, col. 703-705.

indication that a specific office had been established.[31] This arrangement was to last 150 years, till the fall of the exarchate in 751. The duchy of Rome, however, never functioned with the prescribed unification of all powers, civil, legal, and military, in the hands of its commander, precisely because the papacy had assumed a number of important responsibilities— part of the general tendency for ecclesiastical officials to take over when the central government failed. This development was particularly noticeable in the period 555-604 as successive pontiffs tried to protect the city.

Thus Rome was eventually provided with a defensive force commanded by a general who took orders from the exarch of Ravenna. But the main thrust of the administrative reforms benefited Ravenna and the northeast far more than the old metropolis; they confirmed the shift of capital and imperial attention away from Rome. The new Byzantine centre could not entirely replace the old. For instance, when an exarch wished to honour an emperor, he still resorted to the classical custom of raising a column with his statue in the Forum—this was done for the last time by Smaragdus in the reign of Phokas (602-610).[32] For practical purposes, however, Rome was no longer a centre of great importance or significance to the East, and the creation of the exarchate emphasised its decline.

Gregory in Constantinople

Gregory's years in the eastern capital are unfortunately poorly documented. He formed close friendships with a number of ecclesiastics, including Leander of Seville; Constantius, legate of the bishop of Milan; the deposed patriarch Anastasios of Antioch; and Domitian of Melitene. He also got to know members of Maurice's family quite well.[33] But he continued to lead a secluded life, surrounded by monks from his Roman foundation who accompanied him to the East and maintained their familiar routine in the Placidia residence. To them he expounded the Book of Job in commentaries that formed the *Moralia in Iob*, his major theological work. When he wrote it down in 586-90, back in Rome, he dedicated it to Leander, who had participated in the preparatory discussions.[34] Leander, a Catholic

---

[31] B. Bavant, "Le Duché byzantin de Rome," *MEFR, Moyen Age* 83 (1971): 149-58. In Pope Gregory's letters, Castus is always identified as *magister militum* (*Ep.* iii.51; v.30, 36), and is associated with military pay in *Ep.* v.30.

[32] The dedicatory inscription is published in *Corpus Inscriptionum Latinarum*, vol. 6, pt. 1, 251, no. 1200.

[33] Averil Cameron, "A Nativity Poem of the Sixth Century A.D.," *Classical Philology* 79 (1979): 222-32, reprinted in *Continuity and Change in Sixth Century Byzantium* (London, 1981).

[34] Gregory, *Ep.* i.41 (esp. vol. 1, p. 58, with the description of Leander's image in Gregory's heart).

bishop of Seville, had been exiled by the Arian King Leovigild of Spain, possibly for supporting his son's revolt, and sought refuge in Constantinople. He later returned to Spain and was instrumental in the conversion of King Reccared, as well as in the training of his younger brothers and sister, including Isidore, who succeeded him as bishop of Seville in 599-600. Gregory thought very highly of Leander, valued his friendship, and kept in touch with him, although they never met again after leaving the East.

As papal legate to the imperial court, Gregory appears to have taken part in few public events beyond those which his post required. He most probably witnessed the investment of Maurice as caesar and later emperor; he was invited to the marriage celebrations that united Maurice with Constantina, the youngest daughter of Tiberios II, another close friend. Western sources insist that he acted as godfather to their first son, Theodosios, born in 584. He must certainly have assisted at the child's baptism, an important ceremony to which foreign legates were always invited.[35] After a certain amount of theological controversy, he appears to have taken part in a debate with Patriarch Eutychios on the question of the resurrection of the dead. The eastern prelate maintained that the elect who would sit at the right hand of God on the Day of Judgement would not be present in their corporeal bodies but in the spirit. Gregory, however, insisted that the resurrection of Christ provided the model that would be followed. Such debates were common in the East and were frequently arranged by the court on imperial initiatives. In this case, Tiberios II accepted Gregory's objections and ordered Eutychios's work on the subject to be burned.[36]

As Gregory on several occasions states explicitly that he does not know Greek, he probably took part in this debate with the help of translators. Lack of Greek and the cloistered environment in which he lived combined to cut him off from everyday life in Constantinople.[37] Latin, however, was

[35] Gregory of Tours, *HF* 10.1, for the western claim; Theophanes, 385, for an example of the public duties of Roman legates at the Byzantine court (attending the translation of Germanos from the bishopric of Kyzikos to the patriarchate of Constantinople [709]).

[36] Gregory, *Moralia in Iob*, 14.LVI.72-74 (ed. Adriaen, 743-45); cf. Eutychios's work on the Resurrection, *PG* 86 (2), 2373-76. The problem of whether Christ's body was corruptible had occasioned a famous dispute between Severos of Antioch and Julian of Halicarnassos earlier in the sixth century. Justinian had supported aphthartodocetism, the belief that Christ's body must have been incorruptible (*aphthartos*) from the beginning, but this theology satisfied neither the Monophysites, who stressed Christ's one spiritual nature, nor the Chalcedonians, who believed in His consubstantiality. For a florilegium of Monophysite writings that reflect the debate, see M. Richard, "Le florilège du Cod. Vatopédi 236 sur le corruptible et l'incorruptible," *Le Muséon* 86 (1973): 249-73.

[37] G. Cracco, "Uomini di Dio e uomini di chiesa nell' alto medioevo," *Ricerche di storia sociale e religiosa* 12 (1977): 163-202, esp. 191-93; J. M. Petersen, *The Dialogues of Gregory*

still used as the official language of the imperial administration, and was particularly employed in legal affairs. The influx of Roman senatorial and Ostrogothic families from Italy after the first campaign (540) had brought the western classical tongue into greater literary use in the East. In 565 the accession of Justin II was celebrated in a long Latin poem, recited in public by the orator Corippus.[38] Gregory could communicate directly with his friends Rusticiana, a noble lady of Roman descent, and Domitian and Anastasios, who translated some of his writings into Greek. He also kept in touch with Eulogios, patriarch of Alexandria, and members of the imperial family, despite language problems. The affectionate letters he addressed to this circle of friends after 590 suggest that Gregory had found a warm welcome in the East. He moved, of course, amongst aristocrats, where common traditions of education and culture preserved a Mediterranean worldview. This was perhaps the last of the living embodiments of Late Antique cultural unity.

Had he been exposed to the beliefs of the uneducated inhabitants of Constantinople, however, he might have recognised features of his own purely western formation. For in addition to the commitment to doctrinal purity and orthodox theological exposition, Gregory too believed in the power of the divine to perform miracles, in the efficacy of material aids in worship, and in the punishment of sinfulness and wrongdoing by apparently supernatural forms. He probably would have approved of the harsh judgement given by Patriarch John against a sorcerer, accused of conversing with apostate powers over a silver bowl containing the blood of human sacrifices. (The sorcerer and his son were tortured and put to death, a punishment recorded by Gregory himself in a parallel western case of a wizard called Basilius.)[39] Interestingly, the infected silver bowl had been empowered to stop, temporarily, the miraculous flow of oil from the tomb of St. Glykeria, patron saint of Herakleia, when it had unwittingly been substituted for the regular bronze one. Only when it had been removed did the flow recommence, which might well have impressed Gregory as much as the Byzantines. In his collection of miracle stories, the four books of *Dialogues*, written in 593-94, Gregory includes several similar accounts, presented without the slightest shade of doubt. The miracles of the thief whose escape

---

the Great in Their Late Antique Cultural Background (Toronto, 1984), 189-91, modifying earlier claims made in D. Baker, ed., *The Orthodox Churches and the West*, SCH 13 (1976): 121-34.

[38] Averil Cameron, ed., *Corippus, In laudem Iustini Augusti minoris* (London, 1976); cf. idem, "A Nativity Poem," and the works of J. J. O'Donnell: *Cassiodorus* (Berkeley, 1979), and "Liberius the Patrician," *Traditio* 37 (1981): 31-72.

[39] Theophylact Simocatta 1.11; Gregory, *Dialogues*, ed. A. de Vogüé, 3 vols. (Paris, 1978-80), 1.4.3-6 (vol. 1, pp. 38-43).

was prevented by the tomb of a presbyter, or the vestment of Saint Euty-
chius that produced rain in time of drought (3.22 and 3.15) are typical.
The power of saints and holy men and their relics was deeply appreciated
in both West and East, and formed an integral part of Christianity. And it
was as the author of the *Dialogues* that Gregory was remembered in the
East. A mid-eighth-century translation, attributed to Pope Zacharias,
added them to the popular genre of miracle stories widely read.[40] In contrast, Gregory's *Moralia* and *Liber regulae pastoralis*, though available in
Greek translations prepared in Gregory's lifetime, were not much read.

IN ABOUT 585 or 586 Gregory was replaced as legate by Honoratus and
returned to his monastery of St. Andrew with relics of Saints Andrew and
Luke, gifts from the Emperor Maurice. Pelagius seems to have recalled him
to help deal with the obstinate Istrian defenders of the Three Chapters and
other pressing papal matters. The arguments previously employed against
Tuscan bishops had had no effect on Archbishop Elias and his subordinates,
so Gregory now turned to a direct confrontation of their interpretation of
the Fifth Oecumenical Council as a denial of Chalcedon and the *Tomus* of
Pope Leo. He was no more successful; neither sophisticated theological reasoning nor brute force (exercised by the exarch, Smaragdus) persuaded the
Istrians to end their schism. It continued into the seventh century, denouncing Pope Vigilius and Justinian equally for distorting the orthodox
faith, and was only finally ended by the synod of Pavia in 698.[41]
   Gregory might have continued to act as Pelagius's secretary and abbot of
his monastery for some years but for another disaster in Rome. In the winter of 589-90, incessant rainfall and flooding again destroyed those parts of
the city close to the Tiber and spread a serious epidemic of plague in its
trail. The papal granaries were badly affected. The pontiff died. In these
difficult circumstances, Gregory was acclaimed as Pelagius's successor. Although he expressed extreme reluctance to give up the monastic life, he felt
obliged to do everything possible to relieve suffering, to calm the inhabitants in the days of mass burials and collective hysteria. His brother Pal-
atinus, who was then prefect, may have worked with him, putting the
family resources at the service of Rome. So while awaiting imperial confirmation of his election, Gregory struggled to repair the damage. It seems
unlikely that he tried seriously to evade consecration on 3 September

---

[40] G. Cracco, "Uomini di Dio"; Petersen, *The Dialogues*; P. Boglioni, "Miracle et nature
chez Grégoire le Grand," *Cahiers d'études médiévales I: Epopées, Légendes et Miracles* (Montreal/
Paris, 1974), 11-102; E. Auerbach, *Literary Language and Its Public in Late Latin Antiquity
and in the Middle Ages* (London, 1965), 95-103; *LP* 1.435.
   [41] Pelagius II, *Epistulae*, in *MGH, Ep.* 2 Appendix 3, nos. 1-3; cf. Paul the deacon, *HL*
3.26; Gregory, *Ep.* i.16, 16a, 16b; xiii.36 to Smaragdus.

590.[42] However much he identified episcopal office as a burden, it was the natural culmination of his career, and he must have recognised the likelihood of such a prospect. He was certainly a fitting candidate for the office: a Roman by birth, known and liked by the Romans, even if they were not attracted by his reputation for ascetic self-deprivation; a trained administrator with experience of both the papal curia and the imperial court; and a writer and theologian of considerable standing.

POPE GREGORY I

In the East Gregory's elevation was welcomed. His lengthy synodical letter—the customary announcement of appointment accompanied by a personal declaration of faith—was sent to the four eastern patriarchs (and to his friend Anastasios, restored to the see of Antioch in 593).[43] It made clear that he accepted the four Oecumenical Councils as the four books of the Gospels, and greatly revered the fifth. From Constantinople's point of view, he should have been an ideal leader of the western churches. Gregory, however, acted far too independently to please the imperial administration. He was extremely energetic in his control over church lands and property; he intervened in secular affairs, against the exarch's orders (for example, by paying subsidies to the Lombards); and he had a coherent and well-supported theory of the honour due to the see of St. Peter, which made him very critical of patriarchal or episcopal attempts to increase their status. In particular, he would not tolerate Constantinople's claim to the title "oecumenical" or Ravenna's indiscriminate use of the pallium, slippers, and saddle bags—all privileges granted by Rome for a few restricted ecclesiastical ceremonies. There was, therefore, no shortage of grounds for disagreement between the new pontiff and other church leaders.

If we were to judge solely on the basis of the *Life* of Gregory written shortly after his death, possibly by a monk of his own monastery, we would form a very limited picture of his pontificate. To contemporaries, although he was the author of many works, his most remarkable achievement seems to have been the mission to the *gentem Angulorum*, the Anglo-Saxons of Kent.[44] Gregory's other activities are rapidly listed: the provision of a pure silver *cyburium* and additional gold and silk hangings for the altar of St. Peter's; the rededication of a church, previously used by Goths for Arian services, to the martyr Agatha and the Catholic cult; the addition of a partic-

---

[42] Gregory of Tours, *HF* 10.1, records this reluctance later exaggerated; cf. Richards, *Consul of God*, 41-43.

[43] Gregory, *Ep.* i.24 (esp. vol. 1, p. 36: *"sicut sancti evangelii quattuor libros, sicut quattuor concilia suscipere et venerari me fateor. . . . Quintum quoque concilium pariter veneror"*).

[44] *LP* 1.312.

ular canon to the established prayers of the liturgy; the successfully negotiated return of some cities captured by the Lombards; and the conversion of his home into a monastery. Only the introduction of the "Dies que nostros in tua pace dispone" is an unusual feature of this list. The notices of the *Liber pontificalis* usually record in great detail the buildings and rich decorations endowed by Roman bishops, often to the exclusion of their initiatives in other fields. But this account of Gregory's thirteen years is especially barren. Despite his standing as a leader, theologian, and diplomat, the brief notice was considered an adequate testimonial until the ninth century, when John the deacon was commissioned to write a much fuller one. (In about 713 an anonymous monk of Whitby had composed a *Life*, which Bede utilised in his *Ecclesiastical History* finished in 731, to amplify Gregory's important role in the conversion of the Anglo-Saxons.) In the late eighth century, Paul the deacon, a Lombard historian, had also recorded Gregory's *Life* and a useful account of his actions as pope, which is found in the *Historia Langobardorum*.[45] Clearly the record of the *Liber pontificalis* did not attempt to draw on Gregory's own writings, as later biographers did. It represents an immediate impression rather than a scholarly appreciation and thus fails to document a pontificate generally judged to be outstanding in the history of the Late Antique and early Medieval periods. Before discussing Gregory's episcopate, it is useful to consider why this is so and what it implies about the situation in early seventh-century Rome.

The Position of Rome

Firstly, Rome was isolated. The exarch who had responsibility for the battle against the increasing southward movement of the Lombards was too far away to come to Rome's assistance. With Gregory's personal wealth and close supervision of papal estates, particularly those in Sicily, still a relatively peaceful and prosperous area, the city's inhabitants were kept supplied with essential foodstuffs. But the environs of Rome were not secure; hostile forces were settling close by, and towns were passing under Lombard control. The *Liber pontificalis* does not mention Gregory's Roman synods, but these reveal the disastrous extent of Lombard disruption to Italian bishoprics and confirm the much-reduced number of cities still under

---

[45] John the deacon, *Vita Gregorii Magni*, PL 75, cols. 59-242; an anonymous monk of Whitby, *The Earliest Life of Gregory the Great*, ed. and trans. B. Colgrave (Lawrence, Kansas, 1968; reprinted Cambridge, 1985); Paul the deacon, *Vita Gregorii Magni*, PL 75, cols. 41-60, and *HL*. K. Harrison, *The Framework of Anglo-Saxon History to* A.D. 900 (Cambridge, 1976), claims that Bede did not know the "anonymous of Whitby's" *Life*.

Catholic control.[46] As for papal influence abroad, the triumphant mission of Augustine to Canterbury is rightly given prominence; other instances of Roman influence are not mentioned. Gregory's wide contacts with western and eastern church leaders, monastic communities, and secular authorities are all ignored.

Local events clearly take precedence in the biographer's mind. His account of the tomb of St. Peter, appropriately decorated and now made the focus of the mass, exemplifies Roman and papal pride in its foundation. In addition, Gregory's role in founding monasteries and converting churches within the city to Catholic use is stressed. His Roman descent and concern for the city is very evident. In the late sixth century, when Rome was no longer an imperial capital, these were qualities greatly appreciated. Pride in its ecclesiastical history served to support the population in the troubled period of imperial withdrawal to the territory of the exarchate. Rome had no obvious military protector comparable to the Kentish king who received Augustine. And the Roman church still needed such protection; it did not have the resources to defend itself. In his curt notice, the anonymous biographer has revealed something of this growing anxiety and tension while avoiding any discussion of political realities.

With hindsight we tend to assume that the decay of imperial political authority in the West and the related development of ecclesiastical power based on Rome was inevitable, and that contemporaries could understand and take account of it. This approach overlooks the very real fragility of Christian institutions in the early medieval West—their dependence on secular power. Only those monastic communities that had chosen to place themselves almost beyond lay control could claim to be autonomous and self-sufficient. They were nonetheless equally helpless in the face of sudden military attack; witness the devastation of Monte Cassino by the Lombards in the 580s and of many other houses in the late sixth century.[47] Only those shrines and places of pilgrimage that were already established as the sites of miracles and thus had a claim on more than local devotion could ignore shifts in ecclesiastical or secular leadership. Most bishops relied on princely or regal defences; most new monastic foundations, such as those made by St. Columbanus, sought royal patronage to ensure their survival.[48] The or-

---

[46] F. H. Dudden, *Gregory the Great: His Place in History and Thought*, 2 vols. (London, 1905), 1:261-64; L. Duchesne, "Les évêchés d'Italie et l'invasion Lombarde," *Mélanges d'archéologie et d'histoire* 23 (1903): 83-116; 25 (1905): 365-99.

[47] Paul the deacon, *HL* 4.17, describes the expansion of the duchies of Benevento and Spoleto under Zotto and Farwald, which disturbed many ecclesiastical foundations.

[48] In the case of St. Columbanus's foundations, both Luxeuil in Burgundy and Bobbio in northern Italy required additional secular support to survive the death of their founder in 615; see F. Prinz, "Columbanus, the Frankish Nobility and the Territories East of the

ganised structures of the church in early seventh-century Christendom were precarious, and time and again their growth or decay would be decided by military engagements. Although it is generally recognised that Gregory strengthened those aspects of the papacy that would eventually make it possible for his successor and namesake to humble an emperor, his contributions were made at the onset of this development. In 604, Rome was centuries away from a self-sufficient authority to manage the spiritual life of the West. As Gregory's biographer makes clear, beyond the walls of Rome its bishop had little power. The papacy was still an almost exclusively local organisation.

Turning now to the documents that signal Gregory's reputation as a great theologian and administrator—his own writings, particularly the register of his 800 surviving letters—we can evaluate the contemporary *Life*. These confirm the impression of Rome's isolation from the main political centres of the late sixth century. Gregory was dependent on odd travellers and mendicants for information about the situation in Ravenna; he employed a visiting doctor from Egypt and pilgrims to transmit messages to other churches. One of his greatest difficulties as pope was the absence of reliable information. Although he was in contact with the chief ecclesiastics of Africa, and seems to have appointed Columbus of Nicivibus as his unofficial vicar, he felt inadequately informed and worried about local tolerance of Berber Donatists, for example.[49] In Constantinople he maintained Honoratus as official legate, and later Sabinian, Anatolius, and Boniface were all *apocrisiarii*. Similarly, in Illyricum, the vast dioceses embracing most of the Balkans, Greece, Crete, and Thrace, Gregory followed the established custom of naming the metropolitan of Thessalonike as his vicar. He thus had another close contact in the East and was more able to maintain his position as the supreme authority in Illyricum, despite its proximity to the emperor and patriarch of Constantinople.

In Gaul, repeated charges of simony reflected a persistent scandal, which Gregory tried to correct both through local bishops and Roman priests. At King Childebert's request, Vergilius of Arles was appointed papal vicar in 595 and urged to stop priests from buying their consecration. In the same year, Gregory took advantage of the retirement of Dynamius, rector of the

Rhine," in H. B. Clarke and M. Brennan, eds., *Columbanus and Merovingian Monasticism* (Oxford, 1981), 73-87, esp. 77-79.

[49] Unless a formal embassy was to be sent, pilgrims and merchants generally provided the best means of sending letters, even sometimes the most urgent appeals. Few people ever travelled long distances, and when they did they frequently carried messages. On Columbus of Nicivibus, see Richards, *Consul of God*, 198-200; and on the revival of Donatism, see W. H. C. Frend, "Donatist and Catholic: The Organisation of the Christian Communities in the North African Countryside," *Settimane* 28 (1982): 601-634, esp. 630-34.

papal patrimony in Provence, to appoint Candidus, a trusted Roman cleric. This was part of his policy of employing deacons trained in his own chancery wherever possible. Later the papal pallium was granted to Syagrius, a favourite of Queen Brunhild, on condition that he would hold a reforming council.[50] But despite continuing pressure, no council was held. And even with these established channels of communication, Gregory was frequently misled. Part of the problem was due to the fact that deposed or disgruntled clerics often appealed to Rome, producing evidence biased in their own favour. Ascertaining the facts was often a delicate business. And despite explicit instructions to the relevant authority, Gregory found that these were not always implemented: for instance, the clergy of Catania made persistent use of special sandals, *campagi*, to which they were not entitled.[51] The hierarchy of ecclesiastical costume was considered an important matter.

Relations with Secular Authorities

This lack of information and inability to impose decisions taken in Rome rankled with Gregory. He tried repeatedly to involve civilian officials in his support but found Byzantine exarchs and praetorian prefects generally unhelpful. In one case Crementius, an African bishop, had been prevented from going to Rome for trial by a *magister militum*, although the Emperor Maurice had correctly referred the case to the pope.[52] In matters of jurisdiction Gregory was especially sensitive to any reduction in Rome's position. He therefore paid great attention to appeals from southern Spain (603), Thessalonike and Constantinople (595), Corinth, Thebes (592), and Salona, an appeal inherited from the pontificate of Pelagius II.[53] The same zeal for Petrine authority motivated his battles with Patriarch John of Constantinople over the oecumenical title, and brought him into conflict with the emperor.[54] That his friend should now support the patriarch was bad enough; but Maurice then exacerbated matters by instructing Gregory not

[50] Gregory, *Ep.* v.31, 58-60; viii.4; ix.213, 214, 222; cf. Richards, *The Popes and the Papacy*, 316-17.

[51] Gregory, *Ep.* viii.27; footwear would not have been of such significance had it not denoted particular status, a common aspect of medieval clothing. As these sandals were reserved to the Roman diaconate, Gregory was anxious to prevent their use by other clerics. John the deacon records Gregory's distribution of imported materials and foreign clothing to the clergy of Rome at Easter, when they customarily received a gold coin, in *Vita Gregorii* 2.24-28.

[52] Richards, *Consul of God*, 200.

[53] Ibid., 199-218.

[54] Ibid., 217-21; the quarrel was undoubtedly exacerbated by the successful appeal of two eastern clerics to Rome. They were acquitted of the charge of heresy (which had been upheld in the patriarchal court in Constantinople) and were restored to their sees.

to put undue pressure on the Istrian schismatics, who refused to recognise the Fifth Council. They had appealed to Constantinople against Rome, claiming that "emperors had always shown themselves just arbiters and restorers of peace in the church."[55] There is evidence that the pope felt this as a personal betrayal. Persistent opposition to 553, shared by Catholics like Theodolinda, the Bavarian princess who became Lombard Queen, and the Celt Columbanus, founder of Luxeuil and Bobbio, distressed Gregory. Through his friendship with the Queen, he did at least have the satisfaction of witnessing the baptism of her son, Adoald, according to the Catholic rite (603). But this did not produce a permanent change in Lombard affiliation, as Arian practice was again favoured by mid-seventh-century monarchs.

While channels of communication with the northern Lombards were thus kept open, similarly cultivated ladies do not appear to have presided over the courts of the dukes of Benevento and Spoleto, and Gregory had no allies there. Not only were these centres of Arian Lombard power much closer to Rome, but they had also revealed their lack of respect for Catholic foundations by the sack of St. Benedict's monastery, Monte Cassino, which had brought the surviving monks as refugees to Rome. It was Gregory's determination to resist these dukes in central Italy that brought him into conflict with imperial agents. By paying them subsidies, he was able to save Rome from siege and possible capture, but such independent action was deplored in Ravenna. Because the exarchs did not take sufficient pre-emptive action, the natural alliance between Rome and Ravenna, Catholic and imperial, against the common Arian enemy fell apart. This can only have increased the isolation of Rome and the papacy.

Because Gregory was aware of the value of political support for the church, he took steps to ensure good relations with those secular authorities who might be persuaded to provide it. His use of one of the supreme Roman relics, filings from the chains of St. Peter, reveals a sensitivity to temporal problems: on ten occasions such gifts were sent to secular leaders, kings, and officials, not clerics. He acceded to Childebert II and Brunhild in granting the pallium of papal vicar to Vergilius of Arles and Syagrius of Autun, an unprecedented promotion of a non-metropolitan bishop made at the Queen's insistence. Although conditions in the Frankish churches remained the same, Gregory continued to communicate with the Queen over the necessity of reforms and commended to her his nominee, Abbot Kyriakos, who was sent to investigate complaints. He sensed that there was no possibility of instituting Roman traditions and used whatever secular assistance he could to obtain local improvements. Such a policy in-

[55] Gregory, *Ep*. i. 16a and 16b.

volved dealing with the authorities in place regardless of their particular characters. Far from trying to introduce Roman customs into churches under Merovingian control, he could only encourage what was best and curb what was uncanonical within given circumstances.

Regional Variety Within the Western Churches

Gregory's sense of isolation, however, was deepened by the number of independent regional customs in use, for instance, over the celebration of Easter. At his continental foundations, Columbanus had naturally established the Celtic system of calculating the date of Easter based on a cycle of 84 years and wrote to the pope criticising the Roman method.[56] He ridiculed the errors in the Easter tables of Victor of Aquitaine and put forward the Celtic method as *the* ancient tradition, supported by no less a figure than St. Jerome, suggesting that anyone who opposed Jerome could only be a heretic or reprobate. This letter was probably never received. In a later one Columbanus persisted, requesting permission "to maintain the rite of Easter as we have received it from generations gone before." He also justified this proposal by reference to the Third Oecumenical Council, which "decreed that the churches of God planted in pagan nations should live by their own laws."[57] While Gregory did not concur, he may have recognised the impact of Luxeuil's example in Gaul when he instructed Frankish bishops to follow the practice of Rome and Alexandria as opposed to the Celtic. Since Columbanus, who was later patronised by Queen Theodolinda and debated with Arian theologians at her court, was known as a Catholic, his method could not simply be dismissed. Uniformity, however, was not achieved; Gregory roundly condemned Sardinian laxity in the observation of Easter.[58] And the problem continued to vex his successors.

Unity of faith was clearly paramount, but unity of ecclesiastical government was also important. This was the motive behind Gregory's attempt to regulate the primacy of Numidia among African bishops. The local custom of a revolving primacy, held by each metropolitan in turn, disquieted the popes, who preferred to deal with one see established as the leading bishopric. Despite the support and help of a Numidian bishop, Columbus, who served as an unofficial papal vicar, the tradition persisted, and Gregory

[56] *Sancti Columbani Opera*, ed. G. S. M. Walker (Dublin, 1957), 2-13 (letter no. 1).

[57] Ibid., Introduction, xxv-xxvi; 24 (letter no. 3), regretting the fact that earlier letters were apparently not delivered.

[58] Gregory, *Ep.* ix.202, but this was only one of the many charges levelled against Bishop Januarius. Gregory sent Abbot Kyriakos to investigate the disorders reported from Sardinia, as a result of which the bishop was excommunicated.

turned his attention to more serious problems, such as the purchase of ecclesiastical office (simony). The Numidian church not only needed reforming in several respects, more seriously it tolerated a level of Donatist belief
that Gregory found incomprehensible.[59] While urging its bishops to enforce orthodoxy through local councils, and sending his rector Hilarius to
assist Columbus in the task, he tried to restrain Dominicus of Carthage
from interfering in Numidian affairs. But Numidia remained one of those
regions about which Gregory had insufficient evidence to intervene effectively: the exarch of Carthage refused to let bishops visit Rome, and scandals continued to shake the diocese. Two years after his excommunication,
Bishop Paul had still not been allowed to travel to Rome to plead his case.[60]
But even after this, when he finally arrived, Gregory could not ascertain the
full circumstances of his dismissal, and permitted him to take the dispute
to Constantinople. Maurice then referred it back to Numidia, where its
fate is unknown. Although this may have been unusually prolonged, pro-
crastination and unnecessary obstacles were typical of the pope's dealings
with the church in Africa.

In other parts of the West, while Gregory continued to urge churches to
adopt Roman habits, he remained quite tolerant of local variety. He combined a respect for ancient tradition with an adaptation to regional variety,
which may reflect an awareness of the diverse historical circumstances that
had given the Christian communities of the West their distinctive characters. The pope stressed that different customs were not harmful to the
church provided that there was unity of faith. His pleasure at learning of
the Spanish return to Catholicism, effected by the Arian Visigoths in 589,
was not reduced by their particular triple form of baptism. As he wrote to
Leander of Seville in 591, it was the abandonment of Arian belief that mat-
tered most.[61] In other respects also, the church of Spain followed its own
autonomous development, of which Gregory remained generally ignorant.
In his one intervention on the Iberian peninsula, he resolved a dispute between clerics in the Byzantine province of the south.[62] Baptismal rites used
in Sardinia also provoked his disapproval, but as we have seen, the church
there was criticised on other grounds as well. While single or triple im-
mersion at baptism was a relatively minor point, any change in central
matters of faith was firmly opposed.

[59] Gregory, *Ep.* i.72; vi.59; ii.46; iv.35; Frend, "Donatist and Catholic."
[60] Richards, *Consul of God*, 199-200; Gregory, *Ep.* iv.32, 35; vi.59, 61; vii.2; viii.13,
15.
[61] Gregory, *Ep.* i.41: "*in una fide nil officit sanctae ecclesiae consuetudo diversa*" (vol. 1, p. 57).
[62] Gregory, *Ep.* xiii.47, 49, 50, quoting imperial laws from Justinian's *Novels*, the *Codex*,
and *Digest*.

The Conversion of the Anglo-Saxons

This commitment to Roman tradition in conjunction with a flexible approach to regional variety is most evident in Gregory's detailed instructions to the monks who led the papal mission to Kent.[63] Through Queen Bertha, daughter of Charibert of Paris, Christian worship had already been introduced to the Anglo-Saxons, but her Frankish bishop had not made many converts. Augustine and the forty monks who landed at Thanet in 597 came to meet King Ethelbert in solemn procession, bearing an icon of Christ and a silver cross and chanting the Roman litany.[64] Through Frankish interpreters they conveyed the purpose of their mission—to bring the promise of the kingdom of heaven to all who believe in Christ—and prepared to persuade the Saxon leader of the superiority of their faith to his own traditional religion. Example rather than argument was the key to their success. Ethelbert was baptised on Whit Sunday, and by the following Christmas (597) large numbers were converted. Augustine then had to consult Gregory about the organisation of the church in this new diocese; how many suffragan bishops, their method of consecration, and the ritual to be observed in English churches were just some of the points. The pope eventually responded by sending extra missionaries, including four monks who became the first bishops of London, Rochester, and York and abbot of St. Augustine's monastery at Canterbury. They also took with them service books, liturgical vessels and vestments, ornaments, relics, presents, and letters for the king and queen.[65]

Augustine received the pallium of his office and three important letters: a set of answers to his questions (the *Responsa*), an outline for the development of the church under his supreme authority, and a personal communication on his alleged power to work miracles.[66] While Gregory did not doubt Augustine's power, he urged the archbishop to remember with awe that it was God who acted through him. The first two letters reveal the pope's capacity to adapt and tolerate non-Roman customs. Most strikingly, he instructs Augustine to select rites from any church, guided by the principle of providing a liturgy that is suitable for the English.[67] The archbishop was thus at liberty to combine aspects of the Gallican rite familiar

[63] H. Mayr Harting, *The Coming of Christianity to Anglo-Saxon England* (London, 1972).

[64] Bede, *EH* 1.25.

[65] Gregory, *Ep.* xi.35, 37, 39.

[66] Some historians have seen in the *Responsa* an eighth-century forgery, but on balance it seems more likely that they are original; see M. Deansley and P. Grosjean, "The Canterbury Edition of the Answers of Pope Gregory I to St Augustine," *JEH* 10 (1959): 1-49. For an interesting discussion of their significance throughout the Germanic regions, see J. Goody, *The Development of the Family and Marriage in Europe* (Cambridge, 1983), 35-47.

[67] *Responsa*, in Bede, *EH* 1.27, and 2; cf. Gregory, *Ep.* xi.36, 56a to Augustine.

to Bertha with his own eastern and Roman traditions; there was no question of imposing one single superior ritual. But neither was there in Gregory's advice any awareness of the Celtic services in use throughout the west of England, and in parts of Wales, Scotland, and Ireland. And it was the existence of these churches with their own monk-bishops, monasteries, and cult that was to give Augustine so many problems. In spite of the spirit of compromise, explicit instructions concerning Augustine's supremacy over the entire Christian community and all bishops of England made it hard for him to deal with the stern Celtic authorities.

In a separate letter to Mellitus, who became the first bishop of London, Gregory reversed his position on heathen temples in an interesting example of adaptation.[68] Rather than destroying their existence by pulling down their buildings, as had originally been urged, the pope recommended a cleansing purification of such structures and their conversion into churches. The reason for this change of mind was that a "step-by-step" approach was more suitable for "savage hearts," who might be won to the new religion by its use of familiar pre-Christian buildings. Idols had to be destroyed, of course, but the customary sacrifice of animals was to be transformed into an ecclesiastical feast to celebrate the nameday of the martyr whose relics would consecrate the new church. By the emplacement of altar and relics and the sprinkling of consecrated water, Gregory felt that Christian services could be held in ancient buildings.

A certain amount of compromise with Anglo-Saxon tradition was thus permitted in the new diocese, while a free choice of suitable texts determined the actual rite. On the one occasion when Gregory might have imposed Roman traditions unequivocally, he chose not to. But by the selection of Augustine and his monastic companions for the mission, he ensured that a fair degree of Roman influence would guide the church. Material equipment sent from Rome and monastic discipline and learning, of which Gregory was himself a product, were thus installed. By directing an appeal to King Ethelbert himself, a necessary secular protection was also gained. An unforeseen though perfectly understandable result was the devotion of both the Anglo-Saxon church and its princely defenders to the pope and the see of St. Peter.[69] A concomitant hostility to all vestiges of the older Christian tradition maintained by Celtic monks produced Augustine's failure of 602-603. The issues dividing the two groups were thus deepened in a manner which meant that ultimately one would have to give way. The synod of

[68] Gregory, *Ep.* xi.56.

[69] J. M. Wallace-Hadrill, "Rome and the Early English Church: Some Questions of Transmission," *Settimane* 7 (Spoleto, 1960): II, 519-48.

Whitby (664) merely concluded this division by sealing the fate of the Celtic church in England.[70]

Efforts to Remove Pagan Superstition. Gregory's sense of compromise with Anglo-Saxon paganism was particular, not general. When he learnt of tree worship, heathen idols, or pagan celebrations in nominally Christian areas, he urged bishops and secular officials alike to deal harshly with offenders. Persuasion through preaching, missionary work, threats, bribes, and finally direct force were recommended in letters to Sicily, Sardinia, Corsica, and Terracina.[71] He does not appear to have known of a similar attempt to stamp out pagan survivals in Spain, which had been made by Martin of Braga a few years before. Martin's sermon, *On the Correction of the Peasantry*, was written in response to an episcopal appeal for help in dealing with the frequent back-sliding among Christians. It provides additional evidence of the failure to attend church on Sundays, or playing dice and talking through the service, as well as consulting soothsayers and diviners. While such skin-deep Christianity is often attributed to rural areas and a backward peasantry, one must remember that the great majority of people lived in the countryside and were engaged in agriculture. As city-dwellers made up only a tiny fraction of the entire population, and bishops were still based in cities, most people were poorly served by Christian leaders. Village churches, parish priests, and rural monasteries were thinly scattered throughout the Mediterranean world, where the vagaries of nature, of importance to all farmers, had for centuries been mitigated by time-honoured customs and superstitions. Even in Italy, which boasted the highest number of episcopal sees, relatively developed standards of education, and a thriving monastic tradition, recurrent idolatry was common. Christianity as practised by Gregory the Great was the religion of an elite; the mass of believers were nothing like so confident in God's power to save them and frequently sought extra- and non-Christian protection and assistance.

Yet although the pope's faith was based on a sophisticated theology, nourished on the western church fathers, especially St. Augustine, his writings reveal an understanding and appreciation of the beliefs of ordinary Christians. Like Martin of Braga, he knew their doubts and fears and tried to combat them. His step-by-step approach to the Anglo-Saxons may have been influenced by the "savagery" that he recognised hidden in Christian hearts. The precision, repetition, and exhortation of his letters indicate an awareness of the abysmal ignorance and gullibility of most people and

---

[70] M. Deansley, "The Anglo-Saxon Church and the Papacy," in C. H. Lawrence, ed., *The English Church and the Papacy in the Middle Ages* (London, 1965), 29-62.

[71] Gregory, *Ep.* iii.59; iv.23, 26, 27, 29; ix.204; xi.12 (Sardinia); viii.1 (Corsica); viii.19 (Terracina).

many of their leaders. It is a practical approach developed to improve within given limits, rather than to remove the limits altogether. As a product of late sixth-century culture and with a grasp of its vulnerability, Gregory seeks to come to terms with Christians as they are, to strengthen their faith, however restricted its theological orbit.

Gregory's Guide for Bishops

In doing so, Gregory provided some of the means whereby this rudimentary belief would be gradually transformed and the church built up into a serious international organisation. This can be seen in his *Liber regulae pastoralis* (Book of pastoral care), addressed to John of Ravenna, on the functions of a bishop.[72] Gregory here stresses the importance of clerical leadership within his model of church administration, while advising the bishop on a variety of matters. The harmonious relations of masters and servants, united by their common faith, are presented as an earthly concord reflecting the greater peace of heaven. Monastic virtues—humility, chastity, obedience—are emphasised. Marriage is permitted to those who cannot face the tempests of virginity. As the bishop has been selected by God to administer this Christian society, he must strive to set an example in his own life. The subordination of lay to clerical elements is assumed, giving the ecclesiastic a heavy responsibility. This text was widely distributed amongst Gregory's friends in the years 591-94. Copies were made for Leander of Seville and Licinianus of Carthagena, as well as Italian prelates and the Emperor Maurice. Anatolius, the papal legate, got it translated by another close friend, Anastasios. Seven early Latin manuscripts show that it was frequently copied and much read in the West, yet it never circulated widely in the East.[73] Several reasons for this unequal appreciation may be suggested.

Firstly, and most obviously, the churches of the West needed such a text and had reason to go back to it in the seventh and eighth centuries. Buffeted by political hostilities, their Christian traditions were not powerful enough to maintain unbroken links with the unswerving devotion of the early church. Their constant exposure to traditional beliefs, heretical and non-Christian practices, as well as secular manipulation and regulation, had a detrimental influence that could be countered by Gregory's beatific image. The church here below as a model of God's heaven above was presented in a tangible manner, to be emulated by following prescribed guide-

---

[72] The text is in *PL* 77, 13-128; cf. A. Guillou, "L'évêque dans la société méditerranéenne des VIe-VIIe siècles: Une modèle," *Bibliothèque de l'Ecole des Chartes* 131 (1973): 5-19.

[73] Guillou, "L'évêque." One manuscript, *Troyes 581*, shows signs of apparent correction by Gregory himself. The popularity of the work among the laity is clear: in the ninth century Dhuoda and Eccard both owned copies; see P. Riché, "Les bibliothèques de trois aristocrates laïcs carolingiens," *Le Moyen Age* 69 (ser. 4, vol. 18) (1963): 91, 102.

lines. Although St. Augustine's *City of God* was a far more glorious vision, Gregory's *Regula pastoralis* gave bishops direct instructions with unparalleled clarity and simplicity; these had a practical application quite lacking in earlier Christian writings. This quality made the text a most important guide to the organisation and management of new bishoprics, a second reason for its continued use in the West. Not only was Gregory's world full of pagans and non-believers, but on its northern and northeastern borders there were numerous clans and tribes ignorant of Christianity. As we have seen, the conversion and incorporation of these outsiders was considered a primary duty, as revealed in Gregory's attention to the Anglo-Saxon mission. His text provided indications as to the manner of extending the faith to non-Christian lands.

A third reason for the regular consultation of the *Regula pastoralis* lay in the dignity and authority vested by the pope in his model bishop. Gregory's own actions as bishop of Rome confirm the basic outlook: his stress on monastic virtues, especially celibacy, and the significance attached to preaching. In 591-93, two series of his Homilies were delivered from different pulpits in Rome (sometimes by deacons, as Gregory himself was frequently ill). The series of 22 on the Book of Ezekiel had such a reputation as theological exegesis that Columbanus asked Gregory for a copy in 603.[74] But they had been written as sermons intended to inspire and encourage the congregations of Rome. Like the *Dialogues*, they do not assume a great knowledge of Scripture, although they comment in the standard fashion, verse by verse. The morals drawn from this source were designed for a late-sixth-century lay audience, ill-educated, prone to superstition, and bereft of adequate physical protection. By placing the bishop in this position of guiding from within, fully integrated with his flock, Gregory laid the basis for future Christian strength in the West, while at the same time he enhanced the role of the leader.

The Eastern Churches in the Late Sixth Century

Although the qualities of the *Regula pastoralis* might have made it useful, accessible, and even popular in the East had it become known, it did not. No Greek manuscripts are known, and the ninth-century polymath and theologian, Patriarch Photios, was unaware of it, though familiar with the *Dialogues* and a *Life* of the pope in translation.[75] The reasons for this lack of

---

[74] There are 40 homilies on the Gospels and 22 on the Book of Ezekiel, described by Richards as "an extended lamentation over the destruction of Rome," *Consul of God*, 54. Columbanus's letter, no. 1, para. 9 (see Walker, *Sancti Columbani Opera*, 10).

[75] Guillou, "L'évêque," 18; contra Richards, *Consul of God*, 261, claims a wide dissemination in both East and West.

appreciation do not lie in the existence of alternate Greek manuals on the same subject, but in a different ecclesiastical situation in the East, as we have seen in the previous chapter. By the late sixth century, the three apostolic foundations of Jerusalem, Antioch, and Alexandria had established durable institutions throughout their vast sees, in which they justifiably took some pride. Close contact with extensive and equally ancient monastic communities provided a supply of well-formed administrators, while the range of eastern theological interpretation, sometimes verging on heresy, sharpened doctrinal debates. Ancient relics, in material remains, books of exegetical writing, and a less tangible spiritual legacy, strengthened the ties between these churches and their founders. In addition, imperial patronage and protection had assisted in the physical extension of the churches and their endowment. Centuries of fairly regular government had established a certain confidence in Christian institutions, while the example of holy men and women inspired individuals to commit themselves to ascetic ideals.

Although Constantinople did not fit this pattern and had to create a legendary, quasi-apostolic foundation by St. Andrew, its prestige as the bishopric of the capital was successfully built up from the time of Constantine I onwards.[76] It shared in the increasing wealth of the eastern church, receiving many imperial donations, and benefited from the venue of three of the five oecumenical councils (381, 451, and 553). As well as participating in these major gatherings, the churches of the East held diocesan and patriarchal synods, exercised a legal authority over subordinates, maintained discipline and church doctrine, and regulated disputed successions or clerical conflicts according to a recognised body of canon law. This does not mean that they enjoyed a virtuous prosperity devoid of error. But it suggests that in comparison with the West, the mechanisms of control were far more developed and integrated with other forms of authority; the machinery of church government existed and could maintain Christians in the faith despite resurgent paganism and heresy, schism and violence.

With these diverse and firmly implanted traditions, the eastern churches tried to act autonomously within imperial restraints. Yet in spite of flagrant secular interference, emperors recognised the general right of patriarchs to administer their own churches. In the battle against non-believers and heretics, imperial and ecclesiastical officials had to work together; for mutual benefit, a mutual respect was necessary. There were thus two hierarchies in East Mediterranean society, civil and clerical, each clearly defined and equally influential. For aristocratic families, to educate one son

[76] F. Dvornik, *The Idea of Apostolicity in Byzantium and the Legend of the Apostle Andrew* (Cambridge, Mass., 1968).

in a prominent law school for an administrative career and another in a patriarchal school for theological training was quite normal. Both paths
might lead to positions of power—if they produced a senior civil servant
and a patriarchal official, the family would command an important degree
of patronage and probably wealth. The maintenance of higher education in
the East and the quasi-meritocratic system of recruitment meant that tal-
ented students could rise up an established ladder of post and rank. Because
of a slightly competitive relationship between civil and clerical, educational standards remained high and the leading families of the East were
drawn into both. Although Christianity had been resisted by certain senators and representatives of the curial classes, by the late sixth century a
nominal allegiance to the faith was required even for civilian careers, and
punishment for non-observance was severe. The settled nature of the
church and its force in Mediterranean society had created a legitimate ecclesiastical structure in parallel with that of the imperial bureaucracy.

A dual system of this type was completely lacking in the West. In addition, the "patriarchate" of Rome was nothing like as strong as its eastern
equivalents, while the "national" churches were barely established in comparison. Gregory's *Regula pastoralis* attempted to compensate for the inherent weaknesses in western Christianity by indicating what basic duties
were required of bishops and by stressing the honour of the position. It was
both an encouragement to spiritual leadership and a means of imposing ecclesiastical discipline, for Gregory emphasised that bishops should advise
the Christian rulers of the West on all topics, not only church matters,
while clarifying the exact position of bishops within the Christian community. He ordained 62 bishops and took great care in their selection.[77]
He also used synods to provide guidance in awkward situations, such as
episcopal abuse of monastic independence or of church property. In the
canons of his second Roman synod (601), Gregory spelled out the objections to bishops treating ecclesiastical lands as their own or interfering in
monastic successions, which were the preserve of the monks.[78] Thus the
enhanced dignity of episcopal office was tempered by the superior authority
of the whole church and by an awareness of the particular role of monastic
communities within it.

Monastic Influence in Papal Organisation. To strengthen the faith of the western churches, Gregory also drew on monastic traditions in a manner that

[77] *LP* 1.312; Richards, *Consul of God*, 141-43.
[78] *PL* 77, 1340-42; comparable sentiments are expressed in many letters to individuals,
see for instance, *Ep.* v.2, 49; vi.44; viii.12 and viii.17 on the privileges of the monastery of
Sts. John and Stephen at Classis, which Bishop Marianus had failed to respect. Cf. *Ep.*
ix.216 on the privileges of Arles.

incorporated many features of celibate withdrawal from the world into the secular church. This was immediately felt in Rome itself and later spread to other areas. Previously there had been a wide gap between the priests, deacons, and other clergy who officiated in the four major churches of the city and the monks who took no part in public services. From Gregory's pontificate onwards, this monastic population became directly involved in such matters, bringing a more vigorous training, personal humility, and spiritual discipline to them. The development mirrored the pope's own formation and determination to maintain an ascetic routine as bishop. His example, combined with the recruitment of other monks to important roles in papal administration, spread a monastic style of work among the secular clergy. In particular, it profoundly influenced the diaconate of the Roman church.[79] At Gregory's accession in 590 there were 19 deacons, some serving abroad as papal legates or rectors of papal property, others attached to specific churches or charitable institutions. Gregory ordained only five more but greatly extended their functions. And as bishops, including bishops of Rome, were frequently recruited from the diaconate, by incorporating monastic features into the training of deacons, Gregory ensured their greater influence in the life of the church as a whole.

Roman deacons thus became a valuable weapon in the papal struggle to impose control and justice on the papal patrimonies and to resolve clerical disputes. In Provence, Dalmatia, and Africa, Roman clerics administered the papal patrimonies as rectors and attended to local matters; Roman rectors were also appointed to Sardinia and Corsica, throughout Italy, and in Sicily, where the deacon Cyprian was elevated to the most senior position based on Syracuse. Although the rectors' chief task was the administration of papal estates, they sometimes filled additional roles more akin to diplomacy. Like the legates at the imperial court, their official activity also involved a very important duty of finding out what was really going on. When necessary, Gregory also sent personal investigators; for instance, Abbot Kyriakos went to Sardinia to ascertain the level of paganism and was later appointed as envoy to the Frankish church.[80] By insisting on loyalty and devotion to the church of Rome, Gregory effectively spread a more Roman mentality through areas remote from the city, bringing a greater unity to its scattered possessions.

[79] Detailed discussion of diaconal influence and papal personnel is given in Richards, *Consul of God*, 132-39; see F. Prinz, *Askese und Kultur: vor und frühbenediktinisches Mönchtum an der Wiege Europas* (Munich, 1980), 19, on the important consequences of Gregory's integration of monks and monastic values within the established church.

[80] Gregory, *Ep.* iv.23, 25, 26-27; v.2; ix.1, 2, 11. Kyriakos is frequently mentioned in letters to the Frankish church, e.g. *Ep.* ix.208, 213, 218, 219.

Gregory's Attitude to Iconoclasm and Ecclesiastical Art

While this constituted a structural change in ecclesiastical organisation of great import for the future, a more direct and immediate index of Gregory's influence on the churches of the West lies in his correspondence. From his letters we can see and sense the impact of his personality, specific training, attention to detail, and defence of the ancient traditions of the church as contemporaries would have felt it. His criticism of Serenus of Marseille, who wanted to throw all the religious images and decoration out of his church into the sea, is a pertinent example of his power to chastise:

Word has since reached us that you, gripped by blind fury, have broken the images of the saints with the excuse that they should not be adored. And indeed we heartily applaud you from keeping them from being adored, but for breaking them we reproach you. Tell us, brother, have you ever heard of any other bishop anywhere who did the like? This, if nothing else, should have given you pause. Do you despise your brothers and think that you alone are holy and wise? To adore images is one thing; to teach with their help what should be adored is another. What Scripture is to the educated, images are to the ignorant, who see through them what they must accept; they read in them what they cannot read in books. This is especially true of the pagans [gentibus]. And it particularly behooves you, who live among pagans [gentes], not to allow yourself to be carried away by just zeal and so give scandal to savage minds. Therefore you ought not to have broken that which was placed in the church not in order to be adored but solely in order to instruct the minds of the ignorant.[81]

Here a good many of Gregory's favourite allusions are combined. The bishop must not act independently without consulting his brothers, nor should he presume to know best in matters where no precedent is available. Humility and action in accordance with established tradition is stressed. Rather than take argument with Serenus over the question of idolatry, which must have been the bishop's grounds for such forceful action, Gregory proceeds to justify the use of images in church in the formulation that became classic: pictures are the Bibles of the illiterate. He urges Serenus to consider the dangers of his violent example; people will think that such measures are permissible if their bishop behaves thus. And as he happens to live in a region inhabited by uneducated people, what will their "savage minds" make of such destruction? The importance of the bishop's social role is clear: he must preserve order and calm disturbance by teaching the

---

[81] Gregory, Ep. xi.10 (translation by C. Davis-Weyer, Early Medieval Art, 300-1150 [Englewood Cliffs, N.J., 1971], 48), cf. ix.208. Serenus was not only an iconoclast; a few months later Gregory wrote again condemning his conduct, which had to be investigated by Vergilius of Arles, xi.38.

ignorant about the faith through pictures. The civilising mission of the church is performed in this way by its obedient servants, the bishops.

While there is no record of what images of saints were destroyed by Serenus, the practice of using pictures in church was clearly well established. Indeed, it may have been seen as a necessity for the education of *gentes*, a term that probably indicates recently arrived settlers of barbarian origin rather than full-fledged pagans. Augustine's mission to Kent displayed an icon of Christ at its first procession to meet the king, one of the first recorded uses in the West of what was an essentially eastern type of religious art. But of course, western styles of ecclesiastical art were well developed by the sixth century and included narrative histories in fresco and mosaic, representations of individual saints and members of the Holy Family, as well as allegorical ones such as the Good Shepherd. A famous building in Clermont Ferrand, constructed by Bishop Namatius in the early fifth century, had decoration in mosaic and many varieties of marble, while his wife's foundation dedicated to St. Stephen had coloured frescoes. According to local tradition, reported by Gregory of Tours, "She used to hold in her lap a book from which she would read stories of events which happened long ago, and tell the workmen what she wanted painted on the walls."[82] The Late Antique custom of commissioning elaborately carved sarcophagi had produced magnificent Christian sculptures, which also appeared on other sorts of tombs. Episcopal portraits and images of holy men reinforced the commemorative function of religious art.[83]

During his stay in Constantinople, Gregory appears to have noticed the growing cult of icons and their use in churches, together with eastern silks and rich gold and silver decoration. After his return to Rome, his friend Rusticiana sent him an image from the East, which he erected in the monastery of St. Andrew with an accompanying poem. The latter survives both in an inscription from the monastery and in manuscript versions. It commemorated Christ's birth, and therefore probably described an icon of the Virgin and Child.[84] As such images were becoming more common in the East in the late sixth century, Rusticiana probably selected one for her Christmas gift to Gregory. He also thanked her for special curtains sent to St. Peter's, additional evidence that eastern hangings were being intro-

---

[82] Gregory of Tours, *HF* 2.17, 18 (English translation, 131-32).

[83] Bede records the use of the icon, *EH* 1.25, which probably did become a possession of the cathedral or monastery at Canterbury. There are no grounds, however, for identifying it with a copy of the Kamouliana icon of Christ, as is claimed by C. P. Kelley, "Canterbury's First Ikon," *Bulletin of the Friends of Canterbury Cathedral* (1977): 41-44. On artistic developments, see J. Hubert, J. Porcher, and W. F. Volbach, *Europe in the Dark Ages* (London, 1969); and for the growth of iconophile devotion, see R. A. Markus, "The Cult of Icons in Sixth Century Gaul," *JTS*, n.s., 29 (1978), 151-57.

[84] Averil Cameron, "A Nativity Poem."

duced to western churches. In turn, Gregory himself selected the most luxurious style of decoration for the binding of the Gospels that he presented
to Queen Theodolinda.[85] He does not appear to have felt any disquiet at
the use of gems, precious metals, and silk binding for a religious book.
That he also understood the desirability of using the best building materials for church construction is clear from his efforts to get suitably strong
beams from southern Italy for Eulogios, patriarch of Alexandria.[86] Despite
the lack of proof, we may conjecture that Gregory appreciated the excellence of eastern artefacts and their use in church. (One of the few extrava-
gances he permitted himself after returning to the West was the import of
resinated wine, a taste which must go back to his stay in the East.)[87] But
the approval of eastern objects and products stands in sharp contrast to
Gregory's rebuttal of the accusation, made by Sicilian bishops, that he admitted eastern features of the liturgy to the Roman church service.[88] Bor-
rowing in the artistic field could never be extended to ecclesiastical ceremonies.

Relations Between Rome and Constantinople

This ambivalence dominated papal dealings with the authorities in the
East, both civil and ecclesiastical. Gregory's direct knowledge of past problems inevitably coloured his attitude towards Constantinople. As his predecessor, Pelagius II, had already criticised the patriarch's use of the term
"oecumenical," and had ordered the papal legate to abstain from communion until it was dropped, Gregory inherited a serious disagreement in
590.[89] Whether the title had been adopted with a positive intent to belittle
the supreme rank of Rome within the entire church, or as seems more
likely, it reflected the supremacy of the patriarch of Constantinople within
his own diocese, Gregory perceived it as an attack on his own apostolic
foundation. In his frequent attempts to persuade Constantinople to abandon the title, he wrote to the emperor and his friends Anastasios, restored
to the see of Antioch in 593, and Eulogios of Alexandria.[90] Neither saw the
use as a claim to universality above and beyond the defined authority of the

---

[85] The gold, jewelled cover is preserved in the Cathedral treasury of Monza, see Hubert,
Porcher, and Volbach, *Europe in the Dark Ages*, plate 241. Cf. Paul the deacon, *HL* 4.5,
which records that Gregory sent Queen Theodolinda a copy of his *Dialogues*.

[86] Gregory, *Ep.* vi.58; vii.37; viii.28; ix.175; x.21, etc.

[87] Ibid., *Ep.* vii.37 (the *cognidium* imported by Roman traders was not as good as what
the pope could obtain from Eulogios in Alexandria). In exchange he sent Eulogios "*sex minora Aquitanica pallia et duo oraria*," ibid. (vol. 2, p. 486).

[88] Ibid., *Ep.* ix.26 to John of Syracuse.

[89] Pelagius II, *Epistulae*, no. 6, *PL* 72, 738-44.

[90] Gregory, *Ep.* v.41, cf. the very similar protests to Emperor Maurice and Empress Constantina, v.37, 39.

patriarch, and therefore did not understand Gregory's anxiety. They could point to the fact that when the pontiff insisted on hearing an appeal from two priests from Asia Minor, already tried and condemned for heresy by Patriarch John, he was successful in restoring them to their positions, absolved of the charges.[91] And as this case did not spring from an area where Rome had established rights of appellate justice, it was an extraordinary event that boosted papal prestige. Gregory, however, saw this as a recognition of Rome's role as the ultimate court of appeal for the entire Christian world.

Another factor that undoubtedly influenced the course of relations between Constantinople and Rome was Gregory's acquaintance with Maurice and Constantina, dating back to the period of his stay in the East. The pope clearly expected this to assist his principled opposition to certain imperial measures, which perhaps it did. Given his understanding of imperial authority in the church, which is amply illustrated in his tactful letters to the court ("our most pious lord has the power to do whatever he pleases," *Ep.* xi.29), he was very careful in his criticism. When Maurice tried to restrict the rights of imperial officials to enter the church or retire to monasteries (593), Gregory presented his arguments against this in diplomatic letters sent to the emperor and to the emperor's doctor, asking the doctor to raise the matter at an appropriately peaceful moment.[92] Four years later a modified version of the law was promulgated, permitting officials to join monasteries when they had completed their public duties, and soldiers after a three-year novitiate.[93] This success in shifting imperial opinion was, however, matched by a number of issues on which Maurice persisted in policies considered detrimental to the church: the handling of the Istrian schismatics, the treatment of episcopal disputes, and the correct method of dealing with a metropolitan suffering from senility, among others. In all, Gregory recognised the rights of an emperor to intervene in religious matters, but tried to deflect laws deemed too harsh. This understanding of the reality of church/state relations may explain why Gregory felt it necessary to greet the usurper Phokas in 602.[94] To condemn the new emperor for his barbarous treatment of Maurice and his family could only harm the church; to try and communicate with Constantina, imprisoned in a nunnery with her daughters, would be seen as treason. The damage was done and Gregory had to deal with a new source of imperial authority. The imperial portrait of Phokas and his wife, Leontia (which had been sent from the eastern capital) was therefore acclaimed by the whole clergy and Senate, and then

---

[91] Ibid., *Ep.* iii.52; v.44; vi.14-17, 62.
[92] Ibid., *Ep.* iii.64 (cf. iii.61 to Maurice).
[93] Ibid., *Ep.* viii.10.
[94] Ibid., *Ep.* xiii.34 (and xiii.42 to Leontia Augusta).

placed in the chapel of St. Caesarius inside the Lateran for safekeeping.[95] Modern historians who have found Gregory's action unworthy perhaps underestimate the pope's worldly sense of "Realpolitik."

Yet underlying all his relations with authorities in the East there lay a fundamental ambiguity. Gregory recognised the supreme temporal power of the emperor and the role of Constantinople in Rome's survival. A military duke and garrison had been provided to protect the city against attack. Yet time and again these measures proved inadequate, and additional assistance failed to materialise. Gregory himself had to pay the troops before they would fight. His distress at the poor conditions and potential dangers stemmed in part from a longing for Rome to revive and re-create the prosperous days when the schools were full of students and all powers thronged to defend the city.[96] His criticism of both Constantinople and Ravenna was obviously related to their favoured status in the empire, for in contrast to Rome they benefited from imperial patronage even though they were not apostolic foundations. Because he resented the concomitant decline in Rome's status, Gregory jealously guarded what authority he could muster for the see of St. Peter and elevated this aspect of ecclesiastical superiority to a guiding principle.

Gregory's Role in the Early Medieval Papacy.

This understanding of the political realities of the late sixth century also influenced Gregory's attitude towards the culture of the East, specifically those aspects of Greek theology and classical learning that were not available to a Latin-speaking scholar. While he may have consulted Patriarch Eulogios on the nature of some obscure heresies,[97] there is no evidence that he was ignorant of the major theological disputes of the time—his debate with Eutychios seems to suggest the reverse. But as a product of mid-sixth-century Roman education, Gregory was not trained in Greek patristic literature; he knew those writings that had been translated into Latin and was aware of others not yet available. His western formation gave him access to only half the heritage of Late Antiquity, unlike scholars of an earlier generation (Cassiodorus, for instance) whose knowledge was broader. And this shrinking of the field of learning was accompanied by a stricter subordination of knowledge to the service of the church, very clear in Gregory's

---

[95] John the deacon, *Vita Gregorii Magni* 4.20, *PL* 75, 185B; also in Norberg, *CCL*, 140A, Appendix 8, p. 1101.

[96] Gregory, *ep.* v.39 (*"sacellarius ego sum,"* vol. 2, p. 328), vi.58; Courcelle, *Histoire littéraire des grandes invasions germaniques*, 257-58.

[97] Gregory, *Ep.* viii.29; vii.31.

disapproval of Bishop Desiderius of Vienne.[98] Over-zealous enthusiasm for classical subjects, whether verse, rhetoric, or philosophy, was bound to lead to secular, non-Christian, even immoral considerations, quite inappropriate for a cleric. Since the primary task of bishops was to teach and spread the faith, Christian learning obviously took precedence over non-essential topics. So while Gregory's combination of Roman background and Christian education was typical of Late Antiquity, his use of classical scholarship was particular: he directed it solely to the service of the church, to the greater glory of Christ and the faith of the West. In this respect he embodied certain elements of the transitional character of the late sixth century. While drawing on the traditions of Late Antiquity, he was the harbinger of a purely Latin and clerical culture of the medieval West.

This is not to suggest that the pope had some preconceived notion of the church of Rome as the leader of western Christendom. Such an idea reads back into the late sixth century what developed very slowly and hesitantly in the course of several hundred years. What Gregory's letters do reveal, however, is a constant attempt to strengthen Christian authority over the rulers of the West; to establish bishops as leaders of Christian communities; to remove crass superstition, idolatry, and other ancient habits; and to promote the cult of St. Peter and Petrine authority. These measures were adopted in a piecemeal fashion, as and when opportunity arose, often in response to appeals from unfamiliar persons. In no way could they be construed as a master-plan to build up Roman supremacy. Yet they served as the foundation of the medieval papacy. Gregory's stubborn defence of papal authority not only elevated the position of subsequent bishops of Rome vis-à-vis eastern church leaders, it also concentrated the attention of the West on its legitimate apostolic claim. Similarly, the links generated by Gregory facilitated the development of a systematic western organisation in support of the spiritual independence of the papal see. In the 200 years following his death, popes aided by the same machinery would gradually develop the means to claim an equivalent temporal independence. From the days when an instruction from Maurice might inhibit Gregory from prosecuting the Istrian schismatics, we pass to the action of Pope Leo III in crowning Charlemagne emperor. It is a formidable achievement whose foundations were undoubtedly laid in Gregory's time.

[98] Ibid., *Ep.* xi.34; cf. V. Paronetto, "Gregorio Magno e la cultura classica," *Studium* 74, fasc. 5 (1978): 665-80; N. Scivoletto, "I limiti dell' 'ars grammatica' in Gregorio Magno," *Giornale italiano di filologia* 17 (1964): 210-38; and the acute observations of G. Cracco, "Uomini di Dio," 163-202, esp. 199-202.

Byzantium Confronted
by Islam

The Failure of Ecclesiastical Reconciliation

WHILE GREGORY the Great was laying the basis for a united Latin faith, conscious of its own western identity and directed to its specific needs, Justinian's successors in the East struggled to unite opposing factions within the churches. The heritage of the Fifth Council and behind it the fourth, at Chalcedon, cast a long shadow over the seventh century in all parts of Christendom. Long after 553, the Nestorian (East Syrian), Monophysite (West Syrian), and Istrian churches remained out of communion with both Constantinople and Rome. Debates were held, meetings arranged, and tracts published, often at imperial or patriarchal initiative, with a view to reconciling one or another dissident group, but none was crowned with notable success. A fixed pattern inauspiciously similar to that of the late fifth century seemed to condemn such efforts. When Zeno and Anastasios had devised formulae to reunite obdurate opponents of Chalcedon, they had achieved nothing but schism with Rome and had provoked eastern clerics to take their appeals to the see of St. Peter, a dangerous precedent.[1] This procedure, however, was to be much used during the seventh century, when individuals or whole sectors of the eastern churches who received an unsympathetic hearing in Constantinople found it expedient to seek support in the West.

Christendom remained disunited, with non-observant and non-orthodox groups looking more like a permanent feature than a temporary aberrance. The authorities in Constantinople might choose to ignore rather than accept an entire hierarchy of Severan Monophysite bishops, who commanded the loyalty of Christians in Syria, Mesopotamia, and parts of

---

[1] P. Bernakis, "Les appels au Pape dans l'église grecque jusqu'à Photius," *Echos d'Orient* 6 (1903): 30-42, 118-25, 249-57, esp. 249-51. W. H. C. Frend, "Eastern Attitudes to Rome During the Acacian Schism," *SCH* 13 (1976): 69-81, reprinted in *Town and Country in the Early Christian Centuries* (London, 1980).

Egypt.[2] In its key period of creative theology (the early sixth century), this church had established an unshakeable hold on these areas, which effectively removed them beyond the control of any other patriarch. Imperial attempts to impose its own orthodox (i.e. Duophysite) leaders generally foundered, partly no doubt because Antioch resisted the ecclesiastical pressure of Constantinople, but also because the theological differences were passionately held and vigorously defended. Anastasios of Antioch, Pope Gregory's friend, tried actively to overcome these obstacles, promoting the theory that there was only one energy in the Word (Monoenergism).[3] He believed that on this basis some factions could be reconciled. But the position was acceptable only to a few, as later Monotheletes (believers in one will) were to find. A series of debates and exchanges between Neo-Chalcedonians and leaders of various Monophysite sects, primarily the *tritheites* (who held that there were three Gods within the Trinity) achieved little.[4] Loyalty to particular wordings and local clerics produced bitter hostility. Not even greatly respected leaders like John the Faster or Domitian of Melitene could make headway. Doctrinal divisions were apparently too ingrown for changes to be more than a temporary accommodation. One hundred and fifty years of opposition to the formulations of Chalcedon could not be obliterated.

In addition, the central government faced problems of a different order, which may be illustrated by a story recorded both by the Monophysite chronicler, John of Ephesos, and by the Chalcedonian layman, Evagrios.[5] After the defeat of a revolt of Baalbek in ca. 579, certain "heathens" revealed under torture the names of high-ranking officials involved in pagan cults, including Anatolios, the governor of Edessa. As the governmental party arrived to arrest him, the feast of Zeus was being celebrated in a private house. When identified, one participant committed suicide on the spot, but Anatolios himself fled to the local bishop, "to consult him on a

---

[2] R. Devréesse, *Le patriarchat d'Antioche* (Paris, 1945); E. Honigmann, *Evêques et évêchés monophysites d'Asie mineure antérieure au VIe siècle* (Louvain, 1951); W. H. C. Frend, *The Rise of the Monophysite Movement* (Cambridge, 1972).

[3] *Chronikon Paschale*, 692; Devréesse, *Le patriarchat d'Antioche*, 98-99, 118-19.

[4] John of Ephesos, *Ecclesiastical History* 5.1-2, 8-12; P. Allen, "Neo-Chalcedonism and the Patriarchs of the Late Sixth Century," *B* 50 (1980): 5-17; J. Meyendorff, *Le Christ dans la théologie byzantine* (Paris, 1969), 113-20.

[5] John of Ephesos, *Ecclesiastical History* 3.27-34; J. Bidez and L. Parmentier, *The Ecclesiastical History of Evagrius* (London, 1898, reprinted Amsterdam 1964), 5.18, 6.7. The discrepancies in their two versions are obviously due to theological differences, and in addition Evagrios greatly admired Gregory of Antioch and served as his legal adviser, or *ekdikos*. On the date of the trial (588), which is also noted by Pope Gregory I, see P. Allen, "A New Date for the Last Recorded Events in John of Ephesus's *Historia Ecclesiastica*," *Orientalia Lovaniensia Periodica* 10 (1979): 251-55.

point of Scripture." This ruse was uncovered, and he was arrested and taken back to Antioch for questioning. Both the governor and his secretary there implicated Gregory, patriarch of Antioch, and Eulogios, representative of the patriarch of Alexandria, in human sacrifice. The deed had been held responsible for an earthquake at Daphne, outside Antioch, and popular disquiet about the matter had allegedly prevented Gregory from celebrating the liturgy during Holy Week.

Following these revelations, the whole matter was transferred to Constantinople. Evagrios here presents an entirely different chronology, placing Gregory's visit to the capital later and for reasons unconnected with Anatolios. John, however, persists in the intimate association of the two men and details the patriarch's method of perverting the course of justice. He describes how Gregory arrived laden with gifts of gold, silver, costly outfits, and other presents, which were distributed lavishly to the emperor (now Maurice), leading men of the court, and people of influence. The whole aristocracy was thus bought off and the patriarch returned to Antioch, not only exonerated, but also in possession of funds for the construction of a hippodrome for public entertainment there! Building a "church of Satan" was John of Ephesos's comment. Whether Gregory had been correctly branded as a pagan or not, his ability to sway the course of justice in the capital indicates considerable independence. Anatolios had nothing like the same power and was condemned to a most horrible death after his trial. He was accused not only of celebrating the outlawed cults of the ancient gods, but also of commissioning a portrait of Christ that actually represented Apollo. In this way he would have maintained his devotion to the old gods while appearing to venerate a Christian icon.[6]

With such unreliable representatives of imperial authority in charge of major centres like Antioch and Edessa, it is hardly surprising that Constantinople made little headway in winning over regions with a long history of separatist tendencies. Faced with such opposition, the central government began to make conformity to a stricter canon of belief and behaviour one of its prime demands. By the end of the seventh century, Justinian II would have developed the means of obtaining at least a nominal conformity from both civilian and ecclesiastical officials. But the suppression of dissent and the generation of broader theological agreement remained constant problems.

---

[6] John of Ephesos, *Ecclesiastical History* 3.29, cf. *The Ecclesiastical History of Evagrius*, 5.18 (p. 213), where the proof of Anatolios's paganism is documented by an icon of the Virgin that turned away from him as he pretended to pray to it. This is probably one of the last instances of such a subterfuge; cf. similar stories preserved by Theodore Lector, in C. Mango, *The Art of the Byzantine Empire, 312-1453* (Englewood Cliffs, N.J., 1972), 40-41.

TERRITORIAL LOSSES

The traditional theory of a universal church protected by an empire that also embraced the entire known world became increasingly unconvincing towards the end of the sixth century. In the secular sphere, particularly, the hollowness of New Rome's claims was underlined by the imperial government's failure to check non-Roman advances and conquests of border regions. The reorganised exarchate of Ravenna also failed to prevent the establishment of Lombard duchies in central Italy and the southward advance of those forces permanently settled in the Po valley, while in the Balkans, repeated Avar and Slav devastation was followed by occupation. Against these *Sklaviniai*, documented from the last two decades of the century, reinforcements sent out from the capital were initially successful, but as a never-ending stream of settlers crossed the Danube in search of fertile territory, Byzantine forces began to falter. Military pressure was exacerbated by financial problems, which made it necessary for Maurice to reduce military pay. In his earlier and highly successful campaign against the Persians, the emperor had had to face mutinies among the troops, provoked by similar difficulties. His generals had been rejected, a rival emperor was even proclaimed at one stage, but in the end (and in part due to the persuasion of Gregory of Antioch, no less) the campaign was brought to a brilliant conclusion. In the spring of 591, an "everlasting" peace between Byzantium and Persia was signed, and Chosroes II assumed the Sasanian throne as a grateful ally of the emperor.[7]

A similar solution to the Balkan troubles was not possible. Not only were the Avar-Slav invaders difficult to negotiate with, being loosely organised under individual leaders, but in addition their very disparate nature meant constant unpredictability and contradictory military thrusts. Byzantine inability to adapt to this disorganised threat was symbolic of a more general military and political weakness, which manifested itself in dissatisfaction among the fighting forces. For a decade, from about 592 on, as successful raids across the Danube were balanced or cancelled out by unexpected Slavonic inroads, this frustration accumulated. Then in the autumn of 602, faced with the prospect of another futile winter campaign north of the Danube without bread rations and regular pay, certain army

---

[7] Sébéos, *Histoire d'Héraclius*, French translation by F. Macler (Paris, 1904), chs. 2 (pp. 14-15) and 3 (pp. 22-23); M. J. Higgens, *The Persian War of the Emperor Maurice* (Washington, D.C., 1939), 42-54; John of Nikiu, *Chronicle*, ch. 96:13-15, describes how Bishop Domitian of Melitene and General Narses were deputed to accompany the young Chosroes home to Ctesiphon, attired in full regal costume and with the appropriate insignia. On the inscriptions that were erected on the Sasanian/Byzantine border to commemorate the peace, see C. Mango, "Deux études sur Byzance et la Perse sassanide," *TM* 9 (1985): 91-118, esp. 101-104.

detachments raised their commander, Phokas, on a shield.[8] By this well-established custom they thereby declared their lack of confidence in Emperor Maurice and demanded a more effective leader. Phokas assumed the title of exarch and began a triumphant march on the capital. News of the coup provoked a popular uprising in Constantinople, where the circus factions of Blues and Greens appear to have galvanised every element of opposition. Although they took their names from the colours worn by the teams that originally organised chariot racing in circuses and hippodromes throughout the Roman world, by the early seventh century the two factions of Constantinople had additional ceremonial and military duties. They attended the emperor on certain public occasions and could be deployed as a fighting force when necessary. In 602 Maurice entrusted them with the defence of the city walls, but they betrayed him.[9] The emperor also sent his eldest son, Theodosios, to the Persians to request immediate assistance and prepared for flight. But he and his family were caught and returned to Constantinople, where Phokas had been welcomed as emperor. It may have been a scuffle between Blue and Green partisans at a special ceremony, which he clearly misunderstood, that provoked the new ruler's determination to have Maurice and the imperial princes murdered. Constantina and the daughters were confined to a nunnery, and the half-barbarian army officer, Phokas, became undisputed emperor of the East.[10]

The Reign of Phokas (602-610)

His brief reign symbolises the disintegration afflicting Byzantium in the early seventh century. While his elevation followed a traditional military path to the throne, Phokas was a singularly inept choice, devoid of strategic or administrative capacities. Notable failures in both civilian government and military activity quickly reduced the confidence of even his most enthusiastic supporters, chiefly his fellow soldiers and members of the Green faction. And almost from his accession, partisans of the late emperor plotted with Constantina, utilising Chosroes's support and the threat of a Persian invasion. Popular riots in 603 and 605, a revolt in Edessa, and an alliance between Narses, the rebel commander, and the Persians, bear witness to the immediate antagonism to Phokas.[11] But the new ruler commanded enough loyalty to uncover and repress these plots. Constantina herself, tortured to name accomplices, was finally put to death together

---

[8] Theophylact Simocatta, 8.6.10, 8.7.7.

[9] Ibid. 8.8-11; *Chronikon Paschale*, 693-94; Theophanes, 288; Alan Cameron, *Circus Factions* (Oxford, 1976), 121-22.

[10] Theophylact Simocatta, 8.10.4; John of Nikiu, *Chronicle*, chs. 102-103; Alan Cameron, *Circus Factions*, 251-53.

[11] *Chronikon Paschale*, 695, 696-97, 699; Theophanes, 291-93.

with her three daughters and many senators, thus completing Phokas's slaughter of the family.[12] Numerous military officers had similarly been mutilated, killed, or forced into ecclesiastical positions. Phokas employed his brother, son-in-law, and few remaining supporters in unsuccessful campaigns against the Persians, and tried to buy off the Avars with increased tribute. But he failed to secure a greater measure of security for Thessalonike, and after 604 many Slavs were able to settle unopposed in its environs.[13]

Only in the West did Phokas maintain successful relations with both Byzantine administrators and foreign allies. And this was achieved largely by concession. To the exarchate of Ravenna he appointed Smaragdus, who had previously been removed for insanity. In the 580s this exarch had mounted a punitive raid against the Istrian schismatics, which captured the leading ecclesiastics under Severus of Grado, and forced them to accept the imperial position.[14] The return of such an official can hardly have augured well for the region, but it was accompanied by policies designed to placate. Lombard aggression, provoked by the kidnapping of King Agilulf's daughter, was assuaged by her return (603), and Roman hostility to eastern patriarchal claims to the title "oecumenical" lessened by a confirmation of papal primacy (607).[15] During Phokas's reign the most isolated Byzantine garrison at Cremona was withdrawn, and a series of truces left Agilulf free to consolidate his northern kingdom. Smaragdus commemorated the emperor by erecting his statue on a column in the Forum, but none of his policies in the West would appear to justify such an honour.[16] The emperor's authority in Rome was, however, acknowledged by Pope Boniface IV (608-615), who requested imperial permission to convert the Pantheon into a Christian church dedicated to the Virgin and all martyrs.[17] This marks the beginning of an important process of creating more Christian monuments in the predominantly pagan centre of Rome. But there is no evidence that Phokas took the initiative in it. During his reign neither the Istrian schism, nor the row over ecclesiastical titles, nor the Lombard

[12] Theophylact Simocatta, 8.15.1; Theophanes, 295.

[13] *Chronikon Paschale*, 695 (Maurice's brother-in-law, Philippikos, banished to his own monastery, other supporters of the late emperor tonsured). The surprise night attack on Thessalonike described in the *Miracula S. Demetrii* 1.12 probably occurred in 604.

[14] Paul the deacon, *HL* 3.26 (pp. 105-107); 4.28 (p. 126); J. Richards, *The Popes and the Papacy in the Early Middle Ages, 476-752* (London, 1979), 38-39.

[15] Paul the deacon, *HL* 5.28.36 (pp. 125-26); C. Wickham, *Early Medieval Italy* (London, 1981), 31.

[16] The column still stands, and the inscription recording its erection is published in *Corpus Inscriptionum Latinarum*, vol. 6, pt. 1, 251, no. 1200; see also V. von Falkenhausen, *I Bizantini in Italia* (Milan, 1982), plates 7 and 8, and Wickham, *Early Medieval Italy*, 33.

[17] *LP* 1.317.

threat was solved; rather, they all persisted and continued to dominate Byzantine problems in the West.

The Senatorial Coup Against Phokas

After six years of terror, undirected government, unchecked Persian and Slav raiding, manipulation of the church, and continuing economic decline, the Senate of Constantinople took steps to remove the emperor.[18] A secret letter was sent to Herakleios, exarch of Carthage, asking for his direct intervention. The invitation went in the name of Priskos, count of the *exkoubitors*, who had married the emperor's daughter (thus becoming the most likely successor) but now turned against him.[19] By this appeal to an elderly Armenian general, associated with the Emperor Maurice and with a period of successful anti-Persian campaigning in the East, the metropolitan aristocracy expressed its unprecedented dissatisfaction. No other military commander could assist in this coup, for Theodoros, eparch of Cappadocia and the East, the generals Narses, Germanos, and Philippikos, and many other leaders had already been killed or removed by the emperor, whose appointees governed Ravenna and the major eastern provinces.[20] It was therefore a last and slim chance, which indicates the desperation in Constantinople. Senators were prepared to run the risk of treasonable activity and certain death if discovered.

The man to whom they appealed may have been appointed to the exarchate of Africa by Maurice, possibly after the death of Gennadios, exarch until ca. 598-99. (The fact that Herakleios was not apparently known to Pope Gregory the Great, who corresponded with Gennadios and the prefect Innocent, does not provide a decisive date.) Together with his brother Gregory, Herakleios directed the joint civil and military administration of the prosperous province. The export of natural foodstuffs (grain and oil) as well as manufactured objects (pottery) testify to Africa's continuing role in the traditional sea-borne Mediterranean economy. It was certainly by withholding the annual grain fleet in 608 that Herakleios registered his agreement with the senatorial plot.[21] At that time his wife and future daughter-in-law were in fact in Constantinople, perhaps in touch with his

---

[18] G. Ostrogorsky, *History of the Byzantine State*, 3rd ed. (Oxford, 1968), 83-86, characterises the anarchy of Phokas's reign, drawing on contemporary sources that condemn the emperor, and cites the passage from the *Miracula S. Demetrii* 1.10, para. 77. More specific charges against Phokas are levelled by Theophylact Simocatta, 8.15.8-9, and John of Nikiu, *Chronicle*, chs. 104-105.

[19] Theophanes, 295-96; John of Antioch, frags. 109 and 110.

[20] *Chronikon Paschale*, 696; Theophanes, 295, 297. On the origins of Herakleios's family, see Mango, "Deux études," 114, 118 (genealogical table).

[21] *Chronikon Paschale*, 699; Theophanes, 296.

allies. Instead of participating in the plan himself, however, the exarch appointed his son, also called Herakleios, consul, thus designating him as leader of the Senate, a position traditionally held by a consul. In this way the younger Herakleios became a rival to Phokas with the highest title in the imperial hierarchy after that of ruler. In Carthage coins were struck with portraits of the two, father and son, exarch and consul.[22] Whether or not this constitutional move was actually suggested by those in the capital, it established the young Herakleios's claim and gave him a formal position, from which he could be elevated to the throne. The 610 coup was thus quite different from Phokas's; it was achieved primarily by the Senate with military cooperation, not by a forceful revolt of dissatisfied soldiers.

The exarch appreciated the problems involved in mounting a coup from such a distance and planned the approach to Constantinople carefully. First his nephew Niketas (son of Gregory) was sent with the land forces of the exarchate to occupy Tripoli and the Pentapolis (modern Libya) and then Egypt. Only when Alexandria had been taken after fierce fighting with Phokas's general Bonosos, and the Egyptian fleet brought under control (November 609), was it possible for Herakleios the consul to embark for the capital.[23] He commanded the fleets of Mauretania and Africa manned by *Mauroi*, local Berbers, and protected by the Virgin, whose icon was displayed on their mastheads.[24] Constantinople had not only been deprived of grain from Africa and Egypt after 609, but the winter of 608-609 had been unusually harsh, causing bad harvests, famine, and even freezing the sea.[25] Phokas's murders and high-handed treatment of ecclesiastics compounded with shortages of bread and food made the capital rebellious. Few stood by the emperor as Herakleios's fleet approached. At Abydos, the southernmost point of the Propontis, the consul was welcomed by customs officials and informally crowned by the metropolitan of Kyzikos before sailing on to the city. There Phokas was found defenceless and alone in one of the palace churches by two senators, who arrested him. A legendary conversation between the two emperors on board ship may preserve some echo of a personal confrontation, in which the consul accused Phokas of gross misman-

---

[22] John of Nikiu, *Chronicle*, ch. 106, suggests that Phokas had the exarch's wife brought to the capital from Cappadocia and tried to trap Fabia, who was betrothed to Herakleios the younger, in incriminating circumstances, which she adeptly avoided using her menstruation as an impeccable excuse. John of Antioch, frag. 110 confirms that the women were in the capital when Herakleios approached. G. Rösch, "Der Aufstand der Herakleioi gegen Phokas (608-10) im Spiegel numismatischer Quellen," *JÖB* 28 (1979): 52-62.

[23] John of Nikiu, *Chronicle*, chs. 107.12-13, 20; 108.1-12; 109.17. Nikephoros, 3-4; Theophanes, 298.

[24] Theophanes, 298.

[25] Ibid., 297.

agement, and the latter replied, "You do better!"[26] But Herakleios met no organised opposition and was soon raised from the position of consul to emperor, crowned by Patriarch Sergios and acclaimed by the Senate, factions, and people in St. Sophia. After this traditional Byzantine accession, he was also reunited with Fabia/Eudokia, his fiancée, who was crowned empress immediately after their marriage.[27] One treasury official was killed with Phokas and burned in the bronze ox at the Forum Tauri, traditionally used for the cremation of tyrants and criminals. Phokas's brother, Domentziolos, and General Bonosos also died, while symbols of the Blues and the exarch of the city were burned in the Hippodrome with a portrait or statue (*eikôn*) of the deceased emperor. Phokas had adopted the habit of having his image paraded in the Hippodrome for people to make their obeisance.[28]

Problems Facing Herakleios

The coup was thus completely successful. But from the provinces, opposition flared up. A general identified as another brother of Phokas marched his loyal troops towards Constantinople and was only checked by an Armenian assassin.[29] In Italy John Lemigios replaced Smaragdus as exarch but was unable to prevent a revolt against new taxes. Herakleios's new exarch, Eleutherios, was initially more successful. Only a few years later, however, the same official rebelled (619) and was in turn killed by the Roman militia.[30] While the African exarchate, now governed by the new emperor's uncle, Gregory, remained calm and proud of their own consul's success, Ravenna displayed a tendency to independence, which increased throughout the seventh century. In conflicts with both Constantinople and with Rome, its metropolitans and local nobility attempted to win more autonomy.[31] The same hostility to Byzantine control was manifested by certain sectors of the eastern population, who welcomed the Persians into their cities. Economic pressures and differences of belief may account for some of this opposition. But in addition, traditional imperial administration, civil,

---

[26] John of Antioch, frag. 110; *Chronikon Paschale*, 700, for the arrest also reported by Nikephoros, 4; cf. Theophanes, 298-99.

[27] *Chronikon Paschale*, 701; Theophanes, 299.

[28] *Chronikon Paschale*, 701; John of Nikiu, *Chronicle*, ch. 107; Nikephoros, 5.

[29] W. E. Kaegi, Jr., "New Evidence on the Early Reign of Heraclius," *BZ* 66 (1973): 308-330. The evidence comes from the *Life* of Theodore of Sykeon (ed. A. M. J. Festugière [Brussels, 1970], Subsidia Hagiographica 48).

[30] *LP* 1.319, 321; cf. P. Classen, "Der erste Römerzug in der Weltgeschichte: Zur Geschichte im Kaisertums im Westen und der Kaiserkrönung in Rom zwischen Theodosios der Grosse und Karl der Grosse," in *Historische Forschungen für W. Schlesinger* (Cologne, 1975), 325-47.

[31] Theophanes, 301, on the strength of Carthage's fortifications; T. S. Brown, *Gentlemen and Officers* (London, 1984), 159-63.

military, and ecclesiastical, was clearly failing to sustain the loyalties of many groups and sects. Naturally, external enemies determined to take advantage of the situation.

Coming from Carthage and with a tradition of military leadership in his Armenian family, Herakleios represented the provincial aristocracy rather than the senatorial leaders of the capital, who had promoted him. He appears to have accepted a greater degree of guidance from the Senate than was usual, as well as its participation in government, perhaps in order to share responsibility for the weakened state of which he now had charge.[32] The contrast between Africa and the East must have been striking. In Constantinople there was hunger, inadequate funds to finance the court and administration, and a lack of regular troops. On 20 April 611, a great earthquake shook the city, a terrifying event that had to be mitigated by special litanies and prayers.[33] In Asia Minor the Persians were capturing major cities like Caesarea while the Avars devastated Europe. Herakleios, then about 35 years old, had no previous experience of central government; his chief allies were his cousin, Niketas, who arrived from Egypt after the coronation, and his brother Theodore, both young men from Africa like himself. Hardly a single competent general was available to assist him, so he probably needed senatorial advice and help. At this time the Constantinopolitan Senate probably included representatives of the provincial aristocracy who sought refuge in the capital from rural disorders. Priskos, who had issued the original suggestion to Herakleios, might have been a most useful ally. But the emperor distrusted his designs on the throne and sent him off to recapture Caesarea.[34] Patriarch Sergios, on the other hand, put his authority behind Herakleios, and it was to prove very important. One of the emperor's first legal acts concerned the clergy attached to the Great Church (of St. Sophia, Holy Wisdom); their numbers and ranks were clearly established.[35]

The Alliance Between Church and State

The scale of problems facing the new emperor may perhaps be gauged by the fact that during the first decade of his reign he contemplated moving

[32] A. Pernice, L'imperatore Eraclio (Florence, 1905), 25; I. Shahid, "The Iranian Factor in Byzantium During the Reign of Heraclius," DOP 26 (1972): 308-312; H.-G. Beck, Senat und Volk von Konstantinopel: Probleme der byzantinischen Verfassungsgeschichte, Sitzungsberichte der Bay. Akad. der Wissenschaften, Phil-hist. Kl. 6 (1966), esp. 56-60; Rösch, "Der Aufstand."

[33] Chronikon Paschale, 702.

[34] Nikephoros identifies Priskos as Krispos (Crispus, like the son of Constantine I), but correctly reports his imperial aspirations, 5-6.

[35] Zachariae von Lingenthal, Jus graeco-romanum, vol. 3 (Leipzig, 1857), 35-37.

his capital to Carthage, a plan vigorously opposed by the metropolitan population and the patriarch.[36] Sergios's argument against leaving Constantinople may have been supported by the promise of ecclesiastical assistance for the depleted financial resources of the empire. Although no agreement is recorded officially, every known action of the patriarch appears to confirm this decision to help Herakleios in his daunting tasks.[37] The alliance appears to have been based on a close friendship, which was tested by a disaster in the emperor's family. In August 612 Empress Fabia-Eudokia died and was buried in the imperial mausoleum at the Holy Apostles. For the court ceremonies to be continued, the little princess Epiphaneia (then aged 15 months) was crowned empress, but the emperor quickly sought another bride.[38] Unfortunately, his choice of Martina, his own niece, provoked popular protest at a marriage deemed incestuous and declared uncanonical by Sergios. However, once it became evident that Herakleios could not be moved, despite his recognition of the prohibited degree of consanguinity, the patriarch decided to make the best of the situation and stood by the emperor. He duly blessed the couple, crowned Martina as empress, and baptised their son, Constantine, born one year later.[39]

Another element in the new alliance was welded in 619, when the Avars raided the suburbs of Constantinople, causing great terror and panic among the local population. Sergios agreed to a loan of church plate to provide silver for a new coin, struck to buy a peace treaty with the Chagan.[40] At this time supplies of other metals, even bronze in the form of antique statues, were collected and melted down to be minted as coin. But normally the gold and silver in church liturgical vessels was only sold to ransom Christian prisoners, and Sergios's innovation clearly represented an unusual measure of support for secular matters. It was probably during the same Avar threat that the patriarch arranged for the precious relic of the Virgin's robe, which was kept at Blachernai outside the city walls, to be transferred to St. Sophia for safe-keeping.[41] Once peace returned, Sergios

[36] Nikephoros, 12.

[37] J. L. van Dieten, *Geschichte der griechischen Patriarchen von Konstantinopel* (Amsterdam, 1972), 5-10; F. Winkelmann, "Kirche und Gesellschaft in Byzanz vom Ende des 6. bis zum Beginn des 8. Jahrhunderts," *Klio* 59 (1977): 477-89, outlines the background of closer relations; cf. his study. *Die östlichen Kirchen in der Epoche der christologischen Auseinandersetzungen* (Berlin, 1980), 131-35, 137-38.

[38] *Chronikon Paschale*, 703; Theophanes, 300.

[39] Nikephoros, 14-15; Theophanes, 300-301. For an explanation of the emperor's motivation, see Mango, "Deux études," 114.

[40] *Chronikon Paschale*, 706; Theophanes, 301-303; Nikephoros, 13-14, 15.

[41] On the date, see Averil Cameron, "The Virgin's Robe: An Episode in the History of Early Seventh Century Constantinople," *B* 49 (1979): 2-56, esp. 43.

had the church at Blachernai restored and devised a ceremony involving the emperor, as his "assistant," the clergy, and the entire population of Constantinople in the relic's return.[42] First it was transferred to the church of St. Lawrence, where an all-night vigil was held. Then, on the appointed day, a procession set out carrying the precious casket to Blachernai, where its seals were broken and the relic itself displayed, "completely intact, whole and indestructible," although the imperial purple silk in which it was wrapped had perished. Once it had been reinstalled in the shrine, a service was held and a new festival decreed to commemorate the event, which confirmed popular conviction that the Virgin ensured the city's defence. The episode prefigured the highly successful mobilisations that Sergios would organise later, which constituted a significant part of the new alliance between church and state.

The patriarch also revealed his support for the emperor in a practical fashion when the traditional free distributions of bread had to be abandoned, a highly unpopular measure.[43] After the loss of Egypt in 619, the price of a loaf was set at three *folleis* (bronze coins). When the official in charge of the new system, John (nicknamed "the Earthquake") tried to more than double the price to eight *folleis*, a crowd of protesters, led by some of the palace guards (*scholai*), advanced to St. Sophia in riotous ill-humour. Sergios got to the bottom of the problem quickly; he ordered the city prefect to arrest John and take over bread distribution at the old price, thus preventing a serious popular revolt.[44]

THE PERSIAN MILITARY CHALLENGE: THE CAPTURE OF JERUSALEM

While the Avaro-Slav menace to the European provinces of the empire preoccupied the emperor during the first decade of his reign—indeed, it nearly resulted in his death at Herakleia[45]—this period was marked by an

---

[42] This ceremony forms an addition to the accounts of the fifth-century discovery of the robe and its installation in Constantinople, and is clearly written by a contemporary, see C. Loparev, "Staroe svidiatelstvo o Polozhenii ruzibogopoditsi vo Vlachernach v novom istolkovanii," *VV* 2 (1895): 592-612. An English translation of this document may be found in Cameron, "The Virgin's Robe."

[43] *Chronikon Paschale*, 715-16 (possibly entered incorrectly under the year 626; on the alternative date, see K. Ericsson, "Revising a Date in the Chronicon Paschale," *JÖBG* 17 [1968]: 17-28, esp. 19-20).

[44] As note 43 above; cf. van Dieten, *Geschichte der Patriarchen*, 7.

[45] *Chronikon Paschale*, 712; Nikephoros, 12-13; Theophanes, 301-302. The Avars tricked Herakleios into attending a meeting without sufficient military protection. On the date, see N. Baynes, "The Date of the Avar Surprise," *BZ* 21 (1912): 110-28, though Averil Cameron argues convincingly for 619 (rather than 617), "The Virgin's Robe," 43 n.7.

even more dangerous Persian assault. Chosroes II, to whom Maurice had appealed in 602, continued to use this as a pretext for expansion into imperial territory in the East. Neither Phokas nor Herakleios were able to check these advances, which resulted in a severe defeat for the new emperor in 613 and the loss of Antioch. In the following year, a two-pronged attack against Syria and Armenia routed imperial defences; Damascus and then Jerusalem fell, with the catastrophic destruction of Christian monuments and the removal of the True Cross from its shrine in the church of the Holy Sepulchre. An eyewitness account by Strategikos, a monk of the Mar Sabas monastery, describes the slaughter, looting, and burning and the patriarch's efforts to console and strengthen those who remained alive and faced exile in their captors' homeland:[46] "When the holy Zacharias saw the congregation of people in this lamentation . . . he said to them, 'Blessed is the Lord, who makes this chastisement to come upon us. . . . Do not lament, my children, because of this captivity, for even I, the sinner Zacharias, your father, am with you in captivity. . . . Behold we have His cross in our protection and He, who is exalted over us is with us, the True Father who inhabits the heavens. . . . And now, lift up your voice and call upon the Lord and do not cease from prayer, that he may save us from the hands of your enemies. . . .' As the Persians began to drive them away from the Mount of Olives, where this sermon was given, Zacharias bade farewell to Jerusalem: 'Peace to you, Sion, bride of Christ, peace to you, Jerusalem, holy city; peace to you, Holy Anastasis, illuminated by the Lord . . . this is the last peace and my final greeting to you; may I have hope and length of days that I may eventually gain your vision again?' "[47] Then the column of prisoners moved off, 35,000 according to the Armenian bishop Sebeos, leaving behind many thousands of dead. Sebeos says 57,000; Strategikos, relying on Thomas, one of the unfortunate survivors who had to bury the bodies, claims 66,509, and gives a detailed breakdown of the figures by location.[48] To contemporaries, the capture of the holy places by the pagan Zoroastrians was an unparalleled disaster. For the Persians, however, Jerusalem constituted the base from which Egypt could be conquered, and from 619 the entire province passed under Persian rule for almost a decade. Imperial resistance was not effective, and Chosroes repeatedly spurned the embassies sent by Herakleios to negotiate a peace settlement. Nor was Asia Minor spared, for it was during the long campaign of 613-19 that many of

---

[46] *Chronikon Paschale*, 704-705; Theophanes, 300-301; G. Garitte, ed., *La Prise de Jérusalem par les Perses en 614*, 2 vols. (Louvain, 1960) (Georgian text and Latin translation).

[47] Garitte, *La Prise de Jérusalem*, chs. 13 and 14, 2:22, 30.

[48] Ibid., ch. 23, 2:50-54, cf. the partial English translation by F. C. Conybeare, "Antiochus Strategicus' Account of the Sack of Jerusalem in A.D. 614," *EHR* 25 (1910): 515-16; Sébéos, ch. 24 (pp. 68-69).

the oldest urban centres were overrun. The classical way of life was brought to an abrupt end; survivors took refuge in citadels and new mountain settlements more like fortified villages than ancient cities.

Faced with destruction on this scale, and with the appearance of the Persians as far west as the Bosphoros on more than one occasion,[49] Herakleios set about reorganising and training Byzantine military forces. Among the professional troops, the *exkoubitors* represented a capable regiment, but it was commanded by Priskos, whom Herakleios had reason to distrust as Phokas's son-in-law.[50] After the debâcle at Caesarea, when the Persians broke through the Byzantine siege and made good their retreat after a 12-month occupation, Priskos was summoned to stand trial before the Senate of Constantinople. The emperor stripped him of his wealth and titles and forced him to enter a monastery. His personal retainers, however, were enrolled as soldiers of the state, *oikeiakous tes basileias*, and issued with the traditional army rations of grain, though bread was in short supply.[51] At the same time Herakleios appointed his cousin Niketas to lead the *exkoubitors* and placed other supporters in key military positions: Philippikos, one of his father's associates and Maurice's brother-in-law, was brought out of a monastery to assume the title of count, and Theodore, the emperor's brother, was named *kouropalates*, the highest imperial position, and sent to replace Priskos.[52] The chief reform of Byzantine forces, however, concerned the regrouping of palatine soldiers as a fighting force called the Opsikion. It seems to have been effective by 615, when a count of Opsikion is recorded in the position previously held by the count of the domestics (*comes domesticorum*). The Opsikion troops probably accompanied the emperor on his military campaigns in the East and formed the nucleus of a new regiment later based in Bithynia, the westernmost point of Asia Minor, opposite Constantinople.[53]

By making military recovery his priority, Herakleios intensified those currents tending towards an increasing militarisation of the empire. All exploitable institutions and resources were used, even when their subjection to military ends produced economic hardship and popular opposition. The lengths to which the emperor was prepared to go may be illustrated by the

[49] *Chronikon Paschale*, 706 (ca. 616); Nikephoros, 9, 11, 15 (ca. 622).

[50] On the *exkoubitors*, see J. F. Haldon, *Byzantine Praetorians* (Bonn, 1984), 136-39, 161-62.

[51] *Chronikon Paschale*, 703 (Priskos's soldiers may be identified as the troop of *boukellarioi* [from the Latin *bucellarii*] who served as his private guard; see John of Antioch, frag. 110, and Haldon, *Byzantine Praetorians*, 101-102); Nikephoros, 6-7, records the trial in greater detail.

[52] *Chronikon Paschale*, 703; Nikephoros, 7.

[53] Haldon, *Byzantine Praetorians*, 144-45, 174-82.

decision to abolish free distributions of bread (*politikos artos*). After attempts to raise the price, the new principle was imposed, not without trouble. But at the same time, grain was sent to Thessalonike under siege (617-19).[54] To bring an end to the Avar threat to the Balkans, a truce was purchased in the new silver coin struck from church treasures. The same coin was also forced onto the administration, even though it represented an effective salary cut of 50%.[55] The other metals melted down for coinage went to finance the treasury of the *exkoubitors*, who were responsible for recruitment, and to the pay packets of new recruits.[56] In thus putting Byzantine society on a war footing, Herakleios secured a more centralised mobilisation of the entire population during the 620s. He also prepared for the offensive against Persia by studying military manuals and strategy, for like Maurice, Herakleios was determined to lead his own forces into battle.[57]

Although this personal involvement of the emperor was deplored by some members of the Senate, there can be no doubt that it was Herakleios's leadership that guaranteed a greater measure of success than could have been anticipated in 622 when he left the capital. After the peace treaty with the Avars (620), he had transferred what remained of the imperial troops in Europe to Asia, despite evident Slavonic activity. New recruits had been enrolled in the lists, armed, trained, instructed as to their Christian role, and prepared for serious action. But to the contemporary poet, George of Pisidia, it was the emperor's piety and faith that proved decisive in the defeat of the pagan Chosroes.[58] Carrying icons of Christ and the Virgin, a mark of Byzantine belief and a guarantee of holy protection, the troops advanced into Asia Minor, where they trained for several months under their

[54] *Chronikon Paschale*, 711, 715-16; *Miracula S. Demetrii* 2.4, describes Herakleios's efforts to make sure that the city would survive the siege. Although no troops could be spared, the granaries inside the city were filled, and the population could have withstood the attack had not certain merchants sold grain to trading ships at almost double the normal price. Further supplies had to be sent from Constantinople to relieve the famine that broke out the following summer. The Slavs finally withdrew.

[55] *Chronikon Paschale*, 706; cf. M. F. Hendy, *Studies in the Byzantine Monetary Economy c. 300-1450* (Cambridge, 1985), 625-26 n.307.

[56] *Parastaseis syntomoi chronikai*, para. 42; W. E. Kaegi, Jr., "Two Studies in the Continuity of Late Roman and Byzantine Military Institutions," *BF* 8 (1982): 87-113; cf. Haldon, *Byzantine Praetorians*, 436 n.341, 439 n.344.

[57] The emperor's military exploits are recorded by a contemporary, George of Pisidia, in epic verses edited by A. Pertusi, *Giorgio di Pisidia, Poemi I: Panegirici Epici* (Ettal, 1959). Although accuracy may give way to rhetoric due to the purpose and form of these writings, they constitute an invaluable record. For Herakleios's preparations and personal leadership, see George of Pisidia, *Heraclias*, 2.83.118-43; idem, *Expeditio persica* 1.112-31; cf. Theophanes, 303.

[58] George of Pisidia, *Expeditio persica* 1.104-29, 139-44; Theophanes, 302; cf. Haldon, *Byzantine Praetorians*, 169-73.

supreme commander. Thus strengthened, they then marched east, deep into Armenia, achieving a notable victory in the winter of 622-23.[59] For the next five years Herakleios remained in the East, even during the 626 Persian campaign, which advanced nearly to the walls of his capital. The decisive victory finally occurred late in 627, when Byzantine forces met Persian near the ancient city of Nineveh: the Zoroastrians suffered a total defeat. Early in 628, Chosroes was forced to flee from Dastagerd deep inside his empire.[60] The humiliation provoked a coup in which he was killed and his son proclaimed ruler. Through the peace that followed immediately, Herakleios regained all the disputed eastern territory occupied during the previous 15 years. The Persian challenge was finally and decisively answered, but in the same process, both Iran and Byzantium were left weakened and ill-prepared to meet further external threats.[61]

The Siege of 626

Prior to his departure from Constantinople at Easter 622, the emperor had made arrangements to secure its safety. These reflect the alliance between church and state and the degree to which Herakleios respected Sergios's advice. For the emperor entrusted his young son to the care of the patriarch and a general, Bonos, who were to form a council of regency in his absence.[62] He also relied on Sergios to plan the ceremonies that preceded the army's departure: sermons emphasising the crusading mission against the fire-worshipping Persians and the most holy task of returning the Cross to Jerusalem, and blessings on the soldiers who marched behind an icon of Christ "not made by human hands."[63] This trust was not misplaced. When the regents were faced by major problems during the emperor's long campaign in the East, they did not falter.

In 625-26 a large force of Avars and Slavs, led by the Avar Chagan in person, advanced through Thrace towards the capital, while a Persian army approached Chalcedon, the Asiatic city on the Bosphoros opposite Con-

---

[59] George of Pisidia, *Heraclias* 2.12-18 (on the icon of the Virgin); idem, *Expeditio persica* 1.139-53. On the first stage, see N. Oikonomides, "A Chronological Note on the First Persian Campaign of Heraclius," *BMGS* 1 (1975): 1-9. Theophanes, 306-327, gives a detailed account of the campaign; cf. Nikephoros, 19-22.

[60] The victory is described in the emperor's letters to Constantinople, which were read out from the ambo of St. Sophia; see *Chronikon Paschale*, 727-34.

[61] As both the *Chronikon* and George of Pisidia conclude their praise of Herakleios with this defeat of the Persians, and the last decade of his reign is very poorly documented, the degree of exhaustion suffered in both states can best be indicated by their complete failure to withstand Arab attacks in the 630s and 640s, as discussed below.

[62] George of Pisidia, *In Bonum patricium*, in Pertusi, *Giorgio di Pisidia*, 163-70; *Chronikon Paschale*, 718, 720, 726, 726-27; Nikephoros, 15; Theophanes, 303.

[63] George of Pisidia, *Expeditio persica* 1.139-44; cf. Theophanes, 303.

stantinople.[64] The threat of a combined and coordinated siege became clear after the failure of several diplomatic initiatives; this time the enemy was confident of victory. With the Slavs poised to ferry the Persians to the European side of the Bosphoros, the city was in a precarious state. Patriarch Sergios nonetheless addressed the besiegers with confidence: "Oh strange peoples and daimonic hoards, you have undertaken this whole war against these [places] of ours. But the Lady Theotokos will put an end to your presumption and arrogance by her single command. For she is truly the mother of Him who immersed the Pharaoh and all his army in the middle of the Red Sea, and who will prove this daimonic hoard listless and feeble."[65] He took a major part in the defence, organising processions of icons of Christ and the Virgin, which were carried round the walls accompanied by the city population, now increased by large numbers of refugees.[66] They chanted hymns and prayers for divine intervention, while General Bonos led military sorties and planned the naval attack that destroyed the Slav ships (*monoxyles*, single-trunk canoes).[67] This energetic mobilisation of the ordinary people undoubtedly contributed to the city's success in withstanding a brief but terrifying siege, when the emperor was hundreds of miles away in Armenia. After eleven days, the Avaro-Slav forces retired; their failure to capture the Queen City provoked a crisis within the alliance and eventually the collapse of the Danubian Empire of the Avars. The Persians remained encamped on the Bosphoros, within sight of their objective but unable to cross over to it, until the winter of 626-27.[68]

In the folklore of Constantinople, this double victory held a very special place: according to a contemporary source, the Virgin herself had been seen fighting from the walls beside the defenders, a belief that increased common faith in her protective powers.[69] This faith in the Virgin was enhanced

[64] The eyewitness account of the siege, by Theodoros, *synkellos* of the church of St. Sophia, was published by L. Sternbach, *Analecta Avarica*, in *Dissertationum philologicarum Academiae Litterarum Cracoviensis*, ser. 2, no. 15 (Krakow, 1900): 298-320. The Greek text is reprinted (with a French translation) by F. Makk, in S. Szádeczky-Kardoss, *Acta Antiqua et Archaeologica 19* (Szeged, 1975). Cf. *Chronikon Paschale*, 716-26; Nikephoros, 17-19; Theophanes, 315-16; F. Barišić, "Le siège de Constantinople par les Avares et les Slaves en 626," *B* 24 (1954): 371-95; P. Speck et al., *Zufälliges zum Bellum Avaricum* (Munich, 1980).

[65] Sternbach, *Analecta Avarica*, 304.9-13.

[66] Van Dieten, *Geschichte der Patriarchen*, 12-13, and Exkurs I, 174-78.

[67] Sternbach, *Analecta Avarica*, 303-304, 307-308 (monoxyles); van Dieten, *Geschichte der Patriarchen*, 13-17.

[68] George of Pisidia confirmed that the Slavs turned against the Avars, see Barišić, "Le siège de Constantinople," 395; cf. 392, for the view that it was the Avaro-Slav lack of food that provoked their failure. On the Nestorian sources, which attribute the Persians' inactivity to the treachery of their leader, who allied with Herakleios, see Mango, "Deux études," 107-109.

[69] Sternbach, *Analecta Avarica, passim*; Averil Cameron, "The Cult of the Theotokos in

by the introduction of her four feasts into the calendar of the Constantino-politan church. Sergios certainly took the initiative in encouraging the cult, which confirmed popular belief in the "God-guarded" character of Constantinople. He also introduced a separate feast for the elevation of the True Cross when Herakleios returned it in triumph from the East. In addition, during the emperor's absence, two new liturgies were adopted, probably to mark victories in the East. In 624, Sergios's new hymn for the celebration of the Eucharist was first sung, and two years later a new liturgy of the Presanctified, a rite for Lent, which later spread to other seasons.[70] In this way the patriarch not only contributed to the belief that Constantinople was destined to withstand attack because divine powers had ordained that it should remain a Christian bulwark against non-believers; he also composed new rituals that marked the Constantinopolitan church off from others, reinforcing the sense of its historic role.

The patriarch's personal contribution to the city's defence was highlighted when General Bonos died (in May 627) and Sergios remained sole regent and effective head of government. His success in this civilian role conformed to the emperor's high expectations. It was thus as the hero of the siege that Sergios accompanied young Herakleios-Constantine to welcome his father home in 628. The victorious emperor entered his capital in triumph and celebrated the Christian empire's supremacy over its pagan enemies with the patriarch beside him. Herakleios later returned the True Cross to Jerusalem, a symbol both of God's favour to devout believers and of restored Byzantine authority in the East Mediterranean world.[71]

Herakleios's Innovations

While George of Pisidia may have been confident in the emperor alone, twentieth-century historians must ask how such a remarkable reversal of Byzantine fortunes was realised. In particular, what meaning should be given to the terms *nea strateia* ("new army") and *tas ton thematon choras* ("the lands of the themes"), descriptions that occur for the first time in the *Chronographia* of Theophanes in the years 622-23 and have occasioned

---

Sixth-Century Constantinople," *JTS*, n.s., 29 (1978): 79-108; Averil Cameron and Judith Herrin, eds., *Constantinople in the Early Eighth Century: The Parastaseis Syntomoi Chronikai* (Leiden, 1984), 36, on the importance of the Virgin in the Christian history of the city.

[70] Van Dieten, *Geschichte der Patriarchen*, 12; *Chronikon Paschale*, 705-706, 714.

[71] George of Pisidia, *In restitutionem S. Crucis*, in Pertusi, *Giorgio di Pisidia*, 225-30; Sébéos, *Histoire d'Héraclius*, ch. 29 (pp. 90-91); Garitte, *La Prise de Jérusalem*, ch. 24, 2:54-55; Nikephoros, 22-23; Theophanes, 327-28. V. Grumel, "La réposition de la Vraie Croix à Jérusalem par Heraclius," *BF* 1 (1966): 139-49; cf. Mango, "Deux études," 112-13.

much commentary.[72] Do they indicate some major reform undertaken by the emperor prior to his departure on the Persian campaign?

Although the precise meaning to be attached to *strateia* is disputed, in this context it seems reasonable to identify this new army with the body of recruits enrolled by the emperor's officers and *exkoubitors* at this time.[73] The evidence of temporary provincial mints, coupled with the imperial decision to increase funds by a variety of measures (as mentioned above), confirms the importance of this recruiting drive and indicates one area in which Herakleios's reorganisation had lasting effects, namely currency reform. By making additional money available, a large number of new soldiers could be enlisted. But this inexperienced force must have been stiffened by mercenaries hired for the campaign, such as the Lombards who participated. In addition, the regular troops (*stratopeda*) attached to the armies of the Orient, Armenia, Thrace, and the Obsequium also took part. This motley collection of troops was trained by the emperor personally prior to the departure from central Asia Minor. While it proved quickly successful, the key role in defeating the Persians may have been played by Herakleios's foreign allies, the Khazars. The new army, assembled before the campaign, is never again referred to as a separate unit and presumably dispersed on its return to Byzantium in 628.[74]

As far as the term *thema* is concerned, an even greater obscurity sur-

---

[72] Theophanes, 303. N. Oikonomidès, "Les premières mentions des thèmes dans la chronique de Théophane," *ZRVI* 16 (1975): 1-8, uses these references to support the idea of a major Herakleian reform, an interpretation championed by Ostrogorsky, *History of the Byzantine State*, 95-101. But recently the problems of this text have led to highly critical interpretations and even to a determination to avoid using it; see, for example, R.-J. Lilie, "Die Zweihundertjährige Reform: Zu den Anfängen der Themenorganisation im 7. und 8. Jahrhundert," *BS* 45 (1984): 27-39, 190-201, with references to the vast bibliography on this subject.

[73] J. F. Haldon, *Recruitment and Conscription in the Byzantine Army c. 550-950: A Study on the Origins of the Stratiotika Ktemata*, Sitzungsberichte der Bayerischen Akademie 357 (Vienna, 1979), 35-38, but cf. the review by R.-J. Lilie, *BS* 41 (1980): 241-47. It is curious that Theophanes uses exactly the same formulation, *nea strateia*, of the troops enrolled by Chosroes II of Persia in the penultimate year of the war; Theophanes, 315. If this Persian force was new (i.e. genuinely different from older armies), as is sometimes claimed, then it would seem that Theophanes meant to designate Herakleios's new army in the same way; see J. Karayannopoulos, *Die Entstehung der byzantinischen Themenordnung* (Munich, 1959), 52-54. But possibly these passages in the *Chronographia* imply that both sides were desperately trying to enlist additional forces. The formation of an elite professional force is a lengthy business.

[74] Theophanes, 328, records that in Jerusalem in 630 or 631 the emperor "and his army" were welcomed by the patriarch. It probably included the Opsikion forces, who were most likely to accompany such a ceremonial journey; see Haldon, *Byzantine Praetorians* 175-76, and 169-73 on the forces reorganised for the 622 campaign. I am especially grateful for the author's help on this subject.

rounds its origin and meaning.[75] Later in the seventh century, the *themata* (plural) are known as administrative units in Asia Minor, designed to centralise large areas under military command, somewhat in the manner of the western exarchates. The development from "the lands of the themes" to these well-documented "provinces" endowed with their own fighting forces is what causes such problems, although nearly every aspect of the history of *themata* is difficult. One area of agreement concerns the origin of the forces attached to the four original *themata* of Asia Minor, the Anatolikon, Armeniakon, Thrakesion, and Opsikion: this origin is to be sought in the four chief armies of Late Roman times (of the Orient, Armenia, Thrace, and the Obsequium).[76] But was Herakleios responsible for their transformation into military contingents settled in specific regions to which they gave their names? In particular, could such a reorganisation have been undertaken before 622 and did it contribute to the success of the campaign? The paucity of sources and unreliability of the *Chronographia* of Theophanes make it extremely unlikely that a definitive answer can be given. But the absence of references either to the very considerable upheaval in traditional provincial organisation, which would have been entailed, or to the existence of such new organs prior to the reign of Constans II, make a Herakleian reform appear inherently improbable. After the campaign of 622-28, Byzantine forces proved singularly ineffectual, and no troops identified as those of *themata* appear active. But Herakleios did undertake a reform of the Obsequium force, which he later settled in northwestern Asia Minor, a region known as the *thema* of Opsikion, in about 640.[77] This move may well have provided the model for the dispersal of other units in different areas: the remaining forces of the Orient in that area later known as Anatolikon; those of Armenia in the Armeniakon; and those from Thrace in what became the Thrakesion. Whether such a supposition can support a theory that claims a Herakleian origin for the *themata* is another matter. To those prone to cite the tenth-century Emperor Constantine VII on the subject, it is worth pointing out that Constantine says that Herakleios *and his successors* were responsible for the new system.[78] With this broad statement of a gradual development throughout the seventh century most historians would agree.

[75] Karayannopoulos, *Die Entstehung*, 89-97; cf., most recently, J. Howard-Johnston, "Thema," in A. Moffatt, ed., *Maistor: Classical, Byzantine and Renaissance Studies for Robert Browning* (Canberra, 1984), 189-97.

[76] Lilie, "Die Zweihundertjährige Reform," 36-39; Hendy, *The Byzantine Monetary Economy*, 621-23; Haldon, *Byzantine Praetorians*, 165-66.

[77] Haldon, *Byzantine Praetorians*, 174-78, 179-80.

[78] Constantine Porphyrogenitus, *De thematibus*, ed. A. Pertusi (Vatican City, 1952), Preface, 20; 1.48; 2.3.

Herakleios, however, was the emperor who defeated the Zoroastrian fire-worshippers, regained the True Cross, and returned it to Jerusalem. His example of military leadership, personal training, and involvement was to prove an important one for later Byzantine rulers. And behind this informed direction of the defence of the empire lies the emperor's subordination of all imperial resources to military purposes. The variety of means used to increase monetary supplies, the centralisation of economic control, and the use of provincial mints to facilitate recruitment and pay, all reflect Herakleios's innovation in the issue of coinage. Currency reform may have been the factor on which all other changes turned.[79]

THE EFFECTS OF THE PERSIAN INVASION

Despite the final victory in 628, when the Byzantine forces marched back to Constantinople they traversed areas of the empire that had been permanently and severely affected by the Persian campaign of 613-19. In particular, the spacious classical cities of antiquity had been destroyed and abandoned, marking a complete change in living patterns. The same process had taken place in the European provinces, producing new settlements such as Monemvasia (so called because it had only one entrance in a defensive wall atop a near-island site off the southeast tip of the Peloponnese).[80] Other communities fled from their cities to islands. According to the *Chronicle of Monemvasia*, the bishop of Patras arranged for his flock to sail to safety in Sicily, where they remained for over 200 years. Only in the early ninth century did they return to Greece.[81] While urban communities sometimes managed to preserve a certain cohesion, even as refugees, many fled in disorder. Everywhere life was ruralised, localised, and restricted. Provincial nobles and wealthy landowners may have sought refuge behind the walls of their fortified villas; those with houses in the capital maintained their aristocratic ways and added to the permanent membership of the Senate. In the confusion that afflicted the countryside, tied serfs and slaves probably tried to break free from their owners' estates, to become independent in new village or castle communities, where they could occupy and farm their own lands. The disruption of large-scale estate cultivation and regular agricultural activity, plus the lack of contact between different regions, gradually reduced the economy to a subsistence one. In

[79] M. F. Hendy, "On the Administrative Basis of the Byzantine Coinage, c. 400-c. 900, and the Reforms of Heraclius," *University of Birmingham Historical Journal* 12 (2) (1970): 129-54; idem, *The Byzantine Monetary Economy*, 625, 643.

[80] P. Schreiner, "La fondation de Monemvasie en 582/3," *TM* 4 (1970): 471-76.

[81] P. Lemerle, "La Chronique improprement dite de Monemvasie: le contexte historique et légendaire," *REB* 21 (1963): 5-49.

place of organised exchange through markets with imported goods available for sale, self-sufficiency became close to the norm—in manufactured goods as well as foodstuffs.

Even in a reduced state, some cities continued to exist. Thessalonike resisted repeated sieges under the energetic leadership of its bishops, supposedly aided by the protection of its patron saint, Demetrios. The ruling people (*kratountes*) there may have been merchants involved in the grain trade of the city.[82] Similarly, Athens, Corinth, Pergamon, Sardis, Ephesos, and others remained urban centres, though confined to their citadel walls and very much reduced in regular population. The sharp decline in coin finds at Asian sites from 617-18 reflects a suspension of normal economic activity and the beginning of their slow transformation into fortified medieval towns.[83] Thus they became very different centres, organised as garrisons and provincial capitals for the protection of the surrounding villages; the bases of *thema* administration under the control of a central government rather than autonomous urban organs of a world united by international trade.

Byzantine Adaptation

In urban terms, only Constantinople retained its ancient character as a metropolitan centre with its fora, arcades, public buildings, and statues. Similarly, the imperial court became the sole source of patronage, and the patriarchate developed into the most important religious centre in the East. Both adapted their ritual with new ceremonies and liturgies that emphasised their uniqueness.[84] Even the circus factions (Greens and Blues) were gradually tamed by these changes to become more of an ornament of the court and its appearances in public. Their independent power was not entirely curbed, however, and would still play a significant role in political and military affairs in the eighth century.[85]

As the empire shrank into increasing isolation, Latin was forgotten and Greek became the only *lingua franca*. Herakleios's official employment of the term *Basileus* from 629 in place of *Imperator* reflects this shift, which

---

[82] *Miracula S. Demetrii* 2.4 documents the council (*boulè*) of ruling people and citizens of Thessalonike, who decided to send ten boats in search of supplies during the long siege and famine.

[83] P. Lemerle, "Invasions et migrations dans les Balkans," *RH* 216 (1954): 264-308; C. Foss, "Archaeology and the 'Twenty Cities' of Byzantine Asia," *AJA* 81 (1977): 469-86.

[84] C. Mango, *Byzantium: The Empire of New Rome* (London, 1980), 73-74, 78-79.

[85] *Parastaseis syntomoi chronikai*, chs. 3, 36, and Cameron and Herrin, *Constantinople in the Early Eighth Century*, 209-210; Alan Cameron, *Circus Factions*, 249-58.

symbolises the passing of an epoch.[86] The same dominance of Greek is visible in court titles and in the new *thema* administration under a *strategos* and *krites*. Despite a tendency to preserve archaic military forms, during the seventh century army offices were hellenised if not completely transformed, and the new rank of imperial *spatharios* was created. Under the impact of Herakleios's militarisation of the empire, aristocratic forms of address, rank, and function changed, and court positions previously reserved for eunuchs were bestowed on bearded men.[87] It was probably from the capital that Herakleios recruited his generals and *thema* administrators. Certainly the Senate of Constantinople, which retained considerable influence throughout the century, was the sole remnant of curial autonomy and the only aristocratic body. This concentration of the well-born and the wealthy must have formed an important s urce for imperial advisers, court dignitaries, and bureaucrats.

Outside the capital, in the void caused by the breakdown of traditional provincial administration, bishops were sometimes forced to play an entirely civilian and military role. This extension of their previous participation in local government was emphasised by the chaotic conditions but was not noticeably different. The monks and bishops of the Tur Abdin in southeast Anatolia resisted the Persians for two years; Amida held out for three.[88] In those parts of Syria where hostility to Chalcedon still dominated relations with the church of Constantinople, there were incidents of dissident Monophysites welcoming the invaders. But such a defiant anti-imperial gesture was generally reserved to Jewish communities, for example in Antioch in 609 when Patriarch Anastasios II was lynched. This revolt was provoked as much by Phokas's efforts to convert the Jews as by the proximity of the Persians, who did not succeed in capturing the city until

[86] G. Rösch, Ὄνομα Βασιλείας—*Studien zum offiziellen Gebrauch der Kaisertitel in spätantiker und frühbyzantinischer Zeit* (Vienna, 1978); cf. I. Shahid, "On the Titulature of the Emperor Heraclius," *B* 51 (1981): 28-96, restating the author's interpretation of the change as an instance of Christian influence on ancient, essentially pagan titles. But cf. O. Kresten, "Iustinianos I, der 'christusliebende' Kaiser: Zum Epitheton φιλόχριστος den Intitulationes byzantinisches Kaiserurkunden," *Römische Historische Mitteilungen* 21 (1979): 83-109, proving that the ancient name *Flavius* continued in use.

[87] On the development of Greek, see R. Browning, *Medieval and Modern Greek*, 2nd ed. (Cambridge, 1983); on the imperial *spatharioi*, see Haldon, *Byzantine Praetorians*, 182-85; and on court positions, see T. S. Brown, *Gentlemen and Officers*, 133-43.

[88] John of Nikiu, *Chronicle* 97.11, describes the new responsibilities assumed under pressure by Eulogios in Alexandria, which were extended when Patriarch Kyros was made prefect of Egypt during the Arab conquest. This was quite exceptional, however; bishops had no fixed political duties and only undertook such tasks in moments of crisis; see A. Hohlweg, "Bischof und Stadherr im frühen Byzanz," *JÖB* 20 (1971): 51-62. For the civilian and monastic resistance to the Persians, see Devréesse, *Le patriarchat d'Antioche*, 99-100.

611.[89] It was, however, in Jerusalem that the Jews were later held responsible for betrayal. In 614, Patriarch Zacharias had prepared for a long siege, confident in the city's walls and in the hope of imperial assistance. But after only six months the Persians entered by a secret passage and inflicted the worst recorded devastation of the holy places. According to Strategikos and Sebeos, the Jews openly rejoiced at the slaughter of Christians, and even participated in it by ransoming individuals, who were pressured to abandon their faith and killed if they refused. While such accusations resound with stock charges from a long tradition of conflict, stories of Jewish treachery in Jerusalem certainly coloured later church dealings with the synagogues, as the Byzantine authorities attempted to persuade adherents of the Old Testament to accept the evident truths of the New.[90] Although neither theological pressure in the form of Dialogues between Christians and Jews nor outright persecution succeeded in this aim, it was pursued by Constantinople as a continuous ideal to the end of the empire.

Renewed Efforts for Ecclesiastical Unity . . .

Among the Christians, however, Herakleios, like all previous emperors, insisted that there should and could be greater uniformity of belief. He supported Patriarch Sergios's attempt to find common ground via the doctrine of one energy in Christ (Monoenergism), which avoided discussion of His nature. During the Persian campaign he also made contact with the Cypriot Monophysite community, whose leader was in Armenia in the 620s. The issue of Christian disunity was posed in a heightened form by the reoccupation of the eastern provinces, largely Monophysite, after 628. So when the emperor returned the True Cross to Jerusalem, he had talks with the Nestorian community and some dissidents at Edessa, and met Athanasios, the Monophysite Patriarch of Antioch, at Hierapolis.[91] At the same time, Bishop Kyros of Phasis was appointed to Alexandria, where a moderate group of Monophysites called Theodosians seemed interested in re-establishing communion with Constantinople. Armed with a patristic florilegium attributed to the sixth-century Patriarch Menas (later proved to

[89] Sébéos, *Histoire d'Héraclius*, ch. 23 (p. 62) (cf. p. 63 where the Jews are said to have welcomed the Persians into Caesarea); *Chronikon Paschale*, 699.

[90] Sébéos, *Histoire d'Héraclius*, ch. 24 (pp. 68-70); Garitte, *La Prise de Jérusalem*, ch. 10, 2:17-18; cf. the partial English translation by F. Conybeare, "Antiochus Strategicus' Account," *EHR* 25 (1910): 508-509. Theophanes, 300-301, also reports that Jews participated in the slaughter of Christians; R. Devréesse, "La fin inédite d'une lettre de S. Maxime: un baptême forcé de Juifs et de Samaritains à Carthage en 632," *Revue des sciences religieuses* 17 (1937): 25-35.

[91] Theophanes, 328-29. On the preparatory work towards greater unity, see van Dieten, *Geschichte der Patriarchen*, Exkurs III, 219-32.

be a forgery), he was able to win them over and issued a document to celebrate the union in June 633.[92] Monoenergism thus appeared to succeed in uniting Christians of very different persuasions.

In Palestine, however, antagonism to the one-energy doctrine found a vociferous exponent in an elderly monk, Sophronios, who was acclaimed as patriarch of Jerusalem by the clergy there, late in 633 or early in 634.[93] He had already travelled to Alexandria and Constantinople in an effort to prevent the agreements reached by Kyros and Sergios, who denounced him as a troublemaker. But his defence of the Chalcedonian position, backed by considerable popular support, proved sufficiently impressive for Sergios to have second thoughts about the emphatic statement of Monoenergism employed in the Alexandrian union. He issued a new formulation that stressed the unity of the Word (Logos) as the force responsible for directing both the human and spiritual aspects of Christ, and forbade debate over His energy or energies. This brief document, the *Psephos* (Decision), also endorsed the theory of Monotheletism, Christ's one will, a doctrine acceptable to many Monophysites as well as Chalcedonians.[94]

Monotheletism—The Doctrine of One Will. Although the problems of Christ's nature, energy, and will were all interrelated and had been addressed by many theologians before, Sergios now attempted to resolve the central problem raised by Gospel stories of the Gethsemane prayer.[95] If Jesus could have appealed to His Father, saying, "Not my will but thine be done," was there not an opposition between His human will and the divine will of God? The answer provided in the *Psephos* was that Jesus manifested an instinctive movement of the flesh in this moment of weakness, which created a tension between His one divine will and apparent human desire. Sts. Athanasios and John Chrysostomos had offered the same explanation, so Sergios could justifiably stress that Jesus had one will corresponding to the hypostatic unity of His person. The Gethsemane incident was interpreted as evidence of the one divine will in the Trinity of three persons.

[92] Mansi, 11.564-68; cf. F.-M. Léthel, *Théologie de l'Agonie du Christ: La liberté humaine du Fils de Dieu et son importance sotériologique mises en lumière par saint Maxime le Confesseur* (Paris, 1979), 25. Nearly all the documents written during the controversy were read out at the Sixth Oecumenical Council held in 680-81 and can be studied in the acts as published by Mansi. There are French translations by F. X. Murphy and P. Sherwood, *Constantinople II et III* (Paris, 1974). For the following account of Monotheletism, I am very much indebted to Father Kallistos Ware and Dr. Sebastian Brock, whose lectures on East Christian theology (spring 1984) were extremely helpful.

[93] C. von Schönborn, *Sophrone de Jérusalem* (Paris, 1972), 81-84.

[94] Mansi, 11.533E-536A; Léthel, *Théologie de l'Agonie*, 25-26, 37-38: the text of the *Psephos* is included in the longer letter from Sergios to Honorius.

[95] This is the subject of F.-M. Léthel's book, *Théologie de l'Agonie*.

This new formulation was immediately circulated to the eastern patriarchs and the pope, then Honorius I (625-38), with a letter describing the
union achieved at Alexandria.[96] Sergios clearly hoped that by respecting
the Chalcedonian wording "in two natures" and supporting the idea of
Christ's "theandric" energy, derived from the writings of Pseudo-Dionysios, he could gain general acceptance for the *Psephos*. He also recommended a ban on further debate and condemned as a "war of words" (*logo-
machia*) the anxieties expressed by Sophronios. Unaware of the strength of
feeling in the East, Pope Honorius responded favourably to the patriarchal
formula and agreed with the need to silence discussion. In this, his first
letter to Sergios, he also declared his belief in Christ's one will (*voluntas*).[97]
Another distinguished monastic leader, Maximos the Confessor, praised
the patriarch in lavish terms. Even Sophronios appeared satisfied by the
withdrawal of the Alexandrian statement of Monenergism. Thus union
seemed definite, and Sophronios was confirmed as patriarch of Jerusalem
(634).[98]

Some lingering doubts remained, however, for in the synodical letter announcing his election as patriarch, Sophronios recapitulated the Chalcedonian doctrine of the unity of the human and divine in Christ.[99] In this
long, dogmatic statement, the contradictions of Monotheletism were
forcefully revealed in a way that cast heavy theological suspicion on the
union devised and so ardently desired in Constantinople. The document
was dispatched to Constantinople and Rome, though not to Alexandria,
already committed to the one-will doctrine by Patriarch Kyros, or to Antioch, irredeemably Monophysite. But it met with no success. Sergios of
course rejected it, and Honorius found himself bound by his own statement
on the will of Christ. In his failure to convince any of the other church leaders, the new patriarch of Jerusalem thus opened a schism over Monotheletism. It was with a sense of increasing isolation that Sophronios tried to get
the theological arguments debated at a church council. He persuaded
Bishop Arkadios of Cyprus to convene a synod, which met in the mid-630s
and brought together 46 bishops.[100] Under cover of the *Trisagion* issue (a

[96] Mansi, 11.529-38; van Dieten, *Geschichte der Patriarchen*, 38-39.

[97] Mansi, 11.537-44, the crucial word appears at 539C; Jaffé, no. 2018; cf. G. Kreuzer,
Die Honorius Frage im Mittelalter und in der Neuzeit (Stuttgart, 1975), 32-47, 56-57.

[98] Von Schönborn, *Sophrone de Jérusalem*, 83-84, 91; van Dieten, *Geschichte der Patriarchen*,
37-38; Maximos's approval is indicated in his letter to Pyrrhos, *PG* 91, letter 19, cols. 589-
98; cf. Léthel, *Théologie de l'Agonie*, 59-64.

[99] *PG* 87(3), 3147-3200; also Mansi, 11.461-508; cf. von Schönborn, *Sophrone de Jérusalem*, 199-224.

[100] M. Albert and C. von Schönborn, eds., *La lettre de Sophrone de Jérusalem à Arcadius de
Chypre, Patrologia orientalis* 39 (2), no. 179 (Turnhout, 1978), Syriac edition with French
translation. See also the commentary, pp. 170-73. The synod's activity is also recorded in

formula that had become the hallmark of Monophysite belief),[101] Sophronios's defence of the Chalcedonian definitions were discussed. One of Maximos the Confessor's disciples, Anastasios, put the case for Christ's two wills and two energies, but without success. The bishops were unable to conclude and decided to refer the matter to the emperor, a procedure that could not possibly advance Chalcedonian theology against Monotheletism. Realising that he had lost the battle for correct belief in the East, Sophronios decided to appeal directly to Rome and sent his personal envoy, Stephen of Dora, to the West.

Honorius, however, had already given his allegiance to the theory of one will, which was further used by Sergios in his final attempt to elaborate the official theology of Monotheletism. This was issued by Herakleios in 638 as an imperial edict, the *Ekthesis* (Statement), to be observed by all Byzantine subjects.[102] Constantinople's theology was thus given the force of imperial law. But like so many other compromise doctrines, it failed. In a brief three-paragraph definition, too little was expounded and too much omitted. The fierce and inevitable opposition of Sophronios and Maximos encouraged others, generally monks with a rigorous theological training. But in the course of unforeseen military and political events in the East, the centre of hostility to Constantinopolitan Monotheletism shifted to Rome. The doctrine developed to achieve Christian unity instead had the effect of driving another wedge between Old and New Rome.

Although a contrast is frequently made between pliable episcopal acceptance of Monotheletism and obstinate monastic opposition, this does not explain the division. Moderate Monophysite monks in Alexandria and Antioch appear to have welcomed the possibility of rejoining the Chalcedonian church;[103] other monks, such as Pyrrhos, abbot of the monastery of Philippikos, supported the doctrine from the Chalcedonian side. Obviously these favourable forces were exploited by the patriarch and emperor, and one way of doing so was to place monastic supporters in positions of ecclesiastical authority as bishops, where they could influence and win over opponents. Pyrrhos, for instance, was appointed to the patriarchate of Constantinople on Sergios's death in 638. It was much easier for

a Syriac *Life* of Maximos; see S. Brock, "An Early Syriac Life of Maximus the Confessor," *AB* 91 (1973): 299-346, esp. chs. 10-14.

[101] The *Trisagion* continued to identify Monophysite belief, for instance among Syrians moved to Thrace, who spread the heresy there; see Theophanes, 422.

[102] Mansi, 10.993E-996C; cf. Léthel, 48-49, comparing the wording of the *Psephos* with the *Ekthesis*.

[103] As Anastasios of Sinai reported, the Jacobites in Syria were gleeful over the compromise: they claimed that Chalcedon had come to them, rather than the other way around, *PG* 89, 1156A. On the importance of the sermon *"kat'eikona"* for the history of Monotheletism, see van Dieten, *Geschichte der Patriarchen*, Exkurs II, 179-218.

the emperor to manipulate bishops selected through his patronage than abbots chosen by their often very independent communities. So the church hierarchy was bound to play a noteworthy role in the attempt to impose this, as other definitions of belief supported by the secular authorities.

. . . And Their Failure

Conversely, members of the ecclesiastical hierarchy who had misgivings about the new doctrine were not necessarily prepared to challenge it and thereby lose their positions. But monastic opposition could sometimes be voiced without provoking direct imperial retaliation. In this case, however, the uproar against both one-will and one-energy theories (Monotheletism and Monoenergism) came from an unusual and distinctive monastic circle created in the first quarter of the seventh century against a background of continuous military unrest. Sophronios and his spiritual father, John Moschos, had adopted the practice of rootless wandering from one community to another, *xeniteia*—a choice that became a necessity during the Persian and Arab invasions from about 604 onwards.[104] From Palestine to Egypt, Syria, the Aegean islands, and Rome they journeyed, staying for longer periods in Sketis, at Mount Sinai ca. 580-90, then under the direction of one of its most famous abbots, St. John Klimakos, and in Alexandria with Patriarch John the Almsgiver, assisting his Chalcedonian campaign ca. 604-614. After John Moschos's death, or during his final years in Rome, Sophronios visited North Africa, where he met Maximos, a refugee from the Asiatic coast of the Bosphoros, occupied by the Persians in 626.[105] The two shared a Syro-Palestinian background, an intense commitment to the council of 451, and the intellectual training and access to doctrinal books to counter Sergios's innovations. They personified a Chalcedonian diaspora of monks, forced to move from one centre to another, welcomed in their travels by communities respectful of their ascetic experiences, learning, and monastic faith. They apparently took books with them and found other resources in Africa and Rome. And wherever they went, they debated with their opponents, arranging public discussions of which the most celebrated was that between Maximos and Pyrrhos, the ex-patriarch of Constantinople, in Carthage in 645. John Moschos, author of the *Spiritual Meadow*, Sophronios, Maximos, and his faithful assistant Anastasios were probably the last generation of eastern monks to practice the tradi-

---

[104] H. Chadwick, "John Moschus and His Friend Sophronios the 'Sophist'," *JTS*, n.s., 25 (1974): 41-74; von Schönborn, *Sophrone de Jérusalem*, 56-71.

[105] Von Schönborn, *Sophrone de Jérusalem*, 72-78; Brock, "An Early Syriac Life," chs. 18-19.

tional *xeniteia*.[106] Thereafter, the aimless wandering of errant monks without resources and dependent solely on a shared experience would become impossible. One of the richest elements in primitive Christianity, the asceticism of the Desert Fathers, was thus consigned to history, to be revived after a long break by St. Francis of Assisi, whose dedication to poverty drew on this tradition.

THE EXPANSION OF ISLAM

Following the Byzantine victory of 628, Persian forces were obliged to evacuate Egypt, Syria, and parts of Mesopotamia that they had occupied for many years. Into the vacuum caused by their withdrawal, Herakleios appointed city governors and military commanders who attempted to revive the old imperial administration.[107] In this process bishops often assisted but might also frustrate, when doctrinal differences made them antagonistic to Constantinople. Monastic opposition of the sort led by Sophronios and John Moschos did nothing to ease the Byzantine recovery of the eastern provinces. It was against this background of divided loyalties and uneasy compromises that the Muslim advance took place.

The Arab tribesmen who began to wage a holy war on all Christians during the 630s, inspired by the revelations of Muhammad, were no strangers to the eastern provinces of the empire. In 611-12 they had pillaged areas north of the Arabian peninsula, even extending into Syria to attack camel trains and prosperous settlements.[108] But the new creed of Islam and the relative simplicity of conversion transformed the desert tribes who adopted it. Byzantine administrators appear to have been quite unaware of this change and were also inconsistent in their treatment of those Arabs who guarded the desert areas of Sinai for a small subsidy. After a victory in Egypt in the early 630s, a certain official refused to pay the customary subsidy, insulting the Arabs as dogs. They then went over to other Arabs, who led them north into the fertile areas of Gaza, where they settled.[109] In these circumstances the forces of Islam made rapid advances into both Persian and Byzantine territories, capturing Damascus (634) and Jerusalem (638), which was surrendered by Patriarch Sophronios to avoid a repetition of the

[106] A. Guillaumont, "Le dépaysement comme forme d'ascèse dans le monachisme ancien," *Annuaire de L'Ecole Pratique des Hautes Etudes (Ve section)* (1968-69): 31-58.

[107] Haldon, *Byzantine Praetorians*, 173-74.

[108] Theophanes, 300; P. Crone, *Slaves on Horses* (Cambridge, 1980), 22-26 on the background to Arab expansion; cf. F. Donner, *The Early Islamic Conquests* (Princeton, 1981), 20-49; M. Ruthven, *Islam in the World* (Harmondsworth, 1984), 49-55.

[109] Theophanes, 335-36. On the transformation of the Arab tribes, see Ruthven, *Islam in the World*, 82-85; Donner, *The Early Islamic Conquests*, 55-90, 250-67.

bloodshed of the Persian entry in 614.[110] Despite the efforts of Byzantine generals, the emperor's brother Theodore among them, there was no success in checking the Arabs. From his base at Antioch, Herakleios learned of the crushing defeat of his troops at the River Yarmuk (636) and probably witnessed the disorderly flight of some of his contingents pursued by the Muslims far to the north.[111] The unreliability of some Christian Arab recruits, the betrayal by some non-Islamic tribes, even the understandable hostility of some strict Monophysites enrolled in the imperial army, may all have contributed to this defeat. But it seems more likely that the superior coherence of the Islamic side proved decisive. In a similarly speedy campaign against the Persians, all Iraq was brought into the orbit of the new religion.[112] The traditional empires of the East Mediterranean collapsed in the face of this novel Arab force within one decade, 634-44.

While disaffected Christians and Jews are frequently held responsible for assisting the Arab advance, there is more evidence that the whole population was terrified by the appearance of the desert nomads and fled to whatever refuge they could find, Alexandria and Jerusalem as well as smaller fortified towns. As Herakleios had tried to enforce baptism on the Jews, it is hardly surprising that they felt no loyalty to the empire. As John, bishop of Nikiu in Egypt, records in his contemporary account of the invasion, there were some who welcomed the forces of Islam, evidence confirmed by the earlier testimony of Sebeos and Strategikos.[113] But it is only in later Byzantine sources that the accusation of wholesale betrayal and a positive aid for the invaders is made; and these were written at a time when Christians were familiar with the relatively tolerant aspects of life under Islam, which were not at all evident in the 630s.

Clearly, doctrinal arguments alone cannot be held responsible for the Byzantine defeat. Imperial weakness stemmed from the exhausted state of the empire, the inadequate form of provincial administration recently im-

---

[110] Theophanes, 339; von Schönborn, *Sophrone de Jérusalem*, 89-91; A. J. Butler, *The Arab Conquest of Egypt* (Oxford, 1902), rev. ed. by P. M. Fraser (Oxford, 1978); Donner, *The Early Islamic Conquests*, 91-220; D. J. Constantelos, "The Moslem Conquests of the Near East as Revealed in the Greek Sources of the Seventh and Eighth Centuries," B 42 (1972): 325-57.

[111] Theophanes, 338; W. E. Kaegi, Jr., "Heraklios and the Arabs," *Greek Orthodox Theological Review* 27 (2) (1982): 109-133.

[112] R. Frye, *The Heritage of Persia* (London, 1962), 240-42; Donner, *The Early Islamic Conquests*, 173-220.

[113] J. Moorhead, "The Monophysite Response to the Arab Invasions," B 51 (1981): 579-91; John of Nikiu, *Chronicle*, chs. 111-21 stresses the general panic rather than treachery, though see 111.12; 113.2; 114.1; 115.9 for particular cases, and cf. Butler, *The Arab Conquest of Egypt*.

posed, and the general tendency for resources to be centred on Constantinople first and foremost. There is no evidence that Herakleios tried to make any radical changes in the local organisation of the reoccupied eastern regions. No new armies or military governors are recorded. Instead, the old civilian system was revived, with the traditional hierarchy of army commanders under praetorian prefects. And this was the machinery that failed so conspicuously to defend Syria and Palestine against Arab attacks, inspired by the theory of holy war (*jihad*) and encouraged by the prospect of booty. On the Islamic side, the guarantee that those killed in battle against the infidel would go straight to Paradise as martyrs to the faith combined with quite material aspirations to effect a striking transformation of fighting capacity. It was perhaps this novel force behind Islamic expansion that brought to an end the great civilisation of Persia and reduced the empire of East Rome to a tiny fraction of its sixth-century size.

Official Monotheletism

Doctrinal arguments may, however, have played a part in prolonging Byzantine failures to recover the provinces lost to Islam after 638. For in this year, when Sophronios was forced to admit the Muslim victors to the Holy City, and while Maximos was rallying the church in North Africa to Chalcedonian rather than Sergian positions, Constantinople issued a document known as the *Ekthesis* (Statement).[114] It proclaimed a new definition of Christ's one will, *en thelema*, based on the hypostatic union of Father and Son, and thus launched upon the Christian world a developed statement of Monotheletism. It also banned any further verbal disputes over Christ's will or natures—a directive that overlooked its own reliance on precisely the type of formula guaranteed to provoke such debate.

Since 633-34, when Maximos had first welcomed the *Psephos* with such approval, he had been reconsidering Monothelete theology.[115] Following Sophronios, who had compiled a list of 600 patristic citations against it, he criticised Sergios's analysis of the Gethsemane prayer. By denying Christ's human will, the Monotheletes reduced His saving role in the redemption of humankind; Maximos therefore stressed the full humanity of the Word made flesh. But Christ's human will did not operate in opposition to His divine will—the two might be distinct but would always co-

---

[114] The *Ekthesis* is preserved in the form in which it was read out at the Lateran Synod eleven years later, R. Riedinger, ed., *Concilium Lateranense a.649 Celebratum* (Berlin, 1974); also in Mansi, 10.993-96. Riedinger also shows, in "Aus den Akten der Lateran-Synode von 649," *BZ* 69 (1976): 17-38, that the *Ekthesis* includes a paraphrase of Justinian's *Expositio de recta fide* (551).

[115] Léthel, *Théologie de l'Agonie*, 103-121.

operate. By 641 Maximos had completed his Chalcedonian theology of the two natural wills of Christ and employed it with great philosophical skill against proponents of the *Ekthesis*. His denunciation of Monotheletism may also have been strengthened by the fear that previously unflinching Monophysite heretics, only recently condemned, would be brought back into the church. After the fall of Alexandria to Islam, Christian refugees, both Chalcedonian and Monophysite, fled from Egypt in great numbers, many to Africa and Italy. The western churches had only just, after considerable persecution, accepted the compromise with Monophysite belief represented by the Three Chapters, so they were hardly likely to welcome another that forced them to admit their erstwhile opponents to communion.

Pope Honorius died (October 638) without formulating a response to the *Ekthesis*, and Isaac, the exarch of Ravenna, occupied the Lateran palace to ensure the selection of a favourable successor.[116] Patriarch Sergios also died in 638 and was replaced by Pyrrhos, another close friend of the emperor and an enthusiastic Monothelete. The situation at the beginning of 639 was therefore as follows: the Arabs were consolidating their control over Palestine and Syria, poised on the brink of a conquest of Egypt, while Byzantine forces had effectively withdrawn behind the Taurus range in southeastern Asia Minor. Simultaneously, the imperially-sanctioned doctrine of Monotheletism had been confirmed in an attempt to quell theological speculation about the natures and wills of Christ.[117] As it was essentially another compromise, its failure to satisfy either convinced Chalcedonians or committed Monophysites gave it little chance of success. In order to pre-empt opposition in Rome, imperial forces took charge. But they could not prevent Maximos's campaign for orthodoxy in the African church, a warning that the Chalcedonian monks would not accept Monotheletism without a struggle. In this respect, the one-will theory not only deepened the divisions dating back to 451 and 553, but also permitted Islam to become established in previously Christian territory. Thus 638 symbolises another milestone in the disunity of Christendom.

Even in his efforts to secure Roman support for the doctrine, Herakleios was unsuccessful. For after 18 months of negotiations between the Byzantine authorities and papal legates in the capital, Severinus was finally consecrated as bishop of Rome and then suddenly died. His successor, Pope John IV, proceeded to condemn the *Ekthesis*, with western support, an act that revealed to the emperor that his ecclesiastical as well as his military plans had failed.[118] The death of Herakleios in February 641 unleashed yet

[116] *LP* 1.328-29.
[117] Mansi, 10.1002-1003.
[118] *LP* 1.328-29 (Severinus's pontificate lasted from 28 May to 2 August 640); for John

another crisis for the empire, this time of a constitutional variety engendered by the late emperor's determination to make his two eldest sons joint heirs. Since the principle of co-emperors was not a new one, a short detour is necessary to explain why this provision should have provoked such problems.

The Succession Crisis (641)

Herakleios's first wife, Eudokia, had borne him two children before she died of epilepsy in 612. The boy, Herakleios, also called "New Constantine," was 28 years old in 641 and thus perfectly capable of taking over the government. But his father had also wanted to provide for the eldest child of his second marriage to Martina—Herakleios, called Heraklonas, then aged 15. Trying to devise a method for their co-operation, he established that Martina should be regarded by both sons as "mother and empress," a title implying considerably greater power than the Senate of Constantinople was likely to accord to a female regent.[119] In addition, Martina commanded little affection in the capital, where rumours that she was plotting to get rid of Herakleios-Constantine appeared to be confirmed by his sudden death after only three months as emperor. In fact, he probably suffered from consumption. The charge of poison was quite unproved but did nothing to endear Martina to the city population.[120] Devotion to the Herakleios-Constantine branch of the family became clear, however, when his two young sons, aged about eleven and nine years, were acclaimed, together with their uncle Heraklonas. The empress-mother had won power for her own branch but was hedged by competitors.

Of this opposition to the unpopular Martina we learn very little from the sparse contemporary sources. But it must have been well organised and entrenched in the Senate, which now represented not only the aristocratic home of landed wealth, but also the court, the central bureaucracy, and the army. The extent to which the provincial nobility had been concentrated in the metropolis may be illustrated by the case of Theodore of Koloneia, a senator of Constantinople, identified by his place of origin in eastern Asia Minor.[121] He was partly responsible for the peaceful succession of Constantine IV in 668. As the old forms of Roman family names had entirely dropped out of use by the late sixth century, individuals tend to be poorly identified until a new medieval system of naming develops. One of the first

---

IV's letter, see Mansi, 10.607-610, and the condemnation issued by the council of Orléans, ibid., 759-62.

[119] Nikephoros, 27-28; Beck, *Senat*, 42-44.

[120] Theophanes, 331, 341; Nikephoros, 14-15 on the unpopularity that dated back to Herakleios's incestuous marriage to Martina.

[121] Theophanes, 351-52.

indications of greater attention to genealogy and personal relations occurs in this field, where people gradually become identified either by their fathers, their place of origin, or a nickname, frequently unflattering (as in the case of John "the Earthquake," who attempted to raise the price of bread). Theodore of Koloneia undoubtedly represents one of the Anatolian families who had sought refuge and patronage in the capital during the turbulence of the early seventh century.

The Senate had thus come to include a variety of interests, and when it decided to move against Martina, she found few sectors of support. It was nonetheless an unprecedented step for the Senate to depose Heraklonas and his mother in favour of the youngest Herakleios, grandson of the founder of the dynasty. In September 641, when the eldest son of Herakleios-Constantine was proclaimed emperor, Heraklonas and Martina were mutilated and sent into exile on Rhodes.[122] The new emperor was known in the city as Constans, a diminutive of Constantine, and reigned as Constans II (641-68), although he wielded no effective power until about 650.

This aristocratic revolt against Martina was a constitutional innovation that enabled supporters of the rival branch of the family to govern in the name of Constans. His mother Gregoria, daughter of Herakleios I's cousin, Niketas, may have played an important part in the regency. As the widow of Herakleios-Constantine she represented the legitimate line of descent and the North African branch of the dynasty. Those senators who supported her sons' claim could use popular dislike of Martina to impose their choice. They are curiously anonymous, however. One known champion was Patriarch Paul, who replaced Pyrrhos (a firm ally of Martina) in 642.[123] Some may have been drawn from the circle of Patriarch Sergios, who had acted as regent for Herakleios-Constantine during his minority; others from among those who advised him during his brief reign, for instance, Philagrios, an official exiled by Martina and Heraklonas.[124] Whatever its access to ruling circles, this aristocratic clique appears to have clung to its newfound authority throughout the seventh century. Senatorial pressure and direct intervention were felt in 662, when Constans II abandoned the capital for the West, leaving his ten-year-old son and family in Constantinople; and in 668 and 685, when minors came to the throne. So although Byzantium was ruled by the same dynasty from 610 to 695, the power of the Senate undoubtedly increased during the period. In contrast, the military coup of a general such as Leo III in 717 would present these circles

[122] Ibid., 331, 341; Nikephoros, 30-31.
[123] Theophanes, 331, 342; Nikephoros, 30-31 on the tumult that forced Pyrrhos to abandon Constantinople; van Dieten, *Geschichte der Patriarchen*, 71-75.
[124] Nikephoros, 29.

with a mature claimant to the throne and one with fewer past debts to individual senators.

Western Rejection of Monotheletism

The senatorial regency that ruled in the name of Constans II was apparently
committed to the Sergian compromise of the *Ekthesis* and selected the Monothelete Paul to pursue its policies from the see of Constantinople. As the
patriarchs of Alexandria, Antioch, and Jerusalem now had to contend with
an Islamic army of occupation as well as their own internal disputes, the
chief object in Paul's plan was to win Rome over to the one-will doctrine.
But in his brief pontificate (640-42), the Dalmatian John IV had already
voiced western opposition, which was to be repeated by his successors.[125]
In addition, the activities of the Chalcedonian monks in Africa, notably
Maximos, made matters even more difficult for Paul. By his constant
preaching, writing, and debating, Maximos not only aired the most subtle
and well-informed theological opposition to Monotheletism, he also kept
correspondents all over the Mediterranean world aware of his success.[126]
His voluminous letters and tracts reveal contacts with many other Chalcedonians, a community of nuns who had fled Asia Minor during the Persian
invasions, monks displaced from Egypt who passed through Carthage on
their way to Rome, or bishops in Cyprus or Crete who sought his advice on
doctrinal matters. The high point of this campaign against Constantinopolitan error occurred in 645, when the exarch of Africa, Gregory, organised a public debate on Monotheletism between Maximos and Pyrrhos, the
deposed patriarch.[127] From the minutes of this confrontation, the inner coherence and solidity of the Chalcedonian position are very evident. Pyrrhos
was quite incapable of countering it. And his miserable showing signed the
fate of Monotheletism in the West.

In 646, councils were held in Africa and Rome to condemn the doctrine.[128] When Pyrrhos recanted temporarily, Pope Theodore (642-49)
went so far as to excommunicate Patriarch Paul, as an illegal occupant of
the see of Constantinople. Paul took his revenge on the papal legates, Ser-
icus and Martin.[129] But the potential danger of persistent division over

---

[125] Mansi, 10.702, 705-706, 706-708.

[126] In addition to his purely theological writings in *PG* 90 and 91, see his letters to Cosmas, deacon of Alexandria (no. 15); Julian, *scholastikos* of the same city (no. 17); John, archbishop of Kyzikos (no. 6); the bishop of Kydonia (no. 21); Marinos, a monk of Cyprus (no.
20); and the secular dignitaries Peter (*illustris*, nos. 13 and 14) and John *koubikoularios* (nos.
10 and 12); all in *PG* 91.

[127] *PG* 91, 287-362; also in Mansi, 10.709-760.

[128] Mansi, 10.918, 919, 925-28, 929-42, 943; Theophanes, 331.

[129] Theophanes, 331; *LP* 1.333; Mansi, 10.1019-26.

Monotheletism was made plain when Gregory, exarch of Carthage, proclaimed his independence from Constantinople, using popular Chalcedonian support. This 647 revolt was crushed not by imperial troops but by the
Arabs, who invaded the exarchate from Libya and killed Gregory.[130] The
fact that they retired, leaving the Byzantine province a further half-century
of political existence, permitted Constantinople to strengthen its presence
there. But the marked hostility to Monotheletism in the West may have
prompted a slight change of tactic. In 648, Patriarch Paul issued an order—*Typos*—in the name of the emperor, which suspended all discussion
of the energies and wills of Christ.[131] Again the attempt to impose silence
was totally unsuccessful; indeed, it may have promoted more stringent
condemnation in Rome. Under Theodore, plans were made for a synod to
produce the theological proof that Monotheletism was a heresy, grounds
for a real schism. This reaction may also have been hastened by the news
that imperial officials were attempting to force ecclesiastics to sign their
agreement to the *Typos*. One of the papal legates, Anastasius, who refused
to do so, was promptly exiled to Trebizond, and thus began a long period
of deportation and deprivation, which was to be visited upon all staunch
opponents of Monotheletism.[132]

The Lateran Synod of 649. In 649, however, when Pope Theodore died, antagonism was at a high level in Rome, and Martin, previously legate in the
East, was elected and consecrated without waiting for imperial confirmation. Learning of this development, of which it could not but disapprove,
the regency dispatched Olympios as exarch to counter the illegal assumption of papal authority. But he arrived too late to prevent the Lateran Synod
of 105 bishops from meeting.[133] Pope Martin opened the proceedings with
a firm denunciation of both Byzantine theology and treatment of the faithful. After five sessions, which discussed the theological basis of Monotheletism in detail, an anathematisation of the doctrine as heretical together
with its three main exponents, Patriarchs Sergios, Pyrrhos, and Paul, was
drawn up. By this vigorous statement of their own orthodoxy, the churches
of Italy and Africa liberated themselves from eastern tutelage and defined
their own position in the Christian *oikoumene*. It was a momentous development in the separation of East and West, an important step in the division of Christendom.

At this point Byzantium had barely come to terms with the eruption of
Islam in the Near East, let alone the divisive impact of its own Monothelete

---

[130] Theophanes, 343.
[131] Mansi, 10.1029-33.
[132] Ibid., 10.879.
[133] *LP* 1.337-38; for the acts, see Chapter 7.

theology in the West. To the regents in the capital, the Muslim mastery of naval skills was further proof of the seriousness of Arab rivalry. Cyprus had already been overrun and the southern coast of Asia Minor was exposed to raids. Even within the newly established Taurus border, Byzantine territory was not safe, as the attacks on Isauria were to show.[134] Worse, the inhabitants of these threatened areas had no faith in the power of Constantinople to defend them. A revolt by Armenian troops indicated military unrest and an anxiety to come to terms with the Arabs, through a joint alliance against Constans II.[135] In other words, the now greatly reduced empire had not yet found an effective means of resistance to Islam. The forces mobilised by Herakleios against the Persians had not been institutionalised in permanent form. In particular, his military innovations had not withstood the onslaught of the 640s. For most of the seventh century, the traditional forms of provincial administration continued in place, albeit weakened and rendered ineffective by repeated defeats. Only from the last years of Constans II and his son, Constantine IV (668-85), would the effects of military and administrative reforms become evident. The transformation of Byzantium was underway but by no means achieved in 649, when Pope Martin challenged Constantinople's capacity to define orthodoxy.

[134] Theophanes, 343-44.
[135] Ibid., 344.

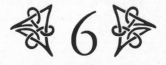

The Visigothic Alternative

WHEN POPE MARTIN set his face against the heresies of the East and thus confirmed the most serious schism of the seventh century, the clergy in Transalpine Europe remained unaffected, almost entirely ignorant of the causes dividing the Christian *oikoumene*. In few areas of the West was this isolation more pronounced than in Spain, where from its earliest days the church had developed along largely independent lines. (For convenience I shall use the term "Spain" to refer to the Iberian peninsula.) In the sixth century this tendency towards autonomy was reinforced by such leaders as Martin of Braga, Licinianus of Carthagena, and Leander and Isidore of Seville, who directed their communities with a self-confident authority. Their intellectual and spiritual training as bishops was reinforced by a remarkable monastic culture, a familiarity with early Christian writings, and a self-sufficiency that marked the Spanish church off from others in the West. To understand how this rather unusual aspect of Iberian Christianity had come about, it is necessary to go back to the last quarter of the sixth century, when Justin II ruled as emperor in Constantinople and Pelagius II was bishop of Rome. At this time particular Visigothic Christian institutions developed, institutions that were to have long-term consequences far beyond the peninsula. As we shall see, what may appear to be a diversionary turning into the parochial aspects of Spanish history is an essential step in tracking the growth of a Latin Christianity.

THE GOTHS IN SPAIN

From the mid-sixth century, the Iberian peninsula was divided politically into three very unequal areas—in the northwestern corner, the Germanic Sueves occupied Galicia; in the southeast a Byzantine province, created by the last of Justinian's western campaigns (552), was governed by officials from Constantinople; and in the centre, a Visigothic kingdom was established early in the fifth century and consolidated after the 507 defeat at Vouillé. At that point the Franks drove the Visigoths from their capital at Toulouse and forced them to retreat over the Pyrenees. From Spain they continued to control the province of Septimania, which extended north of the eastern Pyrenees as far as Narbonne. While it is generally agreed that the Visigoths were few in number—200,000 is one of the more frequently quoted figures, though all are guesswork—the corresponding number of Hispano-Romans was probably lower than the estimate of 8 million.[1] However, it is clear that the Goths always formed a very tiny fraction of the overall population of the peninsula, and they settled chiefly in the central and northern plateau area.

With them the Goths brought their commitment to the Arian form of Christianity, which dated back to the fourth century. Both the East (Ostro-) and West (Visi-) Goths, as well as the Vandals, had embraced Arianism in the Danube region before they set out on their long wanderings into Gaul, Spain, Italy, and Africa. But of all the successor states, the Visigothic maintained its traditional and heretical religion longest, establishing a dominant Arian episcopacy in central Spain, which was flanked by small enclaves of Catholic faith in the two outer regions of Galicia and Carthagena. By the last quarter of the sixth century, the Burgundians had abandoned Arianism, the Sueves had adopted Christianity in its Catholic form, and Justinian's campaigns had removed Arian belief from Vandalic Africa and Ostrogothic Italy. Awareness of this general conversion to the majority faith may well have added to the Visigothic sense of isolation and detachment from other Christian institutions in the West.[2]

In particular, the recent change of belief among the Sueves of Galicia strengthened the Catholic presence in the peninsula. In 572, St. Martin of Braga had presided over a council that confirmed the earlier condemnation of Arianism (561).[3] Under Martin, an eastern monk who brought an asceticism of the Egyptian desert to northwest Spain as well as knowledge of the

[1] M. Rouche, *L'Aquitaine des Wisigoths aux Arabes, 418-781: Naissance d'une région* (Paris, 1979), 48-49. On the vexed problem of the numbers of Goths, see C. Sánchez Albornoz y Menduiña, "Tradición y derecho visigodos en Leon y Castilla," *Cuadernos de Historia de España* 29-30 (1959): 244-65, especially 249, criticising R. d'Abadal i de Vinyals, in *Settimane* 5 (1958), 2:548, for repeating the figure of 80,000. This derives from Victor of Vita, who claimed there were 80,000 Vandals in the first African campaign. In contrast, Sánchez Albornoz suggests about 200,000, but J. M. Wallace-Hadrill, *The Barbarian West 400-1000*, 3rd ed. (Oxford, 1985), 116, reverts to the earlier size, "upwards of 70,000." My thanks to Alastair Saunders for helpful discussion of matters Iberian.

[2] R. Gibert, "El Reino Visigodo y el Particularismo Español," *Settimane* 3 (1956): 537-83; although the extent to which Arianism defined a "national character of credal cleavage," as claimed by P. D. King, *Law and Society in the Visigothic Kingdom* (Cambridge, 1972), 4, may be doubted.

[3] J. Orlandis and D. Ramos-Lisson, *Die Synoden auf den Iberischen Halbinsel bis zum Einbruch des Islam (711)* (Paderborn, 1981), 77-92; cf. Mansi, 9.773-84, 835-44; E. A. Thompson, "The Conversion of the Spanish Suevi to Catholicism," in E. James, ed., *Visigothic Spain: New Approaches* (Oxford, 1980), 77-92.

earliest church councils, Catholic practice gradually replaced Arian in the bishopric of Braga and monastery of Dumio, which he founded there. The refectory walls were inscribed with his verses exhorting the monks to a virtuous life and reminding them that they would not drink the eastern wines of Gaza, Chios, Falerno, and Sarapteno. Little is known of the methods used to achieve the conversion, but it was certainly assisted by the Suevan King Arimir. Subsequent records suggest that Christianity was not deeply rooted and that the Catholic hierarchy's main efforts were directed to the removal of pagan and pre-Christian customs.[4] This must have been a recurrent pattern in sixth- and seventh-century Europe, judging by the number of enactments against persistent traditions, such as celebrating seasonal changes with pagan festivities, or observing Jove's day (Italian *giovedi*, i.e. dedicated to Jupiter) rather than Sunday as the weekly day of rest. Nonetheless, the Sueves officially discarded Arianism in 561, while the Spanish Visigoths maintained it.

The Byzantine occupation of southeast Spain, especially the port of Carthagena, New Carthage, and related coastal cities, Malaga and Basti, similarly reinforced orthodoxy in this area. Despite renewed support for the Catholic bishops, there is no evidence that the *"Romani"* were welcomed—on the contrary, they were seen as a foreign force, however orthodox. The parents of Leander and Isidore appear to have fled from Byzantine forces to settle further west in Visigothic Baetica, the most fully Romanised province of the peninsula, with its capital at Seville (Hispalis).[5] For help in the ongoing struggle with Arian belief, these Catholics turned to North Africa. Contacts had always been close, as Carthage normally formed the central port of call for shipping between the western and eastern basins of the Mediterranean. In the 560s and 570s, Berber activity in the region seems to have forced some monastic communities to seek a refuge in Spain. Donatus and his 70 companions, together with their library of many volumes, were welcomed by a certain lady, Minicea, who established them

[4] J. Vives, *Inscripciones Cristianas de la España Romana y Visigoda*, 2nd ed. (Barcelona, 1969), no. 353; S. J. McKenna, *Paganism and Pagan Survivals in Spain up to the Fall of the Visigothic Kingdom* (Washington, D.C., 1938); M. Meslin, "Persistances paiennes en Galicie vers la fin du VIᵉ siècle," in J. Bibauw, ed., *Hommages à Marcel Renard*, 3 vols. (Brussels, 1969), 2:512-24. J. N. Hillgarth, "Popular Religion in Visigothic Spain," in James, *Visigothic Spain*, 3-60, reprinted in J. N. Hillgarth, *Visigothic Spain, Byzantium and the Irish* (London, 1985); M. Sotomayor, "Penetración de la Iglesia en los medios rurales de la España tardorromana y visigoda," *Settimane* 28 (1982): 2, 639-70.

[5] K. F. Stroheker, "Das spanische Westgotenreich und Byzanz," in his volume *Germanentum und Spätantike* (Zurich, 1965), 207-245; U. Domínguez del Val, *Leandro de Sevilla y la lucha contra el Arrianismo* (Madrid, 1981), 21-22. R. Collins, *Early Medieval Spain: Unity in Diversity, 400-1000* (London, 1983), 98, suggests that the family may have originated "much further east."

on her land and patronised their Catholic monastery of Servitanum.[6] Its abbot, Eutropius, was later to play an important role in the Visigothic adoption of Catholicism and become bishop of Valencia. Another African monk, Nanctus, and his brethren were granted a treasury estate by King Leovigild, despite the difference between their beliefs.[7] This favourable reception reflected close ties with and respect for the monastic tradition of North Africa. It probably deepened Spanish knowledge of Latin Fathers such as Augustine, and brought sixth-century African theological texts into circulation.

Baetica also maintained maritime contacts with the East Mediterranean. From the number of Greek and Jewish inscriptions preserved in the province, it is clear that Easterners, probably involved in commerce, kept their own identities during the sixth century.[8] Through international trade, eastern silks, liturgical vessels, and ornaments entered Spain; a description of the Catholic bishop of Mérida (Emerita Augusta) processing through the city reflects the wealth of this imported finery.[9] To this inland harbour on the River Guadiana, eastern merchants came in the 540s bringing a Greek doctor, Paul, who eventually became its bishop. Another trading ship taking the same route arrived in the city later with the individual named Fidelis, identified as Paul's nephew.[10] St. Martin of Braga had certainly reached Galicia after a similar voyage. Although Paul provoked opposition by his personal use of funds donated to the church of Mérida and his determination to have Fidelis as his successor, there is no evidence that the "eastern" customs of these prelates were resented in Spain. When John of Biclar returned from Constantinople to settle in northeast Spain in the 570s, where he founded a monastery and wrote its Rule, his knowledge of Greek and of east Christian traditions was deeply respected. In Mérida itself, eastern influence may be traced in the building programme undertaken by its bishops. This was financed largely by local devotion to the patron St. Eulalia, whose tunic constituted a most valuable relic, and may have been inspired by eastern models. A hospital and hospice in which visitors could stay and the sick were treated free of charge, churches, and monasteries were constructed, while a lending bank was set up. The Catholic Goth,

[6] C. Codoñer Merino, ed., El "de viris illustribus" de Ildefonso de Toledo (Salamanca, 1972), 121-22; cf. John of Biclar, Chronicle 212.25, 217.7.

[7] VPE 3 (pp. 154-61); John of Biclar, Chronicle 219.10.

[8] Vives, Inscripciones Cristianas, nos. 418, 425, 426.

[9] VPE 5.3.12 (pp. 196-97), cf. Collins, Early Medieval Spain, 96; J. Fontaine, L'Art Préroman Hispanique (La Pierre-Qui-Vire, 1973); P. de Palol Salellas and M. Hirmer, Early Medieval Art in Spain (London, 1967); H. Schlunk and T. Hauschild, Hispania Antiqua (Mainz, 1978).

[10] VPE 4.1-3 (pp. 160-63); 4.3.1-4.4.7 (pp. 168-75). E. A. Thompson, The Goths in Spain (Oxford, 1969), 21-22.

Masona, who succeeded Fidelis, was chiefly responsible for this enterprise. Such resources were peculiar to the city and represented one of the factors tending to regional separatism in sixth-century Spain.[11]

Not only the Catholic hierarchy of such rich cities as Mérida, but also the old Hispano-Roman ruling class of landowners resisted Visigothic Arian control. The "senators" of Amaia who were killed in 574 had presumably tried to preserve their traditional authority in the region, whether they were really senators in the Roman sense or not. In addition, leading Visigoths were not always loyal to the crown. Despite over a century of established princely rule, the tribal structure of the Gothic occupation tended to throw up local tyrants, "*tyranni*" or simply "*loci seniores*," elders, both Roman and Gothic.[12] The combination of these factors, divergent customs, and local particularities rendered Visigothic regal authority quite nominal in the mid-sixth century. The writers who continued the *Chronicle* of Fredegar and Gregory of Tours characterised the tradition of rebellion, assassination, and rivalry for the title king as a "*morbus Gothicus*" ("Gothic disease") especially developed in Spain.[13] Since the Franks also displayed a persistent tendency towards the same activity, with repeated sibling competition and internecine feuding, the Visigoths appeared more murderous still. Nonetheless, against this pattern of disputed leadership, Leovigild (568-86) strove to unite the kingdom under his monarchy and built a centralised power far more effective than any achieved by his Frankish contemporaries. Interestingly, Gregory accepted the totally unfounded story of Leovigild's deathbed penance and conversion to Catholicism. Perhaps he felt that after praising such a successful ruler, he should show that Leovigild also abandoned his heretical belief. There is no evidence that he did.

The Reign of Leovigild

As the youngest son of a nobleman of Seville, Leovigild acceded to sole rule in Spain after the death of his older brother, Liuva (586-57 1/3). Liuva had been elected at Narbonne by the Gothic notables after an interregnum of several months and quickly associated Leovigild with his rule, giving him authority over the South. Once sole monarch, Leovigild secured his own dynasty by marrying Godswinta, widow of his predecessor, King Athana-

[11] *VPE* 5.3.2-9 (pp. 192-97); R. Collins, "Mérida and Toledo: 550-585," in James, *Visigothic Spain*, 189-217.

[12] John of Biclar, *Chronicle* 213.29-30; cf. Braulio, *Vita Aemiliani*, ch. 26, *PL* 80, 712; Thompson, *Goths in Spain*, 61-62. On the *seniores*, see also C. Sánchez Albornoz, *Estudios Visigodos* (Rome, 1971), 158-64.

[13] *The Fourth Book of the Chronicle of Fredegar with Its Continuations*, ed. J. M. Wallace-Hadrill (London, 1960), ch. 82 (p. 70), "morbum Gotorum"; cf. Gregory of Tours, *HF* 3.30 (English translation, 187).

gild, and introducing his two young sons by a previous marriage as *consortes* (consorts in regal power).[14] For almost fifteen years (570-85), he fought to impose centralised control. His most powerful enemies were those in the Byzantine province, but he also had to deal with local dissidents, those tyrants and elders who led a rebellion in Cordova (572) and in the region of Orense (575), as well as the remoter northern provinces (Cantabria 574, Asturia 575) and the Basques (581), and neighbouring Sueves of Galicia, who were finally defeated and incorporated in 584-85. When faced with persistent resistance, Leovigild used confiscation of wealth and property and exemplary execution to force submission. His military supremacy was achieved by harsh and bloody policies.[15]

These alone would not have united the kingdom; institutional means were also necessary. And here Leovigild appears to have taken ancient Roman traditions and contemporary Byzantine practice as his model. He saw the need for a fixed capital and chose the relatively underdeveloped city of Toledo, well protected by natural fortifications and sited conveniently at the centre of his large realm.[16] At a time when Frankish and Lombard rulers generally moved from one palace or villa to another, or demanded hospitality from local ecclesiastics, the establishment of Spain's capital city prefigured a permanent central government. It permitted the construction of a suitably impressive residence with an organised court and settled institutions of administration. While the household character of Leovigild's palace may have owed much to Germanic tradition, its static position endowed the counts (*comites*) with more regular authority and encouraged the development of a permanent treasury and archive, influenced by the Roman tradition of written documents.[17]

The lack of previous building in Toledo demanded a church to reflect the new status of the city. Leovigild undertook the foundation of the basilica dedicated to St. Leocadia and attempted to obtain ancient relics for its consecration. Not only the building but also the cult of St. Leocadia had to be constructed, as there was little established tradition for this martyr. Her *Life* shows every sign of drawing from other sources, but the fabrication

---

[14] Collins, *Early Medieval Spain*, 40.

[15] K. F. Stroheker, "Leowigild," in his *Germanentum und Spätantike*, 134-91.

[16] E. Ewig, "Résidence et capitale pendant le haut Moyen Age," *RH* 230 (1963): 25-72, esp. 31-36; reprinted in his *Spätantikes und fränkisches Gallien*, 2 vols. (Munich, 1976-79), vol. 1. Cf. Collins, "Mérida and Toledo," 212-14.

[17] King, *Law and Society*, 53-57; C. Sánchez Albornoz, "El Aula Regia y las Asambleas Politicas de los Godos," *Cuadernos de Historia de España* 5 (1946): 5-110; reprinted in his *Estudios Visigodos*; J. Vezin, "L'influence des actes des hauts fonctionnaires romains sur les actes de Gaule et d'Espagne au VIIe siècle," in W. Paravicini and K. F. Werner, eds., *Histoire comparée d'administration (IVe-XVIIIe siècles)* (Munich, 1980), 71-75.

succeeded in giving the capital a local patron.[18] To the new church Leovigild summoned his Arian clergy for a national council held in 580, the first of a series of important meetings, at which the ruler and secular nobility would often be present to discuss regal as well as ecclesiastical matters.[19] Leovigild seems to have favoured a more moderate form of Arian doctrine, perhaps as a bait to win over the Catholic hierarchy. When one bishop did accept this position, he was promptly denounced by Catholics in the Byzantine province.[20] There was no significant progress in reuniting the two rival episcopacies.

In his new capital, Leovigild adopted kingly regalia for the first time in Visigothic history in Spain. He sat on a throne dressed in suitably impressive attire and may also have worn a crown. He founded a new city, Reccopolis, named in the Greek style after his second son, Reccared.[21] The Ostrogoths and Lombards of Italy had used Roman models in a similar fashion, adapting ceremonial and artistic representation, such as the presentation of a son as future king in the Roman circus of Milan in the presence of Frankish ambassadors (done by Agilulf for Adaloald), the use of the name "Flavius," and the image of angels as victories. But unlike his contemporaries in the West, Leovigild developed a novel concept of his kingship in the form of an identified national coinage. Until this date, Spanish kings had followed the custom of issuing imitation coins, usually modelled on Roman types minted in the West or Byzantine ones. They were always anonymous and often poorly struck. Leovigild was the first medieval Gothic ruler to put his own name on the coinage, as *dominus noster*, together with such epithets as *victor* (usually after a successful siege), *pius*, *inclitus*. and *iustus* (pious, famous, and just). He also associated his two sons with him on the coinage, a typical Byzantine step in the development of stable dynastic rule.[22]

In another attempt to regulate the kingdom of Spain in uniformity, Leovigild issued a revision of both Euric's Gothic law code and Alaric's *Bre-*

---

[18] VPE 5.6.2-18 (pp. 208-215); Collins, "Mérida and Toledo," 212-15, cf. idem, *Early Medieval Spain*, 99-100.

[19] John of Biclar, *Chronicle* 216.4-9; K. Schäferdiek, *Die Kirche in den Reichen der Westgoten und Suewen bis zur Errichtung der westgotischen katolischen Staatskirche* (Berlin, 1967), 159-64.

[20] Isidore of Seville, *De viris illustribus*, ed. C. Codoñer Merino (Salamanca, 1964), nos. 28 and 30 (pp. 149-51), on the opposition to Vincent of Saragossa.

[21] John of Biclar, *Chronicle* 215.20; K. Raddatz, "Studien zu Reccopolis 1: Die archäologische Befunde," *Madrider Mitteilungen* 5 (1964): 213-33, cf. D. Claude, "Studien zu Reccopolis 2: Die Historische Situation," ibid. 6 (1965): 167-94. Stroheker, "Leovigild," 224-30.

[22] G. C. Miles, *The Coinage of the Visigoths of Spain. Leovigild to Achila II* (New York, 1952), esp. 22; Collins, *Early Medieval Spain*, 49-50.

viarium of Roman law for Romans.[23] The legal division went back to the earliest days of Visigothic occupation, Euric's code dating from ca. 476 and Alaric's influential compilation from 506. In a marked departure from established practice, however, intermarriage between the two groups was henceforth permitted, a measure that must have contributed to the unity of the inhabitants, rather than their separate awareness as either Gothic or Roman. Separation by ethnic group may not have remained in force until ca. 642, when Chindaswinth's new code was issued.[24]

In 579-80 Leovigild's authority was challenged not by a leader of one of the many peripheral areas of the kingdom but by his own son, Hermenegild, governor (*dux*) of Baetica. Under the influence of his Frankish wife, Ingundis, and of Leander (later bishop of Seville), Hermenegild had converted to the Catholic faith and declared himself independent of his heretical father.[25] Although Leander was not on good terms with the Byzantines in Spain, at Hermenegild's request he went off to Constantinople to elicit imperial assistance and there met the papal legate Gregory, who became a close friend. Leovigild was thus faced by a revolt supported by eastern troops, but he possessed sufficient accumulated strength from his renovated kingship to defeat his son in the same manner as any other rebel. Hermenegild struck coins at Cordova and Seville, the two major cities in the south that supported him through the five-year revolt, but he was finally captured and sent into exile in Valencia. A year later, on 13 April 585, he was murdered at Leovigild's order, and not long after the old Arian king himself died.[26]

The Visigothic Conversion to Orthodoxy

Reccared, the surviving son, was unanimously acclaimed by the Gothic nobility and became king by the institutional rituals of anointing and crowning. His coronation marked a further adoption of Byzantine traditions, for until 586 rulers in the West were generally invested by acts of enthrone-

[23] Isidore of Seville, *History of the Goths*, ed. T. Mommsen, in *MGH, AA*, vol. 11, pt. 2, 51 (p. 288.19-20); also available in an English translation by G. Donini and G. B. Ford (Leiden, 1970); King, *Law and Society*, 13-14.

[24] P. D. King, "King Chindasvind and the First Territorial Law-code of the Visigothic Kingdom," in James, *Visigothic Spain*, 131-57; cf. Collins, *Early Medieval Spain*, 123-25. Against Thompson's insistence on the separate identities of Goth and Roman, and bitter hostility between them (for instance, *The Goths in Spain*, 314), Collins suggests that integration is much more likely, *Early Medieval Spain*, 53, 103; cf. J. Fontaine, "Conversion et culture chez les Wisigoths d'Espagne," *Settimane* 14 (1967): 87-147.

[25] John of Biclar, *Chronicle* 217.1-4 and 13; Isidore of Seville, *History of the Goths*, 48-49 (pp. 287-88); Gregory of Tours, *HF* 5.38, 6.43 (English translation, 301-303, 375-76); Collins, *Early Medieval Spain*, 45-48.

[26] Miles, *Coinage*, 23-24.

ment, being raised on a shield and acclaimed by their subjects. Anointing, however, was not part of the eastern ceremony and reflects the Visigothic development of inherited tradition along Christian lines.[27] In the first year of his rule Reccared declared his conversion to orthodoxy, and on the second anniversary of Hermenegild's death he reconsecrated the church of St. Leocadia in Toledo as a Catholic cathedral. Whether he was really influenced by his brother or felt guilt at having participated in his capture and death is impossible to judge. Reccared was probably impressed by the Catholic clergy such as Leander and Abbot Eutropius of the Servitanum monastery. Once he had decided to impose orthodoxy as the "national" faith of the kingdom, he ordered a council to meet in the capital in May 589. This, the third held at Toledo, gathered representatives of 71 episcopal sees and of all leading families, though not any Christian authority from outside Spain. It was, however, the largest council ever, and it established a particular relationship between monarchy and church that dominated all subsequent Visigothic history. As the acts of the council were carefully recorded and survive, it is possible to follow not only the means whereby the conversion took place, but also the stance taken by individual participants.[28] In a period where historical records are few and far between, these conciliar documents provide "living history." And in studying them we follow the example of those members of the late sixth- and seventh-century church in Spain who preserved and quoted the significant phrases from the acts of 589 and other councils as part of their own Christian heritage.

The council was opened by King Reccared, who pronounced his own declaration of faith, stressing the authority of the first four oecumenical councils and quoting the creeds of Nicaea, Constantinople, and Chalcedon, as well as his own.[29] He denounced Arianism with 23 anathemas, which recapitulated Catholic belief in contradistinction to heretical errors. Then both king and queen signed their agreement with these statements of orthodoxy, Reccared adopting the Roman name "Flavius."[30] Eight bishops recanted their Arian belief, and five leading Gothic noblemen signed their own acceptance—Gussinus *"vir inlustris,"* Fonsa, Afrila, Aila, and Ella,

[27] Isidore of Seville, *History of the Goths*, 52 (pp. 288-89); J. L. Nelson, "Symbols in Context: Rulers' Inauguration Rituals in Byzantium and the West in the Early Middle Ages," in *SCH* 13 (1976): 97-119, esp. 103; R. Schneider, *Königswahl und Königserhebung im Frühmittelalter* (Stuttgart, 1972), 196-99.

[28] Orlandis and Ramos-Lisson, *Die Synoden*, 95-117; J. Vives, ed., *Concilios Visigóticos e Hispano-Romanos* (Barcelona/Madrid, 1963), 107-145, and Mansi, 9.977-1005; cf. Isidore of Seville, *History of the Goths*, 52 (p. 289).

[29] Vives, *Concilios Visigóticos*, 107-116 (112, on the four holy synods); Mansi, 9.977-83 (980C).

[30] Vives, *Concilios Visigóticos*, 116 (signatures), 118-21 (anathemas); Mansi, 9.983C, 984-88.

representatives of all the Gothic elders, *"omnes seniores Gothorum."*[31] Next
Reccared proposed that, following the eastern custom, the creed should be
chanted at services before the Lord's Prayer, as an affirmation of orthodoxy.[32] This innovation was accepted together with 23 disciplinary canons,
some of which dealt with the duties of bishops in secular matters, their cooperation with civilian officials in judicial and financial affairs.[33] After the
signing of 64 bishops and seven deacons or presbyters representing their
episcopal leaders, Leander, archbishop of Seville, delivered a homily of joy
at the conversion and faith of the Spanish church.[34]

This inauguration of Catholic supremacy under royal protection established a practice that owed much to imperial custom. In his *Chronicle*, John
of Biclar compared Reccared to the emperors Constantine I at Nicaea (325)
and Marcian at Chalcedon (451), an analogy also confirmed by the imperial
style of acclamation recorded in the acts.[35] In Spain, however, while regal
initiative in summoning councils remained, the greater frequency of such
meetings and their devotion to secular business as well as ecclesiastical,
rather than strictly theological doctrine, marked a new departure. Councils
became a means of confirming royal power at the transfers of Visigothic
rule and were used to strengthen national unity as much as correct doctrine.[36] At the fourth council of Toledo in 633, the proper method of elect-
ing the monarch was set down (see below), for Visigothic Spain never accepted hereditary rule in one dynasty, though it was sometimes achieved.
While the selection remained the preserve of Gothic nobles, it was the
church under Isidore of Seville that drew up a series of conventions to govern the procedure. In general, however, councils of the Spanish church
functioned as a support and auxiliary to regal power. As in the East, the
king selected bishops, theoretically from a short list prepared by the clergy

[31] Vives, *Concilios Visigóticos*, 123; Mansi, 9.989B.
[32] Vives, *Concilios Visigóticos*, 124, and canon 2, 125; Mansi, 9.990A, 993A.
[33] Vives, *Concilios Visigóticos*, 124-33; Mansi, 9.992-99; John of Biclar, who became
Bishop of Gerona after 589, also fulfilled non-ecclesiastical duties in line with these canons,
see Thompson, *Goths in Spain*, 99-101. It was a tradition later drawn on by the Franks,
particularly Charles the Great.
[34] Vives, *Concilios Visigóticos*, 136-44; Mansi, 9.1000-1005; English translation in C. W.
Barlow, *Fathers of the Church*, vol. 62 (Washington, D.C., 1969), 229-35; P. Courcelle,
Histoire littéraire des grandes invasions germaniques, 3rd ed. (Paris, 1964), 257-58.
[35] John of Biclar, *Chronicle* 219.12-13; Vives, *Concilios Visigóticos*, 108; Mansi, 9.997C;
J. N. Hillgarth, "Coins and Chronicles: Propaganda in Sixth Century Spain and the Byzantine Background," *Historia* 15 (1966): 483-508 reprinted in his *Visigothic Spain, Byzantium
and the Irish*.
[36] C. J. Bishko, "Spanish Abbots and the Visigothic Councils of Toledo," in *Humanistic
Studies in Honour of J. C. Metcalf* (Charlottesville, Va., 1941), 139-50 (now reprinted in his
Spanish and Portuguese Monastic History, 600-1300 [London, 1984]); for a general survey, see
H. Schwöbel, *Synode und König im Westgotenreich* (Cologne/Vienna, 1982).

of each see, but unknown candidates could be imposed, even without the required popular and clerical acclamation.[37] Despite this ultimate secular control over appointments, the church manifested much greater critical awareness of its duties and standards than other western churches. In comparison with that of Merovingian Francia, the Spanish clergy was probably better educated and trained. While other monarchs summoned their own church councils, these enjoyed much less success, whether in reforming clerical and monastic standards or in spreading Christian learning. The alliance between church and state in Spain in its unusual mould remained particular to the Iberian peninsula.

The Creed and Filioque in Spain

At the first "national" council of 589, three theological initiatives were introduced and enshrined in Spanish custom: the use of the creed in the mass; its wording; and the refusal to accept the Fifth Oecumenical Council of 553, which was simply ignored in Spain as among the churches of Africa and the West.[38] The first two initiatives represented a development of considerable import, for the creed was generally learnt by those entering the church for the purpose of baptism, and had not previously been chanted in the mass. The practice seems to have been adopted in 589 as a method of eradicating Arian heretical belief. As for the wording, the inclusion of the *Filioque* clause in the third section of the creed devoted to the Holy Spirit constituted a major change.[39] At the councils of Constantinople I (381) and Chalcedon (451), which had both devoted time to this wording as an aspect of Trinitarian definition, it was agreed that the Holy Spirit proceeds from the Father. The addition, "and from the Son" (in Latin, *et ex Filio* or *Filioque*) represented accepted belief but was not actually included in the East. As St. Augustine *had* inserted the addition, however, Leander could cite the most honoured Latin Father in support of the *Filioque*.[40] Given that most ecclesiastical authorities, eastern and papal, agreed that the Holy Spirit proceeds from both Father and Son, there should have been no dispute. But neither in the East nor in Rome was any change made to the Ni-

[37] King, *Law and Society*, 124-29, esp. 125, characterises royal power as "caesaropapaism"; cf. Collins, *Early Medieval Spain*, 116-23; Wallace-Hadrill, *The Barbarian West*, 122-23.

[38] Vives, *Concilios Visigóticos*, 120; Mansi, 9.980C.

[39] Orlandis and Ramos-Lisson, *Die Synoden*, 109 n.54, on the state of the manuscripts and the possibility of later insertion.

[40] On the complex history of the *Filioque*, see E. B. Pusey, *On the Clause "and the Son" in Regard to the Eastern Church and the Bonn Conference* (Oxford, 1876), 46-49, 184-85; J. N. D. Kelly, *Early Christian Creeds*, 3rd ed. (London, 1972), 358-62; J. Madoz, *Le Symbole du IXe Concile de Tolède* (Louvain, 1938), 49-55.

cene and Constantinopolitan creed, cited as definitive at Chalcedon. This
creed did not include the fateful words, "and from the Son." So Reccared's
use was novel: a change, however well documented, from the established
creed as recited in eastern services since 518 (when Justin I instituted
the public recital of the creed as a useful means of confirming correct doctrine), and as learned in the West.[41] Nonetheless, the first Catholic Visigothic king can hardly have anticipated the extraordinary furore this clause
would provoke. Reccared had cited the eastern creeds with the addition,
apparently under the impression that it was included in them. Such confusions were quite possible given the overall agreement in theological
terms and the paucity of eastern documents available at the time.

Although the 589 council does not decree the fate of Arian works or the
future of obdurate Arian clergy, the *Chronicle* of Fredegar describes how Arian bibles and service books were collected, put in a house, and then
burnt.[42] The destruction appears to have been fairly complete, for not a single Gothic manuscript survives from Spain, unlike the *Codex Argenteus* from
sixth-century Ostrogothic Italy. It is therefore impossible to establish how
much of a change was involved in the adoption of orthodoxy. Arianism
does seem to have been successfully condemned, however, for there were
only a few revivals, quickly subdued.[43] One of the reasons for this relatively
peaceful changeover may lie in the fact that written Gothic, the language
devised by Ulfila, was used only for Arian bibles, homilies, and prayer
books. Once these were all removed, Gothic no longer had any function
and gradually died out. Its chief official exponents, Arian priests, apparently converted to Catholicism and adopted Latin. Whether the Gothic
language continued to be spoken is a conundrum that still taxes specialists
of Visigothic Spain.[44] There is little evidence for its use, and several factors
seem to have worked against it, notably the development of conciliar law,
which applied uniformly to all inhabitants regardless of ethnic origin; the
degree of intermarriage; and the ubiquitous use of Latin for writing. After
the adoption of Catholicism, other Gothic customs, including forms of

[41] The eastern custom of reciting the creed during the mass was in fact introduced by
Patriarch Timothy (511-18) under Justin I; see Theodoros Anagnostes (Theodore the Lector), *Ecclesiastical History*, 501, ed. G. C. Hanson (Berlin, 1971), p. 143; cf. John of Biclar,
Chronicle 211.16-17, attributing the innovation to Justin II. On the change, see B. Capelle,
"L'introduction du symbole à la messe," in *Mélanges J. de Ghellinck*, 2 vols. (Gembloux,
1951), 2:1003-1027, reprinted in his *Travaux Liturgiques de doctrine et d'histoire*, vol. 3 (Louvain, 1967).

[42] *The Fourth Book of the Chronicle of Fredegar*, ch. 8 (p. 7).

[43] Collins, *Early Medieval Spain*, 55-58.

[44] J. Orlandis, *La Iglesia en la España visigotica y medieval* (Pamplona, 1976), 40-60 (articles reprinted in more accessible form); cf. Thompson, *Goths in Spain*, 95, 98, 101-104.

burial and dress, appear to have disappeared, reflecting increased Hispano-Roman influence.

THE SPANISH CHURCH

The decisive mould of church/state relations set up by the 589 council permitted an intense Christian influence to pervade ruling circles. Ecclesiastical authors were responsible for elevating the monarchy to a new level, employing the word *maiestas* ("majesty") of Reccared, a term normally reserved for God in the West, and describing Visigothic rule as an *imperium* ("empire").[45] Although previously persecuted by Arian rulers like Leovigild, the Catholic bishops had not been reduced to a manipulatable quantity: they maintained a strong exposition of orthodox faith, based on broad theological reading and rich library resources. While their knowledge of Greek Christian works was mainly through translations, they read widely in early Christian patristic material and were of course directly familiar with Latin theologians, Sts. Ambrose, Hilary, Augustine, Caesarius of Arles, and so on. A major source of both church and secular learning was Africa: from North Africa, Spanish bishops gained the works of Fulgentius of Ruspe and two defenders of the Three Chapters, Facundus of Hermiane and Victor of Tonnena.[46]

Contacts between Spain and Rome were slight, not institutionalised by any attempt to set up a papal vicariate for the peninsula. After their sojourn in Constantinople, Licinianus of Carthagena and Leander of Seville remained in correspondence with Pope Gregory, who advised Leander on the correct form of baptism (single rather than triple) and intervened in clerical disputes within the Byzantine province. It was of course to Leander, a particular friend, that the *Moralia in Iob*, originally composed in the eastern capital, were dedicated. But this communication between the peninsula and Rome does not appear to have survived Gregory's death in 604—it had been based on personal acquaintance and did not continue under his successors. This did not mean, however, that Gregory's writings were not well known and much studied in Spain. On the contrary, King Chindaswinth's decision to send Taio (later bishop of Saragossa) to Rome to find a copy of Gregory's *Moralia* suggests that his total output was known, admired, and felt to be needed in seventh-century Spain.[47]

[45] Isidore of Seville, *De viris illustribus*, no. 22 (p. 146).

[46] P. Riché, *Education and Culture in the Barbarian West* (Columbia, S.C., 1976), 229-301, on the importance of St. Augustine in Spain and manuscripts from Africa. Isidore's appreciation of sixth-century African theologians is clear from his notices on Facundus of Hermiane and Victor of Tonnena, see *De viris illustribus*, nos. 19 and 25 (pp. 144, 147).

[47] J. Madoz, "Tajón de Zaragoza y su viaje a Roma," in *Mélanges J. de Ghellinck*, 1:345-60.

Besides this well-informed episcopacy, the Spanish church also had a developed monastic tradition, which was similarly enriched by contacts with the East. Both Leander of Seville and John of Biclar returned from Constantinople to write monastic rules, Leander for his sister Florentina's nunnery, John for his own foundation. Isidore of Seville also wrote a Rule for the *"coenobium Honorianensi."*[48] From his even closer knowledge of the eremitic tradition in its original homeland, Martin of Braga founded a monastery at Dumio and taught one of its inmates, Paschasius, sufficient Greek to translate part of the *Vitae Patrum*, "Sayings of the Desert Fathers,"[49] These aphorisms, with their total renunciation of the world and devotion to extreme asceticism, humility, and constant prayer, appear to have been followed quite closely by St. Fructuoso and Valerio of Bierzo in the second half of the seventh century. Fructuoso had been trained in the episcopal school at Palencia, embraced the monastic life, and founded several monasteries, including Compludo and Bierzo in Galicia and northwest Spain. He wrote two Rules, stressed the importance of spiritual studies, and developed the traditions established by Martin.[50] Unlike some of the Desert Fathers, however, the Spanish monks considered learning important; Valerio in particular took pains to instruct the peasantry and their children in basic Christian beliefs.[51]

Intellectual Activity: The Contribution of Isidore of Seville

In this determination Valerio demonstrated another aspect of the Spanish church, which had always stressed the need for adequate clerical education. It can be seen in the training that Leander of Seville gave to his younger brothers and sister. From this curriculum Isidore developed an influential model, described in Books 1 to 8 of his *Etymologies*.[52] He included a basic

---

[48] Leander's *Regula*, ed. J. Campos Ruiz and I. Roca Melia, *Santos Padres Españoles*, 2 vols. (Madrid, 1971), 2:21-71, also in *PL* 72, 873-94; it is translated by Barlow, *Fathers of the Church*, 62:183-228. Isidore's *Regula*, ed. Campos Ruiz and Roca Melia, *Santos Padres*, 2:90-125, also in *PL* 83, 867-94. John's is lost.

[49] J. Geraldus Freire, *A versao latina por Pascasio de Dume dos Apophthegmata Patrum* (Coimbra, 1971).

[50] On Fructuoso, see his *Life*, ed. M. C. Diaz y Diaz, *La Vida de san Fructuoso de Braga* (Braga, 1974); text also in *PL* 87, 459-70; English translation in F. C. Nock, *The "Vita Sancti Fructuosi"* (Washington, D.C., 1946). His *Rules*, ed. Campos Ruiz and Roca Melia, *Santos Padres*, 2:137-62, also in *PL* 87, 1099-1130, are translated in Barlow, *Fathers of the Church*, 63:155-206.

[51] Valerio records his own life in fragmentary autobiographical writings of great interest; see C. M. Aherne, *Valerio of Bierzo, an Ascetic of the Late Visigothic Period* (Washington, D.C., 1949); also in *PL* 87, 422-58. References to his teaching occur in the *Replicatio* 3, 4, 6 (pp. 119, 125, 129).

[52] J. Fontaine, *Isidore de Séville et la culture classique dans l'Espagne Wisigothique*, 2 vols. (Paris, 1959), 1:7-9; W. M. Lindsay, ed., *Isidori Etymologiae sive Origenes*, 2 vols. (Oxford,

knowledge of the pagan classics, for against the dangers inherent in non-Christian learning, Isidore set the even greater risk of ignorance. It was certainly not this sophisticated curriculum that Valerio taught to the Galicians, but the idea that education was essential derived from Isidore's insistence. The more direct fruits of this programme can be observed in the "family" training of Isidore's own pupils (Braulio, Ildefonsus, and others), and in the recruitment of well-educated monks to leading positions within the church.[53] One aspect of the significance attached to learning in seventh-century Spain can be gauged from the number of scriptoria established for the copying of manuscripts and the pride taken in libraries—for instance, Braulio's 450 volumes.[54]

While it is generally recognised that Spain preserved classical learning and educational training in a Christian guise far more than other successor states in the West, even the Lombard kingdom of North Italy, the direction to which this was put is not always understood. As indicated above, part of the motive lay in the glorification of the Christian Visigothic kingdom. And in this process a novel form of Christian rule was devised as a political ideology more suitable to the circumstances of seventh-century Spain.[55] The key spokesman of this development was the indefatigable Isidore, bishop of Seville from ca. 600-636, who was constantly writing and compiling compendia of useful information—useful not only to clerics, monks, and other bishops, but also to rulers, administrators, and practical men concerned with mining, medical knowledge, or accounts (some of these would be clerics too).[56] His output resulted from the same combination of religious and secular purpose that is the hallmark of Visigothic

1911), partially translated by E. Brehaut, *An Encyclopaedist of the Dark Ages* (Ithaca, 1912, reprinted New York, 1966), 89-206.

[53] C. M. Aherne, "Late Visigothic Bishops, Their Schools and the Transmission of Culture," *Traditio* 22 (1966): 435-44; Fontaine, *Isidore of Séville*, 2:736-62, 789-806; Riché, *Education and Culture*, 293-303, 353-55, for Spanish insistence on the monastic study of profane texts.

[54] C. H. Lynch, *S. Braulio, Bishop of Saragossa (631-51): His Life and Writings* (Washington, D.C., 1938), 149-58. Many of these books were inherited from Isidore, Braulio's teacher. Even in the very disturbed existence he led, Valerio took pride in copying manuscripts and bemoaned their theft; see the *Ordo querimoniae* 3, ed. Aherne, *Valerio of Bierzo* (p. 77); *Replicatio* 14 (p. 145).

[55] H. X. d'Arquillière, *L'Augustinisme politique*, 2nd ed. (Paris, 1955), 41-42, 142-44; cf. M. Reydellet, "La conception du souverain chez Isidore de Séville," in M. C. Diaz y Diaz, ed., *Isidoriana* (Leon, 1961), 457-66.

[56] For example, Book 17 of the *Etymologies* is devoted to agriculture, edited with a French translation by J. André, *Isidore de Séville, Etymologies Livre XVII, "de l'agriculture"* (Paris, 1981); cf. W. D. Sharpe, *Isidore of Seville: The Medical Writings* (Philadelphia, 1964). See also Brehaut, *An Encyclopaedist of the Dark Ages*.

Christianity and that provided it with a distinctive political independence within a framework of religious orthodoxy.

The Sixth Age of the World. In his ceaseless activity Isidore consulted many older epitomes and excerpts of ancient wisdom, pagan and Christian, but he wrote specifically for the Iberian Christians of his time. The accession of King Sisebut in 612 may well have encouraged him, for Sisebut appeared an ideal of Christian devotion and Catholic leadership, the new regal force that would lead Spain in the paths of the Lord. From a theological study of the transformation wrought by Christ's birth and death, Isidore developed the idea that the final stage in world history would constitute the *regnum Christi*, reign of Christ.[57] This new emphasis on the Christian culmination of the whole of human evolution meant that Isidore could treat all history as revealed destiny. It also concorded with his view of the Bible as a true historical account, in which the Old Testament prophecies were fulfilled by the Gospel narratives of the New. Taking from St. Augustine the traditional notion of the six ages of the world, which corresponded to the six days of Creation (for on the seventh day God rested), Isidore identified the period from the birth of Christ as the sixth and last age, which he dated from the death of Julius Caesar and accession of Octavian. This Christian event was seen as inaugurating an entirely new age, qualitatively different from all the preceding ones, an age that would continue and endure "as long as Christ wills." While he placed a similar emphasis on the Incarnation, Isidore was not familiar with the A.D. dating system of Dionysios, although he had access to a version of the Easter tables, which he misunderstood.[58] For his world chronology, therefore, he relied on his own calculation of the *Annus Mundi*, though he went right back to the dawn of the first day of Creation as the beginning of recorded time. These calculations were further supplemented by reference to the reigns of temporal rulers, both Byzantine emperors and Iberian monarchs.

In this sixth and final age, which was continuing as Isidore wrote, he realised that all societies would be judged by their practice, and the greatest would be that which lived and acted most clearly in accordance with the

[57] M. Reydellet, *La royauté dans la littérature latine de Sidone Apollinaire à Isidore de Séville* (Rome, 1981), 556-57.

[58] On Isidore's chronology, see T. Mommsen, in *MGH, AA*, vol. 11, pt. 2 (Berlin, 1894), 244-51; and on his efforts to use the Alexandrian system of Easter computation, see C. W. Jones, "The Victorian and Dionysiac Paschal Tables," *Speculum* 9 (1934): 408-421, esp. 415-20. Augustine had placed a similar emphasis on the qualitative difference brought about by Christianity, but he identified the *"tempora Christiana"* with the ending of persecution, the "peace of the church" declared by Constantine I. Cf. A. Borst, "Das Bild der Geschichte in der Enzyklopädie Isidors von Sevilla," *Deutsches Archiv für Erforschung des Mittelalters* 22 (1966): 1-62.

faith. This new moral standard identified all known Christian societies of the seventh century as equals, all limbs of Christ, *membra Christi*.[59] By asserting that Christian belief was the deciding factor, Isidore could posit Visigothic society as the most Christian. But as many different states all share in the reign of Christ, there can be no supremacy by one over the others; none can claim a monopoly of power or make outstanding claims on the others. Isidore recognised the special rights of Rome, which could command the devotion and respect of all Christians as the foundation of St. Peter. He did not go so far, however, as to curtail the independence of the Spanish church by these rights, a situation reflected in the lack of communication between Spain and the papacy.[60]

While certain degrees of equality between churches were acknowledged, Isidore turned his understanding of Visigothic Christianity against Byzantium to even greater effect. For if Constantinople maintained its right as the seat of the empire to rule the whole Christian world, the monarchy of the whole kingdom of Spain, *totius Spaniae . . . monarchiam regni*, could be cited as a legitimate Christian society in its own right.[61] This factor became particularly telling after the reconquest of the Byzantine province, which united the peninsula under Visigothic rule, and the forced conversion of the Jews, which brought the entire population to the true faith. King Suinthila, praised by Isidore as a "most religious prince," achieved the final expulsion of the *"Romani"* in the 620s.[62] Isidore also noted in his *Chronicle* that the empire had recently lost Jerusalem and several eastern provinces to the Persians, while the Huns had occupied Thrace and the Slavs Greece.[63] There is an obvious implication: Byzantium is an old power in decline, while the Spanish monarch represents a new authority, the living rather than the dying limb of Christ. The significance of this distinction lay in the independence thus claimed for the Spanish church. Christian authority in the Iberian peninsula was in no way inferior or subordinate to that in Rome or Constantinople. In its determination to live according to the principles of the faith, it might even come to be judged as more Christian than the older centres. While Isidore's confidence may have been misplaced, it was cer-

[59] Reydellet, *La royauté*, 560-61, 593.

[60] See Isidore's letter to Eugenius, *PL* 83, 908; G. B. Ford, Jr., *The Letters of St. Isidore of Seville*, 2nd ed. (Amsterdam, 1970), no. 8 (pp. 47-49); J. Madoz, "El primado romano en España en el ciclo isidoriano," *Revista español de Teología* 2 (1942): 229-55.

[61] Isidore of Seville, *History of the Goths*, 62 (p. 292); cf. his *Chronicle*, 416, 416b (p. 480).

[62] *History of the Goths*, 60 (p. 291); *Chronicle*, 416. On the forced conversion of the Jews, see King, *Law and Society*, 130-37, 144-45; J. Orlandis, "Hacia una meior comprension del problema judío en el reino visigodo—católico de España," *Settimane* 26 (Spoleto, 1980): 149-78.

[63] Isidore of Seville, *Chronicle*, 409a, 413, 414a (pp. 478-79).

tainly not undermined by what he knew of Christian practice elsewhere. His preface to the *History of the Goths*, titled *In Praise of Spain*, reveals a deep conviction that Visigothic Christianity was to have a great future.[64]

The Christian Monarchy of Spain

In parallel with this view of world history, which justified Spain as an equally Christian state, Isidore revised the accepted notion of regal power. The Eusebian concept of monarchy as a semi-divine state, the ruler acting in imitation of God, *mimesis Theou*, was replaced by the idea of a Christian monarch, the servant of his Christian subjects, more akin to a bishop in the church than to any autocratic emperor.[65] In this fundamental change Isidore denies the claims of a universal and necessarily despotic empire to perpetuity: its demise was pronounced by Christ's birth, which permits many churches to co-exist in His eternal reign.[66] The empire is effectively removed, its place taken by the church, and Christian kings are thereby rendered equal to and as legitimate as emperors. In this new *regnum Christi*, however, the dangers and risks of power demand clemency, justice, service, and duty of its leaders.[67] The church supports this Christian rule but does not dominate it; indeed, in certain cases the king must intervene in the affairs of the church to support ecclesiastical discipline.[68] He too must observe the same discipline. Unlike past emperors, the new rulers share fully in the human condition and must convince their Christian subjects by counsel and good example, rather than by force. In his tentative outline of the image of a good king, Isidore stresses the need to avoid envy, to act with mercy towards conspirators, and to override the sins of his predecessors.[69] This is a far cry from the "Mirror of Princes" of later medieval date, but it does constitute a first attempt to distinguish Christian monarchy from previous imperial and republican forms of domination.

In late sixth- and seventh-century Spain, however, the full force of Isidore's theories of Christian leadership were by no means realised. On the contrary, in their handling of ecclesiastical affairs, kings from Reccared onwards displayed an authoritarian domination similar to past models. Their control over the Spanish church has frequently been likened to Byzantine "caesaropapism," a comparison that may be set beside many other similar-

---

[64] *Laus Spaniae*, p. 267; cf. M. Reydellet, "Les Intentions idéologiques et politiques dans la Chronique d'Isidore de Séville," *Mélanges d'archéologie et d'histoire* 82 (1970): 363-400.

[65] Redellet, *La Royauté*, 557, 592.

[66] Ibid., 556, 567-68.

[67] Ibid., 583-86.

[68] Ibid., 587-90, 594.

[69] Ibid., 590-92, 595.

ities or even direct borrowings by the Visigoths from the eastern empire.[70] But as I have shown earlier, in Chapter 3, "caesaropapism" developed in particular historical circumstances in the East, and the term, so often used as one of abuse, cannot be transplanted without extreme care. That said, however, the Visigothic relationship between secular and spiritual authority did resemble the Byzantine, for the following reasons: Reccared initiated the conversion to Catholicism, summoned the church council that effected it, and presided over the proceedings as a devout adherent of the true faith. A regal directive impelled the official abandonment of Arianism and coloured all later ecclesiastical development. The pattern of church/state relations was thus established on the monarchy's terms, although the episcopacy determined many detailed aspects within it. A Christian monarchy in the sense conceived by Isidore would not become a reality for 150 years or so after his death, and then in a quite different part of Europe. But like so many of his novel Christian concepts, when rediscovered, they were to play a vital part in shaping the development of the West.

Despite Reccared's somewhat despotic approach to the church, he provided an important model for Isidore's idea of the Christian ruler, because he was responsible for uniting the entire population of Spain in a proud and independent kingdom.[71] Further material for the composite image was derived from succeeding kings, Sisebut (612-21), Suinthila (621-31), and Sisenand (631-36). With all three, Isidore was on intimate terms, acting as *orator* at the court of Toledo, dedicating his treatise *On Nature (De natura rerum)* to King Sisebut, and discussing with these rulers the Christian role of a king.[72] He condemned their regular attempts to convert the Jews, which often led to persecution and were obviously unsuccessful, and praised their military campaigns against the Byzantines in the south. In the proceedings of the Fourth Council of Toledo held in the church of St. Leocadia in 633, we probably get an accurate reflection of Isidore's ideal of church/state relations.[73] Sixty-two bishops or their representatives gathered at the order of King Sisenand, who prostrated himself at the first session, requesting the participants to intercede for him, to maintain the laws of the church and destroy abuses. After this act of humility the council proceeded to discuss and regulate a variety of ecclesiastical and secular matters,

---

[70] See King, *Law and Society*, 124-29, esp. 125.

[71] Reydellet, *La Royauté*, 586-87.

[72] J. Fontaine, *Isidore de Séville: Traité de la Nature* (Bordeaux, 1960); Reydellet, "La conception du souverain"; cf. the writings of King Sisebut, ed. M. Gil, *Miscellanea Wisigotica* (Seville, 1972), also in *MGH, Ep.*, vol. 3, and *MGH, SSRM*, vol. 3.

[73] Vives, *Concilios Visigóticos*, 186-225; Orlandis and Ramos-Lisson, *Die Synoden*, 144-71; Mansi, 10.611-43.

including the Visigothic succession, in 75 disciplinary canons. In all these the king, Gothic nobles, and (largely) Roman episcopacy cooperated.

The Council of 633. Many features of the Fourth Council of Toledo repay examination as indices of Spanish autonomy. Sisenand's confession of faith made in the first session stated that the Holy Spirit derived from both Father and Son, a belief firmly supported by Isidore. The clearest exposition of this dual procession occurs in Book 7 of his *Etymologies*, in sections 3 and 4 devoted to the Holy Spirit and the Trinity. On the equality of the Three Members of the Godhead, Isidore writes: "The Father alone is not from anything else, thus He alone is called uncreated; the Son alone is by His nature from the Father, thus He alone is called created; the Holy Spirit alone proceeds from the Father and the Son, thus the Spirit alone is constituted by them both."[74] Given the wide dissemination of this work throughout the West, Isidore's authoritative statement on the matter was very influential. The creed of this council was also known outside Spain and was considered a most pure formula of faith.[75] Thus, through Isidore's significant use and amplification of the *Filioque* clause, it became generally known in other western churches to the exclusion of other wordings.

The canons of the Fourth Council of Toledo also reveal Spanish independence in ecclesiastical discipline. The first 17 canons all concerned the uniformity of church services, especially the celebration of Easter and the service of baptism—Pope Gregory's letter to Leander of Seville was quoted here.[76] Further canons stipulated that monastic communities should insist upon a uniform tonsure for monks, and should set up their *oeconomoi* (i.e. officials in charge of the monastic economy) according to the canons of Chalcedon (451).[77] While these references to authorities such as Rome and the Fourth Oecumenical Council indicate an awareness of the supreme

[74] *Etymologies* 7.3.1; cf. 7.4.4; cf. *De ecclesiasticis officiis*, book 2, 24, *PL* 83, 817; Vives, *Concilios Visigóticos*, 187; Mansi, 10.615-16; cf. *VPE*, 5.9.5 (pp. 230-31), which stresses Reccared's defence of the Catholic faith through "preaching the eternity and the oneness in power and substance of the Holy Trinity, distinguishing Its Persons and affirming Its oneness in nature, declaring the Father Unbegotten, holding the Son to be begotten of the Father, believing in the procession of the Holy Spirit from both" (*Spiritum vero Sanctam ex utroque procedere credens*). The *VPE* was probably composed under Bishop Stephen of Mérida (633-38), see the Introduction by Garvin, p. 3.
[75] J. Madoz, "Le symbole du IVᵉ Concile de Tolède," *Revue d'Histoire ecclésiastique* 34 (1938): 5-20.
[76] Vives, *Concilios Visigóticos*, 188-98 (canon 6, on baptism, 191); Mansi, 10.616-24.
[77] Vives, *Concilios Visigóticos*, canon 41 (on tonsure, 206-207); canon 48 (on *oeconomoi*, 208); canons 49-53 (208-209); Mansi, 10, canon 41 (630), canon 48 (631), canons 49-53 (631-32).

earthly regulators of Christian affairs, it is obvious that the Spanish church was more concerned with its own development. The ten canons passed in 633 against the Jews of Spain and the eight on ecclesiastical freedmen were quite specific to the conditions of the peninsula.[78]

Finally, the 75th canon established the means devised by Isidore and Sisenand, "For the strength of our kingdom and the stability of the Gothic race."[79] As the principle of hereditary rule was unacceptable to the Gothic nobility, and the period 601-612 had witnessed great confusion, Isidore realised that the question of succession had to be regulated by a series of conventions governing election, acclamation, and coronation. These were proposed and accepted in canon 75, which isolated the office of king as a supremely Christian duty, neither Germanic nor Imperial, but a new position. Chintila's first act after his election in 636 according to these principles was to summon another council (the Fifth Council of Toledo) to reaffirm the canon.[80] The significance of kingship was further elaborated in 672 by the addition of a ritual anointing, performed by Bishop Julian of Toledo for King Wamba. Although these measures in which leading ecclesiastics played an important role in no way prevented disputes between rival contenders for the throne, they did ensure the legitimation of the winner.[81] The cooperation between church and state in the institution of serious regal responsibilities and Christian duties, while not always effective in Spain, constituted a high point of Isidore's new theory of Christian leadership and was to have a long life.

Isidore's Antagonism to Byzantium

Although Isidore was concerned primarily with the Visigothic monarchy, his ideas of kingship were probably influenced by what he knew of imperial government. There is no evidence that he was familiar with more than the names of his contemporaries, Emperors Maurice, Phokas, and Herakleios, but from his study of ecclesiastical history he had formed a very unfavourable view of Justinian.[82] As the emperor responsible for forcing through the Fifth Oecumenical Council's condemnation of the Three Chapters, never

[78] Vives, *Concilios Visigóticos*, 210-14 (against the Jews), 214-17 (on freedmen); Mansi, 10.633-35, 635-37; King, *Law and Society*, 133 n.5, 134-39.
[79] Vives, *Concilios Visigóticos*, 217-21; Mansi, 10.637-41; cf. Orlandis and Ramos-Lisson, *Die Synode*, 166-71.
[80] Vives, *Concilios Visigóticos*, 229; Mansi, 10.656A-B.
[81] And could be used in reverse to remove a non-Christian ruler, see R. Collins, "Julian of Toledo and the Royal Succession in Late Seventh-Century Spain," in P. H. Sawyer and I. N. Woods, eds., *Early Medieval Kingship* (Leeds, 1977), 30-49; cf. Schneider, *Königswahl und Königserhebung*, 198-200.
[82] Isidore of Seville, *Chronicle*, 404, 406, 410, 414 (pp. 477-79).

accepted in Spain, Justinian was judged a tyrant who persecuted the orthodox bishops and churches of Illyricum and Africa. In addition, Isidore knew that he was the author of heretical books on the Incarnation (a reference to Justinian's belief in aphthartodocetism) and that he was associated with the *Akephaloi* ("headless ones").[83] This charge was the more serious because Isidore had first-hand experience of at least one of this sect, a Syrian bishop called Gregory, who attended the provincial council of Seville in 619, scandalising everyone present by his erroneous and heretical pronouncements. The 12th and 13th canons of this council record Gregory's position and Isidore's refutation of it with a final condemnation and renunciation of akephalism.[84] The adherents of this heresy are characterised in the treatise *On ecclesiastical offices* as an errant people, clerics without a leader or head (*kephalos*), confused and mixed up like the Hippocentaur (neither horse nor man), who pullulate in great disorder.[85] That Justinian should have supported such muddled theology was clearly proof of his own heretical leanings.

The strongest condemnation of Justinian occurs in Isidore's description of famous men, *De viris illustribus*.[86] The emperor is here contrasted with his opponents, Facundus of Hermiane (who wrote 12 books in defence of the Three Chapters) and Bishop Victor of Tonnena, a martyr for the same cause. Through the close connections with Africa, Isidore was particularly well informed on this opposition; it was a copy of Victor's *Chronicle* that Isidore extended from 558 to 625. His opposition to Justinian on religious grounds led him to minimise the emperor's authority, as if the mid-sixth-century Visigothic monarch, Athanagild, were at least his equal in temporal power.[87] The fact that Justinian's forces had reconquered Africa and Italy and established a Byzantine province in southeast Spain only increased Isidore's hostility, even though Athanagild may have colluded with the arrival of Byzantine troops as a support for his own bid for power. Isidore's suspicion of eastern emperors even extended to Constantine I, condemned for being an Arian despite his role at the First Oecumenical Council of Ni-

---

[83] Ibid., 397a (p. 475); cf. *De viris illustribus*, no. 28, p. 144. For the theology of aphthartodocetism, see above, Chapter 4, note 36.

[84] Vives, *Concilios Visigóticos*, 171-85; Mansi, 10.561-68; J. Madoz, "El florilegio patristico del 11ᵉ Concilio de Sevilla," in *Miscellanea Isidoriana* (Rome, 1936), 177-221.

[85] Isidore of Seville, *De ecclesiasticis officiis*, book 2, 3, *PL* 83, 779; cf. *Etymologies*, 7.5.66 on the *Acephali*.

[86] Isidore of Seville, *De viris illustribus*; no. 18, p. 145; on Isidore's defence of the Three Chapters and approval of Origen, see Fontaine, *Isidore de Séville*, 2:868-69; J. Châtillon, "Isidore et Origène," in *Mélanges bibliques rédigés en l'honneur d'André Robert* (Paris, 1955), 537-47, reprinted in his *D'Isidore de Séville à Saint Thomas D'Aquin* (London, 1985).

[87] Isidore of Seville, *De viris illustribus*, no. 22, p. 146: "*Iustinianus in republica et Athanagildus in Hispaniis imperium tenuere.*"

caea and deathbed conversion.[88] Other emperors, Zeno and Anastasios in turn, were similarly associated with the protection of the heretical *Akephaloi*, while Constantinople was identified as the birthplace of the Macedonian heresy.[89]

In conjunction with this pronounced hostility to the eastern capital, Isidore refused to recognise it as the seat of a patriarchate. Only Rome, Antioch, and Alexandria derive great honour from their aspostolic foundation and deserve special reverence as such.[90] Similarly, Constantinople is merely the capital of the Roman Empire in the East, just as Rome is in the West: a city with a pagan past that Constantine adopted as a refuge, because it provided shelter from both the Aegean and Black seas.[91] The downgrading of both civilian and ecclesiastical claims is pronounced: Isidore concedes neither the political preeminence of the eastern capital as *caput mundi*, the head of the world, nor its episcopal claim to the title of oecumenical patriarch. In the latter he may well have been influenced by Gregory the Great's disagreements with John the Faster, known both through Gregory's writings and from Leander of Seville.[92]

Isidore's preoccupation with the moral standing of Christian Spain rested upon this contrast between Spain and the East, always to the disadvantage of the latter. In answer to a query from the archdeacon Redemptus about what sort of bread should be used in the sacrament, Isidore justified the Roman custom of unleavened bread, to be covered with a white linen cloth, rather than leavened bread and a silk cloth as in the East. "But perhaps you may object that silken cloth is more precious and thus more suited for divine uses. To this we say that in both Testaments the whiteness of garments is especially approved, since sincerity of mind is required by it. . . . Which among cloths is as pure as linen, to which whiteness is increased by frequent washing, whereas with silken cloths the whiteness seems to be more darkened from washing?"[93] The sense of rivalry between Greek and Latin authorities and the essential superiority of the Holy Roman Church were two very significant legacies of Isidore's work.

But it is important to remember that Isidore wrote as a regional archbishop for an exclusively Spanish audience, his diocese, the Catholic population of Spain, and its rulers. He worked within the established environ-

[88] Isidore of Seville, *Chronicle*, 331, 334 (pp. 465-66) (a common criticism among western thinkers).

[89] Ibid., 339, 386a, 389a (pp. 467, 473-74).

[90] Isidore of Seville, *Etymologies* 7.12.5; cf. Reydellet, *La Royauté*, 394-95.

[91] Isidore of Seville, *Etymologies* 15.1.42.

[92] Isidore of Seville, *De viris illustribus*, no. 26, pp. 147-48.

[93] *PL* 83, 905-907 (paras. 7 and 8, 907); G. B. Ford, Jr., *The Letters of S. Isidore of Seville*, 2nd ed. (Amsterdam, 1970), no. 7 (pp. 39-44, esp. 43).

ment, however limited, not trying to change it. For intellectual resources and library facilities he was extremely well provided and had no need to travel, although he did write to other bishops for the loan of texts not immediately available.[94] Neither did he express any desire to move from Seville, not even to make a pilgrimage to the see of St. Peter; certainly not to the Holy Land as St. Fructuoso later tried to do (and was imprisoned for the attempt). A voyage such as Egeria had made in the late fourth century was not only quite impractical but also raised suspicion in the mind of seventh-century Visigothic monarchs.[95] But Isidore did not seem frustrated by his rooted existence in Seville and Toledo, for he was concerned above all with the faith of his parishioners and kings, and the strength of Christian institutions. Information about the councils held in Merovingian Francia, events in Rome, or the new theology being developed in the East under Patriarch Sergios and Emperor Herakleios does not seem to have penetrated the isolated world of Visigothic Spain.

The Isidorean "Family" of Scholars

Thus it was for himself and his pupils, future bishops like Braulio, Taio, and Ildefonsus, that Isidore prepared the *Summa* of ancient learning, which passes under the name *Etymologies*. The *Synonyma* (Synonyms) were sent to Braulio, "not because it may be of some use, but because you wanted it."[96] Part of his exposition of Catholic faith, *De fide catholica, contra iudaeos*, was sent to his sister Florentina. It was for the greater glory of Spain that he brought up to date and revised the *World History* begun by Eusebios and continued by Jerome, Prosper, and Victor. For King Sisebut he wrote the treatise, *De natura rerum*, and for Sisenand the panegyrical *History of the Goths*.[97] It was for the church of Spain that he wrote on ecclesiastical offices, began the great collection of canon law, the *Hispana*, and drew up an important list of papal decretals. He advised that when the acts of past councils gave discordant opinions, "the older or stronger authority is to be observed."[98] His own authority in these matters led later forgers to attribute to Isidore a collection of canons, which circulated widely in Carolingian

---

[94] *PL* 83, 898, 909; Ford, *Letters of S. Isidore*, no. 3 (p. 21), requesting the "sixth decade of Augustine" (from his commentaries on the Psalms); cf. no. 10 (p. 53) asking for a copy of the synodal proceedings "in which Sintharius is found boiled" (a reference to trial by the ordeal of boiling water).

[95] Diaz y Diaz, *La Vida de san Fructuoso*, para. 17.

[96] *PL* 83, 899; Ford, *Letters of S. Isidore*, no. 3 (p. 21).

[97] Fontaine, *Isidore de Séville*, 2:454-56, 868; cf. J. N. Hillgarth, ed., *Sancti Iuliani . . . Opera*, *CCL* 115 (Turnhout, 1976), 1:217-54 (*Historia Wambae*), and p. viii.

[98] On the *Hispana*, see P. Fournier and G. Le Bras, *Histoire des Collections canoniques en Occident*, 2 vols. (Paris, 1931-32), 1:100-106; it included some of the canons translated into

Europe, the *Pseudo-Isidoran Decretals*.[99] Isidore also established a uniform liturgy (later known as the Mozarabic rite), studied the calculation of Easter, and may well have revised the Psalter. For the monks of a monastery, possibly to be identified by its founder, Honorius, he wrote a new Rule, and for them and for many more besides he excerpted the *Moralia* of Gregory the Great, to form a simplified code of moral theology, the *Sententiae*.[100] His pupils studied these texts and in turn taught them to the next generation of aspirant ecclesiastical leaders, creating an unbroken chain from Leander down to Julian and Felix of Toledo in the late seventh century. Thus Braulio revised the *Etymologies*, which were still not in final form at Isidore's death in 636, and Ildefonsus continued his catalogue of famous men. Taio excerpted the works of Pope Gregory in another five books of *Sententiae*, while Braulio of Saragossa and Eugenius of Toledo maintained Isidore's practice of presiding at church councils for 20 years (636-56) and directed six of the national assemblies held in the capital. In 640, when the date of Easter was disputed, Braulio gave accurate advice.[101]

This tradition and institutionalisation of ecclesiastical government was of great importance in Visigothic Spain. High-ranking lay officials and the chief monastic leaders regularly participated at councils and signed their assent to canons passed.[102] Toledo became the recognised metropolitan see of all Spain (681) and was even described as *urbs regia* ("the queen city"), a term reserved by John of Biclar in the late sixth century for Constantinople alone.[103] Under Eugenius, Julian, and Felix, the Catholic faith of Spain was safeguarded by the constant repetition of the definitions of the first four oecumenical councils and the creed established by Reccared in 589. When Popes Leo II and Benedict II in turn communicated news of the 680-81 council held in Constantinople, this was accepted as the Fifth Oecumenical Council by the Spanish church. At the fourteenth Council of Toledo, slight

---

Latin by Martin of Braga, see Barlow, *Fathers of the Church*, 62:123-44. The papal decretals are excerpted in *PL* 84, 627-849; Isidore's advice is in letter 4, *PL* 83, 901D-902; Ford, *Letters of S. Isidore*, p. 27.

[99] H. Fuhrmann, *Einfluss und Verbreitung der pseudoisidorischen Fälschungen*, in *MGH, SS*, 24, 3 vols. (Stuttgart, 1972-74).

[100] The *Sententiae* are edited in Campos Ruiz and Roca Melia, *Santos Padres*, 2:226-525, also in *PL* 83, 557-738.

[101] In 627 a Spanish monk named Leo had expounded the Alexandrian system of computing the correct date of Easter, using the Dionysiac tables but without identifying their author, see Jones, "The Victorian and Dionysiac Paschal Tables." Braulio may have had access to these tables when he was consulted by Eutropius, see D. Ó. Cróinín, " 'New Heresy for Old': Pelagianism in Ireland and the Papal Letter of 640," *Speculum* 60 (1985): 505-516, esp. 512-14.

[102] Bishko, "Spanish Abbots," and Schwöbel, *Synode und König*.

[103] Toledo XII, canon 6, Vives, *Concilios Visigóticos*, 393-94; Mansi, 11.1033-34.

disagreements with the acts of 680 were registered in Julian's *Response and Statement of Our Faith*, later elaborated in a more aggressive document, his second *Apologeticum*.[104] This theological argument occasioned the only important exchange between Rome and Toledo between 604 and 711, a further index of Spain's self-sufficiency and independence under the dynamic leadership of its metropolitan see. Toledan mistrust of Rome was probably increased by the very close association of the papacy and Byzantium, especially in this instance, which represented a joint effort to renew good relations. The Spanish church was certainly not prepared to accept on trust definitions of orthodoxy drawn up in Constantinople.

The Isidorean Inheritance

Isidore's immense productivity, which lay at the base of all later ecclesiastical thought in Visigothic Spain, was prepared by a training in the Late Antique curriculum barely studied elsewhere in the West. It was then moulded by and directed towards local needs and conditions specific to seventh-century Spain. In particular, it was put at the service of a monarchy only recently converted to the Catholic faith after a fratricidal conflict. In these circumstances, his theories, both political and ecclesiastical, developed in a tight symbiotic relationship with Visigothic practice, both in state and church. Yet from these thoroughly Iberian roots and focus, Isidore's works were to enjoy a most remarkable destiny *outside* Spain. Even before the end of the seventh century, the influence of his *Etymologies* was felt in northern Europe, especially in Ireland. The sole extant copy made in this period, MS *S. Gall 1399. a.1*, was probably written in Ireland.[105] The anonymous commentators on the *Catholic Epistles* cite Isidore, with Jerome, Augustine, and Gregory, as their ancient sources, adding the names of five Irish contemporaries, Laidcenn, Manchán, Bercan, Bannbanus, and Brecannus. They also reflect Isidore's fascination with Greek and Hebrew, giving etymologies in the three sacred languages.[106] Isidore was especially famous for the *Moralia in Iob*, which Laidcenn (d. 661) abridged in a version

---

[104] Vives, *Concilios Visigóticos*, 380-410; Mansi, 11.1023-41 (letters of Popes Leo II and Benedict IV); J. M. Lacarra, "La iglesia visigoda en el s. VII y sus relaciones con Roma," *Settimane* 7 (1960): 353-84, esp. 367-68; Orlandis and Ramos-Lisson, *Die Synoden*, 272-93. Julian of Toledo, *Apologeticum*, ed. Hillgarth, *Sancti Iuliani . . . Opera*, 1:129-39; F. X. Murphy, "Julian of Toledo and the Condemnation of Monotheletism in Spain," in *Mélanges J. de Ghellinck*, 1:361-73.

[105] J. N. Hillgarth, "The East, Visigothic Spain and the Irish," *Studia Patristica* 4 (Berlin, 1961): 442-56, esp. 450 n.4; idem, "Visigothic Spain and Early Christian Ireland," *Proceedings of the Royal Irish Academy* 62C, no. 6 (1962): 167-94, both reprinted in his *Visigothic Spain, Byzantium and the Irish*.

[106] R. E. McNally, ed., *Scriptores Hiberniae minores*, vol. 2, *CCL* 108B (Turnhout, 1973), viii-x, xii.

known as the *Ecloga* (Selections). But for pseudo-Cyprian, the authors of the *Famina Hisperica* and the Lorica hymn, Isidore was responsible for the handbook of ancient pagan learning, the *Etymologies (Culmen)*, and was identified not as a Christian bishop but as "Esodir in chulmin."[107] Maritime contacts between the west coast of Spain (Braga) and Celtic Ireland and Brittany may account for this rapid spread. From Ireland, Isidore's works passed to Iona and Northumbria, Wearmouth and Malmesbury, bringing information unavailable elsewhere to Bede and Aldhelm in the early eighth century. By land the writings travelled from Septimania, still a diocese of the Spanish church, to Bobbio, Fleury, Reichenau, and other monastic centres.[108] But their influence was most marked in Ireland, where the Celtic church still observed its own Easter and had an intense curiosity about the classical languages and about ancient pagan culture. Evidence of the importance of Spain in the transmission of eastern material to Ireland is clear from liturgical borrowings and the custom of reciting the creed, albeit at a different place, in the mass. Thence they passed to Northumbria, eventually to become an established feature of the English church.[109]

The enthusiastic reception of the Isidorean inheritance in other parts of the West was due to several factors: the paucity of manuscripts available, the fact that those which did survive were sometimes no longer intelligible, the general decline in educational standards, and the increasing distance from eastern materials and intellectual development, which left the West dependent on its own limited and scattered resources. Through his compendia, Isidore provided access to works and authors barely identified in the eighth century, though occasionally preserved in monastic libraries. He also introduced new ideas and knowledge of ecclesiastical customs quite unknown in the West, for example, through his transmission of early Christian conciliar decisions. And because he gave concise and authorita-

---

[107] M. Herren, "On the Earliest Irish Acquaintance with Isidore of Seville," in James, *Visigothic Spain*, 243-50, esp. 244, 250.

[108] B. Bischoff, "Die europäische Verbreitung der Werke Isidors von Sevilla," in *Isidoriana* (Leon, 1961), 317-44, reprinted in his *Mittelalterliche Studien*, vol. 1 (Stuttgart, 1966), 171-94; M. Reydellet, "La Diffusion des *Origines* d'Isidore de Séville au Haut Moyen Age," *Mélange d'archéologie et d'histoire* 78 (1966): 383-437.

[109] See most recently, J. N. Hillgarth, "Ireland and Spain in the Seventh Century," *Peritia* 3 (1984): 1-16, a firm restatement of his earlier views; D. B. Capelle, "Alcuin et l'histoire du symbole de la messe," *Recherches de théologie ancienne et médiévale* 6 (1934): 249-60 (reprinted in his *Travaux liturgiques de doctrine et d'histoire*, vol. 3 [Louvain, 1967]); Kelly, *Early Christian Creeds*, 352-53; E. Bishop, " 'Spanish Symptoms'," *JTS* 8 (1906/7): 278-94, 430 (reprinted in his *Liturgica historica* [Oxford, 1918]); cf. G. Mercati, "More Spanish Symptoms," *JTS* 8 (1906/7): 423-30, on the mid-seventh-century Mozarabic liturgy (also reprinted in Bishop, *Liturgica historica*).

tive guidance both to past thought and correct Christian response to it, he was uniquely qualified to instruct educated circles in western Europe. As these were dominated by the clergy, his insistence on the Christian regulation of society also found a warm welcome. The Christian authorities of the West were often aware of their duties, of the urgency of saving people from damnation, and some struggled to fulfil them. For all Christians, therefore, whether they were practical missionaries, ecclesiastical advisers to secular leaders, monks in isolated communities, or intellectuals and authors such as Bede, the discovery of Isidore's corpus illuminated their activities in a new way. They studied and copied his manuscripts as never before.[110]

In sharp contrast to this use of Isidorean material in northern Europe, Byzantium appears to have remained entirely ignorant of it. Communication between the eastern and western ends of the Mediterranean was certainly hampered in the early seventh century by Byzantine preoccupations with the Persian threat. Reduced maritime activity was part of Constantinople's shrinking economy and minimal political contact with the West. Nor does Isidore appear to have shown any interest in sending his works out of Spain; he did not even feel it necessary or suitable to inform the papacy of the situation in the Spanish church. If his masterpiece, the *Etymologies*, had reached Constantinople, we may speculate that Byzantine reactions would have been mixed. Had the scholars involved in higher education in the capital been able to make sense of the Latin, they would certainly have recognised the technique, which was well developed in the East, though they might have scoffed at the Greek. Byzantine *lexika*, like the geographical one produced by Stephanos in the mid-sixth century, were constructed on the same principles and perpetuated some of the same fanciful derivations, re-employed by the early eighth-century compilers of the *Parastaseis Syntomoi Chronikai*.[111] But the main criticism of Isidore would probably have been in his use of ancient Greek material, so much more familiar and easily accessible to teachers in Constantinople. Possibly they might have been surprised to learn that such compendia were available in Latin; Byzantium had to wait until the tenth century before such truly

---

[110] B. Bischoff, "Die europäische Verbreitung." By the middle of the seventh century, Fredegar used a copy of Isidore's *Chronicle* for his own history, ibid., 176.

[111] On Stephanos of Byzantium, see N. G. Wilson, *Scholars of Byzantium* (London, 1983), 55-56; and on etymologies in general, see R. Reitzenstein, *Geschichte der griechischen Etymologika* (Leipzig, 1897); for a later example, see Averil Cameron and Judith Herrin, eds., *Constantinople in the Early Eighth Century: The Parastaseis Syntomoi Chronikai* (Leiden, 1984), ch. 84, p. 162: "So the city was called Iconium by Philodorus the *logistes* because Perseus came (ἡκέναι) and saved Andromeda." On the importance of etymologies in the transmission of culture, see Fontaine, *Isidore de Séville*, 2:828-30.

encyclopaedic works were compiled by the scholarly circle of Constantine VII.

The fact that Isidore's synthesis of ancient wisdom was immediately appreciated and put to use north of Spain indicates a growing demand in areas that had always been on the fringes of the Late Antique world. It was in these newly Christian lands that the classical content of the *Etymologies* was particularly respected. The Old High German translations and numerous copies made, one in almost every major monastery in northern Europe as well as Italy, reflect the authority of this, the first medieval encyclopaedia.[112] In contrast to the rapid adoption and diffusion of the *Etymologies*, *Sententiae*, and other ecclesiastical texts, Isidore's theories of Christian kingship and the role of states in the *regnum Christi* remained unnoticed for a long time. The delay of more than a century, no doubt due in part to the political circumstances in northern Europe, meant that when rediscovered and applied they acquired an even greater force as something utterly novel and unusual. Although transformed by the different conditions to which they were adjusted, the references to Christian leadership scattered through Isidore's writings assumed great authority under Charles the Great. In particular, they permitted the king's ecclesiastical advisers to develop an elevated concept of monarchy, while insisting on the church's ultimate authority in a Christian society. The foundations could thus be laid for a different integration of church and state in the medieval West and for a rejection of other forms of authority that also claimed to be Christian. In these developments, Isidore's repeated condemnations of the eastern empire took on additional significance.

This legacy could not be realised in Visigothic Spain because the monarchy of Sisebut, Suinthila, and their successors proved too feeble a form to maintain such powerful content. It is not possible here to trace the causes and results of royal decline in seventh-century Spain, but they must be connected to the restless ambition of great landowners and notables, each vying to become king, entrenched regional loyalties, and inadequate economic and social forces at Toledo's disposal. While kings like Wamba, Ervig, and Egica held positions of great honour, their actual powers were not very great. The description of this monarchy as full of Byzantine finery and ritual but not based on commensurate strength is a useful one.[113] In Spain there was insufficient land, property, and manpower directly attached to

---

[112] F. Saxl, "Illustrated Medieval Encyclopaedias," in *Lectures* (London, 1957), 1:228-46, attributes to Hraban Maur of Fulda the first illustrated copy of the *Etymologies*, ca. 844; cf. Afterword.

[113] Hillgarth, "Visigothic Spain and Early Christian Ireland," 169-70; cf. his even stronger characterisation: The "ephemeral and artificial" Byzantinism of Visigothic monarchs, which lacked "the solid armature of the empire," in his article, "Coins and Chroni-

the crown to provide the necessary taxation that could maintain an effective central government.

When challenged by the Arabs in 711, the immediate cause of collapse lay in the same "Gothic disease" described by Gregory of Tours. On the death of King Witteric in 710, the succession was disputed; Roderick was elected by the "senate" (i.e. palace officials), but certain notables refused to recognise him and proclaimed Witteric's son, Achila.[114] The resultant civil war weakened the kingdom while the Basques took advantage of the quarrel. Roderick was forced to campaign against them in the north of Spain at the time of Tarik's crossing from Ceuta to Carthagena in the south. Rather like the Anglo-Saxon Harold in 1066, he arrived to face the invaders after several days' march to find the Muslims rested and encouraged by disaffected Visigoths. In the engagement that sealed the fate of Visigothic Spain, Roderick was killed and his supporters dispersed. His rival, Achila, retreated to Narbonne; coins were struck in his name there and in northern Spain for a few years. One provincial noble, Theudemir, negotiated a recognition of Arab control as an independent agent and retained his personal, private rule. For the rest of the population, however, Muslim domination was quickly imposed and the traditions of the Visigothic monarchy forgotten.

The Visigoths thus failed to live up to Isidore's high expectations of them as a most Christian people whose rule would set new standards in the sixth age of history. This did not mean that his theories were lost forever; they were simply put into cold storage in the monastic libraries of Spain and northern Europe. Because Isidore was accepted as a master in matters both secular and theological, his writings on the nature of Christian kingship were able to assume a new potential in other regions of the West. But when they eventually did, King Sisebut, the Gothic nobility, and the reasons why Isidore had worked so hard to preserve this monarchy were quite unknown. So the "Visigothic alternative" became a possibility again, but of a quite different sort, only at the end of the eighth century, when more propitious circumstances at the court of Charles facilitated another attempt to put it into practice.

---

cles: Propaganda in Sixth-Century Spain and the Byzantine Background," esp. 500-501. Cf. King, *Law and Society*, 23-39.

[114] C. Sánchez Albornoz, "Donde e cuando murió Don Rodrigo, último rey de los Godos," *Cuadernos de Historia de España* 3 (1945): 5-105. T. F. Glick, *Islamic and Christian Spain in the Early Middle Ages* (Princeton, 1979), 25-29, claims that bitter ethnic division between German-speaking Visigoths and Latin-speaking Hispano-Romans facilitated the Arab conquest, quoting Thompson, *Goths in Spain*, 216-17, an interpretation that appears to ignore the effects of over a century of integration. Collins, *Early Medieval Spain*, 142-45, 151-55, gives an altogether more plausible account, cf. L. A. García Moreno, *El fin del reino visigodo de Toledo: Decadencia y catastrofe* (Madrid, 1975).

The Roots of Christian
Disunity, 649-92

WHILE MANY issues continued to divide Christians in different parts of the *oikoumene* during the seventh century, it was the Monothelete theory of Christ's will that brought theological disagreement to a head in the 640s. Once again Rome confronted successive patriarchs of Constantinople, accusing them of introducing novelties—and wrong ones—into the established faith. Once again, the dioceses of Africa championed this defence of orthodoxy, under the influence and leadership of eastern monastic opponents of the "one will, one energy" doctrine. When these Monothelete errors had been exposed by Maximos's defeat of Pyrrhos in the public debate of 645, the Africans turned to Rome, asking Pope Theodore to excommunicate the heretics.[1] They begged him to anathematise Monotheletism as incorrect theology; they asked for their own criticisms to be forwarded to Constantinople by papal legates—in short, they recognised the institutional position of the apostolic throne as the channel through which a condemnation of the East should be made.

ROME, CHAMPION OF ORTHODOXY

Despite the close links between North Africa, Sicily, and Italy, the respect accorded by Christian leaders in Africa to the papacy indicates a more fundamental realignment of authority. It was not simply due to geographical proximity and the increasing difficulty of regular contact with the East Mediterranean. In their appeal to Rome, they highlighted the see of St. Peter as the sole Christian centre with the historical weight and authority to pronounce on theological definitions of dubious orthodoxy. At an earlier time they might have deferred to the judgements of Alexandria or Antioch, especially when voiced by one of the many Church Fathers who had gov-

---

[1] Mansi, 10.919, 943; cf. J. M. Garrigues, *Maxime le Confesseur: La charité, avenir divin de l'homme* (Paris, 1976), 59-60, tracing the strength of the African church back to St. Augustine.

erned those centres so capably. But in the second half of the seventh century, the eastern patriarchates had sufficient problems coping with their Muslim overlords; moreover, they were deeply implicated in the Monothelete heresy. After Sophronios's departure from Jerusalem, a Monothelete bishop, Sergios of Joppa, resumed the position of patriarch illegally and began to ordain suffragan bishops.[2] Alexandria had similarly been captured by partisans of the one-will belief, instituted by Patriarch Kyros. And no orthodox patriarch resided at Antioch after the lynching of Anastasios II in 609; the last Monophysite patriarch was John (631-49). In a polarisation of loyalties, Rome was left as the only established rival to Constantinople.

The independent church of Cyprus expressed its understanding of this state of affairs in a letter addressed to Pope Theodore sent by Archbishop Sergios in 643.[3] They appealed to the pope as the inheritor of St. Peter, the rock on which Christ had laid His foundation, stating their conviction that it was his duty to oppose the heretics of Constantinople and return them to orthodoxy. Since Cyprus had been the venue of the synod summoned by Bishop Arkadios at the request of Sophronios to discuss the dangers of Monotheletism, the Cypriots were clearly aware of the schism that divided the East. Whether or not they were also conscious of the imminent Arab threat to their existence is not so evident, but they did not allow political considerations to sway their antagonism to Constantinople. Following the first attacks in 649, the church of Cyprus was thrown into disorder by repeated Muslim raids. The capital, Constantia, was captured after fierce resistance. From the 650s onwards, the orthodox inhabitants of the island were scattered, some transported under imperial orders to other regions of the empire. By the end of the century, Islamic control was recognised and Archbishop John was temporarily established on the mainland of Asia Minor, near the capital, at a new see called Nea Justinianopolis (the new city of Justinian).[4] Those with the means to do so sought a refuge in Africa, Sicily, and Italy, from both Monotheletism and the Arabs. In this westward movement, Rome probably became the goal of many, from all parts of the East Mediterranean.

Like John Moschos and Sophronios, earlier refugees from Persian hostil-

[2] As reported by Stephen of Dora in his memorandum to the Lateran Synod, Mansi, 10.900C-D, cf. R. Riedinger, ed., *Concilium Lateranense a.649 celebratum* (Berlin/New York, 1974), 46. Cf. C. von Schönborn, *Sophrone de Jérusalem* (Paris, 1972), 85-89.

[3] Mansi, 10.913-16; Riedinger, *Concilium Lateranense*, 60-64.

[4] Theophanes, 343-44, 363, 365. *DHGE*, vol. 13 (1956), 586-87, on Constantia. In 680-81 Archbishop Epiphanios was represented by Bishop Theodore of Trimithous, but by 691-92 the independent church of Cyprus was replaced by the see of Nea Justinianopolis, compare Mansi, 11.688E and 989A.

ity, vulnerable monastic communities and isolated hermits were among those who fled to Rome. Two bishops, Theodore, later pope (642-49), and his father, made their way from Palestine, and a monastic group from Cilicia brought its name to a monastery at Aquae Salviae, close to the Roman church of St. Paul fuori le mure. Similarly, a community of Armenians, possibly from Palestine rather than Armenia proper, found a welcome in the ancient capital of the West.[5] But in addition to these religious refugees, a large number of lay officials and well-to-do individuals also threatened by the Arabs or the Slavs moved to the western centres of orthodoxy. Those from the Balkans (including Thessalonike, Greece, and Crete) that formed the diocese of East Illyricum might have naturally turned to Rome, for this diocese was governed by Rome rather than Constantinople. Among all the Easterners who settled in the Christian capital of the West, 37 Greek monks, deacons, and presbyters presented an appeal against Monotheletism at the Lateran Synod of 649.[6] Some represented communities that had fled as a body, such as the monastery of Renatus; others are described as long established in Rome; yet others had arrived recently from Africa with Maximos the Confessor, the most distinguished of them all. Their influence in the firm opposition to the "innovations" of Constantinople was decisive.

The Lateran Synod

Pope Theodore took the first steps in organising this orthodox stand; indeed, his election in 642 possibly reflected growing unease in Rome about the direction of Monotheletism. The necessity of criticising the Greek sources of the new doctrine had become apparent during the brief pontificate of John IV (640-42), when papal agreement with the *Ekthesis* of Herakleios was withdrawn (as discussed in Chapter 5). So expertise in the patristic writings and other Greek documents produced by Constantinople was rated highly, a development that brought the newcomers into prominence. While Theodore planned the orthodox case, he was greatly assisted by the arrival of Maximos the Confessor from Africa late in 645 or early

[5] The Syriac *Life* of Maximos provides valuable evidence of this westward movement; see S. Brock, *AB* 91 (1973), paras. 17, 18, 20, 23 (which specifies the Arab control of all the sea). On the eastern communities at Rome, see most recently J.-M. Sansterre, *Les moines grecs et orientaux à Rome aux époques byzantine et carolingienne*, 2 vols. (Brussels, 1983), 1:17-21, 53-61, 115-17.

[6] Mansi, 10.904-910; Riedinger, *Concilium Lateranense*, 48-57. The inclusion of a monk named Maximos in this list has led several commentators to conclude that Maximos himself attended the council. Without further particulars about this signatory, it is impossible to judge. There is no doubt, however, as to the importance of Maximos's role in the preparation of the meeting.

646. After the public dispute with the ex-patriarch Pyrrhos, both participants journeyed to Rome for Pyrrhos to recant his defence of Monotheletism. Maximos's vital contribution to the synod preparations may be
gauged from the fact that before 648 he had already compiled a florilegium
of 27 extracts from orthodox writers. These all featured in the list of 161
presented at the Lateran Synod in 649, a detailed documentation of the theological objections to the one-will doctrine.[7] As only 28 of these quotations came from Latin authors, the preponderantly eastern origin of the refutation is clear. In addition, it became the authoritative rebuttal,
reproduced in part at the Sixth Oecumenical Council in 680-81.

The preparations were probably well advanced when Theodore died in
649, for his successor and ex-legate, Martin, presided over the synod only
three months after his consecration in July. From a minute analysis of the
acts, which survive in both Latin and Greek, it appears that the Greek was
original.[8] The synod's deliberations were compiled in Greek, with the
Latin material to be presented being translated; then they were rendered
into Latin. Even the encyclical letter signed by Pope Martin was composed
in Greek. Although he had lived in Constantinople, there is no suggestion
that he really understood the Greek version, and his suffragan bishops were
probably even less familiar with the eastern language. The main purpose of
the synod, however, was to influence adherents of the Monothelete heresy.
So the 105 western prelates summoned to the Lateran in October 649 listened to a translated Latin account of the arguments. They came from all
parts of Italy, with limited representation from Sicily, Africa, and Sardinia, and none from Transalpine Europe or Spain.[9] A few orthodox clerics
from the East and the large body of eastern monks made up for the lack of
official delegates from the other patriarchates. The gathering was one of the
largest ever assembled in Rome and could have left Constantinople in no
doubt about the opposition to Monotheletism in Italy.[10] The Regency in

[7] Garrigues, *Maxime le Confesseur*, 62-64; F.-M. Léthel, *Théologie de l'Agonie* (Paris,
1979), 107-112; R. Riedinger, "Griechische Konzilsakten auf dem Wege ins lateinische
Mittelalter," *Annuarium Historiae Conciliorum* 9 (1977): 253-301, esp. 254-62; on the florilegium, see R. Devréesse, "La Vie de S. Maxime le Confesseur et ses recensions," *AB* 46
(1928): 5-49, esp. 46-47.

[8] R. Riedinger, "Aus den Akten der Lateran-Synod von 649," *BZ* 69 (1976): 17-38; cf.
idem, "Griechische Konzilsakten." On Pope Theodore's preparations, see E. Caspar, "Die
Lateransynode von 649," *Zeitschrift für Kirchengeschichte* 51 (1932): 75-137. The acts are
published in Mansi, 10, and Riedinger, *Concilium Lateranense*.

[9] Mansi, 10.1161-69; Riedinger, *Concilium Lateranense*, 390-403. Very few participants
spoke at the synod, however, which was entirely dominated by Pope Martin and a few well-
informed bishops; see F. X. Murphy and P. Sherwood, *Constantinople II et III* (Paris, 1974),
178-81.

[10] H. J. Sieben, *Die Konzilsidee der alten Kirche* (Paderborn, 1979), 307-310, on the oecumenical character of the council; Sansterre, *Les moines grecs*, 1:117-19.

the East also knew that Maximos was a moving spirit behind the synod and perhaps suspected the work of Sophronios in his contribution. As patriarch of Jerusalem, Sophronios had produced a vast florilegium of 600 biblical and patristic citations against the heresy.

This suspicion was also well founded, in that one of the most impressive documents read out at the synod was a memorandum submitted by Stephen, bishop of Dora in Palestine, once a suffragan of Sophronios.[11] Stephen, like Theodore, had made his way to Rome in the 640s and had been appointed papal vicar in Palestine. In his memorandum, however, he recalled his teacher's condemnation of Monotheletism; the elderly monk who had resisted the "innovations" from the first was thus a real presence in 649. Stephen described how Sophronios had taken him to the very spot of Calvary outside Jerusalem, made him swear to uphold the true faith, and sent him to Rome. Pursuing that dangerous course, against local Monothelete support and invading Muslims, Stephen had come to the see of St. Peter, "where are the foundations of orthodox teaching." In this way an eastern ascetic tradition, based on a profound respect for the apostolic see, served a novel purpose at a time when the practice of ascetic monasticism in the East was increasingly under threat.[12]

Once the council had accomplished its task, condemned Monotheletism, and anathematised the chief perpetrators (Bishop Kyros and Patriarchs Sergios, Pyrrhos, and Paul of Constantinople), its purpose was made evident. Copies of the acts together with an encyclical letter were dispatched to the emperor and patriarch in Constantinople, to the orthodox in Antioch and Jerusalem, to the Carthaginian church, and to the pope's friend, Amandus of Maastricht, who would communicate it to the churches of Austrasia and Neustria in northern Europe.[13] In his letter, Martin blamed the eastern prelates for leading the church into heresy and invited Constans II to condemn Monotheletism. (This exoneration from personal guilt did not, however, induce any change in imperial policy.) Individuals expected by Rome to oppose official Byzantine doctrine in the East were also informed: the new papal vicar, John of Philadelphia; two bishops, Theodore of Esbus and Anthony of Bacatha; an archimandrite and a civilian official, who were to assist John in this task. The metropolitan of Thessalonike, a Monothelete but nominally papal vicar in East Illyricum,

[11] Mansi, 10.892-901; Riedinger, *Concilium Lateranense*, 38-47; Sophronios's florilegium is mentioned in the memorandum.

[12] On the traditional respect accorded to St. Peter amongst the Desert Fathers, see J. J. Taylor, "Eastern Appeals to Rome in the Early Church: A Little Known Witness," *Downside Review* 89 (1971): 142-46.

[13] Mansi, 10.1169-86; Riedinger, *Concilium Lateranense*, 404-421 (the encyclical and letter to Amandus of Maastricht). Cf. *LP* 1.337.

was anathematised, and his clergy was warned that they would have to elect a new leader unless there were changes. Italian bishops who had been unable to attend the council, like John of Milan, signed the acts later.

Martin also commemorated the synod in fresco panels painted near the apse of St. Maria Antiqua in the Forum. Like other eastern depictions of councils, these proclaimed the decisions taken and portrayed some of the participants.[14] In this way, the pope publicised the results of his orthodox council to all Christians, encouraging those who had not yet protested to Constantinople to hold similar assemblies. Through the acts of 649 they were provided with good grounds for condemning the heresy. By this campaign Rome attempted to regulate the faith of Christendom as a whole. The Lateran Synod therefore constituted a very grave threat to the authorities in the eastern capital who had embraced Monotheletism.

The Byzantine Reaction: Monothelete Persecution

Constans II was 19 or 20 years old when the news of this council reached the East in 650. Although emperor since 641, the government had been organised by a council of regency in his name. According to western sources and Stephen of Dora, he had been persuaded to publish the *Typos* of 648 by Patriarch Paul; it was not his own work. In fact, Paul and other senators on the ruling council were probably responsible for the eastern reaction to Martin's communications, which went in the emperor's name. Unfortunately it is difficult to tell, for the reign of Constans II (641-68) is one of the worst-documented in Byzantine history.[15] In the following attempt to reconstruct the sequence and connection of developments, it may help to bear in mind the emperor's youth—he was 25 when he commanded the Byzantine fleet at Phoinix, 32 on his departure for Sicily, and 38 at his death in 668.

Constantinople issued no theological response to the condemnations of the Lateran Synod. Perhaps under the terms of the *Typos*, which prohibited further discussion of the "one will, one energy" problem, Patriarch Paul simply maintained a silence. But clearly Martin had flouted those same terms by summoning his bishops to debate the issue, and it was decided that he had to be punished. The previous summer (649), a new exarch had been sent to Italy with orders to persuade all the bishops and clergy to adhere to the *Typos*. Olympios was also to win over the armies of Rome and Ravenna and persuade them to arrest the pope, a move suggested by the

---

[14] Mansi, 10.797-850; P. J. Nordhagen, "The Frescoes of John VII (A.D. 705-707) in S. Maria Antiqua," *Acta ad archaeologiam et artium historiam pertinentia* (issued by the Institutum Romanum Norvegiae) 3 (1968): 4, cf. 95.

[15] G. Ostrogorsky, *History of the Byzantine State*, 3rd ed. (Oxford, 1968), 87-92.

ex-exarch Platon and another Byzantine official in the capital.[16] Despite
two attempts, however, Olympios was unable to do anything. After failing
in his tasks, Olympios appears to have set off for Sicily, where he hoped to
establish an independent kingdom. It is unlikely that he died confronting
an Arab attack there; an outbreak of plague probably caused his downfall.[17]

The regency then dispatched a former exarch, Theodore Kalliopas, and
Theodore Pellourios, a *koubikoularios*, with specific instructions to arrest
Pope Martin. The reason given for this was that he had been unlawfully
consecrated without imperial permission, but by the time of his trial the
charges against him were developed to include treason. Although the Roman clergy with strong popular support protected their leader from the Byzantine forces sent to remove him, Martin himself agreed to leave Rome
secretly so as to avoid bloodshed.[18] During his miserable sufferings as a
prisoner, on the long journey to the capital, in the harsh imprisonment
there, and during the trial and final exile to Cherson, the imperial authorities never once permitted discussion of theological matters. When the
pope raised the issue of the *Typos*, he was silenced by the city prefect, Troi-
los, who cried out, "Both the Romans and ourselves are Christians and orthodox."[19] In contrast, Martin was repeatedly questioned about his support
for Olympios during the latter's revolt, or his connivance with the Arabs,
that is, his betrayal of the imperial cause. Also his interrogators asked why
he had been uncanonically elevated, and why Patriarch Pyrrhos had been
favourably received by his predecessor, Theodore. Civilian and military officials presided at the trial, calling soldiers from Olympios's troops as witnesses, periodically consulting the emperor and summoning the Senate to
witness Martin's "confessions" of treason.[20] Eventually the pontiff was sentenced to death, later reduced to exile, much to his dismay. He suffered a
further 21 months of deprivation, humiliation and imprisonment, fol-

[16] *LP* 1.337-38.

[17] Ibid., 1.338; A. N. Stratos, "The Exarch Olympius and the Supposed Arab Invasion
of Sicily in A.D. 652," *JÖB* 25 (1976): 63-73.

[18] *LP* 1.338, the very barest account of Martin's arrest, removal to Constantinople, and
exile to Cherson; cf. the pope's own record of the events as preserved in two letters (nos. 14
and 15) to Theodoros, a monk of the Spoudaios monastery at Jerusalem, *PL* 129, 197-202
(also in Mansi, 10, and *PL* 87). There are also two later accounts, probably by Theodoros,
the *Commemoratio* and *Hypomnesticum*, based on Martin's letters and personal recollections
and originally identified as letters from the pope himself, see letters 16 and 17, Mansi, 10.860-
64; *PL* 87, 201-204. Here letter 16 will be refered to by its Latin title as the *Commemoratio*,
and letter 17 as the *Hypomnesticum*. On these texts, see R. Devréesse, "Le texte grec de l'Hypomnesticum de Théodore Spoudée," *AB* 53 (1935): 49-80.

[19] *Commemoratio*, Mansi, 10.856B.

[20] Ibid., 855D (Martin accused by twenty soldiers attached to Olympios and his *notarios*,
Andreas); 856E-857A (the emperor's indirect and unseen presence, and the participation of
the Senate).

lowed by exile to the northern shore of the Black Sea, dependent for basic necessities on ships coming to collect salt, before he died in September 655.[21]

Byzantium had thus made every effort to ensure that the major doctrinal controversy of Monotheletism was transformed into a political affair, and that a leadership loyal to the East was restored in Rome. Once Martin had been conveyed to Cherson, the regency established to administer the see of St. Peter had decided, under imperial pressure, to elect a new pope. Eugenius, a Roman cleric, was consecrated in August 654.[22] For over a year, therefore, there were two bishops of Rome: Martin, in exile, but still in contact with his followers in the West, whom he urged not to accept a substitute; and Eugenius, officiating in St. Peter's. By September 655, Martin had recognised the latter as his successor, although it grieved him that the Roman clergy accepted the change so readily.[23] The theological issue was also kept alive in this confused period by monks loyal to Martin, primarily Maximos and Anastasius, the papal legate, who coordinated a circle of supporters in the East. From his exile in Trebizond Anastasius kept in touch with two younger disciples, Theodoros and Euprepios, who had been banished to Cherson and were able to console the pope on his arrival in 645. Another source of support came from the Spoudaios monastery and from a group associated with the church of the Anastasis in Constantinople.[24] If Constantinople was to succeed in imposing its doctrine in Rome, it had to silence this anti-Monothelete pressure at home.

Although the sources present contradictory accounts of Maximos's movements after the trial of Pope Martin, it seems quite likely that he decided to return to the East to encourage the opposition to Monotheletism. Certainly by spring 655 he and Anastasios were in Constantinople with a copy of the acts of the Lateran Synod of 649, which they used in public debates with their opponents. It was probably this hostile activity in the Byzantine capital that persuaded Constans II of the necessity of another

---

[21] Ibid., 860-62. The precise chronology is worked out by Devréesee, "Le texte grec": Martin arrived in Constantinople on 17 September 653, left the city in March 654, and spent from May 654 to September 655 at Cherson.

[22] LP 1.341.

[23] Hypomnesticum, Mansi, 10.862-64.

[24] LP 1.335 refers to the persecution of the legate (Anastasius), and details are given in later accounts of the sufferings endured by anti-Monothelete martyrs; see PG 91, 195D, 196B. Anastasius spent the last 20 years of his life in exile, first at Trebizond, then at Mesembria, and after his trial in 662 again in the eastern regions of the empire; see R. Devréesse, "La lettre d'Anastase l'Apocrisiaire sur la mort de S. Maxime et de ses compagnons d'exile," AB 73 (1955): 5-16. During his final exile, Stephen, the son of a priest attached to the Anastasis church in Constantinople, visited him in Lazikè, where he enjoyed a more protected existence under the Duothelete governor, Gregorios.

trial.[25] The case against Maximos did not, however, follow exactly the same pattern: although the charges were again political and were made by the civilian authorities, Maximos managed to enunciate the principle that the emperor should not interfere in the life of the church. He justified his adherence to Roman definitions of faith by reference to the authority of St. Peter, while expressing his love of the Greek tongue. But the exchanges recorded by Anastasios and sent to the West to document this courageous defence of Duothelete faith reveal a deep gulf between East and West, which covered more than abstract theology.[26]

Maximos was subjected to two sessions of interrogation, by civilians in May 655 and again in September 656, when Metropolitan Theodosios of Caesarea tried to find some way of reaching a compromise, on the grounds that all the churches, the entire pentarchy of Rome, Constantinople, Alexandria, Antioch, and Jerusalem, were now in agreement, without success.[27] He was then exiled together with Anastasios and the other Anastasius (the legate). During a six-year period they were moved from one place to another but continued to maintain contacts with the opponents of Monotheletism, both within and outside the empire. It was probably this persistent defiance that finally brought Maximos to trial in 662 at the age of 82. To prevent further opposition, his tongue was cut out and his right hand cut off, then another exile was imposed, in Lazikè on the east coast of the Black Sea. Both Anastasios and Maximos died shortly afterwards; only Anastasius the legate survived until October 666, the last witness to a monastic movement that continued to inspire hostility to Byzantium in the West.[28] Pilgrims to Pope Martin's tomb in Cherson reported in the 680s that miraculous cures occurred at it. By the mid-eighth century, the pope's

[25] The Greek *Life* of Maximos reports that Constans II had Maximos arrested in Rome and brought to Constantinople, *PG* 90, 68-109, paras. 17-18 (85-88). But the Syriac *Life* presents a completely different account, in which Maximos returns voluntarily to Constantinople, "taking advantage of the emperor's absence in Armenia," and there continues the struggle against the *Typos* and Monothelete doctrine; see S. Brock, "An Early Syriac Life of Maximus the Confessor," *AB* 91 (1973), paras. 25-26; cf. pp. 330-32 for a possible explanation of the discrepancies.

[26] Descriptions of Maximos's interrogations and subsequent exiles are preserved in the *Relatio motionis*, Anastasius's letter to Theodosios of Gangra, Anastasios's letter to the monks of Caralis, and the *Scholium* or *Hypomnesticum* by Maximos and Anastasios, all published in Latin translations by Anastasius Bibliothecarius, *PL* 129, 623-90; see also Devréesse, "La lettre d'Anastase." The interrogations are published with a French translation by J. M. Garrigues, "Le martyre de Saint Maxime le Confesseur," *Revue Thomiste* 76 (1976): 410-52.

[27] The Greek *Vita*, paras. 19-25, 27-32, *PG* 90, 89-96, 96-101, cf. Maximos's letter to Anastasios, his disciple, *PG* 90, 132, and Garrigues, "Le martyre de Saint Maxime le Confesseur."

[28] Devréesse, "La lettre d'Anastase."

Life would be written by orthodox monks in Rome.[29] In the doctrinal battles of that time the western martyrs' examples would be recalled, both as proof of papal and monastic orthodoxy in the Monothelete dispute and as a reminder of Byzantine power.

By minimising matters of faith and emphasising political obedience and loyalty to the emperor, Constans II and his advisers tried to silence this well-founded opposition. Instead of recognising the Lateran Synod as a direct challenge, which obviously opened a schism between Rome and Constantinople, they consigned it to oblivion. Other theological points at issue (primarily, the title "oecumenical" as used by Constantinople, which smouldered on) were similarly ignored. In the East, the authorities acted as if the *Typos* aroused no contention; it was simply an imperial edict that had to be observed throughout the empire though clerics in all parts resisted. In the West, of course, copies of the acts of 649 survived (one was taken to England in the 660s), and Martin's condemnation of the heresy was known. Byzantine control over Rome, however, mitigated further opposition. Under the exarch Kalliopas, a submissive pope had been elected, Eugenius (654-57). But when the new patriarch of Constantinople sent his synodical letter to Rome with a vague wording on the questions of Christ's will, the people and the clergy (*populus vel clerus*) forced Eugenius to reject it.[30] In a stormy scene in St. Maria ad Praesepe, they refused to let him celebrate mass until he had promised not to accept the statement of eastern heresy. In Constantinople, the influence of Maximos was detected behind this popular support for an independent Roman theology, loyal to Pope Martin. However generated, it was to prove of immense significance in the struggles ahead.

MUSLIM EXPANSION

During the second half of the seventh century, Muslim forces entrenched their control over Syria, Palestine, and Egypt, and extended their threat from Byzantine land to waters by the construction of a fleet. Although the consequences of this maritime presence may have been exaggerated by Pirenne and other historians, by the end of the century the position of all countries bordering the Mediterranean had greatly altered.[31] Traditional patterns of shipping and types of products transported were revolutionised,

[29] P. Peeters, "Une Vie grecque du Pape S. Martin I," *AB* 51 (1933): 225-62; *LP* 1.340 n.16; on the Roman context, see E. Patlagean, "Les moines grecs d'Italie et l'apologie des thèses pontificales (VIIIe-IXe siècles)," *Studi medievali*, 3rd series, 5 (ii) (1964): 579-602.
[30] *LP* 1.341.
[31] H. Pirenne, *Mohammed and Charlemagne* (London, 1939), 120-28; W. H. C. Frend, "North Africa and Europe in the Early Middle Ages," *TRHS*, 5th series, 5 (1955): 61-80.

resulting in profound changes in northern Europe as well as the Mediterranean world. In the East, the Muslim advance towards Constantinople can be plotted from the raiding and occupation of key islands: Cyprus (from 649 onwards), Rhodes (651-54), and Kos (654-55). And the advance by land continued with repeated raids on Cilicia, Armenia, and Isauria, until the Byzantine authorities negotiated a truce between 650-53.[32] Thereafter, Constans II assumed energetic leadership of the defence of the empire's southern coastline and islands. He ordered the construction of ships and commanded the navy in person at the so-called "Battle of the Mats" off Phoinix in Lycia (655).[33] This engagement, however, developed into a total disaster from which the emperor only just escaped alive.

Although the Muslims could now plan a direct attack on the Byzantine capital, Constantinople was spared by the outbreak of civil war within the caliphate. An internal quarrel, provoked by the assassination of Uthman in 656, pitted his relative, Muawiya, against Muhammad's cousin and son-in-law, Ali. The issues of caliphal descent and whether the theocratic powers exercised by the Prophet should be confined to his family posed the question of Islamic leadership in an acute fashion and developed into the first civil war. Although Ali became caliph, he was murdered after a brief rule (656-61), and Muawiya then succeeded in claiming full authority. Damascus became the seat of government, and one of the most brilliant generals of the Arab expansion inaugurated the Umayyad dynasty.[34] But his hold over the ever-growing Muslim world was not immediately firm enough for him to continue the regular atacks on Byzantium. In the interests of internal consolidation, he therefore negotiated a peace, which relieved the empire of constant pressure.

While Muawiya proved as good an administrator as soldier, and the political unity of Islam was not challenged for nearly another century, the first civil war generated a school of thought that refused to recognise the Umayyad rulers. It stressed the trust placed by the Prophet in Ali, who had married his daughter Fatima, and it believed that only a descendant of this marriage could be a legitimate khalifah ("caliph," successor). (Muhammad's lack of sons proved a serious handicap in the transmission of his God-given authority.) This narrow definition of the hereditability of Muslim leadership set the party of Ali (Shi'is) against those (later called Sunnis) who accepted a broader definition and recognised the first three caliphs. Although the split between the two camps only assumed significant proportions in

[32] Theophanes, 343-44, 345; R.-J. Lilie, *Die byzantinische Reaktion auf die Ausbreitung der Araber* (Munich, 1976), 85.

[33] Theophanes, 345-46.

[34] J. Wellhausen, *The Arab Kingdom and Its Fall* (London, 1927, reprinted 1973), 75-104.

the mid-eighth century, it may be traced back to this moment in the 41st year of the Hijri (A.D. 661).[35] It would remain a lasting problem for Muslims, as unresolved today as in the seventh century.

In these circumstances, Constans II was able to attend to the other major hostile forces threatening the empire—the Slavonic tribes settled in the Balkans. They presented a different and more subtle form of enmity, rarely attacking fortified Byzantine centres (though Thessalonike was besieged at least three times in the seventh century), but depriving Constantinople of effective control over large areas. As the Queen City urgently required alternative sources of food to replace the grain fleet of Alexandria, it was essential to maintain Byzantine authority in the wheat-producing regions of Thrace. These were probably the goals of Constans's campaign of 658, which brought some of the *Sklaviniai* under imperial rule and removed many Slavs as prisoners.[36] From this time onwards a policy of moving people of Slavonic descent to Asia Minor was adopted, in the hope of breaking down their communal identity and integrating them into the empire. From the fact that 5,000 went over to the Arabs in 665, who settled them in Syria, the policy might be deemed a failure. But the movement of different ethnic and regional populations continued under tighter control and gradually contributed to the construction of a stronger imperial loyalty.[37]

Byzantine Military Reorganisation. By the end of Constans's reign, at least two of the new provincial armies appear to have occupied the huge areas of eastern and central Asia Minor, to which they gave their names: the *themata* of the *Anatolikon* and the *Armeniakon*. Those of *Opsikion* and *Thrakesion* were also probably in place. Although the process whereby military government replaced traditional civilian administration must have been a very long one, which remains extremely unclear, it was probably initiated by the final defeat of Byzantine troops in Egypt (636) and Armenia (652-55). What remained of the armies of the Orient and Armenia was withdrawn to Asia Minor and established as the *Anatolikon* and *Armeniakon themata*. Their commanders, previously known as *magistri militum per Orientem* and *Armeniam*, assumed the new title *strategos*, but continued to fill military roles, now chiefly limited to defensive action.[38]

[35] On the development of Shi'ite claims, see R. P. Mottahedeh, *Loyalty and Leadership in an Early Islamic Society* (Princeton, 1980), 7-24, especially 12-16.

[36] Theophanes, 347.

[37] Ibid., 348; the 5,000 who went over to the Arabs must have been settled in the East or enrolled in a military unit that was sent to campaign in the East.

[38] See most recently R.-J. Lilie, "Die Zweihundertjährige Reform: Zu den Anfängen der Themenorganisation im 7. und 8. Jahrhundert," *BS* 45 (1984): 27-39; M. F. Hendy, *Studies in the Byzantine Monetary Economy c. 300-1450* (Cambridge, 1985), 621-23.

Given the paucity of evidence for these new units, it is probably impossible to discover exactly how they were organised. The key problem, over which there is considerable debate, concerns military pay; were the troops "landed" (i.e. given plots of land), from which they could finance their own equipment, or did they receive wages and equipment from the central government in the Roman tradition?[39] In conditions of economic decline and reduced imperial revenues, the former seems more likely. The landed solution is also supported by one element of the civilian administration that continued to maintain non-military aspects of provincial government. Thanks to the work of Michael Hendy, the activity of this element, a group of officials called imperial *kommerkiarioi*, can now be connected with the establishment of *themata* soldiers. These officials, appointed by Constantinople and previously responsible for customs and excise, especially the sale and export of luxury products, took over control of military equipment. From the seals used to authorise such transactions, the extension of military recruitment and equipment to new areas can be traced.[40] While the sale of weapons to new recruits is obviously connected with the *themata* units, the other duties of imperial *kommerkiarioi* also reflect a policy of increasing militarisation. For in a period of dearth, the imperial authorities were evidently concerned to secure tighter control over all resources.[41] Through a combination of economic, military, and ecclesiastical pressures, Constantinople gradually established the new *thema* government throughout Asia Minor, though there is little evidence for its efficacity before the reign of Constantine IV.

Like his grandfather before him, Constans II was anxious to secure the succession of his children, Constantine, Herakleios, and Tiberios, and faced similar problems. There was no constitutional opposition to the principle of joint succession, and all three sons were raised to the position of co-

[39] J. F. Haldon, *Recruitment and Conscription in the Byzantine Army, ca. 550-950: A Study on the Origins of the Stratiotika Ktemata*, in Sitzungsberichte der osterreichischen Akademie der Wissenschaften, philol-hist. Klasse, Heft 357 (Vienna, 1979).

[40] The association of Justinian's settlement of the Slavs with the new *themata* has been known for many years; see for example Ostrogorsky, *History of the Byzantine State*, 130-32; and R.-J. Lilie and others have drawn attention to the continuing activity of civilian officials, especially *kommerkiarioi*, within *thema* administration, as for instance in Lilie, "Die Zweihundertjährige Reform," 32-34. Hendy has now elucidated their precise interaction; see *The Byzantine Monetary Economy*, 631-34. The proliferation of *kommerkiarioi* seals for Cappadocia from the late 650s onwards (ibid., 649) might well reflect the settling of Slavs, such as the prisoners of Constans's campaign of 658, in a strategic area of central Asia Minor. Part of the Thracian army may have been sent to Sardis under Constans to form the core of the Thrakesion *thema*; ibid., 641-42.

[41] Hendy, *The Byzantine Monetary Economy*, 619-20, emphasises the immense loss of imperial revenues; the annual budget was reduced to perhaps only a quarter of its previous level.

emperor in turn (Constantine in 654, the two younger sons five years later). It was Constans's brother, Theodosios, who posed the problem. As the sources for the reign are so sparse—not even the name of the empress is recorded—it is hardly surprising that we do not know why the emperor turned against Theodosios. Possibly he had aspired to be co-emperor in more than name; possibly he had supporters among the Regency Council and Senate, who had ruled in the name of Constans during his minority. Whatever the reason, the emperor did not trust his brother and in ca. 660 forced him to become a cleric, as a step that would debar him from the throne. Shortly after he was assassinated on the emperor's orders, an event that prompted the inhabitants of the capital to brand Constans as Cain, a term of immense disrespect in a society profoundly aware of the Old Testament stories.[42] This hatred may also have been fuelled by popular dislike of the treatment accorded to religious opponents, but it is impossible to judge what ordinary people felt about the official policy of Monotheletism.

CONSTANS II AND THE WEST

Although the trials imply a determination to root out all opposition to official Monotheletism, we remain ignorant of Constans's personal views on religion. After the hostility manifested in Rome at the time of Pope Eugenius, there appears to have been a slight shift away from the utterly rigid division between eastern and western positions. On his election in 657, Pope Vitalian sent a somewhat ambiguous synodical letter to Constantinople, mentioning neither the dispute under Eugenius nor the outstanding differences posed by the *Typos* and the acts of 649, both still in force. Not only was the synodical letter accepted in the East, but Constans II replied to the pope with a renewal of Rome's privileges and a magnificent Gospel book bound with gold and gems.[43] This exchange seems to mark a reduction in hostilities, which both sides would exploit during the emperor's stay in the West.

For in 662 Constans undertook a long campaign in the western provinces of the empire, even (according to a later source) intending to move his court to Rome. Leaving his family in Constantinople, with a regent to rule in the name of his eldest son, Constantine, then ten years old, he marched via Thessalonike and central Greece and then embarked for Italy. The finding of large numbers of his copper coins in the excavated material from Athens and Corinth confirms the visit of eastern troops; so does a rough statue base

---

[42] Theophanes, 347, 351; George Cedrenus, *Synopsis Historiarum*, ed. I. Bekker, 2 vols. (Bonn, 1839), 1:762; cf. Ostrogorsky, *History of the Byzantine State*, 121.
[43] *LP* 1.343.

inscribed to the emperor.[44] These cities were still Byzantine centres though they had shrunk to tiny areas, quite unlike their classical ancestors, and they were familiar with the Slavs in settlements close by. From Tarento in southern Italy, the Byzantine forces began another conquest of Italy, this time from the Lombards, at first with ease but later meeting strong hostility. After an unsuccessful siege of Benevento, Constans was forced to fall back on Naples. At this point (663) he paid a ceremonial visit to Rome for plunder.[45] For twelve days, the emperor made donations to churches and led his troops, all holding candles, to masses conducted by Pope Vitalian, while his officials denuded the city of all its bronze statues, ornaments, and even roof tiles from St. Maria ad Martyres, the ancient Pantheon. Vitalian did not protest at this despotic behaviour and let Constans depart for Sicily, sending his haul of metal objects and statues by sea. (These were later removed by Arab pirates, who sent them to the East to be sold.)[46]

Syracuse now became the imperial residence. It was one of the most flourishing cities of the island, still preserving its classical buildings and public functions, such as racing in the arena. To this new capital Constans summoned his family. But the inhabitants of Constantinople protested at the proposal, as if the removal of the three young co-emperors would signal the end of New Rome. Andreas, who served as regent for Constantine IV, and Theodore of Koloneia, made sure that the imperial family would remain in the East, leaving Constans alone in Syracuse.[47] Despite the wealth of the region, the inhabitants of Syracuse and of Sicily, Calabria, Sardinia, and Africa, and the church of Rome, which owned extensive properties in these areas, suffered under Constans II. Excessive new taxation in various forms, capitation, land, and naval ("per diagrafa seu capita atque nauticatione"), were combined with the plunder of church plate to finance the court and enlarged military budget.[48] The naval tax may possibly be related to a fleet that Constans sent without success against the Muslims in Africa. After the Arab victory over the exarch Gregory in 649, the situation in the region of Carthage was more precarious and Sicily at greater risk.[49] Ceuta (Septem) remained a Byzantine outpost at the extreme western end of the Mediterranean; Sardinia and Corsica maintained garrisons. Although the

---

[44] Theophanes, 348, 351; *LP* 1.343; Hendy, *The Byzantine Monetary Economy*, 661; J. Kent, "A Byzantine Statue Base at Corinth," *Speculum* 25 (1950): 544-46.

[45] *LP* 1.343-44; Paul the deacon, *HL* 5.6-11.

[46] *LP* 1.346; Paul the deacon, *HL* 5.13.

[47] Theophanes, 351.

[48] *LP* 1.344; T. S. Brown, *Gentlemen and Officers* (London, 1984), 28; L. Cracco Ruggini, *La Sicilia tra Roma e Bisanzio*, Storia della Sicilia, vol. 3 (Naples, 1980).

[49] J. B. Bury, "The Naval Policy of the Roman Empire in Relation to the Western Provinces," in *Centenario della nascità di Michele Amari* (Palermo, 1910), 2:21-34.

emperor did not remove the Lombards from southern Italy or the Arabs from Africa, his stay in the West resulted in a consolidation of Byzantine control, especially in Sicily.

Despite the favours shown to Rome, the emperor did not overlook the position of Ravenna, the real capital of Byzantine Italy. In 666, he received an appeal from Archbishop Maurus of the city, who wished to establish its ecclesiastical independence from the bishops of Rome. This request represented an ongoing rivalry between the two centres, which fluctuated according to the personalities involved and arguments deployed until its final resolution in the late eighth century. Under Constans II, Ravenna was granted the right to consecrate its own archbishop without Roman approval, a privilege that effectively established its autonomy and that was deeply resented in Rome.[50] Although it proved to be only a temporary setback for the see of St. Peter, this imperial intervention symbolised an aspect of Byzantine administration that was increasingly disliked in the West. While Ravenna could on occasion use its favoured status to obtain additional privileges, and Rome would similarly draw on its Petrine authority, neither maintained an unquestioning loyalty to the East. And during the course of the seventh and eighth centuries, both would in different ways seek to free themselves from imperial tutelage.

Vitalian's Pontificate (657-72)

The honours accorded to Constans II and the tactful handling of his visit to Rome reflect a delicate moment in Roman-Byzantine relations and Vitalian's clear appreciation of it. After a series of relatively brief pontificates (apart from that of Honorius, 625-38), Vitalian's leadership determined important developments in the papacy. During his fifteen years as bishop, the church of Rome appears to have taken stock of its position and standing in the Christian world, its status emphasised by both western and eastern respect. Vitalian guided his see towards a more elevated spiritual position, stressing the need for Rome to avoid the mundane and sordid elements of routine political life, while resolutely upholding its political privileges and worldly assets. Yet he displayed a good understanding of the city's historic links with Byzantium, not only during the emperor's visit but also at the latter's death in 668. When Constans was murdered in the baths at Syracuse, an Armenian rebel named Mizizios was proclaimed. Pope Vitalian ensured that Istrian, Campanian, and Sardinian forces went to put down the

---

[50] Agnellus, *Liber pontificalis Ecclesiae Ravennatis*, ed. O. Holder-Egger, in *MGH, SSRL*, cc. 110-114; this right was recorded in a mosaic still visible at St. Apollinare in Classe near Ravenna, see V. von Falkenhausen, *I Bizantini in Italia* (Milan, 1982), plate 9; T. S. Brown, "The Church of Ravenna and the Imperial Administration in the seventh Century," *EHR* 94 (1979): 1-28.

revolt, thus indicating a loyalty to the house of Herakleios and helping to secure the succession of Constantine IV.[51]

One of the most striking developments of his pontificate was the growth of papal ceremonial commensurate with the universal respect for St. Peter, including the use of colourful robes and liturgical accessories of precious metals, decorated with jewels, silks, and gold threads. Under Vitalian, the musical side of ecclesiastical services was transformed by the establishment of particular chanters later known as *Vitaliani*. The *Schola cantorum* probably originated in these specially trained singers, recruited from the three junior clerical ranks of acolyte, reader, and exorcist. Later in the seventh century when Leo II, Benedict II, and Sergius performed in this *ordo* as young clerics, it was an institution under a *primus* (chief chanter) devoted to the magisterial splendour of masses both in the papal household and at station services. These were inspired by imperial ritual involving the use of organ and Byzantine antiphony (*diaphonia basilika*), which symbolised papal supremacy and authority.[52]

The results of this peaceful penetration and adaptation of eastern customs can be seen in the earliest description of papal ritual, the first *Ordo Romanus*, which details the protocol to be observed each time the pope celebrates mass in one of the seven stational churches of Rome.[53] As the complete papal court was involved as well as the regional clergy, choir, laity, and soldiers, plus the bishops of the suburbicarian sees, the daily ceremony was a complicated one that required elaborate planning. Even the pope's special portable throne and his liturgical books and vessels had to be conveyed to the appropriate region. There were also judicial and social elements to the events, for the procession that set out from the Lateran palace to the regional church on duty also attended to appeals en route, when any petitioner might approach the pontiff and present his case. Finally, since an invited party dined with the pope after the mass, the prior arrangement of menus and other facilities was also required. Through these very public, colourful, and well-orchestrated appearances in the city, papal authority in Rome and concern for the well-being of its population were highlighted.

[51] *LP* 1.346; Paul the deacon, *HL* 5.12; Theophanes, 351-52; Nikephoros, 31-32; B. Navarra, *San Vitaliano Papa* (Rome, 1972), 9-28; W. Hahn, "Mezezius in peccato suo interiit," *JÖB* 29 (1980): 61-70, on the imperial coins struck by Mizizios before his death. Philip Grierson assures me that these are genuine and are marked with the Constantinopolitan mint mark in anticipation of Mizizios's imperial coronation in the capital.

[52] S. J. P. van Dijk, "The Urban and Papal Rites in Seventh and Eighth Century Rome," *Sacris Erudiri* 12 (1961): 411-87, esp. 465-69 on the *Vitaliani*, and 467-68 on Byzantine influences; idem, "Gregory the Great, Founder of the Urban *Schola Cantorum*," *Ephemerides Liturgicae* 7 (1963): 335-56.

[53] M. Andrieu, *Les Ordines Romani du haut moyen âge*, 3 vols. (Paris, 1931-51), 2:67-108; P. Llewellyn, *Rome in the Dark Ages* (London, 1971), 124-26. The first *Ordo* is translated by E. G. C. F. Atchley, *Ordo Romanus Primus* (London, 1905).

In addition to the Gospel book sent from Constantinople, Constans II brought gifts to many churches of Rome in 663, including a gold cloth that he laid on the altar of St. Peter's. Such Byzantine and oriental textiles, frequently of silk embroidered with gold and silver thread, were greatly prized in the West and became very fashionable at Rome in the later seventh century. Popes Benedict II and Sergius both donated altar cloths and curtains in fine fabrics of this kind.[54] At this time also, eastern icons seem to have been introduced, not as objects of devotion in the Byzantine style but as important representations of Christian figures and beliefs. Some ancient icons of the Virgin still surviving in Rome may well date from the late seventh century, while the definitions of the six oecumenical councils were depicted after 680-81 in an image called the "Botarea."[55] Under Pope Theodore, a typically eastern mosaic decoration was added to the church of Santo Stefano Rotondo. It shows Sts. Primus and Felicianus standing on either side of a jewelled cross, below the bust of Christ and Hand of God. The cross is of a type associated with Jerusalem, while the gold ground and elegant flowers confirm a Byzantine model. An even closer use occurs in the chapel of San Venanzio, where Pope John IV began a new mosaic programme to honour the Dalmatian saints whose relics he transferred to Rome in 640-42. Theodore completed the work, including his own portrait among the saints who surround the Virgin in the apse.[56] Whether these seventh-century pontiffs drew on their own taste or imported styles currently fashionable in the East—as supreme judges of the diocese of East Illyricum, they exercised considerable influence in regions close to Byzantium—they encouraged an appreciation of oriental objects. The plethora of textiles, incense burners, sacred vessels, and clerical costumes employed under their patronage indicated primarily a desire for the most costly and prestigious. It was a question of taste and also deliberate policy, which echoed the growing authority of the apostolic see. Papal confidence in this supreme position was encouraged by the devotion of Christians, particularly the newly-converted believers in northern Europe, who came in increasing numbers on pilgrimage to the tomb of St. Peter.

Anglo-Saxon Pilgrims to Rome

When Benedict Biscop embarked on his first journey to the holy see in 653, accompanied by the younger Wilfrid, it was a most unusual event. Despite the close links between Rome and the church in Anglo-Saxon England, pil-

---

[54] *LP* 1.363, 374.

[55] Ibid., 1.391; Paul the deacon, *HL* 6.34; R. Krautheimer, *Rome: Profile of a City, 312-1308* (Princeton, 1980), 91.

[56] Krautheimer, *Rome*, 90, 97-98 (Santo Stefano Rotondo), von Falkenhausen, *I Bizantini in Italia*, plate 4 (chapel of San Venanzio).

grimages to the see of St. Peter from the north were unknown. Both these pilgrims, however, were intent on visiting other Christian centres in Europe. Benedict was to spend two years at Lérins in southern Gaul, while Wilfrid stayed even longer in Lyon.[57] The idea of learning about ancient Christian traditions at first hand was therefore well established, but northerners had not previously gone to Rome itself. When Benedict arrived, Pope Martin had recently left the city, and the clergy were confused and anxious. One of them, an archdeacon named Boniface, befriended Benedict and taught him a great deal about Roman customs, in particular how to employ the tables of Dionysios to calculate the date of Easter. When Wilfrid arrived some time later, he was also very impressed by this novel method.

Despite their reliability for the five 19-year cycles established by Dionysios (i.e. from 532 to 626), these tables had only been officially adopted in Rome in the 630s. And in many parts of the West, continued use was made of the older tables of Victor of Aquitaine, even though these were faulty in several respects. They did not observe the fundamental ruling of Nicaea (325) that Easter should never fall on the vernal equinox (March 21), and they sometimes offered a choice of "Greek" or "Latin" dates. As two different dates were listed for 641, Irish clerics had written to Pope Severinus in 640, announcing their intention to celebrate on 1 April. The Dionysiac tables, however, indicated that 8 April would be the correct date of Easter in 641, and the Irish were so informed. By chance, an identical anxiety is recorded in Spain, where Bishop Braulio of Saragossa had been consulted. He confirmed that the "choice" in Victor's tables was based on inaccurate calculation and that 8 April was correct.[58] It was against this background of a recent resolution to the problem of computing the date of Easter that Benedict and Wilfrid were introduced to the tables of Dionysios.

Both Northumbrians were equally taken with the new papal ceremonial, the use of icons, stained glass, and the "Roman" style of building. When they returned across the Alps, they shared their enthusiasm and knowledge with other Christian communities and began to adapt their Roman experience for use in northern climes. Wilfrid became an ardent campaigner for

[57] Bede, *EH* 5.19 (pp. 516-20); *Lives of the Abbots of Wearmouth and Jarrow*, ch. 2, ed. J. E. King, in *Bede, Historical Works*, 2 vols. (London, 1954), 2:394-96; *The Life of Bishop Wilfrid by Eddius Stephanus*, ed. B. Colgrave (Cambridge, 1927), chs. 3-6 (pp. 9-15). Cf. P. Wormald, "Bede and Benedict Biscop," in G. Bonner, ed., *Famulus Christi* (London, 1976), 141-69.

[58] C. W. Jones, "The Victorian and Dionysiac Paschal Tables," *Speculum* 9 (1934): 408-412; D. Ó. Cróinín, " 'New Heresy for Old': Pelagianism in Ireland and the Papal Letter of 640," *Speculum* 60 (1985): 505-516.

the Dionysiac system of Easter calculation, as opposed to the method based on an 84-year cycle still used in Celtic regions. Benedict's passion was for the richness of Roman ecclesiastical furnishings, silks, liturgical objects, and colourful decoration. This attachment to things Roman was deepened by their subsequent travels on the Continent, especially Benedict's search for books and skilled craftsmen, and Wilfrid's observation of episcopal authority, which he employed at his consecration by Bishop Agilbert of Paris at Compiègne.[59] Their repeated visits to Rome also made the idea of pilgrimage to the Apostles Peter and Paul more familiar among Anglo-Saxons and led to the regal pilgrimages of the late seventh century.

The Synod of Whitby. The results of increased contact between England and Rome were realised slowly, but they did help to resolve some of the anomalous features of northern Christianity. In the case of Easter calculation, the conflict only became an obvious problem when King Oswy of Northumbria married Eanfled, a royal princess who had been brought up in Kent. Oswy's traditional Celtic observation of Easter meant that he always celebrated on the fourteenth day of Nisan, while Eanfled's training decreed that she should wait a week. The discrepancy was serious, because one would be feasting and celebrating the resurrection while the other fasted in preparation for it. Under Wilfrid's influence, Oswy's son, Alfrith, got both parties together at Whitby in 664 and staged a somewhat artificial debate.[60] The monks of Whitby and Lindisfarne, together with the Northumbrian clerics, represented the Celtic system, while Wilfrid, James the deacon, and Bishop Agilbert argued for the Roman. After enquiring which of the two founding figures, St. Peter or St. Columba, had greater authority in the church, King Oswy agreed to adopt his wife's custom without much argument. Bede implies that it was his fear of displeasing St. Peter on Judgement Day that persuaded Oswy for Rome: "Since he is the doorkeeper I will not contradict him . . . otherwise when I come to the gates of the kingdom of heaven, there may be no one to open them because the one who on your showing holds the keys has turned his back on me."[61] This decision was not acceptable to the Irish monks at Lindisfarne, who departed with their leader Colman to preserve the Ionan tradition in the remote outer reaches of the Celtic world. In the long run, however, the Dionysiac method used in Rome would prevail, bringing even the most peripheral regions of northern Europe under the sway of St. Peter.

[59] Eddius, *Life of Bishop Wilfrid*, ch. 5 (pp. 12-13); ch. 11 (pp. 24-26). Cf. Bede, *EH* 5.522; *Lives of the Abbots*, chs. 4-6, 9, and 11.
[60] Bede, *EH* 3.25 (pp. 294-308); cf. Eddius, *Life of Bishop Wilfrid*, ch. 10 (pp. 20-22).
[61] Bede, *EH* 3.25 (pp. 306-307); cf. Eddius, *Life of Bishop Wilfrid*, ch. 10 (p. 22).

Roman Influence in Anglo-Saxon England. Wilfrid and Benedict's informal contacts were soon deepened by Oswy's decision to send Wigheard, archbishop-elect of Canterbury, to Rome for consecration. When he died there of an attack of plague (an event so common that it is not even recorded for the year 665 in the *Liber pontificalis*), Vitalian had to select a new candidate.[62] At first he wished to appoint Hadrian, one of the many refugees from Africa, who had become abbot of a monastery near Naples and who had twice been on missions to Gaul. But Hadrian declined and suggested instead Theodore, an eastern monk born in Tarsos, also in exile in Rome. When Vitalian finally agreed to consecrate Theodore—once his short hair, which had been tonsured in the eastern style, had grown so that he could be given the Roman tonsure—he insisted that Hadrian accompany the new archbishop to Canterbury. The pope was somewhat worried that Theodore might introduce "eastern" customs into the church of England, which had so far been trained in Roman practices.[63] The two set off in May 668, with Benedict Biscop as guide, thus inaugurating what Bede describes as a golden age in the church of the English people.[64]

Under Archbishop Theodore and Abbot Hadrian, and with the support of an increasing number of monks and secular leaders who made the pilgrimage to Rome, the links between the English church and the papacy became very close. Benedict Biscop, who had been tonsured at Lérins and was abbot of Sts. Peter and Paul, Canterbury, before he founded his own monastery at Wearmouth in 674, made six journeys altogether, each time acquiring books, relics, sacred vessels, icons, and building and artistic skills. On his fifth visit, he begged Pope Agatho to let the archchanter John accompany him back to the communities at Wearmouth/Jarrow. The Northumbrian monks thus received instruction in the Roman style of reading and chanting, as well as in matters of liturgical, artistic, and theological import. John wrote down entire services and left a copy of the acts of the Lateran Synod of 649 with them. He was so much in demand in other parts of the English church that he had to travel around teaching music. This interest in chant was shared by the priest Acca, who collected books with such zeal that his library was noted by Bede.[65]

Whether such individual effort would have succeeded in spreading Roman customs very widely may be open to doubt, but additional institutional methods were to reinforce the process. Nechtan, king of the Picts, for instance, wrote to the abbot of Wearmouth/Jarrow declaring that

[62] Bede, *EH* 3.29 (p. 318); 4.1 (p. 328).

[63] Paul the deacon, *HL* 5.30; Bede, *EH* 4.1 (pp. 328-32).

[64] Bede, *EH* 4.2 (p. 332); *Lives of the Abbots*, ch. 3 (pp. 396-98).

[65] Bede, *EH* 4.18 (p. 388), 5.20 (pp. 530-32) on Acca; *Lives of the Abbots*, chs. 6, 7, 9, 11. On Benedict, see Wormald, "Bede and Benedict Biscop," 141-69.

though "the Picts were remote from the Roman people and from their language," they wished to follow the customs of the Roman church. In particular, he requested information about the calculation of Easter, the shape of the tonsure, and the Roman fashion of building (the first two constituted the outstanding differences between Celtic and Roman traditions). In reply, Abbot Ceolfrith, who had been to Rome with Benedict in 678, sent a long letter and builders who would help to construct the church Nechtan wished to dedicate to St. Peter. In this way, the Celtic Picts received translations of Roman texts to guide their own church, and the cult of the Roman Apostle was adopted in the distant climes of western Scotland.[66] In similar fashion, the special devotion of the West and East Saxons and the Mercians was strengthened by the regal pilgrimages of their kings, Caedwalla (baptised Peter by Pope Sergius), his successors Ine, Offa, and Cenred.[67]

To these institutional means of extending Roman practice in northern Europe, two further aspects of Roman control should be mentioned. Both arose from the efforts of individuals to gain papal sanction for particular monastic foundations or for missionary work. Pope Honorius's charter for Bobbio (628) was requested by Jonas, the biographer of its founder Columbanus, as a guarantee of independence against episcopal interference.[68] As later founders were often bishops, Wilfrid and Earconwald for example, it was not from episcopal control but from general secular authority that they wished to protect their houses. Benedict, Hadrian (of St. Augustine's monastery, Canterbury), and Wilfrid (of Ripon) all obtained privileges from Rome in the 670s, while Earconwald's foundation at Barking had its charter confirmed at the same time.[69] Such papal charters were clearly felt to be the best form of protection and insurance against change. Similarly, with papal sanction, missionaries could undertake their work with enhanced authority. Kilian and Colman requested Pope Conon's permission to preach in the region of Wurzburg in 686-87, and shortly after Pope Sergius consecrated Willibrord as Clement, archbishop of the Frisians, thus opening an important missionary front in northeast Europe.[70] From Utrecht, Clement extended Roman observance to modern Luxembourg, where the monastery of Echternach was founded in ca. 700. These monastic centres, assured an independent existence by papal charter, formed a vi-

---

[66] Bede, *EH* 5.21 (pp. 532-52); *Lives of the Abbots*, chs. 7, 16-21 (pp. 406, 432-42).

[67] Bede, *EH* 5.19 (p. 516); Paul the deacon, *HL* 6.15, 28.

[68] Jaffé, no. 2017; cf. T. P. McLaughlin, *Le très ancien Droit monastique de l'Occident* (Paris, 1935), 187-89.

[69] Jaffé, nos. 2104, 2106, 2111, 2112, 2139, cf. Bede, *EH* 4.18 (p. 388), on Benedict's charter for Wearmouth; cf. McLaughlin, *Le très ancien Droit*, 192-95.

[70] *LP* 1.376.

tal web in the transmission of Roman Christianity to some of the more remote corners of the North. When they needed relics for the consecration of
their new churches, or books for their new libraries, it was to Rome that
they turned.

Eastern Pilgrims to Rome

At the same time, Rome was continuing to receive a stream of pilgrims and
refugees from eastern areas occupied by Islam or dominated by Monothelete authorities. The Greek monastery of St. Erasmus may date from the
last year of Vitalian's pontificate (672); the Boetiana housed a community
of Nestorian monks in 676-78; the Domus Arsicia monastery was in existence before 680—in all, ten new Greek houses were established in the 200
years after 650.[71] This influx of Easterners strengthened the degree of
Greek influence in Rome established by Maximos at the time of the Lateran
Synod. Bilingual ability became more common, facilitating the translation
of ecclesiastical documents and Greek texts, such as Sophronios's *Miracles
of Sts. Kyros and John* (partly rendered into Latin by Boniface, a papal
counsellor). The taste for oriental textiles and liturgical objects, evident
from Vitalian's time, became more pronounced, and they were deployed in
a more sumptuous and glistening rite. Eventually this steady growth of
eastern culture resulted in the election of popes from Sicilian, Syrian, or
Byzantine backgrounds, a development that in turn reinforced the same
process.[72] With two exceptions, the bishops of Rome from Agatho (678-
81) to Zacharias (741-52) were all representatives of this oriental culture.
By the early eighth century, even some of the Italian bishops who attended
the Roman synod to which Wilfrid brought his second appeal (704) chat-
ted among themselves in Greek (to his discomfort).[73]

Rome had never been hostile to the adoption of cults from the East and
welcomed the arrival of new relics, saints, and feasts in this oriental period.
Some of these, such as the veneration of St. Anastasios the Persian, were
introduced by refugees who brought their most prized possessions (in this
case, the saint's head) with them. By the middle of the seventh century,
Anastasios's feast was celebrated at Rome, and his relic had built up a reputation for miraculous cures.[74] Later Pope Sergius (687-701) inaugurated
the four feasts of the Virgin in western use. Like so many of the art forms
and ecclesiastical objects adopted, they were of fairly recent Byzantine or-

[71] Sansterre, *Les moines grecs*, 1:31-39.

[72] C. Mango, "La culture grecque et l'Occident au VIIIe siècle," *Settimane* 20 (1973):
683-70; J. Irigoin, "La culture grecque dans l'Occident latin du VIIe au IXe siècle," *Settimane* 21 (1974), 1:425-46.

[73] Eddius, *Life of Bishop Wilfrid*, ch. 53 (p. 112).

[74] C. Bertelli, "Caput Sancti Anastasii," *Paragone* 247 (1970): 12-25.

igin, but each was to be celebrated in a Roman style in a popular procession from the church of St. Hadrian to that of St. Maria Maggiore, with new verses that stressed the fact of her bodily Assumption. Similarly, the Exaltation of the Cross, a festival probably known at Rome for some time, was developed by Sergius into a greater pageantry associated with a new reliquary housed in the Constantiniana.[75] Several liturgical innovations brought Syrian and Greek hymns into Roman services.

Through this involvement with all parts of Christendom, Rome became a truly international centre in the seventh century, the goal of pilgrims from all regions and the source of ultimate judgement, as Wilfrid and the bishops of Crete and Larissa reveal by their legal appeals. It was also the centre in which authoritative accounts of church history were stored, as Bishop Taio of Saragossa found in his search for the writings of Gregory the Great, and Nothelm proved in his transcription of documents from the papal archive for Bede.[76] To accommodate those visiting the holy see, special monastic *diaconiae* were set up; the first is documented in the pontificate of Benedict II, 684-85.[77] The universal respect accorded to Rome and the fact that such respect found material form and presence meant that the city experienced two divergent influences: the oriental, which made Byzantine attitudes more accessible, and the local, which elevated Roman particularity and stressed the independence of the apostolic foundation. Despite an apparent contradiction, however, the two combined to establish a new position for Rome within the Christian world.

One element in this complex synthesis is reflected in the attempt to regulate secular participation in papal elections. The clergy of Rome naturally made the decision about the succession, but their choice had traditionally been ratified by the civilian population. During this period the people and army were given fixed rights.[78] Which inhabitants of the city constituted the *populus* is unclear. Although the senatorial class had been largely dispersed, families with genealogies going back to those once-famous names probably still had influence. As for the army, *exercitus*, there are suggestions that it was now chiefly composed of local men. While the duke of Rome, a subordinate of the exarch, remained a Byzantine appointment, the troops attached to the city did not normally come from the East and were likely to be loyal to their bishop above all. The sole pope with any associ-

---

[75] *LP* 1.376, 374; Sansterre, *Les moines grecs*, 1:149.

[76] Taio's journey is described in chapters 4 and 6; for Nothelm, see Bede, *EH*, Preface (p. 4).

[77] *LP* 1.364 (and note 7); Llewellyn, *Rome in the Dark Ages*, 137-38.

[78] E. Patlagean, "Les Armes et la cité à Rome du VIIe au IXe siècle et le modèle européen des trois fonctions sociales," *MEFR, Moyen Age* 86 (1974): 25-62; T. S. Brown, *Gentlemen and Officers*, 87-88, 94-101.

ation with Byzantine forces was Conon (686-87), whose father had been enrolled in a Thrakesion detachment, possibly stationed in Sicily earlier in the century. By 695 there is ample evidence that Roman soldiers no longer obeyed commands from Constantinople unquestioningly: when an imperial official, Zacharias, was sent to arrest Sergius for opposing the acts of the council in Trullo, he found the pope well protected. Even more significant, the troops attached to Ravenna were also determined not to let Sergius be arrested and removed, to prevent a repetition of the abduction of Martin or Vigilius.[79]

Although the novel constitutional arrangement did not prevent tension at the key moment of transition between bishops, it did emphasise the local nature of Roman episcopal elections. Such a stress was designed to exclude outside influence and was therefore directed primarily against Byzantium. It was part of the whole movement towards greater political independence for the apostolic see. In conjunction with the evident tendencies towards autonomy manifested by Ravenna, it could not but increase Byzantine difficulties in governing the Italian exarchate.

BYZANTIUM UNDER CONSTANTINE IV (668-85)

Since the departure of Constans II from Constantinople, the Regency Council that ruled for his three sons had been preoccupied by a resurgence of Muslim aggression. In 665-66, Amorion, Pergamon, and Smyrna were captured in a severe campaign; for the first time Muslim troops wintered inside the empire, and 5,000 Slavs fled to the enemy. Such disasters suggest that the *themata* system of government, especially in Opsikion and Thrakesion (western Asia Minor), was not capable of defending the empire; military strength had also been reduced by the Italian expedition. In these straitened circumstances, the regents and senators concentrated on the preservation of Constantinople, preventing the departure of the imperial family and maintaining the court on the Bosphoros, where their own authority had real substance.[80] Since the reign of Herakleios, the Senate of Constantinople had experienced a gradual revival and development of its powers, which it was doubtless reluctant to relinquish. Had the entire metropolitan organisation moved to Syracuse in the 660s, the Byzantine Empire might well have fallen 800 years before it did, and Constantine IV might have ruled only in the West, or not at all. But the many vested interests in the Queen City ensured its survival, and in turn Constantine appears to have enjoyed a great loyalty in the capital.

[79] *LP* 1.368, on Pope Conon.
[80] Theophanes, 353, 348, 351.

Once the body of Constans II had been buried in the imperial mausoleum of Constantinople, the church of the Holy Apostles, and the head of the usurper, Mizizios, displayed in public, Constantine IV took charge of the imperial government. Unlike his father, he seems to have made the transition from minor to emperor without problems (though he too would find it impossible to tolerate his brothers' claims as co-emperors).[81] For over a decade his attention was firmly directed towards the east, as Muawiya's Arab generals made repeated efforts to conquer Byzantium. For five successive summers, 674-78, the capital had to beat off combined land and sea attacks from the Arabs' base at Kyzikos.[82] The final imperial victory was undoubtedly due in part to the invention of "Greek fire," a sulphurous combustible that burned on water, but like all innovations in warfare its success depended upon sustained development and skilful deployment. Constantine deserves credit for this and for the city's defence. In the truce that ended hostilities, the Caliph agreed to pay a ransom to Byzantium, including an annual contribution of 50 horses. After inflicting this humiliating peace on the Arabs, Constantinople celebrated a great triumph and a respite from military activity.[83]

Preparations for Ecclesiastical Reconciliation

Hardly any reference had been made to the Monothelete doctrine in force in the East since the last of the trials in 662. Apart from a regular exchange of mutual condemnation, which appears to have accompanied the succession of most popes and patriarchs, theological debate seems to have been silenced, though the churches remained in effective schism. Constantine, however, realised that the issue had to be resolved. By refusing to allow Vitalian's name to be removed from the diptychs of the capital, he revealed his determination to reconcile the churches of East and West.[84] (It was customary to record past bishops of Rome in official records so that they would be remembered in the prayers of the eastern church. Removal of a name was the normal accompaniment to all conflicts; indeed, since Honorius, who was of course celebrated as a Monothelete, no pontiffs apart from Vitalian had been honoured by inclusion.)

It was to Pope Donus (676-78) that Constantine IV directed his suggestion that the churches of Rome and Constantinople should open discussions

---

[81] Theophanes, 352, 360. First Constantine had his brothers mutilated, then he deposed them and reigned with his son Justinian as co-emperor.

[82] Theophanes, 354-56; Nikephoros, 32-33; Lilie, *Die byzantinische Reaktion*, 77-80.

[83] Theophanes, 355-56 (confirmed later, ibid., 361, 363); Nikephoros, 32-33; Lilie, *Die byzantinische Reaktion*, 80-82.

[84] Mansi, 11.200D, 345B; Navarra, *San Vitaliano Papa*, 101-113.

on the question of Monotheletism.[85] As he mentioned Patriarch Makarios of Antioch in his letter, it seems clear that he intended the doctrine, which was upheld by Makarios, to be the central topic of debate. The emperor also added that he hoped for a settlement of the differences over words no longer used, implying that in the capital the heresy was not accepted. He instructed the pope to select a large number of clerics, bishops, papal staff, and Greek monks from Rome, to form a delegation equipped with the necessary texts and skills to negotiate the desired union. On the eastern side, Constantine deposed Patriarch Theodore, who had persisted in trying to get Pope Vitalian condemned as insufficiently Monothelete; a Duothelete priest, George, was appointed with orders for the suffragan bishops to be summoned for discussions with Makarios.

Pope Donus died early in 678, so when the imperial messengers arrived in Rome, they found Agatho on the throne of St. Peter, a Sicilian, the first of a series of popes with eastern origins or connections, whose elections were part of a growing "Byzantine" influence in the West. While his immediate reaction to the proposed conciliation was positive, Agatho determined to gain complete western support before accepting the invitation. Anxious to avoid any charge of cooperating with heretics, he therefore ordered the churches of the West to discuss the matter in their own councils. Information about two of these survive in the form of letters from the councils of Hatfield (England) and Milan to the emperor.[86] At Easter 680, Agatho summoned his own suffragans to Rome, and 125 signed the decrees that established the considered western response.[87] This gathering elected its own representatives, three bishops, and appointed two Roman deacons and a presbyter to represent the pope. Another subdeacon and a presbyter of the church of Ravenna joined the team, plus four monks from the Greek houses of Rome—in all a party of 12. The council drew up a long letter directed to the emperor, to which Agatho added his own, both a coherent and detailed condemnation of the Monothelete heresy. Although the 649 council was never referred to, its acts, which had vigorously ex-

[85] The imperial *sakra* (proposal) was read at the following council, see Mansi, 11.196-201, reprinted in *PL* 87, 1147-54.

[86] Mansi, 11.175-77, 203-208 (the councils of Hatfield and Milan); Bede, *EH* 4.17-18 (pp. 384-88) gives a full account of the former, and its date—September 679—is elucidated by R. L. Poole, "The Chronology of Bede's *HE* and the councils of 679-80," *JTS* 20 (1919): 24-40. For Archbishop Mansuetus's letter, composed by Damian, later bishop of Pavia, see *PL* 87, 1261-68.

[87] The Roman Council is also noted by Bede, *EH* 5.19 (pp. 522-24); Theophanes, 359-60; Nikephoros, 35-36; the acts are lost, see Mansi, 11.185-86, apart from Agatho's account, preserved in his letter to the emperors and in his authorisation for the Roman legates, ibid., 234-86, 286-315 (including the subscriptions of the 125 bishops); also in *PL* 87, 1161-1213, 1216-29.

amined the alleged doctrinal support for one-will belief, must have proved extremely useful to the papacy. A sense of indebtedness may possibly be implied in Agatho's apology for the number and quality of his theologians: their training in the barbarian regions of the West might leave something to be desired.[88] But again, this may be only a polite formality of deference of Constantinople. There seems no evidence that the western delegates felt out of their depth in the lengthy and detailed discussions that took place in the capital. Their knowledge of eastern theology had probably advanced together with eastern influence in Rome, to a point where there was no need to consult eastern specialists on the more subtle shifts of meaning.

The Sixth Oecumenical Council

The exact steps by which the proposed discussions were elevated to the status of an oecumenical council remain obscure. Possibly Agatho's careful response to the imperial invitation encouraged Constantine to summon representatives from the patriarchates of Jerusalem and Alexandria as well. They attended the proceedings, thereby ensuring the participation of all five patriarchates, an essential quality for councils to be universal. However it happened, the council, which opened in November 680 in the domed hall of the imperial palace (the Trullan basilica), slowly grew from a mere 42 participants to the 157 who attended the final eighteenth session in September 681.[89] From the very beginning, however, it described itself as oecumenical and arbitrated the correct belief of Christendom. The emperor presided at the first eleven sessions, until March 20, accompanied by 13 military, civilian, and judicial officials, representing the highest offices of state. When he was unable to attend, his place was taken by four lay officials, and every session was directed by a secular person, for example Paul, an imperial secretary, or John the quaestor. In comparison with the discussions of 649, those of 680-81 were subjected to a marked degree of non-clerical control.

Despite this evident civilian aspect, the council devoted itself to ecclesiastical business with exemplary seriousness and precision. As was usual in the conduct of general assemblies, the acts of past councils were first read and their decrees reaffirmed. This procedure, however, ran into difficulties in the third session, for the Constantinopolitan version of the Fifth Oecumenical Council of 553 included letters from Pope Vigilius to Justinian and Theodora and a sermon of Patriarch Menas condemned as forgeries. At

---

[88] Mansi, 11.235C, 287D-E, cf. 294C.
[89] R. Riedinger, *Die Präsenz-und Subskriptionslisten des VI oekumenischen Konzils (680/81) und der Papyrus Vind.G.3*, in Abhandhungen der Bayerischen Akademie der Wissenschaften, Phil-hist. Kl., N. F. Heft 85 (Munich, 1979); cf. Mansi, 11.11-12 n.30.

this early stage the Roman legates demanded a verification of the record, and discovered that it had been falsified by Monothelete authors—Patriarch Makarios and his deacon, Stephen, were implicated.[90] From this moment on, every document produced or quotation cited had to be authenticated by reference to an established and accepted text. Whole sessions were devoted entirely to this task of checking and double-checking. The collection of two-will testimonies brought by the Roman delegation and Makarios's three codices with one-will testimonies were solemnly sealed in front of the council (session 7) and the seals only broken in sessions 9 and 10 when the citations were debated. Similarly, Patriarch George subjected the evidence against the Monothelete heresy in Pope Agatho's letter to a thorough check. Only when he was satisfied that the wording of each quotation was identical with patriarchal copies of the same theological writings was the letter accepted (session 8).[91]

This awareness of the importance of authenticity defined the council proceedings and constituted an important intellectual innovation. Codices were compared, insertions and deletions identified, and handwriting analysed. Since the changes of wording involved were sometimes very slight, this was a demanding task that raised the whole level of learning in the assembly. It was to prove a very important occasion in the history of the church. For at a time when complete books were very expensive to copy and bulky to carry around, many basic works of theology were known only through excerpts—epitomes. In the same way, patristic evidence against past heresies survived largely in florilegia, collections of texts.[92] By questioning the context of particular quotes, their precise wording and overall meaning, the 680-81 council was obliged to seek out complete texts and authenticated copies of ancient writings. It heard read aloud and approved a manuscript of St. Athanasios, which was produced by the Cypriot delegation.[93] But in particular, it had recourse to the patriarchal library, one of the few that possessed theological writings in their entirety. In searching for such texts, the archivist, George, even found some unknown Monothelete documents, deemed so dangerous that they were ordered to be

[90] Mansi, 11.225B-229A; cf. J. de Ghellinck, *Patristique et Moyen Age*, 3 vols. (Paris/Brussels, 1948), 2:353; G. Bardy, "Faux et fraudes littéraires dans l'antiquité chrétienne," *Revue d'histoire ecclésiastique* 32 (1936): 290-92.

[91] Mansi, 11.332D (session 7); 11.336D (session 8); 11.381-449 (sessions 9 and 10).

[92] On florilegia, see *RAC* 7 (1969), cols. 1131-60 (by H. Chadwick); F. Diekamp, *Doctrina Patrum* (Munster, 1907, reprinted 1981); C. Mango, "The Availability of Books in the Byzantine Empire, A.D. 750-850," in *Byzantine Books and Bookmen* (Washington, D.C., 1975), 33-34; cf. idem, "La culture grecque," 712-13.

[93] Session 14, Mansi, 11.596E-601B.

burned.[94] Normally, however, when heretical writings were condemned, copies were preserved in the patriarchate.

In the course of the council, Patriarch Makarios of Antioch made a confession of faith that was debated and found heretical. He was therefore expelled in the ninth session, and later replaced by a Greek monk from Sicily, Theophanes, one of the Roman team.[95] The Monothelete doctrine was condemned and its perpetrators, Bishop Theodore of Pharan, Patriarchs Sergios, Pyrrhos, and Paul, and Pope Honorius (not included in Agatho's list) were anathematised. A further supporter, Polychronios, was permitted to test his belief by a sort of ordeal: a corpse was to be revived by his Monothelete prayers. The event took place in the Zeuxippos baths outside the palace in front of a large crowd, and his attempt was entirely unsuccessful. Even after this, a priest from Apamea in Syria was allowed to present his own compromise doctrine, but it too was rejected as heretical. A total of seven unrepentant Monotheletes, including Patriarch Makarios, were permitted to take their case to Rome, where subsequent popes tried hard to persuade them to recant.[96]

On 21 April 681, John, bishop of Portus and a representative of the Roman synod, celebrated Latin mass in St. Sophia in the emperor's presence—an oecumenical event and a sign of progress towards union. This was finally pronounced on 16 September and witnessed by the participants, some of whom only arrived for the last two or three sessions.[97] In all the surviving lists of signatures, the papal envoys (including the Greek bishops of Thessalonike, Corinth, and Gortyna, ecclesiastical capital of Crete) take precedence over the Easterners. Similarly, other ecclesiastics from the diocese of East Illyricum, even suffragans, are given unusually high ranks in the final list. This preferential treatment for participants from a region subject, or sympathetic, to papal authority can be seen in the promotion of the metropolitan of Cyprus (from an original position of fourteenth in the hierarchy to seventh, just ahead of Ravenna) or of Athens (from fifty-sixth to forty-third, ahead of all the autocephalous bishops).[98] The reordering reflects Rome's determination to win a higher status for all the bishops under its jurisdiction and Constantinople's decision to accept this principle. Only ten years later, precedence would return to its traditional form; the concession was temporary. During the Sixth Oecumenical Council, however, the

[94] Ibid., 581E; cf. Mango, "The Availability of Books," 31-33, 43-44.
[95] Mansi, 11.385C-D; *LP* 1.354.
[96] Session 13, Mansi, 11.533D-581E; 609A-612B (Polychronios); 617A-620C (Constantine from Apamea); 621A-B (anathemas).
[97] *LP* 1.354; session 18 (16 September) Mansi, 11.629-40; Riedinger, *Die Präsenz-und Subskriptionslisten*, 7-8.
[98] Riedinger, *Die Präsenz-und Subskriptionslisten*.

three Italian bishops who led the Roman delegation managed to command a much greater respect in both honorific and practical terms; the entire party was accommodated at the imperial government's expense in the Placidia Palace, residence of the papal legates, now restored after the damage inflicted during the 640s and 650s. As the sessions advanced, they sent back interim reports to Rome so that Pope Agatho was kept informed, although he did not live to learn of the successful conclusion of the council.[99]

After the final session, the western legates waited for the official Greek transcript of the acts and the emperor's letter. A long vacancy following Agatho's death in January 681 meant that there was no pope to whom they should report; Leo II was only elected in August 682, after their return. He welcomed the acts, however, and had the concluding sections translated into Latin so that the western churches could be informed.[100] Only his letters to the Spanish church survive, but given the organisation of support by Agatho, it is probable that Christians elsewhere were informed of the union. Leo succeeded in converting two of the Monothelete exiles, and they were received back into the church in January 685, while Makarios and four other supporters remained imprisoned in different Roman monasteries.[101] Apart from these named adherents, the heresy appears to have been a moribund force by 681. The union designed by Constantine IV and approved by Agatho and Leo II obliterated all traces of Monotheletism and ushered in a brief period of cooperation and warm relations between Rome and Constantinople, by now quite evidently the only major centres of Christianity.

Byzantine Policy in the West. The ecclesiastical agreement was marked by several privileges for the Roman church, granted almost as a reward for good behaviour. Constantine IV revoked his father's grant of independence to the church of Ravenna; Rome was once again given its traditional right to ordain the archbishop of Ravenna as his subordinate. Under Benedict II (684-85) the emperor further lifted the customary requirement of imperial confirmation of papal elections, in orders to "the venerable clergy, people and most happy army of Rome." This duty appears to have been bestowed on the exarch of Ravenna, the senior Constantinopolitan official in the West; it eased the process of consecration and reduced long delays. Rome's favoured position was emphasised by an exceptional step: the sending of locks of hair from the imperial princes, Justinian and Herakleios, Constantine's sons, to the clergy and army.[102] As a means of signifying a protective

---

[99] *LP* 1.350, 356 and n. 13; Mansi, 11.728.
[100] *LP* 1.359; Riedinger, *Die Präsenz-und Subskriptionslisten*, 5, 11.
[101] *LP* 1.359-60.
[102] Ibid., 1.363.

role over young children, as well as their acceptance as future rulers, the custom was more common in the West than in the East. The emperor's intention was clearly to win forces in Rome other than the pope himself to a loyal support.

Further marks of favour included the reduction of taxes paid annually by the patrimonies of St. Peter in Sicily, Calabria, Bruttium, and Lucania, granted by both Constantine and his son Justinian II in 686-87. The forced sale of grain at fixed prices and other diverse payments made by the church of Rome to Constantinople were dropped, and Sicilians who had been ill-treated by Byzantine soldiers were returned to their families.[103] Possibly these changes stemmed from a recognition of greater autonomy in Rome and were conceded because it was too hard to try and enforce them. Later concern with these taxes, however, reveals that they were significant; Constantinople was reminded of this in 687, when the Sicilian patrimonies provoked an intense conflict. Although the position of rector of these properties was normally reserved to members of the Roman clergy, Pope Conon had appointed a deacon of Syracuse to the post. This official proved so unpopular that on the pope's death, the citizens and junior officers on these estates (*patrimoniales*) revolted and took a formal complaint to the judge of Sicily. Because of dissensions and complications in the case, the judges referred it to the Byzantine capital for an imperial opinion.[104]

The significance attached by Constantinople to the acts of the Sixth Oecumenical Council was revealed in the demand that they be promptly confirmed at the elections of Popes John V (685-86) and Conon (686-87). The letter by which Justinian II ordered this has survived and sheds a most interesting light on the question of church unity.[105] In February 687, Justinian assembled all the chief provincial governors of the empire in the capital. The list of armies at their disposal provides a valuable picture of the *themata* then in existence—the Anatolian, Thrakesion, Armenian, Italian, Karabisian (a naval force), and African (including Sardinia and Septem).[106] But what is even more important is the record of imperial motivation. Following a similar procedure with palace officials, soldiers, political groups (the demes or factions), and imperial guards (*exkoubitors*) of the capital, the acts of 680-81 were read aloud to these military governors. They were expected to listen attentively and then to sign their agreement, so that the acts would be observed throughout the empire. In this way, detailed information about the denunciation of Monotheletism and the reunion of Constan-

---

[103] Ibid., 1.366, 369.
[104] Ibid., 1.369.
[105] Ibid., 1.366, 368; Mansi, 11.737-38.
[106] On the identification of these units, see R.-J. Lilie " 'Thrakien' und 'Thrakesion': Zur byzantinischen Provinzorganisation am Ende des 7. Jahrhunderts," *JÖB* 26 (1977): 7-47.

tinople and Rome could be communicated to all imperial subjects. Justinian appreciated the danger of permitting individuals to keep copies of such documents, for this was how insertions, corruptions, and changes might creep in. He therefore announced to Pope Conon his intention of preserving the official acts inviolate (in the imperial archive as well as in the patriarchal library) and urged the pope to do likewise. [107]

The First Reign of Justinian II (685-95)

On his father's death in September 685, Justinian was only sixteen, but acceded to the throne without difficulty. Rome had already accepted him as a future overlord, and Constantinople fêted the peaceful continuation of the Herakleian dynasty. From the world of Islam, Caliph Abd al Malik (685-705) made a treaty with the empire on terms most advantageous to Byzantium. The young emperor thus came to power in favourable circumstances. Under Constantine IV, the four *themata* originally established to cover Asia Minor had been consolidated into permanent forms of provincial administration. In addition, the *thema* of Thrace in the European hinterland of the capital had probably been set up following the model of the Asian ones. Justinian inherited this pattern of military government from his father and applied it with varying degrees of success to the European regions of the empire. By the end of the century, there would be eight *themata*, comprising the five above and those of Sicily, Hellas, and the *Kibyrraioton*, a naval unit stationed on the southwest coast of Asia Minor.

It was perhaps partly the existence of extensive papal estates and their potential wealth that persuaded the imperial government to reorganise Byzantine administration in Sicily and Calabria. Between 692 and 695, a *thema* governor, *strategos*, assumed supreme control in a manner similar to the exarchs of Ravenna and Carthage or his counterparts in the East. [108] This extension of *thema* structure to Italy may have been occasioned by a Berber revolt in Africa, which drove the Arabs temporarily from their capital, Kairouan. As the Byzantine authorities worked closely with Berber leaders, they probably took advantage of this victory to strengthen imperial control. Sicily was one of the richest provinces in the empire and required particular attention as an important base against Arab piracy. It remained a point of control for what little shipping took place between the East and both Carthage and Rome, and effectively dominated communication between the papacy and the empire. Subsequent *strategoi* of the island were to illustrate what a key role the *thema* could play in imperial politics.

[107] Mansi, 11.738B: *"ipsas chartas illibatas et incommutabiles semper conservabimus."*

[108] N. Oikonomidès, "Une liste arabe des stratèges byzantins du viie siècle et les origines du thème de Sicile," *SBN*, n.s., 1 (1964): 121-30.

In contrast, the creation of the *thema* of Hellas in central Greece represented an assertion of imperial government in a region that had effectively been "lost" from the late sixth century. Contact between Constantinople and the major coastal cities had been maintained, bringing the central government information about the surviving Greek-speaking and orthodox Christian population of those areas. It was probably as a result of the preparations for his major land and sea campaign to Thessalonike in 688-89 that Justinian considered sending a *strategos* to central Greece. His choice of governor, however, proved unfortunate, for Leontios was clearly ill-disposed towards the emperor. He had previously held the position of *strategos* of the Anatolikon *thema* and had spent three years in prison. In 695, when Justinian appointed him to Hellas, perhaps as a combination of punishment and exile, he preferred to rebel and lead the successful coup against the emperor (see below). If he was intended as the first governor, as seems probable, he may also have resisted a potentially difficult assignment. The *thema* took several years to establish; civilian officials responsible for the infrastructure of provincial government are not recorded for some time, but *kommerkiarioi* involved in the equipment of soldiers were active in 698-99. Their activity at Athens and among the Aegean islands, raising soldiers and crews for the Byzantine naval force of *Karabon* or *Karabisianoi*, is also very evident in the early eighth century.[109]

In addition to the extension of *thema* government, Justinian also pursued another traditional policy by transferring "outsiders" to the empire: the Mardaïtes of Lebanon, part of the population of Cyprus, and large numbers of Slavs taken prisoner during the 688-89 campaign.[110] It is in connection with the latter that a very particular mechanism becomes clear, a procedure that was probably used in subsequent military arrangements for the themata. The Slavs were sent to Asia and settled in the region of the Opsikion *thema*; they were granted a five-year period of tax exemption in which they could farm their land without obligation, and then 30,000 were enlisted as Byzantine soldiers. Justinian himself led the newly formed Slav unit against the Arabs near Sebastopolis. Their performance was disastrous: 20,000 deserted to the enemy. In revenge, Justinian ordered that the rest should be killed, together with their families.[111]

While this particular transfer of population thus proved a complete failure, the procedure involved appears to have been more successful. For from the seals used by *kommerkiarioi* in different parts of Asia Minor, it is evident that this method of endowing families with agricultural land in return for

---

[109] Hendy, *The Byzantine Monetary Economy*, 660.

[110] Theophanes, 363-65; cf. Ostrogorsky, *History of the Byzantine State*, 130-32.

[111] Theophanes, 364, 365-66.

stipulated military duties could increase *themata* army units at very little cost to the central government. The mechanism for granting soldiers sufficient means to provide their own army equipment had been found.[112] Whether this procedure had been used earlier, for example by Constans II, who also transferred Slavs to the East, is unclear. Whether it proved efficient under Justinian II may be doubted. But it seems to have supplied the basic technique for later Byzantine military organisation, the principle of *themata* administration in the ninth and tenth centuries.

The Quini-Sext Council of 691-92

In practice Justianian's first reign was relatively successful. He restored imperial control over the territory linking Constantinople with Thessalonike, the chief Byzantine city in the Balkans, and celebrated this victory over the Slavs in a triumph. Military success was attributed to the intervention of St. Demetrios, whose church in Thessalonike benefited from the imperial grant of a saltpan recorded in suitably grandiose terms: "Divine gift granted to the holy and all-glorious martyr Demetrius by the Lord of the whole universe (*tes holes oikoumenes*) Flavius Justinian, the God-crowned and peace-making Emperor . . . for the purposes of illumination and for the daily sustenance of the God-loved clergy and for all (other) needs of the clergy."[113] Inscriptions in the distant city of Ravenna similarly record imperial attention to aqueducts. The emperor undertook a radical reform of the Byzantine gold coinage. His master mosaicists assisted the Arabs in their decoration of the Dome of the Rock in 691-92 (and again at the Great Mosque of Damascus in 705-711). Byzantium's cultural supremacy, championship of orthodoxy, and "civilising mission" to the less privileged areas of the world was acclaimed.

It was in these confident circumstances that Justinian II resolved to hold a church council to enforce the decisions of 553 and 680-81. As the deliberations of this assembly have not survived, its exact date is not known. But from the final address to the emperor, the 102 canons, and signatures of those who attended, it appears to have taken place between September 691 and August of the following year.[114] Bishops from 211 Byzantine sees, including East Illyricum, took part under the presidency of Patriarch Paul of Constantinople. Despite the Arab conquest, legates from Jerusalem, Alexandria, Antioch, and Rome completed representation of the pentarchy, necessary for an oecumenical gathering, though all were afterwards to com-

[112] Hendy, *The Byzantine Monetary Economy*, 361-64.

[113] Theophanes, 364; Nikephoros, 36; A. Vasiliev, "An Edict of the Emperor Justinian II, September 688," *Speculum* 18 (1943): 1-13, esp. 5-6, lines 1, 11-12.

[114] Mansi, 11.929-88; V. Laurent, "L'oeuvre canonique du concile in Trullo (691-92), source primaire du droit de l'Eglise orientale," *REB* 23 (1965): 7-41.

plain that there had been an inadequate presence from these regions.[115] Since the purpose of the council was to confirm the decrees of the Fifth and Sixth Oecumenical Councils by practical measures, rather than to enact new ones, this gathering is sometimes known as the Quini-Sext. It also took its name from the same domed basilica inside the palace where the Sixth Council had met—the Trullan Council or council *in Trulla*. Clearly its status was not as elevated as that of a universal meeting. But because it provided guidelines to bring ecclesiastical conduct closer to orthodox standards established by 553 and 680-81, it assumed a certain importance. Justinian, then aged 22 or 23, attended the sessions in person and attached great significance to the deliberations, possibly as a reflection of his own prestige.

The 102 canons of this council were intended to legislate for the entire Christian world, but they reveal a preoccupation with matters of church discipline and custom peculiar to the East. As no canons had been formulated since the council of Chalcedon (451), there were many areas of activity. Besides displaying a most fascinating array of non-Christian or pre-Christian practices still in use, the canons reflect three basic aims:

1. To keep bishops in their sees, priests in their churches, and monks in their monasteries; that is, to maintain the hierarchical arrangement and geographical division of the church.
2. To confirm Byzantine, as opposed to Armenian, Jewish, or Roman ecclesiastical customs.
3. To counteract pagan, superstitious, and irreverent activities in society, and to protect the simple-minded who might be taken in by them.

Inevitably some of the measures devised to achieve these aims were suitable for eastern Christians, but not for those in the West. Canons 71 and 76 (Mansi, 11.976A, 977A) directed against the traditional jests and theatrical performances organised by law students in Constantinople (dressing up in foreign clothes, echoed in canon 62 [972 B-C] against transvestism and any sort of disguise), could hardly have applied to the West, now denuded of law schools in this sense. Similarly, canon 81 (977 D-E), which added a phrase to the *Trisagion* ("Holy, Holy, Holy") in the liturgy, could only be enforced in those eastern churches using the *Trisagion*. The effort to censor certain types of art as corrupting (canon 100, 985D) and certain hairstyles as seductive (canon 96, 984E-985B) referred particularly to Byzantine practice. Obviously, in the determination to preserve the correct

[115] H. J. Sieben, *Die Konzilsidee der alten Kirche* (Paderborn, 1979), 349; cf. Y. M.-J. Congar, *L'Ecclésiologie du haut Moyen Age* (Paris, 1968), 377, on the later use made of the canons by iconophiles in the East; F. R. Trombley, "A Note on the See of Jerusalem and the Synodal List of the Sixth Oecumenical Council, 680/1," *B* 53 (1983): 632-38.

usage of the eastern churches, the established habits of others would be criticised. This was the case of Armenian and Jewish customs in Armenia (addressed by canons 32, 33, and 39, 956E-960A, 961A-C).

But in canons 3, 13, and 55 especially (941B-944B, 948B-E, 969A) the church of Rome was openly denounced for maintaining practices dissimilar to Constantinople's. Canon 2 (940B-941B) also raised problems by citing 85 Apostolic Canons—Rome recognised only the first 50.[116] In the other rulings, the thorny problems of clerical celibacy and fasting—aspects of church life that were deeply engrained—were dealt with. Roman celibacy was distinguished from Byzantine respect for the marriage of holy men (canon 13). In the East, priests and deacons continued their married life after ordination; only bishops were obliged to send their wives into distant monasteries (a matter treated in canon 48 [965E]). Canon 55 opposed Roman fasting and declared that western clerics must not fast on Saturdays and Sundays except Easter Saturday. These regulations must have been much more offensive to the church of Rome than canon 36 (960C), which renewed the Chalcedon canon of equality between the two sees; or even than canon 30 (956C-D) which discussed clerical marriage in the lands under barbarian domination (perhaps a reference to Agatho's letter of 680).

Another factor that reflected a lack of concern for western customs was the exclusive reliance on past concilial rulings or traditions vaguely attributed to apostolic times. The Council in Trullo ignored all the papal documents that had assumed an equivalent place in the organisation of ecclesiastical discipline in the West.[117] Over the centuries, appeals to Rome had been settled by official letters carrying definite authority; later disputes had similarly been resolved by consulting established precedent. The churches of the West thus had access to a body of quasi-legal rulings invested with canonical status. For Constantinople to exclude this entire corpus of papal decretals was tactless. And when it cited as authoritative apostolic traditions not recognised by the West, a different approach to ecclesiastical law became very evident. Since the Quini-Sext canons were almost exclusively addressed to the eastern churches, they formed the basis for all later canon law. In contrast, the western body of ecclesiastical rulings depended heavily on papal decrees and had no reason to adopt several of the 691-92 canons. The council therefore marked a decisive separation between East and West in a crucial sphere. From the eighth century onwards, the autonomous development of different bodies of canon law would signal an ever deeper division within the Christian world.

[116] H. S. Alivisatos, "Les canons 13, 30 et 55 du Trullanum," SBN 5 (1939): 581-85, attempts to minimise the divergences.

[117] Congar, L'Ecclésiologie du haut Moyen Age, 374-82.

For the papal legates who attended the Council in Trullo, however, there was a more immediate problem. Since most of the canons related directly to eastern habits, such as the growing practice of celebrating the liturgy in private chapels and homes (nos. 31 and 59), the Romans were apparently unwilling to sign the final list.[118] But they were deceived into signing six copies, bearing the assent of three eastern patriarchs and the emperor, which were then sent to Pope Sergius for his signature. He refused, "because some of the canons were outside the ecclesiastical rite." The acts of the Council in Trullo were repudiated and sent back to Byzantium.[119]

Thus another breach between Constantinople and Rome opened. Justinian II lost no time in trying to determine papal agreement by force: first an official was sent to arrest two of the pope's advisers, John of Portus (who had attended the 680-81 council) and the counsellor Boniface, who had translated some Greek *Lives* and had reasoned with Makarios the Monothelete during his imprisonment in Rome.[120] Both men knew Greek and were perhaps selected as targets to be won round to the imperial position and then sent back to convince Sergius. In Rome, however, nothing further was ever heard of them. Instead, Zacharias the *protospatharios* (a military official with a newly created title and rank) arrived to arrest and deport the pope. Once the armies of Ravenna and the Pentapolis got wind of this plan, they marched on Rome to protect Sergius. In quite the reverse of Martin's arrest, local troops far outnumbered Byzantine forces, and Zacharias took refuge from them in the pope's inner chambers. He was later expelled from the city with contempt while the soldiers of the exarchate and citizens of Rome celebrated Sergius's supremacy.[121] They can hardly have mourned when Justinian II was removed from the throne by a coup in 695; Leontios, ex-general of the Anatolian *thema*, forced Justinian to undergo the public humiliation of mutilation in the Hippodrome of Constantinople. He was then exiled to Cherson (the same place as Pope Martin) in such a state that no one ever believed he could again reign as emperor.[122]

In this they failed to understand the determination of a young man (then aged 26) who knew that he was the legitimate ruler of Byzantium. Through the next decade, as Leontios fell to Apsimar-Tiberios and other military leaders revealed their restlessness at Byzantine defeats, Justinian plotted with newfound allies, the Khazars and Bulgars (who lived respectively north and west of his Black Sea exile). In 705, after great struggles,

[118] Mansi, 11.956E, 969C; T. F. Mathews, " 'Private' Liturgy in Byzantine Architecture," *Cahiers archéologiques* 30 (1982): 125-38.
[119] *LP* 1.372, 373.
[120] Ibid., 1.373; 3.97; Mansi, 12.1035.
[121] *LP* 1.373-74.
[122] Theophanes, 368-69; Nikephoros, 37-39.

he triumphantly resumed his rule, hiding his deformity behind a golden nose-plate. He renamed his Khazar wife Theodora, perhaps following his illustrious predecessor Justinian I, and prepared to govern for the rest of his natural life, designating his son and co-emperor Tiberios as his successor.[123] The violence of his second reign and his insistence on a policy of revenge against the inhabitants of Cherson and Ravenna (two cities that he felt had betrayed him in different ways), ensured that instead he would be murdered after a short six-year reign. But he did succeed in patching up relations between Constantinople and Rome.

In 707 he sent messengers to Pope John VII (705-707), again requesting papal assent to the canons of the Council in Trullo. "Being a timid and cowardly man," the *Liber pontificalis* states, "he sent them back without any change."[124] Whether this means that the pope signed them is unclear. He probably did, but died so soon after that Justinian had to take up the matter again with Constantine I (707-715). In an imperial flourish, he ordered the new pope to journey to the East for discussions. And perhaps surprisingly, in view of the emperor's past behaviour, Constantine embarked for Constantinople with a large retinue in October 710.[125] At every stage of his journey where the papal fleet put in to port, he was welcomed and greeted with gifts. Imperial instructions had clearly been issued to make this an honourable event. At the approach to the capital, the young prince Tiberios, accompanied by the patriarch and the Senate, came to receive him, and he entered the city in triumphal procession. Word was sent to Justinian, then in Nicomedia, who responded by inviting Constantine to sail on to meet him there. In dramatic gestures of reverence, the emperor kissed the pope's feet and escorted him into the provincial capital, which had once been an imperial residence. There, after much debate and altercation, a version of the Trullan canons finally received the papal signature and thus became binding throughout the church.[126] One of Pope Constantine's deacons, Gregory, was closely involved in these difficult negotiations. But what emerged from this historic visit was more of a paper agreement than a lasting ecclesiastical regulation. The canons of 691-92 were never enforced in the West. Even outside the patriarchate of Constantinople their validity was questioned, for representatives of the churches of Jerusalem, Antioch, and Alexandria would later complain that they had not been adequately consulted. The agreement of 711 brought the Christians of East and West together in the reduced circumstances created by Islamic expansion in a demonstration of their shared sense of the Muslim threat.

[123] Theophanes, 373, 374-75; Nikephoros, 40-43.
[124] *LP* 1.386.
[125] Ibid., 1.389.
[126] Ibid., 1.390-91.

Yet, as we shall see in Part III, the two halves of Christendom were obliged to fight Islam separately, not together.

WHILE JUSTINIAN was in exile in the Crimea, Carthage fell to a Muslim fleet (698), and by the end of his second reign the Arabs had crossed the Straits of Gibraltar to begin the conquest of Spain (711). At this time, therefore, Christendom was greatly reduced in extent by the continuous and perhaps "determining" advance of the Muslims. Simultaneously, it was itself more clearly delineated into an East and a West, with the emergence of two spiritual centres of very different characters. The empire had become a purely "eastern" unit, in which the patriarch of Constantinople was the unchallenged religious leader. Although Byzantium retained limited control over the exarchate of Ravenna with outposts in Sicily and southern Italy, Sardinia was abandoned as the Arabs took over the whole western basin of the Mediterranean. The Balkans might yet be won back for the empire—Justinian's campaigns against the Slav settlements would be re-affirmed by later conquests—but Byzantium was now predominantly encircled by the direct threat of Islam. Imperial decline in the period between Justinian's accession and his death, 685-711, reflected the instability of a state undergoing long-term reorganisation (in the form of provincial government), long-term economic decline (in terms of resources), and increasing isolation. It was a crisis at once political, cultural, ideological, and economic, which the caliphate was eager to exploit.

In contrast, the papacy had come out of its struggle with Monotheletism as the victor, enhanced in the eyes of western believers and more firmly established as the acknowledged leader of Latin Christianity. Its own ceremonial and liturgy had assumed a distinctive character; its imported icons, vessels, silks, mosaics, vestments, and even church feasts had been put to a particular Roman use that impressed an increasing number of pilgrims. By persistent persuasion and missionary activity, the Lombards of northern Italy had finally been won to the Catholic rite (by the council of Pavia in 698) so that their Arian bishops no longer rivalled those appointed by Rome. Although this conversion did not remove political hostilities, it was a considerable success for the papacy. Even more than this doctrinal achievement against heretics eastern and western, the widespread cult of St. Peter, especially among Christians in northern Europe, built up loyalty to the church of Rome on a new basis. To the apostolic see came bishops seeking consecration at papal hands, relics of the Apostles for the dedication of their new churches, and Roman styles of decoration to adorn them. To Rome came missionary monks seeking papal confirmation of their efforts to spread the Gospel amongst the non-believers of the north. To Rome also came established abbots who wished to place their monasteries under papal protection, with immunity from secular control. Finally, it was to Rome that these secular potentates came, seeking papal baptism with a Christian name and a retreat from the world. The combination of these different forms of devotion to St. Peter meant that by the late seventh century Rome occupied an elevated position. While the fortunes of the empire sank, those of the Christian institution, which had in a sense replaced the empire in the West, continued to rise, expanding its hegemony.

III

THE THREE HEIRS
OF ROME

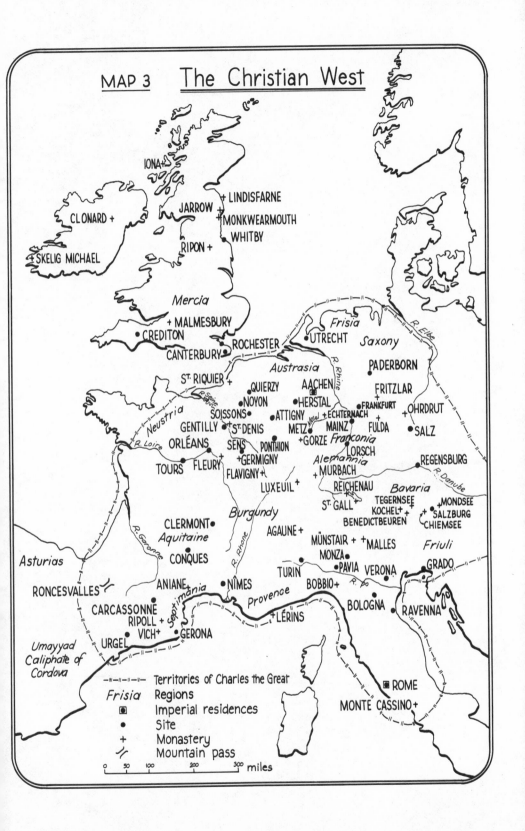

MAP 3   The Christian West

IONA +

CLONARD +

+ SKELIG MICHAEL

+ LINDISFARNE
JARROW +
+ MONKWEARMOUTH
WHITBY
RIPON +

Mercia

+ MALMESBURY
• CREDITON
CANTERBURY•   ROCHESTER•   UTRECHT   *Frisia*   *Saxony*   R. Elbe

ST. RIQUIER +   *Austrasia*   PADERBORN

Neustria   QUIERZY•   AACHEN ▣   FRITZLAR +
•NOYON   •HERSTAL   +FRANKFURT   + OHRDRUT
SOISSONS•   ATTIGNY•   +ECHTERNACH   • SALZ
GENTILLY•   +ST. DENIS   METZ• MAINZ   FULDA
ORLÉANS•   SENS• •PONTHION   +GORZE *Franconia*
R. Loire   FLEURY   +GERMIGNY   LORSCH   REGENSBURG
TOURS•   •   FLAVIGNY +   *Alemannia*   + MURBACH   R. Danube
                LUXEUIL +   REICHENAU   *Bavaria*
                        ST. GALL +   TEGERNSEE +   +MONDSEE
                        Burgundy   KOCHEL + + SALZBURG
CLERMONT•   AGAUNE +   BENEDICTBEUREN   CHIEMSEE
Aquitaine
CONQUES•   MÜNSTAIR + +MALLES   *Friuli*
                        MONZA•
Asturias   TURIN• •PAVIA VERONA•   GRADO+
RONCESVALLES   •NÎMES   BOBBIO+   R. Po
ANIANE•   *Provence*   BOLOGNA•   RAVENNA•
CARCASSONNE•   *Septimania*   + LÉRINS
RIPOLL +
VICH+ •GERONA
URGEL•
Umayyad
Caliphate of
Cordova

–"–"–"– Territories of Charles the Great
Frisia Regions
▣ Imperial residences
• Site
+ Monastery
)(Mountain pass

0   50 100   200   300 miles

▣ ROME

MONTE CASSINO +

FOR MOST MEDIEVALISTS, the eighth century is characterised by the growth of Frankish power in the West and (if they glance eastwards) by the distinctive heresy of iconoclasm in Byzantium. The imperial coronation of 25 December 800 is seen as a watershed between a "Dark Age" and its recognisable successor, "medieval history"; the achievements of Charlemagne (Charles the Great, 768-814) are generally held responsible for "restoring" a unity to "the West." Under a ruler called "The Father of Europe" (*Europae Pater*) by his contemporaries, something occurred that is often known by such textbook phrases as "The Rise of the West" or "The Birth of Europe." The term *Europa* is indeed used for the first time at the turn of the eighth/ninth century for the area over which Charles was nominally sovereign, an area quite restricted, therefore, compared to its modern geographical usage.[1]

A major and novel development did take place at the time. But to comprehend what happened under Charlemagne and his Frankish predecessors, they must be placed within the wider framework that enabled them to pursue their claims. The concluding section of this book will investigate the nature of the specifically "western" development associated with the year 800. Traditional approaches, which often assume that the distinct character of modern Europe was already present in embryonic form in Charles's realm, are distorted by hindsight. A more accurate historical reading will set the "western" development within a Mediterranean context, where it becomes evident that it was one part of a much larger process, whose centre of gravity lay in the East. The "Rise of Islam" and the consolidation of a transformed Byzantine Empire were simultaneous with and related to the advances made by the Franks and their papal allies.[2] The correlation of all three forces, Islamic, Byzantine, and Frankish-Papal, ensured that no one military order or religious culture would again unite the world that had been Rome's.

The familiar western analysis of this period, which views it as a progres-

---

[1] D. Bullough, "Europae Pater," *EHR* 85 (1970): 59-105; D. Hay, *Europe, The Emergence of an Idea*, 2nd ed. (Edinburgh, 1968), 37-55; J. Fischer, *Oriens-Occidens-Europa* (Wiesbaden, 1957), 79-82.

[2] See, for instance, the general account given by G. Cracco in the Italian history of Europe, *L'Europa e il Mondo*, vol. 1, *Dal Medioevo ad Oggi, Europa, Islam, Bisanzio nel Medioevo* (Turin, 1980).

sion from Charles Martel's defeat of the Arabs to his grandson's coronation
as emperor, may be traced to the surviving documentation. In 791, Charles
ordered that the papal correspondence addressed to his family should be
collected together as a valuable record. The resulting *Codex Carolinus*,
which survives in one copy only, does not include all the letters sent from
Rome in the period 739-91, but it preserves nearly one hundred, which
constitute a major source of information, from Rome's point of view.[3] One
of the greatest losses in documentation for the period is the other half of the
correspondence, all the Frankish replies. Another is the twin collection
planned in 791 to bring together all the Byzantine diplomatic correspondence with the Franks for the same period. But it is the absence of Pippin's
and Charles's letters to successive bishops of Rome, from Zacharias to Hadrian, that is most crucial. For this loss has coloured nearly all interpretations of the relationship and alliance initiated in 754. Because we can now
read only the papal appeals for military assistance and protection, often
couched in a language akin to moral blackmail, we tend to overlook the
reciprocal nature of the arrangement.

Pippin may not have been a sophisticated political leader, but he could
understand what advantages Rome's backing might bring to his family—
he did not embark on a policy of expansion into the Italian peninsula to
safeguard the Christian republic of Rome simply out of respect for St. Peter
and his power to loose and bind on Judgement Day. Rome's legitimation
of his dynasty would also assist in consolidating his authority over the
semi-independent regions adjoining his Frankish territories, in establishing Frankish leadership of Christian missionary work among the pagans
and thus his own domination of the emerging political culture of northern
Europe. These ambitions were not greater than those of the papacy: both,
in fact, stemmed from the void left by an over-long decline in ancient and
Roman institutions in the West. There had been many attempts to fill this
void, as we have seen (notably by the Visigothic monarchy of Spain, and
by the churches of the West under Roman leadership). In the second half
of the eighth century, Pope Stephen II and King Pippin embarked on another apparently joint effort, composed of two distinct schemes that could
come together for mutual reinforcement at a critical moment. Each embodied a separate sense of the possible advantage to be gained, but we only
have a record of the papacy's.

Despite intense historical interest in the imperial coronation, this is not
the only reason why the second half of the eighth century is one of the most
studied (and disputed) periods in early medieval history. In comparison
with preceding centuries, there is simply far more evidence available. This

---

[3] *Codex Carolinus*, in *MGH, Ep.*, vol. 3, no. 1, 469-657.

source material does, however, pose very particular problems and has given
rise to a great variety of interpretations. Differences turn especially on the
significance to be given to the terms of the alliance made between the papacy and the Frankish monarchy, the meaning of the title *patricius Romanorum*, and the words *donatio* and *iustitiae* of St. Peter. And upon these hang
each and every understanding of the motives to be attributed to the parties
involved. But a completely new dimension is added by the fact that the
evidence includes a number of celebrated forgeries, notably the *Constitutum
Constantini*, or *Donation of Constantine*.[4] This document purports to record
an arrangement made between Constantine I and Pope Sylvester in the
early fourth century. It states that the emperor entrusted to the bishop of
Rome all the provinces, places, and cities of Italy and the western regions
(*partibus Hesperiae*) when he went off to found his new capital, Constantinople, in the East (*Oriens*). It thus laid claim to a substantial political as
well as spiritual authority for the papacy, while emphasising the idea of a
separation of West from East, which would be used by the Franks to help
justify an independent western imperial authority.

Now one of the most striking features of the eighth century considered
in the wider view is that at precisely the same time Islamic thinkers were
also seeking to consolidate their faith, clarifying the Prophet's inheritance
by similar methods. They relied on oral "traditions," *hadith*, allegedly pronounced by Muhammad himself and preserved in an unbroken oral chain,
which formed a sort of extra-Koranic collection descending from his companions. Systematic use (and abuse) of these sayings created, according to
Ignaz Goldziher, "one of the greatest and most successful literary fictions."
The two societies of the Mediterranean world that functioned independently of Byzantium were thus "inventing traditions" of a politico-religious
nature that helped to secure and consolidate their regional dominance.[5]
While these formative developments remained quite autonomous and took
dissimilar forms, both were responses to the conflicts and crises of rapid
change during the eighth century. Neither can be understood or explained
without regard for their shared context.

This context is broadly defined by the fact that Arab settlement within
the Mediterranean becomes an established political force and assumes a cultural profile in the eighth century. It is further defined by the way that the
massively reduced Christian world of Late Antiquity fails to retain even a

---

[4] *Constitutum Constantini*, ed. H. Fuhrmann, in *MGH, Fontes iuris germanici antiqui* (Hannover, 1968).

[5] I. Goldziher, *Muslim Studies*, vol. 2 (London, 1971), Excursus 2, Hadith and the New
Testament, 346-62; M. Sharon, "The Development of the Debate Around the Legitimacy
of Authority in Early Islam," *Jerusalem Studies in Arabic and Islam* 5 (1984): 121-41, esp.
123-25, on the art of invention.

nominal unity. Several different aspects of the former, the process initiated by Islam, can be isolated—geographic, doctrinal, and artistic. The first may be illustrated by the gradual consolidation of Muslim authority in North Africa and Spain, which completes a southern crescent across the Mediterranean world. From this semi-circular band, maritime communication, island security, and even the activity of ports on the northern shores are threatened. Hostilities now extend from the eastern into the western basin of what had once been a unifying Roman lake, challenging traditional patterns of control in Sardinia as well as Cyprus, on the coast of Provence as well as Crete, in Naples as well as Constantinople. Everywhere Christians find themselves under attack from "Saracen" pirates and raiders.

A second and more substantial aspect of Islamic settlement concerns its specific forms of government. In contrast to previous patterns of administration adopted in different parts of the Muslim world, during the eighth century the Arabs developed their own style, informed by a distinctive body of sacred law (shari'a), with important consequences for secular as well as doctrinal organisation. A greater sense of Islamic culture is reflected in the third aspect: the impressive art forms developed in this period, which enshrine the defining features of an identifiable Muslim civilisation. This is equally visible in the mosques of Cairo, Kairouan, and Cordova, decorated with ornamental wooden carvings, metalwork, painted tiles, silk hangings, and carpets, in the calligraphic art that inspires manuscripts of the Koran and the geometric patterns on their fine bindings.[6] These artefacts and buildings consolidate Arab presence in the same way as the novel social and political forms through which they are promoted.

Following every extension of Muslim control, there seems to be an initial wave of conversion to Islam and then a cooling in contacts between the faiths. Despite periodic outbursts of persecution, the established Jewish and Christian communities generally manage to maintain themselves by paying the stipulated taxes and observing the restrictions that symbolise their inferior status (cutting their hair, not riding with saddle and stirrups, praying quietly, and respecting the public celebration of Islam). Those who refuse to convert are nonetheless guaranteed freedom of worship and are even encouraged to persist in their unbelief for financial reasons. Those who adopt the faith and language of the conquerors (frequently liberated prisoners-of-war or non-Arabs) gain a recognised position as mawali; with other unconverted non-Arabs, they provide the technical and administrative skills for city organisation and Islamic government.[7] Although the ma-

[6] R. Paret, "Die Entstehungszeit des islamischen Bilderverbots," Kunt des Orients 11 (1976-7): 158-81, on the importance of hadith in fixing the ban on human representation.
[7] J. Wellhausen, The Arab Kingdom and Its Fall (London, 1927, reprinted 1973), 71-72,

wali are accepted as Muslims, their Arab overlords and patrons often continue to lead a separate existence, living in their own distinctive urban quarters, marrying among themselves and generally remaining a minority. Such isolation heightens the cultural differences between Islam and other faiths while concentrating Muslim patronage in relatively small circles where new artistic and cultural features can be sponsored.

Yet despite this consolidation of Islam, which strengthened its impact in the Mediterranean world, the eighth century also witnessed the second civil war and an even more serious political split in Muslim allegiance. The Abbasid revolution of 750 and removal of the caliphate from Damascus to Baghdad destroyed Umayyad authority in all but the most western regions. It raised to supreme authority the descendants of Muhammad's uncle, Abbas, who employed Shi'ite ideology in their political struggle and established a theocratic rule. In this attempt to combine spiritual and political leadership in a new dynasty, *hadith* played an important role. "Traditions" both to support and to deny Abbasid claims were fabricated on all sides. Although all were devoted to the same exercise (of justifying political positions), the fundamental differences between Sunni and Shi'ite *hadith* prevented agreement on a single body of traditions. Not one but several were being composed simultaneously.[8] In terms of both moral authority and political dominance, the Arab world was thus severely divided, although this did not detract from the overall growth of Islamic pressure on Christendom and an increased Muslim presence among Christians. The factors tending toward a sharper Islamic profile within the Mediterranean were strong enough to override those generating division.

The variety within Islam became apparent, however, as the Frankish monarchy established diplomatic relations with each independent authority. Under Pippin, a Frankish embassy returned from the Abbasid caliphate of Baghdad, the most distant Muslim capital. Charles's ill-fated expedition to Saragossa (778) brought him into contact with both the Umayyad caliphs of Cordova and various independent emirs in northern Spain. These governors subsequently maintained relations with the court of his son, Louis, king of Aquitaine. In the years 797-98, however, the new Frankish capital at Aachen was the goal of diplomatic missions from a claimant to the caliphate of Cordova and the independent governor of Barcelona, while the Frankish court returned an embassy to Baghdad. King Alfonso II of the Asturias, who maintained a small Christian realm in this

278-79, 298-99, 308-310; I. Goldziher, *Introduction to Islamic Theology and Law* (Princeton, 1981), 33-35.

[8] *Hadith, Encyclopaedia of Islam*, vol. 3 (1970), 25 (by J. Robson); Goldziher, *Muslim Studies*, 2:59-71, 97-103; R. P. Mottahedeh, *Loyalty and Leadership in an Early Islamic Society* (Princeton, 1980), 17-27.

northwest corner of Spain, also presented Charles with diplomatic gifts of booty captured in a raid on Lisbon—including an Arab tent, slaves, mules, and cuirasses. The Muslim embassies came laden with similarly exotic presents—Caliph Harun al Rashid's envoys eventually arrived from Baghdad with an elephant—and each presented individual proposals for peace and friendship with the most powerful ruler of the West.[9] Yet at the same time, all were part of the southern Mediterranean world now controlled by political and religious forces, which, however much they might contend with each other, still owed their existence to the faith of Islam. Christian communities under their administration might occasionally appeal for assistance to their co-religionaries in the northern spheres, but the question of their "liberation" was not raised. On the contrary, the fate of these non-Muslim peoples was left entirely in the hands of their conquerors. By the beginning of the ninth century, Islam had taken over vast territories on a permanent basis. The effective loss of Christian control in the lands of that religion's birth and greatest diffusion was an accepted fact in centres as disparate as York, Rome, Aachen, Aquileia, and Constantinople.

But the impact of this loss was not uniform throughout the Christian world. The most dramatic effects of Islamic expansion clearly lay in the East, where the number of Christians in the ancient pentarchy of five patriarchates (the oldest centres in the Mediterranean) declined rapidly. While Alexandria, Jerusalem, and Antioch still supported Christian communities, their supreme leaders (the patriarchs) resided elsewhere. A system of titular patriarchs and bishops evolved to preserve the apostolic succession of important sees, but these figureheads could not command traditional respect. In Syria, Palestine, and Egypt, Christianity effectively took second place, and its absent leaders experienced an inevitable loss of status. Local representatives of monasteries and outlying bishoprics, which succeeded in maintaining a precarious existence, frequently commanded intense loyalty; some were even respected by the Islamic forces, with whom they negotiated improvements in the daily conditions of the faithful. But the history of these communities is one of progressive decline and atrophy, as the political reality of Muslim rule induced a constant pressure towards conversion. Only amongst the most self-conscious and articulate guardians of Christian traditions—the monks of Mt. Sinai, the White monastery on the Nile, or Mar Sabas near Jerusalem—could these live on, develop, and influence the Islamic environment.[10]

[9] F. L. Ganshof, "The Frankish Monarchy and Its External Relations from Pippin III to Louis the Pious," in *The Carolingians and the Frankish Monarchy: Studies in Carolingian History* (Ithaca, 1971), 162-204.

[10] S. H. Griffith, "Stephen of Ramlah and the Christian Kerygma in Arabic in Ninth-Century Palestine," *JEH* 36 (1985): 23-45.

In contrast to this stranglehold on the ancient centres of Christianity, those within the orbit of Byzantium did not experience a similar decline. Some communities were eclipsed, but others were strengthened by the arrival of refugees from the eastern provinces; many were forced to move from their urban settings to new rural sites and subsequently adopted new, less classical names (e.g. the church of Aphrodisias in Caria became that of Stauroupolis); the new fortified settlement of Monemvasia in southeast Peloponnesos may represent a Christian community from Sparta. Between the late seventh and early ninth centuries, a limited extension of Christianity took place, an indication that the resources of the eastern church were not entirely consumed. Conversion played an important personal if not institutional role in imperial dealings with various Bulgar tribes settled in the northern Balkans. One of their leaders, Tervel, was probably baptised when he was adopted as caesar by Justinian II in the early eighth century; another, Telerig, was given the position of patrician when Leo IV acted as his godfather at the baptismal ceremony of 777.[11] While there is no evidence that large numbers converted at the same time, members of the Bulgar nobility and courtiers close to the tribal leaders probably found it useful to adopt the same belief. By the middle of the ninth century, when Sts. Cyril and Methodios organised the effective spread of Christianity throughout the independent kingdoms of Bulgaria and Moldavia, the faith was by no means unknown. And the Byzantine capacity to render the Greek Bible and liturgy into the spoken language of these peoples (who still use these texts written in Church Slavonic and Russian) ensured that they would remain within the eastern orbit of Christianity, despite rival missionary activity carried on in Latin with Roman support.

Imperial policies also encouraged the adoption of Christianity by the Slavonic tribes settled in the southern Balkans. After Leo III's detachment of the diocese of East Illyricum from Rome, there was a notable increase in episcopal sees in the provinces of Hellas, Peloponnesos, Thessaly, Macedonia, and Thrace. In Greece the number jumped from about 18, recorded in the late seventh century, to the 46 bishops who attended the council of 787.[12] Representatives from Troizen (near the ancient site of Epidauros) or Porthmos and Oreos on the island of Euboia seem to indicate new Christian communities. While at coastal cities like Thessalonike, Athens, and Corinth, the faith had never ceased to be observed, the novelty of eighth-century expansion is that it documents the spread of Christian belief among the Slavonic settlers who had effectively replaced older communities. An

[11] Theophanes, 374, 451; Nikephoros, 41-42.

[12] R.-J. Lilie, " 'Thrakien' und 'Thrakesion': Zur byzantinischen Provinzorganisation am Ende des 7. Jahrhunderts," *JÖB* 26 (1977): 7-47.

important encouragement to missionary work among bishops was probably provided by the Empress Irene, who came from Athens and insisted upon its promotion to metropolitan status towards the end of the century.[13]

But this relatively modest achievement in the lands under Byzantine influence pales in comparison with the immense extension of Christianity in the West during the eighth century. Far from the direct threat of Islam, western communities flourished and expanded energetically. From a developed monastic base in Ireland, Scotland, and Northumbria and an established episcopal hierarchy throughout Anglo-Saxon England, missionary activity penetrated to the extreme West and across the Channel into parts of Europe still pagan. Given the close ties already linking the see of St. Peter with the Christians of northern Europe, Rome's support and encouragement of this extension was to be expected. But the initiative appears to have come from the north, as an injection of determination to follow Christ's instruction to the Apostles: "Be ye fishers of men. . . ." Under Sts. Clement and Boniface (as Willibrord and Winfrith became known), the faith was preached in previously unfished waters, and the catch was often impressive. Nor were the Anglo-Saxons alone in the task. From Septimania (or further south in the surviving Christian areas of Spain) came Pirmin, and from Francia, Emmeram, Rupert, and Corbinian.[14] But it was largely due to the work of Clement and Boniface that a striking improvement occurred between the early and late eighth century in regions now designated as Saxony, Franconia, Bavaria, and Carinthia. Thanks to their intensive missionary work, an entire ecclesiastical network had been set up, with independent monasteries as far east as Fulda, Fritzlar, and Ohrdrut (in the north) and on several of the Austrian and Bavarian lakes, Chiemsee, Mondsee, and Tegernsee (in the south). Many were supported by local notables and Frankish rulers; Pippin's daughter, Gisela, patronised the monastery at Kochel, a daughter house of Benedictbeuren, in the 740s. Within the territories controlled by her brother, Pirmin's foundation at Reichenau (724) was one of the most important, from which a number of other monastic centres were started. Similarly, Chrodegang's later activity at Gorze

[13] J. Herrin, "Aspects of the Process of Hellenization in the Early Middle Ages," *Annual of the British School at Athens* 68 (1973): 113-26.

[14] K. Bosl, "Der 'Adelsheilige': Idealtypus und Wirklichkeit, Gesellschaft und Kultur im merowingerzeitlichen Bayern des 7. und 8. Jahrhunderts: Gesellschaftsgeschichtliche Beiträge zu den Viten der bayerischen Stammesheiligen Emmeram, Rupert, Korbinian," in *Speculum historiale: Festschrift J. Sporl* (Munich, 1965), 167-87, reprinted in F. Prinz, ed., *Mönchtum und Gesellschaft im Frühmittelalter* (Darmstadt, 1976). F. Prinz, *Frühes Mönchtum im Frankenreich* (Munich/Vienna, 1965), 210-18. H. Löwe, "Pirmin, Willibrord und Bonifatius, Ihre Bedeutung für die Missionsgeschichte ihrer Zeit," *Settimane* 14 (1967): 217-61. J. Semmler, "Mission und Pfarrorganisation in den Rheinischen, Mosel- und Maasländischen Bistümern (5.-10. Jahrhundert)," *Settimane* 28 (1982), 2:813-88.

and St. Avold provided the impetus to further foundations at Gegenbach (761) and Lorsch (764). [15]

Christian reaction to the spread of Islam thus varied according to zone; in the East, the older religion experienced a decisive setback, in Byzantium, a limited consolidation, and in the West, a vigorous growth. The major significance of this western expansion lay in the intensification of monastic life, with its stress on celibacy, education, the copying of manuscripts, and the spread of Latin. Through this ecclesiastical training, the clergy could assume a dominant position in western society as a whole. And at a time when society remained very fragmented, such clerical influence acted as an important unifying factor. Indeed, it is possible that the general acceptance both of Latin as the language of secular record and of Christian culture in the West was a precondition for the later development of feudalism. Familiarity with the language of oaths and fealty was certainly assisted by the ubiquitous use of ecclesiastical Latin, while church discipline predisposed those in a weaker position to adopt terms of commendation and vassalage to their stronger superiors.

By the end of the eighth century, therefore, a decisive realignment of forces had taken place within the Christian world under the impact of Islam. A remarkable shift in dominant belief had left the eastern patriarchates weakened and impoverished. Only Constantinople, never accepted as an apostolic foundation of equal authority and antiquity, preserved sufficient resources to expand the faith through missionary work. But now for the first time, the Christians who lived in the West probably outnumbered their brethren in the older centres of the East. While these numbers can not be calculated, the scale of some of the western monastic foundations and the vast, though thinly populated areas brought into the faith imply a considerable increase. By whatever criterion we attempt to measure this growth, it must stand in marked contrast to the evident decrease of Christian observance in the East Mediterranean. But it must not be seen simply as a replacement of East by West; the rapid expansion of the faith in previously pagan regions of northeast Europe was different both in scope and in character. It attempted to implant the basic Christian tenets of belief where systematic theology had previously been unknown and was little appreciated: the results were sometimes ephemeral, marked by only a passing commitment to Christian practice and then a resumption of pagan traditions. Nor was this aspect of the expansion confined to Christianity; within Islam, a comparable situation left many North African tribes with an in-

---

[15] A. Angenendt, *Monachi peregrini* (Munich, 1972); A. Borst, *Mönche am Bodensee 610-1525* (Sigmaringen, 1978), 19-101, with wonderful photographs; idem, ed., *Mönchtum, Episkopat und Adel zur Grundungszeit des Klosters Reichenau* (Sigmaringen, 1974); Prinz, *Frühes Mönchtum*, 218-22. See also the Afterword, below, pp. 481-87.

adequate understanding of the new religion and a tendency to revert to idolatry and other ancient practices. The Arab conquest brought Arabisation, but not necessarily a very profound Islamisation.

In these circumstances of expansive but occasionally superficial growth and of extremely rapid political change, the two faiths of the Mediterranean were both affected by anxieties and confusions. Exercising control throughout the scattered regions won to a nominal observation and ensuring correct observation proved very difficult. Local particularities could easily promote separatist tendencies, which took both religious and political forms. Against these tendencies, leading authorities within each faith tried to buttress their claims to determine future development by reference to past authority. None of them, however, could take the place of Rome in the ancient Mediterranean; they all failed to secure an outright dominance and had to be content with more restricted spheres of influence.

Although, as noted above, the processes whereby both Islamic and Christian claims were established are comparable, they were far from identical. While a particular document was constructed in Rome in support of papal authority, teachers in several Muslim centres elaborated their own "traditions" independently. Islamic and Christian types of tradition so forged (in both senses of the word) were therefore very different, but they all served a similar function in eighth-century society. Each helped religious authorities to systematise their history in a more favourable light, to establish their own supremacy against other interpretations of the faith or against rival political forces. Each represents "the invention of tradition"— a necessary stabilisation at a time of extreme uncertainty and rapid change.[16] In neither case is the political background the sole motor for such developments: both the use of *hadith* and the theory of Petrine supremacy preceded the Abbasid revolution and the Frankish intervention in Italy. But it was in the context of such major upheavals in previously accepted and established political institutions, which shattered the unity of both Muslim and Christian worlds, that these constructions could be put to novel uses. The eighth century therefore marks a very particular moment: with *hadith* and the *Donation of Constantine*, the two faiths, which represent a completely different type of belief-system from that of the ancient world, construct their own histories and lay claim to a past that justifies future dominance.

The same period also marks the final collapse of Constantinople's political claims to an imperial role throughout the known world as the heir of Rome. In place of the imperial tradition of hegemony, the eastern empire

[16] For a general overview, see E. Hobsbawm, "Introduction: Inventing Traditions," in E. Hobsbawm and T. Ranger, eds., *The Invention of Tradition* (Cambridge, 1983), 1-14.

becomes marginalised, while the Islamic and Western polities assert their own place in the Mediterranean world. This tripartite division establishes very different states. In the East, Muslim society represented a new version of that fusion of political, theological, and military authority characteristic of the Greco-Roman world. Yet it did not draw solely on the ancient civilisations; it represented a foreign, external force, inspired by a new faith.[17] Although it might have replaced the imperialism centred on the eastern capital had the walls and defence of Constantinople been less strong, it could not have continued the Byzantine style of domination.

Meanwhile in the West, authority was more clearly divided between secular and religious powers. While Charles might preside over the bishops of the Frankish church, he could not deny the independent moral strength exercised by Rome. The uneasy balance between these two, represented by Leo III's coronation of Charles in 800, presaged an unorthodox development, although one directly inspired by ancient models, both imperial and Christian. But however much it called upon Roman traditions as the "Holy Roman Empire," it in no way restored them unchanged. The later separation of church and state would come to constitute a more fundamental break from ancient traditions in that it opened the way to the parcellised sovereignty of feudalism so antithetical to Roman imperialism.[18]

Only in Constantinople might such a continuity have been possible, and as we have seen, the transformed Byzantine Empire of the late seventh century lacked military and political dominance to make good its traditional claims. It maintained the same style of government, however, if on a smaller scale, and it adapted this machinery to eighth-century challenges. Like Muslim and papal authorities, the Byzantines were not above constructing particular texts that would amplify what they firmly believed to represent ancient tradition. But although the iconoclast controversy provided opportunity for a re-examination of Christian worship, the issue was too narrow to allow the eastern church a possibility of development comparable to that presented by *hadith*. And in the Feast of Orthodoxy (843), which finally restored the icons and guaranteed their revered position, a tradition of only limited significance was manufactured, though it too was justified by a pious fake.[19] The Byzantine church did not emerge from the

[17] Wellhausen, *The Arab Kingdom and Its Fall*, Introduction, esp. 1-10, 24-26, 61-68; cf. P. Crone and M. Hinds, *God's Caliph* (Cambridge, 1986).

[18] P. Anderson, *Passages from Antiquity to Feudalism* (London, 1974), esp. 139-42, 146-53.

[19] J. Gouillard, "Le Synodikon d'Orthodoxie: édition et commentaire," *TM* 2 (1967): 1-316; the fake is the *Letter of the Patriarchs of Alexandria, Antioch and Jerusalem* allegedly written in 836 to petition Theophilos to restore the icons, see L. Duchesne, "L'iconographie

struggle with a more universal claim on the loyalty of Christians everywhere; rather, it secúred a clearer Greek and eastern character, confined
culturally and geographically to the northeast corner of the Mediterranean.
From this base, it was to exercise a very considerable influence over developments in the neighbouring Slav and Muslim territories, as well as in the
West, but never again over that imperial hegemony derived from Rome.

byzantine dans un document grec du IXe siècle," *Roma e l'Oriente* 5 (1912-13): 222-39, 273-
85, 349-66; cf. R. Cormack, *Writing in Gold* (London, 1985), 121-24, 261-62.

Eastern Iconoclasm: Islamic
and Byzantine

SINCE THE EARLY seventh century, the cult of icons had continued to penetrate all levels of Byzantine society, compelling a devotion in emperors and patriarchs, bishops and craftsmen, women and soldiers, monks and peasants.[1] The growth of icon veneration was stimulated by their "official" use as military ensigns and protective devices, during the 626 siege for example, and by a widespread popular faith in their intercessory powers, which increased despite the fact that icons were not consecrated as holy objects.[2] The cult was not confined to urban centres, as many celebrated icons belonged to isolated rural settlements and attracted annual pilgrimages from a wide area. Those of the Virgin at Mousge and Sozopolis were responsible for miraculous cures that brought people from far and near to the wonder-working shrines. Icons also familiarised worshippers with different saints; when a rural patron, St. Platon of Galatia, appeared to some monks taken prisoner near Mt. Sinai, they recognised him because of the similarity to his representation on their own local icons and attributed their liberation to his holy intervention. Similarly, a young girl in Constantinople identified a dream figure by reference to the icons displayed on the screen of St. Artemios's church. Even those who had never seen icons of St. Demetrios were able to understand his miraculous assistance when they reached his shrine in Thessalonike; the image associated with the *kiborion* (canopy) over his tomb protected the city against barbarian attacks, performed miraculous healing, and directed those far away to come to the

---

[1] J. Herrin, "Women and the Faith in Icons in Early Christianity," in R. Samuel and G. Stedman Jones, eds., *Culture, Ideology and Politics* (London, 1982), 56-83; H.-G. Beck, *Von der Fragwürdigkeit der Ikone*, Sitzungsberichte der Bayerischen Akademie der Wissenschaften, Philos.-Hist. Klasse, Heft 7 (1975); idem, *Das byzantinische Jahrtausend* (Munich, 1978), 183-87. I should like to thank Margaret Aston and Robin Cormack for particularly helpful discussions about iconoclasm.

[2] P. Brown, "A Dark-Age Crisis: Aspects of the Iconoclastic Controversy," *EHR* 88 (1973): 1-34, esp. 5-8; R. Cormack, *Writing in Gold* (London, 1985), 9-107.

city's aid. Through collections of such miracle stories, the cult of particular icons and saints extended to all parts of the empire.[3]

Icons as Intercessors

It was in their role as intercessors between man and God that the icons commanded particular devotion. Numerous legends of women, whose inability to conceive a child (or sometimes, more particularly, a son) was removed by prayers directed to icons, reflect an anxiety common to many medieval societies. St. Glykeria, the patron of Herakleia, promised a child to the parents of St. Elizabeth through the medium of her icon; Elizabeth was in due course dedicated to her in front of the same image.[4] Similarly, a childless couple was blessed by the Virgin's icon at Sozopolis, and the mother of St. Stephen had her longing for a son satisfied at the Blachernai shrine in Constantinople. For the cure of disease rather than infertility, the medical saints, Cosmas and Damian, Artemios, Febronia, and others, were frequently invoked and their icons consulted. Incubation for one or more nights in their shrines—the pagan custom of sleeping close to the god— was rewarded by nocturnal visits of the saints (again recognisable in features familiar from their images) and finally by cures.[5] The oil burning in lamps suspended in front of icons also had curative power, as did the miraculous effluents that emerged from the Sozopolis icon or the relics of St. Euphemia in Chalcedon. Icons were also appreciated for their power to move: in the early seventh century, Patriarch Sophronios wrote down the ancient legend of St. Mary the Egyptian, who was allegedly converted by a picture of the Virgin preserved at Jerusalem in his time.[6]

Not only images of the Holy Family and saints gained such power; icons were also painted of the living. Patriarchs sometimes displayed their own images and those of church leaders like Bishop Abraham of Luxor (late sixth century). In the early seventh century, however, a portrait of St. Theodore of Sykeon was painted secretly by a monk for his community in the Byzantine capital. The brothers wished to have a record of the saint who had cured one of them of possession but feared that Theodore might not

[3] A. Papadopoulos-Kerameus, ed., *Miracula S. Artemii*, in *Varia graeca sacra* (St. Petersburg, 1901); P. Lemerle, ed., *Miracula S. Demetrii*, 2 vols. (Paris, 1979).

[4] F. Halkin, "Sainte Elisabeth d'Heraclée, abbesse à Constantinople," *AB* 91 (1973): 249-64, paras. 3 and 4.

[5] L. Deubner, *De Incubatione* (Leipzig, 1903); N. Fernández Marcos, *Los Thaumata de Sofronio, Contribución al estudio de la incubatio cristiana* (Madrid, 1975).

[6] Patriarch Sophronios recorded his own cure from oil obtained from lamps at the shrine of Sts. Cosmas and Damian, *Miracula*, no. 70 (*PG* 87[3], 3669A), cf. nos. 22, 36, and *Miracula S. Demetrii*, 2.6, para. 315 (1:240). The conversion of St. Mary the Egyptian is described by Sophronios, *PL* 75, 682A-C.

approve. The painter was therefore instructed to observe Theodore through a crack. Once the icon was finished, the saint pardoned the painter and blessed the object.[7] Icons were thus displayed in monasteries as well as churches and particular shrines.

Personal and Imperial Icons. Individuals also owned icons and used them in their private devotion at home, particularly when they had special reasons to be grateful for assistance. When Sophia, a widow, took her only son Alexander to ordinary doctors, they told her that she would have to pay for their services. At her protests of poverty, one asked if she didn't own a gold or silver icon, which she could sell to raise the money. She did not, in fact. Fortunately, however, she was directed to the shrine of Artemios, where the cure was effected without payment.[8] For women especially, possession of an icon permitted a most satisfying form of Christian devotion, independent of church liturgy, officials, or environment. In the privacy of their homes, women set up their icons and poured out their distress, prayer, and gratitude to the figure, whom they came to know in a very personal way. The existence of portable icons with covers to protect them in transit—one as small as 20.1 x 11.6 cm.—confirms their use in this form of worship. These icons emphasised the holy person's power of intercession and the personal nature of the prayer, a relationship between the worshipper and worshipped that did away with any ecclesiastical intervention.[9]

In contrast to this very personal function, the most celebrated ancient icons usually served a public and imperial role as well. Tradition attributed to St. Luke a painting of the Virgin and Child, which Empress Eudokia believed she had found in Jerusalem in the fifth century.[10] She sent it to Constantinople for the shrine at Blachernai, which already housed the Virgin's most precious relics, the veil and girdle, as well as a number of other votive images. Other famous icons of Christ from Edessa and Kamouliana derived from the imprint of his face on a cloth. Traditionally, the first had been sent by Christ to King Abgar and served as a miraculous protection for the city during a sixth-century Persian siege. From the second, two

[7] Herrin, "Women and the Faith in Icons," 65; cf. Cormack, *Writing in Gold*, 39. On patriarchal portraits, see John of Ephesos, *Ecclesiastical History* 1.11 (pp. 8-9); 2.27 (134-35), and Theodoros Anagnostes, *Ecclesiastical History*, frag. 57; and on portraits of bishops of Rome who were commemorated in the diptychs of Constantinople, see *LP* 1.354.

[8] *Miraula S. Artemii*, no. 36 (57-59): "*chrysiken eikona e eidos argyrion,*" literally "a gilded icon or an image of silver" (p. 58).

[9] Herrin, "Women and the Faith in Icons," 66-69; on the icons, see K. Weitzmann, *The Monastery of St. Catherine at Mount Sinai: The Icons*, vol. 1 (Princeton, 1976).

[10] C. Mango, *The Art of the Byzantine Empire 312-1453* (Englewood Cliffs, N.J., 1972), 34-35; A. Wenger, *L'Assomption de la Très Sainte Vièrge dans la tradition byzantine du VIe au Xe siècle* (Paris, 1955).

icons had been painted, and their ownership provoked intense rivalry and jealousy in central Asia Minor. After one had been burned in a barbarian raid, Justin II (565-78) had the other brought to the capital, overtly for its safety, but probably to enhance the holy objects of Constantinople.[11] The Blachernai and Kamouliana icons were displayed in special chapels that served as shrines and increased the authority of the cult object. Lamps and candles were lit before them, incense was burned and prayers offered. Once the True Cross had been rescued from Muslim domination and sent to Constantinople, it was housed in St. Sophia in much the same way. In the late seventh century, Bishop Arculf from Gaul witnessed the Feast of the Exaltation of the Cross, in which the relic was solemnly removed from its sumptuous reliquary and presented, on three successive days, to different sections of the population.[12]

The Chalke Icon. Of these imperial icons, the most famous was probably one displayed on the Chalke Gate of the imperial palace.[13] This "Brazen House" was a large structure covered with statuary of imperial significance. It formed the major ceremonial entrance into the vast complex called the Great Palace of Constantinople. From a description that probably dates from the late sixth century, the Chalke seems to have been adorned with many imperial statues, including those of Maurice (582-602), and ancient objects, such as four Gorgon heads from the Artemision at Ephesos, two philosophers from Athens, a cross erected by Justinian, and a statue of his general, Belisarios, with golden rays. It was probably Maurice who commissioned the icon of Christ "in His human form," which was erected above the emperor's statue and which became an important talisman for the capital. Although its design is not known, it may well have resembled the long-haired, bearded Christ depicted on a Sinai icon. (In turn, this sixth-century work may have been ordered by Justinian as a gift for the rebuilt monastery.)[14] Whatever the model, the Chalke icon of Christ assumed a significant public role, intimately connected with the well-being of the imperial palace and whole city of Constantinople.

Towards the end of the seventh century, this human representation of

---

[11] Herrin, "Women and the Faith in Icons," 63.

[12] *Adamnan, De locis sanctis,* ed. D. Meehan (Dublin, 1958), 108-111.

[13] C. Mango, *The Brazen House* (Copenhagen, 1959), 108-112; S.Gero, *Byzantine Iconoclasm During the Reign of Leo III with Particular Attention to the Oriental Sources* (Louvain, 1973), Appendix 5B, 212-17; P. Speck, *Kaiser Konstantin VI: Die Legitimation einer Fremden und der Versuch einer eigenen Herrschaft* (Munich, 1978), 2:606-8.

[14] *Parastaseis Syntomoi Chronikai,* paras. 56, 44a, 77, 78, 80; Averil Cameron and Judith Herrin, eds., *Constantinople in the Early Eighth Century: The Parastaseis Syntomoi Chronikai* (Leiden, 1984), 22-23, 174-75. On the Sinai icon, see Weitzmann, *The Icons,* 1: 13-15, plates I and II.

Christ was established in the highest channels of both church and state in a novel fashion. In his first reign (685-95), Justinian II introduced a radical change in the gold coinage of the empire. For the first time ever, the head of the reigning emperor was removed from the obverse (front) to the reverse (back) to allow a portrait bust of Christ to be displayed.[15] Two types of portrait were used. One showed a bearded Christ with long hair (as on the Sinai icon), while the other used a youthful type with short curly hair. Both emphasised the wonder of the Incarnation and the salvation wrought by God in His human form—a firm statement of Christ's role as intercessor between the world below and heaven above. As such, both can be related to the 82nd canon of the Council in Trullo (691-92), which ordered that Christ should no longer be represented in His symbolic form—as the Lamb of God.[16] The eastern church also wanted to stress a realistic pictorial art, which revealed Christ among men as the human Redeemer. While this canon cannot have taken effect immediately, in conjunction with the Christ images circulating on the new gold coinage it must have encouraged the production of icons and other artefacts displaying the Human Saviour.

Official Control of Art

At the same time, the council recognised the dangers inherent in art that was unclear or in pictures that might be misinterpreted. It therefore decreed (canon 100) that art that could corrupt, deceive, or confuse was to be censored. This ruling should be interpreted in the light of additional canons with similar aims: those to prevent the seduction or deception of the uneducated, such as the 63rd, which ordered the burning of the apocryphal acts of the apostles and lives of the saints. All religious art was held to be of great importance in education—for instance, the definitions of orthodoxy established by the six oecumenical councils, which were displayed in pictorial form on the Milion at the centre of Constantinople. Through icons, the Holy Family became well known, the saints could be identified by their insignia and costume, and the true faith could be taught. In church frescoes, the lives of saints could be depicted as a narrative of holiness, good works, and Christian courage, which would inspire the beholder to emulate such virtues. A developed artistic scheme and routine characterisation was already established; the council sought to ensure that it fulfilled its function.

The imperial use of ecclesiastical art as propaganda went back centuries and had been regularly employed, for example by Herakleios in 610, when

---

[15] A. Grabar, *L'Iconoclasme byzantin: Dossier archéologique* (Paris, 1967), 36-45, 77-80, and plates 11-19.

[16] See Weitzmann, *The Icons*.

he nailed an icon of the Virgin to the masthead of his African fleet. But in the reign of Justinian II, a more systematic attempt was made, presaging a new emphasis in traditional methods. Not that Justinian's innovation in coin types was maintained by his successors—Leontios (695-98), Tiberios III (698-705), and Philippikos (711-13) returned to the usual arrangement of imperial bust (obverse) and cross on steps (reverse). The change does not appear to spring from any aversion to the Christ type in itself, but rather from a desire to resume the most traditional imperial type, which elevated the authority of these short-lived rulers. In other respects, the early eighth-century emperors continued Justinian's emphasis.

Philippikos, who favoured the Monothelete doctrine, altered the Milion depictions of the true faith, substituting portraits of those patriarchs who had championed Monotheletism for the image of the Sixth Oecumenical Council, which condemned it. When news of the event reached Rome, it caused such a stir that a Roman image of the six councils was put up in St. Peter's.[17] Philippikos's name was deleted from the liturgy, his portrait was removed from public places, his coinage refused, and his regnal year not recorded in the dating clauses of papal documents. Since these four privileges constituted the most obvious recognition of imperial authority over Rome, their denial implied a strong condemnation. Only the emperor's rapid demise and the restoration of the Milion decoration by his successor, Anastasios II, prevented a schism over the revival of Monothelete heresy.[18]

The incident reveals, however, that the six universal councils were recorded in composite images or a series of paintings, displayed in Rome as in Constantinople in important public positions. (A similar cycle in mosaic survives in the church of the Nativity at Bethlehem.) A graphic description of the faith was presented to the illiterate and those whose understanding of doctrine was limited. Such images celebrated the collective authority of Christian communities throughout the world and the defining power of general councils. They served as a constant reminder of the breadth of the *oikoumene* and its historic formation.[19] This was particularly important in the West, since no oecumenical council had ever been held there, and in Rome, since the successors of St. Peter had no western rivals and were inclined to press their own apostolic claims to a more universal leadership. In the late seventh and early eighth centuries, however, Rome was endowed with a number of eastern icons, in addition to its own images of St. Peter,

[17] On Philippikos, see A. Grabar, *L'Iconoclasme*, 48-49; Theophanes, 381-82; *LP* 1.391-92, on the Botarea image.

[18] A. Grabar, *L'Iconoclasme*, 48-49; *LP* 1.391-92. The four privileges will be discussed further in Chapter 10.

[19] A. Grabar, *L'Iconoclasme*, 50-61; C. Walter, *L'Iconographie des conciles dans la tradition byzantine* (Paris, 1970).

Christ, and the Virgin, and eastern styles of church decoration, promoted by Greek popes. The outstanding example is provided by St. Maria Antiqua, redecorated by Pope John VII (705-707) with Byzantine frescoes.[20] Much attention has been paid to the possible hidden meanings of these paintings. The fact that Christ is depicted in the flesh, in a Crucifixion scene that is combined with great throngs of Christians in an Adoration of the Cross, seems to indicate that Pope John accepted the 82nd canon of the Council in Trullo against symbolic use of the Lamb. But in the procession of popes, each identified as *papa Romanus*, Martin I is included, thereby recalling his martyrdom in the East. The Lateran Synod of 649 was also commemorated in the enscribed scrolls held by figures in the fresco, which John VII had had painted on the exterior wall of the Oratory of 40 Martyrs. Although the frescoes suffered in an earthquake in 847 and are poorly preserved, they still testify to a thoroughly Byzantine knowledge of the power of ecclesiastical images, employed by the pontiff to strengthen the church of Rome.

Secular art in Constantinople. From a chance remark in an obscure early eighth-century text (the *Parastaseis Syntomoi Chronikai*), it seems that the concern for artistic similitude and realistic depiction at this time was not confined to ecclesiastical art. A portrait of Philippikos in the baths of Zeuxippos was said by contemporaries to be a very good likeness and admired by artists for this quality—its realism was appreciated.[21] This method of evaluating a secular work of art may be set in the context of the Trullan decrees on the necessity of correct identification. In both cases, it was important that there should be no doubt as to the persons or scenes represented. The same concern is moreover borne out by a certain anxiety over pagan statuary manifested in the same text, which parallels ecclesiastical dislike of any ambiguity. By the early eighth century, there was only a slight danger that pagan images might be mistaken for Christian ones. But 100 years earlier, icons purporting to represent Christ had in fact been identified as portraits of Zeus painted by pagan artists, and miraculous intervention and punishment of those responsible was necessary to prevent Christians from venerating the old gods.

[20] P. J. Nordhagen, "The Frescoes of John VII (705-707) in St. Maria Antiqua in Rome," *Acta ad archeologiam et artium historiam pertinentia* (issued by the Institutum Romanum Norvegiae) 3 (1968); J. D. Breckenridge, "Evidence for the Nature of Relations Between Pope John VII and the Byzantine Emperor Justinian II," *BZ* 65 (1972): 364-74; P. Romanelli and P. J. Nordhagen, *S. Maria Antiqua* (Rome, 1964), a brief description in Italian with good colour photographs.

[21] *Parastaseis*, para. 82; cf. Cameron and Herrin, *Constantinople*, 272-73; Mango, *Art of the Byzantine Empire*, 133.

In the case of statuary, however, mistakes were still made, and in Constantinople, which had been decorated by its founder with the most outstanding examples of ancient sculpture, such anxiety was most developed. The bronze Athena from Athens, the tripod and Rhodian chariot from Delphi, the reclining Hercules by Lysippos, and many other remarkable pagan works of art had reached New Rome in this way.[22] While Old Rome had also been plundered to provide many of the imperial statues that adorned Constantinople, it too contained ancient objects little understood. The legendary interpretation of the statues with bells on the Capitol probably originated in the early medieval period. According to this explanation, each statue represented a Roman province, and if that province revolted, the statue would ring its bell.[23] In the midst of such overtly non-Christian imagery, the inhabitants of Constantinople and Rome feared the fanciful powers attributed to statues of ancient gods, a fear apparently shared by the Persians.[24] They were also worried that such statues might be incorrectly understood and mistaken for Christian ones. In Constantinople, it was known that Constantine I had converted an ancient statue (some said of Apollo-Helios, the sun god) to use on his own column in the Forum.[25] Pagan statues were also held to be responsible for natural disasters, such as earthquakes, for the punishment of Christians who got too interested in them, and for predictions of the fate of emperors and of the city itself. In this way, old pagan magic lay inherent in the statuary decorating Constantinople, and people had to be warned not to dabble in it.[26] Such concerns were undoubtedly related to the general tendency noted above, to make sure that Christian art was explicit, realistic, and unambiguous. They reflect an appreciation of the power of images and a desire to safeguard that power against misuse (which might lead to idolatry) or misinterpretation (which might revive the pagan cults).

The Eighth-Century Cult of Icons

In the history of Byzantium, the most significant aspect of the cult of icons was that associated with their power to protect and defend Christian com-

---

[22] *Parastaseis*, paras. 37 (Herakles), 39, 60, 61 (Athena), 69 (tripod of Alexander); Cameron and Herrin, *Constantinople*, 248-49.

[23] The legend is recorded in a Greek work, of the same date as *Parastaseis*, which manifests many of the same attitudes towards ancient statuary, see Cosmas of Jerusalem, *PG* 38, 546.

[24] John of Ephesos, *Ecclesiastical History* 6.23; cf. *Parastaseis*, para. 6.

[25] *Parastaseis*, para. 68a; Cameron and Herrin, *Constantinople*, 263-64.

[26] *Parastaseis*, paras. 4, 28, 41, 64; Cameron and Herrin, *Constantinople*, 25-26, 28, 31-34.

munities. We have already noted the role of the image of Edessa (the *man-dylion*, or towel upon which Christ impressed his features). The very presence of St. Demetrios in his tomb at Thessalonike, his appearance on the city walls, and his alleged refusal to leave the city under siege saved its inhabitants from "enemies of the soul and the body . . . as a wall" (*teichizou-san*).[27] While it was an icon of Christ not made with human hands (*acheiropoiete*) that Patriarch Sergios had carried around the walls of Constantinople in 626, the Virgin herself had been seen fighting beside the defenders. In his homily delivered on the anniversary of the Byzantine victory of 718, Patriarch Germanos makes reference to her repeated, saving role.[28] As with St. Demetrios, this role is not dependent upon icons, for the Virgin dwells in the city and keeps constant guard over it. "She alone defeated the Saracens and prevented their aim, which was not just to capture the city but also to throw down the royal majesty of Christ."[29] Like the column of fire and cloud of smoke, she led the besieged as the children of Israel were guided through the desert. And the Arabs, like the Egyptians, were defeated.[30]

The role of images could also be a vital one and was held responsible for the defeat of the Arabs outside Nicaea in 727. During a 40-day siege, the icons of the Fathers of the First Oecumenical Council, the 318 bishops, were paraded around the walls.[31] Whether these were composite pictures of the council itself or icons of the individual participants, the protection they brought to Nicaea was deemed effective, for the Arabs withdrew. Shortly after this event, Bishop Willibald, who was on a pilgrimage to the Holy Land, made a special visit to Nicaea to witness the site of the council and admire the icons.[32] In the early eighth century, therefore, the spiritual protection available to Byzantine cities was vested in their particular patron saints, relics, and icons. The tradition inaugurated at Edessa in 540 had been enormously strengthened and widely spread by the time the empire faced its most serious challenge. By then, Christians believed not only in the power of icons to intercede, to cure, and to save, but also to defeat the Muslims.

[27] *Miracula S. Demetrii* 1.15, para. 16 (1:165).

[28] V. Grumel, "Homélie de S. Germain sur la délivrance de Constantinople," *REB* 16 (1958): 188-205.

[29] Ibid., para. 11, p. 194.

[30] Ibid., paras. 18-19, pp. 196-97.

[31] Theophanes, 405-406; Nikephoros, 58; D. Stein, *Der Beginn des byzantinischen Bilderstreits und seine Entwicklung bis in die 40er Jahre der 8. Jahrhunderts* (Munich, 1980), 141-55.

[32] *Vita Willibaldi*, ed. O. Holder-Egger, in *MGH, SS*, 15(i), 86-106, esp. 101, lines 23-28, describing his trip to see the "*imagines episcoporum qui erant ibi in synodo.*"

THE RENEWED ARAB THREAT

This belief must be appreciated in relation to the equally developed fear of that conquest—the two increased together as opposite sides of a coin. For the treaty that ratified Constantine IV's triumph of 678 was broken in 694-95 and gave way to a period of regular Islamic campaigning. Every summer, Muslim forces entered Byzantine territory from northern Syria, striking either due north against the eastern frontier and the old Roman province of Armenia IV, or west into central Asia Minor. Frequently, an additional raid by sea sacked coastal settlements and islands. This annual pressure strained Byzantine defences, both frontier garrisons and *thema* army units. As it was hard to maintain the latter as field armies when local resources were scarce due to enemy raiding, a strategy of avoidance was developed to spare the possibility of defeat and preserve military capacity. Cavalry units gradually replaced unmounted troops, as field armies and foot soldiers were divided up between key garrisons and fortresses.

This strategy, which sprang from the military weakness of the *thema* armies, had two disadvantages: it dispersed the fighting forces, making it harder to get a substantial army together; and it effectively abandoned outlying towns and villages to the enemy. Many, with populations swelled by refugees from undefended rural areas, were captured; men were killed, women and children taken off as prisoners. After the attack of 707-708, Tyana was completely deserted; Taranton and Kamachon were similarly emptied.[33] And the fate of those taken prisoner was also highly disadvantageous: Eustathios, son of the patrician Marianos, was killed together with many others at Harran for refusing to deny the Christian faith—an event probably paralleled in many cases.[34]

Byzantine inadequacy in the face of the renewed and confident advance of Islam was partly due to the relatively new structure of *thema* organisation, which co-existed with the older civilian system for most of the seventh century and was not very well integrated. The adaptation of Late Roman methods of administration to the military and strategic demands of the period is poorly documented, but the bureaucratic changeover from twenty-seven provinces to four *themata* can hardly have been made without some disorder and confusion. That civilian officials attached to the praetorian prefects continued to exist is clear. In due course, however, and very gradually, the new military governors (*strategoi*) acquired their own staffs, a hierarchy that included judicial and financial personnel as well as subordinates responsible for military affairs. Among the latter, the *anagra-*

[33] R.-J. Lilie, *Die byzantinische Reaktion auf die Ausbreitung der Araber* (Munich, 1976), 139-40.
[34] Theophanes, 414.

pheis, epoptai, and *praktores,* in charge of the measurement and assessment of land, property and livestock for tax purposes and for the military rolls, assumed a very significant place. Under a chief *chartoularios* (keeper of records), teams of such officials investigated landownership and all relevant resources throughout the *themata*. Although some of these functions were taken over from the older system, others developed through increasing military pressure and under the dominant influence of the new one. The establishment of this "thematic" government, frequently known only from the seals of the officers involved, proceeded slowly, possibly creating friction with the older, established channels of administration. The changeover does not appear to have been completed until about the middle of the eighth century.[35]

Military failures of the late seventh century may also be related to the disruption of economic activity unleashed by the previous 40 years of warfare. But behind all these factors lies the even larger transformation underway—that of the decline of urban life with all its traditions of curial control and local resources. In making the necessary adjustment to a village- and castle-based society, the empire witnessed a tremendous upheaval, in which the central administration experienced extreme strains. In place of a considerable local autonomy and initiative in self-preservation, Constantinople now had to provide for defence throughout the empire.

Byzantine Weakness

Additional factors reducing the effectiveness of imperial defence included a resurgence of Bulgar hostility, which demanded intense military effort in the Balkans. The decade of peace with the Arabs, 680-90, was entirely taken up by this western threat rather than providing a period of recuperation and reorganisation of productive forces. Although Justinian II's campaigns were largely successful, the transfer of units from Asia Minor to the Balkans left the eastern frontier more exposed. In addition to this shortfall in defensive strength, the basic stability of the Herakleian dynasty was broken by Justinian's deposition in 695. A series of soldier-rulers imposed by *thema* units and other interest groups (like the Constantinopolitan factions) captured the imperial office for over two decades.[36] Some were competent militarily, others less so, and all of them proved ephemeral. Only Apsimar-

[35] Lilie, *Die byzantinische Reaktion,* 287-311; idem, " 'Thrakien' und 'Thrakesion': Zur byzantinischen Provinzorganisation am Ende des 7. Jahrhunderts," *JÖB* 26 (1977): 7-47; W. E. Kaegi, "Notes on Hagiographical Sources for Some Institutional Changes and Continuities in the Early Seventh Century," *Byzantina* 5 (1975): 61-70; J. F. Haldon, *Byzantine Praetorians* (Bonn, 1984), 180-81.

[36] J. Herrin, "The Context of Iconoclast Reform," in A. Bryer and J. Herrin, eds., *Iconoclasm* (Birmingham, 1977), 15-27.

Tiberios established himself for more than four years—the others were deposed, mutilated, or murdered by different military cliques or sections of those in ruling circles within two or three.

This persistent change of ruler reflected dissatisfaction with central government and frustration at repeated military defeats. But it was accompanied by a striking aimlessness and lack of preparation. Particular army units behaved in a wild fashion, sometimes intent on making their own leader emperor (as in 695 when the Anatolikon forces imposed Leontios), sometimes simply hostile to a ruler with no idea of a replacement (as in the Opsikion troops' frantic search for a candidate in 715).[37] Against such activity no regular government could be maintained. The imperial bureaucracy ought to have kept essential services going, providing supplies and pay, but it obviously lacked direction. Of the five rulers who replaced Justinian II in 695 and 711, only the civilian Anastasios II (713-15) seems to have been capable of taking coherent measures against the Arab threat. Learning that a siege of the capital was planned, he repaired the city walls, built siege engines and catapults, and stocked the granaries.[38] The Arab armada and double army did not reach Constantinople until the summer of 717, by which time Anastasios was in exile in Thessalonike. But his preparations against a possible siege most probably contributed to the final Byzantine victory.

The chronic instability in ruling circles was further exacerbated by a split in the church, provoked by Philippikos's determined revival of Monothelete belief. Like many soldier-emperors, the Armenian Bardanes justified his bid for power by a holy man's prediction, in this case that he would reign as Philippikos, reverse the Sixth Oecumenical Council, and reinstate the "one-will" doctrine. When he gained the throne in 711 through an alliance of naval and Opsikion *thema* support, he changed the definition of orthodox belief by imperial fiat. Many high-ranking ecclesiastics did not oppose this: Germanos, later patriarch of Constantinople, was promoted to the see of Kyzikos, and Andreas, metropolitan of Crete, accepted it.[39] But others did not approve of a return to the doctrine condemned as heretical by an oecumenical council within living memory. Whether Monotheletism played a part in Philippikos's downfall in 713 is not clear; his brief reign allowed little time to impose the innovation, which remained perhaps in the earliest stages. The contemporary reaction recorded in Rome may not have been confined to the West. And after 713, the changes made to the Milion decoration were naturally reported by the

[37] Theophanes, 383, 385-86.
[38] Ibid., 383-84; Nikephoros, 49-50.
[39] Theophanes, 381-82; Nikephoros, 48.

deacon Agathias as a regrettable matter.[40] Regardless of the degree to which the revived dogma was enforced, it must have divided opinion within the church at a time when Arab raids were particularly severe. The expeditions of 712 to Amaseia, Gangra, and Armenia IV were followed by others to Pisidian Antioch and again to Armenia in 713, devastating large areas of central and northern Asia Minor as well as border towns like Taranton. Ecclesiastical differences and the resulting confusion could only weaken the Byzantine military effort yet further.

The Accession of Leo III and Siege of Constantinople

While the Monothelete dispute was patched up by Anastasios II's restoration of orthodoxy, anxieties remained. When Leo, general of the Anatolikon *thema*, arrived at Constantinople as the leading candidate for the throne, Patriarch Germanos required him to swear an oath of orthodox belief. The danger of another heretical soldier-ruler was clear, and the patriarch evidently wished to protect his own somewhat insecure record. Leo duly made the necessary confession of faith and, after acclamation in the capital, was crowned by the patriarch in St. Sophia.[41] It was March 717, and Arab armies were reported to be not far from the Bosphoros. Since the previous summer, one had been ravaging western Asia Minor, capturing Pergamon; another under Maslama, a renowned Muslim commander, now set out from Syria on the northern route via Amorion to join with the first, while the Arab fleet advanced from the Aegean. In a concerted effort to make Constantinople his own capital and the centre of an Islamic empire, Caliph Suleiman had planned a three-pronged attack.[42] Despite warnings of its serious nature and Anastasios's efforts to prepare the city for siege, the Byzantines were neither ready to withstand the onslaught nor confident of victory. Popular fears of disaster surface in a strange apocalypse composed in the capital during the winter of 716-17 as Islam moved in closer. It describes the end of the world in terms that reflect Byzantine weakness under Theodosios III.[43] The possibility of an Arab victory, heralding the reign of Anti-Christ, lay behind this prophesy of doom and imminent disaster. Such apocalyptic literature had circulated in the seventh century in regions threatened by Islamic conquest, but never before in the Queen City. That it did so now suggests that for the first time, the end of Byzantium was actually contemplated by its inhabitants.

[40] A. Grabar, *L'Iconoclasme*, 48-49.

[41] Theopanes, 390; Nikephoros, 52; Speck, *Kaiser Konstantin VI*, 1:399-404.

[42] E. W. Brooks, "The Campaign of 716-8 from Arabic Sources," *JHS* 19 (1899): 19-33.

[43] K. Berger, *Die griechische Daniel-Diegese* (Leiden, 1976). Cf. C. Mango, "The Life of St. Andrew the Fool Reconsidered," *Rivista di studi bizantini e slavi* 2 (1982): 310-13, on the correct date.

In these circumstances, the defence of the capital against the triple attack assumed a significance clear to contemporaries. Leo III took charge of the military organisation, planning the flotilla of small boats ablaze with Greek fire that would be sent against the Arab navy, while calling on the Bulgars to harry the besiegers. His strategic and diplomatic efforts were assisted by one of the hardest winters known—in the extreme cold and snow (an unfamiliar experience for many of the Muslims), frostbite, disease, inadequate food supplies, and death took their toll among the forces encamped round the walls.[44] The besieged within were meanwhile encouraged by ecclesiastical litanies arranged by Germanos and the clergy. In one, Leo III may have led a procession to the sea walls holding a cross, with which he struck the sea to dispel the invaders (possibly in imitation of Moses during the flight of the Israelites).[45] In others the clergy probably carried holy icons around the walls as they had during the siege of 626.[46] It is important to note that all felt the need for divine intervention and took steps to ensure the spiritual protection of the city. Leo used the cross as a symbol of Christian victory; Germanos later attributed the successful defence to the Virgin alone. Both, however, recognised that the situation required the aid of heavenly forces.

After their gruelling winter before the walls of Constantinople, the Arabs attempted to take the city by force in the late spring. Their assaults were resisted, and in the summer the new caliph, Umar, sent orders for the siege to be lifted. On the Feast of the Dormition of the Virgin (15 August 718), the Arabs withdrew, a coincidence that left Constantinople confident in the certain power of its protectress. While this great victory was celebrated, Leo ordered an additional harassment of Muslim seaborne forces, which successfully destroyed most of the fleet. Every year thereafter, on the eve of the same feast, Germanos led an all-night service of prayer and thanksgiving for the deliverance of the capital, preaching the homily that identified the Virgin's role.[47] He did not mention the emperor or his procession with the cross, nor did he permit the cross to assume any significance in the outcome. In this way, Leo was reminded annually that imperial strategy and skill, as well as his own belief in the authority of the

[44] Theophanes, 395-98; Nikephoros, 52-54.

[45] *Parastaseis*, para. 3; Cameron and Herrin, *Constantinople*, 58, 170-71; Gero, *Leo III*, 36-43, 135-36.

[46] P. Speck, *Artabastos der Rechtgläubige Vorkämpfer der göttlichen Lehren* (Bonn, 1981), 164, 171-3.

[47] Grumel, "Homélie de S. Germain." On some of the legendary stories that circulated after the Arab defeat, see Gero, *Leo III*, 181-85; the miraculous fiery hailstorm that was held responsible for destroying all the Arab ships except ten may preserve an echo of the eruption of 726, which will be discussed below.

cross, had nothing to do with the triumph of 718. He may have celebrated his own victory, however, by erecting an image of the cross flanked by prophets and apostles in front of the palace.[48]

For the inhabitants of the city, the successful defeat of the Arabs must have seemed a real improvement, no matter who took ultimate responsibility. It was evident that both emperor and patriarch had struggled against the infidel who departed in disorder. Byzantine joy at this sight was generated by genuine relief that the end of the world was not yet at hand. This relief was certainly shared by the farmers of Asia Minor who witnessed the Muslim withdrawal; at last their fields and vineyards would be free of Arab armies and destruction. *Their* hope, however, was rapidly shattered. The defeat in August 718 checked only the caliph's ambitions on Constantinople—while Byzantine frontier defence was still weak, raiding could continue as before, even if Arab forces could not mount another major siege for a while. A quick survey of the calendar of Muslim activity within the empire from 719 to 730 reveals how little had changed for the rural population of Byzantium.

Continuing Arab Raids

The summer raid of 719 was followed in 720 by two major incursions: to Pisidian Antioch in central Asia Minor and to Armenia IV in the north. The former took the well-worn route from Syria across the Taurus range, through Isauria close to Mistheia and Ikonion. Antioch was not captured, but its inhabitants were threatened. In the north, in regions destroyed by warfare in 707, 711, 712, 713, and 717, the 720 raid took 700 prisoners. The next year (721), Dalisandos, a city in Isauria, was taken—it had also been besieged in 709 and 713. In 721-22, eastern Asia Minor was raided, and in 722-23, the regular Arab advances north and west of the Taurus again took place. The following year (723-24), Kamachon and Ikonion fell in similar attacks. Muwasa, a fortress on the eastern frontier near Melitene, was taken by storm, its male population killed, and the women and children removed as prisoners to the caliphate. In 725, Caliph Hisham's son, Muawiya, one of the most distinguished Arab generals, led a raid into Byzantine areas where pasture had been burnt, presumably in an attempt to discourage Muslim activity. In reprisal he burnt the remaining crops and took further prisoners. One year later it was the turn of Caesarea, the ancient capital of Cappadocia. As Caesarea had withstood all previous sieges, apart from a very early one in 646, its capture was a major disaster. Nor was naval activity neglected; Muawiya raided Cyprus in 726 and plundered

---

[48] See the letter of Patriarch Germanos to Thomas of Klaudioupolis, *PG* 98, 185A (also in Mansi, 13.124E).

smaller islands. In 727, he commanded the Arab army that took the northern route into Asia Minor and swung west via Paphlagonia, taking Gangra
and advancing to the walls of Nicaea. The 40-day siege failed to secure its
submission, and the army withdrew. But it returned in 728 to Armenia,
capturing Semalouos, and in 729 and 730, attacking western Asia Minor
and the southern littoral in both naval and territorial raids. Caesarea was
again threatened, and the castles of Charsianon and Farandiyya in the far
east were taken. Such annual campaigning constituted an unrelenting pressure on Byzantine garrisons and caused continuous devastation of villages
and agricultural land.[49]

By far the most damaging of these campaigns were those of 720-21,
723-24, 726, and 727, which took the main routes towards Constantinople, reminding the communities in their path of the 716-18 invasion. As
there is no record of serious Byzantine opposition in the form of forces sent
to counter the Islamic advance, it appears that the *thema* armies were unable
to check it. The rural population sought refuge in those fortified castles and
garrison centres that lay furthest from the invasion routes, abandoning
crops and settlements, perhaps taking their flocks with them. They saw the
necessity of putting defensive walls between themselves and the Arabs, and
they probably implored divine protection through the familiar medium of
holy objects. At Dalisandos the famous local relic, the shield of St. George,
promised a suitably warlike security. At Ikonion, Gangra, and Caesarea,
icons may have served the same purpose as at Nicaea in 727. But even with
such invocations these strongholds were not safe. Byzantine troops stationed in or near them could not prevent their fall and the subsequent
slaughter or captivity of their inhabitants augmented by refugees. Not only
had the triumph at Constantinople in 718 failed to drive the Arabs away,
but in addition, the spiritual protection accorded to the capital was denied
to Asia Minor in the 720s. There was no longer any guarantee of safety.

Islamic Culture and Anti-Byzantine Motivation

The Arab attacks of this decade were also motivated by a stronger anti-
Christian ideology developed from the late seventh century, particularly in
the reign of Yazid II (720-24).[50] Although doubt has been expressed about
the decree issued in 721, it seems clear that the caliph did order the destruction of Christian art in both churches and private homes, and that this

---

[49] E. W. Brooks, "The Arabs in Asia Minor from Arabic Sources (641-750)," *JHS* 18
(1898): 182-208; Lilie, *Die byzantinische Reaktion*, 143-49; J. Wellhausen, *The Arab Kingdom and Its Fall* (London, 1927, reprinted 1973), 339-40.

[50] For seventh-century instances of Arab attacks on Christian art and crosses, see S. H.
Griffith, "Theodore Abu Qurrah's Arabic Tract on the Christian Practice of Venerating Images," *Journal of the American Oriental Society* 105 (1985): 53-73, esp. 60.

was carried out.[51] The attack on representations of the Holy Family in Christian institutions under Muslim control was directed against wall paintings, liturgical vessels, and other artefacts, but it must have afflicted icons especially. The sources that preserve information about Yazid's reign attribute the decree to Jewish influence and a prediction that it would permit the caliph to reign for 40 years. Such stories circulated equally in the Byzantine Empire, as we have seen; they were frequently fabricated to justify particular policies or to provide an explanation for otherwise unclear actions.[52] Behind Yazid's attack, however, lies the growth of an autonomous identity for the caliphate and its cultural independence from past models.

This development can be traced back to the reign of Caliph Abd al Malik (685-705), when a nascent form of aniconic Islamic art begins to emerge. It is immediately visible in new coin types. As previous gold issues had been adapted from Byzantine models, with changes such as de-Christianizing the cross on steps motif by removing the horizontal bar, the shift towards a separate Islamic currency marks an important step.[53] The fact that it coincides with major changes in Byzantine coin types can hardly be due to chance. Between 693 and 695 Abd al Malik issued several experimental silver coins, which are now extremely rare: they employ a basic Sasanian type but with Koranic inscriptions around the edge, and images of the caliph standing in prayer, or the mihrah and anaza (lance), on the reverse, with further declarations of the Islamic faith. During the next five years, these types were replaced by the completely aniconic coinage, which displayed no image whatsoever, simply professions of faith and claims for the superiority of Islam over all other religions.[54] These purely Arabic silver coins became more common from about 700 and gradually dominated older issues. The change was most meaningful to literate Muslims who recognised the slogans on them, but it could be understood in a limited way by Byzantine traders, who must have observed the departure from previous

[51] A. A. Vasiliev, "The Iconoclastic Edict of Caliph Yezid II, A.D. 721," *DOP* 9 (1955): 23-47.

[52] P. Crone, "Islam, Judeo-Christianity and Byzantine Iconoclasm," *Jerusalem Studies in Arabic and Islam* 2 (1980): 59-95; Gero, *Leo III*, 62-65, 79-81.

[53] J. Walker, *A Catalogue of the Muḥammadan Coins in the British Museum*, vol. 2, *The Arab-Byzantine and Post-Reform Umaiyad Coins* (London, 1956), 1-42; M. Bates, "The 'Arab-Byzantine' Bronze Coinage of Syria: An Innovation by 'Abd al Malik," in *A Colloquium in Memory of G. C. Miles* (New York, 1976), 16-27.

[54] Walker, *Muḥammadan Coins*, 2: 84-104; A. Grabar, *L'Iconoclasme*, 67-74, and illustrations 65-66; P. Grierson, "The Monetary Reforms of 'Abd al-Malik," *Journal of the Economic and Social History of the Orient* 3 (1960): 241-64; M. F. Hendy, *Studies in the Byzantine Monetary Economy c. 300-1450* (Cambridge, 1985), 632 n. 342.

types and the arrival of a totally non-Byzantine style. The contrast between this non-pictorial Islamic coin form and the new gold coins of Justinian II carrying the bust of Christ could hardly have been more marked.

A similar emphasis on the written word of Islam in the new art of the caliphate is clear from the Dome of the Rock, the mosque of Jerusalem completed by Abd al Malik and dated to the year 72 A.H. (A.D. 691-92) by a lengthy Koranic inscription.[55] While Christian mosaicists living under Muslim rule were partly responsible for the setting of the tesserae, the range of familiar artistic motifs was severely limited. Instead of figural representations such as those which adorned the desert palaces, baths, and private villas of the Umayyad rulers and governors at Qusayr Amra, Mshatta, Khirbat al Minya, or Qasr al Hayr, the craftsmen here executed only floral decorations, trees, foliage, fruits, and urns of flowers against a traditional gold background. In the Great Mosque at Damascus, finished under Caliph al Walid (705-715), who also built Qusayr Amra, the same stress on Koranic texts was added to a vast exterior mosaic of architectural design—palaces, towers, bridges, and castles set in an idyllic pastoral environment.[56] The richness and beauty of this "garden of Paradise" style was a decisive innovation in mosaic work: the ancient technique, though unknown to Muslim craftsmen, was employed to record a purely Islamic scheme, a further sign of the caliphate's new sense of purpose and self-definition in the world of the early eighth century.

It is clearly not fortuitous that at this period Damascus should have created art forms specific to its creed and polity (the two being identical). Despite a dazzling centrifugal conquest, Islam had no distinct artistic expression to impose—the faith enshrined in the written word of the Koran was all. In its first 50 years, therefore, the caliphate displayed few characteristic forms: Byzantine methods of government and civil administration were taken over in Syria, Palestine, and Egypt, Persian methods in Iraq.[57] Only differences between the tribal forces of occupation as well as those between previous imperial systems determined slight variations in cultural expression. But as confidence increased and the goal of making Constantinople

[55] M. Gautier-van Berchem, *The Mosaics . . .* , in K. A. C. Cresswell, *Early Muslim Architecture: Umayyads* A.D. *622-750*, 2nd ed. (Oxford, 1969), I (i), 203-322; cf. H. Stern, "Notes sur les Mosaïques du Dôme du Rocher et la Mosquée de Damas," *Cahiers archéologiques* 22 (1972): 201-220; O. Grabar, "The Umayyad Dome of the Rock in Jerusalem," *Ars Orientalis* 3 (1959): 33-62; C. Kessler, " 'Abd al-Malik's Inscription in the Dome of the Rock: A Reconsideration," *Journal of the Royal Asiatic Society* (1970): 2-14.

[56] O. Grabar, *The Formation of Islamic Art* (New Haven, 1973), 1-44, 48-67; Gautier-van Berchem, *The Mosaics*, I (i), 323-72; cf. Stern, "Notes sur les Mosaïques," For wonderful photographs of Jerusalem, Damascus, and other Umayyad mosaics and monuments, see Cresswell, *Early Muslim Architecture*, I (i) and (ii).

[57] P. Crone, *Slaves on Horses: The Evolution of the Islamic Polity* (Cambridge, 1980), 29-36.

their own capital became realisable, the authorities in Damascus sought ways of distinguishing themselves from their predecessors. Experimentation with new coin types, tax registers kept in Arabic rather than Greek, the use of Koranic inscriptions in mosque decoration, and the attack on Christian art are all part of this slow process of creating a culture peculiar to Islam.[58]

The Muslim forces that marched and sailed against the Byzantine capital in 716-18 may have been slightly aware of this "cold war." But after 721, when they had heard the edict against Christian art read out, they had a clearer idea of their aim: in fighting the Byzantines they were also preventing idolatry—for the Mosaic prohibition of worshipping graven images was observed by Arabs, as well as Jews and Christians.[59] It was with this sense of the profane nature of their enemies' art, which permitted human representation and thereby encouraged the worship of man-made things, that the armies of Islam renewed their annual attempts to destroy the empire in the 720s.

THE REIGN OF LEO III (717-41)

While the victory in August 718 gave Leo III popular support in the capital and strengthened his standing with the regular troops, the new emperor had by no means established his authority before this inspired Islamic challenge resumed. As ex-general of the Anatolikon *thema*, he knew how inadequate that force was in the defence of central Asia Minor and probably recognised the weakness of other Byzantine detachments, for instance, the navy that had so conspicuously failed to protect Constantinople. Military reorganisation and troop improvement were therefore among his most urgent concerns. But in addition, after the disorders of the past twenty years, the entire administration of the empire had to be restored on a regular working basis. Leo also had to take measures to ensure that his reign did not follow the pattern of his predecessors, who had been swept aside by ambitious competitors. Faced by such a range of problems, he adopted a systematic programme of reforms designed to deal with each in turn. The re-

[58] Theophanes, 376, reports that Caliph Walīd instructed that Arabic rather than Greek should be used in financial and government records, which were still kept by Christian officials in Damascus. Cf. Griffith, "Theodore Abu Qurrah's Arabic Tract," 62-63.

[59] R. Paret, "Die Entstehungszeit des islamischen Bilderverbots," *Kunst des Orients* 11 (1976-77): 158-81; idem, "Textbelege zum islamischen Bilderverbot," in *Das Werk des Kunstlers: Studien . . . H. Schrade dargebracht* (Stuttgart, 1960), 36-48; O. Grabar, *Formation of Islamic Art*, 75-89, 97; M. G. S. Hodgson, "Islam and Image," *History of Religions* 3 (1963): 220-60, esp. 226-44.

sults were not immediately apparent and are barely mentioned in the surviving sources.

This is largely due to the nature of the sources, which represent the views of the ultimately triumphant iconophiles. Once they made sure that the "icon-haters" had been discredited and driven out of the church (by the council of 787 and again after 843), all iconoclast writings were also excised. So our understanding of the anti-icon movement in Byzantium is recorded largely through highly antagonistic records put together in devout iconophile circles during the early ninth century. They are not only biased, but also were written 60 or 70 years after the introduction of iconoclasm. In particular, the *Chronicle* attributed to Theophanes, abbot of the monastery of Megas Agros in Bithynia, may be taken as the considered iconophile historiography of its time (811-14). It was probably compiled from notes collected by George the *synkellos*, author of a world history arranged by years from Creation, which relied on an oriental source probably composed in Palestine and is notoriously unclear about historical developments in the West. The other major source for Leo's reign and the first phase of iconoclasm is by the early ninth-century patriarch of Constantinople, Nikephoros; while it is briefer, less biased, and more factual, it also reports the iconophile perspective.[60]

In contrast to these later compilations, there are two sources contemporary with the reign of Leo: three surviving letters by Patriarch Germanos (715-30), and the *Life* of Pope Gregory II (715-31).[61] Both reflect the iconophile convictions of their authors and subjects, but they do so with the spontaneity of immediate reaction to the first wave of concern about icon veneration. Germanos's testimony especially constitutes an invaluable record for the 720s. Of course, at the time official accounts were kept at the court of Leo III. Imperial propaganda was regularly produced by all rulers. But the records kept by iconoclast emperors and ecclesiastics do not survive except in the most fragmentary state, for instance when they were subjected to iconophile condemnation. Echoes of Leo's propaganda may be traced to cerain oriental sources, but in general the iconophile attempt to destroy it was remarkably successful.[62] This must always be borne in mind as we analyse his reign.

[60] C. Mango, "Who Wrote the Chronicle of Theophanes?" *ZRVI* 18 (1978): 9-18; Gero, *Leo III*, xv-xviii, on the bias of surviving sources, which is corrected, in part, by his presentation of the oriental material.

[61] *PG* 98, 148-88 (also in Mansi, 13.92-128); cf. L. Lamza, *Patriarch Germanos I. von Konstantinopel (715-730)* (Wurzburg, 1975); *LP* 1.396-410. The letters are analysed by Stein, *Der Beginn des byzantinischen Bilderstreits*, 4-88, and translated in J. Mendham, *The Seventh Oecumenical Council* (London, 1849), 223-49.

[62] Gero, *Leo III*, Appendices 1, 2, and 4.

The chronic instability of the early eighth century was illustrated almost as soon as Leo gained control of Constantinople. A revolt broke out in Sicily, where the governor took advantage of the proximity of Arab forces to Constantinople and the apparent lack of resistance to put forward his own candidate for the throne. One of Leo's trusted supporters, Paul, who had served as *chartoularios* and held patrician rank, was sent to put down the attempt and to remain as governor.[63] He succeeded in reassuring the people that the capital was not about to fall to the Arabs and that Leo was indeed emperor. The severity of the challenge may perhaps be gauged from the punishments imposed on the rebels: the leaders' heads were sent to Constantinople to be displayed in public, while the other participants were mutilated and exiled. Despite this successful display of imperial authority, unease and disquiet were also evident in Italy, where news of the Arab campaigns was known. In 719, however, it was from Thessalonike that another challenge came. The ex-emperor Anastasios staged a coup in conjunction with certain high-ranking members of the central bureaucracy as well as military officers, including the general of the Opsikion *thema*. As he tried to involve the Bulgars in what might have proved a dangerous attack on Constantinople, written instructions were deemed necessary. And when these letters fell into the emperor's hands, Niketas Anthrax, commander of the walls, and Theoktistos, the first secretary, were implicated. Leo had them beheaded and persuaded the Bulgars to hand over the other conspirators. Anastasios and the archbishop of Thessalonike were also executed, and the heads of all those involved, among them senators, a *magistros*, and Isoes, *strategos* of the Opsikion *thema*, were paraded through the Hippodrome in a show of strength.[64] The emperor then placed his chief military ally and son-in-law, Artabasdos, governor of the Armeniakon *thema*, in charge of the rebellious region. Artabasdos had supported Leo's bid for the throne in an alliance not unfamiliar among disaffected generals.[65] He now became the emperor's trusted second-in-command, gained the high rank of *kouropalates*, and took responsibility for security in the sensitive area of western Asia Minor, which lay closest to Constantinople.[66] In times of need, the capital drew on additional forces from Opsikion, and its loyalty was crucial.

[63] Theophanes, 398-99; Nikephoros, 54-55.

[64] Theophanes, 400-401; Nikephoros, 55-56.

[65] Speck, *Artabasdos*, 49-51.

[66] Ibid., Anhang I, *Der cursus honorum des Artabasdos*, 153-54, overlooks the fact that Isoes was count of Opsikion until this revolt, when he was beheaded, see Theophanes, 400; Nikephoros, 56; Artabasdos's promotion to the position followed. The title of *kouropalates*, mentioned by Theophanes, 395, may have been bestowed earlier, at the time of his marriage to Anna.

Whether or not Artabasdos had also anticipated that by the terms of the alliance with Leo he would eventually accede to power, in 720 the emperor took steps to maximise his own claims to the throne. He crowned his son, Constantine, born in 718, as co-emperor and issued a gold coin with a portrait of the young prince to commemorate the event.[67] This gave notice to any rivals who fancied themselves as potential rulers that a dynastic authority was being set up in Constantinople. Clearly Constantine would not be in a position to rule for many years, but the principle of his succession was established by his official association in imperial authority, sanctioned by acclamation as co-emperor. The correct constitutional measures had been taken to ensure his accession as Leo's heir. No reaction from Artabasdos is recorded, and throughout Leo's reign he appears to have served as a reliable ally. He successfully directed the resistance at Nicaea in 727 and is recorded together with the emperor in an inscription on the city's walls.[68]

Military and Administrative Reforms

Although the surviving sources attribute little imperial activity to the first nine years of Leo's reign, recording the annual Arab campaigns and noting the emperor's attempt to force conversion on the Jews and Montanists, the reorganisation of *thema* forces was probably planned at this time.[69] The creation of the *thema* of Crete seems typical of the effort to provide better defence against Muslim raids.[70] Similarly, Leo established a purely naval *thema*, the Kibyrreot, based on the southern coast of Asia Minor, to replace the detachments of *Karabisianoi*. After the 719 revolt, when Artabasdos was moved to the Opsikion *thema*, a loyal commander of the walls and a new general for the Armeniakon *thema* must have been appointed to replace the rebels.[71] While there is no evidence for substantial Byzantine military opposition to the Muslim forces regularly dispatched from Syria until the stand made at Nicaea, Leo is likely to have considered how best to improve

---

[67] Theophanes, 400 (with the probably apocryphal account of Constantine's baptism), 401; Nikephoros, 56-57. On the commemorative coin, see P. Grierson, *DOC*, vol. 3, part 1 (Washington, D.C., 1973), 227, and plate I, type 3 onwards.

[68] A. M. Schneider and W. Karnapp, *Die Stadtmauer von Iznik* (Berlin, 1938), 49, no. 29; Stein, *Der Beginn des byzantinischen Bilderstreits*, 173, 222.

[69] Theophanes, 401.

[70] J. Herrin, "Crete in the Conflicts of the Seventh Century," in *Aphieroma ston Niko Svorono*, eds. V. Kremmydas et al. (Rethymno, 1986), I:113-126.

[71] Theophanes, 410, first mentions a *strategos* of the *Kibyrraiotoi* in connection with a major attack on Italy; cf. H. Ahrweiler, *Byzance et la Mer* (Paris, 1966), 31-32. But the passage connects this attack with Leo III's fury against Pope Gregory and the revolts in Italy, on which Theophanes is particularly unreliable. While Leo's concern for naval defence is evident, the date of the *thema ton Kibyrraioton* remains problematical. On the 719 revolt, see Theophanes, 400-401; Nikephoros, 55-56.

frontier defence and city protection during this period of harsh and repeated defeats.

In the West, however, Leo had to take measures to consolidate his authority rapidly. The reduction in taxation and payments in kind granted
by Constantine IV and Justinian II in the late seventh century may have
represented a decline in Byzantine administrative efficiency as much as a
favour. The emperor accordingly sent officials to supervise a new assessment of taxable property and land, so that the rates could be revised up-
ward. Paul, the *chartoularios* who had been appointed governor of Sicily in
717-18, probably assisted in the work of recording the population for a
more accurate poll tax.[72] Later in the 720s, the same man may have served
as exarch of Ravenna, extending this activity to mainland Italy. Certainly
it was in Byzantine Italy and Rome above all that opposition to the new
taxation became dangerous to Constantinople. As one of the largest landowners, the church was extremely hostile to any new surveys that would
increase its liability. Pope Gregory II (715-30) was especially concerned at
this prospect. In areas directly under Roman control, he succeeded in preventing the imposition of the new tax burden. In others closer to Ravenna
it was enforced.[73] It was to resolve this discrepancy that Leo sent three missions in turn: Marinos, a *spatharios*, appointed as duke of Rome (who retired with ill health after an unsuccessful attempt on Pope Gregory's life);
a subordinate of the exarch Paul, whose plans provoked the assassination of
Byzantine officials in Rome; and another *spatharios* from Constantinople,
who joined a count from Ravenna in a march on Rome that was checked at
the Salerian bridge by Romans with Lombard help.[74]

The second of these had been sent specifically because of papal opposition to the new tax assessment. Gregory feared that eastern administrators
would "deprive the churches of Italy of their wealth,"[75] and therefore with-
held the taxes due on ecclesiastical property. It was this fiscal matter that
embittered papal relations with Constantinople during Leo's campaign to
tighten Byzantine control over the *thema* of Sicily and other western possessions. While this policy has sometimes been interpreted as an attempt
to double taxation at a stroke, or as a method of financing expensive military reforms, it was probably a general measure imposed throughout the
empire. The extension of *thema* administration, based on accurate surveys
of land, property, and population, was a fundamental part of the effort to
reactivate the normal working of imperial administration. In the West,

[72] Theophanes, 398; cf. 410.10, 413.7.
[73] *LP*, 1.403 (papal prevention of the *censum*), 405 (confusion between the pro-papal and
pro-imperial party at Ravenna).
[74] Ibid., 1.404.
[75] Direct quote from *LP* 1.403, *"suis opibus ecclesias denudare."*

however, it was to provoke serious antagonism as it met the supreme land-owning authority—the church of Rome, led by a native-born pope, Gregory II, whose distinct capabilities were to ensure a continuing and strenuous opposition.

Popular Anxieties

While those in ruling circles might try to frustrate Leo III's attempts to revitalise imperial administration, the great majority exercised no choice in the matter and had to accept whatever was decreed in the capital. It is not clear, however, how far such decisions were effectively imposed. In the eastern regions of the empire, furthest from Constantinople, tax reforms were probably subordinated to the more pressing needs of defence. And as we have seen, the accession of Leo III meant little change in this regard. The inhabitants of border areas and those regularly raided by the Arabs tended to reserve their loyalty for more local powers than any imperial representative. And when it was a question of protection from Muslim attack, a particular icon or relic might command much greater respect than a military commander sent from the capital.

But during the 720s, as the enemy repeatedly attacked without hindrance, captured fortified settlements, and carried off prisoners, Byzantine morale sank. Those who witnessed Islamic violence spread fearful tales amongst any who had escaped direct assault. As in the case of the apocalyptic projections that circulated in Constantinople before the siege of 717-18, continuing Muslim success made the Christian survivors think that their world was coming to an end. They could only "explain" such a calamitous situation in terms of God's anger, anger at their failure as Christians. But if God continued to favour the Arabs, the Byzantines were surely being punished for some dreadful sins. While they may not have been able to identify these offences, they may have begun to doubt their own faith in the divine protection previously attributed to holy objects. In particular, if they had sought refuge in a walled town where the invocation of spiritual aid through icons had *not* guaranteed safety, then they must have cursed their icons.

Precisely because such feelings of frustration and anxiety are generally experienced by those with most to lose, who live at the lowest levels of society, without resources and bereft of book learning, they are most distant from those who record their "official" history (usually ecclesiastical chroniclers and monastic writers).[76] They are also likely to be most deeply af-

---

[76] Obviously these feelings cannot be documented by reference to written sources, but for some indirect evidence for them, see Herrin, "Women and the Faith in Icons"; Beck, *Von der Fragwürdigkeit*; idem, *Das byzantinische Jahrtausend*, 183-87.

fected by failures such as the failure of icon protection. Precisely for these
two reasons, their reactions are never recorded by the surviving iconophile
historians, and their "feelings" have to be reconstructed from implications
and nuances in highly prejudiced sources. It is because they have no "voice"
in the texts that they have so far been written out of the history of Byzantine iconoclasm. Their plight has been ignored and their anxiety dis-
counted. Yet as we shall see, these may have been vital factors in the complex movement that led to the destruction of icons in Byzantium.

Byzantine Iconoclasm in Asia Minor

During the 720s a certain bishop, Constantine of Nakoleia, from the ecclesiastical diocese of Synnada (not far north of Pisidian Antioch), began to
write and preach sermons against the veneration of icons. He was reproved
by his metropolitan, John, who inquired of Patriarch Germanos whether a
local synod should be held to rectify this unusual behaviour. On the basis
of lengthy discussion with Constantine in the capital, Germanos declared
himself satisfied that the matter would not go any further and therefore
needed no disciplinary action. But later he had to write again against Constantine's continuing hostility to the cult of icons.[77] His correspondence
provides a most valuable account of the arguments employed by the first
iconoclasts in their antagonism to an established Byzantine practice. The
fundamental reason lay in the Old Testament prohibition of idolatry, and
specifically in the Second Commandment: "Thou shalt not make unto thee
any graven image. . . . Thou shalt not bow down thyself to them, nor serve
them" (Exod. 20:4-5).[78] Patriarchal reasoning had not persuaded Constantine that icons were not graven images and that venerating them was perfectly lawful. The bishop persisted in his views; worse still, in Germanos's
eyes, his example appeared to be approved and followed by others. For at
Klaudioupolis (which lay directly between Gangra and Nicaea), Metropolitan Thomas had undertaken a thorough removal of icons. In a letter to

[77] PG 98, 155-62, esp. 161B, to John of Synnada (Mansi, 13.100-105); PG 98, 161-
64, to Constantine (Mansi, 13.:105-108).

[78] PG 98, 156C-D, cf. 176D in the letter to Thomas of Klaudioupolis, Mansi, 13.100C
and 117B. The same sentiment is forcefully expressed in the letter identified as a communication from Pope Gregory II to Germanos, PG 98, 147-55; Mansi, 13.91-100; Jaffé, no.
2181. J. Gouillard, "Aux origines de l'iconoclasme byzantine: le témoinage de Grégoire
II?" TM 3 (1968): 243-307, esp. 244-53 (reprinted in La vie religieuse à Byzance [London,
1981]), convincingly argues that this is another of Patriarch Germanos's letters to the early
iconoclast bishops. But Stein, Der Beginn des byzantinischen Bilderstreits, 128-37 claims it is
a letter from Pope Zacharias, 741-52; and Speck, Artabastos, Anhang II, Der Brief Papst
Gregors II., 155-78 identifies only the beginning and end as by Pope Gregory II; cf.
P. Conte, Regesto delle lettere dei papi del secolo VIII (Milan, 1984), 67.

Thomas[79] that appears to be written later than those to Constantine and John of Synnada, patriarchal distress is greatly increased by the evident support commanded by the anti-icon policy: "On this account whole cities and tribes of people have been thrown into a state of the greatest confusion . . . [as a result of which] the enemies of the cross of Jesus Christ may find cause for exultation" (PG 98, 184C). While it is impossible to establish the numbers affected by this movement, Germanos seems to imply that in two dioceses of western Asia Minor, many Christian centres had adopted the new iconoclast teaching. He also makes a significant connection between such activity and the Arabs ("the enemies of the cross of Jesus Christ"), who would say that the Christians had been wrong up to this time, "for they would not have thrown away their icons made by hand unless they had been convinced that it was idolatrous" to have them (184D). The fact that iconoclasm brought into question all past Christian practice and appeared to confirm Muslim tradition was obviously extremely disturbing to the patriarch.

Additional arguments employed by the first iconoclasts can be deduced from this important letter to Thomas. The Jewish taunt that Christians are idolators who worship mere matter, the wood and colour of icons, appears to have influenced a genuine desire to restate the importance of spiritual worship (168A). Similarly, the iconoclasts were embarrassed by Arab accusations of the same type; their own Christian observation of Old Testament law was seriously undercut by such charges brought by exponents of rival monotheist faiths (168C). To obliterate further criticism, the icons should be removed; then there would be no grounds for condemning Christians as idolators. Another aspect of the same problem appears in the anxiety expressed over the deleterious effects of icon veneration, namely that it substitutes a carnal understanding of God for a spiritual conception. It seduces people away from the supreme worship, which is reserved to God alone, and detracts from a true understanding of the Trinity (181C, cf. 180C). In the same vein, the icons are held responsible for infrequent attendance at church services, especially at mass (185A). (This may well reflect the private nature of image veneration, which could be performed in shrines and homes without clerical assistance, and an antagonism to the aristocratic ownership of such shrines and their icons.) The iconoclasts also found it scandalous that candles were lit and incense burned before icons, as if in honour of the images (184B). But their most telling charge was that those icons held to be capable of miraculous cures had ceased to perform them. They cited the image of the Virgin at Sozopolis, which used to exude

---

[79] PG 98, 163-88; Mansi, 13.108-128.

an ointment from its painted hand that had a great reputation as a healing agent. Thomas seems to have interpreted its failure to produce this ointment as proof of the icon's uselessness (185A-B). It could also be seen as an instruction to desist from icon veneration in general, and it appeared to support the contention that the cult was idolatrous and had to be curbed.

Patriarch Germanos does his best to counter these arguments, citing a good many scriptural precedents for the use of images in the church and claiming that icon veneration is an ancient custom. He stresses the importance of not introducing innovations into ecclesiastical life that might cause confusion amongst the faithful (165D). Against the accusation of idol worship, he argues that the Jews frequently slipped into idolatry, they built and adored the Golden Calf, while the Arabs make invocations to a lifeless stone in the wilderness, the Kaaba (168B-C, 172A, 168D). The ancient justifications for religious art are briefly rehearsed, namely that it inspires the worshipper with a desire to emulate the virtues and good deeds of the holy person represented, that it serves an important role in the conversion of heretics, and above all that it demonstrates the wonder of the Incarnation, by which men are saved.[80] This final claim is repeated most emphatically as a reason for depicting Christ in the flesh, a reflection of the church's recent decision to minimise symbolic and encourage human representations of the Saviour.

On the icon of the Virgin at Sozopolis, "which never met with any contradiction or suspicion," Germanos reminds Thomas that just because God no longer manifests His power to heal through it, this does not mean that it never had such power. God simply does not choose to employ this particular medium any more. As the patriarch firmly believes that God works in this way, other icons might be so used in the future (185B). Precisely because image veneration has proved so efficacious in the past, it must be pleasing to God. And he concludes by citing the *Ecclesiastical History* of Eusebios, where a description is given of the statue erected at Paneas by the woman with an issue of blood who was cured by touching the hem of Christ's garment. In the fourth century, a strange herb grew up at that spot and provided a cure for all sorts of diseases. The same authority is quoted for coloured images of Sts. Peter and Paul and of Christ, which although made in the heathen style, were still pleasing to God. If icons like these have been in existence for so long and have performed such important functions, it cannot be right to revile them and try to remove them from the life of the church (185D-188D).

---

[80] The fact of the Incarnation also frees Christians from "all idolatrous errors and impieties": *PG* 98, 169C, cf. 172C-173C.

Iconoclasm in the Byzantine Capital

This evidence of the first iconoclasts in Asia Minor, provided by a firm defender of icons, must be dated to the decade prior to January 730, when the patriarch was forced to resign. It is the sole contemporary account of the outbreak of icon removal, and it documents the serious concern voiced by Constantine and Thomas. Whether it preceded, followed, or occurred immediately after the great volcanic eruption in the Aegean in the summer of 726 is unclear. But nearly 100 years later, Patriarch Nikephoros was to attribute to the terrifying event Leo III's decision to identify the veneration of icons as the cause of divine wrath.[81] This huge underwater explosion was so severe that tidal waves were created, and a hail of pumice and ash darkened the sky as the molten lava was forced up and scattered over the entire Aegean. There is comparative evidence for the destruction caused by such events, for in the very same area, which lies over a geological fault, the island of Santorini, ancient Thera, had been blown up and practically destroyed by a vast eruption in ca. 1500 B.C.[82] All that remained after the explosion was part of a narrow circular formation jutting up around a perfectly round volcanic lake, with a smaller segment (Therasia) beyond. The sea had swallowed the rest. On that occasion, pumice carried by the tidal waves careered right across the Aegean, hitting the prosperous settlement on Crete at Knossos, inland from modern Heraklion. Its effects almost obliterated Minoan civilisation on the island, weakening its centres in a way that facilitated the Mycenaean conquest that followed. Its thriving culture is now recalled in the legends of the Trojan War, the Minotaur in the labyrinth, and the annual sacrifice of young girls, commemorated in the bull-jumping frescoes discovered by Sir Arthur Evans.

In 726, the results may not have been quite so damaging, though they were severe enough to be recalled in an annual litany designed to prevent repetition.[83] Instead of territorial destruction, a new island was thrown up between Thera and Therasia. But the accompanying phenomena—pumice, lava, and ash borne by tidal waves or showered out of the darkened sky— must have been extremely disturbing nonetheless. To the eighth-century inhabitants of the Aegean islands and coastlands, in which Constantinople lies, such natural disasters could only be understood as manifestations of supernatural power, generally associated with heavenly displeasure. God

---

[81] Nikephoros, 57; cf. Theophanes, 404-405, where the display of divine wrath caused Leo to intensify his war against the holy icons, already an established fact, Theophanes, 404.3-4.

[82] J. V. Luce, *The End of Atlantis* (London, 1969), esp. 58-95.

[83] B. Croke, "Byzantine Earthquakes and Their Liturgical Commemoration," *B* 51 (1981): 122-47; G. Dagron, "Quand la terre tremble . . . ," *TM* 8 (1981): 87-103, esp. 96.

was chiding the Byzantines for some sin. As we have seen, the readiness to take parallels from the Old Testament, a source of almost unequalled significance for medieval Byzantium, was highly developed. Germanos naturally turned to the analogy of the Egyptians with the Arabs and the children of Israel with the Byzantine defenders of Constantinople. The 726 explosion was therefore interpreted as a sign comparable to those natural disasters inflicted on the chosen people in their time of tribulation (i.e. as proof of divine disapproval). But of what particular sin? In the iconophile records, it was identified by Leo himself as the sin of idolatry, represented by an excessive veneration of icons. Theophanes also claims that Leo had been antagonistic towards icons even before the 726 eruption, and adds that the emperor therefore ordered the Christ image on the main entrance to the imperial palace, the Chalke Gate, to be taken down.[84] No source indicates that any other sin was considered: idolatry was being punished. And to prevent idolatry, the icons had to be removed.

It is probably impossible to correlate the sequence of events perfectly. The argument that the explosion of 726 inaugurated Byzantine iconoclasm depends in part on a reference in Germanos's letters to an image of the cross with prophets and apostles, which Leo III and Constantine had erected in front of the palace.[85] If this is interpreted as a substitute for the Christ icon on the Chalke Gate, then the emperor not only took down an icon but put up in its place a different sort of icon. This was dominated by the cross, which should be revered by all Christians, and would have had smaller figural decoration and inscriptions identifying the sayings of Old and New Testament leaders. It would therefore have been of a type that would not encourage excessive worship. For the erection of this image, the patriarch praises the emperors as "Christ-loving," the epithet always used of Christian rulers of the East. If the new image had served as a substitute for the Christ image, this praise grates somewhat with those accounts of the violence inflicted on pious people who are said to have protested at the removal of their special protective talisman.[86] But it is also possible that the imperial image of a cross with prophets and apostles was put up in another place "in front of the palace" in thanks for the triumph of 718. As we have seen, Leo found no resonance of his own trust in the power of the cross in Germanos's emphasis on the role of the Virgin.

But a more serious doubt on the theory of image substitution arises from the fact that the patriarch nowhere mentions the Chalke incident. Indeed, the story of the removal of the Christ icon and accompanying brutal treat-

[84] Theophanes, 404.
[85] *PG* 98, 185A; Stein, *Der Beginn des byzantinischen Bilderstreits*, 70-74, 143-55, 197.
[86] Theophanes, 405; cf. the letter of Pope Gregory to Germanos, Gouillard, "Aux origines."

ment accorded to those who gathered to protest occurs first in a highly prejudiced iconophile source, the second letter of Gregory II to Leo III, which
may be a forgery.[87] In exaggerated tones, it relates how an officer, Julian
the *spatharokandidatos*, was stoned to death by "pious women," who were
then savagely punished by other soldiers. Germanos does not associate the
cross image with any icon destruction or loss of iconophile life; rather, it
appears to belong to an earlier period when the emperors could definitely
be portrayed as "Christ-loving" rulers. If this is the case, then his letter to
Thomas in which the cross image is mentioned must predate the Chalke
incident of 726. And it follows that the iconoclast activity in Asia Minor
occurred before the sub-aquatic eruption and may have influenced the emperor's interpretation of it.

Western Reactions. However we construe the chronology of events, the critical debate about icons in Constantinople provoked swift and fierce reactions in Italy, where there was already hostility to the empire over financial
matters. News of the Chalke incident is preserved only in a garbled form
in the *Life* of Pope Gregory II, which describes a huge bonfire of all the
icons of the capital made in the centre of the city—a typical instance of
iconophile inflation and elaboration.[88] But the *Life* correctly records that
the emperor sent orders for the pope to remove icons from the churches under his control or run the possibility of even more serious imperial cen-
sure.[89] This was not an imperial edict against icons everywhere as has been
claimed, for no other officials were so informed, not even Patriarch Germanos.[90] It was a personal threat to the Roman pontiff and was used by

---

[87] The two letters allegedly written by Pope Gregory II to Leo III (Jaffé, nos. 2180 and
2182) have aroused intense interest ever since the authenticity of the first was doubted by
Hartmann (1889). H. Grotz, "Beobachtungen zu den zwei Briefen Papst Gregors II an Kaiser Leo III," *Archivum Historiae Pontificiae* 18 (1980): 9-40, has argued that they are original
and were composed in Greek in Rome. He also documents the two interpolations in the first
letter. Against this, Gouillard, "Aux origines," believed both letters were originally written in Latin and badly translated into Greek in the early ninth century by monastic circles
that wished to condemn Leo III as heresiarch. It is in the second letter, however, that the
graphic description of the removal of the Chalke icon occurs, complete with the name of the
officer sent to take this first step in the imperial attack on holy images; see Gouillard, "Aux
origines," 293, lines 218-26. A similar story is related in the *Life* of St. Stephen the
Younger (*PG* 100, col. 1085C). But the entire episode may be a literary *topos*, lifted from a
much earlier source; see Stein, *Der Beginn*, 197 n. 17; Speck, *Kaiser Konstantin IV*, 2:607-8.
Most recently, Conte, *Regesto delle lettere*, 62-76, has surveyed the letters, expressing doubts
about their authenticity. Nonetheless, it remains clear that Leo III and Pope Gregory II did
exchange letters; the emperor's have not survived, and those of the pope may also be lost.

[88] *LP* 1.409.

[89] Ibid.

[90] See, for instance, M. V. Anastos, "Leo III's Edict Against the Images in the Year 726-

Byzantium as another attempt to secure his agreement to the new census. After repeated non-cooperation over these fiscal matters, Leo now added his own demand for the removal of icons as a means of avoiding idolatry. Naturally, Gregory refused and wrote to inform the emperor that he had no right to intervene in ecclesiastical matters. Backed up by a rising tide of opposition to the empire, the pope rejected the imperial order and maintained his stand against increased taxation. But he tried to dissuade Leo from iconoclasm and curbed local Italian forces from setting up a rival claimant to the throne.[91] His restraint at this point reveals that Gregory had no immediate design to establish Rome's independence of Constantinople. But his authority over those who condemned iconoclasm and taxation created a powerful iconophile force.

The Growth of Eastern Antagonism to Icons

Rather than pursue the minutest details of all possible reconstructions of the events of 726-30, it may be more useful to bear in mind the general tumult in Asia Minor, not only in parts where the Arabs were victorious. At Nicaea in 727, a large refugee and rural population sought shelter as the Muslims advanced from the east. They had devastated Paphlagonia, taken Gangra, and doubtless approached the well-fortified ancient city with confidence, destroying crops, driving off any livestock, and terrifying all before them. As count of the Opsikion *thema*, Artabasdos was responsible for the city. He employed the traditional methods of securing its safety: organised military defence and efforts to gain spiritual protection through the patrons of Nicaea, the 318 bishops who had participated at the First Oecumenical Council in 325. (According to a later iconophile source, the city was indeed saved by their intercession.) But among Artabasdos's soldiers there was an iconoclast, who stoned an icon of the Virgin, which had presumably been added to the others. The ninth-century chronicler records that the soldier had no faith in her power to shield the Byzantines and for his sins lost one of his eyes the next day in an Islamic catapult attack.[92] Obviously the story was only preserved because of its iconophile moral: such disbelief is interpreted as "iconoclast madness" justly punished by divine intervention. But the fact remains that it implies that at least one Opsikion soldier had turned away from icons. Such aggressive antagonism springs from precisely the despair of someone who had previously placed all trust in the power of icons. The greater the commitment, the greater

---

27 and Italo-Byzantine Relations between 726 and 730," *BF* 3 (1968): 5-41; T. F. X. Noble, *The Republic of St. Peter* (Philadelphia, 1984), 30.

[91] *LP* 1.404-405.

[92] Theophanes, 406.

the disappointment and the greater the hatred. Hence this type of attack on an icon of the Virgin, which occurred while not far away Metropolitan Thomas was elaborating his own justification for the removal of icons from churches.

These reactions lay at the relatively well-informed and most unsophisticated extremes of the spectrum of iconoclasm, but they were both part of the same phenomenon. This sought a scapegoat for the humiliation of Arab defeat and found one in the implicit belief that holy images would protect. As soon as the icons failed to guarantee a successful defence, they were despised rather than revered and were held responsible for misleading people. In this respect, excessive icon worship may have been identified by iconoclasts as something likely to deceive the simple-minded. The Council in Trullo had drawn attention to such dangers, mentioning the use of amulets, incantations, and other magic practices. But by its insistence on representing Christ in human form, the council had encouraged iconophile veneration, which was now construed by Constantine and Thomas as a similar danger, for it raised hopes and expectations that could not always be satisfied. The iconoclasts saw how faith in icons was thus reduced to a mystic belief in supernatural aid and condemned it.

Leo III can hardly have remained unaware of this ecclesiastical and possibly military opposition to the cult of icons in Asia Minor.[93] The suggestion that such activity could have been kept from him ignores the fact that the clerics were bishops of crucial areas fairly close to the western coast and directly controlled by Artabasdos as count of the Opsikion *thema*. The disturbances recorded by Germanos could not possibly have remained unknown to the emperor. Whether iconoclasm was already widespread among *thema* soldiers is impossible to judge. The question of different army units' affiliation and sympathy during the iconoclast controversy has been debated at length, the only sure conclusion being that soldiers tended to support effective military leadership regardless of religious considerations.[94] But Leo III would certainly have viewed even an individual case with concern, for he could not afford to ignore unrest in the *thema* armies. If hostility to icons was growing among ordinary soldiers and provincial inhabitants, he had to take account of a movement of loyalties. In the absence of any secure information on the emperor's personal views, it seems more likely that he exploited provincial and military antagonism to icons by adopting the arguments put forward by Constantine and Thomas. In this way he aimed to maintain the support of *thema* soldiers while consol-

---

[93] As claimed by Gero, *Leo III*, 59-93; though he also admits the possibility of another pre-726 iconoclastic grouping responsible for verses, which celebrate the power of the Cross, 119 (note 25), 123.

[94] W. E. Kaegi, Jr., "The Byzantine Armies and Iconoclasm," *BS* 27 (1966): 48-70.

idating his own position as ruler, at a time of extreme peril for the empire as a whole. The shift of attention from icons to the emperor as the figure with prime responsibility for Christian welfare and the means to protect it undoubtedly confirmed his own view of the imperial role.[95]

While such reasoning made sense in the context of war-torn Asia Minor, it was quite irrelevant to the West. In Rome particularly, there was no idolatrous association between icons and their veneration. The dictum of Pope Gregory the Great was well known to his eighth-century successors, who also stressed the pedagogic functions of Christian art. Although icons do not seem to have been used quite so extensively in western religious observance, they were common features of many Roman churches. Gregory II could not possibly have removed them without causing alarm. In any case, he had no grounds for acceding to the imperial order, threat or no threat. As he had already survived several assassination attempts by Byzantine officials (according to the *Life*), he must have been used to such imperial pressure. The last recorded act of his pontificate was the denunciation of pseudo-Patriarch Anastasios's synodical letters, accompanied by further dogmatic epistles to the impious emperor.[96] Though these do not survive, one can surmise that they stressed the emperor's incapacity to adjudicate theological matters (repeating the earlier charge). Leo, however, showed no respect for such clerical claims.

The emperor had already displayed a capacity to utilise the military power base from which he had risen to the throne. Apart from the alliance with Artabasdos, then governor of the Armeniakon, he does not appear to have had significant contacts among ruling circles, a legendary story of his association with Justinian II notwithstanding.[97] Thus he employed reliable military supporters to deal with all the major problems of his early reign and built up his standing in the armed forces through the defence of the capital. Such qualities also commanded a new type of respect and loyalty among civilian officials, who could probably appreciate the effort to systematise resources to meet the Arab threat. So when Leo interpreted the 726 eruption as evidence of God's anger at Byzantine idolatry and took down the Christ icon from the Chalke, he may have acted with considerable support. While the particular icon chosen may have shocked some, *all* knew that something was wrong and that some correction of sin was called for. The news that provincial bishops were preaching against icon venera-

---

[95] Gero, *Leo III*, 48-58, drawing on the preamble to the *Ecloga*, the legal code issued by Leo III and Constantine V, which is to be dated to the year 740, not 726, see L. Burgmann, ed., *Ecloga* (Frankfurt am Main, 1983), 10-12. The preamble, *Prooimion*, is published with a German translation, 160-67, cf. the partial English translation in Gero, *Leo III*, 50-54.

[96] *LP* 1.409-410; cf. Theophanes, 409.

[97] Theophanes, 391-95.

tion, while the active destruction of icons was possibly spreading among *thema* soldiers, may have influenced the emperor. And as Germanos was already engaged in theological debate with the bishops, Leo sought to persuade him that their worries were correct and idolatry was rife. The novelty of their opposition to icons meant that there was no clear-cut understanding of it; it appeared to draw on Old Testament texts well known in the eastern churches and had no previous record as a movement touched by wrong belief. Given this ambiguity, Leo used the issue for his own purposes. Whether he was even aware of the theological problems, let alone a convinced iconoclast, is immaterial. He took advantage of the prevalent disquiet over Christian images to enforce the cult of the cross at their expense.

The Deposition of Patriarch Germanos. Four years later, when he had failed to win Germanos over to the iconoclast way of thinking, Leo gave official imperial support to the party opposed to icons. At a civil assembly (*silention*) that met in January 730, Germanos resigned rather than condone the view that icon veneration could be idolatrous. After warning the emperor that no change could be made in the orthodox belief of the church without a general council, he went into an undisturbed retirement on his family estates. His assistant, Anastasios, who had probably advised Leo on the mechanisms of deposition, was elevated in his place.[98]

No other cleric from the Constantinopolitan church, no one from the court or the imperial administration went into exile with Germanos, a telling fact that seems to indicate that the main civilian, military, and ecclesiastical leaders had already pledged support for the emperor and accepted his action as the traditional imperial right of intervention in church affairs. Among ecclesiastics, the notion of *oikonomia* had conditioned many to acquiesce in such changes. Since deposition, exile, or death was the normal fate of those who refused to adapt, the exercise of a little "economy" frequently governed attitudes toward imperial theology. Indeed, Germanos had given an example of this sort of compromise when he agreed to the reintroduction of Monotheletism by Philippikos. Leo might have expected him to do the same in 730. Instead, the patriarch withdrew from the fray; he had already failed to check the iconoclasts in Asia Minor and perhaps knew that iconoclasm was not unpopular among the people.

In evaluating Germanos's role in the process that led to the adoption of official Byzantine iconoclasm, it is instructive to compare him with his direct contemporary, Pope Gregory II. Both were experienced administrators

---

[98] Ibid., 407-409; Nikephoros, 58 (both sources note that the persecution of iconophiles followed). S. Gero, "Jonah and the Patriarch," *Vigiliae Christianae* 29 (1975): 141-46.

who made successful careers in their respective institutions. Gregory came from an established Roman family, took holy orders under Pope Sergius, and worked his way up through the diaconate, becoming successively *sacellarius* (junior assistant to the papal treasurer) and *bibliothecarius* (librarian), two posts apparently created by Sergius for him. As chief papal adviser, he accompanied Pope Constantine I on his trip to the East and negotiated the re-wording of the Council in Trullo decrees in 711.[99] His election as pope in 715 was the culmination of a typical clerical career in the curia, the only unusual aspect (at that time) being Gregory's Roman birth. For many years the papacy had been dominated by Easterners or men of eastern origin, often from Sicily, who spoke Greek and were familiar with the oriental churches. By his administrative skills and wide-ranging experience, however, Gregory was the natural successor to Constantine and also a very popular choice with the people of Rome.

Germanos, on the other hand, lived all his life in the shadow of imperial condemnation, coming from a family that opposed Constans II and was therefore punished by his successor, Constantine IV. He was castrated and forced into a clerical career, as a priest and deacon of the church of St. Sophia before being appointed to the see of Kyzikos. During the brief reign of Philippikos (711-13), he did not protest against the revival of Monotheletism, although he subsequently agreed to condemn it as heretical. With this promise, Anastasios II (713-15) promoted him to the patriarchate, and a council was then held to re-establish orthodox doctrine.[100] At every stage of his life, Germanos had witnessed the power of the emperor, just as his father had in a civilian capacity, and knew what it meant to oppose a Byzantine ruler. Even as head of the eastern church, he had considerably less freedom of action than Gregory, although probably greater resources at his disposal.

The main difference between the two church leaders, however, remained the degree of secular control to which the Easterner was subjected. In the church of Constantinople, imperial interpretations of theology were as significant as patriarchal views, whereas in Rome the pope's definitions of doctrine were supreme. Conversely, the full authority of the Byzantine Empire could be put at the service of the orthodox, while the papacy had no comparable lay institution in Rome to give force to its sacerdotal leadership. Thus, popes were forced to manage the diplomatic affairs of central Italy and became political negotiators without material strength, and at the same time tried not to tolerate civilian pressure on the terrain of the spir-

[99] *LP* 1.389-91, 396.
[100] Zonaras, 14.20 (cf. Theophanes, 352); Theophanes, 382, 384-85; Nikephoros, 48-49; Mansi, 12.189A-196C; Lamza, *Patriarch Germanos I*, 53-78.

itual. It is hard to say which of the two had the greater problems; but in Constantinople relations were already established within a particular framework, which gave the secular government decisive powers in the running of the church. In Rome, by contrast, no satisfactory framework had been evolved, and the search for a balanced relationship with western civil authorities was to preoccupy the papacy throughout the eighth century.

In 730, when Germanos gave up the unequal struggle against Leo III, he may have known that iconophile resistance was bound to fail. Although later sources claim that a great many clerics, monastics, and well-born people suffered the martyr's crown for their belief, there are no named iconophile heroes of Leo's reign.[101] In contrast, Germanos himself provides indirect evidence of support for iconoclasm in an influential sector of Constantinopolitan society when he describes those at court who made life difficult for the faithful (i.e. the iconophiles). Theophanes similarly refers to those who agreed with the emperor (*oi toutou symphones*) and those who were his comrades in arms (*tous autou synaspistas*).[102] Clearly, any who owed their position to the emperor were always likely to subscribe to imperial theology as well. And for those who had no definite views either way, the case for supporting Leo was well made by his military achievements. So in contrast to Germanos's solitary protest against the emperor's "impiety, wickedness and wrong belief," many in the episcopacy, at court, and in the army "thought like Leo" and supported him.

Such considerations were not readily understood in Rome. But a most remarkable aspect of the western response to iconoclasm is the extent to which Pope Gregory restrained the anti-Byzantine movement, maintaining a political loyalty to the East while denouncing its theology. On the other hand, the Romans rallied particularly to defend their spiritual leader, manifesting a great appreciation of Gregory as one of them, a growing hostility to eastern officials, and a desire for greater autonomy. The pope was at the centre of the storm and seemed in a way to personify the currents in struggle: he represented both the theological independence of the West, which would not accept imperial definitions of faith, and the old political order in which the emperor was still supreme ruler over large parts of Italy. But Gregory was also aware of Leo III's duty to protect Rome from the Lombards, and when that was no longer fulfilled, he felt the need of straightforward military assistance. That the exarch was failing to provide it because of the continuous pressure of Arab invasions in the East could not have been appreciated in Italy, though it was of course one of the chief

---

[101] Theophanes, 409. Nikephoros, 58, does not mention martyrdom—only punishments and tortures.

[102] *PG* 98, 77-80; cf. Theophanes, 405, 408; Gero, *Leo III*, 88-89.

reasons for the plight of the western provinces. Lacking any understanding of the gravity of Arab attacks and of Leo's consequent priority for the defence of Constantinople, those in the West could not sense the necessity of resisting Islam or the jubilation that accompanied victorious campaigns, that is, the context in which iconoclasm emerged and found widespread support. They only felt the growing danger of the Lombards, saw the absence of Byzantine reinforcements as a failure to respond to appeals, and were thus quite unprepared to accept the eastern practice of iconoclasm. When these differences were exacerbated by rumours of plots to kill their pontiff, the Romans strengthened their determination to protect Gregory and to support his stand against the eastern heresy.[103]

FROM THIS analysis it is evident that iconoclasm was born of the crisis generated by the Muslim advance, which set in process a complex reaction, both military and religious. Byzantine victories in the East later assisted the consolidation of iconoclast belief, so that the two gradually became inseparably interrelated. By the second half of Constantine V's reign, it is extremely difficult to identify a purely theological factor. Yet iconoclasm did have a theological root. The concerns of Constantine and Thomas about a possible infringement of the Second Commandment were serious and deeply felt. Their anxieties, however, would not have reached such a point had not the holy images come to assume a highly sensitive and prominent role in Byzantine society, where the faithful could see and venerate their Christian founder, His mother, and His saints as very familiar persons. The danger lay in their adoration of such images and their faith in the power of icons to save—a danger both to the images when they failed, and to those who did not foresee the sin of idolatry.

[103] Noble, *The Republic of St. Peter*, 30-40.

Divergent Paths

THE BYZANTINE church came to terms with iconoclasm with the loss of only one leader—Patriarch Germanos. But from Muslim-occupied Palestine, a fierce hostility emerged with the reaction of St. John of Damascus, who delivered a denunciation in his *Three Orations Against the Calumniators of the Holy Icons*.[1] As a monk of the monastery of Mar Sabas near Jerusalem, he represented that community within the church which refused to give up the veneration of holy images, not least because it was also responsible for their production. Icon painters were frequently monks who worked for their own monasteries as well as other ecclesiastical patrons. John was the son of Sergios Mansour, a local Christian notable, who had been employed by the Arabs in the financial administration of the caliphate of Damascus. He had been well educated in Greek philosophy and theology by a Sicilian tutor, and had followed his father's career before withdrawing to one of the most famous monasteries of the holy land.[2] His *Three Orations* provided a vigorous justification of iconophile practice, which was eventually adopted as the foundation of official Byzantine theology in the East.

This turns on a very careful definition of an icon and its relationship to the prototype represented; on the different sorts of Christian worship, of which the supreme variety, *latreia*, is reserved to God alone; and on the important pedagogic function of images: "and as a book [serves] those who can understand letters, this an icon does for the unlettered."[3] While thus removing the uncircumscribable Godhead from any form of representation, the depiction of the Human Christ is justified as an image of the

---

[1] B. Kotter, ed., *Contra imaginum calumniatores orationes tres, Die Schriften des Johannes von Damaskos*, vol. 3 (Berlin, 1975). In the second oration, John claims that many other bishops and fathers were also exiled with Germanos, but he does not know their names, 2.12.29-30 (p. 103).

[2] D. J. Sahas, *John of Damascus on Islam* (Leiden, 1972), 6-26; Greek wisdom, both secular and theological, was imparted by Cosmas of Sicily (an Arab prisoner-of-war, captured and transported to Syria, cf. Theophanes, 348).

[3] John of Damascus, *Contra imaginum calumniatores* 1.17.5-7 (p. 93).

Word incarnate and a reminder of the salvation of humanity through God's redemptive powers. Through dense philosophical argument, using abstract theological terms (especially in the first oration), icons are identified as an ancient, unwritten tradition of the church (like venerating the cross or praying towards the East).[4] Their ordained and integrated place in Christian worship is established and illustrated by a mass of patristic citations (one florilegium for each oration). The arguments of the iconoclasts are countered one by one, and Emperor Leo III's intervention in matters of faith condemned. John recalls that Christ gave the power to bind and loose to the Apostles, not to the emperor, and rulers have no priestly power that could authorise their direction of spiritual concerns.[5] While these arguments may not have been immediately understood in their entirety, the attack on imperial claims to order Byzantine belief and on the iconoclasts as heretics must have encouraged not only the veneration of holy images but also Christian artistic traditions, particularly in Palestine. Because of the relative isolation of the Mar Sabas monastery, John's *Three Orations* did not circulate very widely until much later in the eighth century. But his fame as a champion of icons spread rapidly through the Byzantine world and provoked his anathematisation at the iconoclast council of 754.

In the West, as we have seen in Chapter 8, Rome inevitably served both as the butt of Byzantine anger and the mouthpiece of western reaction to iconoclasm. There is no evidence that Christian communities outside Italy were even aware of the eastern initiative in regard to artistic representation, which is not surprising in view of Byzantine isolation from Transalpine Europe. The use of icons was not widespread in other western churches: Benedict Biscop had transported the Roman custom to Northumbria together with building skills, the use of stained glass, chanting, and liturgical practices. But in other parts of the British Isles, iconic art appears to have been rather limited. In Francia and the newly converted regions of northeast Europe, patron saints and monastic founders were sometimes commemorated in sculpted or painted tombstones, while the use of icons in the eastern style was not unknown. Christian art concentrated more on familiar Roman traditions, the architectural features of carved capitals, lintels, and architraves, often decorated with non-representational patterns—scroll, interlace, leaf and vine—with only a little painted imagery. Although fresco and mosaic decoration remained part of that traditional Roman repertoire, craftsmen capable of using the media and patrons wealthy enough to insist upon them were rare.

Despite Byzantine pressure to conform to eastern iconoclasm, Roman

[4] Kotter, *Die Schriften*, Introduction, 18.
[5] John of Damascus, *Contra imaginum calumniatores* 1.66.13, cf. 2.12.21 (pp. 167, 103).

bishops of the early eighth century were more concerned with the extension and consolidation of the faith in the West. Following Pope Sergius's consecration of the Northumbrian missionary Willibrord as archbishop of the Frisians, with the Roman name of Clement, papal involvement in the Anglo-Saxon work of conversion was a constant preoccupation.[6] From his base at Utrecht, Clement founded the monastery of Echternach (in about 700) and extended his activity east and north into Denmark, encouraged by Rome and by the arrival of younger pioneers from Britain. Among these, Winfrith of Crediton (Devon) also sought Roman approval of his missionary work; in 718, Gregory II gave him the Latin name Boniface and sanctioned his activity among the Germanic peoples living east of the Rhine. He was later raised to the position of bishop and established his see at Mainz.[7] While eighth-century popes did not direct the work of conversion as closely as Gregory I, their advice on disputed topics of Christian marriage and divorce, diet and ancient customs, guided Clement and Boniface in their struggles.[8] Overall, correspondence with the Anglo-Saxon missionaries and with those secular authorities who were asked to assist and protect them occupies a much larger part of the papal record than that with the East. For the conversion of pagan tribes previously hostile to (or simply ignorant of) the faith was obviously of greater importance than the Byzantine fear of idolatry and resulting attack on icons.

There was also a practical aspect to the papal reaction to iconoclasm. Since Constantinople was responsible for imperial administration and defence of the Ravenna exarchate, duchy of Rome, and large areas of southern Italy and Sicily, Gregory II, Gregory III, and Zacharias (popes between 715 and 752) naturally turned to the Byzantine emperor for protection against the Lombards. Throughout this period, the kings of northern Italy and dukes of Spoleto and Benevento, although divided amongst themselves, kept up a regular pressure on Rome. King Liutprand (712-44) appears to have directed his military expansion chiefly against the duchies, whose independent existence he could not tolerate. But he also tried to conquer the exarchate, occupying the western parts in 726-27 and attacking major cities and Ravenna itself in the 730s and 740s.[9] The threat to Ra-

[6] W. H. Fritze, " 'Universalis gentium confessio': Formeln, Träger und Wege universalmissionarischen Denkens im 7. Jahrhundert," *Frühmittelalterliche Studien* 3 (1969): 78-130; C. H. Talbot, *The Anglo-Saxon Missionaries in Germany*, 2nd ed. (London, 1981).

[7] *LP* 1.397; T. Schieffer, *Winfrid-Bonifatius und die christliche Grundlegung Europas*, 2nd ed. (Darmstadt, 1980); idem, "La chiesa nazionale di osservanza Romana: L'Opera di Williborde di Bonifacio." *Settimane* 7 (1960): 73-94.

[8] W. Kelly, *Pope Gregory II on Divorce and Remarriage* (Analecta Gregoriana, vol. 203) (Rome, 1976).

[9] Paul the deacon, *HL* 6.256-58; J. T. Hallenbeck, *Pavia and Rome: The Lombard Mon-*

venna carried immense significance for bishops of Rome, for without a firm Byzantine presence there and undisputed control of the Apennine corridor joining the exarchate to the duchy, the apostolic see was immediately at risk. Despite the appointment of seven dukes in succession between 724 and 743 and some stability within the duchy, its defence remained dependent on the exarch.[10]

When it failed, and this happened with increasing frequency in the first half of the eighth century, pontiffs had to employ local resources in the defence of Rome. As often as not, these were primarily diplomatic and involved direct negotiations with the Lombards. In the late 720s, for instance, Gregory II appealed over the castle of Sutrium, captured by a Lombard force, and got it returned "to the Apostles Peter and Paul."[11] Not only did this represent a successful intervention in central Italian politics, then highly confused, but it also marked an important development for the papacy. For the first time, bishops of Rome, as the successors of Sts. Peter and Paul, controlled a fortified site in the name of the founders of their church. From this relatively humble beginning, the papal state was to grow throughout the eighth century. Whether Pope Gregory realised the potential of his negotiations with the Lombards or not, later pontiffs were to use the same method to acquire direct control over a much larger area than that previously administered by Constantinople. The dispute over Sutrium and its resolution in favour of the see of St. Peter emphasised Byzantine inability to govern regions threatened by the Lombards and indicated a local power vacuum. Under Gregory III and Zacharias, the papacy began to adapt itself to fill that space.[12]

ROMAN CONDEMNATION OF ICONOCLASM—THE COUNCIL OF 731

Papal reaction to eastern iconoclasm, therefore, combined theological opposition with political loyalty. Gregory II's protests to Constantinople, against the deposition of Patriarch Germanos in 730 and the imperial order to remove icons from Roman churches, were repeated by his successor Gregory III (731-41), whose messengers were imprisoned in Sicily. Un-

---

archy and the Papacy in the Eighth Century (Philadelphia, 1982), 23-39; T. F. X. Noble, The Republic of St. Peter (Philadelphia, 1984), 31-32, 35-37, 40-45, 50-55.

[10] B. Bavant, "Le duché byzantin de Rome," MEFR, Moyen Age 91 (1979), 41-88; T. S. Brown, Gentlemen and Officers (London, 1984), 54-55.

[11] LP 1.407-408; Noble, Republic of St. Peter, 31-32; cf. 25-26, on the case of the castle of Cumae, which Gregory II bought for 70 lbs. of gold in 717-18 from Duke Romuald of Benevento.

[12] The whole process of adaptation is succinctly described by E. Ewig, "The Papacy's Alienation from Byzantium and Rapprochement with the Franks," in Handbook of Church History, ed. H. Jedin and J. Dolan, vol. 3 (New York, 1969), 3-25.

daunted by this political show of force, the new pope summoned a council in November 731, which met in St. Peter's to reject iconoclasm.[13] As the acts of the council are lost, it can only be reconstructed from a later one held in 769, which drew on the earlier gathering and quoted from it. It is clear, however, that a large number of bishops attended the 731 council—93 from all parts of Italy, including the archbishops of Ravenna and Grado.[14] Gregory III compiled a list of extracts from Biblical and patristic texts designed to prove that icon veneration was an established tradition. This was a fairly basic selection drawn from well-known sources. In addition to the Old Testament, Gregory used writings of St. Athanasios, St. Gregory of Nyssa, St. John Chrysostomos, St. Cyril, St. Gennadius of Marseille, pseudo-Ambrose, the petition of the clergy against Severos Antioch, and Gregory the Great's letter to Secundinus, a hermit.[15] As a bilingual scholar of Syrian origin, the pope could use Greek as well as Latin writings, but there is no evidence that he elaborated a sophisticated argument. The eastern texts employed had been regularly cited ever since Epiphanios of Salamis first raised the propriety of icon veneration in the fourth century. Yet the council of 731 represents another important stage in Roman independence from the East and set a model for all later western opposition to iconoclasm.

Gregory also promoted the cult of icons in Rome as part of his lavish building programme. In St. Peter's, images of Christ, the Virgin, and the Apostles were engraved on new silver roof beams, while an icon of the Virgin was added to the oratory of the Saviour. Another icon, of the Virgin and Child, was set up in a new oratory built in St. Maria ad Praesepe. Murals in the Byzantine style were commissioned to decorate the crypt of St. Crisogono, which was also endowed with new furnishings, lights, silk veils, altar cloths, and liturgical vessels; it seems to have been one of Gregory's most favoured foundations. He restored the entire church and established a monastic community there to maintain a pilgrim hostel (*diaconia*) and to perform the church services.[16] But in many other Roman churches and catacomb shrines, Gregory was responsible for necessary repairs and restorations. Indeed, the record of his patronage in the *Liber pontificalis* almost excludes reference to the important political negotiations that dominated his pontificate.

[13] *LP* 1.415; Gregory III, Letter to Antoninus of Grado, in *MGH*, *Ep.*, vol. 3, no. 1, 703 (also in Mansi, 12.300).
[14] Mansi, 12.713-22, cf. 13.759-810, letter-treatise of Pope Hadrian I, quoting from the now-lost acts of 731.
[15] Mansi, 12.720C, 777E, 798D-E, 778A, 785E-786A, 786A-B, 792D.
[16] *LP* 1.417-21.

Byzantine Retaliation

It is difficult to assess Leo III's reaction to the council of 731, for the eastern sources represent a hopelessly confused record of events in the West throughout the first half of the eighth century. Theophanes, the main chronicler, does not distinguish between Popes Gregory II and III, who are not even mentioned by Nikephoros; the 731 council is unknown, and papal opposition to Constantinople takes the form of withholding taxes and writing dogmatic letters against the emperor.[17] A Pope Gregory is held responsible for refusing to accept Patriarch Anastasios's synodical letter (of 730) and for removing Rome and all of Italy from the empire (presumably Gregory II). This is followed by an imperial expedition directed against the pope (unnamed) and against the defection of Rome and all Italy, recorded in ca. 732.[18]

Since the *Liber pontificalis* reports that on several occasions Gregory III's envoys were arrested in Sicily and even held for over a year, it appears that Theophanes's very unclear chronology may represent the imperial response to Roman condemnation of iconoclasm.[19] Obviously the general nature of the papal communications was passed on to the eastern capital by Byzantine officials in Sicily, while their messengers languished in custody. Yet it is impossible to be confident of the motives attributed to Leo III by this hostile witness, which records no other exchanges between Rome and Constantinople. In the absence of any clearer record, we have to interpret Byzantine retaliation in the light of Leo's known preoccupation with the Arab threat and his determination to secure the eastern defence of the empire.

There are three separate aspects to the measures recorded by Theophanes, and they have all caused much debate and commentary.[20] The first concerns a reorganisation of Byzantine taxes already collected in the *thema* of Sicily and Calabria, the second addresses the registering of all male children on official records, and the third (not mentioned in any eighth-century source but definitely related) details the transfer of East Illyricum from papal to patriarchal control.

The crucial aspect of Leo's reorganisation of capitation taxes and the patrimony of St. Peter's in Sicily and Calabria is that *thema* officials were to

---

[17] Theophanes, 404, begins to record bishops of Rome with a Pope Gregory, whose episcopate lasted nine years (ca. 724-25 to 733-34); thereafter Zacharias is noted for 21 years (ca. 733-34 to 754-55), 410, 421. In neither case is the number of years correct. The previous notice on Pope Stephen and his flight to Francia is a ninth-century scholion by Anastasius Bibliothecarius, 402-403. On Pope Gregory's activity, see 404, 408.28-29, 409.14-17.

[18] Theophanes, 408.21-25; 409.17-18; 410.5-6; 413.7-8. But see also Chapter 8 above, note 71, on the problematic nature of this reference to the *Kibyrraiotoi*.

[19] *LP* 1.416.13; 416.21-417.1.

[20] Theophanes, 410. 9-17.

take over their administration; taxes that had previously been paid to the churches were now to go directly to the treasury in Constantinople (*to demosio logo*); ecclesiastical autonomy in the management of papal patrimonies was ended. Guillou has recently elucidated the obscure phrase *to trito merei* by reference to the custom of establishing what proportion of taxes should be covered by the church.[21] In Byzantine Istria at the end of the eighth century, the church paid one-half of the total sum of public taxation; the other half was divided between the lay property owners. In 732-33, the proportion for Sicily and Calabria was set at one-third from the people and two-thirds from the church. If this appears a high rate of taxation on ecclesiastical property, one should recall how many churches owned estates in Sicily (Rome and Ravenna particularly) and how much privately owned land was constantly coming to the churches in the form of pious donations and legacies. The chief innovation in Leo's measures was that connected with the Byzantine administration of the *themata*: papal *rectores* were made redundant, Constantinopolitan *chartoularioi* and their subordinates took over. No new taxes were imposed, although Theophanes's account is often so interpreted.[22] But the very large annual income raised from the papal patrimonies (three-and-a-half talents of gold, with a good deal of provisions and levies in kind) was now appropriated by Greek functionaries from the East. At the same time, instructions were issued for the male children to be registered and inscribed on *thema* records, an essential requirement for raising military forces from Sicily and Calabria and for all *thema* administration.[23] This same procedure was certainly in use in the Asia Minor *themata* and was hardly comparable to Pharaoh's slaughter of the innocents, but Theophanes singles it out for special condemnation as something that even Leo's Arab teachers did not do to the Christians under their control.[24]

These two retaliatory measures, financial and military, were adopted in order to force Pope Gregory to accept imperial policies over taxation as much as iconoclasm. The military element may also have been prompted by news of a Lombard siege of Ravenna, which forced the exarch to flee to

[21] A. Guillou, "La Sicile byzantine: Etat des recherches," *BF* 5 (1977): 95-145, esp. 106-107; idem, *Régionalisme et indépendence dans l'empire byzantin au VIIe siècle* (Rome, 1969), 301-307, document 6, lines 53-54 (pp. 62-63), on the taxes levied on vineyards, which reflects the system of levying taxes by a proportion of the land/crop productive value; cf. T. S. Brown, *Gentlemen and Officers*, 114-115 (on taxation).

[22] Zonaras, 15.4.10, is typical of the later assumption.

[23] Theophanes, 410.14-15.

[24] Ibid., 410.15-17; since Theophanes presents iconoclasm as a heresy developed by Leo III on Islamic models, he frequently condemns the emperor as "Saracen-minded," e.g. 405.14, cf. 406.25.

Venetia,[25] while the fiscal aspect consolidated the new *thema* administration in Sicily, as well as bringing revenues directly to the treasury. Leo's determination to secure a strong imperial base in the island fitted into his overall conception of naval defence against the Arabs, in which Crete was to play a similar role. In northern Italy, the exarch Eutychios was left to fend for himself and managed to hold out, with a good deal of diplomatic support from both Gregory III and his successor Zacharias, until 751.[26] But the shipwreck of the Kibyrreot fleet in the Adriatic (see Chapter 8) proved to be the final Byzantine effort to shore up the exarchate. Imperial investment was then switched to southern Italy, a change that signalled the end of Byzantine authority north of Rome and provoked Gregory into a reconsideration of the papacy's traditional loyalty to Constantinople.

A third aspect of Leo's reform of Sicilian government concerned the churches of those areas. Although contemporary Greek and Latin sources are silent on the matter, it was in this same period that Leo transferred the dioceses of Illyricum, previously under Roman control, to Constantinople. In letters of Pope Hadrian (772-95) and Pope Nicholas I (858-67), this is associated with the "theft" of papal patrimonies and must therefore be dated ca. 732-33.[27] Once the decision to "Byzantinise" southern Italy had been taken, there was no point in leaving the bishoprics there under the control of Rome, and complete dioceses passed under Constantinopolitan authority. These included dioceses in Greece and the Balkans, which had always been Byzantine in name if not in fact, and also Crete. The anomaly by which the pope of Rome could appoint to bishoprics in these purely Greek regions, where Latin was less and less understood, was thus removed, and at a stroke the spiritual as well as the daily life of their inhabitants became the subject of eastern direction. The Balkan dioceses, which had been administered up to this point by a papal vicar based in Thessalonike, included large areas dominated by Slav settlements, where the church had little of its ancient prestige. No great loss can have been felt by the removal of these barely Christian areas. Papal interests in Dalmatia and Istria, at the head of the Adriatic, were not affected, and the patriarchates of Grado and Aquileia remained independent of Constantinople. But Crete,

---

[25] Paul the deacon, *HL* 6.54; cf. Gregory's letter to Antoninus, in *MGH, Ep.*, vol. 3, no. 1, 703.

[26] J. T. Hallenbeck, "The Roman-Byzantine Reconciliation of 728: Genesis and Significance," *BZ* 74 (1981): 29-41, makes too much of Eutychios's diplomatic activity.

[27] *MGH, Ep.*, vol. 5, no. 3, 57 (also Mansi, 13.808D); *MGH, Ep.*, vol. 6, no. 4, 447-51, 553-40 (Pope Nicholas I's letters to Patriarch Photios); M. V. Anastos, "The Transfer of Illyricum, Calabria and Sicily to the Jurisdiction of the Patriarchate of Constantinople in 732-733," *SBN* 9 (1957): 14-31.

however distant from Rome, constituted an important diocese, whose metropolitan ranked high in the eastern ecclesiastical hierarchy. Whenever disputes arose, the pope intervened as supreme arbiter; dissatisfied bishops could appeal to him against the judgement of their metropolitan, and Rome thus benefited from considerable deference and respect.[28]

Similarly, control over the dioceses of Sicily and Calabria increased the pope's standing and authority in areas that were already somewhat hellenised by seventh-century immigration by Greek-speaking peoples from mainland Greece, the Peloponnese, Palestine, and Syria. Since the patrimonies of St. Peter were concentrated in these rich agricultural areas, such direct access was clearly useful to their administration by papal rectors. The right to appoint church leaders also helped to maintain pro-Roman sympathies among the episcopate (one of the privileges claimed by Pope Nicholas I in the ninth century concerned the choice of the metropolitan of Syracuse, chief of the Sicilian bishops).[29] Close links between the island and Rome had been established by the election of several Sicilians to the papacy during the seventh century; the south was recognised as a distinguished educational centre where many ecclesiastics were trained. Its monasteries had greater facilities and frequently more bilingual ability than existed in Rome. All in all, the inclusion of Sicily and Calabria in the orbit of the western church had resulted in increased prestige and theological refinement for the papacy, which now passed to Constantinople.

Gregory III's Appeal to the Franks

In spite of the schism opened by the council of 731, Gregory III considered Byzantine rule one of the facts of life. He maintained a political loyalty to the eastern empire and expected Constantinople to fulfil its duties in the duchy of Rome. But when it became evident that no military force would be sent from Byzantium, the pope tried to make an alliance with the Lombard dukes of Spoleto and Benevento in central Italy that would protect Rome from the Lombard kingdom further north. This strategy proved completely unsuccessful, for it drew the most important Lombard ruler, King Liutprand, into an increasingly hostile relationship with the papacy. When the duchies made common cause with Pope Gregory, Liutprand marched south to threaten Rome. Faced with such a direct challenge and deprived of material aid from the East, the pope was forced to negotiate.

---

[28] J. Herrin, "Crete in the Conflicts of the Eighth Century," in *Aphieroma ston Niko Svorono*, eds. V. Kremmydas et. al. (Rethymno, 1986).

[29] Anastos, "The Transfer of Illyricum, Calabria and Sicily," esp. 23-25.

Gregory did, however, take the unusual step of addressing an appeal to a Transalpine ruler, Charles Martel, leader of the Franks.[30]

As the protector of Boniface in his missionary work, Charles was valued by the papacy, despite depredations of ecclesiastical property and a high-handed manner with church benefices. In the first letter of 739 sent to the *"subregulus"* and *"excellentissimus filius,"* Gregory stressed the spiritual advantages that would accrue to Charles if he came to the aid of the besieged church of Rome.[31] On Judgement Day, St. Peter would not forget this Christian action. By implication, a failure to assist the papacy in this world might damage the Frankish ruler's chances of salvation in the next. It was a powerful combination of promises and veiled threats, frequently repeated in later correspondence between popes and kings. Although Charles returned the embassy, he offered no immediate assistance; his own policy of alliance with the Lombards of northern Italy preempted any overt move against Liutprand. Gregory appreciated the contact, however, and sent a further letter in 740 restating the needs of Rome, which concluded: "Do not despise my appeal or turn deaf ears to my entreaty, that the Prince of the Apostles may not shut the heavenly Kingdom against you."[32] In contrast with Constantinople's silent refusal to take positive steps, Charles was a power to be reckoned with. And in the face of Lombard aggression, the papacy had recognised its weakness and had conceived of the possibility of seeking aid from Francia. This unexpected change of tactic perhaps indicated to both parties the seriousness of conditions in central Italy.

RELATIONS BETWEEN ROME AND CONSTANTINOPLE
UNDER POPE ZACHARIAS (741-52)

When Gregory III died in December 741, King Liutprand was again at the gates of Rome and neither the Byzantines nor the Franks seemed likely to send forces to relieve the city. Yet his successor, Zacharias, opened nego-

---

[30] Schieffer, *Winfrid-Bonifatius*, 172, claims that Boniface suggested the move.

[31] *CC*, no. 1 (476-77); cf. Noble, *Republic of St. Peter*, 45-46, emphasising the desperate situation in Rome and papal use of the keys of St. Peter's tomb, a gift greatly appreciated in Francia; E. Caspar, *Pippin und die römische Kirche* (Berlin, 1914, reprinted Darmstadt, 1973), 1-9.

[32] *CC*, no. 2 (477-79); the Lombard taunt, "Let Charles . . . come with the army of the Franks and help you and rescue you from my hand!" was also reported (477.37-478.1) as if to increase pressure on Charles; cf. the later use of the same device by Pope Stephen II. The Frankish reaction as recorded in ch. 22 of the *Continuation* of the Chronicle of Fredegar, ed. J. M. Wallace-Hadrill, *The Fourth Book of the Chronicle of Fredegar* (London, 1960), 96, included the claim that Gregory wished to place Rome under Charles's protection. This seems to be an interpretation based on later events experienced by the author, who was writing in 768.

tiations and succeeded in forging a twenty-year alliance with the Lombard monarch. In return for a commitment not to ally with the dukes of Spoleto and Benevento, Zacharias obtained the return of four towns recently captured (though this was only made good by another personal intervention at Interamna in 742).[33] Despite this triumph of Roman diplomacy, the new pope did not ignore relations with Constantinople. Following customary practice, he sent legates to the eastern capital after his election, with his synodical declaration of orthodoxy (that is, iconophile belief).[34] Leo III had died in July 741, leaving his son Constantine as heir apparent and victor with him in a decisive defeat of Muslim forces at Akroïnon the previous year. Yet Artabasdos had claimed the throne against his brother-in-law, perhaps in accordance with the alliance that dated back nearly 30 years to the uncertain period before Leo's accession. It seems likely that both contenders had announced their rights to exercise imperial rule to the authorities of the West, Byzantine administrators, and Roman pontiffs alike. Similarly, both appealed to Caliph Walid for support.[35] Western reaction to this disputed succession is not recorded, but clearly Zacharias had to proceed with caution. Constantine had been acclaimed co-emperor in 720 and was evidently the legitimate heir, but Artabasdos established himself in Constantinople and appeared to have the upper hand in 742-43. The papal envoys probably delivered Zacharias's synodica to Patriarch Anastasios and then returned to Rome to report on the situation. Until a clear outcome could be predicted, the pope advised prudence.[36]

But it appears that he may have sent another legate back to the East with a proposal, *aliam suggestionem*, which was to be presented to the eventual winner.[37] This second embassy probably arrived in 743, waited, and then witnessed the end of Artabasdos's revolt in November, when Constantine regained control of the capital and proclaimed his undisputed authority. Once re-established, the emperor sought out the papal envoy and received Zacharias's proposal. The text of the *Liber pontificalis* continues:

And then because the most blessed pontiff had demanded, he [Constantine] arranged the donation in documents of two estates [*massae*] which were called Nym-

---

[33] *LP* 1.427-29; Noble, *Republic of St. Peter*, 51-52, stresses the independent character of Zacharias's negotiations in the name of the republic of St. Peter, and the extent of territory returned "to the blessed Peter, prince of the apostles."

[34] *LP* 1.432.

[35] Theophanes, 416.

[36] P. Speck, *Artabasdos, der rechtgläubige Vorkämpfer der göttlichen Lehren* (Bonn, 1981), 115-18.

[37] *LP* 1.432; O. Bertolini, "I rapporti di Zaccaria con Costantino V e con Artavasdo nel racconto del biografo del papa e nella probabile realtà storica," *Archivio della Società romana di storia patria* 78 (1955): 1-21

pha and Normia, then part of the state domain [*publici iuris*], to be held in perpetuity [*iure perpetuo*] by the same most holy and blessed pope of the Roman church. (*LP* 1.433.6-8)

It is not clear whether Zacharias had demanded these two estates as compensation for the loss of the papal patrimonies or whether he demanded the patrimonies back again. But obviously Constantine V acted in response to a papal request; he did not simply offer the donation. The question of icon veneration was not raised—it is never mentioned in the *Life* of Zacharias—nor was the fact that the churches of Rome and Constantinople were effectively in schism.

Enhanced Papal Authority in Italy

Although Pope Zacharias was probably not aware of the relative strengths of the two parties in the civil war, he had tried to keep on good terms with both until Constantine's victory became evident, and was rewarded with properties in central Italy and an improvement in Roman-Constantinopolitan relations, iconoclasm notwithstanding. Constantine clearly wished to muster support from all quarters, while Zacharias was anxious to persuade the emperor of Rome's dangerous weaknesses and needs. The pope therefore persisted in his predecessor's policy of political loyalty to the East in combination with criticism of its theology, and the emperor took conciliatory steps to strengthen Rome's resources. But as no additional military aid was immediately forthcoming, Zacharias had to continue his diplomatic manoeuvres in Italy. These evidently commanded great respect in Ravenna, for in 743 the exarch and archbishop of the city begged him to intervene with the Lombards on their behalf. Liutprand had attacked the exarchate and seized the castle of Cesena, which controlled the route south to Spoleto. The pope set out to Ravenna and was welcomed by Eutychios at the border of the now-reduced exarchate.[38] Zacharias later went on to the Lombard capital, Pavia, where he managed to persuade Liutprand to restore Cesena to the exarchate and withdraw from occupied territories.[39] In these negotiations the exarch took no part but empowered the pope to act for him. Zacharias made one more ambassadorial journey during his pon-

---

[38] *LP* 1.429-30, records the seizure of Cesena followed by Pope Zacharias's journey to Ravenna and Pavia. The novelty of this intervention is highlighted by the fact that the exarch and people of Ravenna came out to greet the pope. Receptions of this type normally took place at Rome, where the pope went out a stipulated distance to welcome the exarch with acclamations.

[39] *LP* 1.430-31; "*ad partem reipublicae*" is much more likely to refer to the exarchate under imperial government than the duchy of Rome now increasingly under papal control, but see Noble, *Republic of St. Peter*, 31-35.

tificate, to Perugia in 749, then besieged by Liutprand's successor, King Ratchis, and again succeeded in forcing a withdrawal.[40]

Ever since the time of Pope Leo I, bishops of Rome had been involved in such activity, so it should be seen as an integral part of episcopal duty. But with Gregory III and Zacharias, a distinct development is noticeable: their enhanced authority in central Italian politics. This is clear not only from their increasing diplomatic success but also from their ability to replace official representatives of the empire. In contrast with Pope Gregory I's efforts to protect Rome from Lombard attack, which provoked the anger of both Ravenna and Constantinople, the efforts of eighth-century pontiffs were particularly requested—the roles had been effectively reversed as the powers of both emperor and exarch paled in comparison with the papacy's. While this shift reflects the decline of Byzantine military strength in the West and Lombard determination to take advantage of it, Rome had assumed a leading position. And this is a political position based partly, but not solely, on moral standing. Though the Lombard adoption of orthodoxy at the council of Pavia (698) may have elevated papal authority at the regal and ducal courts of Italy, devotion to the see of St. Peter did not override political ambitions. King Liutprand and local leaders of Spoleto and Benevento still cherished plans of territorial aggrandisement that threatened the exarchate and duchy of Rome. So when eighth century pontiffs negotiated with these opponents to maintain the independence of the duchy of Rome, they could not rely on catholic respect alone. Political arguments, diplomatic skills, and the use of extravagant gifts were necessary to convince the Lombards. These were the traditions deployed in novel fashion by Gregory III and Zacharias to obtain the restoration of estates and fortified sites to the Apostles Peter and Paul when imperial military forces failed.

Papal Relations with the Franks

Another important diplomatic event of Zacharias's pontificate concerned the Franks. The question on which Pippin, Charles Martel's son and mayor of the palace, sent his chaplain Fulrad to consult the pope turned on his own authority in Francia. Is it right, he asked, that the man who takes responsibility for government and rules should not be called king? And Zacharias confirmed that this was not right, thus sanctioning the replacement of Merovingian power by the new Carolingian dynasty.[41] This was

---

[40] *LP* 1.434; King Ratchis became a monk. The Lombards then elected Aistulf as king (July 749).

[41] Frankish sources: *Fredegarii Constinuatio*, ch. 33; *Royal Frankish Annals*, a.749; cf. *Annals of Einhard*, a.749. No mention is made of the event in papal sources.

not a matter of recent controversy in Francia. For many years the palace mayors had been kings in all but name. After the death of Theuderic IV (737), Charles Martel reigned alone, and was addressed by Pope Gregory III as *subregulus* "sub-king," "under-king." Pippin had found it expedient to withdraw Childeric III from a monastery to fill the regal position in 743, but there was little doubt that "the Merovingian blood royal was in very short supply."[42] Zacharias therefore gave ecclesiastical cover to a situation recognized as unsatisfactory by the great majority of Frankish nobles. In 751, Pippin was elected king by the nobility, anointed by the bishops, and enthroned. Zacharias's legate, Boniface, may have assisted at the ceremony, although there is no direct evidence that the pope particularly requested him to ensure that papal support would be fully acknowledged by the new dynasty.[43]

Since Pippin's main personal base within Francia was concentrated on Austrasia, the northeast region in which his ancestor, Arnulf of Metz, had accumulated property four generations earlier, one of the immediate benefits of his election as king lay in the acquisition of estates, villas, and monasteries previously controlled by the Merovingians in Neustria and Burgundy. Palaces such as Compiègne, Servais, Quierzy, Ver, Lille, and Soissons passed into his hands, greatly extending his resources. Paris, one centre of Merovingian power, was allowed to decline, even though the famous monastery of St. Denis to the north was greatly favoured by Pippin and his family. Even as king, however, he had no fixed residence, but moved regularly throughout his territories with the entire court, exploiting the products of varied estates and loyal supporters. Diversity rather than unity characterised his kingdom, which had consistently revealed tendencies towards local autonomy, regionalism, and particularism, even under the personal rule of Charles Martel (737-41).[44]

Apart from his family possessions and the support of "all the great men," who had taken an oath of allegiance to him in 751, Pippin derived an important element in his regal authority from the church. Rome had been in contact with previous palace mayors and knew them to be effective rulers, so Zacharias's authorisation of the office of king followed naturally. While the papacy undoubtedly gave added legitimacy to the change, local eccle-

[42] R. McKitterick, *The Frankish Kingdoms Under the Carolingians, 751-987* (London, 1983), 30; Noble, *Republic of St. Peter*, 65-66, on the fragility of the Frankish kingdom at this time.

[43] McKitterick, *The Frankish Kingdoms*, 35-38; Noble, *Republic of St. Peter*, 68-71, and the Frankish sources cited in note 41 above.

[44] McKitterick, *The Frankish Kingdoms*, 37-38; E. Ewig, "Résidence et capitale pendant le haut moyen âge," *RH* 230 (1963): 25-72, esp 49-54, reprinted in *Spätantikes und fränkisches Gallien*, vol. 1 (Munich, 1976).

siastical support was also essential. The bishops and senior clerics who had assisted at the ritual of unction endowed the monarch with a quasi-spiritual power—among them, Chrodegang, bishop of Metz since 742, and possibly the Anglo-Saxon missionary, Boniface, as well as the abbots of the most important monasteries, who frequently acted as royal advisers, ambassadors, and administrators.[45] Both Boniface and Chrodegang in different ways embodied the eighth-century devotion to St. Peter and had recourse to the spiritual authority of Rome to further their work. But they represented two separate strands in the Christian tradition, which together enriched ecclesiastical experience and standing in the Francia of Charles Martel and Pippin.

Missionary Activity and Church Reform

Since the 720s, Boniface had worked to extend the Christian faith to pagan lands in northeast Europe, especially among the Saxons and Frisians who lived beyond Austrasian control and regularly disrupted it. Pope Gregory II and subsequent pontiffs down to Stephen II supported and praised his achievements, as well as recommending them to the Austrasian mayors of the palace. Charles Martel and Carloman, Pippin's brother, had patronised and protected Boniface and his disciples, who seemed to prefer the challenge of an insecure existence among non-believers to the more settled life of bishops and abbots within an established church. Nonetheless, in true Anglo-Saxon and Irish tradition they succeeded in founding monasteries, winning converts, spreading the Gospel through wide areas, while insisting on the high standards and rigorous asceticism associated with their background. The foundation of Fulda, an outpost of the faith far to the east of Mainz, symbolised not only this successful missionary activity, but also its close connection with Rome, for like St. Augustine in Kent, Boniface regularly consulted the apostolic see as to the best means of proceeding.[46] It is perhaps not suprising, therefore, that he reported most unfavourably to Gregory II, Gregory III, and Zacharias on standards among the Frankish clergy. No doubt these were low, but in addition Boniface came from an environment intolerant of laxity, where devotion to the cause might well demand the ultimate sacrifice of death as a martyr (as it did in his case).[47]

[45] *Fredegarii Continuatio*, ch. 33, on consecration "by the bishops"; J. L. Nelson, "Symbols in Context: Rulers' Inauguration Rituals in Byzantium and the West in the Early Middle Ages," in D. Baker, ed., *The Orthodox Churches and the West, SCH* 13 (1976), 97-119; R. Schneider, *Königswahl und Königserhebung im Frühmittelalter* (Stuttgart, 1972).

[46] Schieffer, *Winfrid-Bonifatius*, 222-25, 226-67, 274-75: J. M. Wallace-Hadrill, *The Frankish Church* (Oxford, 1983), 150-58.

[47] Wallace-Hadrill, *The Frankish Church*, 158-61; McKitterick, *The Frankish Kingdoms*, 53-55.

In contrast, Chrodegang had been educated at the court of Charles Martel and served as *referendarius*, a senior lay official, before he took holy orders and became a bishop. With an insider's view of Frankish problems, he undertook the task of reforming clerical discipline, education, and practice, an equally challenging if less dangerous task. His efforts were concentrated mainly within the Frankish realm in close conjunction with both Roman advice and regal support. It included the foundation (with relics from Rome) of an exemplary monastery at Gorze (from which Gegenbach and Lorsch were established in the 760s); the composition of a rule for the cathedral clergy at Metz (the *Regula canonicorum* of 755), and the more uniform regulation of liturgical practices in accordance with papal traditions.[48] While both Boniface and Chrodegang held reforming church councils that significantly improved internal standards, in the 740s and 750s respectively, it was largely under Chrodegang's influence that in 746 a combined lay and clerical gathering decided to appeal to Pope Zacharias for advice on a number of contentious issues—topics such as the subordination of lower clergy to metropolitan and episcopal control, Christian marriage, the conduct of nuns, and the control exercised by lay patrons over their own church foundations, which vexed all eighth-century churchmen. Zacharias's lengthy reply indicates one of the most obvious means whereby Roman interpretations and traditions entered the Frankish church. Canons of past councils and of the holy apostles are cited together with decrees of Popes Leo I and Innocent I, to provide a secure basis for judging errors and establishing rules.[49] Although Zacharias was severely critical of Frankish customs, his advice appears to have been accepted. In the following year, a synod of bishops under Boniface, then titled *"legatus Germanicus catholice apostolice Romane aecclesiae"* (legate of the catholic apostolic church of Rome for Germany), sent its declaration of obedience to Rome, promising to maintain orthodoxy and ecclesiastical unity while accepting the ultimate authority of St. Peter and his successors.[50] A strong reforming party had thus emerged within the Frankish church before Zacharias gave his blessing to Pippin's assumption of regal power.

While the papacy thus succeeded in influencing developments north of the Alps, it was powerless to prevent a final Lombard triumph in Italy. Despite Zacharias's courageous negotiations, King Aistulf gained control of

[48] E. Ewig, "Saint Chrodegang et la réforme de l'église franque," in *Saint Chrodegang* (Metz, 1967), 25-53, reprinted in *Spätantikes und fränkisches Gallien*, vol. 2 (Munich, 1979); C. Vogel, "S. Chrodegang et les débuts de la romanisation du culte en pays franc," in *Saint Chrodegang*, 91-109.

[49] *CC*, no. 3 (479-87); Wallace-Hadrill, *The Frankish Church*, 164-65.

[50] *Concilia*, pt. 1, no. 6, 46-48, 48-50, reveals the acceptance of Zacharias's guidance and the subjection of the Frankish church to Rome.

Ravenna by July 751, adding the prize so long sought after to his territorial base. During the campaign, Byzantine officials in the West were notable for their absence or lack of loyalty—the last exarch, Eutychios, went over to the Lombards and gained a safe retirement in Naples. The pope found no support in his lonely opposition to Lombard expansion, and in March 752 he died.[51] Yet the consummate skill with which he delayed the process, thus preserving and strengthening surviving Roman territories, left the papacy in a not-desperate situation. In particular, Zacharias's administration of the patrimonies of St. Peter and his development of *domuscultae*, new farms established on abandoned land, provided greater resources for the city and churches of Rome. His building activity had also been directed to the refurbishing of the Lateran palace, begun by Gregory III, which was redecorated in mosaic. And in the field of theology, Zacharias was responsible for commissioning, if not executing, the Greek translation of Gregory the Great's *Dialogues*.[52] As the last in a long line of popes of eastern origin, this effort was a more than worthy conclusion to nearly 70 years of Greek influence in Rome.

THE REIGN OF CONSTANTINE V (741-75)

Meanwhile, among the Greeks of the East, Constantine V was trying to consolidate his own authority after two-and-a half years of civil war. The first years of his personal rule were marked by continuing hostilities with the Arabs and by an extremely severe outbreak of bubonic plague. The disease had spread from Sicily and Calabria to Greece and the Aegean islands, carried presumably by rats on ships. Its effects in Constantinople were devastating and have been held responsible by modern historians for reducing the metropolitan population to an all-time low.[53] In graphic descriptions, the horrific results of this attack are stressed by later chroniclers, but in addition to the usual problem of insufficient living to bury the dead, they record that as the aqueduct of Valens had ceased to function in the seventh century, there was no regular supply of fresh water in the city; cisterns were used for mass graves, and people suffered hallucinations that increased the

[51] *LP* 1.441 (a very vague allusion only, and recorded under Pope Stephen II, rather than Zacharias); *Chronicon salernitanum*, ch. 2, ed. U. Westerbergh (Lund, 1956), 4. Cf. O. Bertolini, *Roma di fronte a Bisanzio e ai Longobardi* (Rome, 1941), 498-99.

[52] *LP* 1.435; J.-M. Sansterre, *Les moins grecs et orientaux à Rome aux époques byzantine et carolingienne*, 2 vols. (Brussels, 1983), 1:139-40, 153-56; Noble, *Republic of St. Peter*, 58-59, claims Zacharias completed the creation of an independent papal republic begun by Gregory II and III. The pope's attention to the city's basic needs may, however, have been of greater importance.

[53] Theophanes, 422-23; C. Mango, *Byzantium: The Empire of New Rome* (London, 1980), 78-81.

confusion and violence. In Greece also, the plague left such a trail of deaths that Slavs from the north were able to infiltrate and settle on abandoned lands.[54] After two years (745-46) it began to decline and, unlike the attacks of the mid-sixth century, apparently did not recur. So despite its very harsh consequences, by the 750s the task of reconstruction could commence.

While the plague was taking its toll in the capital, the young emperor was campaigning annually against the Arabs in an effort to secure the eastern frontiers. Continuing his father's policies, he was concerned to revitalise Byzantine *thema* forces as well as to strengthen those units stationed in the capital who served as an imperial guard (the *tagmata*). In 745 (or 746), an expedition into northern Syria captured Germanikeia and Doulichia, while the governor of the Kibyrreot fleet checked an Arab attack on Cyprus.[55] The northeastern frontier was then secured with the help of an Armenian ally, Kouchan, who assisted in the lengthy siege of Melitene and the surrender of Claudias and Theodosioupolis, all major border fortresses. At Melitene, once the population had been evacuated, the fortifications were razed and the city completely destroyed to prevent its use as an enemy base. Similarly, Constantine devastated the region around Arsamosata so that it could no longer protect Arab operations against the empire.[56]

These activities of the late 740s and early 750s were largely successful and brought a period of relative freedom from Muslim counter-attack to the frontier areas. They were greatly assisted by dissension within the Arab world, which came to a head in the Abbasid revolt against Umayyad authority in 750. Once the new caliph, Abul Abbas, had established his centre further east and south, Damascus was rapidly eclipsed and with it the Syrian stronghold of anti-Byzantine campaigns. His new capital, Baghdad, constructed in the 760s, was carefully planned and rapidly became a very populous capital city.[57] It was not the first time that Muslim division had permitted imperial consolidation. But in addition, Constantine took advantage of the lull in hostilities to develop Byzantine military strengths and to impose new settlement policies on the civilian population. By these two means, he deployed the resources available in a most effective manner.

[54] Theophanes, 423-24; Nikephoros, 62-63.

[55] Theophanes, 422, 424; Nikephoros, 62, 64; J. F. Haldon, *Byzantine Praetorians* (Bonn, 1984), 228-35.

[56] Theophanes, 427; Nikephoros, 65; R.-J. Lilie, *Die byzantinische Reaktion auf die Ausbreitung der Araber* (Munich, 1976), 164-65, 245-47.

[57] The Abbasids took their name from the Prophet's uncle, Abbas, and claimed descent from him, I. Goldziher, *Introduction to Islamic Theology and Law* (Princeton, 1981), 44-47; P. Crone, *Slaves on Horses: The Evolution of the Islamic Polity* (Cambridge, 1980), 46-48, 62-65; Theophanes, 424-26 (garbled accounts that note the decline of Damascus, 425).

Internal Reorganisation

Although the reorganisation of military forces is not recorded until the mid-760s the emperor evidently started work on it much earlier. The main objective of his overall plan was to curtail the powerful *thema* of Opsikion, which Artabasdos had commanded during the civil war. As noted above, this area close to the western coast of Asia Minor had always served as a reserve of military strength for the capital and had developed firm military traditions exploited by Constantine's rival over a long period. It was to prevent a recurrence of such a challenge that the emperor demoted the *thema* in the hierarchy of military command, elevating the Thrakesion force instead. The count of Opsikion appears to have been reduced in rank and status and a new officer of the same rank, called *topoteretes*, was appointed as second-in-command, to make sure that no further plots were hatched against the emperor.[58] Later the whole area of Opsikion was divided to create three smaller units: a reduced Opsikion, Boukellarion, and Optimaton. At the same time, Constantine reformed the crack troops based in the capital and western Asia Minor, the *scholai* and *exkoubitors*, to create an effective imperial field army under his own control. The new post of *domestikos ton scholon* (general of the Schools) was established to train and direct this centralised and more professional fighting force.[59] As a court official based in the capital, he was under constant imperial surveillance and had to work closely with Constantine in constructing a military unit of impeccable loyalty. The emperor thus ensured that the *tagmata* of Constantinople could be rapidly mobilised for action and could be counted on in the implementation of imperial policy. With these two elements guaranteed, his own position became much more secure.

As regards the civilian population of the eastern regions, Constantine imposed another radical change, one also related to the reorganisation of military forces. In his policy of rendering the border areas uninhabitable, the emperor removed the people of Germanikeia and Doulichia to Byzantium. Among them were many Syrian Monophysites, who spread their heretical beliefs in Thrace. Similarly, after the capture of Melitene in 751, the Arab inhabitants taken prisoner were dispersed in other frontier cities, and the Christians (largely of Syrian or Armenian extraction) were transported to the western half of the empire and settled in Thrace.[60] Such large-scale movements of population had taken place before but never in quite such a systematic fashion: since the fortress of Melitene was flattened, there could

---

[58] Haldon, *Byzantine Praetorians*, 205-210, 212-14.

[59] Ibid., 222-27, 228-32.

[60] Theophanes, 422, 429; Nikephoros, 65, 66; A. Lombard, *Constantin V, Empereur des Romains* (Paris, 1902), 33-36.

be no question of a return—the people resettled in Europe were uprooted and set down in a completely new environment. There was, however, one similarity between their old and new homelands: both were frontier regions prone to insecurity and enemy activity. The chief difference lay in the substitution of Bulgar for Arab raiders. On the other hand, Thrace had not been regularly devastated; it was a fertile wheat-growing area where the new inhabitants could farm and raise flocks. Although threatened by Bulgar attacks after 755, when Constantine refused to pay the customary tribute, the transplanted population probably had an easier life in the West than on the war-torn eastern frontier.

Another aspect of Constantine's civilian policy is visible in his determination to restore the dominance of Constantinople after the plague. As the capital had been the sole urban centre capable of resisting the general decline of cities noticeable from the sixth century onwards, such an effort was required for the economic, social, and ceremonial life of the empire. In the 750s, the metropolitan population was increased by forced resettlement; inhabitants of central Greece (from the *thema* of Hellas), the Aegean islands, and parts of southern Peloponnesos (and even Sicily?) were moved to Constantinople.[61] A decade later it was necessary to rebuild the Valens aqueduct, which brought water supplies from distant sources to the capital. For this task construction workers were summoned from all parts of the empire, including builders and plasterers from Asia and Pontos, potters, other ceramic craftsmen, and workers from Hellas, the islands, and Thrace.[62] Whether they were all allowed to return after successfully completing the restoration seems very unlikely, as their skills were probably in demand in the metropolis. Although there is little evidence for secular building at this time, the concentration of imperial attention on Constantinople and the very gradual beginnings of an economic revival combined to increase such activity in the capital. And from the limited archaeological record, ecclesiastical construction seems to have been centered in the capital.

Constantine's Patronage of Art

Although artistic policy under Leo III and Constantine V before the 750s is barely recorded, the surviving evidence suggests that both emperors had decided to elevate the life-saving symbol of the Cross in place of iconic representation. This did not involve the destruction of icons, merely the more public use of another equally holy and meaningful Christian image. Leo III displayed the cross on steps instead of his own imperial portrait on the obverse of the new silver coin, the *miliaresion*, with an inscription on the

[61] Theophanes, 429.
[62] Ibid., 440; Nikephoros, 75-76.

reverse.[63] (There would be no return to the bust of Christ used by Justinian II until the "Triumph of Orthodoxy" in 843.) After a severe earthquake in 740, which destroyed many monuments in the capital as well as a section of the walls, the church of St. Irene was rebuilt and its apse decorated with a large jewelled Cross on a gold ground, with verses from Psalm 65 around the arch. From traces of similar monumental Crosses in St. Sophia of Constantinople, St. Sophia of Thessalonike (where the same text was used), and the Koimesis church of the Virgin at Nicaea, it is clear that this constituted the general scheme adopted.[64] Unfortunately there is no firm indication as to the date of the changes, but it seems reasonable to suppose that they followed the redecoration of St. Irene. In the 760s, however, there were still iconic pictures in the patriarchal palace in Constantinople, which were then altered to crosses, so the process must have been a slow and gradual one.[65]

It is important to note that redecoration occurred. Ecclesiastical art did not cease even when iconoclasm became official and when the destruction of artefacts with figural representation was sanctioned (by the council of 754). Icon painters were obviously directed towards different styles of artistic production such as fresco decoration; new churches were constructed and adorned with suitable iconoclast ornamentation. Far from simply destroying art, iconoclast rulers and bishops patronised new forms and encouraged the use of the Cross and non-human patterns of decoration, such as the vegetal and floral designs preserved in image-free Islamic monuments of the late seventh and eighth centuries.[66]

Similarly, it may have been under iconoclast patronage that some of the most spectacular surviving Byzantine silks were produced. While these hangings are notoriously difficult to date, the fact that silk production continued during the eighth century and that certain silks depict secular subjects known to have been favoured by Constantine V suggests that he may

---

[63] DOC, III(i), plates II and III, type 22 onwards; cf. S. Gero, Byzantine Iconoclasm During the Reign of Leo III (Louvain, 1973), 113-26; cf. idem, Byzantine Iconoclasm During the Reign of Constantine V (Louvain, 1977), 162-64.

[64] W. S. George, The Church of Saint Eirene at Constantinople (London, 1912), 5-6, 48-51, 54, and plate 17; R. Cormack, "The Arts During the Age of Iconoclasm," in A. Bryer and J. Herrin, eds., Iconoclasm (Birmingham, 1977), 35-44, esp. 35-37, 41.

[65] Nikephoros, 76; cf. R. Cormack and E. Hawkins, "The Mosaics of St. Sophia at Istanbul: The Rooms Above the South West Vestibule and the Ramp," DOP 31 (1977): 177-251.

[66] Mansi, 13.427C-D; canon 7 of the council of 787 orders that iconoclast churches founded without relics should be reconsecrated with them. Cormack, "The Arts During Iconoclasm," 44, concludes that it was imperial patronage that marked the iconoclast period.

have encouraged their production.[67] These subjects include scenes from the Hippodrome—charioteers racing, the imperial quadriga (of four horses pulling a chariot), wild beast fights, and animal tamers—and the depiction of unusual animals, frequently displayed to the public during Hippodrome events—elephants—or imaginary beasts. Several silks preserved in the West reveal these very complex secular scenes and may have originated in the Byzantine capital. The purple imperial quadriga silk that served as Charles the Great's shroud is one of the most outstanding; others include the Vatican silk of an animal tamer with a wild beast (the so-called "Samson" silk), the Gilgamesh silk at Sens, and a number of fragments of elephant silks.[68] As Constantine instructed that scenes depicting his favourite charioteer should be displayed in the redecorated Blachernai church, and continued the traditional use of silks as diplomatic gifts and as partial payment for the ransom of Byzantine prisoners of war, his association with both the medium and the subjects employed is clear.[69] But there were many other centres of silk production in the eighth-century Mediterranean world, notably the ancient Sasanian silk workshops and those of Christian origin in Alexandria and Syria, which continued in production after the Arab conquest.[70] And silks were highly prized in the West, where the silkworm remained unknown for many centuries. Until silks of Byzantine manufacture can be distinguished from Islamic ones and more securely dated, it is impossible to be confident about the origins of those preserved in countless western cathedral treasuries. Nonetheless, iconoclast patronage and Constantinopolitan production may account for some of the eighth-century examples.

The Theological Development of Byzantine Iconoclasm

Since there is no record of any iconoclast activity or debate between 730 and ca. 752-53, it is impossible to reconstruct the history of Byzantine icons in this period. Constantine V's views on the image question were, however, clarified in the early 750s when he ordered that meetings (*silentia*) should

[67] The evidence of *kommerkiarioi* seals confirms that a tight imperial control was exercised over the production and sale of silks, see M. F. Hendy, *Studies in the Byzantine Monetary Economy c. 300-1450* (Cambridge, 1985), 630-31.

[68] W. F. Volbach, *Early Decorative Textiles* (London, 1969), 78-80, 87-121 and plates 48, 55, 56, 60; but see also the doubts expressed by H. Wentzel on the dating of these and other Byzantine silks, "Das byzantinische Erbe der ottonischen Kaiser: Hypothesen über den Brautschatz der Theophano," *Aachener Kunstblätter des Museumsvereins* 43 (1972): 11-96, esp. 19-37.

[69] *Life* of St. Stephen the Younger, *PG* 100, 1120; Nikephoros, 76.

[70] M. Lombard, *Les textiles dans le monde musulman* (Paris, 1978), 12-16, 93-95, 101-103; cf. Volbach, *Early Decorative Textiles*.

be held in all cities of the empire. The nature of these gatherings is probably reflected in a dialogue preserved in one document called "The Advice of the Old Man Concerning Holy Icons," which was recorded by an eyewitness, Theosebes.[71] Here an iconoclast bishop, Cosmas, questions an elderly monk, George, who was opposed to the denigration of images. In the second section their argument summarises the issues at stake between the old and new schools of thought.

Cosmas attacks the iconophile justification of icon veneration as a form of resistance to divinely inspired imperial decrees. These must be obeyed because Constantine is the true imitator of Christ and destroyer of idols. His views are shared by the entire Senate and its leaders.[72] The battle is one against idolatry because representations of Christ, the Virgin, and the Saints are impiously venerated. Idolatry is a grave sin condemned both in the Old and New Testaments, and this written proscription must be obeyed.[73] (This last charge is aimed against the belief that icon veneration is an established though unwritten tradition in the church.) Against this assault George appeals to the *imperial* tradition of erecting statues of Christ, which is said to go back to Constantine I. He cites unrecorded traditions, the apocryphal stories of images of Christ such as that associated with King Abgar.[74] Cosmas protests that witnesses from canonical sources must be produced; George obliges by quoting the New Testament emphasis on faith by seeing. He counter-attacks, accusing the iconoclasts of using the testimony of Epiphanios of Salamis, George of Alexandria, and Severos of Antioch, heretical authors, or worse (in the case of Epiphanios), Novatian forgeries. George expresses his amazement that such works should be studied in the imperial palace by Constantine V and his advisers, rather than the writings of the Apostles and Church Fathers.[75]

Throughout the dispute, each side appeals to authority as the key to justification, and each accuses the other of misusing texts and employing unacceptable sources. There is no treatment of the Trinitarian or Christological problems of representing Christ, nor is there any discussion of the eucharistic concept developed by Constantine V. As in the reign of Leo III, the argument remains at rather a low level and is fairly blunt; it turns essentially on the question of "tradition," and the relative authority of Old

[71] B. M. Melioransky, ed., *Nouthesia gerontos peri ton hagion eikonon*, in *Georgii Kipryanin i Ioann Ierusalimlyanin* (St. Petersburg, 1901), v-xxxix. On the *silentia*, see ibid., 67-71; Theophanes, 427; on Theosebes and his teacher, the monk George, see Gero, *Constantine V*, 25-27.

[72] *Nouthesia*, viii, xxviii.

[73] Ibid., ix-x, xx.

[74] Ibid., xxv, xxi-xxii.

[75] Ibid., xxvii-xxviii.

and New Testament "tradition."[76] Whoever has ecclesiastical tradition on his side and can convince the other of it is most likely to "win." Such debates, however, did air the basic issues and could act as a preparation for more sophisticated argumentation. This seems to be the motive behind the meetings organised throughout the empire in the early 750s.

Leo III had taken the first important step in establishing that image veneration was wrong: installing an adherent of the new doctrine as patriarch of Constantinople. Over 20 years later, Leo's son prepared to take the next step, which was to order an official ecclesiastical condemnation. This could only be achieved by an oecumenical council. In the preparation of this council, Constantine's commitment to iconoclasm became apparent for the first time. As we have seen, the study of relevant texts was already being undertaken in the imperial palace at the time of Cosmas's debate with George. At the emperor's orders, imperial officials were assisting ecclesiastical authorities in combing the Bible and patristic sources for authoritative condemnation of icons as man-made objects, no more than wood and paint, and certainly not worthy of true veneration.[77] Many of these citations later formed an iconoclast florilegium.

A further stimulus to the development of iconoclast theology was provided by the emperor himself. Constantine composed a series of tracts called *Enquiries (Peuseis)*, devoted to particular aspects.[78] There may have been 13 originally, though only two survive. The first attacks the concept of a true representation of Christ on the grounds that a true image must be of the same substance as the original, since Christ's divine nature cannot be circumscribed or in any way depicted, and the human cannot be separated from the divine: He can not be represented in an image. The idea that the "theandric" Christ (i.e. God and Man) can be delineated is therefore a theological impossibility.[79] The second proposes a new concept of the true image of Christ, which is said to be embodied in the Eucharist. As a symbol of the sacrifice made on behalf of humanity and the Resurrection achieved by it, the Eucharist is a true representation of Christ, which all should worship. Like the Cross, it recalls the Human Christ without sublimating the Divine and thus preserves the mysterious union between both the Saviour's

---

[76] Throughout the *Nouthesia*, iconoclast reliance on the Old Testament prohibition of making and worshipping graven images is condemned as Judaising by iconophiles, who stress the entirely new situation created by the Incarnation. Claims for the ancient use of Christian icons in the church tend, however, to rely on unwritten traditions, a weak link in iconophile argument.

[77] Mansi, 13.268B-C, 269C-D, the iconoclasts refused to revere icons because they were unconsecrated objects and in no way holy; cf. Gero, *Constantine V*, 78.

[78] G. Ostrogorsky, *Studien zur Geschichte des byzantinischen Bilderstreites* (Breslau, 1929, reprinted Amsterdam, 1964), 7-45; Speck, *Artabasdos*, 245-59.

[79] Gero, *Constantine V*, 41-45.

natures.[80] In these two tracts Constantine advances iconoclast theology to new levels, raising issues not previously discussed and elaborating sophisticated arguments against the iconophiles.

Since most of the evidence for this textual preparation was later systematically destroyed by the victorious icon venerators, we are dependent on fragmentary extracts for our understanding of iconoclast thinking. The chief proof-texts survive only because they were cited and denounced at the iconophile council of 787. This claimed that they were produced on single sheets out of context and were therefore unverifiable and liable to misinterpretation.[81] While the later council went to great lengths to cite iconophile texts from complete manuscripts, sometimes in more than one codex, its own treatment of sources was very similar to the iconoclasts'. The lessons of the Sixth Oecumenical Council of 680-81 had not yet been mastered, and polemic frequently influenced doctrinal purity.

The Council of Hiereia (754)

Patriarch Anastasios died late in 753, and the emperor did not appoint a successor immediately. Orders had already been sent out for a universal church council to gather in the palace of Hiereia near the capital in February 754, and Constantine concentrated on its organisation. According to the much later Life of St. Stephen the Younger, the eastern patriarchs were asked to attend and refused because they understood its purpose.[82] Whether the pope was similarly instructed is unclear; no western source records his knowledge of the council, and there is no indication that the Roman legates who were in Constantinople shortly before had been briefed about it. Therefore, of the five patriarchal sees, the ancient pentarchy, none was represented at the iconoclast council of Hiereia. The see of Constantinople was vacant; the three Easterners refused to attend, and the Roman pontiff was possibly unaware of the gathering.[83]

As many as 338 bishops from the eastern churches are reported to have participated, however, deliberating from 10 February to 8 August 754.[84]

[80] S. Gero, "The Eucharistic Doctrine of the Byzantine Iconoclasm and Its Sources," BZ 68 (1975): 4-22.

[81] Mansi, 13.37B; C. Mango, "The Availability of Books in the Byzantine Empire, A.D. 750-850," in Byzantine Books and Bookmen (Washington, D.C., 1975), 30-31.

[82] Mansi, 13.204A; Theophanes, 427; Life of Stephen the Younger, PG 100, 1118, 1142-46.

[83] Theophanes, 427.33-34; LP 1.442, 444.17-445.1; papal legates accompanied John the silentiarios back to Constantinople in 752, and returned to Rome by September 753. Of the eastern sources familiar with the council of Hiereia, only Michael the Syrian mentions western participation, "from the province of Rome and those of Dalmatia, Hellas, Cilicia, and Sicily," Michael the Syrian, Chronicle 2. 520-21.

[84] Mansi, 13.232E.

At this final session the new patriarch of Constantinople was acclaimed and enthroned; he was a monk, Constantine, previously bishop of Syllaion. The proceedings had been directed by the emperor and his chief theological advisers, Theodosios of Ephesos, Sisinnios of Perge (called Pastillas), and Basil of Pisidia (called Trikkakabes).[85] Although the number of participants seems very large in contrast to the 174 who attended the Sixth Oecumenical Council, Leo III and Constantine V had obviously appointed candidates sympathetic to iconoclasm since 730. Some were rewarded for their support—for example, the iconoclast bishop of Gotthia (in the Crimea), who was translated to the prestigious see of Herakleia (in Thrace).[86] Many felt justified in following the imperial line or simply exercised the traditional economy. When cross-examined in 787 about their support, several pleaded ignorance or claimed that they had been deceived.

In 754, however, the council recorded unanimous agreement in its iconoclast theology, summarised in the final Definition (*Horos*), and its canons against icons.[87] These decrees and the formal anathemas against leading iconophiles—Patriarch Germanos, George of Cyprus, and John of Damascus—were read out in the Forum of Constantine and acclaimed by the inhabitants and troops of the capital.[88] Icons were thus condemned as idols; possession of them or other objects decorated with religious images was to be punished; true veneration was to be reserved for God alone, and iconophile texts were to be burnt. At the same time, the honoured position of the Virgin and her powers of intercession were stressed; Christians were ordered not to destroy churches, only iconic decoration and then only with express permission.[89] There was, apparently, no immediate spontaneous iconoclast activity.

By the council of 754 an essential stage in the alteration of official church dogma was reached, for it was generally recognised that without "universal" ecclesiastical agreement, no "innovation" could be introduced into church "tradition." As the definition of all these terms was open to dispute,

[85] Ibid., 13.1010B-1011B, where they are singled out for special condemnation by Basileios of Ankyra, a former iconoclast, cf. 14.397E-400A; Theophanes, 427. On their names, see Gero, *Constantine V*, 55-56, n. 10.

[86] *AASS*, June, vol. 7, 168.

[87] The *Horos* is preserved in the form in which it was read out at the sixth session of the council of 787, see Mansi, 13.204-354; English translation in Gero, *Constantine V*, 68-94; cf. M. V. Anastos, "The Argument for Iconoclasm as Presented to the Iconoclastic Council of 754," in *Late Classical and Medieval Studies in Honor of A. M. Friend, Jr.* (Princeton, 1954), 177-88.

[88] Theophanes, 428. On the possible identification of George of Cyprus (otherwise unknown) with George the monk of the *Nouthesia*, see Mango, "The Availability of Books," 30.

[89] Mansi, 13.329D, 332B, 332D-E, 345A-B.

each church council had to justify its own use. In this case, the assembled bishops identified themselves as the Seventh Oecumenical Council, argued that icons had never been an ancient tradition of the church, and therefore condemned their veneration and exalted position as an innovation.[90] But these definitions of tradition and innovation, the Council's understanding of the six previous councils, and especially its failure to secure the agreement of the pentarchy, would later form the grounds on which iconophiles and western opponents would both condemn iconoclasm.

The Fall of Ravenna to the Lombards

To publicise the decrees of the council of 754, Constantine ordered that the Definition and anathemas should be read out in annual commemorations.[91] But news of the official adoption of iconoclasm probably spread faster by word of mouth. In the autumn and winter of 754, when western reaction might have been expected, however, none is recorded, for the very good reason that Pope Stephen II was not in Rome. In November 753 he had taken the unprecedented step of making an official visit to the Frankish court. It is now necessary to examine the background to this unparalleled innovation in papal activity, provoked by the fall of Ravenna to the Lombards.

While the exact date of the city's capture remains unknown, the fact that King Aistulf issued an official act dated 7 July 751, at "*Ravenna in palatio*," indicates the change.[92] The chief centre of Byzantine authority in the West for centuries was now part of the Lombard kingdom of northern Italy and served as one of Aistulf's royal residences. In addition to sealing an end to imperial aspirations in what had been the exarchate, the Lombard capture of Ravenna marks a turning point in the history of Europe; it is a crucial pivot upon which the whole future development of the West turns. Not that Byzantine authority was completely removed, for forces loyal to Constantinople remained in Rome, Sicily, and Calabria, as well as Venetia and Istria at the head of the Adriatic, but they were put to no concerted effort to check Aistulf. From the eastern capital, Constantine V could do no more than send an embassy to the Lombard king demanding the return of Ravenna to imperial control.[93] Since Ravenna had for many years been the

[90] Ibid., 13.1010B; 14.205A-B, 209C-D, 349D-E, etc. on the oecumenical character of the council of 754; the third, fourth and fifth parts of the *Horos* deal with icon veneration as an idolatrous innovation, ibid., 14.245-325.

[91] Gero, *Constantine V*, 109, n. 183.

[92] C.-R. Brühl, ed., *Codex Diplomaticus Langobardiae* 3.1, no. 23 (Rome, 1973), 111-15; cf. C. Wickham, *Early Medieval Italy* (London, 1981), 45-46.

[93] Dölger, *Regesten*, no. 312; cf. many later embassies of this character, nos. 313-20. No Byzantine sources record any of these comings and goings.

great prize in Lombard ambitions, this diplomatic opening was doomed to failure. Aistulf had absorbed the duchy of Spoleto into his kingdom; he now commanded the Apennine corridor from Ravenna to Rome and looked forward to unimpeded progress in his domination of Italy.

He embarked on this policy almost immediately, attacking the northern cities of the duchy of Rome. In the apostolic see, Zacharias had died in March 752, and a presbyter named Stephen had been elected, only to die after four days in office. The city population then gathered at the shrine of the Virgin ad Praesepe in the church of St. Maria Maggiore where the deacon Stephen was acclaimed.[94] He came from an established Roman family, had been orphaned and brought up in the Lateran palace with his younger brother Paul. Both were ordained to the Roman diaconate by Zacharias before 744. Stephen's election thus marks a distinct turn away from the seventh- and eighth-century pattern of eastern popes to a reliance on native-born bishops, often of well-known local families. Whether this can be interpreted as a conscious development among the constituent forces involved in papal elections, clergy, army, and people is hard to judge. It certainly does not represent a rejection of the Greek party in Rome, which continued to exercise considerable influence in the life of the city and provided later candidates for the papacy. But the indigenous Roman population may have seen this moment of extreme danger as a time to close ranks behind one of their own, on whom they could rely to put local interests first.[95] If so, they were not disappointed in their choice.

According to the pope's biography in the *Liber pontificalis*, written by a contemporary, Stephen II at first tried the methods used to such effect by Zacharias in his dealings with the Lombards. He sent his brother, the deacon Paul, and Ambrose the *primicerius*, armed with many gifts, to negotiate a truce. They signed an agreement that was supposed to last 40 years, but it was broken after only four months.[96] Another embassy composed of abbots from Benevento was then prepared. At this time an envoy arrived from Constantinople, John the *silentiarios*, bearing two orders, one for the pope and the other for Aistulf, demanding the return of the usurped *"reipublicae loca"* (literally, "places of the republic" by which the empire generally designated what had been imperial territory in the West—the exact meanings attached by the eastern capital and subsequently by the papacy to the term "republic" are difficult to determine). When John failed to persuade the Lombard king to comply with this order, Stephen sent his own legates back to the East beseeching Constantine to send help for the liberation of Rome

[94] *LP* 1.440.

[95] Ibid., *"natione Romanus."*

[96] Ibid., 1.442 (first embassy to Aistulf); the treaty was signed in June and broken in September/October.

and all Italy. This was his first recorded communication with Constantinople, and it made no reference to the new pope's recent election or the
customary exchange of synodica.[97]

It was in this highly insecure situation that the pope organised a new
ritual: in this, the Roman clergy and populace accompanied their bishop
barefoot and with ash on their heads in a procession to St. Maria ad Praesepe, carrying the icon of Christ "not made by human hands." They
chanted prayers for Christian safety and for the death of Christ's enemies.
Every Saturday, similar processions were arranged to the shrines of Sts. Peter and Paul, so that at three major points in the city the local inhabitants
could join a regular appeal for divine intercession against the Lombard
peril.[98] In this public demonstration of iconophile practice, Stephen emphasised Roman antagonism to iconoclasm and extended the use of Rome's
ancient icons in a manner that had been very developed in the East prior to
730. Prayers and faith in icons alone, however, were not going to prevent
Aistulf from trying to realise his projected conquest of the duchy of Rome.

In the words of the papal biographer, "When Stephen realised that no
help would come from the imperial power, he recalled the actions of his
predecessors, Gregory II, Gregory III and Zacharias," who had appealed to
Charles, king of the Franks, and "inspired by divine grace" he sent a secret
message to King Pippin by a Frankish pilgrim.[99] A complete realignment
of political influence in central Italy was thus initiated. Pippin replied favourably to Stephen's appeal and later sent two envoys, Chrodegang of
Metz and Duke Autcharius, to escort the pope on a proposed visit to Francia. Before their arrival, and while the Lombards were capturing Ciccana,
a castle where the Roman church had estates, the Byzantine ambassador
returned to Rome with another instruction. Constantine V now ordered
the pope to negotiate directly with Aistulf as an imperial official, empowered to receive back Ravenna and the cities belonging to it in the emperor's
name.[100] The coincidence of both Frankish and Byzantine missions at the
apostolic see symbolised Stephen's dilemma: should he persist in what had
been a dismal history of Byzantine failure to wring concessions from the
Lombards, and should he accompany the Franks to Pippin, who held out

[97] Ibid.; Paul the deacon, *Continuatio Casinensis* 4 (in *SSRL*, 199). Noble, *Republic of St. Peter*, 72, says that Stephen appealed to the Byzantines "several times" for aid early in 752, but the record of the *Liber pontificalis* is silent on these requests.

[98] *LP* 1.443.

[99] Ibid., 1.444; G. Tangl, "Die Passvorschrift des Königs Ratchis und ihre Beziehung zu den Verhaltnis zwischen Franken und Langobarden vom 6.-8. Jahrhundert," *Quellen und Forschungen aus italienischen Archiven und Bibliotheken* 38 (1958): 1-66, esp. 60-61; L. Levil-lain, "L'avènement de la dynastie carolingienne et les origines de l'état pontifical (749-757)," *Bibliothèque de l'école des chartes* 94 (1933); 225-95, esp. 230.

[100] *LP* 1.445.

the possibility of more effective assistance? Given the past 18 months of military hostilities, his decision to opt for the latter should not surprise us.

So on 14 October 753, after special benedictions for the city, Pope Stephen left Rome accompanied by a great throng of local people, who only turned back at the northern limit of the duchy, 40 miles on the route to Pavia. There both the Byzantine and Frankish envoys added their efforts to the final papal appeal for Aistulf to return the lands illegally assumed. To no avail—the king refused them all. But neither did he accede to the subsequent proposal for Stephen to proceed to Francia. This too was opposed. After further negotiations, however, a somewhat unwilling agreement was given, and on 15 November the papal party left Pavia. It was an impressive gathering of bishops, priests, Roman and clerical officers, including Ambrose (previously ambassador to the Lombards), George of Ostia, and Wilcharius of Nomentanum (both later legates).[101] Although nowhere expressly stated, it seems likely that Stephen had put his brother Paul in charge of the see of St. Peter during this crucial journey.

For the first time ever and in inauspicious and inclement conditions, a bishop of Rome crossed the Alps by the Val d'Aosta and the Great St. Bernard pass, and rested at the famous monastery of St. Maurice (at Agaune), which had been designated as the meeting place.[102] While they waited for Pippin's envoys, Fulrad (now abbot of St. Denis) and Duke Rotardus, the papal entourage may have elaborated the protocol to be observed at what was an unprecedented ceremony. Although Pippin was indebted to the papacy for dynastic legitimacy, there is no evidence that he had much sense of how to handle his relations with the supreme western church leader. Stephen, on the other hand, probably had very clear ideas of his own status and how this should be reflected in his negotiations with the Frankish king. It appears that elements of the papal-regal relationship embodied in the famous forgery, the *Donation of Constantine*, had been settled before the two parties met (although scholars disagree).[103] This historic event took place outside the royal palace of Ponthion (near Châlons) at Epiphany (6 January 754). Pippin had sent his eldest son, Charles, then aged 11, to welcome the pope at Langres, 100 miles to the south, and escort him to the palace. But he himself led Stephen's horse into Ponthion (in the manner ascribed in the *Donation* to Constantine I, who is alleged to have served as Pope Sylvester's squire).[104]

[101] Ibid., 1.445-46; Cf. Noble, *Republic of St. Peter*, 78-80, on the length of stay at Pavia, 10-14 days; Tangl, "Die Passvorschrift," 53-62.

[102] *LP* 1.447; one of Stephen's advisers died at St. Maurice after the very cold and strenuous experience of crossing the Alps at the onset of winter.

[103] On the *Donation*, see pp. 385-87 below. Levillain, "L'avènement de la dynastie carolingienne," 232, indicates the possible significance of the rest at St. Maurice.

[104] *LP* 1.447; *Fredegarii Continuatio*, ch. 36 (p. 104). For a figure of such later impor-

Negotiations Between Pope Stephen and King Pippin (754)

The following day the pope dressed in sackcloth and prostrated himself before the king in an act of supplication. By extending his hand and helping the pontiff to rise, Pippin engaged himself to negotiate some form of protection for the see of St. Peter.[105] But as it was mid-winter and the ecclesiastics had just made a long and tiring journey, he invited them to rest at the monastery of St. Denis. Although neither the *Liber pontificalis* nor the Frankish sources reveal clearly how the alliance was agreed, the major steps consisted of a meeting at the royal palace of Quierzy in April 754 and the consecration of Pippin as king at St. Denis in July, when he and his two sons, Charles and Carloman, were all invested with the title of *patricius Romanorum*, and Queen Bertha was blessed. At this ceremony the nobles were enjoined never to choose a king from another Frankish family because that of Carolus (hence Carolingian) had been honoured by the vicar of St. Peter. Pippin promised to maintain the rights of St. Peter and in particular to restore to the leader of the Apostles those church lands conquered by the Lombards.[106]

In addition, a very significant element of the alliance lay in the spiritual relationship established between the two men. After 754, Pope Stephen invariably refers to Pippin as *"spiritalis compater"* (literally, "spiritual co-father"), Bertha as *"spiritalis comater,"* and their sons as his spiritual sons. This indicates that the bond of *compaternitas*, which united natural and spiritual or godparents at a child's baptism, had been assumed.[107] As the children concerned had probably already been baptised, the ritual by which this shared responsibility was evolved may have related to their anointing as patricians, or to their confirmation. A sacramental bond of a personal

---

tance, it is curious that the precise date of Charles's birth is not known, see K. F. Werner, "Das Geburtsdatum Karls des Grossen," *Francia* 1 (1973): 115-57, where 2 April 742 is proposed; cf. the same author's article, "La date du naissance de Charlemagne," *Bulletin de la Société des Antiquaires de France 1972* (Paris, 1975): 116-42.

[105] *LP* 1.447-48; *Fredegarii Continuatio*, ch. 36 (a contemporary witness); cf. the much later *Chronicon Moissiacense*, 293.1-7; Levillain, "L'avènement de la dynastie carolingienne," 236.

[106] *LP* 1.448; *Royal Frankish Annals*, a.754. On the sources for the St. Denis ceremony, see A. Stoclet, "La 'Clausula de unctione Pippini regis': mises au point et nouvelles hypothèses," *Francia* 8 (1980): 1-42, who proves that the text is most likely to date from the late tenth century (the *Clausula* is translated in B. Pullan, *Sources for the History of Medieval Europe* [Oxford, 1966], 5-8). W. Affeldt, "Untersuchungen sur Königserhebung Pippins," *Frühmittelalterliche Studien* 14 (1980): 95-187. On the meaning of the title *patricius Romanorum*, see Stoclet, "La 'Clausula de unctione Pippini regis'," 26-33; H. Wolfram, *Intitulatio I* (Vienna, 1967), ch. 8; idem, *Intitulatio II* (Vienna, 1973), 19-22; cf. Noble, *Republic of St. Peter*, 278-91.

[107] A. Angenendt, "Das geistliche Bündnis der Päpste mit den Karolingern (754-796)," *HJ* 100 (1980): 1-94, esp. 10-16, 40-43.

character had been initiated, but it was also designed to pass to Pippin's heirs and Stephen's successors. It imposed duties on the papacy that became visible in later arrangements for the Franks to be honoured in St. Peter's, where the pope said prayers for them and for their victories. Pippin further consolidated his new proximity to the apostolic see by sending a gift of an altar table for St. Peter's and also requesting the transference of the relics of St. Petronilla, supposed daughter of the Apostle, from the catacombs into the same basilica. The Carolingians became particularly devoted to the cult of St. Petronilla.[108]

These rituals, both in Francia and later in Rome, had one major aim from the papal point of view: to elevate Pippin's status while binding him more closely to the defence of St. Peter. From the Frankish side, the king swore by the most solemn oaths to fulfil the role of papal protector and gained in prestige and authority from it. Although the agreement is sometimes misleadingly referred to as the "Donation of Quierzy" and records may have been kept by both parties, there was probably no written account of it as such.[109] The novel ceremonies performed by the participants would have created a much greater impression than signatures at the bottom of a contract. Another factor in the arrangements made in 754 concerned potential Lombard hostility, for Aistulf had suspected that the papal visit would produce changes not necessarily to his liking. He had therefore forced Pippin's brother, Carloman, to leave his monastic retreat at Monte Cassino in order to dissuade the Franks from supporting the pope. So in the summer of 754, Pippin had to deal with two proposals from Italy relating to the dominant authorities in the peninsula.[110] Papal consecration and legitimisation of the Carolingians, associated with the spiritual benefits of *compaternitas*, must have influenced his decision to oppose Aistulf and reject his brother's appeal.

Roman Influence in Francia. The pope's presence north of the Alps had other results also: in the field of ecclesiastical reform it strengthened the pro-Roman party in several notable ways. The alliance itself inevitably brought

[108] Ibid., 45-49; cf. Sansterre, *Les moines grecs et orientaux,* 1:159-62, on the growth of the cult of St. Petronilla and other local saints.

[109] L. Saltet, "La lecture d'un texte et la critique contemporaine," *Bulletin de littérature ecclésiastique* 41 (1940): 176-206 and 42 (1941): 61-85; cf. E. Griffe, "Aux origines de l'Etat pontifical," ibid. 53 (1952): 216-31. Noble, *Republic of St. Peter,* 83-86, argues for a document that was no longer in the papal archives twenty years later when Charles visited Rome, see *LP* 1.498. Charles then confirmed his father's promise made at Quierzy, which is translated by the biographer of Pope Hadrian I into geographical terms—the so-called Luni-Monselice line.

[110] Paul the deacon, *Continuatio Casinensis* 4, in *SSRL,* 199; *continuatio tertia,* c. 35, in *SSRL,* 210; Leo, *Chronica monasterii Casinensis,* in *MGH, SS,* 7, 585; *Royal Frankish Annals,* a.753; *LP* 1.448-49.

the ruling family into closer relations with the holy see and encouraged the cult of St. Peter. In addition, Pope Stephen appointed Chrodegang of Metz as archbishop, with responsibility for the consecration of bishops. Since Chrodegang had been sent to accompany the papal party from Italy, he would have had ample opportunity to consult with Roman clerics as to the best ways of achieving higher standards in the Frankish church. Abbot Fulrad of St. Denis, Remedius of Rouen (Pippin's brother), and other prominent "reformers" probably also discussed matters with the pope while he was at hand.

The most significant change associated with this period was the official adoption of Roman liturgical practice (specifically chant), which was intended to replace the varied "Gallican" forms in use. In 760, Bishop Remedius went to Rome and returned with Simeon, *secundus* of the *schola cantorum*, who gave expert instruction in Francia. This gradual changeover entailed the corresponding necessity of establishing a uniform sacramentary (service book), and harmonising the other mass books with it. A syncretic version, known as the "Gelasian Sacramentary of the eighth century," was produced, perhaps at Flavigny, a Benedictine monastery founded by Pippin.[111] But it did not succeed in reducing the variety of mass books used in Francia, as Charles's later reform reveals. The movement towards greater uniformity in church liturgy and discipline was encouraged by Pope Paul I's gift of a Roman antiphonal and responsal in 760 and by Pope Hadrian's collection of canon law, the *Dionysio-Hadriana*, sent in 774. Under Charles, Paul the deacon was commissioned to draw up a standard Homiliary (of Biblical, patristic, and hagiographical readings),[112] and the pope was asked to provide Charles with a copy of the service book authorised by Pope Gregory I, a measure of the Frankish desire to import established Roman tradition. This request embarrassed the papacy, for no sacramentary employed in Rome went back to a late sixth-century original.

---

[111] R. E. Reynolds, "Image and Text: A Carolingian Illustration of Modifications in the Early Roman Eucharistic *Ordines*," *Viator* 14 (1983): 59-75; C. Vogel, "Les échanges liturgiques entre Rome et les pays francs jusqu'à l'époque de Charlemagne," *Settimane* 7 (Spoleto, 1960): 185-295, esp. 240-42; idem, "S. Chrodegang et les débuts de la romanisation du culte en pays franc," in *St. Chrodegang*, 91-109, esp. 94-98; idem, "Les motifs de la romanisation du culte sous Pépin le Bref (751-68) et Charlemagne (774-814)," in O. Capitani, ed., *Culto cristiano e politica imperiale carolingia* (Todi, 1979), 13-41.

[112] Homiliaries supplied select passages from the Bible, patristic writings, and stories of the saints, which were to be read at the Mass and at choral celebration of the Office. Normally two separate collections were used, both linked to the liturgical year, with specific readings for each Sunday. Frequently these were sermons, by St. Augustine or St. Caesarius of Arles for instance, hence their name (*homilia = sermo*), see R. Grégoire, *Les Homéliaires du Moyen Age* (Rome, 1966), 1-13, and 71-114, for the one drawn up by Paul the deacon and dedicated to Charlemagne.

So Hadrian decided to send his current Roman stational service book, parts of which probably did go back to Gregory's time, and once this had been provided with the essential additions it became known in Francia as the Gregorian Sacramentary.[113] While variety persisted in Frankish church services and much "hybridisation" occurred, Pope Stephen's visit gave an impetus to the movement towards Roman dominance that continued into the ninth century.

Pippin's Italian Campaigns

It was not easy to win over the entire Frankish nobility to the political and military alliance with Rome. Loyalty to Carloman and doubts over the advantages to be gained may have caused hesitation and delay. Only after the general assembly of 1 March 755 at Berry did Pippin secure agreement for an anti-Lombard campaign. So one month later, after Easter, the Franks set out on the promised Italian expedition, another first of its kind (for the previous attempt of the 590s had been unmemorable).[114] They crossed the Alps, routing the Lombard defences at Susa, and besieged Aistulf in Pavia. Aistulf quickly sued for peace, and a treaty drawn up and sworn by solemn oaths provided that all lands usurped should be returned "to St. Peter, the holy church of God and republic of the Romans." In addition, a substantial tribute was to be paid to Pippin. Despite papal warnings that Aistulf's promises meant nothing, by July 11 Pippin was back in Francia. He nominated his brother Jerome and Abbot Fulrad to accompany Stephen back to Rome.[115] The expedition seemed to have been entirely successful.

After an absence of nearly two years, there must have been great rejoicing when the papal mission re-entered the city. But whatever celebrations commemorated its triumph, Aistulf was to confound them almost immediately. As predicted, his lack of respect for oaths nullified the terms of the treaty. Far from returning any territory, he launched further attacks on the duchy. By the New Year (756), Rome was again besieged, this time by three separate Lombard armies. Stephen had already sent a letter to Pippin by Fulrad, reminding him of his duties towards the holy see.[116] In claiming

---

[113] J. Deshusses, "Le Supplément au Sacramentaire Grégorien, Alcuin ou Benoît d'Aniane," *Archiv für Liturgiewissenschaft* 9 (1965): 48-71; idem, *Le Sacramentaire grégorien: I Le supplément d'Aniane* (Fribourg, 1971); C. Vogel, "La réforme liturgique sous Charlemagne," in W. Braunfels, ed., *Karl der Grosse*, 4 vols. (Dusseldorf, 1965), 2:217-32, esp. 231-32; E. H. Kantorowicz, *Laudes Regiae* (Berkeley, 1958), 60-62.

[114] Levillain, "L'avènement de la dynastie carolingienne," 271-74; on the date, see the discussion in Noble, *Republic of St. Peter*, 88.

[115] Einhard, *Vita Karoli*, ch. 6 (English translation, 61); *LP* 1. 450-51; *CC*, no. 6 (489). For the terms used to describe the papal state, see Noble, *Republic of St. Peter*, 96-97.

[116] *CC*, no. 6 (488-90); cf. *LP* 1.451-52.

that the intercessions of Christ Himself would grant Pippin immense victories in the defence of His church, the pope seeks to put pressure on the Frankish monarch. "This good work (to restore the usurped lands to St. Peter) is reserved to you and through you the church will be exalted and the Prince of the Apostles will obtain his rights [*iustitiae*] . . . You are called to render justice to that Prince without any delay, as it is written—faith is justified by works."[117] Further hints at the eternal salvation that Pippin would receive on the day of judgement are directly linked to the fulfilment of his donation, confirmed by his own hand, which he had ordered to be offered to "our lord, St. Peter, to him your protector."[118] The same points are made in four more letters carried through the enemy lines by four ambassadors after eight weeks of the siege. The stronghold of Narnia had been taken, and Stephen clearly feared that Rome could not hold out. He quoted to Pippin Aistulf's jeer: "Let the Franks come and get you out of my hands now."[119]

The mention of a written donation (*cyrographum donatio*) in the first of these four letters has prompted historians to assume that the alliance concluded in 754 was indeed recorded. Yet in the context of these desperate appeals, the reference appears to stem from an image of the Keeper of the Keys on the day of judgement rather than from an actual document that had been formally presented to the church of St. Peter. The pope develops the veiled threat that Pippin's salvation is at stake: "For you know that the Prince of the Apostles holds your signed donation firmly and it is necessary for you to fulfil it, lest when the day of judgement comes it is discovered to have no foundation." If on the other hand Pippin does what he has promised, he will obtain eternal life and the Prince of the Apostles will make Pippin and his descendants his own.[120] In the final letter of this group, Stephen adopts the literary ruse of speaking for St. Peter himself, in the first person singular, "I, Peter the Apostle. . . ." Again the consequences of not heeding this appeal are spelled out—the risk of the eternal and inextinguishable fire of Tartarus with the devil and his pestiferous angels, and dispersal like the dispersal of the children of Israel.[121] But there is no mention of Pippin's donation. Nor does the previous implication of a written document signed by Pippin himself feature in any later correspondence. It is as if Stephen refers to this when he needs to put most pressure on the Frankish king. And although Charles's later donation was said to be based on his father's earlier prototype, the fact that this had not survived to the 770s

[117] *CC*, no. 6 (490.12-18).
[118] Ibid. (489.42-490.1).
[119] Ibid., no. 8 (495.42-43 and 40-41); *LP* 1.452. Cf. the same taunt in 740, *CC*, no. 2 (477.37-478.1).
[120] *CC*, no. 7 (492.34-493.1), cf. no. 6.
[121] Ibid., no. 10 (501-503).

suggests that it may never have existed. Stephen possibly used the treaty of 755 drawn up after Pippin's first campaign and interpreted it in the light of verbal promises made in 754.

Whatever their basis, these papal appeals clearly moved the king, though his answers to Stephen's letters are unfortunately not preserved. In 756, however, he seems to have had less difficulty in organising the Frankish host, which set out again after Easter (28 March). When Aistulf learned of the fact, he lifted the siege of Rome to block the Frankish advance at the Alps. But his preparations were ineffective; by another rapid march, Pippin's forces proved victorious once more.[122] And this time the king made sure that his terms would be observed. Not only was a list made of the 22 cities and their territories to be returned to St. Peter and the holy Roman church in perpetuity, but Abbot Fulrad was empowered to receive the keys from the *primatos* (elders) of each one. These symbols of Roman control were then to be laid on the altar of St. Peter, while the document (the so-called "Donation of Pippin") was deposited in the papal archive.[123]

Pope Stephen's policy thus appeared totally successful; his commitment to the Carolingian dynasty had brought Rome both territorial security and strong military protection. As he wrote to Pippin in the spring of 757, "The mother and head of all the churches of God . . . the foundation of the Christian faith" (i.e. the Roman church) had been restored thanks to Frankish virtue.[124] In this letter he orders prayers to be directed to God for Pippin's immense goodness. The Frankish monarch is identified as a new Moses and David, and his wife and sons as most blessed. In addition, God favours Pippin and his descendants as the leaders of the Franks in perpetuity (an even stronger statement of Carolingian authority than previous ones). With evident pleasure, Stephen next reports to Pippin Aistulf's impious end and the election of Desiderius as king. With Fulrad's help, divine providence, and the power of St. Peter, the new Lombard leader has returned six more cities to the apostolic see. And not only is there peace between the new Roman state of St. Peter and the Lombard kingdom, but even the dukes of Spoleto and Benevento have commended themselves to Pippin and to the service of God.[125]

Roman and Frankish Relations with Constantinople

The next matter to be settled concerned the "part of the Greeks," the first direct reference to Byzantium in any of Stephen's letters to the Franks. He requests Pippin to dispose of this part so that the apostolic and holy cath-

---

[122] *LP* 1.452-53.
[123] Ibid. 1.453-54.
[124] *CC*, no. 11 (504.16).
[125] Ibid. (505-507).

olic faith will remain united and unharmed forever, the holy church of God secure from the interference of others and liberated from the Greeks' "pestiferous wickedness."[126] Whether this refers to territory still under Byzantine control, areas loyal to Constantinople, or to the activity of pro-Byzantine agents in central Italy is impossible to tell. South of Rome, Naples had provided a retreat for several exarchs under stress and may have harboured figures who distrusted the new papal-Frankish alliance. In Istria also, Byzantine suzerainty was nominally accepted, though local autonomy prevailed. Pro-Greek factions might well have found a sympathetic refuge from both Lombard and Carolingian power in the coastal regions at the head of the Adriatic that remained in maritime contact with the East Mediterranean and preserved a good deal of independence in their inaccessible lagoons. The foundation of Venice early in the ninth century revealed a firm antagonism to the newly-established Frankish authority in northern Italy and a long-standing and beneficial friendship with Constantinople, which may date back to this troubled time.

Though the pope's passing reference to a "Greek part" in the letter of 757 is not identifiable, the reason for its inclusion becomes clearer in the light of the next paragraph. An imperial official, John the *silentiarios*, has arrived in Rome with a letter from Constantine V. Stephen is sending him on to Pippin, in the knowledge that the Franks and Romans see perfectly eye to eye on the question of Byzantine authority. As if this total harmony were not sufficient, Fulrad will also report to the king on the subject. Stephen again praises the abbot of St. Denis lavishly—not only for his handling of the treaty by which the cities gave up their keys, but also for his part in securing good relations with Desiderius.[127] From this it appears that Fulrad had been instructed to keep Pippin to the agreed anti-Byzantine line, which simply assumed that the entire territory of the exarchate now belonged as of right to St. Peter, the holy church and republic of the Romans.

As Pippin too had benefited from the developments of 754-57, he was unlikely to permit eastern claims to undermine his new position. So the Byzantine embassy was welcomed neither in Rome nor in Compiègne. A flurry of eastern officials had been coming and going since early 756, monitoring the situation in Italy and Francia, always reiterating the Byzantine position that the lands of the exarchate should return to the emperor, their rightful overlord. This argument made little impression. The papal-Frankish alliance had already revealed its potential and was to hold sway in Europe for a long time to come. After a particularly frosty reception at Pavia

[126] Ibid. (506.38).
[127] Ibid. (506.42-507.3, and 506.6).

in 756, when the Byzantine envoys learned bluntly that Pippin had no intention of acting on behalf of the empire—he had already promised to return the exarchate to the Apostle Peter—Constantine adopted a different tactic. The following year he sent George the *protoasekretis* (first secretary) to Pippin with an organ, an extraordinary gift by eighth-century diplomatic standards.[128] Thereafter, eastern embassies were regularly sent to Francia, but not to Rome. As if to punish Pope Stephen II and his successor (and brother) Paul I for their failure to support imperial claims to the exarchate, Constantine V ignored the papacy and tried to court the Franks. One embassy even proposed a marriage alliance between the emperor's son, Leo, and Pippin's daughter, Gisela, though it did not come to fruition.[129] But it reflected the shift of Byzantine attention to a new centre of power in the West, a recognition of Pippin's ability to influence developments in Italy. While Constantinople did not cease to claim the exarchate for Byzantium, the possibility of making good that claim must have dwindled to negligible.

Byzantine Iconoclasm After 754

During the decade of Paul I's pontificate (757-67), the consequences of the council of Hiereia became clearer both in the East and the West. Constantine V used its Definition to try and persuade overt iconophiles to abandon their faith in holy images, resorting to violent persecution when argument failed. News of humiliating measures imposed on monks and nuns, punishment, exile, and even martyrdom reached the West, brought by refugees such as the Greek monks, who were installed by Paul I in the monastery established in his family house.[130] Iconoclast activity appears to have been concentrated in and near Constantinople, or in areas firmly under the control of committed supporters such as Michael Lachanodrakon, governor of the Thrakesion *thema*. Figural decoration in churches, on ecclesiastical furniture, icons, hangings, liturgical objects, and in holy books were undoubtedly destroyed. Evidence survives, however, for the existence of many regions of the empire where the persecuting forces of the capital did

---

[128] Dölger, *Regesten*, no. 320, again only recorded in western sources; *Fredegarii Continuatio*, ch. 40; *Royal Frankish Annals*, a.757; *LP* 1.452. Only the later *Annales Mettenses*, a.757 (in *MGH, SS*, I, 333), specify that this embassy brought the organ, "which had not previously been seen in Francia."

[129] *Royal Frankish Annals*, a.767; *CC*, no. 45 (560-63); F. L. Ganshof, "The Frankish Monarchy and Its External Relations from Pippin III to Louis the Pious," in his volume *The Carolingians and the Frankish Monarchy: Studies in Carolingian History* (Ithaca, 1971), 162-204.

[130] *LP* 1.465; Sansterre, *Les moines grecs et orientaux*, 1:36, 159-60; 2:90-91, 187.

not reach.[131] In general, the iconophile sources preserve an exaggerated account both of the extent of iconoclasm and of the number of victims. More refugees came to the West as a result of the Arab conquests of the Near East than under the threat of official Byzantine iconoclasm.

The numbers of named iconophile martyrs and of persecuting iconoclasts remain small, implying perhaps a considerable exercise of "economy" by clerics, a less-than-fervent loyalty to image veneration, and a tendency to follow official policy among the populace at large. But there were those, chiefly monks, who resisted all attempts to make them abandon their icons: St. Andreas Kalybites, from a community at Blachernai; St. Stephen the Younger, from the St. Auxentios monastery in Bithynia; Peter the Stylite; and St. Andreas the Cretan.[132] Although St. Stephen was betrayed by one of his own disciples, in general the monastic brethren stood by their leaders and suffered with them. In the highly coloured accounts of their deaths, Constantine V is given a prominent role as iconoclast interrogator. But there are few named officials who actively pursued iconophiles, and the total of iconoclast bishops recorded is not much above a dozen. More significant, perhaps, as an index of the meaning of iconoclasm for ordinary people is the adherence of the *tagmata* of Constantinople to the doctrine.[133] Among these crack troops Constantine V had his greatest supporters. But whether their loyalty to the emperor sprang from a shared commitment to iconoclast practice or from an appreciation of his military leadership and his victories is hard to tell.

THE PONTIFICATE OF POPE PAUL I (757-67)

It is unlikely that the evidence of iconoclasm made Paul I such a determined critic of Byzantium. The new pope shared many of his brother's pro-Frankish and anti-Byzantine preconceptions and continued his hostility to the East. In correspondence with Pippin, Paul regularly stresses the devious activity of Constantinople's ambassadors, held responsible for stirring up Lombard and Neapolitan forces against Rome and threatening papal control over its patrimonies in southern Italy, but he rarely mentions

---

[131] The *Life* of St. Stephen the Younger, *PG* 100, 1117-20, lists regions that provided a haven for iconophiles. Their geography is disputed, see H. Ahrweiler, "The Geography of the Iconoclast World," in Bryer and Herrin, eds., *Iconoclasm*, 21-27; cf. M.-F. Rouan, "Une lecture 'iconoclaste' de la Vie d'Etienne le jeune," *TM* 8 (1981): 415-36.

[132] Gero, *Constantine V*, 122-25.

[133] *PG* 100, 1125C; Haldon, *Byzantine Praetorians*, 231-35; P. J. Alexander, *The Patriarch Nicephorus of Constantinople* (Oxford 1958, reprinted 1983), 111-16, 118, on iconoclast garrison soldiers in the early ninth century.

eastern persecution.[134] On the contrary, his almost obsessive concern in the 760s is with the rumour of a Byzantine invasion, which is supposed to land in the south or on the Adriatic coast to restore the exarchate with Lombard support. This will remove from papal administration the cities recently won, if not Rome itself—that is, Paul is most anxious about the independence of the newly created Roman republic. Among the torrent of appeals against this alleged danger, Paul also warns of the untrustworthy nature of the Greek envoys.[135] As he probably knew that Pippin was maintaining diplomatic relations with Constantine V, he may have feared some agreement between the two.

Other factors also contributed to papal worries over the stability of the Frankish alliance. Archbishop Sergius of Ravenna's rival claim to authority over the exarchate deprived Rome of some of the cities that Pippin had handed over to St. Peter; King Desiderius conspired with the Byzantine ambassador, George, and forces in the south to reconquer Ravenna; and in Rome a number of older families appeared to regret the demise of imperial power in Italy and therefore proved critical of papal links with Francia.[136] Pippin meanwhile failed to respond to any of the pope's urgent appeals for help—he even refused to send a permanent ambassador to the papal court, who would act as a counterpart to Paul's representative Wilcharius. The latter failure may have been interpreted as a particular slight, for in a break with tradition the papacy had effectively switched its permanent legate from the court of the eastern emperor to that of the Frankish king. After the pontificate of Zacharias there is no further evidence for the long-standing institution of papal *apocrisiarii* in Constantinople. In contrast, that pope's correspondence with Boniface reveals a very similar delegation of apostolic authority, which developed by 748 into the establishment of a "legate of the Apostolic see," the personal representative of the pope in Francia.[137] When Stephen II bestowed the archiepiscopal pallium on Chrodegang of Metz, the role of apostolic legate was also inherited. From that date onwards the institution had become a fixed part of the Frankish court, although no reciprocal arrangement had brought a permanent Frankish representative to Rome.

[134] The heretical Greeks are condemned as *nefandissimi, odibiles*, and *perversi*, e.g. in *CC*, no. 32, cf. no. 34, but without any details of the specific heresy.

[135] *CC*, nos. 17, 20, 25 (514-17, 521.12-14, 529-30).

[136] Ibid., nos. 16, 30, 36 (513-14, 536-37, 544-47); P. Llewellyn, *Rome in the Dark Ages* (London, 1971), 217-20; D. H. Miller, "Byzantino-Papal Relations During the Pontificate of Paul I: Confirmation and Completion of the Roman Revolution of the Eighth Century," *BZ* 68 (1975): 47-62.

[137] *LP* 1.416; cf. S. Boniface, letter no. 82 of 1 May 748, in *MGH, Epistolae selectae*, vol. 1, 182-84; translated by E. Emerton, *The Letters of Saint Boniface* (New York, 1940), 151.

Since Paul had also taken steps to reassure Pippin of the fundamental change of alliance, by sending the announcement of his election to the king and not to the emperor, and by communicating his pleasure at continuing the spiritual relationship established by his brother, Frankish lack of enthusiasm may well have occasioned a sense of insecurity in Rome. Pippin did intervene with Desiderius in 760 after one of Paul's more desperate appeals for military pressure to restrain Lombard ambitions. But he showed no sign of leading a Frankish army into Italy, or even of visiting Rome to confirm the bond of *compaternitas*. It was perhaps to overcome feelings of papal isolation in 763-64 that Paul instructed his own envoys to accompany Pippin's to Constantinople, where they learnt of Constantine V's efforts to form a closer alliance with the Franks.[138] In this way Byzantium certainly "punished" the papacy for Stephen's "treachery" in securing the cities of the exarchate for St. Peter, and for Paul's maintenance of the break in diplomatic relations between Old and New Rome.

This break had obviously been strengthened by the iconoclast council of 754, although Paul made no direct response to it. By not announcing his election or sending his synodica to the patriarch, he expressed Rome's opposition, which was later communicated by papal messengers who urged Constantine V to resume the veneration of icons. But in the West, while he denounced the wicked and heretical Greeks to Pippin, the pope did not dwell on the crimes of iconoclasm or its theological falsehoods. He did, however, forward to the Frankish court evidence of continued iconophile practice among Christian communities under Islam, which had been sent to Rome by Patriarch Cosmas of Alexandria.[139] Whether the Frankish church was seriously concerned about icons is unclear; the episcopal authorities were probably more anxious to stamp out the abuses condemned at the reforming councils of the 750s and 760s. So the cause of the schism between Constantinople and Rome was not aired in Francia until 767, when a Byzantine embassy to Pippin attended a synod at Gentilly near Paris.

The Synod of Gentilly (767)

As the acts of this synod are lost, it is almost impossible to reconstruct the event, a singular misfortune for the historian of ecclesiastical division. According to two later western sources, it took place before Easter 767 and

---

[138] Pope Paul's announcement of his election to Pippin in 757, *CC*, no. 12; his appeal, *CC*, no. 34 of 761, cf. no. 14 of 758; on the spiritual ties, Angenendt, "Das geistliche Bündnis," 57-60; *LP* 1.464.

[139] *LP* 1.477 (the first reference to the official Byzantine iconoclast council in Roman sources); *CC*, no. 40 (552-53), cf. no. 99 (652-53), a very similar use of the eastern patriarch's letter by pseudo-Pope Constantine II.

was the occasion for a set-piece debate between the eastern and western churches over the Trinity and the holy images. The Byzantines had accompanied a Frankish embassy back from Constantinople, and Pope Paul sent his own delegates together with a statement of his support for Pippin's orthodox stand and a letter for the leading Frankish nobles who also attended.[140] Clearly, the issue of icon veneration could also raise Trinitarian problems, as Constantine V's denunciation of the possibility of representing the Human Christ had shown. But the suggestion that the synod also discussed the problem of the procession of the Holy Spirit, made only in one additional account, does not necessarily follow. The *Filioque* clause of the creed did not become a contentious issue in Francia until after 787 and may have crept into this source erroneously.[141]

If, as seems likely, the synod of Gentilly brought together a large number of ecclesiastical and secular dignitaries for a theological disputation in the king's presence—a practice much favoured by Charles later—it represents a purely Frankish occasion. The Byzantine and Roman participants appeared as expert witnesses, so to say, in what was an independent meeting organised by Pippin. Although the outcome is nowhere explicitly stated, it is evident that the iconophile party succeeded in convincing the Franks. After 767, Constantine V made no further efforts to win support in the West, nor did he pursue the proposed marriage alliance with Pippin's daughter. And Pope Paul recorded his pleasure at the failure of the Gentilly negotiations in one of his last letters to Pippin. The Frankish king is compared to Moses and praised for repudiating the "schism of the heretics and the authors of an impious doctrine."[142] But he did not live to enjoy the consolidation of the papal-Frankish alliance, and after his death in June 767 it collapsed temporarily. The anti-Frankish party in Rome collaborated in the election of a layman imposed by Lombard forces, Constantine II, who held office for 13 months.

The Donation of Constantine

During Paul's pontificate, however, the Roman curia paid attention to the theoretical underpinning of the alliance with the Franks. The desire to justify papal claims to lead the churches of the West was by no means new in the mid-eighth century, but as a result of Pope Stephen's transalpine journey it gained a greater urgency. Under Stephen and Paul, the basic ele-

---

[140] *Royal Frankish Annals*, a.767; *Annals of Einhard*, a.767; *CC*, no. 37 (549.1-13); cf. L. Olsner, *Jahrbücher des fränkischen Reiches unter König Pippin* (Leipzig, 1871), 404-405.

[141] *Chronicon Adonis*, PL 123, 125 (a mid-ninth-century world history by Ado, bishop of Vienne).

[142] *CC*, no. 42 (554-55).

ments in an elaborate forgery were prepared to boost the moral authority of the successors of St. Peter. In this, the so-called *Constitutum Constantini* (*"Donation of Constantine"*), a fictitious fourth-century alliance between Pope Sylvester and Emperor Constantine I was endowed with ceremonial, religious, and political form.[143] Baptism was associated with political investiture, as the pope presided over the emperor's adoption of the faith in the Lateran baptistery and received from him full authority over the western parts of the empire. This authority was symbolised in the crown that Roman bishops could bestow on worthy Christian rulers. Through this implied superiority of ecclesiastical standing in the West, based on the New Testament story of Christ's reliance on St. Peter—"Thou art Peter, and upon this rock [*petra*] I will build my church; and the gates of hell shall not prevail against it" (Matthew 16:18)—eighth-century bishops of Rome sought to increase their fragile position in dealings with secular powers.

While the quite inaccurate tradition of Sylvester's role in the conversion of Constantine was well known in Rome and elsewhere during the Late Antique period, the genesis of the *Donation of Constantine* is much debated. Those responsible for drawing up the document, first written in Greek and then translated into Latin, carefully omitted any trace of their own context.[144] So it is necessary to examine the use made of the forgery, which is first cited as a historical document in a letter of Pope Hadrian I, dated May 778. The pope there expresses his hope of performing the baptismal rite for Charles's newborn son; the ceremony had been planned for Easter 778 but had been put off because of the Frankish campaign into Spain.[145] The same connection between papal authority and baptism was of course an integral part of the bond of *compaternitas* established between Stephen II and Pippin. Hadrian repeated it in 781 when he baptised the two Frankish princes, Carloman, renamed Pippin, and Louis, and crowned them as kings of Lombardy and Aquitaine respectively. The ceremony took place in the Lateran in direct imitation of Sylvester's original rite. In 788 an even closer identification was made, when the pope acclaimed Charles as a new Constantine and therefore himself, by implication, as a new Sylvester.[146] And a final clarification occurred in the events of 800, especially in the visual form of

[143] *Constitutum Constantini*, ed. H. Fuhrmann, in *MGH, Fontes iuris germanici antiqui* (Hannover, 1968), English translation in Pullan, *Sources for the History of Medieval Europe*, 9-14.

[144] H. Fuhrmann, "Das frühmittelalterliche Papsttum und die Konstantinische Schenkung: Meditationen über ein unausgeführtes Thema," *Settimane* 20 (Spoleto, 1973): 257-92, esp. 269.

[145] *CC*, no. 60 (586-87).

[146] Angenendt, "Das geistliche Bündnis," 87-89.

mosaics put up by Pope Leo III in the Lateran palace and the church of St. Susanna.

Obviously the theories underlying this forgery take time to become identifiable factors in papal politics; some historians have been unwilling to date the document before 806, others prefer to place its emergence in the last decade of the eighth century. But in seeking a context for the fabrication, the pontificate of Paul seems to fit particularly well.[147] As we have seen, Stephen's success in persuading Pippin to take military measures to defend the papacy could not be repeated by his brother. On the contrary, from 757 to 767 the Franks maintained friendly relations with Constantinople and tended to ignore Lombard agression in central Italy. Pippin did not return to Rome, and he left it extemely isolated. The pope's repeated appeals for protection and exaggerated fears of imminent destruction reflected both his anxiety about the alliance and his utter dependence on it. In such circumstances, the confection of a text that purported to establish the rights of Roman bishops over the entire West could provide an unanswerable justification for papal authority. The pressures behind such a production increased during Paul's pontificate and resulted in a theory of Petrine supremacy, in worldly as well as spiritual affairs, that met the pope's needs. It proved that the successors of St. Peter had a historic claim on the loyalty of truly Christian rulers and could be used to put pressure on the Frankish dynasty.

That Pippin resisted such pressure is evident; he also wished to extend his own authority in the West; but he did not deny the spiritual and political alliance made with the papacy. His daughter, Gisela, baptised in Francia, became Paul's spiritual godchild when Pippin sent her baptismal towel to Rome, as did his son later. This affirmation of Frankish *compaternitas* with the pope kept the spiritual bond alive.[148] It was only the military aspect of the alliance that Pippin failed to maintain. And in this respect particularly, the *Donation of Constantine* constituted an ambitious attempt to enforce reciprocal benefits.

IN SEEKING to understand the mid-eighth-century developments initiated by Pope Stephen II, which resulted in such a profound change in international relations, it is not sufficient to cite the theological schism of iconoclasm or Stephen's Roman background. While the pope may not have shared Zacharias's sense of political loyalty to the East, there is no indication in the surviving sources that Byzantine iconoclasm was a serious issue

---

[147] Noble, *Republic of St. Peter*, 135-36 and note 173, for a recent, rapid survey of the arguments. Casper, *Pippin und die römische Kirche*, 185-89, argued that Paul I's pontificate was likely.

[148] *CC*, no. 42 (554-56); Angenendt, "Das geistliche Bündnis," 60-61.

in 752. Neither hostility to eastern theology nor attachment to iconophile practices is sufficient to explain the reorientation of papal politics. But it is interesting to note that Stephen's own use of icons reveals their adaptation for western use in precisely the same circumstances of impending external threat that had brought them to such prominence in seventh-century Byzantium. There is, however, no trace of any attempt to promote this and condemn iconoclasm. The schism that he inherited was now 20 years old; it had not forced his predecessors to reconsider their customary loyalty to Constantinople; no dramatic acts of iconoclasm had been reported from the East—so Stephen could have continued as before.

A major change had occurred in Italy, however. Since the very first days of Stephen's pontificate, Rome had been challenged by King Aistulf, whose demand for an annual poll tax would have drained the duchy of gold resources as well as removing all papal independence of action. To submit to such a "protectorate" was inconceivable for the supreme spiritual leader of the West. Instead, Stephen would try by all means within his grasp to maintain Rome's independent identity. And after the fall of Ravenna, that meant finding an alternative military defender. From the Byzantine point of view, there is no hint that the political realities of central Italy were understood. For many decades bishops of Rome had been coping with the Lombard activity—indeed, Zacharias's success with Liutprand cannot have prepared the imperial court for Stephen's desperate appeals. The loss of Ravenna was seen as a temporary setback, and the city would be regained by negotiation, not force of arms. As before, the pope would act as chief Byzantine negotiator, and these traditional means of exerting Byzantine authority in the West would prevail. Such reliance on ancient patterns of political dominance only strengthened Aistulf's determination to hang on to his military conquests. But even if a Byzantine force had been sent against the Lombards, it is not clear whether it would have succeeded.

Finally, the Frankish response to Pope Stephen's appeal fitted into the Carolingian effort to extend and consolidate dynastic control in Europe. Pippin showed no intention of remaining in Italy longer than was necessary to accomplish his part of the agreement. But if by a relatively brief campaign he could re-establish the bishop of Rome's independence, this was not a high price to pay for the reciprocal blessings on his family. The succession of his sons and the support of the church were thus assured—two factors of considerable weight to a new, and some might claim illegitimate, ruling dynasty. The later complication raised by Constantine V's direct appeal to the Franks to return the exarchate to the empire could be countered by the assertion that the holy see "owned" large areas of central Italy, a fact that had become a reality in the eighth century. In addition,

Pippin could support the theory that the successors of Sts. Peter and Paul had "rights" to territory that Constantinople had ceased to defend.

It was, therefore, the Byzantine failure to protect Ravenna and Rome from the Lombards and the ensuing military crisis that sparked off a complete reorientation of the western church's political alliances. And having decided to seek Frankish support in order to survive, successive pontiffs justified their policy in terms of eastern heresy. The theology and use of icons played only a small part in what was a turning point in East/West relations: small but significant, for it was a means of expressing and legitimising western authority. At the same time, it ensured the specific value of representational art in the West. [149] Rome, once ancient capital and now a small walled town under papal administration, was removed from the traditional orbit of imperial and Byzantine continuity and plunged into a new world, ex-barbarian, self-taught, Christian, Latin-speaking, and totally western. This movement seals the north/south axis of western Europe emphasising one unit—Italy, the Frankish territories, and the British Isles—which constitutes the new reserve of Christianity. By this realignment, the authority of the eastern churches and of the eastern emperor, together with their heretical beliefs and non-Latin languages, were put aside. The Christian *oikoumene* was thus divided into two hostile sections, and when the schism of 754 ended, officially in 787, unity between the two proved impossible.

[149] F. Masai, "La politique des empereurs Isauriens et la naissance d'Europe," *B* 33 (1963): 191-221; cf. G. Ostrogorsky, "Rom und Byzanz im Kampfe um die Bilderverherung," *Seminarium Kondakovianum* 6 (1933): 73-87, esp. 85-86.

🖋 10 🖋

The Carolingian Innovation

IN THE HISTORY of early medieval Europe there is one figure of sufficient renown to be widely recalled today: Charlemagne, *Carolus magnus*, Charles the Great. Claimed by both France and Germany as a founding father, the inspiration of the Holy Roman Empire, commemorated in the romantic legends of his *Pilgrimage to the Holy Land* and the *Song of Roland*, his role has often been exaggerated. In the following account of his reign to 794, I shall attempt to get round the assumed "greatness" by concentrating on one major achievement, the synod of Frankfurt. The reform movement that led up to this council had much greater importance and lasting significance than the imperial coronation on 25 December 800, which is treated in the concluding chapter. Here I shall try to set aside the prejudices of Charles's ninth-century eulogists so as to give due weight to the many factors that structured the Carolingian innovation and the many other individuals who contributed to it.

The process must begin with an evaluation of the reign of Charles's father, Pippin, the third of that name, but the first to rule as king and thus the first Carolingian monarch. It was through his efforts that the new dynasty came to dominate such large regions of what we now call Western Europe. In a series of carefully planned campaigns, he had extended the power base of his father, Charles Martel, westwards into Maine (748-53), east into Saxony (753) and southwest to Aquitaine and Septimania (760-68). Within his own kingdom also he faced rivals in Bavaria, Auxerre (an over-mighty episcopal centre), and Burgundy. During the last decade of his reign, when he refused to return to Italy despite papal pleas, he was preoccupied by annual expeditions to Aquitaine, one region that had obstinately resisted Frankish rule. By the assassination of Duke Waifar and the *Capitulare Aquitanicum* issued in April 768, his success appeared assured within the limits of the Garonne and Bordeaux. And in the same year, the return of his embassy to the caliph of Baghdad with proposals of friendship symbolised the enhanced standing of Carolingian authority not only in the West but also beyond.[1]

---

[1] *Capitularia* no. 18 (42-43); *Fredegarii Continuatio*, chs. 30-32, 35, 41-51; this last

In another respect also Pippin continued his father's policies, supporting missionary work among the non-Christian peoples within and outside the ill-defined eastern frontiers of his territory. But his attitude to the church was significantly different; he encouraged ecclesiastics to organise and direct reforms of the Frankish church. This relative independence of the spiritual sphere is evident from a series of councils held under Chrodegang's leadership to regularise ecclesiastical practice and resolve disputes between 755 and 767.[2] Pippin attended some of these meetings in person and issued laws to authorise the enforcement of their decisions: an insistence on Roman liturgical forms, baptismal and marriage rites, Sunday observance, and uniform penance for ecclesiastical offences. Both at the local and the international level of church organisation, the new dynasty drew on religious support, which underlay the consolidation of its rule.

The new prologue added to a revised version of the Salic Law, completed in 763-64, reflects some of the sense of achievement registered under Pippin. In place of their legendary descent from the heroes of the Trojan War, which had been invented in the seventh century to cover an obscure origin, the Franks were now defined as a most Christian people. "Noble, brave, wise, pure, courageous, strong and free from heresy," are some of the adjectives used to justify their dominant position in the West.[3] In this grandiose eulogy, the Frankish nobility was elevated with the king, for Pippin remained dependent on his nobles and needed their cooperation. He also admitted non-Frankish legal traditions in his territories; for instance, the *lex patriae* (in fact, Roman law) was to be used in Aquitaine. Thus, despite an emphasis on regal authority, the administration of justice was far from uniform. The extent to which written law was observed is also unclear; local custom and pressure exerted by powerful landowners may have settled most disputes.[4] So the claims made for the Frankish people in the prologue are probably more important as a reflection of the self-conscious strength and role adopted by Pippin than as evidence of a legal system uniformly administered.

chapter also describes the return of Pippin's embassy to Baghdad, with Saracen envoys who spent the winter at Metz and then presented their gifts to the king before sailing from Marseille back to the East. Cf. M. Borgolte, *Der Gesandtenaustausch der Karolinger mit den Abbasiden und mit den Patriarchen von Jerusalem* (Munich, 1976), 40-45.

[2] E. Ewig, "Saint Chrodegang et la réforme de l'église franque," in *Saint Chrodegang* (Metz, 1967), 25-53, reprinted in his *Spätantikes und fränkisches Gallien*, vol. 2 (Munich, 1979); J. M. Wallace-Hadrill, *The Frankish Church* (Oxford, 1983), 170-74.

[3] *Lex Salica*, Prologue, 1.4; K. A. Eckhardt, ed., *Die Gesetze des Karolingerreichs 714-911*, 3 vols. (Weimar, 1953-56), 1:82.

[4] On the problems of early medieval law, see C. P. Wormald, "*Lex Scripta* and *Verbum Regis*: Legislation and Germanic Kingship, from Euric to Cnut," in P. H. Sawyer and I. N. Wood, eds., *Early Medieval Kingship* (Leeds, 1977), 105-138.

Charles and Carloman (768-71)

The extent to which the king was himself bound by tradition was revealed in the arrangements made for his sons to succeed him. The Frankish territories were divided into two rather unequal shares: Carloman the younger was allotted a central region, comprising "the kingdom of Burgundy, Provence, Septimania, Alsace, and Alemannia," with perhaps the eastern half of Aquitaine and parts of southern Neustria and Austrasia, including the key cities of Paris, Soissons, Sens, and Bourges. Charles received most of Austrasia, the northeast core of Pippin's home base, lands further north and east, plus the northern parts of Neustria and western and frontier regions of Aquitaine. After their father's death at St. Denis in September 768, the two sons were both proclaimed kings of the Franks, and each entered into his inheritance in his respective "capital" on October 9, Carloman at Soissons, Charles at Noyon.[5] Although Pippin might have foreseen a certain rivalry between them, Frankish tradition, like Merovingian, demanded that he divide the territories. The idea of primogeniture to designate an heir was as inconceivable as the eastern principle of establishing a co-emperor according to imperial tradition, though neither guaranteed the peaceful transfer of authority or removed the possibility of a disputed succession.

Meanwhile, in Rome the tumult that followed Pope Paul's death in 767 was resolved just over a year later by the arrest of Constantine II and the defeat of the pro-Lombard party. The legal election of Pope Stephen III was engineered by Christopher the *primicerius* (chancellor in charge of the record office, *scrinium*, in the Lateran palace), who was one of the most important supporters of the Franks within Rome.[6] His son, Sergius, and nephew, Gratiosus, also held posts in the local administration. Stephen's election coincided with the accession of Charles and Carloman after Pippin's death (20 September 768). Three new principals thus entered the already complicated Italian arena, where the Lombard king Desiderius resolutely opposed both the Frankish monarchy and the new pope. Stephen immediately announced his election to the two Frankish kings, requesting their assistance at a council to be held to review Constantine II's pontificate.[7] Although both replied favourably and arranged for bishops from their territories to attend the Lateran Synod, which met in April 769, they did not act as one and appeared disenchanted with the division imposed by their father.

---

[5] *Fredegarii continuatio*, chs. 53, 54; *Royal Frankish Annals*, aa.768, 769; Einhard, *Vita Karoli*, ch. 3 (English translation, 57-58).

[6] *LP* 1.468-71.

[7] *CC*, no. 44 (558-60).

The Lateran Synod (769)

The twelve Frankish participants, five from Charles's territories and seven from Carloman's, joined 39 Italian bishops, mainly from the duchy of Rome—the area previously known as the exarchate, Pentapolis, northern Italy, and Lombard Tuscany were less well represented.[8] In the first session they heard a report by Christopher the *primicerius* on the disorders introduced by Constantine II and his brother, the Lombard duke Toto of Nepi. Constantine was excommunicated as an anti-pope and those prelates he had consecrated were condemned. Particular attention was paid to his uncanonical election from lay status, an irregularity shared by Sergius of Ravenna and Stephen of Naples as well as several deacons similarly advanced to high ecclesiastical rank (session two). In the third session they were deposed, re-elected, and consecrated by Stephen III. Finally, the synod recorded its emphatic support for the veneration of sacred images as a tradition maintained by all past bishops of the apostolic see and all the Fathers of the church.

This statement in favour of iconophile practice is the first direct reference to official Byzantine iconoclasm recorded in the *Liber pontificalis*. Previous mentions of eastern heresy had not alluded to the 754 council of Hiereia, although knowledge of it is implied in Pope Paul I's letters ordering Constantinople to restore the icons. Now, 15 years after the event, Rome refuted and condemned the "execrable council recently held in the regions of Greece for the removal of the holy images."[9] The Lateran Synod also confirmed the Roman Council of 731 that had been called by Gregory III to repudiate iconoclasm and added several important documents to its list of texts. The first was a declaration of iconophile belief sent to Rome by the three eastern patriarchs and forwarded by Constantine II to Pippin (it was probably a copy of the document received by Paul I). Stephen III cited the evidence of this text in his own defence of icon veneration, using the Edessa image of Christ as a very ancient example.[10] The second was a fuller and different version of Pope Gregory the Great's letter to Secundinus; this was provided by Herulphus, bishop of Langres. The third was St. Ambrose's description of the finding of the relics of Sts. Gervasius and Protasius, revealed to him in a dream; Archbishop Sergius of Ravenna sent this to the synod as indirect proof of the value of icons, for messengers of God who

[8] Mansi, 12.713-22, the participants are listed at 714-15; cf. *Concilia*, pt. 1, 80-81; *LP* 1.473-77.

[9] *LP* 1.477.

[10] Mansi, 12.720B-D (this is the barest account of the fourth session); Pope Hadrian's letter-treatise of 791 to Charles (the so-called *Hadrianum*) gives more detail, *MGH, Ep.*, vol. 5 (*Epistolae Karolini Aevi* 3), 5-57; also in Mansi, 13.759-810 (and *PL* 98, 1247-92); Pope Stephen III's use of the Edessa icon, *Epistolae Karolini Aevi* 3, 23 (Mansi, 13.720B-722C; *PL* 98, 1256B-1257A).

appear to people in visions could be recognised as such by their resemblance to icon portraits.[11]

The importance óf the Lateran Synod, however, did not reside in its theological expertise, but rather in its composition. The fact that nearly a quarter of the participants came from Francia marked a new departure for western ecclesiastical organisation and symbolised the strength of the papal-Frankish alliance. For the first time, a pope summoned bishops not only from the "respublica Romana" and other parts of northern Italy, but also from Frankish dioceses over which he had no immediate jurisdiction. By involving these non-Italians, Pope Stephen accomplished several aims: first, his own election and the condemnation of his predecessor was confirmed by ecclesiastics north of the Alps, a measure that brought him greater security and prestige, as well as giving a stern warning to the Lombard faction within Rome; second, the Frankish bishops assented to a firm statement of iconophile practice that effectively consolidated the western position on icons and debarred further dealings with the heretical authorities in Constantinople; and third, the claim for Rome's absolute independence in all matters pertaining to papal elections was made clear—no secular power, Lombard or Frank, would be able to attempt a repeat of Constantine II's illegal seizure of the apostolic see without provoking opposition.

From the Frankish point of view also, the 769 synod was an important event. Previously bishops of the reformed Frankish church had not participated as equals with Roman clerics, but now they contributed to the debate and were involved in the definition of the faith of the western churches, against the heretical belief of the East. Their presence in Rome had the result of incorporating them into the orthodox Christian universe, which included communities subject to the eastern patriarchs. Through the declaration of iconophile doctrine, accompanied by the eastern creed, which was also read out in translation, they gained a broader vision of Christianity, which included little-known Greek texts as well as the more familiar extracts from pseudo-Dionysios, which had been sent to Francia by Pope Paul I.[12] This stressed that orthodoxy was defined only by oecumenical councils and recapitulated the basic declarations of the first six. In

[11] For Pope Gregory's letter, see Mansi, 13.792D-793E, 798A-B; cf. Gregory the Great, *Registrum epistularum*, ed. D. Norberg, 2 vols., CCL 140-140A (Louvain, 1982), 2:1104-1111 (appendix 10); for the text of St. Ambrose, Mansi, 13.794A-B.

[12] Mansi, 13.764A-C. The Greek texts, drawn from Saints Gregory of Nyssa, Sophronios of Jerusalem, Cyril of Alexandria, and John Chrysostomos, were familiar enough in Rome, where florilegia of such citations were translated and copied; see for instance the original manuscript from which the Paris copy, *B.N. graecus 1115*, was made, C. Mango, "The Availability of Books in the Byzantine Empire A.D. 750-850," in *Byzantine Books and Bookmen* (Washington, D.C., 1975), 33-34; cf. idem, "La culture grecque et l'Occident au VIIIe siècle," *Settimane* 20 (1973): 683-721, esp. 711-13.

addition, the Franks also witnessed at first hand the full official ceremonial employed on important pontifical occasions, with the attendance of all the Roman clergy, monks of Greek and Latin monasteries, the militia and army leaders, and the entire population of the city. And this full secular participation occurred at all four sessions of the synod and at the subsequent ritual in St. Peter's. After a barefoot procession to the basilica, with everyone singing hymns, the *scriniarius*, Leontius, read the synodical acts from the ambo, and three bishops repeated the anathemas in a collective demonstration of orthodoxy (against heretics) and correct ecclesiastical practice (against uncanonical election).[13]

By the synod of 769, therefore, the Roman church righted itself after many months of internal disturbance, and the Frankish church came into its own. Although neither the iconoclast definition of faith prepared by the council of 754 nor the developed iconophile theology of John of Damascus appear to have been discussed formally, the West closed its ranks against the eastern heresy. And with this theological decision, both the papacy and the Frankish monarchy abandoned official contacts with Constantinople. In the last years of Constantine V's reign (767-75) no embassies were recorded. This stand-off in diplomatic relations coincided with the Byzantine policy of not pursuing potential western allies, which followed from the Gentilly discussions. It seems to have marked a period of coming to terms with the loss of Ravenna and concentration on imperial defence in the East, when the emperor successfully defeated a Bulgar threat to imperial settlements in Thrace and continued his military and administrative reforms.

In the summer after the Lateran Synod, the Frankish territories were threatened by a major revolt in Aquitaine and Gascony. Carloman, however, refused to assist Charles in two campaigns against the rebels, a decision that did nothing to improve relations between the brothers. Their mother, Bertha, tried to effect a reconciliation; she also went to Bavaria and Italy, possibly hoping to win allies. At the court of Desiderius she arranged for one of his daughters to be betrothed to Charles, who had not yet been married. Pope Stephen protested in no uncertain terms: how could a Frank, one of God's chosen leaders, anointed and blessed by the vicar of St. Peter, even consider marrying a Lombard? The proposal would obviously undermine the papal-Frankish alliance, something the pope could not countenance.[14] In the event it proved short-lived, for within a year Charles repudiated his Lombard bride and married Hildegard, daughter of a Swa-

[13] *LP* 1.477.

[14] *CC*, no. 45, cf. M. V. Ary, "The Politics of the Frankish-Lombard Marriage Alliance," *Archivum Historiae Pontificae* 19 (1981): 7-26.

bian noble. But this alliance brought no amelioration of relations between the two Frankish kings, which continued to be strained until Carloman's death (December 771). Carloman's widow, Gerberga, then fled to King Desiderius with her two young sons, indicating that she certainly felt the need for a powerful protector and had little confidence in her brother-in-law. Carloman's chief supporters, Wilcharius, bishop of Sens, Fulrad of St. Denis, and Counts Warinus and Adalhard swore oaths of loyalty to Charles, who thus overrode the claims of his young nephews and assumed full control of his brother's share of the Frankish territories.[15]

Italy at the Accession of Pope Hadrian (772)

King Desiderius, however, welcomed Gerberga and took her sons' claims very seriously, for their arrival presented him with an opportunity to set Frank against Frank. On the death of Pope Stephen III and the election of Hadrian (24 January 772), he opened a novel type of campaign to pressure the papacy into recognition of the princes' rights by anointing them as kings.[16] Through his chamberlain, Paul Afiarta, the Lombard party in Rome had already secured the deaths of Christopher (the *primicerius*) and his family, who led the pro-Frankish faction. He now ordered that the bishop of Rome should be brought to Pavia to perform the ceremony of consecration for Carloman's sons.[17] At the same time, Desiderius continued an aggressive policy within the Italian peninsula, designed to unite the dukedoms of central Italy with his own northern kingdom. His successful campaigns were confirmed by a marriage alliance that united his daughter, Adelperga, with the ruler of Benevento. In the north also, Lombard influence was extended by the marriage between another daughter, Liudbirc, and Tassilo of Bavaria.[18] Had Bertha's arrangement for Charles been satisfactory, Desiderius would have drawn the older Frankish brother into the same web of alliances. But Charles realised the dangers of leaving his nephews in Lombard hands, while Pope Hadrian also resisted pressure to con-

---

[15] *Royal Frankish Annals*, a.771; Einhard, *Vita Karoli*, ch. 18 (English translation, 73). Some of Carloman's supporters, however, went over to Desiderius and encouraged the anti-Frankish party in Italy.

[16] *LP* 1.488. In this he may have been continuing Carloman's policy, for Dodo, an envoy of the king, had tried to persuade Pope Stephen III to recognise the young princes as his godsons.

[17] Desiderius's agent in Rome, Paul Afiarta, is alleged to have boasted that he would bring the pope to Pavia for this purpose "even if I have to hobble him with a rope round his feet," *LP* 1.489; cf. A. Angenendt, "Das geistliche Bündnis der Papste mit den Karolingern (754-796)," *HJ* 100 (1980): 66-67.

[18] *Chronicon Salernitanum*, ch. 9, ed. U. Westerbergh (Stockholm/Lund, 1956), 11; J. T. Hallenbeck, *Pavia and Rome: The Lombard Monarchy and the Papacy in the Eighth Century* (Philadelphia, 1982), 119-25.

secrate them. In a classic display of the principle of allying with one's enemy's enemy, the pope doubtless sensed that he could increase his own authority through the Franks, and together they checked Lombard hopes.

Since 757 the interplay of diplomatic contacts, occasionally followed by military intervention, had bound Frankish, Byzantine, Lombard, and Roman interests into a complex network. Although the alliance between the papacy and the Frankish monarchy may be seen as the one stable factor in this pattern, King Pippin had been noticeably absent from Italy, and neither of his sons had ever shown particular concern to use their title of "patrician of the Romans." In addition, the variety of different forces at work in Italian politics—which involved the Lombard dukes of Benevento and Spoleto, the Byzantine dukes of Naples and governors of Sicily, Arab rulers in northern Africa and independent pirates, and local notables, both iconophile and iconoclast, all subject to considerable inconsistency—inevitably produced confusion. At every turn the surviving sources leave room for ambiguity, lack of clarity, and diverse interpretation. So the following analysis will attempt to draw out a few lines of development, rather than trying to fit all the details and conflicting evidence into one consistent picture.

On the election of Pope Hadrian early in 772 the situation was as follows: the Franks were divided into two parties represented by King Charles, who appeared the undisputed ruler of Transalpine Francia, and by those loyal to Carloman's young sons, supported by the Lombard king in Pavia. Lombard alliances also meant increased pressure on the Roman republic. The papal city was split between pro-Frankish and pro-Lombard factions, while Hadrian may have come from an aristocratic tendency favourable to imperial tradition. The new pontiff appears to have delayed announcing his election to any secular authority (which would have indicated his choice of external alliance) in order to concentrate on improving his position in Rome. To clear up the violence that had dogged Pope Stephen's brief pontificate, he ordered an investigation into the deaths of Christopher the *primicerius* and his relatives, which revealed Paul Afiarta's responsibility.[19] This Lombard involvement further justified Hadrian's hesitation about cooperating with Desiderius. But the longer he resisted the king's demands for the recognition of Carloman's inheritance, the more Lombard forces threatened different parts of the papal republic.

His problem was resolved by an appeal from Ravenna for Roman assistance against Lombard occupation of three neighbouring towns, which had formed part of the Roman republic since 756. This provoked Hadrian into direct opposition to the Lombards. Since Afiarta's complicity in the murder

---

[19] *LP* 1.489-90; D. S. Sefton, "Pope Hadrian I and the Fall of the Kingdom of the Lombards," *Catholic Historical Review* 65 (1979): 206-220.

of Roman clerics was evident, the pope ordered that he should be arrested and sent to Rome to stand trial. But Archbishop Leo of Ravenna had the Lombard chamberlain tried and condemned to death in his own city. (In Hadrian's plan, Afiarta would have been given an opportunity to express contrition and then sent into exile in Constantinople.)[20] Thus his peremptory execution crystallised the relation of powers in northern Italy: it emphasised Ravenna's continuing desire for autonomy and independence from Rome, it stiffened Desiderius's efforts to expand Lombard authority, and it probably revealed to Hadrian that respect for imperial judicial traditions no longer existed and that the papacy had to defend its lands by military force. In 772 the only source of effective aid was Francia.

It was this combination of factors which persuaded Hadrian to renew the alliance with Charles. He was also prompted by the arrival of Frankish envoys, sent to check whether the Lombards had returned the cities of St. Peter. As they had not, and showed clear signs of preparing another blockade of Rome, the pope sent an urgent request for military assistance, recalling the terms of the past alliance.[21] At first Charles offered 14,000 gold coins if Desiderius would return the cities illegally usurped; he was not keen to embark on an immediate military campaign. But when the Lombards refused, an expedition was agreed, and in the summer of 773 the Frankish host was summoned to cross the Alps. It probably numbered "hundreds rather than thousands" and succeeded in getting through the Alpine defences by ruse rather than superior strength, while the Lombards retreated in disarray.[22] Desiderius fled to Pavia, his son Adelgis to Verona, and their support in central Italy collapsed—the duchy of Spoleto and other occupied cities offered their loyalty to Rome. So the Franks settled down to besiege the Lombard strongholds into submission, confident of victory. Sometime in the winter of 773-74, Prince Adelgis abandoned Verona, though it was protected by the best surviving fourth-century fortifications, and sought refuge in Constantinople, where he was received with honour. Pavia, however, continued to hold out.[23]

Charles's First Visit to Rome (Easter 774)

In these circumstances, Charles decided to celebrate Easter at the tomb of St. Peter. Since the Frankish monarchs always kept the most important

---

[20] *LP* 1.488, 490-91; on the term *consularis*, see ibid., 515 n.15, and T. S. Brown, *Gentlemen and Officers* (London, 1984), 140-43.

[21] *LP* 1.494; cf. P. Llewellyn, *Rome in the Dark Ages* (London, 1971), 233-34.

[22] *LP* 1.494-95; *Royal Frankish Annals*, a.773; D. Bullough, *The Age of Charlemagne*, 2nd ed. (London, 1973), 46-50.

[23] *LP* 1.495-96; *Annales of Einhard*, a.774; Theophanes, 449 (Adelgis is identified as Theodotos, king of the Lombards).

church feasts with a public demonstration of faith, this pilgimage to Rome fitted an established custom. But there is no evidence that Pope Hadrian had much advance warning. Charles was nonetheless received with ceremonies appropriate to an official of patrician status (i.e. equivalent to those for an exarch), although the Frankish king had not used his title *patricius Romanorum* prior to the visit. These ceremonies included a formal welcome outside the city by clerical and municipal officers, accompanied by the local militias with their banners, lay patrons, and young boys to chant the customary acclamations. At St. Peter's, Pope Hadrian greeted Charles, and they entered the basilica together to pray at the Apostle's tomb.[24] After this devotional act of fundamental significance to every pilgrim, the king was granted permission to enter the city with his entourage and witnessed the baptism of catechumens at the Lateran (a traditional Easter Saturday ritual).

His brief five-day stay in Rome, when he lodged at the Frankish foundation of St. Petronilla, not at the old imperial residence on the Palatine, was marked by attendance at Easter services in the appropriate stational churches and by several important meetings with Pope Hadrian.[25] The accuracy of the *Liber pontificalis* record of these meetings has been questioned. As in the forged *Donation of Constantine*, papal expectations of precise Frankish duties are given emphasis, repeated in later correspondence. Hadrian clearly used the occasion to press Charles to renew his father's promises to protect the church of Rome. And for the first time, these Frankish undertakings appear to have been written down in a document (the earlier record of Pippin's "Donation" could not be found in the papal archives). In the three copies made, one for each party—bishop, monarch, and the Apostle himself, which in accordance with superstitious practice was laid on his tomb—the territory of the "respublica Romana" was more fully delineated than previously.[26] Areas that had never formed part of the exarchate were now claimed by Rome or promised by Charles (for example, Istria, which was still independent). Both Hadrian and Charles agreed to conditions they did not subsequently fulfil. While the cities usurped by Desiderius were returned to Rome, the Frankish king had no intention of making over to the papacy large tracts of northwest Italy, as his later actions showed. Immediately after his pilgrimage to Rome he returned to Pa-

---

[24] *LP* 1.496-97; cf. O. Bertolini, *Roma di fronte a Bisanzio e ai Longobardi* (Rome, 1941), 688-98.

[25] *LP* 1.497-98.

[26] Ibid., 1.498. P. Classen, "Karl der Grosse, das Papsttum und Byzanz," in W. Braunfels et al., eds., *Karl der Grosse: Lebenswerk und Nachleben*, 4 vols. (Dusseldorf, 1965-67), 1:537-608, esp. 551-52. This important study has been reprinted with additional notes and corrections (Dusseldorf, 1968).

via and negotiated its submission and Desiderius's exile in a Frankish monastery. He then entered the city in triumph and crowned himself king of the Lombards. Frankish control over Lombardy was to persist for a century.[27]

During the 774 visit, however, the spiritual alliance of *compaternitas* between the papacy and the monarchy was not renewed. Only after the birth of Charles and Hildegard's third child, Carloman (777), was the idea revived and planned for the following Easter. But in May 778, Pope Hadrian expressed regret that Charles had not come to Rome because of a Spanish campaign—this was the ill-fated expedition to Saragossa, destroyed at Roncesvalles on its return through the Pyrenees.[28] His wish was realised only three years later when the ceremony eventually took place and Carloman was baptised Pippin. (The delay suggests that both sides wanted the ceremony to take place, however belatedly.) On the same occasion, Hadrian also anointed Pippin and his younger brother, Louis, as Kings of Lombardy and Aquitaine respectively.[29] (Louis had been born in 778 and immediately baptised because his twin had died at birth.) The renewed link of spiritual paternity was again connected with the investiture of regal power (as in 754), and through it Charles's conquest of two previously independent areas received papal legitimation. In addition, the legend of Pope Sylvester's baptism of Emperor Constantine I, as preserved in the *Donation of Constantine*, was realised in eighth-century terms.

Cultural Development in Francia

That the 773-74 campaign marked a significant stage in Charles's regal "career" is evident from the new title employed on his official documents— "*Carolus gratia dei rex Francorum et Langobardorum atque patricius Romanorum.*"[30] His conquest of Lombardy and pilgrimage to Rome extended and established his authority more securely. But he also had to pay attention to the administration of his new territories, in which dukes and bishops had previously exercised a large measure of autonomy. While Lombardy's in-

---

[27] *Royal Frankish Annals*, a.774; *Annales of Einhard*, a.774; *LP* 1.499; K. Schmid, "Zur Ablösung der Langobardenherrschaft durch die Franken," *Quellen und Forschungen aus italienischen Archiven und Bibliotheken* 52 (1972):1-35; Hallenbeck, *Pavia and Rome*, 157-73; Sefton, "Pope Hadrian I."

[28] *CC*, no. 60 (586-88). The 778 campaign into Muslim Spain not only provided the historical background for the later *Chanson de Roland*, it also stimulated the flight of Christians and their manuscripts from Spain into Frankish territory, for example the northern movement of Theodulf of Orléans and Benedict of Aniane.

[29] Angenendt, "Das geistliche Bündnis," 71-74.

[30] Classen, "Karl der Grosse," 552-54; with additional notes in the reprint [74], which emphasise how un-Byzantine the title *patricius Romanorum* is.

dependence as a separate kingdom was preserved together with its own secular and ecclesiastical legal system, Frankish counts took over responsibility for the administration. Charles also took advantage of the resources available at the Lombard court to strengthen his own.

Since the late seventh century, Pavia had served as the established centre of Lombard power. It was one of only a few cities in northern Italy that maintained the urban traditions of Roman times: aqueducts, baths, palaces, mints, and markets, all within strong city walls. Successive kings had patronised court scholars and rhetoricians, teachers, lawyers, and doctors, employing a host of educated administrators in their chancelleries.[31] When Charles captured the city, its population had been weakened by famine and plague, but it revived and its best scholars were quickly re-employed in Francia. From about 774-76, Peter of Pisa is known as Charles's personal teacher of letters (*grammatica*); after 776 Paulinus (a master of the art of grammar, later appointed archbishop of Aquileia) became an ecclesiastical adviser, and in 782 Alcuin was summoned from York. The king had met him in Parma and now invited him to teach at court. In the same year, Paul the deacon arrived to beg Charles for the release of his brother, who had been imprisoned in Francia after a Lombard revolt in 776. At the king's insistence he remained seven years, writing poems, a homiliary, and the history of the archbishops of Metz, before he returned to Monte Cassino.[32] There he composed his most famous work, the *History of the Lombards*. This pattern of employing the most cultivated scholars also attracted other non-Franks. Before 780, Arno, later abbot of St. Amand, left Bavaria and sought out Charles's patronage. He later became archbishop of Salzburg. Similarly, Theodulf, a Spanish scholar of Visigothic extraction, moved north in the 780s in hopes of finding employment at court. He too served as an abbot and bishop, as well as royal envoy (*missus*) after 802.[33]

The tradition of drawing on foreign expertise was by no means new. Under Charles Martel and Pippin, Anglo-Saxon missionaries and their disciples had been supported; the Irish monk Virgil spent two years with the Frankish court before being appointed bishop of Salzburg, and Roman

[31] D. A. Bullough, "Urban Change in Early Medieval Italy: The Example of Pavia," *Papers of the British School at Rome* 34 (1966): 82-131; esp. 94-102; E. Ewig, "Résidence et capitale pendant le haut Moyen Age," *RH* 230 (1963): 25-72, esp. 37-47, reprinted in *Spätantikes und fränkisches Gallien*, vol. 1 (Munich, 1976).

[32] R. Folz, *The Coronation of Charlemagne* (London, 1974), 63-69; H. Fichtenau, *The Carolingian Empire* (Oxford, 1968), 79-103.

[33] On the use of such scholars as administrators, see H. Liebeschutz, "Theodulf of Orleans and the Problem of the Carolingian Renaissance," in *Fritz Saxl 1890-1948*, ed. D. J. Gordon (London, 1957), 77-92; K. F. Werner, "Missus-Marchio-Comes," in W. Paravicini and K. F. Werner, eds., *Histoire comparée d'administration, IVe-XVIIIe siècles*, Beiheft der *Francia*, no. 9 (Munich, 1980), 191-239.

prelates such as George of Ostia and Wilcharius of Nomentanum, who acted as papal legates, ended up as Frankish bishops.[34] But Charles's effort to bring Alcuin and other outstanding scholars to his court from all regions (including those like Ireland and Northumbria, far beyond his political control) had important consequences. Representatives of the broadest range of learning who might otherwise not have met congregated around a monarch renowned for his intellectual curiosity. They arrived with their own texts, books of reference, and teaching aids, and sent for works that were not available at court or in the chief monastic libraries.[35] Through the common medium of their Latin culture, the diverse heritages of Septimania, Ireland, Visigothic Spain, Northumbria, Lombardy, and Rome could be shared with Francia. And all these sources of knowledge were also put to a practical use with Charles's encouragement. Medical, astronomical, agricultural, musical, architectural, and military manuscripts were studied for immediate guidance; the writings of Priscian, Donatus, and others for a training in grammar; the *Psychomachia* of Prudentius possibly for moral standards.[36]

Many of the classical authors studied with the king's express encouragement had been known in different areas for centuries (for instance, Suetonius). What was novel in the late eighth century was the degree of intellectual exchange and interaction generated by the court and monastic centres. It helped in the establishment of definitive texts of important works, scholarly editions, accurate copying, translations, and informed exegesis. Completely unfamiliar writings were also "discovered": the Greek works of pseudo-Dionysios (sent to Charles by Pope Paul I in about 760), Pliny's *Natural History* (known to Bede), or Martianus Capella (used by Gregory of Tours in the late sixth century); rare manuscripts were lent from one centre to another to facilitate rapid diffusion. Confraternity books link-

[34] P. Riché, "Le renouveau culturel à la cour de Pepin III," *Francia* 2 (1974): 59-70; J. Hubert, "Les prémisses de la Renaissance Carolingienne au temps de Pepin III," ibid., 49-58. But see D. Bullough, "*Aula Renovata*: The Shaping of the Carolingian Court, 768 to 794," Sixty-seventh Raleigh Lecture on History (1985), to be published in the *Proceedings of the British Academy*.

[35] On Alcuin, see W. Edelstein, *eruditio et sapientia: Weltbild und Erziehung in der Karolingerzeit* (Freiburg-im-Breisgau, 1965); P. G. Godman, *Alcuin: The Bishops, Kings and Saints of York* (Oxford, 1973). B. Bischoff, "Die Hofbibliothek Karls des Grossen," in *Karl der Grosse*, 2:42-62. The effects of all this activity are, however, minimised by Bullough, "*Aula Renovata*."

[36] B. Bischoff, "Die Bibliothek im Dienste der Schule," *Settimane* 19 (1972): 385-415; R. McKitterick, *The Frankish Kingdoms Under the Carolingians, 751-987* (London/New York, 1983), 144-45, 152, 158-59. D. A. Bjork, "The Frankish Kyrie Text: A Reappraisal," *Viator* 12 (1981): 9-35, esp. 13, points to the late eighth century as an important period in musical development, although the documents are of much later date.

ing groups of monasteries and bishoprics in liturgies for the living and the dead, library catalogues, as well as individual volumes, also circulated.[37] The great majority of these were of course of Christian origin and were read as much for their moral value as for intellectual stimulation. But occasionally pagan authors were closely studied, especially poets such as Virgil, masters of classical Latin prose like Cicero and Suetonius, even the major Greek philosophers, Aristotle and Plato (though only very small parts of their corpus were known in translation).

While Carolingian scholarship did not prize originality greatly, and some of the commentaries produced by the court scholars were dull, it served a very important purpose. By insisting upon a basic understanding of correct Latin grammar, classical prose style, and the range of poetic forms, educational standards were raised and access to the western cultural inheritance ensured. The accurate copying of ancient manuscripts also preserved texts for future study. So however constrained, Charles's efforts to further learning had a profound impact on intellectual activity and laid the basis for a "renaissance," which finally blossomed in the ninth century.[38]

Two particularly important developments were encouraged. The first concerned the Christian system of dating. It had been evolved by the Venerable Bede, whose works were studied throughout Charles's territories, and was based on the year of the Incarnation. In place of the many different methods of computing dates, this calculation forward from the first year of our Lord provided a clearly Christian system of chronological measurement. Counting from the year one, events could be dated in the year of the Lord's Incarnation, *anno dominicae incarnationis*, or in the year of the Lord, *anno Domini* (whence A.D.). The value of such a standard had been effectively illustrated by Bede in his *Ecclesiastical History*.[39] It was now encouraged by Charles, who employed it in several of his own court documents and helped to spread its use in Europe, although other methods also continued. While Arabic numerals were not yet known and the Roman system of capital letters continued for counting, the A.D. dating system facilitated accurate record-keeping and a comparison of time-spans. It provided a

[37] Bullough, *The Age of Charlemagne*, 99-128; McKitterick, *The Frankish Kingdoms*, 210-13; for the Reichenau confraternity book, see J. Autenrieth, D. Geuenich and K. Schmid, eds., *Der Verbrüderungsbuch der Abtei Reichenau, MGH, Libri memoriales et necrologia*; Nova series, vol. 1 (Hannover, 1979), and see the Afterword, pp. 484-85, below.

[38] H. Liebeschutz, "Wesen und Grenzen des Karolingischen Rationalismus," *Archiv für Kulturgeschichte* 33 (1950): 17-44; J. Marenbon, *From the Circle of Alcuin to the School of Auxerre* (Cambridge, 1982).

[39] Bede, *EH*, historical introduction, xviii-xix; W. Levison, *England and the Continent in the Eighth Century* (Oxford, 1966), 269-77; H. Fichtenau, " 'Politische' Datierungen des frühen Mittelalters," in *Intitulatio II*, ed. H. Wolfram (Vienna, 1973), 453-548, esp. 516-17.

wider sense of the historical past and Carolingian continuity with previous European dynasties. It also broke from the parochial time-system still in use in Rome.

The second was related to the development of a new minuscule script, which became the hallmark of Carolingian learning. The aims of the new minuscule were to increase the legibility of texts, correctly copied, carefully laid out, and written with an alphabet of distinct letter forms and hierarchy of scripts. Text, scholia, and heretical comment could thereby be separated, a consideration of importance when the text was to be used for teaching converts. Since correct Latin was a difficult language to master, especially for those familiar with vulgar Latin, it is hardly surprising that grammatical texts were some of the first to be copied in minuscule; five survive from the period before A.D. 800. Similar improvements in presentation and legibility had already been made in the insular minuscule practised at the Wearmouth-Jarrow scriptorium, which probably influenced the Carolingian script. Another impetus derived from Pippin III's concern for better Latin charters, manifested as early as 769.[40] Again, the emphasis was on correct word division and punctuation, correct Latin, and improved legibility. Charles also understood the value of good writing for good administration, for a universal application of law was dependent on a universal script. Prior to the dissemination of Carolingian minuscule, such an aim was impossible, because so many local styles existed. Thus, with Charles's support, two major technical advances were widely promoted and came to hold a dominant position in the intellectual life of the West.

The Eastern Revival of Learning. By a coincidence, which seems to be related to the equally unsatisfactory character of Greek uncial script, a similar process was to result in an almost contemporary revival of learning in the East. This was also marked by a minuscule script; indeed the need for technical improvements in manuscript production appears as an essential prerequisite for intellectual change.[41] Although the origin of the script (first

[40] For much help with the problems of Carolingian minuscule I thank David Ganz, who supplied the evidence for the five early grammatical texts: *Bern 207, Paris B.N. Lat.13025, S.Gall 876, Vat.Pal.Lat.1746,* and *Berlin Dietz B 66.* He also directed me to the splendid lecture by M. B. Parkes, *The Scriptorium of Wearmouth Jarrow* (Jarrow Lecture, 1982), and to R. Schneider, "Schriftlichkeit und Mundlichkeit im Bereich der Kapitularien," in P. Classen, ed., *Recht und Schrift im Mittelalter* (Sigmaringen, 1977), 257-79. See in addition, B. Bischoff, "Panorama der Handschriftenüberlieferung aus der Zeit Karls des Grossen," in *Karl der Grosse* 2:233-54, reprinted in his *Mittelalterlichen Studien*, vol. 3 (Stuttgart, 1981); F. L. Ganshof, "The Use of the Written Word in Charlemagne's Administration," in his collected essays, *The Carolingians and the Frankish Monarchy* (Ithaca, 1971), 125-42.

[41] N. G. Wilson, *Scholars of Byzantium* (London, 1983), 63-68; P. Lemerle, *Le premier*

used in a dated manuscript in 835) is still disputed, it was probably due to a combination of factors: increasing iconophile pressure to counter the arguments against icon veneration, and the need for a speedier and more economical method of writing official documents issued by the imperial chancellery. The development took place against the background of declining papyrus imports from Egypt and higher costs of parchment, the main substitute.

Mango has correctly emphasised the role of Syro-Palestinian monastic communities in both the technical and intellectual aspects of this revival.[42] Their isolated situation and reduced means under Islam may have stimulated a fundamentally new approach to manuscript production, as they sought to copy iconophile writings and to find a more sophisticated justification for image veneration. Communities like that of Mar Sabas near Jerusalem, where John of Damascus had prepared his *Three Orations*, maintained scriptoria and libraries and regarded the copying of manuscripts as an integral part of monastic life. So the eastern monks faced a daily problem of producing texts with greater speed and more economic use of resources, which they took with them when forced to move to Byzantium towards the end of the eighth century. Scholars like George, from the St. Chariton community, who became assistant (*synkellos*) to Patriarch Tarasios shortly after 784, probably had an influence out of all proportion to their number.[43]

A second stimulus to the development of a more rapid and economical method of writing may have derived from the imperial chancellery in Constantinople, although it was probably bound by convention and the conservatism usually found in central bureaucracies. Official records and written documents were, however, produced in very large numbers in Byzantium. And it is striking that some of the leaders of the iconophile revival of learning were trained as imperial administrators. They mastered a notarial cursive hand in their secular careers, which may have influenced the practice of monastic scriptoria. The link becomes significant in the case of Platon, abbot of the Sakkoudion monastery from 781, and Patriarchs Tarasios and Nikephoros (786-806, 806-815), who are all known to have

---

humanisme byzantin (Paris, 1971), 109-121; B. L. Fonkič, "Scriptoria bizantini: Risultati e prospettive della ricerca," *SBN* 17/19 (1980-82): 73-118.

[42] C. Mango, "La culture grecque et l'Occident au VIIIᵉ siècle," 716-17; cf. his "L'origine de la minuscule," a later contribution to the international colloquium, *La paléographie grecque et byzantine* (Paris, 1977), 175-79.

[43] C. Mango, "Who Wrote the Chronicle of Theophanes?" *ZRVI* 18 (1978): 9-18; G. L. Huxley, "On the Erudition of George the Synkellos," *Proceedings of the Royal Irish Academy* 81C (1981): 207-217.

copied many manuscripts.[44] Through their example and the influence of
Syro-Palestinian monks, copying became for the first time an expected part
of monastic life in Bithynian and Stoudite foundations. And by the early
ninth century, these monasteries had scriptoria that produced a large number of iconophile texts.

However it occurred, Greek minuscule encouraged the study and copying of manuscripts in exactly the same way as Carolingian. But within Byzantium it had even greater force because writing had not previously been
an established part of monastic routine. This is another reason for seeking
its origin in an iconophile centre beyond the imperial frontiers—Rome as
well as Palestine has been proposed. An even more fitting environment,
however, is provided by the monastery of St. Catherine on Mt. Sinai, where
close investigation of the medieval library has recently revealed a wealth of
unknown material.[45] Until this is published, the question of both the origin and date of Byzantine minuscule must remain "frozen." But on the evidence available at present, the 780s and 790s would seem to mark the first
use of minuscule in monasteries near Constantinople and in contact with
the foundation of Stoudios in the capital, where St. Theodore became abbot
at the very end of the century.

Minuscule was not, however, immediately adopted and promoted in official circles, as it was in the West. A variety of other scripts remained in
use for many years, while minuscule was confined to monastic and intellectual milieux. Similarly, although the method of dating from the Incarnation was known in the East, the traditional combination of calculating by
indiction and from the year of Creation continued to be used in official documents.[46] The court and chancellery made no effort to take advantage of
the innovations.

In the sphere of scholarly activity, however, official support from ruling
circles was forthcoming, as in the West. By the middle of the ninth century

[44] Lemerle, *Le premier humanisme*, 8-35; B. Hemmerdinger, "La date du papyrus de
S. Denis et la minuscule grecque," in *La paléographie grecque et byzantine* (Paris, 1977), 519-
21 (correcting his earlier articles); see also Fonkič, "Scriptoria bizantini," 83-92, on Stoudite copying.

[45] For the as yet largely unpublished archive from Mt. Sinai, see D. Harlfinger et al.,
eds., *Specimina Sinaitica: Die datierten griechischen Handschriften des Katharin-Klosters auf dem
Berge Sinai 9. bis 12. Jahrhundert* (Berlin, 1983). I am particularly grateful to Cyril Mango
for his help on this matter.

[46] On Byzantine chronology, see H. Gelzer, *Sextus Julianus Africanus und die byzantinische
Chronologie*, 2 vols. (Leipzig, 1880-85); F. K. Ginzel, *Handbuch der mathematischen und tech-
nischen Chronologie*, 3 vols. (Leipzig, 1906-1914). The more recent study by V. Grumel, *La
Chronologie* (Paris, 1958), is confusing for dating methods, but useful for lists of rulers,
earthquakes, etc. For the seventh century in particular, see J. Beaucamp et al., "La Chronique Paschale: le temps approprié," in C. Pietri et al., eds., *Le temps chrétien de la fin de
l'Antiquité au Moyen-Age (IIIe-XIIIe siècles)* (Paris, 1984), 451-68.

the Magnaura school, founded in part of the imperial palace, provided encouragement for the secular research undertaken by Leo the Mathematician and his pupils in the fields of philosophy, geometry, astronomy, and arithmetic.[47] This intellectual curiosity about ancient learning had developed in centres like the monastery of Stoudios, where the philosophical influence of Aristotelian thought informed iconophile image theory. It is particularly striking in Patriarch Nikephoros's rebuttal of iconoclast doctrines, but was shared by iconoclasts such as John *grammatikos*, patriarch under Emperor Theophilos (829-41).[48] Although the Stoudios scriptorium produced mainly theological works and remained rooted in questions of christology and artistic representation for many years, its activity prepared the way for the revival of secular traditions. For in contrast to the Carolingian circle of scholars, the Byzantine milieu had more direct access to the pagan inheritance of ancient Greece. This permitted the hesitant late-eighth-century movement to flower in the ninth-century encyclopaedic activity of Patriarch Photios, the philosophical and mathematical investigations of Arethas, and the so-called "Macedonian Renaissance" of the tenth century.[49]

Byzantium in the 770s

In isolation from western contacts and preoccupied with the Bulgar threat, the Byzantine Empire in the final years of Constantine's long reign (741-75) displays little evidence of iconoclast fervour. Active persecution of icon venerators appears limited; much greater attention is given to the organisation of *thema* administration and new military formations (the *tagmata*). Officially, iconoclasm remained the doctrine of the church of Constantinople, denounced by the three eastern patriarchs in their letters to Popes Paul I and Constantine II and by Rome in 769, as we have seen. At Constantine's death, which Pope Hadrian reported to Charles with satisfaction, his son Leo IV succeeded.[50] Since he had been raised as an iconoclast, it seemed likely that the same religious policy would persist. Recent research, however, has shown that Leo had a less obsessive concern with theological doctrine than his father. He immediately undertook structural reforms in the army and the church, designed to counter traces of active iconoclasm and to build up a broader range of support, based on those who

---

[47] Lemerle, *Le premier humanisme*, 158-65; P. Speck, *Die Kaiserliche Universität von Konstantinopel* (Munich, 1974), 1-13.

[48] P. J. Alexander, *The Patriarch Nicephorus of Constantinople* (Oxford, 1958, reprinted 1983), 188-213; Lemerle, *Le premier humanisme*, 132-35; cf. Wilson, *Scholars of Byzantium*, 68-84.

[49] Lemerle, *Le premier humanisme*, 177-241; Wilson, *Scholars of Byzantium*, 90-135; but cf. the quite different interpretation of P. Speck, "Ikonoklasmus und die Anfänge der Makedonischen Renaissance," in R.-J. Lilie and P. Speck, *Varia I* (Bonn, 1984), 175-210.

[50] *CC*, no. 58 (583-84).

had gone along with Constantine's dogma but not out of a profound conviction. Speck has identified this "indifferent class," to whom the divisive effects of persecution seemed more harmful than their dogmatic value, as a key component of the gradual shift from official iconoclasm to the restoration of icons.[51] Minimising the numbers of those seriously committed to either iconophile or iconoclast practice, he traces a growing faction of neutral character, drawn from all sectors of Byzantine society, which Leo IV and his successors needed to court.

In the affairs of Italy Leo barely intervened, and he showed no knowledge of the transformed situation. Although the Lombard prince Adelgis, who fled from Verona in 773-74, was given a haven in Constantinople and the title of *patricius*, this was not an alliance of great importance. Far more significant was the ceremony of 777 in which Leo stood godfather to Telerig, a Bulgar chieftain who was baptised and granted the same honour. This combination of family association and patrician status represented the ancient imperial method of building alliances through a "family of kings." It was the means adapted to a new end by Pope Stephen II in his 754 alliance with Pippin.[52] Since Adelgis was already a Christian, he did not benefit from such a meaningful association with the emperor and was forced to spend a dozen years in exile before his attempted return to power (788). Meanwhile, in southern Italy, the activity of a governor of Sicily in collaboration with the Lombard duke Arichis of Benevento, who had assumed the mantle of Desiderius, was repeatedly denounced by Pope Hadrian. Between 776 and 778, attacks on Terracina were reported to Charles, plus the illicit trading of Greek merchants in enslaved prisoners and the usurpation of papal patrimonies in Naples, as if Byzantine forces were actively involved.[53] Whether this was correct, and if so whether Leo IV ordered such harassment or ignored what was undertaken independently, is unclear. But papal anxieties appeared exaggerated.

THE REIGN OF CONSTANTINE VI "WITH HIS MOTHER" (780-90)

Leo also tried to ensure the accession of his son, Constantine, born in January 771 and crowned co-emperor in 776. As in the case of Herakleios and

[51] P. Speck, *Kaiser Konstantin VI: Die Legitimation einer Fremden und der Versuch einer eigenen Herrschaft* (Munich, 1978), 1:54-55, 70-71, 72-73, 99-101.

[52] Theophanes, 451; F. Dölger, "Die 'Familie der Könige' im Mittelalter," *HJ* 60 (1940): 397-420, reprinted in *Byzanz und die europäische Staatenwelt* (Ettal, 1953); A. Angenendt, *Kaiserherrschaft und Königstaufe: Kaiser, Könige und Papste als geistliche Patrone in der abendländischen Missionsgeschichte* (Berlin/New York, 1984), 7-9.

[53] *CC*, nos. 59 (584-85), 61 (588), 64 (591-92), 65 (592-93). Cf. the very similar fears expressed by Pope Paul I.

Constans II, he wished to prevent disputes, but his own half-brothers, the five caesars, grown men with experience of government, presented a constant threat. While he reigned they could be restrained. But when he suddenly died (in September 780) and Constantine VI and his mother Irene were acclaimed as joint rulers, a struggle was probably inevitable. Not that the role of female regent was considered unconstitutional: it was perfectly legitimate for Irene to act on behalf of her ten-year-old son; imperial protocols for such an occasion existed and were smoothly put into effect. But 40 days after their accession, a plot among army and navy leaders to establish the caesar Nikephoros as emperor was discovered—an indication of the unrest foreseen by Leo IV. All the brothers were forced to take holy orders (a disqualification) and to serve as priests in the Christmas mass at which Irene and Constantine performed the normal imperial roles. Those who had supported the attempted coup were all banished.[54] These measures did not remove all potential rivalry to the new rulers, but they permitted Irene to promote her own men to key positions: Staurakios became "foreign minister" (*logothetes tou dromou*), John the *sakellarios* took over the post of commander-in-chief of the armed forces, and Theodore the patrician (later governor of Sicily) assumed a more prominent role. In addition to these three eunuchs, loyal supporters were placed at the head of the Armeniakon *thema*, the *exkoubitors*, and the Dodecanese naval force.[55] The empress-mother thus gave notice that she would not tolerate alternate claims on the throne.

Imperial Control in Greece

As a member of the Sarandapechys family based in Athens, Irene devoted considerable attention to the problems of the European provinces of the empire. Since the late sixth century, Slavonic tribes had been moving southwards through the Balkans, settling on fertile land and putting Christian communities to flight. Although coastal cities like Thessalonike, Corinth, and Athens, and well-fortified centres such as Thebes and Larissa, were never captured, imperial control was very greatly reduced. Coinage almost ceased to circulate, many ecclesiastical sees were overrun, and contact with Constantinople was severely restricted. Previous emperors had led successful expeditions against the *Sklaviniai* blocking the main highway from the capital to Thessalonike, but under Irene and Constantine VI a more sustained effort was made. In 783, Staurakios headed a campaign

---

[54] Theophanes, 454-55; Speck, *Kaiser Konstantin VI*, 1:105-114.

[55] Theophanes, 455, 456; on the traditional influence of "beardless men" at court, particularly at times of female rule, see K. Holum, *Theodosian Empresses: Women and Imperial Dominion in Late Antiquity* (Berkeley, 1982).

into those parts of Thrace repeatedly threatened by Bulgar activity and proceeded through Thessalonike and central Greece into Peloponnesos, where he inflicted heavy losses and captured prisoners and booty.[56] His victory was celebrated in a triumph in the hippodrome at Constantinople, and the following year the empress and her son made an official tour of the pacified region of Thrace. Accompanied by musicians and members of the court in ceremonial attire, they processed inland to Berroia, which was refounded and renamed Irenopolis, went even further west to Philippopolis, and then returned to the capital via Anchialos on the Black Sea coast, in an unusual display of imperial authority.[57]

Byzantine *thema* administration had been established in Thrace and Hellas (central Greece) in the last two decades of the seventh century but had been disrupted by subsequent Slav and Bulgar infiltration. As a result of the renewed central presence brought by Staurakios's expedition, both became more secure and supported an increased number of episcopal centres. Some of these new or revived bishoprics were at inland sites previously occupied by non-Christian tribes, indicating an extension of the faith that may have involved missionary work and conversion. In the diocese of Herakleia (Thrace), Tzouroulon, Charioupolis, and Hexamilion may reflect this growth; also the sees of Develtos, Boulgarophygon, and Pamphylon (under Adrianople), Troizen, Porthmos, and Oreos (under Athens and Corinth).[58] Before 802, Irene secured the promotion of Athens to metropolitan status, thus creating a third archbishopric in Greece in addition to Thessalonike and Corinth. She also employed members of her family to strengthen provincial administration there, used Hellas as a place of exile, and established the *thema* of Macedonia.[59]

Under Irene's successor, Nikephoros I, forces stationed at Thebes (the administrative centre of the *thema* of Hellas) or at Corinth were available to the general sent to put down a Slav revolt in 805-806. As a result of this victory at Patras, which also involved an Arab attack by sea, Nikephoros I not only set up the *thema* of Peloponnesos but also rebuilt the churches of that city, raised it to metropolitan status, and established suffragans at Methone and Lakedaimonia. By an imperial chrysobull, the Slav families who had participated in the revolt were expropriated and made dependent

[56] Theophanes, 456-57.

[57] Ibid., 457.

[58] R.-J. Lilie, " 'Thrakien' und 'Thrakesion': Zur byzantinischen Provinzorganisation am Ende des 7. Jahrhunderts," *JÖB* 26 (1977): 7-47, esp. 35-46; J. Darrouzès, "Listes épiscopales du Concile de Nicée (787)," *REB* 33 (1975): 5-76, esp. 22-26.

[59] Theophanes, 473-74; N. Oikonomidès, *Les Listes de préséance byzantines des IXe et Xe siècles* (Paris, 1972), 349; J. Darrouzès, *Notitiae Episcopatuum ecclesiae Constantinopolitanae* (Paris, 1981), no. 2.

servants of the newly endowed church of St. Andreas.[60] The same emperor extended *thema* government to the area of Thessalonike, the island of Kephalonia, and Dyrrachion in Epeiros, on the west coast of Greece.[61] Thus the combination of military and ecclesiastical policies, inaugurated by Irene, brought large areas of the Balkans under firmer imperial control. In conjunction with the unofficial missionary activity of holy men and the evangelical work of bishops, these policies won not only the Slav settlers but also later Bulgar raiders to the faith. A lasting Christian domination resulted, which is represented by the myriad Byzantine churches surviving to this day.[62]

Because Irene presided over the Seventh Oecumenical Council (787), which restored the icons to their place of veneration in the eastern church, it has often been assumed that she must have been a convinced iconophile from birth, and that Greece must have remained an iconophile stronghold. This is patently false.[63] Constantine V would never have allowed his son and heir to marry into a known iconophile family, and probably chose the Sarandapechys bride from central Greece as a useful iconoclast alliance. But it does appear that during Leo IV's short reign and Irene's subsequent period as regent, she realised that iconoclasm no longer commanded substantial support. As official dogma it was of course observed on pain of death and was still promoted by those sections of the army who cherished Constantine's memory. But among the population at large, the removal and destruction of icons had not generated a permanent and lasting passion. Feelings possibly ran higher among those who had resisted iconoclasm— monks who had sought refuge in outlying parts of the empire, even as far as Rome, and those who clung to their icons as the most meaningful way of worshipping (notably women who felt themselves excluded from a valid Christian role in the organisation of the church and liturgy).[64] Like her husband, Irene must also have noticed the tendency for Byzantine officials to exercise a traditional "economy" in respect of the established faith—

---

[60] Constantine Porphyrogenitus, *De Administrando Imperio*, vol. 1, ed. G. Moravčsik (Budapest, 1949), ch. 49, 228-33; vol. 2, *Commentary* (London, 1962), 182-85.

[61] Oikonomidès, *Les Listes*, 352 and note 366.

[62] G. Millet, *L'école grecque dans l'architecture byzantin* (Paris, 1916, reprinted London, 1974). A. H. S. Megaw, "The Chronology of Some Middle Byzantine Churches," *Annual of the British School at Athens* 32 (1931-32): 90-130.

[63] Speck, *Kaiser Konstantin VI*, Anhang III, "Griechenland blieb orthodox," 1:405-419; J. Herrin, "Women and the Faith in Icons in Early Christianity," in R. Samuel and G. Stedman Jones, eds., *Culture, Ideology and Politics* (London, 1982), 56-83.

[64] K. Ringrose, "Monks and Society in Iconoclastic Byzantium," *Byzantine Studies/Etudes byzantines* 6 (1979): 130-51; P. Brown, "A Dark-Age Crisis: Aspects of the Iconoclastic Controversy," *EHR* 88 (1973): 1-34, reprinted in *Society and the Holy in Late Antiquity* (London, 1982); Herrin, "Women and the Faith in Icons," esp. 70-74.

those whose positions depended on a public declaration of support for iconoclasm might nonetheless remain uncommitted to the doctrine and could
therefore be won to another with care. It is difficult to say whether she actively sought to further a return to icon veneration or to reverse official
iconoclasm as a barrier to her consolidation of power. In either event, her
course was the same—to undo the established iconoclast structure and replace it by one that would gain the adherence of both disaffected iconophiles and people indifferent to either dogma.[65]

Irene's Alliance with Charles

When was this course adopted? And did the decision influence Irene's initiatives in Italian politics, which date from the first year of her joint rule
with Constantine VI? Since these ended the hostile silence that had been in
force since 767 by proposing a peaceful alliance with Charles, they seem to
reflect an acceptance of both Frankish assumption of imperial lands in
northern Italy and also western condemnation of iconoclasm. In this case,
Irene had realised that in order to secure Byzantine positions in Sicily and
southern Italy, she would have to gain Charles's support. She therefore
abandoned Constantine V's policy and instead sent an embassy to negotiate
an alliance to be sealed by the marriage of her son with Charles's daughter,
Rotrud.[66] This implied that the two contentious issues, Ravenna and iconoclasm, could be settled amicably. Pressing for a neutral religious policy
would have the added advantage of winning Rome's good will—a factor
that may have weighed in her calculations. So when she learnt that Charles
was in Italy early in 781, she instructed ambassadors to meet him. (They
may have travelled west with the new governor of Sicily, Elpidios, who was
appointed at the same time.) The fact that Charles went to Rome at Easter
for the delayed baptism of Carloman-Pippin and coronation of both sons as
kings confirmed the accuracy of Irene's predictions. Unless this Frankish
monarch, whose *compaternitas* with Pope Hadrian must have been fully appreciated in Byzantine circles, could be won over, he might prove a dangerous enemy, particularly to imperial possessions in southern Italy.

As the western and eastern sources for this initiative present contradictory chronologies, it is difficult to determine how it developed. Possibly
the idea of any rapprochement between the Byzantine emperors and the
Franks provoked the Sicilians to revolt, proclaiming Constantine VI's uncles, the caesars, as alternative rulers, but it may have been the proposed
marriage that sparked off their hostility. A revolt simply to secure greater

[65] Speck, *Kaiser Konstantin VI*, 1:115-16.
[66] Theophanes, 455; *Minor annals*, a.781 (in *MGH, SS* 16.497); cf. Dölger, *Regesten*, no. 339.

autonomy for the Byzantine territories in the West can not be ruled out either. The insurrection, however, was put down by a large military and naval expedition led by the patrician Theodore, and the marriage negotiations went ahead.[67] Since no Frankish or western princess had ever married into the imperial family, Irene's proposal brought great prestige and honour to the Carolingians. A Byzantine official, Elissaios, accompanied Charles from Italy back to the Frankish court, where he was to instruct Princess Rotrud in Greek letters and language.[68] As Constantine was only 11 years old in 781 and Rotrud 6 or 7, their union was designed (as in so many medieval alliances) to take effect when the prince reached his majority, in about six years' time.[69] Until then Rotrud would be prepared for her life as empress in Constantinople, to step into the position once the marriage was celebrated.

Roman Reaction to the Byzantine-Frankish Alliance. In the papal correspondence of the time, the alliance between Charles and Constantinople is not recorded, but a number of other related developments are noticeable. The hostile characterisation of the Sicilians dating from 779-80 as "Greeks hateful to God," and their governor as "the most wicked patrician of Sicily," disappears, presumably as a result of Theodore's victory and increased restraint in Byzantine activities in southern Italy.[70] But sometime between 781 and 783 Hadrian relates the news from Constantinople to Charles: a "Persian" invasion of the empire has advanced to within 60 miles of Constantinople and captured "Amoria" with great booty.[71] (This probably reflects an account of the campaign of Harun, son of Caliph Mahdi, who besieged Nakoleia, defeated Michael Lachanodrakon, and in a three-pronged strategy brought the Arabs to Chrysopolis on the Bosphoros. Irene sued for peace, which proved expensive but effective.[72]) In recounting such a humiliating experience for Byzantium, Hadrian alerted his spiritual son to imperial weakness.

Other elements of growing papal hostility to the empire are visible in a

---

[67] Theophanes, 454-55; Speck, *Kaiser Konstantin VI*, 1:116-22, cf. Classen, "Karl der Grosse," 558-59.

[68] Theophanes, 455.24-25; Einhard, *Vita Karoli*, ch. 19 (English translation, 74).

[69] On the importance of such marriage alliances, frequently planned years in advance, see D. Herlihy, "Land, Family and Women in Continental Europe, 701-1200," *Traditio* 18 (1962): 89-120; and the brilliant comparative treatment by J. Goody, *The Development of the Family and Marriage in Europe* (Cambridge, 1983).

[70] *CC*, nos. 64 (591-92) and 65 (592-93).

[71] *CC*, no. 74 (605).

[72] Theophanes, 456; Speck, *Kaiser Konstantin VI*, 1:123-27. This was the first appearance on Byzantine territory of Harun al Rashid, caliph from 786 to 809, whose rule is generally characterised as the golden age of Abbasid power.

gradual process of change in Roman administration, notably record-keeping and minting, and in the protocol relating to the eastern emperors (prayers said for their well-being and the public display of their portraits). For centuries it had been traditional for Roman bishops to remember the emperors in official prayers, to honour their images in public and on imperial coinage, and to date records from the rulers' assumption of consulship and actual reign.[73] Allegedly, these four privileges had been accorded to Pope Sylvester by Constantine I. They had been withdrawn from Philippikos (711-13) when news of the revival of Monothelete heresy reached Rome. And under Hadrian, two at least were replaced by new methods particular to Rome. Between 772, when official documents were dated by Constantine V's regnal year, and 781-82, the pontifical year under the general rule of Jesus Christ became the established system of dating. Hadrian's successor, Leo III, omitted the reference to Christ and added the year of Charles's assumption of authority in Italy, thus completing a transference from eastern to western secular power. Similarly, Hadrian's silver coinage carried his own name and St. Peter's rather than the emperor's (no gold was minted in Rome after 775).[74] The tradition of displaying imperial portraits in the city and major churches died out over a longer period; by the eighth century, popes were more frequently depicted. And emperors continued to be named in official prayers (unless condemned as heretics). But from 754, Frankish monarchs were also mentioned in regular prayers as part of the spiritual alliance, and there is evidence that these had a special significance for both Pippin and Charles.[75] The major shift in public acclamation occurred when Charles first visited Rome and was greeted with *laudes* appropriate for a patrician (this might also have happened earlier, when Pope Paul I dedicated an altar table sent by Pippin).[76] While each measure on its own might be seen as an adjustment to changing circumstances, taken all together they add up to a substantial rejection of imperial privileges. This may reasonably be linked to Hadrian's desire to establish a greater independence from the East.

Papal misgivings about Charles's new peace with Byzantium were, however, rather undercut by the letter he received in 785 from Irene and Constantine VI, and the synodica from Tarasios, the new patriarch of Constan-

[73] J. Deér, "Die Vorrechte des Kaisers in Rom (772-800)," *Schweizer Beiträge zur Allgemeinen Geschichte* 15 (1957): 5-63, esp. 42-54, reprinted in G. Wolf, ed., *Zum Kaisertum Karls des Grossen* (Darmstadt, 1972).

[74] Ibid., 8-18; Classen, "Karl der Grosse," 554-55, and 559, on the context in which Pope Hadrian may have decided to establish greater papal independence.

[75] Angenendt, "Das geistlichte Bündnis," 45-46, 75-76.

[76] E. H. Kantorowicz, *Laudes Regiae* (Berkeley, 1953), 53, 75-76; Folz, *The Coronation of Charlemagne*, 82-83; Angenendt, "Das geistliche Bündnis," 51-52.

tinople. These announced the emperors' intention of calling an oecumenical council to restore orthodoxy. The participation of the eastern patriarchs and support of Pope Hadrian were requested. Plans to facilitate his journey to the East were also laid down—these highlighted the crucial position of Sicily in West/East communication and the importance of its governors and bishops in imperial diplomacy. The Byzantine rulers admitted that innovation and error had crept into the eastern church and proposed to restore the ancient traditions (i.e. icon veneration). Irene had prevailed on Patriarch Paul to retire into a monastery, leaving the way clear for her to raise a loyal, iconophile civil servant to the post. Tarasios had duly taken holy orders and been promoted through the entire scale of clerical offices to be consecrated head of the church at Christmas 784. He defended this rapid elevation from lay status in his letter to Hadrian.[77]

The change by the Constantinopolitan authorities could not but please the pope, who responded warmly. While he declined to make the journey himself, he appointed two legates to represent the apostolic see at the council—his *oeconomus* (chief administrator), Peter, and the abbot of the St. Sabas monastery at Rome, also called Peter. They left for the East on 26 October 785, taking with them the pope's lengthy reply.[78] This demanded that the pseudo-synod of 754 be condemned in the presence of his envoys, and that the emperors send their declaration of faith with the assurance that it was supported by the patriarch and the entire senate. Hadrian further requested the return of the papal patrimonies removed by Irene's predecessors and of the ancient papal right to consecrate bishops and archbishops in East Illyricum. After a firm statement of Roman primacy, Hadrian objected to Tarasio's use of the epithet "universal" (as in the title "oecumenical patriarch") and demanded that the new patriarch send his own declaration of faith to Rome, allegedly to quell disquiet over his promotion from lay status.

Finally, Hadrian stated that Rome must be recognised as the head of all the churches of God.[79] This blunt declaration of Roman primacy was based

---

[77] Theophanes, 458-60, records the demission of Patriarch Paul, Tarasios's elevation and consecration, and the dispatch of his synodica and declaration of faith together with Irene's invitation, the imperial *sakra divalis*. The patriarchal records are cited but not read in full at the council of 787, see Mansi, 13.986-90, cf. 1055-71; the *sakra* was also read, ibid., 984-86; 1002-1007.

[78] Pope Hadrian's replies, his synodica (Jaffé, no. 2448), and his letter to Tarasios were partially read at the council, Mansi, 12.1055-84 (Greek translation); also in *PL* 96, nos. 56 and 57, 1215-42. On the full Latin texts, see L. Wallach, "The Greek and Latin Versions of II Nicaea and the Synodica of Hadrian I (JE 2448)," *Traditio* 22 (1966):103-125, reprinted in his *Diplomatic Studies in Latin and Greek Documents from the Carolingian Age* (Ithaca, 1977).

[79] The last section of Hadrian's letter, containing this claim, was omitted from the Greek

on the papal belief that the church of Constantinople had placed itself out-side the unity of the Christian *oikoumene* by its adoption of iconoclast her-esy, which had been condemned by Pope Gregory III in 731 and again in 769. Orthodoxy had been upheld in Rome while incorrect dogma was sup-ported in the eastern capital. The successors of St. Peter (*vices gerens Petri*) could therefore claim to have maintained the true faith unchanged, which justified their superior position at the head of all the churches.[80] Despite this assertion, which was bound to cause hostility in Byzantium, and the other conditions that were imposed, the papacy was clearly favourable to the move to reestablish orthodoxy in the East. Yet there is no evidence that Hadrian reported his reaction to Charles.

In planning the council, Irene and Tarasios followed established eastern practice. Since 325, the participation and agreement of all five patriarchs (the pentarchy of Alexandria, Antioch, Jerusalem, Rome, and Constanti-nople) was considered essential to any universal definitions of faith. At sub-sequent councils the custom of reaffirming previous oecumenical deci-sions—anathemas and canons—developed as a means of preserving correct doctrine.[81] In the light of these traditions, critics of the council of 754 stressed the fact that the pentarchy was evidently not represented; worse still, far from agreeing with these church leaders, the council had anathe-matised and persecuted them. This alone constituted sufficient grounds for invalidating its claim to universal authority. But in addition, its rulings did not accord with those of the previous six oecumenical councils. In 785-86, therefore, the Constantinopolitan organisers tried to make quite sure that these criteria would be met. Tarasios's attempt to gain the support of the eastern patriarchs was resolved by the participation of two monks, probably members of the Christian communities under Islam, who had sought refuge in the Byzantine capital.[82] Together with the papal legates

---

translation. It is further developed in the pope's letter-treatise to Charlemagne, the *Ha-drianum*.

[80] For the text of the *Hadrianum*, see *Epistolae Karolini Aevi*, 3 (in *MGH, Ep.*, vol. 5), 5-57, also in Mansi, 13.759-810 and *PL* 98, 1247-92. The claims for Roman primacy, scattered throughout, are concluded at the end, where Rome is identified as the "head of all the churches of God," and Charles is reminded of his duties towards the see of St. Peter, *Epistolae Karolini Aevi*, 3.57. Cf. Y. M.-G. Congar, *L'ecclésiologie du haut moyen âge* (Paris, 1968), 190-92, 358.

[81] H. J. Sieben, *Die Konzilsidee der alten Kirche* (Paderborn, 1979), 318-20.

[82] Theophanes, 460-61. The status of these monks was later questioned, see S. H. Grif-fith, "Stephen of Ramlah and the Christian Kerygma in Arabic in Ninth-Century Pales-tine," *JEH* 36 (1985): 23-45, esp. 30-31. Relations between Constantinople and the Chris-tians under Islam appear to have been severed by the Abbasid caliphate, see S. H. Griffith, "Theodore Abu Qurrah's Arabic Tract on the Christian Practice of Venerating Images," *Journal of the American Oriental Society* 105 (1985): 53-73, esp. 71.

they would ensure the representation, however nominal, of the pentarchy. Then documents were prepared that justified icon veneration as one of the ancient traditions of the church. Agreement with the rulings of past oecumenical councils would thus be confirmed.

But Constantinople failed to orchestrate majority support for the proposed restoration of icons among the bishops who were summoned. So when the council opened on 7 August 786, in the church of the Holy Apostles in Constantinople, a well-planned iconoclast intervention, spearheaded by troops of the guards and *tagmata* loyal to Constantine V, prevented orderly debate.[83] A group of iconoclast bishops, which may have included those of Nicaea, Rhodes, Pessinous, Ikonion, Pisidia, Ierapolis, and Karpathos, singled out as ringleaders in 787, denounced the meeting. General pandemonium was only partially resolved by an imperial official, who arrived to close the proceedings. Whilst most participants left, some iconoclasts remained in the church reciting the iconoclast definition of faith, as if determined to prevent any change in official doctrine.[84]

THE SEVENTH OECUMENICAL COUNCIL (787)

Irene was not to be dissuaded, however. She instructed Staurakios to order the iconoclast troops into Asia Minor on the pretext of an Arab attack, and in May 787 recalled all the bishops and legates. The Roman party had reached Sicily before it received this second summons.[85] On September 9 the council reconvened in the Bithynian city of Nicaea, chosen partly in imitation of the first oecumenical meeting but also because untoward opposition could be more effectively controlled outside the capital.

As Tarasios and Irene were agreed that iconoclasm was a heretical belief, both the chief issue and the procedure to be adopted by the council were clear: penitent iconoclasts who genuinely regretted their past error should be readmitted to the church and the heresy condemned. The first three sessions were therefore devoted to matters of ecclesiastical discipline and organisation; only in the fourth did a serious examination of iconoclasm commence. Since this approach in effect excused the Byzantine church of embracing a heresy and imposing it for over 50 years, it would not have met with Pope Hadrian's approval. But as he was not there to object and had not foreseen this tactic, his legates were unable to influence the careful stage-management of the council.

At the opening of the first session, the Sicilian bishops invited Patriarch

[83] Theophanes, 461-62; the events are referred to at the opening of the council of 787, Mansi, 12.990-91, 999-1002; cf. Speck, *Kaiser Konstantin VI*, 1:153-56.

[84] Mansi, 12.1015D; Theophanes, 461-62.

[85] Theophanes, 462; *Epistolae Karolini Aevi*, 3.57.

Tarasios to address the assembly on the reasons for the change of venue, and
the military officials present (Petronas, count of Opsikion, and John, minister responsible for the central military bureau) ordered the imperial *sakra*
to be read.[86] This was the letter from Constantine VI and Irene addressed
to the council. It gave another account of the decision to summon the council and its purpose, mentioning the synodica of Pope Hadrian, which had
been brought by his two representatives and which would be read out later.
But first, the known iconoclasts prepared to acknowledge their heresy were
examined. There were two groups: three distinguished metropolitans—
Basil of Ankyra, Theodore of Myra, and Theodosios of Amorion—and
seven bishops. Basil had submitted a written account of his errors to clear
himself of the charge of heresy and to return to communion with "Rome,
Constantinople and all the other orthodox bishops" (Mansi, 12.1007D-
1011B). Theodore read the same confession, while Theodosios had prepared his own (1014A-1015B). After discussion it was agreed that all three
were truly penitent and should be readmitted to the church. They then assumed the seats appropriate to their metropolitan rank (1015D).

For the second group of bishops, however, no such clear-cut procedure
was available. The seven who came from those parts of Asia Minor and islands especially threatened by the Arab attacks of the 720s were closely associated with the disruption of the 786 meeting. After cross-examination
by Tarasios and lengthy discussion of the canonical rulings that governed
the readmission of heretics, the patriarch recommended forgiveness (1015-
1051). But the eastern and papal legates remained very critical, while
many of the monks present were totally opposed, especially to the admission of those who had been ordained bishops during iconoclasm (1022D,
1031C-D). Abbot Sabas of the Stoudios monastery in Constantinople
proved a vociferous hardliner, whose strict application of canon law was
only overruled by evidence adduced by the papal legates. Peter cited the
examples of Makarios, the Monothelete patriarch condemned at the Sixth
Oecumenical Council and sent to Rome to be won over, and of Meletios,
who had received ordination from Arian clerics but became a saint of the
early church nonetheless (1034C, 1035E, 1038B). Even so, the session
continued to debate the relevance of past instances in ecclesiastical history
for some time. Finally the issues of readmission and reordination were
agreed, and the seven read out their confessions of faith (1050D-E).

The same problems dominated the second session, however, when Gregory of Neocaesarea was introduced to the council by an imperial official as

[86] Mansi, 12.999, 1002C. The directing role of these two civilian figures is a very notable feature of the council. On numerous occasions their interventions forced a resolution
of problematic issues, always affirming the "imperial" position against western or monastic
opposition.

another penitent iconoclast (1051E-1054C). After further cross-examination, he was ordered to return later with his confession. Leontios, another secular officer, then announced that he had brought the letters of the pope and of the eastern patriarchs, which would be read so that the council would learn what these authorities thought would be "suitable in the present circumstances" (1054D). Greek translations of Pope Hadrian's synodica to the emperors and his letter to Tarasios were read and approved by all (1055-71, 1077-84). Tarasios commented that Hadrian had confirmed the ancient traditions of the Catholic church, which the East also acknowledged, including the relative worship of icons, true worship being reserved to God alone (1086B). John of Jerusalem, one of the eastern delegates, praised Irene for arranging this council, which brought together Mercy and Truth in an identical declaration of faith (i.e. Hadrian and Tarasios) (1086D). No one commented publicly on the fact that the translation of the papal synodica was highly defective; it omitted large sections from the original Latin text.

In the third session, Gregory of Neocaesarea and the other iconoclast bishops were finally readmitted, though not until John the *logothetes*, the presiding secular official, intervened in support of Tarasios's plea for charity (1118B). Again it was the non-Constantinopolitan patriarchal legates and the monastic community that objected to any relaxation of discipline, but some of the Sicilian bishops took a milder line. Once they had been re-seated, Tarasios's declaration of faith was read, as was the eastern patriarchs' letter to the council (1119-27, 1127-46). This was not written for the occasion, but had been drafted to express opposition to the 754 council. It stressed the desire of all Christians in Syria and Egypt living under "the enemies of the cross" (1130E) to make known their own orthodoxy and condemnation of "the other [council] called by some the seventh, as a destruction of the Apostolic and Patristic traditions and the extinction and abolition of the holy and venerable icons" (1134C). The letter went on to apologise for the non-attendance of the patriarchs themselves, Theodore of Jerusalem, Cosmas of Alexandria, and Theodore of Antioch, and their bishops who could not make any public move in support, for fear of "horrible threats and deadly penalties of those who rule over us" (1134D). It reminded Tarasios that the Sixth Oecumenical Council had also taken place without their participation (on account of the "tyranny of the accursed") but that this had not denied its universal character (1134E-1135A). The patriarchs thereby confirmed their belief in the pentarchy as the decisive force behind doctrinal changes and sought to obviate any objection to their absence from the council. The session concluded with a general agreement that all the churches held the same faith, and the participants concurred with their signatures.

This basic agreement achieved one of the major aims of the council and must have been as pleasing to the Roman legates as to the eastern authorities, though the procedural means adopted for the readmission of past heretics was not entirely to Rome's liking. Pope Hadrian would have preferred an explicit condemnation of iconoclasm as a heresy, wrongly approved by the eastern church. This was required to induce a sense of shame and humility before Rome's orthodoxy. With this exalted sense of his authority, Hadrian had demanded the total restoration of holy images as the only measure that could remove the great error and scandal caused by Constantine VI's great-grandfather's destruction—"the madness of heretics which overthrew the venerable images and led into error . . . all the people who live in the East" (1055E). He had further recommended to the eastern emperors the example of his spiritual son and *compater*, Charles, who had subdued all of *Hesperia* and *Occidua*, establishing the rule of Christians over barbarian nations (1058A). This part of Hadrian's letter to the emperors was so full of the primacy of Rome that it was omitted in the Greek translation. In Constantinople, those responsible for this version dwelt instead on the pope's promise that when the images had been reinstated in their former dignity, "then Constantine and Irene shall be renamed the New Constantine and the New Helena and praised throughout the universe" (1058A).

The eastern authorities thus realised that Hadrian was staking a claim to superior orthodoxy and resisted it. The crucial element of this theoretical debate turned on the precise significance to be attributed to the key Petrine text—"*Tu es Petrus.*" While the primacy of St. Peter himself was recognised in the East, there was no agreement on its transmission to his successors.[87] In their official letters to the council, the emperors and the patriarch stopped short of accepting that Rome still exercised an absolute authority throughout the entire church. Tarasios stressed Christ's role as head of the church and of the council; Irene, the imperial right to summon such a gathering without ecclesiastical authorisation. The direction of the proceedings, while under Tarasios's control, was guided by lay officials, as usual— a factor that constituted one of the major differences between oecumenical and western councils. The traditional role of the emperor as "equal of the apostles," their "partner," had no direct parallel in Latin Christianity.[88]

While the papal legates were always given primacy of honour as representatives of Rome, being seated and signing every sessional record first as well as proposing the final ceremony of icon restoration, Hadrian's argu-

---

[87] Congar, *L'ecclésiologie du haut moyen âge*, 363-70; W. de Vries, "Die Struktur der Kirche gemass dem II. Konzil von Nicäa (787)," *Orientalia Christiana Periodica* 33 (1967): 47-71, esp. 59-60.

[88] As claimed at Nicaea, see Mansi, 13.408, for instance; cf. de Vries, "Die Struktur," 62-63.

ments for iconophile practice were treated quite roughly in the fourth session. In contrast, the eastern patriarchs' letter was acclaimed without further ado (Mansi, 12.1135-46). Some of the citations adduced by the pope in favour of icon veneration were verified by reference to eastern copies of the same works and the traditions of the entire church (as in 680-81). Others were simply ignored, among them, interestingly, his two main *testimonia*, which derived from the legendary account of Pope Sylvester's baptism of Constantine I and Pope Gregory the Great's letter to Serenus of Marseille. While the first had been branded as apocryphal by no less an authority than Pope Gelasius (in the late fifth century), its value for iconophile theory depended on the identification of visionary figures from their portraits, an argument admitted by the council in a whole range of eastern examples. The second may simply have been unknown in the East; the papal legates made no effort to spell out its pedagogic significance, though again similar evidence was adduced from a number of other Greek texts. In this rather casual treatment of Hadrian's considered position on iconophile theory, the council of 787 paid little respect to apostolic claims to universal leadership. Rome was treated as one of the five patriarchates; its presence and authority was as necessary and important as that of the others, but not decisively more so.

This stress on the collective authority of the pentarchy took on a physical form in the carefully orchestrated discussion of iconophile miracles and iconoclast wickedness recorded in the fourth and fifth sessions. While the underlying argument had been decided in the patriarchate of Constantinople and was enunciated by Tarasios's staff with support from those secular officials representing the emperors, many other participants intervened with their own evidence on numerous occasions.[89] John of Jerusalem, one of the "eastern" legates, brought several books with him and read from others kept in Constantinople; he also commented on many statements in an authoritative fashion (Mansi, 13.9E, 20C, 53E, 72A-D, for instance). Individual bishops and monks presented their own copies of iconophile writings and confirmed the veracity of others. The papal legates produced two texts and approved a reference to the *Miracles* of the holy martyr Anastasios (the Persian saint), whereupon a Sicilian bishop confirmed that a woman had recently been cured at the saint's Roman shrine (24C-D). Similarly, the existence of icons responsible for miraculous cures was proved by sworn testimony: Theodore of Seleukeia vouched for the evidence of Manzon, another bishop, healed by an icon of Christ only one year previously; the bishop of Kition confirmed under oath the power of a mo-

---

[89] P. van den Ven, "La patristique et l'hagiographie au concile de Nicée de 787," *B* 25-27 (1957): 325-62, esp. 332-41; Mango, "The Availability of Books," 30-33.

saic image of the Virgin (possibly the apse mosaic in his own church) (65D-E, 77D). Although these textual contributions may well have been solicited, the verbal ones preserve an air of spontaneity, which appears to draw on the widespread belief in miraculous powers associated with icons.

Constantinople, however, provided the largest number of proof-texts, in part due to the resources of the patriarchal library. As we have seen, it was in this library that theological texts, both orthodox and heretical, were stored. Against its holdings the authenticity of other manuscripts was tested and the use of brief quotations correctly interpreted in their context within complete works. The difference that this procedure could make is amply illustrated by one short episode in the fourth session of the 787 council (33A-37C). A brief extract from one of the letters of St. Neilos of Sinai had been quoted with approval at the iconoclast council of 754. It was now read in its entirety so that the iconophile message could be appreciated. By consulting the whole work, rather than an isolated quotation on a separate sheet (*pittakion*), Theodore of Myra was convinced, though he also claimed that one word had been changed at the 754 council. To make sure that St. Neilos had argued in favour of images, another text was read from a different book. In addition to the wealth of patristic sources produced by the patriarchal library, it also supplied copies of the famous letters of Patriarch Germanos to the first iconoclast bishops of Asia Minor; these were read at the end of the fourth session (100-128A).

In contrast to the spontaneous participation witnessed in the fourth and fifth sessions, the sixth lacked any unplanned aspects (202-364). This was devoted to a refutation of the iconoclast Definition (*Horos*) of 754. Gregory of Neocaesarea was forced to read the document section by section, and after each iconoclast claim, Epiphanios, a deacon of the Great Church read the iconophile response. The entire session is a dialogue culminating in the official Constantinopolitan justification of image veneration. No one else participated; no additional arguments were adduced. Thus, when it came to the formal denunciation of iconoclasm, nothing was left to chance; Tarasios had carefully prepared the Byzantine position, which was firmly imposed on the council.

At the second oecumenical council held at Nicaea, therefore, the Byzantine church attempted to return to orthodoxy on its own terms, ignoring the critical judgement of Pope Hadrian, and making no response to his requests concerning the papal patrimonies. It is often supposed that the account of the origins of iconoclasm read out in the fifth session by John of Jerusalem, which identified Constantine of Nakoleia as the arch-heretic, was devised to spare Constantine VI and Irene any embarrassment (13.197A-200B). But as we have seen, it incorporated many of the factors that underlay the first manifestations of doubt in icon power. In the face of determined imperial action to restore veneration, all those iconoclast bishops of 786 bent with the prevailing wind and anathematised the doctrine they had so recently championed. At the close of the fourth session, 335 bishops and 132 abbots, clerics, and monks signed their adhesion to iconophile theology (133-56), including Elias, priest at the Blachernai church in the capital, who admitted that "no one was more active than I in the late persecution" (41A). He read out some of the canons passed at the Sixth Oecumenical Council, especially number 82 on the human representation of Christ, and reported that this had persuaded him to change his mind about the holy images (40E-41B). After the seventh session at Nicaea, when the iconophile Definition of faith was proclaimed, the iconoclasts anathematised, and (probably) 22 disciplinary canons decreed (364-439), one final meeting was held at the Magnaura palace in New Rome at the emperors' request. There, in the presence of the whole city and the military orders, the patriarch reported on the council's work; its Definition was read and acclaimed by all together with the anathemas and the testimonies to icon veneration.[90] With a final Glory to God, the Seventh Oecumenical Council concluded its work (417A-B).

While the icons were officially restored with the approval of all present, it is very doubtful whether the soldiers who had participated at the 786 gathering felt equally convinced of the heretical content of their belief. Iconoclast currents were not completely removed by the Seventh Council; they disappeared into an underground stream of popular memories closely associated with Emperor Constantine V and his many military victories. In their partial but coherent interpretation of his reign, imperial triumphs, the low price of grain, and a general sense of well-being were inseparably connected (while iconophile martyrs and the destruction of artefacts were conveniently overlooked). Despite Irene's successful reversal of iconoclast doctrine, these associations were not expunged and would survive a generation of iconophile practice to re-emerge in the second decade of the ninth century.

Within Byzantium, however, the immediate reaction to 787 appeared generally positive.[91] Monastic communities and devout iconophiles, who had returned to the capital in expectation of rewards for their constancy, were established in influential positions by Irene. With the approval of Hadrian's legates, no further antagonism was expected from the West,

---

[90] Theophanes, 462-63; on the significance of the final session and the justification of the council as the true Seventh Oecumenical Council, see J. A. Munitiz, "Synoptic Greek Accounts of the Seventh Council," *REB* 32 (1974): 147-86, esp. 175-76.

[91] P. Henry, "Initial Eastern Assessments of the Seventh Oecumenical Council," *JTS*, n.s., 25 (1974): 75-92. The acts of 787 remained unknown to Christians living under Arab rule, see Griffith, "Theodore Abu Qurrah's Arabic Tract," esp. 58.

though the pope did not express his satisfaction at the outcome of the council. As several of thé conditions listed in his 785 letter had not been met—specifically, the return of papal patrimonies and rights associated with papal control over East Illyricum—this is not entirely surprising. In Constantinople, the only cloud on the horizon that might reduce the empress's pleasure at successfully concluding the council concerned the alliance with Charles. And this does not seem to have been influenced by matters of faith; on the contrary, it stemmed from a clear difference of political interest, and once again southern Italy provided the troubled context.

Lombard Benevento

After the deposition of King Desiderius in 774, Duke Arichis of Benevento had assumed the title *"princeps gentis Langobardorum."* He began to date his official documents by his own regnal year and had his own initials overstruck on the Byzantine coinage in circulation. He wore a crown and kingly regalia (as had earlier Lombard rulers of Pavia) and refounded Salerno as his capital.[92] In this extremely independent manner he allied with the governor of Sicily in attacks on Gaeta and Amalfi (786) and usurped papal estates in the Naples area. It was in response to Hadrian's urgent appeals for these lands to be returned and the renewed Lombard threat checked that Charles arrived in Italy late in 786.

Rather than risk a military confrontation, Arichis negotiated a peace with the Frankish monarch, to whom he swore allegiance and handed over his son Grimoald and twelve other hostages, the normal guarantee of such a treaty.[93] Outside Capua, a Byzantine embassy caught up with Charles before Easter 787, and talks were held. Whether the Franks Witbold and John had already returned from the East (they had been sent to Constantinople to finalise plans for the proposed marriage) is unknown. At this meeting in southern Italy, however, the alliance was definitely broken off, both sides claiming responsibility.[94] Clearly, neither wished to admit the humiliation of being repudiated. On balance it seems more likely that

[92] *Chronicon Salernitanum*, ch. 19 (23), relating a story of how the young Arichis aspired to the title; Classen, "Karl der Grosse," 554; H. Belting, "Studien zum Beneventanischen Hof im 8. Jahrhundert," *DOP* 16 (1962): 141-93; E. Garms-Cornides, "Die langobardischen Fürstentitel (774-1077)," in Wolfram, *Intitulatio II*, 341-452, esp. 342-61; P. Bertolini, *Figura velut qua Christus designatur* (Rome, 1978), 112-18.

[93] *Annals of Einhard*, aa.786, 787; *Chronicon Salernitanum*, chs. 9-13 (11-19). For Hadrian's numerous appeals, see *CC*, nos. 57, 61, 64, 65 (582-83, 588-89, 591-92, 593, 630-31); these letters form the basis for O. Bertolini's very convincing reconstruction of Charles's relations with Benevento, see "Carlomagno e Benevento," in *Karl der Grosse*, 1:609-671, esp. 633-36.

[94] Theophanes, 463; *Royal Frankish Annals*, a.787; Speck, *Kaiser Konstantin VI*, 1:164-65, cf. Noble, *Republic of St. Peter*, 176-77.

Irene had already taken the decision on the grounds that the marriage would exalt Charles's authority in the West and bring an overmighty political ambition into Constantinopolitan circles. The careful division of Byzantine and Frankish influence in Italy might be disturbed, with dangerous consequences for Sicily and Calabria.

While Charles celebrated Easter 787 in Rome, the alliance most feared by Hadrian and his predecessors began to take shape, as Arichis broke all his oaths to the Carolingians and requested Byzantine aid. Irene decided to employ the Lombard prince Adelgis in the service of Constantinople and planned a double attack to coordinate activity in both the south and north of Italy. In response to Arichis, a high-ranking embassy was sent to Salerno in summer 787 to invest him with the honour of patrician (the insignia and official costume described in relation to this embassy reveal what a grand business the ceremony would be). At the same time, Adelgis was promised the opportunity to restore Lombard authority in Pavia. But by one of those quirks of history, the embassy to Benevento arrived too late—Arichis was dead and his sole surviving son, Grimoald, was held hostage at Charles's court.[95] Although Charles had been obliged to move north against Tassilo of Bavaria, a further conflict between Franks and Byzantines appeared inevitable, quite apart from ecclesiastical or dynastic differences.

It broke out in the autumn of 788, when a large force was sent from Constantinople to support Adelgis's claims. Grimoald had been allowed to assume his inheritance on condition that Charles's name was used on the coinage and in the dating of official documents of Benevento.[96] He was also provided with limited Frankish military assistance, supplemented by forces from the duchy of Spoleto. Despite an apparently inferior army, Grimoald was able to drive the Byzantines back into Calabria and Sicily. Charles's protégé thus defeated Irene's, and Adelgis returned to Constantinople, where he died.[97] This final obliteration of Lombard hopes for a restoration also sealed Carolingian possession of the title "king of the Lombards" and confined Byzantine control in the Italian peninsula to the extreme south and Sicily.

Another quite striking outcome was the role Lombard Benevento would play in European culture. For not only did Grimoald maintain a delicate

[95] CC, no. 83 (617); Dölger, Regesten, no. 348; J. Gay, L'Italie méridionale et l'empire byzantin, 2 vols. (Paris, 1904), 1:36-37; Garms-Cornides, "Die langobardishen Fürstentitel," 372-74.

[96] Erchempert, Chronicon, ch. 4 in SSRL, 236; cf. Belting, "Studien zum Beneventanischen Hof," 147; Chronicon Salernitanum, ch. 29; cf. Bertolini, "Carlomagno e Benevento," 648-53.

[97] Royal Frankish Annals, a.788; Bertolini, "Carlomagno e Benevento," 653-56; Noble, Republic of St. Peter, 177-80.

balance between the two great powers, but his court developed into one of the most important intellectual centres in the West. Its proximity to the Greek south and the ancient civic traditions of the Mediterranean world gave it a bilingual base and a developed concept of urban life, which made Salerno a leading city in cultural as well as commercial terms.[98] The centre of advanced medical studies, which attracted students from as far away as Armenia, it may be seen as one of the western regions that shunned imperial control but adapted the cultural heritage of Byzantium. In this contradictory process, a significant element of eastern and Greek influence was incorporated into decisively "western" states. But in addition, Salerno did not ignore the advances made in scientific, medical, and philosophical knowledge in the Islamic world, and promoted translations from the Arabic. It thus contributed decisively to the twelfth-century rediscovery of classical learning in the West that preceded the Renaissance.[99]

Frankish Reaction to the Seventh Oecumenical Council

When Pope Hadrian received the Greek *acta* of 787 (with the imperial *sacra* and Tarasios's declaration of faith), he commissioned a Latin translation. This was made in Rome in about 788-89 and was an inaccurate version of the Greek, which as we have seen did not include the complete documentation furnished in Hadrian's original Latin synodica of 785. Whether this was noticed or not, a copy of the translation was made for Charles and sent to him (as notification of the correction of the eastern heresy).[100] By 789-90 at the latest, therefore, the Frankish court was in possession of a version of the 787 proceedings. The text of a new oecumenical council with its definition of the correct Christian approach to holy images must have been of considerable fascination, not only to Charles but also to his circle of court theologians: Alcuin, Theodulf of Orléans, Paulinus of Aquileia, and Angilramnus of Metz amongst them. Their curiosity was probably tinged by a slight prejudice against the Byzantine claim to arbitrate for the entire Christian world. It was as a self-conscious group of western intellectuals

[98] Belting, "Studien zum Beneventanischen Hof," esp. 175-93 (on the church of St. Sophia, built by Arichis); Gay, *L'Italie méridionale*, 1:39-48 (on the bilingual traditions, which permitted Benevento to link West and East).

[99] C. H. Haskins, *The Renaissance of the Twelfth Century* (Cambridge, Mass., 1927), 53-54, 322-23, 326-29; P. I. Kristeller, "The School of Salerno," *Bulletin of the History of Medicine* 17 (1945): 138-94, esp. 151-53 on Constantine the African's translations from Arabic; F. Gabrieli, "La cultura araba e la Scuola medica Salernitana," *Rivista di studi salernitani* 1 (1968): 7-21; U. Westerbergh, *Ninth Century Beneventan Poetry* (Lund, 1957); E. A. Loew, *The Beneventan Script* (Oxford, 1914), revised with a second volume by V. Brown (Rome, 1980); B. Lawn, *The Salernitan Questions* (Oxford, 1963), esp. 1-15.

[100] Wallach, "The Greek and Latin Versions"; A. Freeman, "Carolingian Orthodoxy and the Fate of the *Libri Carolini*," *Viator* 16 (1985): 65-108, esp. 77-81.

with the highest standards and standing in the Frankish territories that they first studied the Latin translation of the 787 acts.

Reconstructing their immediate reaction is rendered very difficult by the loss of the *Capitulare adversus synodum*, a document prepared in Charles's name and directed against the acts, including Hadrian's synodica of 785 (as it appeared in the incomplete and incorrect record of the second session). Angilbert, abbot of St. Riquier and court chaplain, took the *Capitulare* to Rome, and the pope responded with a vigorous defence. The essential parts of this reply—if not the whole—are preserved in a "letter-treatise" of ca. 791, known as the *Hadrianum*.[101] Frankish criticism in the *Capitulare* is summarised and then refuted point by point. Evidently Charles's theologians found fault with a great many aspects of the council, but did not order their condemnation very succinctly (to judge by the *Hadrianum*). They criticised Irene's role on the grounds that it was improper for a woman to preside at a council (c. 53); Tarasios's orthodoxy and elevation from lay status (and here the issue of the procession of the Holy Spirit was explicitly raised) (cc. 1, 12); and the use of past conciliar decrees and of a large number of texts adduced in favour of icon veneration, which they found not pertinent (c. 35). But the most fundamental attack on the acts sprang from the question: Where in the Old or New Testament are orders given to make or adore images (c. 19)? The Franks claimed that one of the earliest instances adduced, the story of Christ's image sent to King Abgar of Edessa, was preserved in no Gospel (c. 18). In addition to this basic objection to the veneration of icons, they stated that images were not equal to the relics of martyrs or saints (c. 59). They also dismissed all the evidence of nocturnal visions as an indirect confirmation of the value of icons (c. 13) and much more evidence produced by the council. There was thus no shortage of issues on which they took an antagonistic stand.

At this stage Hadrian had not made any official response to Constantinople, and he consulted the Franks in order to present a united western approval.[102] Clearly he was not anticipating continuing hostility. In this he underestimated both the theological expertise available at court and Charles's idea of a Christian monarch's duty to maintain orthodoxy. For far from accepting the *Hadrianum*, Charles commissioned a more detailed examination of both Roman and Byzantine arguments.

This was the origin of the famous *Libri Carolini* (literally, "*Charles Books*"), which defined an independent Frankish theology.[103] While they

---

[101] *Epistolae Karolini Aevi*, 3, 5-57.

[102] Ibid., 57; cf. Classen, "Karl der Grosse," 563.

[103] *Libri Carolini sive Caroli Magni Capitulare De Imaginibus*, in *Concilia*, III, Supplement II (Hannover/Leipzig, 1924), also in *PL* 98, 999-1248. A new edition for the *MGH* is being prepared by Ann Freeman.

were drafted by a group and were issued in the king's name, two of the outstanding intellectuals of the time, Alcuin and Theodulf, probably took a large responsibility; and as Alcuin was away in York during the vital period, 790-93, the preparatory work was mainly Theodulf's.[104] His very particular Visigothic heritage is revealed in numerous quotations from the Mozarabic liturgy and, perhaps, in the close reading of Isidore of Seville's work, which influences every aspect.[105] The text provides evidence of the Carolingian capacity for self-confident theological reasoning, which marks another stage in the estrangement of West from East.

The Reign of Constantine VI

While the Seventh Oecumenical Council was receiving such intense investigation in the papal curia and the Frankish court, a very different drama was developing in the Byzantine capital. Although the empress-mother had directed the restoration of icons, throughout the council meetings Constantine had been referred to as the senior emperor, as was customary. The pope had even identified him as a New Constantine, as if to recall the Christian ruler who presided over the First Oecumenical Council. And he had celebrated his sixteenth birthday in January 787 and thereby attained his majority. Although the arranged marriage with Charles's daughter Rotrud had been broken off, in November 788 (or earlier), his mother selected Maria of Amnia, granddaughter of a wealthy Paphlagonian landowner, St. Philaretos, as his wife.[106] He therefore required his own private family quarters as well as official imperial rooms in the palace. Clearly he had

[104] Theodulf's authorship is championed by A. Freeman, "Theodulf of Orleans and the *Libri Carolini*," *Speculum* 32 (1957): 663-705; "Further Studies in the *Libri Carolini*, I and II," ibid., 40 (1965): 203-289; "Further Studies in the *Libri Carolini*, III," ibid., 46 (1971): 597-612. L. Wallach, on the other hand, argues that Alcuin was responsible, see "The Unknown Author of the *Libri Carolini*: Patristic Exegesis, Mozarabic Antiphons and the *Vetus Latina*," in *Didascaliae: Studies in Honour of A. M. Albareda*, ed. S. Preta (New York, 1961), 471-515; "The *Libri Carolini* and Patristics, Latin and Greek: Prolegomena to a Critical Edition," in *The Classical Tradition: Studies in Honor of H. Caplan*, ed. L. Wallach (Ithaca, 1966), 451-98. Wallach's attack on Freeman culminated in "Theodulph of Orléans's Alleged Authorship of the *Libri Carolini*: On Fictions and Facts," in his *Diplomatic Studies*, part 3; Freeman was defended by P. Meyvaert, "The Authorship of the *Libri Carolini*," *Revue Bénédictine* 81 (1979): 29-57. See also G. Arnaldi, "La questione dei *Libri Carolini*," and F. Mütherich, "I *Libri Carolini* e la miniatura carolingia," both in O. Capitani, ed., *Culto cristiano e politica imperiale carolingia* (Todi, 1979), 63-86, 283-301.

[105] Freeman, "Theodulf of Orleans"; E. Dahlhaus-Berg, *Nova Antiquitas et Antiqua Novitas* (Cologne/Vienna, 1975), 190-201; Wallach, *Diplomatic Studies*, 52-53, 63, 139, 176, 207.

[106] Theophanes, 463; M.-H. Fourmy and M. Leroy, "La vie de S. Philarète," *B* 9 (1934): 85-170; Speck, *Kaiser Konstantin VI*, 1:203-204, analyses the background of this hagiological compilation and indicates why it may have been written in 821-22.

reached man's estate and could anticipate acting as the senior emperor in deed as well as name. These feelings were manifested in his desire to have his own men hold office in place of Irene's trusted eunuchs. In particular, he resented the power wielded by Staurakios, who controlled the entire government through the foreign ministry.[107] Yet Irene showed no intention of withdrawing from her position as regent, or making over any aspect of imperial authority to Constantine.

Meanwhile, icons were gradually returned to their place of honour. Portable icons that had survived the destruction were again displayed in churches, on iconostasis screens, and in public places—a mosaic panel of Christ was restored to the Chalke Gate of the imperial palace (possibly not before 797-802).[108] Several new churches were constructed or reconstructed on the site of older ones: St. Sophia in Thessalonike, dated by mosaic roundels with the monograms of Constantine and Irene; St. Sophia at Bizye in Thrace (which may recall the triumphal tour of 784); and several monastic churches in Bithynia, which had become a centre of iconophile activity under the influence of St. Platon of Sakkoudion, the disciples of St. Stephen the martyr, and some of the eastern monks who settled in the empire in the 780s. In Constantinople, imperial patronage was responsible for the refitting of the church of the Virgin of the Fountain, where Irene believed she had received a miraculous cure. The emperors presented their own portraits in mosaic to commemorate the cure, showing themselves endowing the church with new golden veils and curtains, a crown, and liturgical vessels decorated with precious stones and pearls. Sculptures of the emperors were also made, probably for public display.[109] The return to figural art appears to have proceeded slowly, and many crosses remained (in the church of St. Irene for instance). While monastic artists may have received imperial commissions for illustrated manuscripts and icons, there is, as I have noted above, far more evidence for the revival of scriptoria devoted to non-illustrated manuscript production of a theological nature.

At first Constantine's efforts to assert his own power were unsuccessful, but his mother's obstinate refusal to recognise his imperial rights except in the most formal terms provoked disquiet in certain military quarters. The costly and humiliating peace signed with Harun al Rashid represented a distinct contrast to the victories of Constantine V and Leo IV, and *thema*

---

[107] Theophanes, 464-65; Speck, *Kaiser Konstantin VI*, 1:190-91.

[108] The iconophile Definition of faith (Mansi, 13.377C-D) stipulated that icons should be put up in houses, on walls and doors, and beside highways (as well as in churches), as a constant reminder. C. Mango, *The Brazen House* (Copenhagen, 1959), 121-22; cf. A. Grabar, *L'Iconoclasme byzantin: Dossier archéologique* (Paris, 1957), 130-31; Speck, *Artabasdos*, 245-59.

[109] R. Cormack, "The Arts During Iconoclasm," in A. Bryer and J. Herrin, eds., *Iconoclasm* (Birmingham, 1977), 40; Mango, *The Art of the Byzantine Empire, 312-1453*, 156-57.

commanders were anxious to restore the high status of the army. For two or three years, it seems, maternal and filial factions engaged in a war of nerves and diplomacy within the empire, each trying to reduce the other's base of support and win an outright acknowledgement of superiority.[110] This was not influenced by the icon question directly, though hardened military officers (especially those responsible for the newly formed crack troops) may have tended to support Constantine. After 787, no more official acts of iconoclasm are recorded, but generals such as Michael Lachanodrakon continued in office, and the associations lingered on, encouraging hopes of greater military security and pride in Byzantium.[111]

In another way, however, the condemnation of iconoclasm had an immediate bearing on the struggle. The council had prompted loyal iconophiles to return to the capital, hopeful of ecclesiastical positions and greater influence. Among these were a number of monks who represented the cutting edge of rigorous canonical observation and strict discipline within the church. From their isolated, celibate existence and recent experience of persecution, they brought new concepts of religious devotion to the church.[112] These inevitably drew attention to the underlying tensions between episcopal and monastic clergy. Needless to say, the monks found much to criticise in the past iconoclast direction of the eastern church; they had voiced several substantive points during the 787 council. Sabas of the monastery of Stoudios led the opposition to the readmittance of self-confessed iconoclasts to their former posts and pursued any suspicion of irregular ordination. Afterwards this party concentrated on those accused of paying to obtain bishoprics (simony).

The fourth and fifth canons passed at the council had reiterated the rulings against simony, and Patriarch Tarasios decreed that clerics guilty of the sin should purge it by one year's penance. At a ceremony designed to restore peace and unity, those who had done so were readmitted in January 789. Tarasios had reported on the matter to Pope Hadrian and clearly felt that his procedure had adequately corrected the offences.[113] Though there is no evidence of continuing protest, the monastic party does not seem to have been convinced. From 787 onwards a certain distrust between the monastic and secular clergy militated against ecclesiastical unity within the empire. This was worsened by Irene's determination to elevate the layman Tarasios to the patriarchate. Against this symbol of imperial and worldly

[110] Theophanes, 465-66, 464.

[111] Ibid., 456, 466, 468.

[112] J. Leroy, "La réforme studite," in Il monachesimo orientale, Orientalia Christiana Analecta, vol. 153 (Rome, 1958), 181-214; Alexander, The Patriarch Nicephorus, 80-93.

[113] Mansi, 13.421E-426D; Tarasios's letter to Pope Hadrian, PG 98, 1441-52; cf. Speck, Kaiser Konstantin VI, 1:193-201.

direction of the church, the most powerful abbots asserted their independence and passed severe judgement on the slightest patriarchal deference to secular pressure. The restoration of icons did not, therefore, bring a lasting peace to the eastern churches; it encouraged the growth of a monastic party that took every opportunity to chastise defects among other clergy.

In 790, when Constantine VI finally established his own authority and banished Irene to her newly constructed Eleutherios palace in western Constantinople, he was 19 years old. He exiled Staurakios, Aetios, and all his mother's other eunuchs and installed his own advisers.[114] For the next seven years he reigned as sole emperor, leading Byzantine forces in regular campaigns (with occasional successes, but not with the strategic skill of his father and grandfather). Both Arab and Bulgar armies inflicted heavy defeats during this period. Constantine also divorced his wife, Maria, by whom he had at least one daughter, Euphrosyne, and married one of the palace "ladies-in-waiting," Theodote, who was related to the family of Platon and Theodore of Stoudios.[115] Despite the kinship, the strict monastic party protested immediately, on the grounds that while Maria lived it was illegal for the emperor to take another wife. As head of the church, Tarasios was held responsible for curbing this licentiousness; he imposed a canonical punishment on the couple and the priest, Joseph, who had blessed the marriage. The lightness of this penance led to a complete schism between the patriarch and the monks over the divorce.[116] Constantine, meanwhile, had Platon of Sakkoudion imprisoned in one of the palace chapels and exiled the other vocal critics to Thessalonike. Such high-handed action did nothing to ease the tensions, which were exacerbated the following year when Theodote gave birth to a son, christened Leo. Unfortunately, he survived only seven months.[117] Had he lived to be recognised as Constantine's co-emperor and heir, the scandal over his parents' wedding might have died down. As it was his untimely death was interpreted as proof of an illegal union; it confirmed the monks' righteous hostility. It also enabled Irene to mobilise her own supporters and move against her son. On 15 August 797, at her command, they arrested Constantine, incarcerated him in the purple chamber of the palace where he had been born, and blinded him.[118] The intention was doubtless to cause his death, although the loss of his sight was sufficient to disqualify him from exercising imperial authority.

[114] Theophanes, 466-67; Speck, *Kaiser Konstantin VI*, 1:209-219.

[115] Theophanes, 469, 470.

[116] P. Henry, "The Moechian Controversy and the Constantinopolitan Synod of January, A.D. 809," *JTS*, n.s., 20 (1969): 495-522, esp. 496-503.

[117] Theophanes, 470-71.

[118] Ibid., 471.28; but cf. Speck, *Kaiser Konstantin VI*, 1:306-309.

Ecclesiastical Reforms in Francia

As we have noted in Chapter 9, liturgical uniformity within the Frankish territories was regarded as a pressing concern by both Pippin and Charles. A further stimulus to ecclesiastical discipline was provided by Pope Hadrian's gift of a collection of canon law, the so-called *Dionysio-Hadriana,* handed over to Charles in Rome in 774.[119] But since the 770s and 780s were largely occupied by Frankish efforts to conquer Saxony and to consolidate control over Aquitaine, Lombardy, and Septimania, while preventing the recurrence of internal revolts, the king had little opportunity to put the collection into use. Only after the baptism of Duke Widukind of the Saxons (785), a raid against Brittany (786), the suppression of a rebellion in Thuringia (785-86), and the forced annexation of Bavaria (788), was it possible to look forward to a period that might not be totally dominated by annual campaigning.[120] And as Charles's court was then at the height of its intellectual powers, he decided to try and devote greater attention to strengthening Christian rule throughout his lands.

In the revised edition of the Salic Law, issued in 763-64 by Pippin, the Christian calling of the Franks "established by God the Creator" and their chosen role of extending "the Catholic faith, free of heresy," had been extolled. Several of the 100 chapters emphasised religious duties and matters of faith. But it was not until Charles began to issue capitularies, collections of particular rulings decided by individual assemblies of secular and ecclesiastical officials, that specific methods of improving Christian teaching and clerical standards were evolved. The Capitulary of Herstal (779) opens with six chapters dealing clearly with the supreme authority of bishops within their dioceses, to whom clergy and monks are both to be subject. The seventh decrees that all Christians shall pay the tithe, one-tenth of the products of their labours, to the church where they receive the sacraments.[121] What had previously been a moral duty now became legally binding and would be enforced by the king's administrators. The remaining chapters, however, deal with secular matters decided at the Herstal assembly.

This mixture of worldly and spiritual topics is typical of the capitularies

[119] D. A. Bullough, "Roman Books and Carolingian *renovatio*," in D. Baker, ed., *Renaissance and Renewal in Christian History, SCH* 14 (Oxford, 1977), 23-51; H. Mordek, "Dionysio-Hadriana und Vetus Gallica, historisch geordnetes und systematisches Kirchenrecht am Hofe Karls des Grossen," *Zeitschrift der Savigny Stiftung für Rechtsgeschichte,* Kanonistische Abteilung 55 (1969), 39-63; F. L. Ganshof, "The Church and the Royal Power in the Frankish Monarchy Under Pippin and Charlemagne," in *The Carolingians and the Frankish Monarchy* (Ithaca, 1971), 205-239.

[120] *Royal Frankish Annals,* aa.783, 784, 785, 786, 787; on the conversion of the Saxons, see Angenendt, *Kaiserherrschaft und Königstaufe,* 207-212.

[121] *Capitularia,* no. 20 (46-51); McKitterick, *The Frankish Kingdoms,* 78-105.

and may well have reduced their universal and lasting application. Some clearly have only a local significance, because they are designed to correct a particular abuse or rectify a unique situation. With the *Admonitio generalis* of 789 and the letter *de litteris colendis* written between 781 and 791, however, a general reform is initiated, one intended to improve Christian learning throughout the Frankish territories, to provide universally binding legal proscriptions and guidance in resolving all manner of ecclesiastical disputes.[122] The *Admonitio* consists of 85 chapters, clauses, or sections, the first 59 incorporating a summary of the canons of the *Dionysio-Hadriana* collection, the rest devoted to Christian instruction for the clergy and laity. Many of the canons selected were rulings of past church councils, others originated in papal decretals; all concerned the duties and responsibilities of clerics, starting with bishops but not forgetting the humbler parish priests, and the duties of ordinary Christians. Thus, the basic regulations against simony, intrusion by a bishop into the affairs of another's diocese, failure to observe Sunday as a day of rest, or the sanctity of a consecrated building were repeated, although these had been recorded by many earlier councils of the church in Gaul and ought to have been well known in Francia.

A novel element lies in the stress on educating the clergy, so that Christian services, prayers, and rituals are correctly understood and properly performed. The value of accurately copied texts is emphasised, and copying is defined as an important and difficult task not to be left to inexperienced young boys. The importance of teaching them is, however, repeated in several chapters concerning the provision of schools (usually attached to religious institutions). A similar spirit pervades the *de litteris colendis* addressed to Baugulf, abbot of Fulda, which was probably drawn up by Alcuin or Angilramnus of Metz. In this important official document on education, Charles urges that monasteries and bishoprics shall establish schools, not only for their own clergy but for boys from their environs.

Although a good start was made in the field of ecclesiastical reform and the development of Christian education by these two measures, Charles was soon forced to resume the pattern of annual military campaigns that characterised the early part of his reign. From 791, his primary concern was to secure the southeast frontiers of his lands, now extended by the incorporation of Bavaria (788). In one of the last of Tassilo's attempts to resist Frankish overlordship (despite his oaths of loyalty to Charles), he had approached the Avars. It was against this people, established between the Alps and the Danube, that Charles campaigned in 791-93.[123] Although his military

[122] *Capitularia*, no. 22 (53-62); R. McKitterick, *The Frankish Church and the Carolingian Reforms, 789-895* (London, 1977), 1-21.
[123] *Royal Frankish Annals*, a.791; *Annals of Einhard*, a.791; *Annales Laureshamenses*, a.791. The last two note that Charles ordered a fast and special prayers for victory before

strategy displayed great brilliance, it was not immediately successful. In 792 his own son, Pippin the Hunchback, was involved in an internal rebellion, which appears to have involved many Frankish aristocrats. Charles had most of them put to death and rewarded those who remained loyal, while Pippin entered the monastery of Prüm.[124] But all his plans were undermined by the floods that destroyed the harvest of 792 and 793 and brought famine to many areas. The king ordered that special services should be held in all churches, psalms extolling penance should be recited, and clerics should fast and say prayers for the king, army, and food supply. All were to give alms and exercise Christian charity to placate divine displeasure. Yet these measures were ineffective, for in the summer of 793 the Saxons rebelled again, reneging on their fealty to Charles and the most solemn Christian oaths.[125]

These reverses did not prevent the Frankish court theologians from working on their critiques of two heresies. The first, Adoptionism, was of limited regional significance (being confined to Spain and Septimania), but flourished close to Francia. The other was very distant but had been adopted by an entire state as the true faith. The condemnation of both was an interrelated process. The Adoptionist heresy claimed that Christ was the Son of God only by adoption and thus denied the unity of the Trinity; it drew on a number of early Christian movements of dubious orthodoxy and was firmly supported by Archbishop Elipand of Toledo. Despite Pope Hadrian's efforts to curb the belief, it spread and came to Charles's attention when propounded by Bishop Felix of Urgel, one of the towns in the Spanish border region that had requested Frankish overlordship in 785. At a council in Regensburg held in 792, Felix was condemned.[126] Alcuin and Paulinus identified Adoptionism as a form of Nestorian belief, and each prepared a detailed treatise against it, which was to be approved at the councils of Frankfurt and Aquileia in 794 and 796.

THE SYNOD OF FRANKFURT (794)

Like all Frankish assemblies, the synod of Frankfurt dealt with both theological and practical matters (in this case, relating to the recent floods and

---

the battle, see M. McCormick, "The Liturgy of War in the Early Middle Ages: Crisis, Litanies and the Carolingian Monarchy," *Viator* 15 (1984): 1-23, esp. 8-9.

[124] *Royal Frankish Annals*, a.792; *Annals of Einhard*, a.792. The *Annales Laureshamenses*, aa.792, 793, provide greater detail, including the rewards given to Charles's supporters.

[125] *Royal Frankish Annals*, a.793; *Annals of Einhard*, a.793; *Annales Laureshamenses*, a.793; Bullough, *The Age of Charlemagne*, 96; cf. McCormick, "Liturgy of War," 9-11.

[126] W. Heil, "Der Adoptianismus, Alkuin und Spanien," in *Karl der Grosse*, 2:95-154; Pope Hadrian's letter to the bishops of Hispania, *CC*, no. 95, also in *Concilia*, pt. 1, 122-30; *Royal Frankish Annals*, a.794; Bullough, *The Age of Charlemagne*, 62.

devastation caused by them). What distinguished it from other reforming councils of the 790s was the very careful documentary preparation that went into the anti-Adoptionist tracts and the *Libri Carolini*, and the claim for a totally independent theology set out in the latter, which Charles had personally approved. At Frankfurt, the churches of Charles's territories realised an autonomy, which separated them from both Rome and Constantinople. When they subscribed to the *Libri Carolini*, they condemned both the council of 787 and Pope Hadrian's support for it, and thus gained a voice in ecclesiastical affairs, critical of the papacy though still respectful of Petrine authority. "Europa" for the first time denied Rome's right to speak on its behalf and aggressively denounced Constantinople's assumed leadership of the entire Christian world. It was a development sponsored by Charles and articulated by a group of western clerics assembled at his court. And although many of the participants at Frankfurt cannot have followed the complex theological, political, and methodological arguments used, their assent gave notice to the older centres of Christianity of significant changes in the medieval world order.

In the absence of any record of the proceedings, we cannot trace the detailed organisation of the synod. But from the capitulary drawn up at the conclusion and other documents issued, it is clear that Charles took a leading role.[127] He summoned and presided over the meeting, which appears to have included representatives of all the bishops in his far-flung territories, including those from Aquileia, and two papal legates sent by Hadrian. These ecclesiastics met separately in the great hall of the palace at Frankfurt and were directed by Charles to listen to Elipand's statement on Adoptionism and then to discuss it. He himself reserved judgement. The *Libri Carolini* were probably read out in similar fashion so that Frankish objections to both icon veneration and destruction, as well as a number of other matters, could be made public. In this capacity Alcuin believed that Charles was acting as the "rector of the Christian people," the divinely commanded leader of the churches within his dominions. He was acclaimed as "king and priest" (*rex et sacerdos*). His sacerdotal character developed from the fact that he was "anointed by God" (*christus Domini*) and charged with responsibility for the salvation of his people as a New David.[128] In these unusually exalted terms, Charles was identified as the

---

[127] *Concilia*, pt. 1, no. 19, *Capitulare Francofurtense*, 110-71; the actual Capitulary is also in *Capitularia*, no. 28 (73-78); F. L. Ganshof, "Observations sur le synode der Francfort de 794," *Miscellanea Historica in honorem A. de Meyer* (Louvain, 1946), 1:306-318. The evidence for Charles's personal intervention in the final text of the *Libri Carolini* is preserved in Tironian notes, see Freeman, "Further Studies in the *Libri Carolini*, III: The Marginal Notes in *Vaticanus Latinus* 7207."

[128] *LC*, Preface to Book 1 (p. 2); 1.17, 19; cf. H. Fichtenau, *The Carolingian Empire* (Oxford, 1957), 49-59.

moving spirit behind the synod, which assumed greater significance as a result.

Unlike previous councils that had claimed the epithet "universal" although they clearly did not fall into the same category as the first five—for example, the Lateran Synod of 649 (the Sixth) or the iconoclast council of 754 (the Seventh)—the Frankfurt Synod recognised its local character. While it denied that the gathering held at Nicaea in 787 constituted the Seventh Oecumenical Council, it never claimed this title for itself.[129] Instead, it tried to show that the traditional method of representing the Christian universe at a general council was no longer valid. "Universality" was not to be achieved through the representation of Christianity by its leaders (patriarchs and bishops), but through the representation of the entire faith. A spiritual universality defined by correct faith should replace any notion of territorial universality.[130] The inadequacy of this old theory was proven by the fact that the pentarchy of five patriarchates failed to speak for the majority of Christians. Now that Antioch, Alexandria, and Jerusalem were under Islamic control, the local churches of the West had effectively replaced those of the East as the centre of the faith. And at Nicaea no authority had represented these western communities; Rome had not even consulted them.

Against the ancient conciliar theory of the pentarchy as guardians of the faith, a different theory was espoused at Frankfurt. It claimed that there were two crucial aspects to a truly universal gathering: the first lay in the assent of all Christians (a horizontal consensus), the second in the continuity with previous councils, their deliberations, traditions, and canons (a vertical consensus). In neither respect did 787 qualify as oecumenical, for it had not consulted with all churches on the question of icon veneration, nor had it upheld the decisions of past councils. Had the patriarch of Constantinople sent out letters to enquire what Christians everywhere thought on the problem, a real consensus (*plures consentientes*) throughout "the churches of the whole world" could have been reached. And then the council would have been in a position to rule which communities were in agreement with ancient traditions and universal practice, and both types of consensus would have been achieved. Instead, at Nicaea a regional agreement, of one part of the church (the Greek), had been adopted, and was now to be imposed on all the others on pain of excommunication. Nicaea thus fell

---

[129] *LC*, Preface to Book 1 (p. 5), cf. Preface to Book 3 (p. 102); 4.13 (pp. 197-98); *Royal Frankish Annals*, a.794; *Annals of Einhard*, a.794; cf. *Annales Laureshamenses*, a.794, which does report the meeting as a "universal synod." H. Barion, "Der kirchenrechtliche Charakter des Synod von 794," *Zeitschrift der Savigny Stiftung für Rechtsgeschichte*, Kanonistische Abteilung 19 (1930), 139-70, esp. 166-67; Sieben, *Die Konzilsidee der alten Kirche*, 330.

[130] *LC* 4.28; Barion, "Der kirchenrechtliche Charakter," 149-50.

into the category of a local synod rather than a genuinely universal council.[131]

Paradoxically, the Frankish theologians had arrived at this novel concept of the Christian *oikoumene* partly through past Roman practice. Since the time of Pope Martin, the different churches of the West had been asked to give their considered opinion on major issues dividing the faithful. They had also consulted the apostolic see for clarification of practical problems encountered in their immense extension of Christianity in northern Europe. Their desire to act according to established traditions could not be faulted, and their rightful place within the universal community could not be denied. So it was with the knowledge of their part in ending the Monothelete heresy (680-81) or in condemning iconoclasm (769) that the Franks refused to accept the decisions of Nicaea. For at Nicaea, western orthodoxy was confirmed. And having been proved correct, the Frankish churches were not going to embrace a different eastern heresy.

The example of the Spanish church at the Fourteenth Council of Toledo in 684 may perhaps have influenced them.[132] The decisions of this gathering would have been known to Theodulf of Orléans, if not Alcuin and other theologians. At this meeting, Pope Leo II's response to the Sixth Oecumenical Council was subjected to a very careful scrutiny in three stages: receipt, reading, and approval. Although the council did support the condemnation of Monothelete heresy, four years later Metropolitan Julian presented a treatise to the Fifteenth Council, which was slightly critical. The Spanish ecclesiastical community had often exercised independent judgement in matters of faith, and in this as in many other aspects of Visigothic practice set a precedent for the Franks to follow.

In other respects, however, the hostility displayed at Frankfurt was a product of intense theological debate at Charles's court. On the matter of vertical consensus (agreement with church tradition as embodied in past councils), the *Libri Carolini* found Nicaea wanting in several parts, for instance, not maintaining the established position of Rome in the Christian world (*LC* 3.1). But more fundamental was the claim that icon veneration was not a matter of true faith, a subject "necessary and profitable for believers" (*LC* 3.12,17). In the Frankish view it did not merit sufficiently serious consideration to justify a council. Since the veneration of images was useless (in regard to the much more important matter of salvation), its

---

[131] *LC* 3.11; 4.13; Sieben, *Die Konzilsidee*, 328-30. The six oecumenical councils are held up as shining gold coins, against which the so-called seventh council appears as dull bronze. Interestingly, Theodore, abbot of the Stoudios monastery, had come to the same conclusion on the character of the 787 council, see Henry, "Initial Eastern Assessments," and idem, "The Moechian Controversy."

[132] Sieben, *Die Konzilsidee*, 339-41.

regulation was a matter of indifference. Therefore, the Byzantine motive for summoning a council was itself reprehensible—councils should be reserved for vital matters of theological definition (*LC* 3.11). In this case a local synod would have been quite adequate. This argument reflected western ignorance both of the passions aroused by iconic art in the East and of the sophisticated theological discussions that it generated. Given such a basic difference of approach, it is hardly surprising that the *Libri Carolini* should display little sympathy for the testimonies adduced at Nicaea to prove that the council accorded with past oecumenical rulings.

In its examination of these citations, the Frankish text frequently found the 787 use of scriptural and patristic writings "not pertinent" (*non ad rem*). An uncritical quotation was not only interpreted as irrelevant but also condemned as incorrect and equated with a wrong quotation. For such a citation to be usefully employed, its precise meaning had to be established and then its relevance to the problem. [133] The Frankish theologians dismissed a number of apocryphal texts used, citing the Decretal of Gelasius on received books as their authority. This applied particularly to the eastern reliance on stories of dream revelations, and equally to Pope Hadrian's use of the Acts of St. Sylvester (*LC* 2.13). By extension it also applied to the Lateran Synod of 769, which had accepted the evidence of St. Ambrose submitted by Archbishop Sergius of Ravenna.

But even in its discussion of correct and relevant citations from the Old Testament, for example, the western theologians stressed an allegorical interpretation, which had little in common with the philosophical and Platonic currents that informed eastern exegesis. Here two different schools clashed—a medieval Latin one, heavily dependent on the symbolism of Sts. Augustine, Gregory the Great, and Isidore of Seville, and a Late Antique one, still indebted to classical philosophy and Greek mystical expression. [134]

Although the Frankish court did not admit that icon veneration constituted a serious problem, the *Libri Carolini* defined a middle way, *via regis*, between two extremes: total destruction (iconoclasm) and gross adoration (iconophilism), represented by the two councils of 754 and 787. By insisting on the pedagogic function of all aids to correct faith, the Frankish document revealed its debt to Pope Gregory I, whose dictum on images as Bibles of the illiterate was emphasised. (It was also scandalised by the mistranslation of this text from the Greek version of Hadrian's synod-

[133] Ibid., 332-33.
[134] See the chapter by H. Liebeschutz, *Cambridge History of Later Greek and Early Medieval Philosophy*, ed. A. H. Armstrong (Cambridge, 1967), 565-71.

ica.)[135] As any image was no more than the wood and paint of which it was made, mere profane materials, unconsecrated and with no inherent holy quality, to worship it only led to idolatry. In addition, the eastern justification for honouring images owed much to pagan reverence for imperial portraits, as Byzantine theologians from St. Basil onwards had repeatedly claimed (LC 2.19). But to the Franks this was an association that had to be uprooted from Christian practice. The eastern use of religious images was thus branded as an essentially non-Christian one and the entire theory of intercession dismissed. Icons were to be permitted only as a useful means of instruction for the unlettered. And to reinforce this pedagogic function, the persons or scenes depicted were to be "correctly" identified in writing. The superiority of word over image was repeatedly stressed (e.g. LC 2.13, 30).

Over the content of the acts of Nicaea there was, therefore, a fundamental disagreement. This also extended to the form in which it was presented, for the Franks were horrified by many eastern assumptions of a non-religious nature. They took particular exception to the claims made for imperial authority and to the elevation of Tarasios from lay status. That the eastern emperors "reigned with God" and presided over the council with an authority equal to that of the apostles (isapostolos) was an intolerable arrogance in the West (LC 1.1, 3; 3.14, 15, 19). Charles's role as "defender of the church" reflected a more appropriate humility. By an unfavourable comparison Charles was also identified (in terms taken verbatim from papal correspondence) as a New David and his subjects as the New Israel, leaving aside the eastern rulers as relics of a defunct world order, pagan emperors rather than true Christians (LC, Preface, pp. 2, 3, 7; 1.17, 19). Constantinople was attacked in terms very similar to those used by Isidore of Seville (as a den of heresy), while the kingdom of the Franks was praised as one endowed with most Christian virtues. The sense of a new Christian practice in Europe was contrasted with the pagan superstition of lifeless objects observed in the East. Even allowing a woman to exercise control over a church gathering was harshly criticised (from the eighth session the Franks thought that Irene had presided throughout the council). In short, the Libri Carolini lost no opportunity to distinguish the Christian rule of Charles from the imperial and essentially pagan government of Constantinople.

The Filioque Clause

Tarasios's declaration of faith and justification of his rapid promotion to the position of patriarch provided additional ammunition for the Frankish at-

---

[135] G. Haendler, Epochen Karolingischer Theologie: eine Untersuchung über die Karolingischen Gutachten zum byzantinischen Bilderstreit (Berlin, 1958), 24-25.

tack (*LC* 3.2). Since many laymen were appointed to high ecclesiastical office in the West, by Charles no less, the doubts cast on Tarasios's suitability were fairly slight. But his doctrine was found to be in error when he cited the procession of the Holy Spirit "from the Father through the Son" (*ex Patre per Filium, LC* 3.3). According to the Franks, this reduced the Holy Spirit to a lesser position within the Trinity, where it was no longer equal and consubstantial with the Father and the Son. They condemned this as pernicious error, a *virus*, related to the incorrect Arian dogma that the Holy Spirit had been created. Here they produced a long series of Old Testament citations to illustrate the uncreated nature of the Spirit and its own creative power.[136] From patristic sources as formulated by Isidore of Seville, they quoted his briefer statement on the procession of the Holy Spirit, rather than the more complex one of St. Augustine. The same wording had been used by Alcuin and Paulinus in their treatises against Adoptionism, also approved at Frankfurt. Paulinus's *libellus*, read at the synod, contained a strong defence of the dual procession of the Spirit, which he developed further at the 796 synod of Aquileia.[137]

At Aquileia, Paulinus tackled the basic problem, which was that the *Filioque* clause involved an addition to the text of the creed as preserved by the oecumenical councils of Nicaea and Constantinople. He pointed out that at the 381 council, the precise wording agreed at Nicaea had been changed in order to clarify the creed, producing the accepted formulation that the Holy Spirit proceeds from the Father. Change for the purpose of clarification was then used in 796 to justify the additional clause "and from the Son."[138] This was how the creed came to be taught and recited in the mass, for Paulinus, like Alcuin, was convinced that the public declamation of faith banished heretical belief. The innovation was first introduced in the royal chapel and then spread throughout the Frankish lands. The educational value of such a practice was obvious and may have been copied from the Visigothic church. For in the way that the creed had been used in Spain from 589 onwards to remove the Arian heresy, so the Frankish church now sought to defeat Felix of Urgel and Elipand of Toledo through the same custom and in the same wording. The final triumph over Adoptionism in 800, when Felix renounced it, strengthened the *Filioque* clause and brought it into even broader use.[139]

---

[136] R. G. Heath, "The Schism of the Franks and the 'Filioque'," *JEH* 23 (1972): 97-113.

[137] On numerous occasions the *LC* cite patristic commentary and exegesis from Isidore rather than from the original sources, see for instance 3.3; cf. Dahlhaus-Berg, *Nova Antiquitas et Antiqua Novitas*, 190-201. For the 794 *libellus* of Paulinus, see Mansi, 13.873-83.

[138] Mansi, 13.833, on the addition made in 381, "*suppleverunt quasi exponendo sensum*," cf. Paulinus's use, ibid., 342C-E, and his exposition, 842-45.

[139] Felix's *Confession* in *MGH, Ep.*, vol. 4, no. 2, 329.28-38 (Ep. 199); cf. Wallace-Ha-

Once the synod of Frankfurt had approved these condemnations of Spanish and Greek heresies, it established a number of canons to ensure correct practice in the western churches. Most of the disciplinary measures had already been issued in the *Admonitio generalis* of 789 and drew their authority from the *Dionysio-Hadriana* collection. That they required repetition reflects the constant struggle against backsliding among Frankish clergy and monks and the difficulty of instituting a regulated and stable hierarchy of dignitaries and functions in ecclesiastical life. One group of canons (11-18) on monastic discipline reiterates the need for all monks and nuns to live according to the Rule of St. Benedict. Charles had asked the abbot of Monte Cassino to send him a text of this monastic rule and thought that the manuscript he received was a copy of the saint's original document. As the royally authorised text, it was treated with great respect. In the early ninth century, two monks from Reichenau were sent by their librarian, Reginbert, to study the manuscript and make a very careful copy, noting all the discrepancies between this version and others in use. The copy they made constitutes the first "edited" text of the Rule, and the oldest surviving manuscript, now in the monastery of St. Gall, goes back to this very copy.[140] Of course, other interpolated versions continued to circulate, and many monasteries preserved traditions stemming from their original "mixed" rules, which they were reluctant to give up. Another group of canons (19-54) tackled problems in the organisation of the secular clergy and popular observance, for instance, canon 21 on keeping Sunday as the Lord's day, canon 42 on restricting the cult of saints to the accepted and established holy figures—here the educative role of bishops was stressed. Canon 53 stated that all bishops and priests should know the sacred canons, canon 29 ordered bishops to instruct their subordinates so that they would all be qualified to be canonically elected and worthy of the house of God,

drill, *The Frankish Church*, 209-211; D. B. Capelle, "L'origine anti-Adoptionist de notre texte du symbole de la messe," *Recherches de Théologie ancienne et médiévale* 1 (1929): 7-20 (reprinted in his *Travaux liturgiques de doctrine et d'histoire*, vol. 3); W. Heil, *Alkuinstudien*, vol. 1 (Dusseldorf, 1970).

[140] J. McCann, *St. Benedict* (London, 1979), 117-28, summarises the fundamental study by L. Traube, *Textgeschichte der Regula S. Benedicti*, Abhandlungen der Königlichen Bayerischen Akademie der Wissenschaften, Band 25 (Munich, 1910), esp. 63-78; cf. J. Semmler, "Karl der Grosse und das fränkische Mönchtum," in *Karl der Grosse*, 2:255-89; G. Moyse, "Monachisme et réglementation monastique en Gaule avant Benoît d'Aniane," in *Sous la règle de S. Benoît* (Geneva/Paris, 1982), 3-19. On Reginbert, see Afterword, below. Despite the emphasis placed on correct observance of the Rule of St. Benedict in 794, this had to be repeated in 802 at the council of Aachen, vividly described in the *Annales Laureshamenses*, a.802; cf. *Capitularia*, nos. 36-41 (105-118); and was not considered adequate. Only under Charles's son, Louis the Pious, was the reformer, Benedict of Aniane, more successful.

canon 33 demanded that all Christians should be taught the Catholic faith of the Holy Trinity, the Lord's Prayer, and the Creed, and canon 52 reassured believers that prayers might be directed to God in any language provided that the heart was pure—an innovation against the old theory of three sacred languages, Hebrew, Greek, and Latin, clearly related to the growth of devotional prayers in the vernacular.[141]

In several respects the Frankish rulings of 794 may be compared with the canons issued at Nicaea in 787.[142] Simony, or the purchase of ecclesiastical office, and any notion of charging for a candidate to enter a monastery were condemned at Frankfurt (canon 16) and Nicaea (canons 4, 5, and 19). The movement of clerics from their appointed place of service without superior permission was similarly denounced (Frankfurt, canons 7, 24, 27; Nicaea, canons 10, 21), as was the abuse of ordaining clerics before they had reached the stipulated age (Frankfurt, canons 46, 49; Nicaea, canon 14). While the West ordered that abbesses should live according to the canons or be removed (Frankfurt, canon 46), in the East it was the continuing existence of double monasteries (condemned at Nicaea, canon 20) and the possibility of women mixing with monks that required additional rulings (canons 18 and 22). On the question of private ecclesiastical foundations, a comparable concern is expressed in Frankfurt (canon 54) and Nicaea (canon 13); both stress that the original function of divine services must be maintained in these buildings.

But in other ways the synod of Frankfurt illustrates the relative instability and weakness of the Frankish church. This is especially evident in the provisions for judicial procedures, mentioned in several canons.[143] Canon 6 stipulates that while bishops are to administer justice over all their junior clerics, and irreconcilable differences are to go to the archbishop, counts (*comites nostri*) are also to assist the bishops. In the last resort, disputes are to be brought to Charles himself with letters relevant to the case from the archbishop. Both in the association of secular officials in episcopal courts and in the insistence on written documents, this represents an advance.[144] But canons 30, 38, and 39, which deal with quarrels between clerics or between the laity and the clergy, reveal a degree of uncertainty in regulating ecclesiastical life, while the repetition of four chapters from the *Admonitio generalis* relating to the treatment of sins and crimes (canons 34-37)

[141] Bullough, *The Age of Charlemagne*, 116-18; Wallace-Hadrill, *The Frankish Church*, 377-89. Latin remained the sole language of the liturgy.

[142] For the following comparison, reference can be made to the sources: Mansi, 13.417-39 (Nicaea); *Concilia*, pt. 1, 165-71 (Frankfurt).

[143] Ganshof, "Observations," 313-14.

[144] But the same emphasis on judges presenting their conclusions in writing appears in the council of Aachen (802), another indication that progress was slow.

suggests that uniformity of judicial administration was far from complete. In contrast, the eastern church possessed a longer and more continuous tradition of canonical judgements, which were generally known, though not necessarily better observed. The tendency to record all judgements and to legislate for novel situations was also more developed. And the custom of holding local ecclesiastical councils was well established, though it needed repeating at Nicaea (canon 6, citing the Sixth Oecumenical Council ruling). None of these factors can be interpreted as ensuring better standards in church organisation, but they indicate a more ingrained mechanism for resolving disputes. The discussion recorded at Nicaea over the treatment suitable for contrite heretics, for example, reveals an informed awareness of canonical legislation on the subject, while the monastic party's objections to too charitable an interpretation illustrate an inveterate legalism harboured in certain Byzantine circles. In comparing the eastern and Frankish churches at the close of the eighth century, the latter's youthful character marks an obvious difference. But the lack of continuity with ancient Christian institutions was a significant factor, which meant that Charles and his ecclesiastical advisers had to devise new methods and adapt Roman traditions for the church's administration. In contrast, Irene, Tarasios, and the monastic groups of the East inherited a developed system and debated its future development in the light of shared traditions.

While the results of the synod of Frankfurt were clear enough—two heresies had been officially condemned by the assembled Frankish bishops and lay leaders—the implication of the meeting was not so evident. Two papal legates had concurred in the decisions, thus placing Pope Hadrian in the untenable position of supporting both the council of Nicaea and the synod of Frankfurt. He welcomed the firm action against Adoptionism. But the 794 denunciation of iconophilism opened a schism between the Frankish churches and the East, which made him look foolish. Although his death in 795 may have brought slight relief to the apostolic see, his successor Leo III inherited an impossible situation.[145]

Frankfurt thus established a breach not only between West and East, but also within the West. For the separation from Constantinople of the churches under Charles's control, encouraged by the example of independent Visigothic practice and theory, also reduced Rome's control over the West. The synod witnessed the end of an era of papal hegemony over the western churches. Thereafter, Frankish leaders assumed a less humble and more directive relationship with the papacy. They had discovered an autonomy that would structure subsequent Christian development in Europe. Although Rome would reassert its authority under more powerful

[145] Classen, "Karl der Grosse," 564-65.

ninth-century leaders, the Frankish initiative of 794 had created an alternative focus of religious expertise and judgement. It had set a precedent for secular rulers backed by their own ecclesiastics to challenge papal interpretations of purely theological matters, a dangerous threat to previous acceptance of Petrine supremacy.

The synod also marked an end to the early Christian sense of the *oikoumene*, the universal church. For while Charles assumed responsibility for correct observance of the faith in his most Christian empire, Constantinople reiterated and emphasised its own different, yet equally Christian and imperial traditions. Icon veneration, justified by the use of ancient models adapted from the pagan to the Christian world and amplified by philosophical analysis in the classical style, became an integral part of these traditions. This prepared the way for a new context in which artistic models derived from ancient Greece, the Hellenistic world, and Rome could be revived. A wealth of classical resources were thus available to Byzantium that were denied to the West. They created a living link back to the ancients, which determined much of the East's political direction and coloured its sense of purpose. In this development, the debate over holy images had played an important role and had confirmed those classicising tendencies particular to the world of New Rome.

In contrast, when the West drew on its own fund of ancient traditions, it created something quite different. All the roots of classical culture, the learning of Late Antiquity as it had been preserved by individual commentators and encyclopaedists like Isidore of Seville, imperial ideals, and Roman concepts of law influenced the new, conscious identity of Charles's Europe. Yet Carolingian society was bound by oaths of loyalty and structured on relations of dependence and limited authority, quite at variance with ancient practice. While Charles's advisers may have called it the "renovation of empire" (*renovatio imperii*), there was no doubt about the qualitative difference between their own world and that of Old Rome. And one of these differences lay in its thoroughly functional attitude towards religious art, so distant from the devotional involvement current in the East.

The Two Emperors of Christendom

IN 1776, when Edward Gibbon published his first volume of *The Decline and Fall of the Roman Empire*, he outlined the general scheme of his undertaking. It fell into three periods: from the second to the fifth centuries A.D.; from the age of Justinian to the elevation of Charlemagne; and from the revival of the western empire to the fall of Constantinople to the Turks in 1453. He hoped to complete his study of the first period in a second volume but dared not "presume to give any assurances . . . with regard to the subsequent periods."[1] In the event it took him five years to complete the first period, which filled another two quarto volumes, and in 1782 Gibbon could announce his "serious resolution of proceeding to the last period(s) of my original design," reassuring the reader that "it is not my intention to expatiate with the same minuteness on the whole series of Byzantine history."[2] Nonetheless, the two periods from the sixth to the fifteenth century required another "three ponderous volumes," the same number as he had devoted to the first period, and were not published until 1787. It was 23 years since he had first conceived the idea of writing such a history.

One of the first things any historian who follows in Gibbon's footsteps, as I have in this study, can learn from him, is how hard it is to stop. In particular, once the decision is made to concentrate on the transitional period between Late Antiquity and the medieval world, all subsequent European history seems to unfold to link our own times with those distant centuries. But an end has to be made somewhere. And for this study I have decided to close at the final restoration of icon veneration in the East in 843. This happens to coincide with the Treaty of Verdun, by which Charles's grandsons, Lothar I, Louis the German, and Charles the Bald, tried to divide up the Frankish territories in a more satisfactory way than

---

[1] Edward Gibbon, *The Decline and Fall of the Roman Empire*, vol. 1 (London, 1776), Preface. This first edition comprised 16 chapters, of which the last two were most critical of Christianity. Gibbon's great work is here cited in the edition prepared by J. B. Bury, 7 vols. (London, 1909-1914).

[2] Gibbon, *Decline and Fall*, 1:xxxix-xli.

that devised by their father, Louis the Pious. It is an interesting coincidence, as we shall see later.

The choice of date, however, means that the half-century that follows the synod of Frankfurt will be given a rather compressed treatment. This period will be discussed as an appendage to the synod rather than as a celebration of western imperial power. For the coronation of Charlemagne, although regarded as one of the most crucial (and memorable) dates in early medieval history, marks the culmination of the process just examined more than the opening of a new imperial phase in the West. What the Carolingian dynasty had accomplished before 800 proved of greater significance in the later history of Europe than the ninth- and tenth-century achievements worked out by Charles's heirs. Of course, in certain particulars they were able to improve on his efforts, in the reform of monastic life and the study of classical authors, for instance. But they were primarily inspired by the grandeur of his ambition, rather than being able to realise what he had set in motion. There is a sense, therefore, in which the imperial coronation should be seen as the final point of a long gestation. It represents the uneasy alliance of two different kinds of heirs to Roman power in the West, papal and Carolingian. Each was striving to make the inheritance of imperial traditions, however transformed, its own. This interaction of vicars of St. Peter with claimants to the imperial title was to become one of the determinants of western European development thereafter.

While both sides were thus to look back to 800 as a founding moment, they did so in order to endow it with mystical significance and precedence for superior ecclesiastical or secular authority—manifesting another attempt to "invent tradition" as a means of securing legitimacy. In fact, a combination of peculiar circumstances had permitted the two original parties to create a hybrid ceremony cobbled together for an immediate purpose in December 800. I shall now, very briefly, survey the circumstances that resulted in this event and created the two emperors of Christendom.

OLD ROME, NEW ROME, AND SECOND ROME

Since Charles had inherited the tradition of an itinerant court and had spent all his reign in movement between one palace or villa and another, the decision to construct a more permanent residence constituted a break from Frankish tradition. In about 796, however, the small settlement at Aachen (Aquis Grana) was chosen for this honour.[3] It was already a favourite bath-

[3] There is an immense bibliography on the Carolingian capital, see for instance, R. Folz, *The Coronation of Charlemagne, 25 December 800* (London, 1974), 102-106; H. Fichtenau, *The Carolingian Empire* (Oxford, 1957), 67-69; W. Kaemmerer, "Die Aachener Pfalz Karls des Grossen," in W. Braunfels et al., eds., *Karl der Grosse: Lebenswerk und Nachleben*, 4 vols.

ing place on account of its hot springs and had served as a royal villa in Pippin's time. Charles now planned the new buildings with great care using ancient columns, capitals, and other materials transported from Ravenna and Pavia, whose imperial, Late Antique, and Lombard buildings served as models. Old Testament descriptions of Solomon's constructions and Duke Arichis's church of St. Sophia at Benevento may have given Charles particular ideas, for instance in his palace chapel, a centrally planned octagon. The position of Charles's throne in the gallery, from which he could look down on the altar of the Virgin, endowed with numerous relics and liturgical vessels in gold and silver, may have imitated arrangements in St. Sophia, Constantinople. There, too, the ruler had direct access to the gallery of his cathedral church from the palace. St. Sophia was also decorated with imperial portraits, as were later Carolingian foundations. Although the original decoration of the Aachen palace chapel is not precisely known, the most costly materials appear to have been used: coloured marbles, precious metals, and mosaics in the ancient style still visible in Rome and other Italian cities. In the vault of the chapel, Christ and the Elders were depicted in mosaic with the Beasts of the Apocalypse, in a scene reminiscent of manuscript illustrations of Christ in Majesty. An additional parallel with contemporary book painting is found in the columns of canon tables in a Gospel book still in the cathedral of Aachen, which can be identified as different antique marbles used in the chapel.[4]

The central structure of the Second Rome, also called *Roma Ventura* ("the future Rome"), consisted of a vast royal residence, the sacred palace (*sacrum palatium*). This term had also been used of the Lombard palace at Pavia, but Charles's building may have been designed to compete with Constantinople. Since its internal decoration probably resembled the glittering reception halls of the Great Palace on the Bosphoros, which would have been described by Frankish ambassadors, some historians have pressed this rivalry too far, implying that Charles consciously intended to better the By-

---

(Dusseldorf, 1965-7), 1:322-48; cf. the contributions by G. Bandmann, F. Kreusch, and L. Hugot in vol. 3. These are now critically reviewed by L. Falkenstein, "Zwischenbilanz zur Aachener Pfalzenforschung," *Zeitschrift des Aachener Geschichtsvereins* 80 (1970): 7-71; cf. M. Cagiano de Azevedo, "Note archeologiche riguardo al Sacramentario inviato da Adriano I a Carlo Magno," in *Studia Storica O. Bertolini* (Pisa, 1972), 1:73-79. Interestingly, Einhard devoted equal attention to the long bridge over the Rhine, a technological achievement, and to the Aachen church, see *Vita Karoli*, para. 17. Later in the ninth century, Notker, in his *Life of Charlemagne* (para. 27), recorded the monarch's conscious imitation of Solomon. Both lives are translated by L. Thorpe, *Two Lives of Charlemagne* (Harmondsworth, 1969), see esp. 71, 125-27.

[4] D. Bullough, *The Age of Charlemagne*, 2nd ed. (London, 1973), 149-59, 166; H. Belting, "Studien zum Beneventanischen Hof im 8. Jahrhundert," *DOP* 16 (1962): 141-93, esp. 175-93.

zantine emperors. It is more likely that he was determined to adorn his new capital with the most extravagant and impressive designs obtainable, and spared no expense in gathering craftsmen and materials from all parts of his territories. Nonetheless, from the very end of the eighth century, Aachen was being referred to in the West as a Second Rome, in terms that challenged the chief city of the East, traditionally known as New Rome. Later it contained three silver tables decorated with a *mappa mundi*, a map of Rome and a map of Constantinople, respectively, another indication of Aachen's claim to equality with the other two.[5] At his now-permanent centre of government, Charles strengthened his international standing by concluding diplomatic alliances with the Spanish emirate of Cordova, the Kingdom of Asturias, and the caliphate of Baghdad. The silk tents, carpets, and exotic spices, which reached Aachen from both the Arab and Christian rulers of Spain, proclaimed Charles's exalted status in far distant places and consolidated his prestige in the West.[6]

Meanwhile, in the East, Constantinople had revived after the outbreak of plague in the mid-eighth century and was functioning as a capital city once again. Large areas within the walls had been abandoned or given over to additional vineyards and orchards, but the rebuilding initiated by Leo III and Constantine V was maintained by their successors. Not only were the triple walls and water supplies repaired, but attention was paid to the needs of a growing population. Empress Irene installed new public bakeries in a disused ancient hippodrome near the Amastrianon and built many hostels, hospitals, and shelters for the poor and elderly, while Patriarch Tarasios is known to have distributed free meals to the poor, part of a renewal of public charity.[7] Economic activity had increased in the capital to the point at which the empress's remission of taxes paid by city traders brought her considerable popular support. Secular construction, encouraged by

---

[5] For the term *sacrum palatium*, see Bullough, *The Age of Charlemagne*, 166; for the tables, see Einhard, *Vita Karoli*, para. 33 (Thorpe, *Two Lives*, 89). On the use of New Rome, see *Karolus Magnus et Leo Papa*, ed. H. Beumann, F. Brunholz, and W. Winkelmann (Paderborn, 1966); English translation by P. Godman, *Poetry of the Carolingian Renaissance* (London, 1985), no. 25 (197-206), where the poem is attributed with a query to Einhard, following D. Schaller, "Das Aachener Epos für Karl den Kaiser," *Frühmittelalterliche Studien* 10 (1970): 134-38. Cf. also Godman, *Poetry*, no. 24 (190-97), the *Ecloga* by Moduin of Autun, esp. 192.24-27 and 192.31, where Aachen is called New Rome and associated with a renovation of classical Rome.

[6] Einhard, *Vita Karoli*, para. 16 (Thorpe, *Two Lives*, 70) (including an emphasis on the great respect accorded to Charles by the kings of the Irish); F. L. Ganshof, "The Frankish Monarchy and Its External Relations from Pippin III to Louis the Pious," in *The Carolingians and the Frankish Monarchy: Studies in Carolingian History* (Ithaca, N.Y., 1971), 162-204.

[7] *Patria Constantinopoleos*, ed. T. Preger, in *Scriptores Originum Constantinopolitanarum*, 2 vols. (Leipzig, 1901-1907, reprinted New York, 1975), 3:85, 173; cf. John of Ephesos, *Ecclesiastical History* 2.43; 3.14; C. Mango, *The Brazen House*, 50-51.

Constantine V at the suburban palace of St. Mamas, was continued by Irene, who built herself a new palace, the Eleutherios, close to her bakeries.[8] Similarly, imperial patronage of deluxe objects such as the elaborate silks produced in the state workshops of Constantinople stimulated the activity of skilled craftsmen. New Rome was gradually reasserting its legendary prosperity, not only within the empire but also among neighbouring lands.

In contrast to these two political capitals, which drew their inspiration from Old Rome, that city had become an entirely ecclesiastical centre. But by the end of the eighth century it also controlled a large part of central Italy, the expanded duchy of Rome, now generally designated as the "holy Roman republic."[9] It was administered by a secular and religious staff appointed by the pontiff, whose chief task was to ensure its loyalty and wellbeing. It also had to supply an adequate stock of provisions for the city and all its visitors. Basic foodstuffs were largely cultivated on the papal *domuscultae*, farms established by Pope Zacharias and greatly extended by his successors as "apostolic farmland." These estates were administered by clergy and held charters that decreed them to be "forever and absolutely inalienable."[10] Under Pope Hadrian, existing *domuscultae* were expanded and seven more were added at sites close to the major roads leading to Rome, to facilitate the transport of produce. At his own family estate of Capracorum he established that all the resources available should be devoted to the poor of the apostolic see. Every day one hundred (or more) were to be fed "in the portico next to the stairway leading up to the Lateran palace, where are the paintings of the poor; fifty loaves, each weighing two pounds, and two ten-gallon jars of wine, weighing sixty pounds, and cauldrons of soup shall every day be distributed to the poor by one of our faithful cellarers; each pauper will receive a ration of bread and one measure of wine, that is two cupfuls, and a bowl of soup."[11]

In conjunction with this extension of papal charity, the city's *diaconiae* were also increased. Near St. Peter's, three were provided for local poor and foreign pilgrims, not only with substantial daily rations but also with washing facilities (baths), which all were instructed to use once a week. For

[8] Theophanes, 467, 472, 476 (on the Eleutherios palace); ibid., 475 (on taxes); ibid., 419, 432, on St. Mamas; cf. *Parastaseis*, para. 15, and *Constantinople in the Early Eighth Century: The Parastaseis Syntomoi Chronika*, ed. Averil Cameron and Judith Herrin (Leiden, 1984), 23-24. On Irene's bakeries, see C. L. Striker, "The *Coliseo de Spiriti* in Constantinople," in O. Feld and U. Peschlow, eds., *Festschrift F. W. Deichmann* (forthcoming).

[9] T. F. X. Noble, *The Republic of St. Peter* (Philadelphia, 1984), 138-83; R. Krautheimer, *Rome: Profile of a City, 312-1308* (Princeton, 1980), 109-114.

[10] *LP* 1.502, "*in usu et propria utilitate sanctae nostrae Romanae ecclesiae perenniter permaneant.*"

[11] Ibid., 1.501-502; P. Llewellyn, *Rome in the Dark Ages* (London, 1970), 243-44.

regular baths to be practicable it was necessary to improve the water supply for St. Peter's, so Hadrian undertook major repairs to the vast Sabbatina aqueduct and water pipes that had been non-functional since Aistulf's siege twenty years before. The water mills on the nearby Gianiculo also required attention. Nor did the pope neglect the needs of the city within the walls; the Claudian aqueduct and great pipes of the Aqua Jobia and Vergine were repaired and towers in damaged parts of the walls rebuilt.[12] Again, three *diaconiae* near the Forum, installed in ancient buildings, not only had guaranteed supplies of food but also of water for washing. And the churches attached to all sixteen welfare centres were endowed with new altar covers and six curtains. Hadrian and his successor, Leo III, were exceptionally generous in their gifts of luxurious hangings to many churches of the city: in St. Peter's alone, a set of 65 to hang between the columns of the nave and a large one for the main west door. Necessary repairs were also paid for by Charles: one thousand pounds of lead for the roof of St. Peter's and 84 huge beams to replace those in the four major basilicas.[13]

Charles's position as protector of the apostolic see was commemorated in the city. Under Pope Leo III, the dining room of the Lateran palace, the Triclinium Maius, was enlarged and redecorated. In its apse he depicted a mosaic of the Mission of the Apostles, and on either side a trio of figures representing the alliance of secular and ecclesiastical authority that had developed in the eighth century. On the right was St. Peter enthroned, bestowing the pallium on Pope Leo and the banner of Rome on King Charles; on the left (probably), a corresponding illustration of the *Donation of Constantine*: Christ endowing Pope Sylvester with the pallium, and Constantine with the labarum. As the Triclinium was partially demolished in 1589, and the mosaics totally restored in 1625, only to be transferred to a new niche in the following century, their original condition is lost irrecoverably.[14] But they appear to have celebrated Charles's role as the counterpart to Constantine, and Leo's as the successor of Sylvester. A similar decoration adorned the church of St. Susanna, where Leo had been priest before his election. The whole building was remodelled, and Leo and Charles were shown as donors in the apse mosaic (lost since the late sixteenth century).[15]

---

[12] *LP* 1.503-505, 510; cf. Krautheimer, *Rome*, 110-11.

[13] *LP* 1.499.10-15; Hadrian's letters record Charles's help, see *CC*, nos. 65 (592-93) and 78 (609-610). Leo III subsequently presented another set of 65 curtains to St. Peter's, and 96 for the altar and presbytery (*LP* 2.13.14-15). These are, however, just a tiny fraction of the endowments of both popes, see ibid., 1.499-514; 2.1-3, 9-33.

[14] *LP* 2.3-4 (although the apse decoration is not specified); cf. H. Belting, "I mosaici dell'aula leonina come testimonianza della prima 'renovatio' nell'arte medievale a Roma," in *Roma e l'età carolingia* (Rome, 1976), 167-82; Krautheimer, *Rome*, 115-16.

[15] *LP* 2.3.12-29 (again the subject of the mosaic is not mentioned; in contrast, the papal endowments in liturgical objects, gold and silver, precious hangings, and other extravagant

Of the three cities that traced their traditions back to the foundation of Romulus and Remus, Constantinople most resembled the ancient capital of the caesars, precisely because it still functioned as the centre of an empire. Aachen, despite its imitation of antique buildings, remained a very small settlement entirely dominated by the Frankish court, which had not adopted the stiff, ceremonial ritual associated with imperial customs. The grand plans and ambitious role implied by Alcuin in his identification of the city as a Second Rome were thwarted by the danger of earthquakes. Before 803 Aachen had to be abandoned, and although it was reoccupied once the damage had been repaired, its instability compared unfavourably with the permanency of Constantinople and symbolised the gulf between the eastern and western successors of imperial Rome.[16] In contrast, the oldest of the three foundations experienced a very considerable growth in prosperity, due largely to the Frankish conquest of Lombardy. Under pontifical rule, the Roman Republic furnished materials and funds to rebuild city institutions in their new ecclesiastical guise. While entire regions within the circuit of the walls had become agricultural or waste land, and ancient senatorial villas and palaces were no longer maintained, papal ceremonial and largesse had taken over the imperial role, and at the end of the eighth century, the city of St. Peter enjoyed considerable prestige. The resources of Old Rome had been revitalised in preparation for the coming struggle for dominance with its younger rivals.

The Aftermath of Frankfurt

With his own position enhanced by the synod of 794, Charles proceeded to campaign against the rebellious Saxons. The conquest and forced conversion of these independent people and other non-Christians appears as one of the practical consequences of Frankfurt. After legislating for the Christian education of his own subjects in such detail, to ignore the needs of the heathen would have been a failing in Charles's primary duty. Equally, other policies adopted after 794 seem to be related to the synod: a changed attitude towards the papacy, and an even firmer hostility to the East.

The first, military, consequence was immediately realised in elaborate plans to defeat the pagan Avars, established in a strong central European state. This undertaking against an experienced and crafty enemy presented the greatest strategic difficulties to date. Early in 795, Charles began to organise the accumulation of baggage trains, mounts, fodder, and all the

decorations are carefully listed). On the ideology of the mosaics, see P. Classen, "Karl der Grosse, das Papsttum und Byzanz," in *Karl der Grosse*, 1:537-608, esp. 575-76; Belting, "I mosaici."

[16] Einhard, *Vita Karoli*, para. 32 (Thorpe, *Two Lives*, 85).

necessary military equipment for a three-pronged attack along very extended supply lines. His care was rewarded later that year when one army broke into the Avar ring (the central encampment) and plundered it of a huge collection of treasure, some of which dated back centuries.[17] Missionary work began immediately. Charles established a protectorate over the Danubian regions and incorporated the westernmost parts into his territories of Bavaria and Friuli. After another campaign in 796, one of the Avar chiefs came to Aachen to secure an alliance. Charles stood godfather to him at his baptism and presented him with many gifts, in a ceremony typical of medieval alliances offered by "the family of kings."[18] Although the complete subjugation of the Avar Kingdom and reorganisation of the Danube area was not achieved until the early ninth century, the 795-96 campaign was one of the most brilliant and successful in both military and Christian terms.

While Charles had mourned Pope Hadrian's death as the loss of a faithful family friend, and had a striking tombstone carved for him in Francia, the event presented the possibility of resolving Rome's awkward Janus-like support for both Nicaea and Frankfurt.[19] The year 796 therefore opened a new epoch in Frankish-papal relations. Immediately after his election, the new pontiff, Leo III, dispatched the keys of St. Peter and the *vexillum* (city banner) of Rome to Charles. His ambassadors met those of the king bringing part of the Avar booty to "the celestial city," where it was to be distributed among the churches.[20] In Charles's response to Leo, he requested a renewal of the inviolate treaty of faith and charity, and the pact of paternity and spiritual protection that had existed between himself and Hadrian. But a new tone was struck in his statement on regal and papal responsibilities for Christian defence. While kings fight for the church of Christ, both against unbelievers and against inadequate knowledge of the Catholic faith, popes should provide support by standing with their arms upheld like Moses (a reference to the posture that was taken to ensure triumph).[21] The larger pedagogic role undertaken at Frankfurt was also

---

[17] Ibid., para. 13 (Thorpe, *Two Lives*, 67-68); *Royal Frankish Annals*, a.795; *Annals of Einhard*, a.795; *Annales Laureshamenses*, a.795; cf. J. B. Ross, "Two Neglected Paladins of Charlemagne: Erich of Friuli and Gerold of Bavaria," *Speculum* 20 (1945): 212-35.

[18] *Royal Frankish Annals*, a.796; *Annals of Einhard*, a.796; A. Angenendt, *Kaiserherrschaft und Königstaufe* (Berlin/New York, 1984), 232-33; Ross, "Two Neglected Paladins," 220-22.

[19] Einhard, *Vita Karoli*, para. 19 (Thorpe, *Two Lives*, 75); *Annales Laureshamenses*, a.795 (section 28); cf. Bullough, *The Age of Charlemagne*, plate 19.

[20] *Royal Frankish Annals*, a.796; *Annales of Einhard*, a.796.

[21] *Epistolae Karolini Aevi* 2, no. 93, pp. 136-38; the crucial passage occurs at 137.27-138.2. The letter has occasioned much commentary and analysis, see for example, J. M. Wallace-Hadrill, *The Frankish Church* (Oxford, 1983), 186-87.

translated into specific instructions for the pope (to curtail simony, for instance), as Charles fulfilled his title "rector of the Christian people." This sense of supreme guardianship influenced his relations with Pope Leo. For his part, the pontiff began to date his documents from the Carolingian conquest of northern Italy and bestowed his blessing on the reorganised Bavarian church, which obtained a metropolitan see (Salzburg) at the king's insistence in 798.[22] Within the now-traditional alliance, Charles was claiming a senior and dominating position.

Since Constantinople made no official contact with Charles between 788 and 797, and neither Pope Hadrian nor the Frankish court informed the East of the synod of Frankfurt, it is impossible to tell if Constantine VI learnt of it. When the emperor finally sent an envoy to Aachen (in 797), there is no indication that it was directed toward differences raised by the synod. Possibly, the continuing problem of disputed territories in Istria/ Venetia and Benevento formed the main subject. Following Grimoald's 788 defeat of Byzantine forces in southern Italy, prisoners, including Patriarch Tarasios's brother, had been held in Frankish prisons. Their liberation was sought and finally obtained by another embassy sent in 798.[23] Constantine, however, was not able to witness this success as he had been removed from power in August 797.

During her brief reign as sole emperor (797-802), Irene pursued the desirability of peaceful relations not only with Charles, but also with the Arabs. Under Harun al Rashid, the caliphate aspired to far-reaching domination, which threatened Byzantium directly. This foreign policy was compounded by internal revolts (again from the partisans of the caesar Nikephoros and his brothers) and by the dangerous ambitions of Irene's two chief advisers, Staurakios and Aetios. As both were eunuchs, they conspired to promote their own male relatives in open rivalry.[24] Irene played one off against the other and resisted the general pressure for her to remarry and thus raise a man to the position of ruler (the normal action for a widowed empress). Her position might be anomalous, even unprecedented, but she revealed no obvious desire to permit any man to protect or control her. On the contrary, her use of the masculine form of address, *basileus*, rather than the feminine, *basilissa* (employed during her joint rule with

[22] See Leo III's letter to Charles, no. 4, and to the clergy of Salzburg, no. 3, *Epistolae Karolini Aevi* 3, 58-60; cf. Classen, "Karl der Grosse," 568-69, and the additional notes in the reprint [76] (Dusseldorf, 1968); Angenendt, *Kaiserherrschaft*, 234-36.

[23] *Royal Frankish Annals*, a.798; *Annals of Einhard*, a.798, report the liberation of Sisinnios; cf. the extremely curt notice of Constantine's embassy of 797, *Annals of Einhard*, a.797.

[24] Theophanes, 473, 474, 475; P. Speck, *Kaiser Konstantin VI. Die Legitimation einer Fremden und der Versuch einer eigenen Herrshaft* (Munich, 1978), 1:329-32.

THE THREE HEIRS OF ROME

Constantine VI), suggests that she was quite determined to rule alone. The same is implied by her gold coinage, which carried her portrait on both obverse and reverse in a departure from imperial custom.[25]

The claim made in one contemporary western source, that Irene's embassy to Charles in 798 proposed to hand over to him the empire in the West, assumes that Irene could only operate from a position of weakness. Several modern historians accept that this must have been the case; others believe that the embassy represents an unofficial approach made by her enemies, who wished to see the Frankish king as ruler in Constantinople.[26] If this could possibly be the case, which I very much doubt, Charles saw through the pretence. The record was probably written in the heady atmosphere of 798-800, when the term *imperium* was taking on new meanings and the *Donation of Constantine* had spread the idea of an imperial division. For Irene, peaceful alliances with powerful neighbours were one thing, and perfectly regular; a plan to make Charles emperor over the West (or in the East) was quite another.

CHARLES'S CORONATION

As many substantial books have been written on the imperial coronation, here I will merely sketch some of the relevant factors bearing on the division of Christendom—primarily the relations between Constantinople and Aachen, and between Charles and Leo III. Both of these should be set against the background of schism traced above, that is, the denunciation of Nicaea at Frankfurt and Hadrian's contradictory acceptance of both.

The basic chronology of the ceremony can be briefly recapitulated: Charles arrived in Rome in November 800 to investigate charges against Leo III's conduct as pope and the physical attacks on him. On December 23 the pontiff cleared himself of all accusations by an oath of compurgation, accepted by all parties.[27] Two days later at Christmas evening mass,

[25] J. Herrin, "Women and the Faith in Icons," in R. Samuel and G. Stedman Jones, eds., *Culture, Ideology and Politics* (London, 1982), 69-73, with plate 9; Speck, *Kaiser Konstantin VI*, 1:323-26.

    [26] For instance, Fichtenau, *The Carolingian Empire*, 72-73; cf. Classen, "Karl der Grosse," 566-67. On the importance of this contemporary reference, see H. Löwe, "Ein Kölner Notiz zum Kaisertum Karls des Grossen," *Rheinische Vierteljahrsblätter* 14 (1949): 7-34.

    [27] This *sacramentum* is preserved, see *Epistolae Karolini Aevi* 3, no. 6 (63-64); cf. H. Adelson and R. Baker, "The Oath of Purgation of Pope Leo III in 800," *Traditio* 8 (1952): 35-80; L. Wallach, "The Roman Synod of December 800 and the Alleged Trial of Leo III: A Theory and the Historical Facts," *Harvard Theological Review* 49 (1956): 123-42; M. Kerner, "Der Reinigungeseid Leos III vom Dezember 800: Die Frage seiner Echtheit und frühen kanonistischen Überlieferung," *Zeitschrift des Aachener Geschichtsvereins* 84/5, (1977-78): 131-66.

Leo III placed a crown on Charles's head as he rose from prayer (or came up from the tomb of St. Peter): the Roman clergy and people then acclaimed him as Augustus (emperor), in a revised and extended version of the imperial *laudes*, and Leo made the eastern sign of reverence (*proskynesis*) by prostrating himself before Charles. Thus a Frankish king became emperor.[28]

What part, if any, did Constantinople play in this imperial coronation, which clearly owed much to Byzantine ceremonial? As there are plenty of purely western motives for the event (even if they may not all be in agreement), is there any need to seek an eastern role? Traditionally, western medievalists have limited this to a ritual element. But some Byzantinists have sought to identify a much greater initiative behind the proceedings, even going so far as to suggest that Irene was responsible for the entire event.[29] Against such a claim, I believe, on the contrary, that the empress had no intention of sharing her supreme power with anyone. Indeed, it seems unlikely that she could have conceived of the notion of reviving the western empire in order to win Charles's alliance.

A more plausible explanation for the imperial coronation lies in the combination of factors of western origin, which were all in some way satisfied by it. Pressures for some recognition of Charles's status had been developing at his court, in the curia of Pope Leo III, in the monastic and episcopal libraries of such writers such as Alcuin, Paulinus, Theodulf, and probably in the minds of a number of the participants. Despite some degree of planning, pope and monarch may not have been in complete agreement as to the precise nature of the ceremony. But even in this case we can be sure that the particular arrangements made for mass on 25 December 800 had nothing to do with an official Byzantine coronation ritual.[30] It was experienced and interpreted in various ways, which are preserved in the different accounts: Pope Leo's in the *Liber pontificalis*, Charles's in the *Royal Frankish Annals*. Other descriptions indicate what contemporaries made of the ceremony. So although there is no sense of unanimity among the Latin sources, it is possible to analyse some of the motives and pressures behind

[28] For an introduction to the sources and their problems, see B. Pullan, *Sources for the History of Medieval Europe* (Oxford, 1966), 11-14; R. Sullivan, *The Coronation of Charlemagne: What Did It Signify?* (Boston, 1959); Folz, *The Coronation of Charlemagne*, esp. 43-50.

[29] J. B. Bury, "Charles the Great and Irene," *Hermathena* 8 (1893): 17-37, esp. 21-37; cf. Speck, *Kaiser Konstantin VI*, 1:332-33. This is not the place to discuss a fascinating hypothesis, which demands a lengthy examination.

[30] Einhard, *Vita Karoli*, para. 28 (Thorpe, *Two Lives*, 81), alone records that Charles was surprised and disapproved of the pope's action, an addition that is sometimes assumed to be a "classical" embellishment, see Folz, *The Coronation of Charlemagne*, 149; English translation of the passage, ibid., 239.

the event, some ideological, others purely practical. It was their convergence that proved decisive.

As we have noted, Charles's conduct at the synod of Frankfurt, its new "universal" character, and the practical consequences of his role as guardian of the faith, drew attention to Aachen's directive force in western orthodoxy. Similarly, the condemnation of Nicaea, which branded eastern practice as idolatrous and thus in severe breach of Old Testament law, also allowed Charles to assume a more righteous position. Whether disapproval of Irene's presidency over the false council was compounded by her later assumption of sole rule, her claim to reign as emperor was used as an additional western argument against Constantinople.[31] Charles's political aims, ecclesiastical duties, and religious convictions all tended towards greater rivalry rather than accommodation with the East. This is clear from the construction of Aachen as Second Rome, whether consciously based on descriptions of Constantinople or planned to resemble ancient imperial buildings in the West.

To this sense of rivalry must be added the fact that some of Charles's contemporaries noted the similarity between the territories under his control and the provinces of the ancient Roman Empire in the West. Alcuin, in particular, used the concept of *imperium* and developed the idea of *renovatio*, a revival.[32] Since the British Isles, Spain, North Africa, Sicily, southern Italy, and Dalmatia were entirely omitted from the Carolingian kingdoms, it was more of an imaginary than a real reconstruction of ancient Roman power. But this does not mean that the idea was any less meaningful for all that. It was combined with a sense that the name bestowed on a ruler carried a significance over and above its limited meaning. Thus when Pippin asked Pope Zacharias about the regal title, his real powers and responsibilities were recognised. Correspondingly, the extension of most Christian administration to many parts of Europe before 800 demanded a titulature for Charles grander than that of monarch. The reality of his powers endowed the Carolingian kingdoms with an imperial aura, which required a

---

[31] The account of the *Annales Laureshamenses*, a.801 (English translation in Folz, *The Coronation of Charlemagne*, 237), stresses that Irene's use of the imperial title was improper and led Charles to assume the position of emperor, as if there was no eastern ruler. Cf. Bullough, *The Age of Charlemagne*, 167-68. On Charles's coronation as the culmination of a series of attempts to renew the Roman Empire in the West, see P. Classen, "Der erste Römerzug in der Weltgeschichte: Zur Geschichte der Kaisertums im Westen und der Kaiserkrönung in Rom zwischen Theodosios der Grosse und Karl der Grosse," in *Historische Forschungen für W. Schlesinger* (Cologne, 1975), 325-47.

[32] F. L. Ganshof, *The Imperial Coronation of Charlemagne* (Glasgow, 1949); L. Wallach, *Alcuin and Charlemagne: Studies in Carolingian History and Literature* (Ithaca, 1959), 15-27; C. Erdmann, *Forschungen zur politischen Ideenwelt des Frühmittelalters* (Berlin, 1931), 16-31; Wallace-Hadrill, *The Frankish Church*, 207-209.

new status. The imperial title reflected that substance—name and content were aptly matched.[33]

Local Problems in Rome

In these circumstances of increasing rivalry and tension, Pope Leo III's appeal to Charles in 799 emphasised the Carolingian monarch's duty to protect the holy see of St. Peter. And unlike past calls for military assistance against the Lombards, this rested on Charles's rights within Rome as *patricius Romanorum* and presented him with the opportunity to exercise an authority not solely derived from military conquest.

Leo's problems stemmed from the "family" style of pontifical administration developed by his predecessor: Hadrian had employed his nephews in positions of considerable influence. Both Paschalis and Campulus had also served as legates to the Frankish court. Under Leo III, these aristocratic officials lost their power. The new pope also appointed rapacious administrators whose determination to extract maximum produce from the *domuscultae* and other papal estates may have curtailed the rights and privileges of Roman landowners and noble families. Although the precise grounds for discontent are not made clear in the *Liber pontificalis* (a record favourable to Leo), in April 799 the pope was attacked by a gang hired by Hadrian's nephews as he rode through Rome to celebrate mass. They imprisoned him, threatened to blind him and cut out his tongue, accusing him of the stock crimes, adultery and perjury. But he was rescued by loyal attendants who called on Charles's nearest local official, Duke Winichis of Spoleto, for assistance. In the company of an armed guard, Leo escaped from Rome and was escorted via Spoleto, over the Alps and down the Rhine to Charles's remote residence at Paderborn in central Saxony.[34]

These disturbances brought the pontiff to the monarch in the guise of a hapless fugitive, insecure in his own bishopric and accused of relatively serious crimes—chiefly secular, since those of adultery and perjury were regularly brought against any cleric under suspicion. Messengers from the opposition also arrived in Paderborn to press these charges. The situation obviously demanded Charles's arbitration, for his authority as *patricius Romanorum* was recognised by all parties. After Leo's honourable reception, negotiations began over the correct means of re-establishing him as bishop

---

[33] H. Beumann, "Nomen Imperatoris: Studien zur Kaiseridee Karls des Grossen," *HZ* 185 (1958): 515-49, reprinted in G. Wolf, ed., *Zum Kaisertum Karls des Grossen* (Darmstadt, 1972); Classen, "Karl der Grosse," 586-709.

[34] *LP* 2.4-6; *Annales Laureshamenses*, a.799 (section 32); *Royal Frankish Annals*, a.799; *Annals of Einhard*, a.799. Folz, *The Coronation of Charlemagne*, 234, 236, 237-38; W. Mohr, "Karl der Grosse, Leo III und der römische Aufstand von 799," *Archivum Latinitas Medii Aevi* 20 (1960): 39-98.

of Rome. A verse account of these discussions is preserved in the Paderborn epic, probably written by Einhard early in the ninth century.[35] It implies that Charles's willingness to assist Leo's return in triumph was matched by the pope's desire to bestow on him the more prestigious title of emperor: both wished to elevate the terms of the alliance dating back to 754 to a superior level. For Charles the step corroborated all the other tendencies noted above; for Leo it corresponded to the procedure described in the *Donation of Constantine*. Writing about six years after the event, Einhard presents it as a potential gain for both parties; his epic also indicates that Leo's two-month visit to Charles in Saxony marked another significant step towards the imperial coronation.

In October 799, the papal party returned to Rome augmented by the Frankish archbishops of Cologne and Salzburg, appointed as Charles's legates (*missi*) to investigate the charges. Some sort of trial was held, and Paschalis and Campulus were found guilty, but it was decided to defer judgement until the king could evaluate the situation.[36] During the next twelve months, Charles was under increasing pressure, from Alcuin in particular, to go to Rome and settle matters. In the same period he received an embassy from the patriarch of Jerusalem, and sent Zacharias, a palace presbyter, back to the Holy Land with many gifts, thus initiating a Carolingian presence in the East.[37] The problem of Saxon prisoners-of-war also demanded Charles's attention, and he decided to resettle whole families with women and children in different parts of his lands, dividing Saxony between his *fideles*, bishops, presbyters, counts, and other vassals. A large church was dedicated in the new Carolingian centre of Paderborn to commemorate his victory over the Saxons and to further their conversion. In 800 he made a pilgrimage to the shrine of St. Martin at Tours, where his wife Liutgard died and was buried. On this occasion he spent some time with Alcuin, abbot of the monastery, but what they discussed is not recorded.[38]

Eventually, Charles announced that he would celebrate the following Christmas in the eternal city. He knew that it would be the 800th anniversary of the birth of Christ and wished to mark this important A.D. date by observing the festival in Rome. As a further tribute to Christian influence in Carolingian dating, Alcuin urged Charles to adopt December 25 as

---

[35] *Karolus Magnus et Leo papa*, and see Schaller, "Das Aachener Epos."

[36] *LP* 2.6-7 (the passage is translated in Folz, *The Coronation of Charlemagne*, 238).

[37] *Royal Frankish Annals*, a.800; *Annals of Einhard*, a.799.

[38] *Annales Laureshamenses*, a.799; *Royal Frankish Annals*, a.800; *Annals of Einhard*, a.800; *Capitularia*, nos. 26-27 (68-72). Cf. the similar technique for resettlement employed in Byzantium by Justinian II, discussed here in Chapters 7 and 8. For the death of Liutgard, see Alcuin's letter to Charles, *Epistolae Karolini Aevi* 2, no. 197, 325-26.

the start of the year, a proposal that found favour especially with his son, Louis the Pious, and was only rejected two generations later.[39] Whether the immediate significance of Charles's anniversary trip was also appreciated by the pope is unknown, but Leo realised that the king, his spiritual *compater*, patrician of the Romans, and personal protector would be coming, and planned the visit accordingly. From the evidence of all the surviving sources, arrangements were made to cover Charles's welcome (at the twelfth milestone from the city), his subsequent visit to St. Peter's, and his entry into Rome. It seems not unreasonable to assume that provision was also made for suitable honorific rituals to be performed in the course of his stay—his presidency at the court that finally absolved the pope of all the accusations, and his attendance at Christmas mass at St. Peter's rather than the usual stational church. Certain preparations lay behind this special service at which the actual coronation took place and the new *laudes* were chanted.[40]

Consequences of the Imperial Coronation

In the absence of records by different participants and witnesses, it seems safer to examine the consequences of the Christmas ceremony rather than attempting to assess its significance to each in turn. Charles remained in Rome until after Easter 801, longer than ever before, and exercised his judicial rights in the city by condemning Hadrian's nephews, Paschalis and Campulus, to death, commuted at Leo III's intervention to imprisonment and exile in Francia. His imperial stature is reflected in official papal documents, dated by Charles's imperial year and consulate, though the pope continued to put his own name first, a departure from both Byzantine and Frankish practice. Coins were minted with Charles's name as well as the papal monogram. The emperor's name also preceded that of the pope in official acclamations and prayers, and his portrait was given the place of honour.[41] In other words, those rights traditionally reserved to eastern rulers were thus unequivocally transferred to the new western emperor. But

---

[39] H. Fichtenau, " 'Politische' Datierungen des frühen Mittelalters," in H. Wolfram, ed., *Intitulatio II* (Vienna, 1973), 513-17; cf. the discussion of dating in Chapter 10.

[40] *LP* 2.7; *Annales Laureshamenses*, a.800 (section 33); *Royal Frankish Annals*, a.800; *Annals of Einhard*, a.800, all translated in Folz, *The Coronation of Charlemagne*, 234-39; cf. 231-33, the *laudes*. On these new *laudes*, which acclaimed Charles emperor, see E. H. Kantorowicz, *Laudes Regiae* (Berkeley, 1958), 63-64, 84-85, 103-104. On the discrepancies between individual accounts, see P. Schramm, "Die Anerkennung Karls des Grossen als Kaiser (bis 800)," *HZ* 172 (1951): 449-515, reprinted in his *Kaiser, Könige und Päpste*, 4 vols. (Stuttgart, 1968-71), vol. 1; Classen, "Karl der Grosse," 592-93 (and additional notes in the reprint [78]); cf. Folz, *The Coronation of Charlemagne*, 143-50.

[41] *LP* 2.7-8; *Royal Frankish Annals*, a.801; *Annals of Einhard*, a.801.

this did not imply a reduction in papal authority in the government of the city. Immediately before the coronation, Charles's role as defender and protector of Christians everywhere had received emphatic confirmation in the arrival of legates from Jerusalem, bringing him the banners of the city.[42] It was this universal responsibility for the faith, rather than a localised Roman one, that seems to have been expanded and intensified by the new honours assumed in 800.

Charles issued no official documents from Rome. The first use of the imperial title occurred at Reno, near Bologna, on 29 May 801, and in a very particular form. As analysed by Classen, the lengthy description combined several purely eastern features with novel ones.[43] Charles was identified in traditional Byzantine terms as "most serene Augustus [Majesty], crowned by God, the great pacific emperor"; in a new formulation, "governing the Roman Empire"; in a devotional formula possibly derived from Frankish or Lombard use, "by the mercy of God"; and finally, "king of the Franks and the Lombards," titles held since 774, which Charles wished to retain. The unusual element, "governing the Roman Empire," may have been found in Ravenna; it had had a long life in imperial documents from the sixth century onwards and did not correspond exactly to any formula in Greek used by seventh- or eighth-century eastern rulers. As for the inclusion of his long-established regal titles, it may well reflect Charles's concern to incorporate the Franks and Lombards in his larger and grander unit of empire. The only attribute he was willing to drop was that of "patricius Romanorum"—evidently supplanted by the supreme imperial dignity.[44]

In contrast to the role of patrician, which had been rather narrowly restricted to the city of Rome and its surrounding area, that of "emperor" applied in a worldwide sense to the entire Christian West. The formulas "governing the Roman Empire" or "renovation of the Roman Empire," which feature on the seal used to authenticate imperial documents, lay claim to this universalist tradition.[45] Yet not only did Charles's empire fail

---

[42] *Royal Frankish Annals*, a.800; *Annals of Einhard*, a.800; J. Deér, "Die Vorrechte des Kaisers in Rom, 772-800," *Schweizer Beiträge zur allgemeinen Geschichte* 15 (1957): 5-63 (reprinted in Wolf, ed., *Zum Kaisertum Karls des Grossen*). Noble, *Republic of St. Peter*, 298-99, puts a highly negative interpretation on Carolingian "rights" inside the Roman Republic, and stresses papal autonomy.

[43] P. Classen, "*Romanum gubernans imperium*: Zur vorgeschichte der Kaisertitulatur Karls des Grossen," *Deutsches Archiv* 9 (1951): 103-121, reprinted in Wolf, *Zum Kaisertum Karls*; cf. Classen, "Karl der Grosse," 588-92, and [78] in the reprint.

[44] *Royal Frankish Annals*, a.801; *Annals of Einhard*, a.801; cf. Wolfram, *Intitulatio II*, 19-22.

[45] Folz, *The Coronation of Charlemagne*, 152-55, and plates 12 and 13; cf. Classen, "*Romanum gubernans imperium*," 119-20. D. Bullough, "*Imagines regum* and Their Significance

to recreate the old western Roman Empire, in addition it was conceived in a completely different fashion. Rome did not become its capital but remained an ecclesiastical city governed by its bishop, with an increasingly large area of surrounding countryside. Within the new unit created by his previous conquests, Franks and Lombards had their own place as Romans, together with all the other different ethnic groups—one Christian people under Charles's government. In this stress on the emperor's role as vicar of God, which pervades Charles's later legislation, there is a distinct break from ancient traditions.[46]

The suggestion that Pope Leo III was not fully aware of the new symbolism and titulature employed in the Christmas ceremony is contradicted by his role in the preparations. His concept of the alliance between monarch and pope is also made clear by the mosaic decorations that he commissioned prior to 800. These reflect a clear pontifical aim: to recreate in the already established spiritual relationship a cooperation based on the model of Pope Sylvester and Emperor Constantine I (as "documented" by the *Donation of Constantine*). The coronation also drew on the practice employed by popes from Zacharias onwards, the sanction of temporal authority by pontifical unction. Charles had been anointed three times before the coronation ceremony (in 754, 768, and 771). And in 800 his eldest son Charles was thus designated as his heir.[47] Obviously Leo III relinquished certain powers when Charles became emperor (in fields where Hadrian had acted with considerable independence), but in his somewhat compromised situation the 800 ceremony restored his sacral authority as bishop and associated him in a new stage of the alliance. Since the emperor showed no inclination to remain in Rome or move his northern capital to the "ancient home of the caesars," the pope was left as undisputed master in his ecclesiastical metropolis.[48]

Finally, from the evidence of Charles's courtiers, advisers, and scholar-poets, the imperial coronation rationalised a familiar situation. The name of emperor formalised their ruler's elevated dignity. They gladly swore the revised oath of fealty, served as *missi* in the investigation of imperial justice and protection of the poor, and celebrated the revival of empire in new

---

in the Early Medieval West," in G. Robertson and G. Henderson, eds., *Studies in Memory of David Talbot Rice* (Edinburgh, 1975), 223-76, esp. 244-45.

[46] Wallace-Hadrill, *The Frankish Church*, 187-90.

[47] *Royal Frankish Annals*, a.800; cf. Folz, *The Coronation of Charlemagne*, 145-47. Alcuin's letter to Charles, no. 217, singles out the unction of the emperor's son for particular congratulation, *Epistolae Karolini Aevi* 2, 360-61.

[48] *Annales Laureshamenses*, a.801. This source again justifies Charles's imperial title with a particular claim, that because he controlled the ancient home of the caesars he should be an emperor like them.

buildings, decorative programmes, and manuscripts inspired by ancient models.[49] The tower-gateway of Lorsch monastery and the miniature silver arch that Einhard presented to the Maastricht monastery of St. Servais both appear to have been inspired by the Arch of Constantine in the Roman Forum. Similarly, the rebuilt tomb of St. Boniface, consecrated in 819 at his foundation of Fulda, copied the basilica of St. Peter and was constructed in the Roman fashion (*Romano more*, as were many of Charles's buildings at Aachen and Einhard's foundation at Seligenstadt).[50] Another source of important models was found in the description of Solomon's constructions, equally an inspiration for eastern imperial churches. From the Old Testament, Theodulf of Orléans derived the mosaic decoration for the apse of his small personal chapel at Germigny-des-Prés.[51] Here the symbolic treatment of a religious subject in the manner recommended by the *Libri Carolini* may be detected. For the central feature is the Ark of the Covenant watched over by two cherubim and two angels, and designated by the Hand of God descending from the sky. The villa of Germigny, however, was decorated with figures representing the Seven Liberal Arts, the Four Seasons, and a world map in antique style.[52]

The Filioque Dispute

So while the imperial coronation meant different things to different parties involved, all drew on models (real or imagined) of the Roman past to "explain" it and agreed on its significance for the West. In one respect, however, Charles's assumption of a universal protectorate over Christians everywhere reopened the schisms of Frankfurt. As noted above, the city of Jerusalem had sent its Christian representatives to Rome late in 800. The following year, news of the return of Charles's embassy to the Caliphate of the East was brought to the new emperor at Pavia. Harun al Rashid's legates were accompanied by Isaac the Jew, the only one of three Carolingian envoys to survive the journey, and a much-prized gift, an elephant named Abulabaz. Charles instructed that the Abbasid ambassadors should be es-

---

[49] Bullough, *The Age of Charlemagne*, 189-91.

[50] Ibid., 185-86; C. Heitz, " 'More romano': Problèmes d'architecture et de liturgie carolingiennes," in *Roma e l'età carolingia* (Rome, 1976), 27-38. On Fulda, see D. Heller, "Das Grab des hl. Bonifatius in Fulda," in *Sankt Bonifatius* (Fulda, 1954), 139-56. At Aachen, Seligenstadt, and Reichenau, the Roman foot of measurement was used, see Afterword, 486.

[51] A. Grabar, "Les mosaïques de Germigny des Prés," *Cahiers archéologiques* 7 (1954): 171-83; P. Bloch, "Das Apsismosaik von Germigny-des-Prés," in *Karl der Grosse*, 3:234-61; M. Vieillard-Troiekouroff, "Nouvelles études sur les mosaïques de Germigny des Prés," *Cahiers archéologiques* 17 (1967): 103-112; A. Freeman, "Theodulf of Orleans and the *Libri Carolini*," *Speculum* 32 (1957): 663-705, esp. 692, 699-703.

[52] *LC* 1.15, 20 (pp. 35, 48); Bullough, *The Age of Charlemagne*, 189 and plate 76; idem, "*Imagines regum*," 241-42.

corted at once to Aachen, though the elephant had to wait until the next summer to cross the Alps. Its arrival in Aachen is noted in many sources as a great wonder, and it survived the change of climate, travelling around with Charles until its death in 810.[53] The success of the mission to Baghdad and its safe return after an absence of four years was interpreted as another sign of Charles's increased authority. With Harun al Rashid's permission, he now ordered a community of Benedictines to establish a Carolingian monastery in Jerusalem, as a symbol of his concern for the holy places.[54] As representatives of the reformed Frankish clergy, they naturally employed the form of the Latin creed adopted at Frankfurt. But in the sensitive atmosphere of Jerusalem, where Greek monks had maintained their Christian faith through over 150 years of Muslim occupation, the additional *Filioque* clause was immediately noticed and condemned. Eastern protests against the Latin "innovation" resulted in such battles that the western monks appealed to Pope Leo III to settle the matter. Since the creed was not recited in the Roman mass and Leo still followed his predecessor's position on the clause, supporting the eastern wording, the whole question had to be re-examined.[55]

At the council of Aachen held in 809, Charles commissioned Theodulf of Orléans to prepare a florilegium of patristic testimonia in favour of the addition.[56] Once the council had discussed the problem, it was decided to send a mission to Rome to explain the Frankish position. Abbot Smaragdus, who went with the embassy, composed a treatise on the procession of the Holy Spirit. The ensuing debate, which took place in Leo's presence, turned on the delicate business of altering the words of the creed. While the pope agreed that the procession of the Spirit from the Father *and* the Son was doctrinally correct, he refused to sanction the change adopted in

[53] *Annals of Einhard*, aa.801, 802; *Annales Laureshamenses*, a.802; Einhard, *Vita Karoli*, para. 16 (Thorpe, *Two Lives*, 70).

[54] On the background to Charles's activity in the holy places, see F. W. Buckler, *Harunu'l Rashid and Charles the Great* (Cambridge, Mass., 1931); M. Borgolte, *Die Gesandtenaustausch der Karolinger mit den Abbasiden und mit den Patriarchen von Jerusalem* (Munich, 1976).

[55] See the letter from the monks of the Mount of Olives, *Epistolae Karolini Aevi* 3, no. 7, 64-66 (also in *PG* 94, 206-208), and Leo III's letter to Charles, ibid., no. 8, 66-67; B. Capelle, "Le Pape Leo III et le 'Filioque'," in his *Travaux Liturgiques de doctrine et d'histoire*, vol. 3 (Louvain, 1967), 35-46; cf. the important Greek source, the *Life of Michael the Synkellos*, translated by V. Peri, "Leone III e il 'Filioque': Echi del caso nell'agiographia greca," *Rivista di storia della chiesa in Italia* 25 (1971): 3-58; and most recently, M. Borgolte, "Papst Leo III, Karl der Grosse und die Filioque Streit von Jerusalem," *Byzantina* 10 (1980): 401-427.

[56] *Royal Frankish Annals*, a.809; Theodulf's florilegium, *PL* 105, 239-76; *Concilia*, part 1, no. 33, 236-39; cf. E. Dahlhaus-Berg, *Nova Antiquitas et Antiqua Novitas* (Cologne/Vienna, 1975), 13, 175, 177.

the Frankish church and urged that the chanting of the creed at mass be abandoned.[57] In this he supported the eastern church, which continued to regard the Franks as in error and resolutely opposed any addition to the creed. The alliance between Rome and Aachen, renewed and developed by the coronation ritual, therefore failed to resolve a major theological disagreement. Throughout the ninth century, the creed with the *Filioque* was chanted in Carolingian lands, while in Rome it was not even used in the mass. Pope Leo, however, commemorated the "correct" wording of the creed in both Greek and Latin on silver plaques erected in St. Peter's.[58]

Eastern Reaction to the Coronation

Meanwhile, in the East, no formal notification of the ceremony of 800 was received, and its precise import remained unknown. Two independent notices of the coronation are recorded in the *Chronographia* of Theophanes. One gives Charles's title as Emperor of the Romans (*basileus Romaion*); the other reverts to the usual King of the Franks (*rex Fraggon*). The first mentions unction from head to foot by the pope and associates the action with the wearing of imperial clothes and a crown; the second laconically records the crowning only.[59] Both, however, stress Leo's role. In the longer account, which clearly derives from a Roman source, papal activity is directly related to Charles's intervention in restoring Leo to his throne. The coronation becomes a *quid pro quo*, and is placed here in the *Chronographia*, because it follows from the attack on the pope and his flight to Charles.[60] No reaction to the event is noted, but after the second, brief notice comes a reference to Charles's intention to invade Sicily, and then, as if it were part of the invasion plan, another reference to his plan to marry Irene.[61] The idea is repeated in the following year, when Frankish and papal ambassadors arrived in Constantinople together, the former proposing not only marriage but also a plan to unite the lands of the East and the West.[62] Had Irene been in any doubt about the nature of Charles's coronation, this embassy would presumably have clarified his new imperial status. But by October 802, she had already been ousted from power in a palace coup that installed her finance minister as Emperor Nikephoros I.[63]

[57] Smaragdus, *De Spiritu Sancto, PL* 98, 923-29; *Colloquium Romanum,* in *Concilia,* part 1, 240-44.

[58] *LP* 2.26, lines 18-22, cf. 2.46, note 110; Mansi, 14.18-22; *PL* 145, 635.

[59] Theophanes, 473, 475 (both translated in Folz, *The Coronation of Charlemagne,* 239-40).

[60] Speck, *Kaiser Konstantin VI,* 1:359 and note 245c (2:781).

[61] Theophanes, 475.13-14 (translated in Folz, *The Coronation of Charlemagne,* 240).

[62] Theophanes, 475.27-30 (translated in Folz, *The Coronation of Charlemagne,* 240).

[63] Theophanes, 476-79; Byzantine history from the death of Irene to the accession of

Neither the coup nor western clarification of the ceremony of 800 entailed a rupture of diplomatic relations, however. Since the Frankish threat to Sicily did not materialise, negotiations over spheres of influence in southern Italy could continue. A Byzantine embassy returned to the West in 803, met Charles in Salz, and returned to Constantinople with proposals for peace. Thereafter, diplomatic contact was severed, though the cause of failure was not immediately clear.[64] While it is generally assumed that Charles's insistence on using the imperial title gave offence, there were so many other areas of tension between the new emperor's territory and older imperial claims in the West that it is hard to extricate one specific point. Byzantine understanding of the coronation ceremony may perhaps have played a part. But it was not recorded as the grounds for breaking off normal contacts. Three years later, however, Nikephoros I prevented Patriarch Nikephoros (806-815) from sending his synodical letter to Rome, because Pope Leo had crowned Charles and supported the Byzantine monastic party led by Theodore Stoudites in its criticism of the emperor and the patriarch.[65] In Constantinople, Leo's actions were considered tantamount to a form of self-exclusion from the Christian community. East/West relations were thus rendered extremely uneasy.

It was in fact the status of the Venetia and Dalmatia that provoked a resolution of the imperial title problem, but not until 812. From 804 onwards, Carolingian/Byzantine rivalry for control over these regions brought naval battles and many changes of authority. Throughout, Nikephoros and his successor, Michael I (811-13), seem to have been concerned to restrict Charles's political influence to areas that had never (or not for centuries) formed part of the Eastern Empire.[66] Thus they were anxious to retain Byzantine administration over the maritime centres and trading posts on the east and north coastline of the Adriatic. New *themata* were established in Kephalonia and Dyrrachion. Further north, Dalmatia and the

Basil I (867) is well covered by J. B. Bury, *A History of the East Roman Empire* (London, 1912).

[64] *Royal Frankish Annals*, a.803 (translated in Folz, *The Coronation of Charlemagne*, 241); Dölger, *Regesten*, no. 361; P. Grierson, "The Carolingian Empire in the Eyes of Byzantium," *Settimane* 27 (1981): 885-916.

[65] See Patriarch Nikephoros's letter to Pope Leo III, which was finally sent after the emperor's death in 811, *PG* 100, 169-200, esp. 197A-B (also in Mansi, 14.29-56); Alexander, *The Patriarch Nicephorus*, 73, 93-96; J. Gouillard, "L'Eglise d'Orient et la primauté romaine au temps de l'iconoclasme," *Istina* 21 (1976): 25-54, esp. 37-46, reprinted in *La vie religieuse à Byzance* (London, 1981). On Theodore's criticism, see R. Devréesse, "Une lettre de S. Théodore Studite relative au Synode moechien," *AB* 68 (1950): 44-57, esp. 48-53; cf. Gouillard, "L'Eglise d'Orient," 46-52.

[66] Classen, "Karl der Grosse," 598-604 (and additions [78]-[80]); cf. O. Bertolini, "Carlomagno e Benevento," in *Karl der Grosse*, 1:665-69.

Venetia were kept firmly in the Byzantine orbit, although Venice itself had more of the status of an independent duchy under a powerful family closely allied to Constantinople.[67] In return for secure control over these areas (confirmed in written treatises), the Byzantine embassy sent to Aachen by Michael I in 812 recognised Carolingian claims to Croatia and acclaimed Charles as emperor. According to western sources, the *laudes* were chanted in Greek, and Charles therefore had the satisfaction of hearing the term *basileus* used.[68] What the concession meant in Constantinople is not recorded. As Charles took no steps to make his surviving son Louis emperor until the following year (813), the eastern emperor had no way of evaluating the potential of the title in the West.

Interestingly, the ceremony whereby Charles passed on his most prestigious title reduced ecclesiastical participation to a minimum. Although it took place in the palace chapel at Aachen, neither Pope Leo nor the leading Carolingian archbishops were permitted a role: the old emperor simply instructed his son to take the crown from the altar, and Louis put it on in front of the entire court.[69] The prayers that accompanied this transfer of authority gave ecclesiastics no greater presence than was normal at ceremonial events. After an extremely long and exceptionally successful reign, Charles retired from active government to devote himself to the correction of Biblical texts, according to Thegan, with the help of Greek and Syriac specialists.[70] But subsequent use of the imperial title among his descendants was to reveal how little it could change the engrained patterns of Carolingian inheritance. And although some who held it undertook visits to Rome, where papal consecration was occasionally repeated, the close spiritual link that had characterised eighth-century Frankish-papal relations died with Charles.

THE SECOND BYZANTINE ICONOCLASM (815-42)

Both Nikephoros I and his son-in-law Michael I fell from power because of failures to defend Byzantium from Bulgar forces led by an energetic chieftain, Khan Krum. And these military disasters revived a sense of frustration among *thema* commanders and other army officers. Although it would not be correct to attribute to this disaffected constituency alone the revival

[67] A. Carile and G. Fedalto, *Le origini de Venezia* (Bologna, 1978), esp. 223-37, 365-91.
[68] *Royal Frankish Annals*, a.812; cf. Charles's letter to Michael I, *Epistolae Karolini Aevi* 2, no. 37, 556 (both translated in Folz, *The Coronation of Charlemagne*, 241-43); Dölger, *Regesten*, no. 385; Kantorowicz, *Laudes Regiae*, 27 n.45.
[69] Thegan, *Vita Hludowici*, para. 6, in *MGH, SS*, 2, 591-92; *Royal Frankish Annals*, a.813; Folz, *The Coronation of Charlemagne*, 175-76.
[70] Thegan, *Vita Hludowici*, para. 7.

of iconoclasm, it was from the armed forces that a significant pressure came. It combined with a deep-rooted dislike of the strict monastic party that exercised great influence over Michael I.[71] In an episode that reveals both some of the mythical associations generated by Constantine V and the myth of iconoclasm itself, soldiers of the *tagmata* garrisoned in the capital broke into the tomb of their hero, calling on him to lead them once again to victory and prosperity through iconoclasm. By carefully stage-managed preparations, the tomb in the imperial mausoleum of the Holy Apostles appeared to open.[72] Those behind this ploy appear to have been three relatively junior officers, Leo, Michael, and Thomas, who had all had their future imperial roles predicted by an old hermit. In the traditional manner they had formed an alliance (*phratria*), like that between Leo III and Artabasdos, to ensure that these triumphs might be realised.[73]

The first to succeed was Leo (813-20), an Armenian, governor of the Anatolikon *thema*, who refused to support Michael I's anti-Bulgar policy. With expert theological assistance he prepared for the renewal of iconoclasm at a council held in 815. Exactly the same procedures were adopted as for the first introduction of iconoclasm. The iconophile Patriarch Nikephoros was deposed, sent into exile with St. Theodore and other monks, and replaced by a pliant figure. A purely eastern gathering of bishops was then summoned to condemn the veneration of icons. Although the arguments presented at this council, which survive in its Definition (*Horos*), were not exactly the same as those of the earlier phase, the acts of the 754 council provided the fundamental evidence.[74] No significant attention was paid to western doctrine. As no Greek version of the *Libri Carolini* has ever come to light and the eastern theologians of 815 would have found the original Latin text extremely difficult to understand, they were probably unaware of its existence. After the council, an iconoclast cross again replaced the mosaic icon of Christ, put up by Irene on the Chalke Gate. Once more, the episcopal and secular clergy of the empire appear to have bent with the prevailing wind, while the monastic party, firmly led by St. Theodore Stoudites, dominated a forceful opposition. From exile the iconophiles attacked

[71] Alexander, *The Patriarch Nicephorus*, 85-101; R. Browning, *Byzantium and Bulgaria* (London, 1975), 49-50, 127-29.

[72] Theophanes, 501; Alexander, *The Patriarch Nicephorus*, 76, 111-25.

[73] P. Lemerle, "La révolte de Thomas le Slav," *TM* 1 (1965): 255-97; H.-G. Beck, *Byzantinisches Gefolgschaftswesen*, Sitzungsberichte der Bayerischen Akademie der Wissenschaften, Phil.-Hist. Klasse (Munich, 1965), Heft 5.

[74] P. J. Alexander, "The Definition of the Iconoclast Council of St. Sophia (815)," *DOP* 7 (1953): 35-66; cf. M. V. Anastos, "The Ethical Theory of Images Formulated by the Iconoclasts in 754 and 815," *DOP* 8 (1954): 151-60; P. J. Alexander, "Church Councils and Patristic Authority: The Iconoclastic Councils of Hiereia (754) and St. Sophia (815)," *Harvard Studies in Classical Philology* 63 (1958): 493-505.

the new iconoclasm: Theodore in his correspondence with iconophile monks in exile and Pope Pascal I in Rome, as well as in his theological works and refutation of iconoclast verses; ex-Patriarch Nikephoros in his *Refutatio et Eversio*, a sophisticated theological criticism of the 815 council and Constantine V's iconoclasm.[75] Thus, eighth-century divisions were reproduced, though they did not result in an identical outcome.

The second of the military trio to claim his destiny was Michael II (820-29), who had his erstwhile brother-in-arms murdered at Christmas mass. His own reign was in turn bedevilled by the challenge of Thomas the Slav, the third of the trio, who led an indefatigable campaign to win the throne. After a highly destructive civil war ending in a year's siege of the capital, the rebel forces of Thomas were finally defeated. In opposition to Michael II's neutrality on the question of icons, within the moderate iconoclasm described in a letter to Louis the Pious, Thomas had declared his iconophile sympathies. But there is little evidence that the issue determined political loyalties. In two instances, eighth-century patterns were reversed: Thomas was supported in his bid for power by the Arab caliphate, and Michael II chose Euphrosyne, daughter of Constantine VI and Maria of Amnia, as his second wife.[76] Muslim support could therefore be extended to a declared iconophile if necessary, and an iconoclast who committed his heir to a firm anti-icon education at the hands of John the Grammarian could marry an iconophile if this would strengthen his hold on imperial power.

Under Theophilos (829-42), who succeeded his father Michael without challenge, the iconoclast party gained a much stronger position in the empire, while Muslim culture exercised a genuine influence. Greater attention was paid to the administration of justice and the establishment of Byzantine control in disputed frontier regions of northeastern Asia Minor and Cherson (on the northern coast of the Black Sea). But these measures did not succeed in checking Arab military activity, and in 838, Amorion, the hometown of Michael II and one of the strongest in Asia Minor, fell. Among those taken prisoner by Caliph Mutasim, 42 refused to convert to Islam and were murdered, the 42 martyrs of Amorion.[77] From 837 on-

---

[75] The iconophile theories of this period require detailed analysis, which is not possible here. For Theodore's verses, see P. Speck, *Theodoros Studites, Jamben auf verschiedene Gegenstände* (Berlin, 1968); for Nikephoros's writings, P. O'Connell, *The Ecclesiology of St. Nicephorus I (758-828)* (Rome, 1972), and Alexander, *The Patriarch Nicephorus*. On the development of icon veneration, see J. Gouillard, "Contemplation et imagerie sacrée dans le Christianisme byzantin," *Annuaire de l'Ecole Pratique des Hautes Etudes*, Ve section, 86 (1977-78), 29-50, reprinted in *La vie religieuse à Byzance* (London, 1981).

[76] Lemerle, "La révolte de Thomas le Slav," 287-88; Herrin, "Women and the Faith in Icons," 70.

[77] Bury, *East Roman Empire*, 259-72; on the 42 martyrs of Amorion, see F. Halkin, *Bibliotheca hagiographica graeca*, 3rd ed., 3 vols. (Brussels, 1957), 2:99-100.

wards, when John the Grammarian was made patriarch, iconophiles were actively persecuted, especially monks of foreign origin. But this policy was effective mainly in the capital; elsewhere, antagonism to icon veneration was very limited. After the death of Theophilos, his widow Theodora, who had maintained her own iconophile practice in secret, managed to reverse the official position without too much difficulty.

Western Reaction to the Second Phase of Iconoclasm

In the West, however, the eastern renewal of iconoclasm reported to Louis the Pious by Michael II in 824 had helped to provoke another serious discussion of the issue. The latter's imperial letter described some of the idolatrous and superstitious practices that had led to the council of 815. These included using icons to stand as godparents to children at baptism and to serve as portable altars for the celebration of the Eucharist in private homes, abuses that were held to justify the moderate iconoclasm now decreed in the East.[78] Against such perverse uses, pictures were permitted but only to serve as Scripture—a statement of Gregorian principle of which Charlemagne would not have disapproved. The Byzantine emperor then requested Louis's assistance in combatting the influence of eastern iconophile monks who had fled to Rome and were spreading their false beliefs and practices in the West.[79]

The Synod of Paris (824-25). Louis reacted to this appeal by sending two bishops to Pope Eugenius to investigate the situation: their report was presented to a select gathering of bishops summoned to Paris late in 824. Permission to examine the issue was granted with the proviso that the Frankish clerics should not attempt to teach or instruct the pope, who reserved to himself all the prerogatives claimed by Rome in the realm of theology.[80] Within these restrictions the Frankish bishops proceeded to survey the past 36 years of controversy over religious images. Their conclusions are documented in the *Libellus synodalis Parisiensis* (825), which recapitulates the whole history of Frankish opposition to the veneration of icons, Pope Ha-

---

[78] *Concilia*, part 2, no. 44A, pp. 475-80; also in Mansi, 14.417-22; Dölger, *Regesten*, nos. 408 and 409; A. Freeman, "Carolingian Orthodoxy and the Fate of the *Libri Carolini*," *Viator* 16 (1985): 65-108, esp. 100 (a translation of part of Michael II's letter to Louis the Pious).

[79] *Concilia*, part 2, 479-81, esp. 479.18, 19-20, forbidding the use of incense and lamps at holy pictures, and emphasising their value as a visual form of Scripture.

[80] This forms part of the *Libellus synodalis Parisiensis, Concilia*, part 2, no. 44B, 481-532 (also in *PL* 98, 1299-1350); esp. 481-84, on the meeting of bishops; their request for Pope Eugenius's permission to re-examine the question of images (482.30-31, 522.41); and papal authority in questions of belief (522.25-27).

drian's role in the council of 787, his erroneous or not pertinent *testimonia*, and Charles's condemnation of Nicaea.[81] The *Libri Carolini* are not mentioned, however. But papal support for image worship is identified as a major obstacle to orthodoxy, an "ill-advised defence, contrary to divine authority and to the teaching of the Holy Fathers."[82] The bishops had therefore embarked on their own investigation in order to convince the papacy of the truth. *Testimonia* were collected and taken to Rome by legates instructed to persuade Eugenius of the need to maintain "a measure of moderation in the possession of images." Louis even prepared for the eventuality of a papal embassy to Constantinople in support of the 815 council; his own envoys would sail from the same port in a joint delegation.[83] But the *Libellus* had no greater success with Eugenius than the *Capitulare* with his predecessor. Both papal approval of the council of 787 and Carolingian approval of moderate iconoclasm remained unchanged.

A further element in the continuing debate developed from a spontaneous recurrence of hostility to religious images initiated by Claudius, bishop of Turin (818-ca. 827).[84] Claudius was a pupil of Felix of Urgel, the Spanish Adoptionist with strong Nestorian tendencies. Despite this suspicious background, he was appointed chaplain at the court of King Louis of Aquitaine and later served as imperial *missus*. In 818 he was consecrated in Reims as archbishop of Turin and ordered to extend the Frankish liturgical reforms to northern Italy. Close links had been established between the two sees; Louis had given Archbishop Ebbo of Reims funds for the reconstruction of the double church, which formed Turin's cathedral. In addition to his instructions to reform ecclesiastical life in his diocese, Clau-

---

[81] See the partial translation and useful commentary in Freeman, "Carolingian Orthodoxy," 101-103.

[82] *Libellus synodalis Parisiensis*, no. 44B, 482.26-30, translated by Freeman, "Carolingian Orthodoxy," 102. Among the "Holy Fathers" cited in the *Libellus*, there is a reference to Dionysios, the bishop allegedly sent by Pope Clement to Gaul, frequently identified as Dionysios the Areopagite. The complete Greek corpus of Pseudo-Dionysian writings did not arrive in Paris until 827, but this reference may indicate growing interest, see D. Luscombe, "The Reception of the Writings of Denis the Pseudo-Areopagite into England," in D. Greenway et al., eds., *Tradition and Change, Essays in Honour of Marjorie Chibnall* (Cambridge, 1985), 115-44, esp. 116-17.

[83] *Concilia*, part 2, no. 44C, letter to Jerome of Sens and Jonas of Orléans, 533.19-20 (translated in Freeman, "Carolingian Orthodoxy," 103-104); cf. 483, on the need to persuade Pope Eugenius by subtle flattery. The proposed travel arrangements, 533, were repeated in Louis's letter to the pope, no. 44D, 534-35.

[84] On Claudius, see his letters, *Epistolae Karolini Aevi* 2, 590-613, esp. no. 12, 61-63 (excerpts from a longer work on the cult of images, which was refuted by Theudemir); S. Casartelli Novelli, "La Cattedrale ed i Marmi carolingi di Torino nelle date dell'episcopato di Claudio l'iconoclasta," *Cahiers archéologiques* 25 (1976): 93-100; E. J. Martin, *A History of the Iconoclast Controversy* (London, 1930), 264-66.

dius also arrived with a personal knowledge of Theodulf of Orléans and with the attitudes towards religious art enshrined in the *Libri Carolini*. These conflicted with the Italian devotion to images, relics, the cult of saints, and belief in penitential pilgrimages to Rome. The new archbishop therefore began to remove images and even crosses from the churches under his control, and commissioned non-figural marble sculptures for his new cathedral.[85] As a result of this activity, iconoclasm once again became a pressing issue in Carolingian circles. Claudius's views were repudiated in two treatises by Dungal and Jonas of Orléans, which firmly restated the middle way between idolatrous worship and total destruction.[86] But Emperors Louis the Pious and Lothar continued to support the archbishop, whose views received wider dissemination through the *Capitulare Olonense* (825). Thereafter, Carolingian tradition reasserted its emphasis on the motive of the Christian believer, who might learn from pictures as from the cross, relics, and pilgrimages. Against both extremes of iconophile adoration and fervent iconoclasm, the positive benefit of religious images was confirmed and remained the governing principle behind ninth-century art in the West.[87]

For a permanent testimony to the iconoclast position of Claudius and Theodulf, one must turn to northwestern Spain, where several ninth-century monuments with aniconic decoration survive. In Oviedo, the capital of the Asturias, artists painted the large church of San Julián de los Prados (Santullano) with a totally non-figural scheme.[88] In the upper registers, fresco panels imitate the polychrome marbles and *opus sectile* inlay found in early Christian buildings, in Spain as in all Mediterranean centres. Below these, decorative vases with floral or vegetal display look surprisingly like the early Umayyad mosaics at the Dome of the Rock, which in turn draw on early Christian models. Since the Christian kingdom of Asturias lay so close to Muslim Spain, the question of Islamic influence is immediately posed. But as other Asturian churches of the same period have figural decoration (San Miguel de Lillo, for example), it is not so easily answered. The Santullano frescoes cannot be described as very successful—individual panels are dwarfed by the scale of the building—but they present a curious

[85] Casartelli Novelli, "La Cattedrale," 96, 99-100; idem, "L'intreccio geometrico del IX secolo, scultura delle cattedrali riformate (forma simbolia) della rinascenza carolingia," in *Roma e l'età carolingia* (Rome, 1976), 103-114.

[86] Dungal's *Responsa*, PL 105, 468-70; Jonas's *De cultu Imaginum*, PL 106, 305-388; cf. Martin, *History of the Iconoclast Controversy*, 266-68.

[87] *Capitularia*, no. 164, 328-29.

[88] A. Grabar and C. Nordenfalk, *Early Medieval Painting* (New York, 1957), 65-68; H. Schlunk and M. Berenguer, *La pintura mural asturiana de los siglos IX y X* (Madrid, 1957), 14-105.

tribute to an iconoclasm developed by Theodulf and Claudius, both Christians from Muslim Spain. Whether the iconoclast model is Carolingian or Islamic remains unclear, and in monumental painting the Asturian churches are a solitary witness to the stormy debate over the propriety of representing holy persons in western art.

The idea that it was wrong to adore man-made objects thus failed to take root in the West. By the end of the ninth century, under Charles the Great's grandson, the first statue reliquaries were produced in Francia, inaugurating a cult that would have been considered completely idolatrous and scandalous by Charles, Theodulf, and the others responsible for the *Libri Carolini*. [89] It is a striking testimony to the power of three-dimensional sculpture that these statues, like the golden, seated St. Foy at Conques, became established in regions where the force of eastern icons had never been experienced. They were, however, an exact parallel to the painted images of Byzantium, and inspired an equal devotion. In this respect, traditions of figural representation drew on a common source that satisfied the religious needs of people in all parts of medieval Christendom.

Iconophile Support for Rome

Paradoxically, it was the church of Rome that gained most from the second outbreak of iconoclasm in Byzantium. The eastern iconophile monastic party sought and found considerable support in the apostolic see during the 820s and 830s. Under the leadership of St. Theodore Stoudites, it reaffirmed the crucial role of arbiter that popes had played in Monophysite and Monothelete controversies from the mid-seventh century onwards. Building on this eastern tradition of appealing to Rome against Constantinopolitan heresy, the banished iconophiles formulated arguments about the particular qualities of Roman bishops, inheritors of St. Peter and therefore representatives of a higher authority than eastern patriarchs. With this welcome, if opportunistic, declaration of support for Petrine supremacy, Leo III and his successors provided sustenance for refugees like Methodios, while laying claim to an independent theology. [90]

In this process the popes were assisted by the eclipse of the three eastern patriarchs under Arab rule, who lost all semblance of their original authority in the first half of the ninth century. Islam, therefore, in only a partially successful expansion, strengthened the autonomy of Rome, and the ancient

[89] M.-C. Hubert and J. Hubert, "Piété chrétienne ou paganisme? Les statues-reliquaires de l'Europe carolingienne," *Settimane* 28 (1982): 235-68; P. Riché, *Daily Life in the World of Charlemagne* (Liverpool, 1978), 234, on the scandal they caused.

[90] F. Dvornik, *Byzantium and the Roman Primacy* (New York, 1966), 101-105; Gouillard, "L'Eglise d'Orient," esp. 42-44, 48-52.

Christian pentarchy gave way to two centres of Christian power, Constantinople and Rome, now set on an antagonistic course. During the second iconoclast dispute, the papacy acquired a heightened authority in doctrinal matters. Secure in the loyalty of iconophiles in the East, Roman pontiffs staunchly defended their own practice against innovations as varied as moderate Carolingian iconoclasm and the *Filioque* clause. In this way they gradually asserted their control over all the Christian communities of the West, demanding an obedient submission from even the most independent among them. Basing their claims to supreme authority on the primacy of the chief apostolic foundation and their position as direct successors of St. Peter himself, popes expressed vindication at the final restoration of icons in 843, but did not allow it to remove the friction that had developed between Rome and Constantinople. Outstanding disagreements, therefore, prepared the way for Pope Nicholas I's quarrel with Patriarch Photios in the 860s. In turn, many of these ninth-century differences between eastern and western traditions would surface again during the great schism of 1054, notably the *Filioque* clause.

From this sense of continuity in an anti-Byzantine posture and from the strength of customs handed down over centuries, the papacy drew cumulative strength and staying power. Petrine authority also extended beyond the ecclesiastical sphere, as bishops of Rome asserted their indispensable power of sacral unction, sought by temporal rulers in the West. Their permanent presence in an unbroken chain from the chief Apostle onwards contrasted with the rapid changes registered in secular power, as imperial families and entire dynasties came and went from the arena of western political struggles. The roots of this stability had been laid in the early Christian period. But between the pontificates of Gregory the Great and Leo III a great consolidation had taken place. The developed papacy of Gregory VII (1073-85) owed much to its predecessor of the seventh and eighth centuries.[91]

The Restoration of Icons (843)

Once Theophilos was dead, the pattern of returning the holy icons to their honoured position assumed an uncanny similarity to the events of 785-87. Like Irene, Theodora was proclaimed empress-regent for her son Michael III (who was only three years old); she ruled in his name until 856, using

[91] W. Ullman, *The Growth of Papal Government in the Middle Ages*, 3rd ed. (London, 1970); G. Arnaldi, "Il Papato e l'ideologia del potere imperiale," *Settimane* 27 (1981): 341-407; for an indication of the problems caused by the *Filioque* in the ninth century, see B. Laourdas, "The Letter of Photius to the Archbishop of Aquileia," *Kleronomia* 3 (1971): 66-68; J.-M. Sansterre, *Les moines grecs et orientaux à Rome aux époques byzantine et carolingienne*, 2 vols. (Brussels, 1983), 1:141-44.

her own male relatives as advisers and generals. Unlike her iconophile predecessor, she did not have to wait to reverse iconoclasm.[92] Theophilos's policies had run their course; the close connection between iconoclasm, military success, and imperial well-being was no longer convincing, particularly after the loss of Amorion. Theodora's co-regent and chief minister, Theoktistos, who had previously served Theophilos, headed civilian pressure for a return to icon veneration, in conjunction with those iconophiles who had suffered persecution. As in 785, the first step was to depose the iconoclast patriarch, John the Grammarian in this case, and replace him by an iconophile, Methodios. This was arranged by Theoktistos and several high-ranking court officials and relations of the empress, who appear to have taken the initiative in ending iconoclasm.[93]

It was left to Methodios to devise a suitable ecclesiastical conclusion. Under his direction a special ceremony was enacted on the first Sunday in Lent, 843, to be repeated annually as a new feast of the church, the Triumph of Orthodoxy.[94] In it, the detractors of icons and older heresiarchs were named and anathematised in turn, while iconophile heroes and other orthodox leaders were celebrated and their writings read out. This was a purely Byzantine occasion; Rome was not invited to participate. Icon veneration was of course justified as an ancient tradition of the church, and for the first time the more sophisticated arguments of St. John of Damascus received an enthusiastic approval. Methodios also wrote a long iconophile epigram about the image of Christ, which was again restored to the Chalke Gate.[95] Although the redecoration of churches proceeded slowly, the iconoclast repertoire of non-figural, floral, and geometric patterns retreated to its traditional place in the borders and corners of religious pictures. The Chludov Psalter, painted in Constantinople in the late ninth century, displays an artist's appreciation of the threat iconoclasm had posed to the practice of painterly skills; the burning, whitewashing, and mutilation of figural art is depicted with lively condemnation.[96] While some of the crosses put up by iconoclasts remained as an equally important symbol of iconophile faith, after 843 iconic art forms reasserted a firm hold in Byzantium.

Despite continuing criticism of Patriarch Nikephoros by followers of Theodore Stoudites, Methodios insisted that both these iconophile saints who had died in exile should be commemorated in the capital. So the relics

[92] Herrin, "Women and the Faith in Icons," 69-70, 73, and plate 90.

[93] C. Mango, "The Liquidation of Iconoclasm and the Patriarch Photios," in *Iconoclasm*, ed. A. Bryer and J. Herrin (Birmingham, 1977), 133-40.

[94] J. Gouillard, "Le Synodikon d'Orthodoxie: édition et commentaire," *TM* 2 (1967): 1-316.

[95] A. Grabar, *L'Iconoclasme byzantin: Dossier archéologique* (Paris, 1958), 136-42.

[96] M. Shchepkina, *Miniatourii Khloudovskoe Psaltirii* (Moscow, 1977).

of Theodore and Nikephoros were translated to the monastery of Stoudios and the church of the Holy Apostles respectively, in January 844 and March 847.[97] In honouring its heroes, the victorious iconophiles dedicated themselves to expunge the memory of iconoclast persecution and the theology that had justified it. This was achieved most notably by Patriarch Photios's eloquent justification and defence of the power of holy images, delivered as a sermon at the dedication of the apse mosaic of the Virgin and Child in St. Sophia.[98] In this way the formal history of Byzantine iconoclasm came to a close, although Photios continued to worry excessively about recurrent outbreaks of what he considered a highly dangerous heresy. But the supporters of iconoclasm offered little resistance and barely reappear in later ninth-century sources.[99] The issue of icon veneration had not managed to instill a permanent fear of idolatry among the Byzantine population at large, and the iconophile party drew on deeper roots to vindicate its triumph. The eastern church thus reaffirmed its belief in the power of holy images to intercede and established them in a permanent and prominent position, which they continue to hold today.[100]

THE TWO EMPERORS OF CHRISTENDOM

Returning to the coincidence noted at the beginning of this chapter, the situation in 843 draws attention to one of the most striking contrasts between East and West. While in Constantinople the empress-mother Theodora inaugurated the Triumph of Orthodoxy and united Byzantium under the authority of her young son, Michael III, Charles's descendants sought a way of establishing their own separate kingdoms under Lothar's overlordship. The eastern principle of succession by primogeniture had no parallel in the Carolingian West. It was facilitated by the fact that Michael was Theodora and Theophilos's only surviving son, whereas the Carolingians from Charles onwards all produced numerous male heirs. But behind the tripartite western division of Verdun lay centuries of non-Roman traditions of power-sharing, which could not easily be replaced by the notion of one

---

[97] J. Pargoire, *L'église byzantine de 527 à 847* (Paris, 1923), 274; for the *Translatio* of Nikephoros, see *PG* 100, 163-68.

[98] C. Mango, *The Homilies of Photius Patriarch of Constantinople* (Cambridge, Mass., 1958), no. 17, 286-96, esp. paras. 2-6, 289-95; R. Cormack, *Writing in Gold* (London, 1985), 146-58, with good photographs.

[99] See Mango, "The Liquidation of Iconoclasm"; H. G. Thümmel, "Die Disputation über die Bilder in der *Vita* des Konstantin," *BS* 46 (1985): 19-24; cf. J. Featherstone, "An Iconoclastic Episode in the Hesychast Controversy," *JÖB* 33 (1983): 179-98.

[100] J. Gouillard, "Art et littérature à Byzance au lendemain de la querelle des images," *Cahiers de civilisation médiévale* 12 (1969): 1-13, reprinted in *La vie religieuse à Byzance*; L. Ouspensky and V. Lossy, *The Meaning of Icons*, 2nd ed. (New York, 1982).

emperor ruling over a variety of kingdoms united in one unit.[101] Imperial traditions were weak, barely developed, in comparison with those of the East.

The office of western emperor also lacked the institutional stability built up by the church of Rome, and would over time become almost dependent on the pontiffs, who made their sacral authority an essential element in the assumption of imperial power. Despite the successful transference of the title from Charles to Louis and from Louis to his son Lothar, the imperial name could not guarantee substance in the manner conceived by contemporaries. The Carolingian concept of shared sovereignty was not without its own destiny, however. For within the traditions of territorial division and limited authority nestled the principles of feudal organisation, which were to characterise the medieval West. And through their hierarchy of reciprocal duties—social, economic, and military—the West would eventually realise a greater potential than that locked within the Byzantine imperial system.

For a millenium the idea of a Holy Roman Empire in the West, a continuation of one founded by Charles in A.D. 800, proved just as tenacious as the imperial tradition in the East. Western monarchs, generals, and aristocrats competed for a papal coronation in order to reign over an empire variously defined. In 1804, however, Napoleon adopted the title "Emperor of the French" in a coronation attended by Pope Pius VII at Paris. Two years later Francis II relinquished the title of Holy Roman Emperor, becoming Emperor of Austria instead, and thereafter no secular ruler obtained sufficient domination in Europe to revive the concept engendered by Charles. In contrast, after the fall of Constantinople to the Ottoman Turks in 1453, when Constantine XI died, Byzantine traditions were assumed by the grand princes of Moscow, and sealed by the marriage in 1472 between Sophia, niece of the last emperor, and Ivan the Great. Their grandson, Ivan IV (more commonly known as "the Terrible"), was crowned *Tsar* (from the Greek *kaisar* = *caesar*), adopted Byzantine court ceremonial, which he transferred to the recently constructed Kremlin in Moscow, and perpetuated the autocratic elements of eastern imperial rule in a dynasty that lasted until 1917. Thus the notion of two emperors of Christendom persisted for centuries after the reigns of Irene and Charles, and inspired many different attempts to impose Christian rule in areas far beyond the boundaries of either Frankish or Byzantine dominion.

[101] T. Mayer, ed., *Der Vertrag von Verdun, 843* (Leipzig, 1943); F. Dölger, "Europas Gestaltung im Spiegel der frankisch-byzantinischen Auseinandersetzung des 9. Jahrhunderts," in Mayer, *Der Vertrag*, 203-273; reprinted in his *Byzanz und die europäische Staatenwelt* (Ettal, 1953); F. Ganshof, "On the Genesis and Significance of the Treaty of Verdun (843)," in *The Carolingians and the Frankish Monarchy*, 289-302.

Conclusion

HISTORY does not come to conclusions. But books must, and by way of conclusion I would like to stress two distinctive aspects of my account of the formation of Christendom. The first emphasis, a temporal span, highlights the importance of the transitional period between Late Antiquity and the Middle Ages; the second, geographic, insists upon the eastern Mediterranean as the centre of that world.

I have presented Byzantium as an essential factor in the development of both the West and Islam, for it was at one and the same time the power that frustrated the Muslim challenge to Christianity, even while it failed to confine Islam to Arabia. This combination resulted in deadlock in the East. Neither the emperors in the Queen City of Constantinople nor the caliphs, successors of the Prophet, were able to lay claim to the Mediterranean area as a whole. It was this check that allowed a separate medieval Christendom to exist in the West, where spiritual loyalty to Rome became transformed into a supranational authority independent of any secular power. The energy of episcopal rulers of Rome itself and the growth of Carolingian military strength ensured a Christian faith that persists even today. In this process, Byzantium, the caliphate, and *Europa* "found" their own cultures, creating traditions to meet their needs. Within the context of the Mediterranean and the inheritance of Greco-Roman civilisation that they all shared, each laid claim to the past in different ways.

In *Europa*, the mode of conserving these varied traditions was to lead to a quite spectacular development, which has marked off the once-peripheral West. While its roots undoubtedly lie in the particular economic relations that encouraged the extension of mercantile practices beyond the autonomous towns of northern Europe, an ecclesiastical impulse is also at work. For the church insisted on the use of Latin, making it an international language understood by rulers and their advisers, who otherwise spoke different vernaculars. This helped to stabilise and incorporate the division of authority, in a hierarchy of fealty and allegiance, civil *and* clerical, which engendered the parcellised sovereignty characteristic of feudalism. Without the special role and function of the church, it is doubtful whether feudal relations would have spread so extensively through western societies. Of course, ecclesiastical feudal lords made their own considerable direct contribution to medieval development, while substantial church wealth was devoted to the organisation of charity, an indispensable part of medieval urban development. Christianity was thus a crucial catalyst in the amalgamation of Roman and "barbarian" authority, and in the West it was to have unique results.

Furthermore, as the guardians of Latin as a learned language, western churchmen played an important part in the rediscovery of the classical world. Through the language of ancient Rome, however transformed, a link back to the empire of Caesar and the culture of Cicero could be realised, when Europe wished to explore its past. Among the first post-Carolingian scholars to exploit this connection was a "professional" ecclesiastic, Gerbert of Aurillac. Educated in a small French monastery, he was sent by its abbot in 967 to the region on the border of Muslim Spain, ancient Septimania. There, in the monasteries of Vich and Ripoll, and in the company of clerics familiar with both Greek and Arabic, he mastered ancient science, astronomy, and mathematics in their Islamic guise. Although dependent upon translations, Gerbert studied texts of Aristotle with an introduction by Porphyry, Ptolemy's astronomy, and ancient Greek arithmetic and medicine in manuscripts long available in the Arab caliphate. The knowledge he acquired of the abacus, the astrolabe, and the sphere gave his learning a practical function, which was eagerly sought after in late tenth-century Europe.[1]

Gerbert's sole surviving philosophical work, *Of Rationality and the Use of Reason*, was written for his imperial pupil, the young Emperor Otto III.[2] While Gerbert begged and borrowed copies of interesting manuscripts on a variety of topics (for instance, Demosthenes on ophthalmology), his personal preference seems to have been for logic and philosophy; he particularly enjoyed Boethius's *Consolation*. Yet Gerbert remained a cleric and followed a traditional ecclesiastical career, first as bishop of Reims, later as abbot of Bobbio and as Pope Sylvester II (999-1003). He was appointed to these final honours by the emperor, a prince of Byzantine and German parents, who tried to emulate both Constantine I and Charles the Great in his brief rule over the Holy Roman Empire. With Gerbert's encouragement, Otto was identified as "a man, Greek by birth, Roman by empire," who,

---

[1] P. Wolff, *The Awakening of Europe* (Harmondsworth, 1968), 172-89.

[2] Gerbert's writings are divided into mathematical and ecclesiastical works, with a large collection of letters, all in *PL* 139. The *Liber de rationali et ratione uti*, cols. 157-68, was originally sent to Otto III in a letter, see H. P. Lattin, *The Letters of Gerbert, with His Papal Privileges as Sylvester II* (New York, 1961), no. 232 (297-99). Cf. U. Lindgren, *Gerbert von Aurillac und das Quadrivium* (Wiesbaden, 1976), 78-79, 89-94.

"as if by hereditary right, seeks to recapture for himself the treasures of Greek and Roman wisdom."[3] These two embarked on an adventurous cultural programme, which consciously nurtured the myth of Constantine I and Sylvester I, preserved in the *Donation of Constantine*. Gerbert's choice of papal name must be seen in the context of this document's continuing significance in educated circles. Their plans did not come to fruition, and Otto III died aged 22, just 15 months before his teacher. Their efforts, however, reveal two ways in which the Church made the ancient world of Greece and Rome accessible to the medieval West: through Arabic transmissions, as well as through the reworking of classical traditions.

The fruits of clerical concern with Latin learning would be reaped only in the twelfth century and the later Renaissance. And by the fifteenth century, the classical harvest heralded the collapse of Christendom, as the concept had been understood in medieval terms. The ecclesiastical cocoon in which medieval people lived had been broken. Thereafter, for some at least, the dominance of religion became a matter of choice. This qualitative change marks a frontier between the medieval and the modern.

In the field of art it was experienced early on, when the discovery of classical sculpture in particular provided the inspiration for completely new depictions of the naked human body, which ran counter to medieval conventions. Scientific observation of human anatomy and the practice of dissection, as pioneered in the medical school of Salerno, here played an important role. Renaissance paintings of both pagan deities and secular patrons rendered obsolete an entire tradition of art arbitrated by the church. Later, the Reformation's attacks on wonder-working images and statue reliquaries opened a new phase in the history of iconoclasm, reasserting eighth- and ninth-century fears of idolatry, and quoting from the same texts. Both religious and secular art developed styles previously inconceivable, as medieval Christendom came to an end.

Following the Renaissance and Reformation, as the West was transformed into the Europe of the modern capitalist world, the other two heirs of classical antiquity did not remain unchanged.[4] The cultures of both Islam and Orthodox Christianity spread far beyond their original base in the eastern Mediterranean. Yet they remained fixed—they had been more decisively formed—by the period of the seventh and eighth centuries. In the eighteenth century, for instance, the notion of dating events before Christ's birth in reverse sequence, which could extend backwards indefinitely, was developed in Europe to complement the A.D. system.[5] The Orthodox and

---

[3] Lattin, *Letters of Gerbert*, no. 231 (296-97).

[4] For a broad comparison, see J. Hall, *Powers and Liberties: The Causes and Consequences of the Rise of the West* (Oxford, 1985).

[5] O. Cullmann, *Christ and Time*, 3rd ed. (London, 1965), 17-18, 32-33.

Islamic faiths, however, continued to be measured by their established timescales, which could not admit of a history prior to the earth's creation as inscribed in the Book of Genesis. Although this is only a symptom of the differences that had opened up between Europe and its neighbours, it draws attention to the secular possibilities embedded in the West from the period of Charlemagne.

Despite the fact that this western potential was at first developed entirely by clerics, it was certainly related to the existence of separate, independent authorities, civil as well as ecclesiastical. The mutual antagonism and rivalry of these authorities, which rarely led to the passive subordination of "church" by "state" or vice versa, created a tension and a competitive focus in society that had no parallel in the East. Its significance has often been noted, generally in terms of a division between power and culture. But Christendom was also a polity in the West, not just a religious order. The intellectual, institutional, and artistic tenacity and influence of its faith played a decisive role in the emergence of the modern world.

Afterword

IN THE SUMMER of 1971, long before this study was envisaged, Norbert Elias took me to visit the island of Reichenau in Lake Constance. It was a warm, sunny afternoon with a slight breeze that ruffled the tall trees against an unclouded blue sky. As he told me about the history of the monasteries built on this tiny promontory attached by a causeway to the lake's southern shore, I began to realise why he liked the place so much. Although he in no way shared the Christian devotion of its monks, he loved the peace of their environment, which has not changed radically since the Middle Ages. We wandered slowly from one church to another, enjoying the welcome contrast of cool interiors after the heat outside, and admired the frescoes at Oberzell, each scene with its neat Latin inscription, in a series narrating miracles from the Gospel stories. Norbert's eyesight was poor, but he knew the iconography from many previous visits and made sure I did not miss anything he particularly liked. So we spent a very peaceful afternoon in one of the most beautiful spots on Lake Constance, also one of the most important centres of Carolingian learning.

It was only many years later, after the bulk of this study was written, that I remembered reading about a ninth-century library catalogue from Reichenau, and went back to Lehmann's great work on medieval libraries to look it up. To my surprise, the catalogue appeared to illustrate almost perfectly the significance of Late Antique scholarship. It contained a list of 415 codices that formed the monastery's collection in 821; these included all the major western thinkers who had contributed to that formative culture. As I glanced down the entries I realised that they named virtually all the major Latin sources I had used in this study, and that these were gathered under one roof in the mid-ninth century on an island in a lake in the Alpine foothills.

The catalogue was made by Reginbert, a monk of Reichenau who served as librarian and scribe for 50 years before his death in 847. Of the manuscripts listed, some with dedicatory verses typical of Carolingian scribes, 42 can be attributed to his activity. The copying accounted for the most recent additions to a library that had been built up over a century. It included all the Church Fathers of the West, who dominated the ecclesiastical approach of later writers: Saints Cyprian, Hilary, Jerome, Ambrose, Augustine, and Caesarius of Arles; Popes Leo I (represented by 55 sermons) and Gregory the Great (40 sermons, the *Moralia in Iob, Dialogues*, and 53 letters). Only a few of the corresponding Greek patristic writings existed at Reichenau, in translations mainly by Rufinus: the *Rule* of St. Basil, St. Athanasios's *Dialogue with the Arians*, two collections of sermons by St. John Chrysostomos, and Eusebios's *Ecclesiastical History*, with Rufinus's commentary on it. Earlier in the eighth century, however, Abbot Peter had acquired a Greek Psalter with the Septuagint from Italy; it had been lent to Bishop Egino of Constance and was never returned. Among hagiographic sources, there was also a Latin translation of the *Life* of Antony, with more familiar western biographies of Saints Hilary, Martin, Augustine, Columbanus, Gregory I, and Emmeram, and the lives of the popes, *Gesta pontificum romanum*. In the collection of monastic rules was one of Pachom, together with those attributed to Caesarius, Ambrose, Augustine, Columbanus, another Irish rule, and the *Regula Benedicti*. Prosper was represented by his *De vita activa et contemplativa*, Cassian by his *Institutes* and *Conferences*.

The main portion of the library was devoted to biblical and liturgical texts, of course: several copies of books of the Old and New Testament (usually in small units); a large number of Mass books (58 sacramentaries and 50 psalters, for instance); collections of canon law, books of decretals, and a Roman liturgical book. Bible exegesis also accounted for many volumes, not only the authoritative studies by Jerome, Augustine, Gregory the Great, Isidore of Seville (on the books of *Genesis* and *Kings*), and Bede (on *Proverbs*, the *Epistles* of Luke and Mark, and *Acts of the Apostles*), but also Bishop Justus on the *Song of Songs* and Primasius on the *Apocalypse*. The most recent exegist represented was Alcuin, whose commentaries on the *Song of Songs* and the *Gospel* of St. John confirm his stature in early ninth-century scholarship. In the Reichenau library, Cassiodorus was known only from his commentary on the Psalms, but his initiative may be traced behind several other works, all profane: the Latin translation of Josephus's *Antiquities* and *Jewish War*, and perhaps in parts of the six medical codices in the monastic collection.

Cassiodorus's great contemporary, Boethius, was better known: three codices contained parts of his *De arithmetica, De geometrica, De dialecta* (preserved with Alcuin's *Rhetoric*); the *Consolation of Philosophy*; and the *Art of Medicine* with another copy of the *arithmetica*, and Bede's treatise on time. Post-sixth-century writers at Reichenau were basically two: Isidore and Bede, both well represented—the Visigoth by his *Etymologiae*, two copies of the *Sententiae*, the *De natura rerum, Differentiae*, commentaries on Augustine's *City of God*, and a book of computistical calculation (bound with Bede's treatise on the same subject); the Northumbrian by his *Ecclesiastical History*, his book on time bound up with his treatise on the dialectics of Aristotle and the Sibylline *Dicta* (oracles), his study of metre transmitted with Alcuin's grammar, his *De natura rerum* with a harmonised Gospel version attributed to Gregory the Great, his own *De orthographia*, great Easter cycle, commentary on the Old Testament tabernacle and on the books of *Tobias* and *Esdra*. Not a complete record of either scholar's works, but a good sample for later generations to study.

It is hardly surprising that the Reichenau collection contained a good many works on grammar, since that discipline had become fundamental to the preservation and teaching of correct Latin, a necessary basis for any other study. Priscian and Donatus were known, together with many later commentators, Sergius, Isidore, Eucherius, and Alcuin among them. Late Antique verse was also well represented by the Easter hymns of Sedulius; Juvencus on metre; Arator's versified *Acts of the Apostles*; and verses by Prudentius, Venantius Fortunatus, Dracontius, and Virgilius Maro. For a correct appreciation of classical poetry, metrical analysis was essential. Bede's was explained by Alcuin, and Aldhelm of Malmesbury's *Regula pedum* was augmented by his own example of verses in praise of the Virgin. A collection of *carmina* in German provided a change from Latin verses, but this part of the collection concentrated on classical Latin poetry. With a copy of Virgil's *Georgics* and the *Aeneid* available at Reichenau, students could work up to the *fons et origo* of the western tradition.

A small number of profane writings completes the list: of historical works, Reichenau had (in addition to Eusebios, Josephus, and Bede) a copy of Gregory of Tours's *Historia Francorum* and Orosius's *World History* (surprisingly, there was no copy of the *Tripartita*). It also owned a copy of Dares of Phrygia's history of the Trojan War, and his work on the origin of the Trojans. There was a copy of Apollonius's *De architectura* (i.e. Vitruvius) and a map of the world. For secular biography there was Einhard's *Life* of Charlemagne. And in addition to the little bit of Aristotle and the Sibylline oracles mentioned above, Reichenau contained several books of laws—Roman and non-Roman—including an important copy of the *Lex Langobardorum*.

According to the generally accepted tradition, the monastery at Reichenau was founded in 724 by Pirmin, a monk of Franko-Irish or Spanish origin, who was responsible for establishing many communities in Alemannia and Alsace. In most of them he encouraged the practice of writing and learning that would later blossom into famous centres of copying and scriptoria. Pirmin himself may have composed a highly influential work, the *Scarapsus* or *Dicta Pirmini*, which provided a guide for Christian conduct, especially among monks in the newly converted regions of northeast Europe. Whether he also brought books to Reichenau that formed the nucleus of the library is still debated. But both the foundation of Reichenau and the later development of its library symbolise the importance of Late

Antiquity in the history of the West. For Pirmin, even if he was not among
the Christians who fled north beyond the Pyrenees as Arab military conquest put an end to Visigothic domination over Spain, represents the preservation of ancient culture in a non-Mediterranean, medieval environment.
The 821 catalogue not only encapsulates the specifically western inheritance of this culture, but also points to the significance of Spain, Ireland,
and Northumbria in the great arch of intellectual transmission, which
brought learning, liturgy, and art from the East to northern Europe, and
thence to Lake Constance. Reichenau may thus be seen as one of the northern outposts of Christian faith, through which Late Antique culture persisted, to form the basis of ninth-century education.

The particular contribution made by Reichenau to this process is very
clear from its translations of Latin works into vernacular German. In this
relatively novel task, glossaries and collections of glosses (marginal com-
ments and word equivalents) were extremely important. Many early ones
originated at Reichenau, where native skills were encouraged by Walafrid
Strabo's connection with Fulda. Through his knowledge of Hraban Maur's
glosses on the Old High German translation of Isidore of Seville, an authoritative collection was issued, including glosses on the book of *Genesis*
and Tatian's *Diatessaron*, both translated into German at this time. Long
before this, however, scribes working under Reginbert had produced the
interlinear translation of the *Rule* of St. Benedict (which survives at the
monastery of St. Gall, *MS 916*). This German version in Alemannic dialect
is entered between the lines of the Latin text, though only the Prologue and
first fourteen (of 73) chapters are completed. The *Hymns* of St. Ambrose
were also made available in German at Reichenau in a translation of higher
quality than the *Rule*. From a later manuscript made in about 842, the purpose of this translating activity is clarified; this is a collection of verses entitled, "For the purpose of teaching the German language." It displays a
concern with German glosses of works in Latin and was probably used for
teaching Latin to those whose native tongue was the local Alemannic German. At a time when Latin was becoming less and less a spoken language,
and the stress on correct church Latin demanded higher standards, it was
vital that converts and novices entering the monastic life should acquire an
accurate knowledge of the language of the faith, the medium in which culture was transmitted.

One of the most unusual manuscripts written at Reichenau in the early
ninth century is the justly famous confraternity book, which combines the
commemoration of spiritual brotherhood between monastic communities
with the commemoration of their deceased members and patrons. It is a
liturgical book of special prayers for the living and the dead. While the
type of association may go back to Anglo-Saxon precedents, as well as the

Frankish prayer confederation of Attigny (762), by the 820s when the first entries were made, Reichenau's links were unusually widespread. Monasteries as far away as Monteverde in the south (Tuscany), Conques and Jumièges in the west, Salzburg and Mondsee in the east, and Fulda to the north were all conjoined in prayer. But the core of the 50 communities listed lay nearby and included many other foundations by Pirmin, as well as the three diocesan cathedrals of Constance, Basel, and Strasbourg. The serious aims of the confraternity have recently been confirmed by a quite surprising discovery: a stone altar slab inscribed with names, about 300 of them legible, which was excavated from Bishop Egino's church of Sts. Peter and Paul at Niederzell. Among the monks, abbots, and lay patrons thus recorded, 212 are known from written lists incorporated in the Reichenau confraternity book in the tenth and eleventh centuries. This so-far unique archaeological find reveals that the sense of confraternity at Reichenau extended beyond the liturgical precepts enshrined in the book, to the very altar at which those prayers for the living and the dead were said.

While the Reichenau scriptorium, active from the 750s, did not produce illuminated manuscripts comparable to those of Charles's court, Fleury, Reims, or Tours, Reginbert and his pupils were responsible for a number of important texts. Not only the "edited" version of the *Rule* of St. Benedict (*St. Gall 914*), but also copies of Vitruvius (architecture), ancient medical writings, and the original medieval version of the Einsedeln collection of classical inscriptions from Pavia and Rome were produced at Reichenau. When Walafrid Strabo wrote his *Hortulus*, verses on the monastic garden, in which plants and herbs were cultivated for medicinal purposes, he used a copy of Quintus Serenus (and might have consulted the selections from Hippocrates, Soranus, Democritus, and Caelius Aurelianus, also in the library).

Illustrated manuscripts from Reichenau are rare until the late ninth century, when the Bern Prudentius (if correctly ascribed to Reichenau) depicts female warriors in "classical" dress, the personified virtues and vices. This is not the best Carolingian copy of a much-studied poet of Late Antiquity, but the pictures are finely drawn and well coloured. Abbot Grimald of St. Gall (841-72) commissioned artists from Reichenau to decorate his new residence, a sure sign that their work was appreciated. And from the mid-tenth century they began to rival even the most outstanding scribes, with their illuminated Gospels for Bishop Gero (pre-969) and the Homiliary for Bishop Egino (ca. 980). These fine manuscripts culminated in the Gospel book made for Henry II between 1002 and 1014.

It is from this period in the history of Reichenau that the sole surviving frescoes date: those in the nave of the church of St. George, Oberzell (originally all three churches would have been painted). Over a very large area, the artists depicted eight scenes of Christ's healing, four on each wall, framed with complex decorative bands. Above, between the windows, a row of prophets, and below, a series of roundels of priests, much less grand in scale and execution, do not distract from the dignified presentation of the familiar Gospel stories, the raising of Lazarus, the healing of Jairus's daughter, the curing of the man blind from birth, and so on. Each is labelled by a quotation, perhaps an indication that Charlemagne's insistence on the correct identification of pictures was followed. Although faded, the predominance of browns, pinks, and the plentiful use of white on their pale blue background still make a surprising impact. The careful, uncluttered layout and distinguished figures of Christ compare favourably with those at the Johannes church, Münstair, similarly decorated with Gospel stories, but in a cramped scheme, with a plethora of frowning figures crowded together.

Apart from the careful identification of each scene at Oberzell, there is no sign of the iconoclastic tendencies that influenced Carolingian court life in the 790s and again in the 820s. The Fleury Gospels, with symbols of the Evangelists and the Hand of God (perhaps a tribute to Theodulf's principled objection to human representation), find no parallel at Reichenau. The architecture of Egino's original building at Niederzell was clearly inspired by Verona, where he was previously bishop, and by the Roman church of St. Maria in Cosmedin, rebuilt by Pope Hadrian I. Similarly, the present cathedral at Mittelzell, built by Abbot Heito in 816, was constructed in Carolingian style like Aachen and Seligenstadt, according to a Roman foot of measurement, and with Roman roof tiles. But the late tenth-century fresco painters did not share this determination to do things the Roman way; their concern, as at nearby Goldbach, was to present visual instruction in clear, unambiguous forms. They followed in the tradition of western aesthetics moulded by the Gregorian dictum that religious art should provide Bibles for the illiterate. Their art was designed to educate and was congruent with a feudal world of divided powers, in which individual benefactors (lay and ecclesiastical) took responsibility for the correct faith of their dependents. At Malles, another Carolingian foundation in the Alps, the church of San Benedetto contains portraits of both the secular and priestly donors of the church, who announce their role in this important task.

While I do not want to exaggerate the significance of Reichenau, it does nonetheless typify the vigour characteristic of eighth- and ninth-century missionary activity, which brought much of northeast Europe into the realm of Christendom. Its concern with vernacular German and the translation of classical works was matched by a high standard of Latin, the language of both religious life and intellectual activity. Its frescoes present an impressive example of Carolingian didactic art, otherwise very poorly preserved, and its magnificent library draws together a number of important strands that made up the early medieval heritage of Late Antiquity. As a symbol of the monastic refuge, which sheltered this culture through the vicissitudes of medieval history and into the service of renaissance Europe, Reichenau stands apart. It remains one of the most attractive emblems of the formation of Christendom.

Abbreviations

AA   See *MGH, AA*.

AASS   *Acta Sanctorum*, third edition (Paris/Rome, 1863-70).

AB   *Analecta Bollandiana*.

AJA   *American Journal of Archaeology*.

Annales Laureshamenses   In *MGH, SS*, vol. 1, 22-39.

Annals of Einhard   In *MGH, SSRG*, vol. 6; also in *MGH, SS*, vol. 1, 13-89.

B   *Byzantion*.

BF   *Byzantinische Forschungen*.

BMGS   *Byzantine and Modern Greek Studies*.

BS   *Byzantinoslavica*.

Buildings   Procopius, *Buildings*, ed. J. Haury, revised G. Wirth (Leipzig, 1964); English translation by H. B. Dewing and G. Downey, *Procopius*, vol. 7 (Cambridge, Mass., 1940).

BZ   *Byzantinische Zeitschrift*.

Capitularia   In *MGH, Legum sectio 2: Capitularia regum Francorum*, vol. 1, ed. A. Boretius (Hannover, 1883).

CC   *Codex Carolinus*, in *MGH, Ep.*, vol. 3.

CCL   *Corpus Christianorum series Latina* (Turnhout).

Chronicle (John of Biclar)   Ed. T. Mommsen, in *MGH, AA*, vol. 11, pt. 2, 207-220.

Chronicle (John of Nikiu)   *Chronique*, ed. H. Zotenberg (Paris, 1883), with French translation.

Chronicle (Michael the Syrian)   *La Chronique de Michel le Syrien*, ed. J.-B. Chabot, 2 vols. (Paris, 1904), with French translation.

Chronicon Moissiacense   In *MGH, SS*, vol. 1, 280-313.

Chronikon Paschale   *Chronicon Paschale*, ed. L. Dindorf, vol. 1 (Bonn, 1832).

Concilia   In *MGH, Legum sectio 3*: vol. 2, *Concilia aevi Karolini*, pts. 1-2, ed. A. Werminghoff (Hannover, 1906-1908).

DACL   *Dictionnaire d'Archéologie Chrétienne et de Liturgie*, ed. F. Cabrol and H. Leclercq (Paris, 1903-1953).

DHGE   *Dictionnaire d'Histoire et de Géographie ecclésiastiques*, ed. A. Baudrillart, A. Vogt, U. Rouzies (Paris, 1912-), in progress (vols. A-G).

DOC   P. Grierson, *Catalogue of the Byzantine Coins in the Dumbarton Oaks Collection* (Washington, D.C., 1966-), in progress.

DOP   *Dumbarton Oaks Papers*.

Ecclesiastical History (John of Ephesos)   *The Third Book of the Ecclesiastical History of John of Ephesus*, trans. R. Payne Smith (Oxford, 1860).

EH   Bede, *Ecclesiastical History of the English People*, ed. and trans. B. Colgrave and R. A. B. Mynors (Oxford, 1969).

EHR English Historical Review.

Ep. See *MGH, Ep.*

Epistolae Karolini Aevi See *MGH, Ep.*

Epistolae Selectae See *MGH, Epistolae Selectae.*

GRBS Greek, Roman and Byzantine Studies.

HE   Eusebios, *Historia Ecclesiastica*, ed. E. Schwartz, in *Eusebius Werke*, Band II, 3 vols. (Berlin, 1903-1909). Trans. by A. C. McGiffert, *The Church History of Eusebius* (Oxford/New York, 1890), and by K. Lake and J. E. L. Oulton (London, 1926-32).

HF   Gregory of Tours, *Historia Francorum*, in *MGH, SSRM*, vols. 1-2. English translation by L. Thorpe, *Gregory of Tours, The History of the Franks* (Harmondsworth, 1974).

HJ Historisches Jahrbuch.

HL   Paul the Deacon, *Historia Langobardorum*, in *MGH, SSRL*, 45-187. English translation by W. D. Foulke (Philadelphia, 1907).

HZ Historische Zeitschrift.

IGLS Inscriptions grecques et latines de la Syrie, ed. L. Jalabert, R. Mouterde et al., Institut français d'Archéologie de Beyrouth, Bibliothèque archéologique et historique, 6 vols. (Paris, 1929-67).

JAC Jahrbuch für Antike und Christentum.

Jaffé   P. Jaffé and G. Wattenbach, eds. *Regesta Pontificum Romanorum* (2nd revised edition), vol. 1, *From S. Peter to A.1143 (Innocent II)* (Leipzig, 1885).

JEH Journal of Ecclesiastical History.

JHS Journal of Hellenic Studies.

JÖB and *JÖBG Jahrbuch der österreichischen Byzantinistik* (formerly *Jahrbuch der österreichischen byzantinischen Gesellschaft*).

John of Antioch   John of Antioch, *Excerpta de insidiis*, ed. C. de Boor (Berlin, 1905).

JRS Journal of Roman Studies.

JTS Journal of Theological Studies.

LC   *Libri carolini*, ed. H. Bastgen, in *MGH, Concilia*, vol. 2, Supplementum (Hannover, 1924).

LP   *Le Liber pontificalis*, ed. L. Duchesne, 2 vols. (Paris, 1884-92), with a third volume of additions, corrections, and indices published by C. Vogel (Paris, 1957).

LRE   A. H. M. Jones, *The Late Roman Empire, 284-602*, 3 vols. (Oxford, 1964).

Mansi   J. D. Mansi, *Sacrorum Conciliorum nova et amplissima collectio* (Florence/Venice, 1759-98, reprinted 1901-1927).

MEFR Mélanges de l'Ecole française de Rome.

MGH Monumenta Germaniae Historica.

MGH, AA Auctores Antiquissimi, vol. 11, pt. 2, *Chronica minora saec. IV, V, VI, VII*, ed. T. Mommsen (Berlin, 1894, reprinted 1961).

MGH, Ep. Epistolae,
    vols. 1-2, *Gregorii I papae, registrum epistolarum*, ed. P. Ewald and L. M. Hartmann (Berlin, 1887-91);

vol. 3, *Epistolae Merowingici et Karolini Aevi*, no. 1, ed. W. Gundlach (Berlin, 1892);

vol. 4, *Epistolae Karolini Aevi*, no. 2, ed. E. Dummler (Berlin, 1895);

vol. 5, *Epistolae Karolini Aevi*, no. 3, in 2 pts., ed. E. Dummler, K. Hampe, A. de Hirsch-Gerenth (Berlin, 1898-99).

MGH, Epistolae selectae vol. 1, *Die Briefe des heiligen Bonifatius und Lullus*, ed. M. Tangl (Berlin, 1916, reprinted 1955).

MGH, SS Scriptores in folio (Hannover, 1826 onwards).

MGH, SSRG Scriptores rerum Germanicarum,

vol. 6, *Annales regni Francorum* . . . 741-829 (Royal Frankish Annals and Annals of Einhard) ed. G. H. Pertz and F. Kurze (Hannover, 1895, reprinted 1950);

vol. 25, *Einhardi Vita Karoli Magni*, ed. O. Holder-Egger (Hannover, 1911, reprinted 1965).

MGH, SSRL Scriptores Rerum Langobardicarum et Italicarum saec. VI-IX, vol. 1, ed. G. Waitz (Hannover, 1878, reprinted 1964).

MGH, SSRM Scriptores Rerum Merovingicarum,

vol. 1, *Gregorii Turonensis opera*, ed. W. Arndt and B. Krusch (Hannover, 1884-85):

pt. 1, *Historia Francorum* (reprinted 1966);

pt. 2, *Miracula* . . . (reprinted 1968).

Miracula S. Demetrii Les plus anciens recueils des miracles de saint Demetrius, ed. P. Lemerle, 2 vols. (Paris, 1979-81).

Nikephoros Nikephoros, *Breviarium*, in *Nicephori opuscula historica*, ed. C. de Boor (Leipzig, 1880).

PG J. P. Migne, *Patrologiae Cursus Completus* . . . *series graeca*, 162 vols. (Paris, 1857-66).

PL J. P. Migne, *Patrologiae Cursus Completus* . . . *series latina prima*, 221 vols. (Paris, 1846-63).

RAC Reallexikon für Antike und Christentum, ed. T. Klauser (Stuttgart 1950-) (vols. A-G).

REB Revue des études byzantines.

Regesten F. Dölger, *Regesten der Kaiserurkunden des oströmischen Reiches*, vol. 1 (Munich/Berlin, 1924).

RH Revue historique.

Royal Frankish Annals Annales Laurissenses, in *MGH, SSRG*, vol. 6; also in *MGH, SS*, vol. 1, 134-88; English translation by B. W. Scholz, *Carolingian Chronicles* (Ann Arbor, 1970).

SBN Rivisita di studi bizantini et neoellenici.

SCH Studies in Church History.

Settimane Settimane di studio del Centro italiano di Studi sull'alto Medioevo (Spoleto).

SS See *MGH, SS*.

SSRG See *MGH, SSRG*.

SSRL See *MGH, SSRL*.

SSRM See *MGH, SSRM*.

Theophanes   *Theophanis Chronographia*, vol. 1, ed. C. de Boor (Leipzig, 1883, re-
    printed Hildesheim, 1980); partial English translation by H. Turtle-
    dove, *The Chronicle of Theophanes* (A.D. *602-813*) (Philadelphia, 1982).

Theophylact Simocatta   Theophylact Simocatta, *Historiae*, ed. C. de Boor (Leip-
    zig, 1887); revised ed. P. Wirth (Stuttgart, 1972); English translation
    by Michael and Mary Whitby, *The "History" of Theophylact Simocatta*
    (Oxford, 1986).

TM   *Travaux et mémoires.*

TRHS   *Transactions of the Royal Historical Society.*

Vita Karoli   Einhard, *Vita Karoli*, ed. O. Holder Egger, in *MGH, SSRG*, vol. 25;
    also in *SS*, vol. 1, ed. G. Pertz; English translation by L. Thorpe, *Ein-
    hard and Notker the Stammerer, Two Lives of Charlemagne* (Harmonds-
    worth, 1969).

VPE   J. N. Garvin, ed., *The "Vitas Patrum Emeretensium"* (Washington, D.C.,
    1946).

VV   *Vizantiiskii Vremennik.*

Wars   Procopius, *History of the Wars*, 2 vols., ed. J. Haury, revised G. Wirth
    (Leipzig, 1963); English translation by H. B. Dewing and G. Downey,
    Procopius, vols. 1-5 (Cambridge, Mass., 1914-28).

Zachariah   *The Syriac Chronicle . . . of Zachariah of Mitylene*, trans. F. J. Hamilton
    and E. W. Brooks (London, 1899).

Zonaras   Zonaras, *Epitome Historiarum,* ed. M. Pinder and T. Büttner-Wobst,
    vol. 3 (Bonn, 1897).

ZRVI   *Zbornik Radova Vizantološkog Instituta* (Belgrade).

Index

Aachen, 299–300, 446–48, 451–53, 456, 462–64, 466; royal chapel at, 440, 447, 466; sacred palace, 447–48; council of (802), 441n; council of (809), 463

Aba, Mar (patriarch of Nestorian church), 108

Abbas (uncle of Muhammad), 299, 361n

Abbasid: revolt, 140, 304, 361; Caliphate, 413n, 416n; ambassadors to Charlemagne, 462

Abd al Malik (caliph [685–705]), 9, 282, 323–24

Abedrapsas, 50

Abgar (king of Edessa), 309, 366

Abraham, 92

Abraham (bishop of Luxor), 308

Abul Abbas (caliph of Baghdad [750–54]), 361

Abydos (map 2), 190

Acca, 270

Achila (Visigothic king), 249

Acts of the Apostles, 55n, 57, 92; versified by Arator, 84, 483

Adalhard (count), 396

Adam, 4

Adelgis (Lombard prince), 398, 408, 425

Adelperga, 396

administration, Roman imperial, 34; adopted by non-Romans, 51; developed by Justinian, 40; Gothic dual system of, 35; Cassiodorus serves in, 42; Arator in, 84; Byzantine imperial, 137, 192, 197, 211, 213, 317, 324, 405; Islamic, 137, 324-25, 344; Persian, 137, 324; Frankish administration of justice, 391, 404, 442–43; Carolingian, 404; papal, 414

Admonitio generalis, 433, 441, 442

Adoald (Lombard prince), 166, 226

adoption: of other rulers' sons, 39; of non-Christian rulers at their baptism, 301

Adoptionism, 434–45, 440, 443, 470

Adrianople (map 1), 410; Visigothic victory at (378), 25

Adriatic Sea, archipelago of, 22, part of the "West," 22, 121, 351, 380, 465

Adventus, 36

Aegean: sea, 22, 242, 319; littoral, 135; islands, 135, 210, 283, 360, 363; earthquake, 334

aera, 3

Aesclepius, 54

Aetios, 431, 453

Aetius (Roman general), 30

Afghanistan, 124

Africa, 210, 214, 251–53, 265, 456; diocese of (map 1), 23; grain from, 20, 44, 189, 190; Vandal conquest of, 33–4, 221; parts occupied by desert nomads, 36; reconquered by Justinian, 41; refortified by Justinian, 43; schools restored, 44; landowners of, 47; Berber attacks on, 71, 154; decline of classical cities, 134; exarchate of, 154–56; fleet of, 190; idolatry in, 304; conquered by Arabs, 136; Arab rulers of, 397

Africa, church of, 98, 102, 107, 214, 218; monks of, 121–23, 154, 217; and council of 646, 217; Augustinian traditions of, 223; refuses to recognise Fifth Oecumenical Council, 230; bishops of, persecuted by Justinian, 241

Agapetos (monk and bishop of Apamea), 67

Agapitus (pope [535–36]), 80, 119

Agatha (martyr), 161

Agathias (deacon), 319

Agatho (pope [678–81]), 125, 270, 272, 276–77, 280

Agilbert (bishop of Paris), 269

Agilulf (king of the Lombards), 188, 226

Agnellus (archbishop of Ravenna), 148

Aistulf (Lombard king), 359, 370–73, 375, 377–79,

Akephaloi (Severan Monophysites), 120, 123, 125, 241–42

Akroïnon (map 2), 137, 354

Alans, 27

Childebert II (king of the Franks [d. 595]), 51, 164, 166
Childeric III (Merovingian king), 357
Chilperic (king of the Franks [d. 584]), 51
China, 7, 37
Chindaswinth (Visigothic king), 227, 232
Chintila (Visigothic king), 240
Chios (map 1): wine from, 222
Chlotar I (king of the Franks), 84, 115
Chludov Psalter, 474
Chosroes I (Persian emperor [531–79]), 39
Chosroes II (Persian emperor [590–628]), 136, 186–87, 195, 197–98
Christ, 60, 65, 118, 345, 378, 420; birth date of, 4–5, 235, 458, 480; nature(s) of, 55, 102, 107–108, 208, 367–68; will(s), of, 208, 213–14, 218, 259; energy of, 208, 218; essence of, defined at Nicaea, 56; unity of, 208; crucifixion of, 313; resurrection, of, 158, 367; reign of, 235–37; general rule of, 414. *See also* icons of Christ
Christendom, 7–8, 13–14, 22, 103, 141, 164, 255, 277, 477, 480; disunity of, 214; division of, 10, 218, 250–59, 286–87, 454; Rome as centre of, 273; Muslim pressure on, 134, 299–300; two emperors of, 445–46, 454–62, 464–66, 485–76; collapse of, 479
Christian church, 10, 53, 55, 84; hierarchy of, 51, 56, 57–59, 72–73, 75, 171, 285; parish priests in, 171; early history of, 81; institutions of, 12, 143, 163–64, 171, 172–73; in Spain, 220; early Christian conciliar decisions, 246, 359; early traditions of, 305, 369, 415, 417, 474. *See also* bishop(s); canon law; council(s); liturgy; Oecumenical Council; traditions
Christian faith, 7, 89, 126, 134–35
Christianitas, 8
Christianity, 8–9, 12, 144, 235n; rivalry with Islam, 8–9; as state religion of empire, 21, 51, 58; protected by emperors, 118, 126; becomes dominant faith of non-Roman world, 22; adopted by non-Romans, 37, 43; as a spiritual challenge to paganism, 38, 126; senatorial patrons of, 49; as a new belief, 54; growth of, 54–78; variety within, 90–99, 106–114; regional loyalties of, 141; western devel-

opment of, 389, 448; as a universal faith administered by uniform law, 100, 119; intolerance in, 78, 138; Orthodox, 479
"Christ-loving," 335–36
Christmas: mass, 409, 468; of A.D. 800, 454, 459; as the start of the year, 458
Christology, 101, 125, 366–67, 407
Christopher (*primicerius*), 392–93, 396–97
Christotokos ("Mother of Christ"), 108
Chrodegang (bishop of Metz), 303, 358–59, 372, 376, 383, 391
Chronicle of Fredegar, 224, 231
Chronicle of Isidore of Seville, 236
Chronicle of John of Biclar, 229
Chronicles, book of, 3
Chronikon Paschale, 112
chronology. *See* dating
chrysobull, 410
Chrysopolis, 413
churches, private, 113, 442
church plate, 193
Ciccana, 372
Cicero (author of *Hortensius*), 75, 402, 478
Cilicia, 252, 260, 368n
circus factions, 187, 191, 204, 281, 317
Classis (port of Ravenna), 26, 149
Claudias, 361
Claudius (archbishop of Turin), 470–72
Clement, St. (missionary) (Willibrord), 139, 271, 302, 346
Clement of Alexandria [d. after 215], 58, 79, 94, 97, 98
Clermont (map 3), 178
Clonard (map 3): monastery of, 106
Clovis (king of the Franks [481–511]) 35, 36; adopts Christianity, 105; death of, 115
Codex argenteus (Gothic Bible), 31, 231
Codex Carolinus, 296
co-emperor, 215, 262–63, 275; established by Diocletian, 23; failure of 24
coemptio, 146
coenobium (*koinobion*), 62
coinage: Roman imperial, 34, 46; Roman, imitated in West, 52, 226; Byzantine imperial, 37, 414, 454; struck in Syracuse, 266n; issued by Justinian II, 311, 312, 324, 364; silver, 193; *miliaresion*, 363; and Byzantine currency reform, 201, 203; overstruck in Benevento, 424;